Economic Analysis

of

Agricultural Projects

EDI SERIES IN ECONOMIC DEVELOPMENT

Economic Analysis
of
Agricultural Projects

Second Edition,
Completely Revised and Expanded

J. Price Gittinger

PUBLISHED FOR
THE ECONOMIC DEVELOPMENT INSTITUTE
OF THE WORLD BANK

The Johns Hopkins University Press
BALTIMORE AND LONDON

The Johns Hopkins University Press
Baltimore, Maryland 21218, U.S.A.

EDITOR   James E. McEuen
PRODUCTION   Christine Houle
FIGURES   Raphael Blow
INDEX   Ralph Ward and James Silvan
BOOK DESIGN   Brian J. Svikhart
COVER DESIGN   Joyce C. Eisen

Photo credits: World Bank photographs (facing pages) by Hilda Bijur, 437; William Graham, 431; Per Gunvall, 188; Yosef Hadar, 242; Edwin Huffman, papercover, 298; Jaime Martín-Escobal, 42, 411; Peter C. Muncie, 64; James Pickerell, 286; Tomas Sennett, frontispiece, 362, 445, 457; and Ray Witlin, 2, 84, 214.
Frontispiece: Milking tethered sheep in Syria.

• Karya ini tersedia pula dalam Bahasa Indonesia dengan judul *Analisa Ekonomi Proyek-Proyek Pertanian* diterbitkan oleh Penerbit Universitas Indonesia (Jln. Salemba Raya 4, Jakarta).

• Une version en français de cet ouvrage a été publiée sous le titre *Analyse économique des projets agricoles*, Editions Economica (49, rue Héricart, 75015 Paris, France; distributeur au Canada: Le Diffuseur, C.P. 85, Boucherville, Québec J4B 5E6).

• Esta obra también ha sido publicada en español bajo el título *Análisis económico de proyectos agrícolas*, por la Editorial Tecnos (distribución en España: Grupo Editorial, S.A., Don Ramón de la Cruz 67, Madrid 1; distribución en otros países: GSR Internacional, Villafranca 22, Madrid 28, España).

طبعت نسخة من هذه الدراسة باللغة العربية في مطبعة الاهـرام
بعنوان " التحليل الاقتصادى للمشروعات الزراعية " ـ الاهـرام،
شـارع الجلاء، القـاهرة، جمهورية مصر العربية .

本书中文译本「农业项目的经济分析」由中国财政经济
出版社出版（北京市大佛寺东街8号）

First hardcover and paperback printing July 1982
Second paperback printing April 1984

Library of Congress Cataloging in Publication Data:
Gittinger, J. Price (James Price), 1928–
   Economic analysis of agricultural projects.
   (EDI series in economic development)
   Bibliography: p. 445
   Includes index.
   1. Underdeveloped areas—Agriculture—Cost effectiveness.   2. Agriculture—Economic aspects.
I. Title. II. Series.
HD1417.G58   1982   338.1'3   82-15262
ISBN 0-8018-2912-7   AACR2
ISBN 0-8018-2913-5 (pbk.)

Foreword

To INCREASE THE GROWTH AND EFFICIENCY of the agricultural and rural sectors of the developing countries is of prime concern to the international community. More rapid progress is crucial not only to improve the quality of life of the 60 percent of the world's population earning its living from rural labor, but also to ensure adequate food supplies for all nations in the face of rapid worldwide population growth and rising incomes that lead people to want more and better-quality food. Unless domestic food production in developing countries steadily increases, these requirements will place unbearable strains on the world's food production and distribution system—threatening widespread malnutrition in the poorest countries and adding to inflationary pressures in the industrial nations.

In the next few years, agriculture and rural development will be a priority in the lending programs of The World Bank and International Development Association (IDA). The World Bank will maintain its support of member governments with technical expertise and a continuing flow of resources. It will help governments to expand irrigation systems, provide more effective extension services, increase food storage capacity, disseminate agronomic technology, and improve the marketing and distribution of agricultural goods.

This effort will require large quantities of scarce resources—both people and money—from our member nations and from the Bank itself. We must use these resources efficiently.

Since its founding the Bank has encouraged, indeed insisted upon, the responsible preparation of the development projects for which it lends. This book is one more implement by which the agricultural work of the Bank is carried out.

The Bank shares its experience and skill with member governments and their technical and administrative staffs so that wise and careful investment decisions will yield higher national incomes and a better quality of life for the people of the developing world. In no sector is this sharing of information more important than in agriculture and rural development, where sound investment has such effects on the lives of millions.

The Economic Development Institute (EDI) has played an important role in disseminating the Bank's experience. Since its founding in 1954, more than 10,000 senior officials from member governments have attended EDI courses both at headquarters in Washington, D.C., and overseas. EDI has helped dozens of institutions throughout the world to provide courses in economic management and project analysis in their own curricula.

Economic Analysis of Agricultural Projects derives from the Bank's concern to hasten agricultural and rural development and from the course activities of EDI. The book presents a sound, careful methodology for project analysis based on the efforts of agricultural specialists in the Bank and throughout the world. Care has been taken to make the technical topics discussed understandable to those without advanced training in economics. The book was written to be used either in individual study or in the classroom.

We are pleased that the first edition has enjoyed such wide acceptance. Since it was published in 1972, it has become a standard text for those planning agricultural projects and teaching project analysis. In offering this revised edition, with expanded coverage and the addition of more recent experience, we hope to make its contribution even more effective.

A. W. CLAUSEN
President
The World Bank

Washington, D.C.
June 1982

Contents

Appendixes

Preface

THIS BOOK was written to provide those responsible for agricultural investments in developing countries with sound analytical tools they can apply to estimate the income-generating potential of proposed projects.

Scope and Methodology

The book has not been written only for a narrow grouping of agricultural economists. Rather, it is intended for all who must share in shaping agricultural projects if these undertakings are to be high-yielding investments: agronomists, livestock specialists, irrigation engineers, and many others. All these people are meant when the term "analyst" is used. To the existing resources of these diverse professionals, the book adds a tool for multidisciplinary use so that many with many skills can work together in applying their knowledge to analyze proposed projects.

The formal economic theory underlying the analytical system outlined here is not complicated; it certainly is not so technical as to cause problems for noneconomists. For those not already familiar with it, I have discussed the necessary economic theory in the course of the presentation and have defined technical terms both in the text and in the glossary-index at the end of the book. The mathematical techniques used are also simple; they are limited to addition, subtraction, division, multiplication, and the simplest algebra. The computations needed for project analysis, however, are too tedious to be done by hand. A simple electronic calculator is a virtual necessity (see chapter 10 under "Calculator Applications in Project Analysis"), but there is no need for advanced calculators or computers.

The analytical system outlined in this book is a consistent statement of the general methodology currently employed by the World Bank for all but a few of its project analyses (Gittinger, Garg, and Thieme 1982). (The details of World Bank analyses vary somewhat according to the sector and the views of individual analysts.) With minor variations, the system is also used by most international agencies concerned with capital transfer, including the African Development Bank, the Asian Development Bank, and the Inter-American Development Bank. The economic analysis in this system is based on "efficiency prices"—prices that show effects on national income broadly defined. The system enables us to judge which among project alternatives is most likely to contribute the largest amount to national income. The system underlies millions of dollars of investment decisions made every year. Thick volumes of economic analysis backing up proposed investments usually involve nothing more complicated than what is discussed in the following pages—although large investments may require much elaboration and may involve intermediate steps to accommodate all the "ins" and "outs" of a complex agricultural project.

In recent years several analytical systems have been proposed that extend the methodology outlined here to take into account not only the contribution a project makes to national income but also the effect of a project on income distribution and saving. Most notable are those of Little and Mirrlees (1974), the United Nations Industrial Development Organization (UNIDO) (1972a), and Squire and van der Tak (1975). These analytical systems, which remain the subject of much professional discussion, are far more complex than the one I have presented. The system outlined here, however, is compatible with these more complex systems; in fact, Squire and van der Tak recommend the same methodology for project identification and valuation. The difference is that, once Squire and van der Tak have determined economic values on the basis of efficiency prices, they then proceed to weight those values to account for income distribution and saving. In the analytical system given here, we will stop with the efficiency price analysis. We will then suggest making a subjective decision to choose among the high-yielding alternatives the one that has the most favorable effects on income distribution, saving, and other national objectives. The system outlined here is not immediately adaptable to the Little and Mirrlees or the UNIDO systems, but there are no major conceptual differences up to the point we carry the analysis. Both Little and Mirrlees and UNIDO recommend further refinements to allow for the effects on income distribution and saving that are not incorporated in the formal analytical scheme recommended here.

The Revised Edition

Compared with the first edition, published in 1972, this second, revised edition has an expanded discussion of the project approach that incorporates more recent experience and provides more detailed and rigorous treatment of identifying, pricing, and valuing costs and benefits. The basic analytical system, however, is unchanged. Much additional material has been added on farm budgets and other aspects of financial analysis, and a bit more on the methodology of comparing costs and benefits.

In the Economic Development Institute (EDI), the first edition has been extensively used for teaching project analysis. The sequence of topics taken up in EDI courses on agricultural and rural development, rural credit, livestock, and irrigation projects generally follows the order found here. Thus, the overall concept of a project is presented first, followed by farm budgets and financial analysis, and then by economic analysis. (For a more detailed description of the process of project analysis, and of the organization of the chapters in this book, see the last section of chapter 1, "Steps in Project Analysis.") In practice, however, the methodology of comparing costs and benefits discussed in chapters 9 and 10 is usually taught in parallel with the topics on financial and economic analysis. This both permits a change of pace in the teaching and gives course participants more time to practice using methodological tools before proceeding to case studies in which they are asked to apply their knowledge of financial and economic analysis and their methodological skills. EDI has prepared a number of case studies and other training materials to teach agricultural and rural development project analysis, and these are available to others teaching these subjects. (See the last page of this book for information about how to obtain these materials.)

Acknowledgments

I could never have written a book such as this without extensive help from many, many people. The book grows out of lectures and training materials prepared for EDI courses, and its style reflects its origin. I have benefited enormously from, and this revised edition has been informed by, participants in these courses both at EDI headquarters and in developing countries. Readers will note I have made liberal use of training materials prepared by my colleagues.

It is impossible to acknowledge all the individuals who have helped me, but special appreciation should be expressed to Hans A. Adler, George B. Baldwin, Maxwell L. Brown, Colin F. M. Bruce, Orlando T.

Espadas, F. Leslie C. H. Helmers, P. D. Henderson, William I. Jones, Klaus Meyn, Frank H. Lamson-Scribner, David H. Penny, Walter Schaefer-Kehnert, Arnold von Ruemker, Jack L. Upper, and William A. Ward, all presently or formerly with the EDI; to numerous present and former staff working with agricultural projects in the World Bank, especially Graham Donaldson, Lionel J. C. Evans, John D. Von Pischke, Gordon Temple, Willi A. Wapenhans, and A. Robert Whyte; and to Frederick J. Hitzhusen, Ohio State University, and John D. MacArthur, University of Bradford.

J. PRICE GITTINGER

Using This Book

THE ORGANIZATION, conventions and notation, and special features of this book are briefly explained here at the outset for the reader's convenience.

Organization of Chapters

Chapters are presented in an order that in general follows the process of preparing an agricultural project analysis. The sequence of this process is described in the last section of chapter 1, "Steps in Project Analysis." Because the analytical process is iterative, chapters frequently contain cross-references to appropriate sections and subsections in other chapters.

Computations

Project analyses rest on many assumptions that by their very nature are only approximate. The final results of computations, therefore, should be rounded with this limitation in mind and presented appropriately with only significant digits included—say, in millions or thousands of currency units, thousands or hundreds of tons or hectares, or the like. To make methodological points more apparent, however, many illustrative computations in this book have been carried out much further than called for by such a rule. Hence, they should not be taken as a model for presentation. (See the section in chapter 9 entitled "How Far to Carry Out Computations of Discounted Measures" for a discussion of this topic.)

Decimals and commas in numbers

Throughout this book, a decimal is indicated by a point set level with the bottom of the line of type (.). In numbers of 1,000 or greater (except those designating the year), a comma (,) distinguishes groupings of thousands. Thus, 1 million would be written 1,000,000.0. Whenever a decimal fraction appears that is less than 1, a zero appears before the decimal point to avoid misreading the fraction; thus, one-fourth appears in decimal form as 0.25.

Rounding convention

For all computations in this book, the following rules have been used for rounding:

1. When a value of less than 5 is to be dropped, the digit to the left is unchanged.

2. When a value of more than 5 is to be dropped, the digit to the left is increased by 1.

3. When a value of *exactly* 5 is to be dropped, the digit to the left, if *even*, is left unchanged; if *odd*, it is raised by 1. Under this rule, all numbers that have been rounded by dropping an *exact* value of 5 are reported as even numbers.

Thus, in the first illustrative tabulation in the "Compounding" subsection of chapter 9, the following rounding will be found:

$$1,050 \times 1.05 = 1,102.50 \text{ } rounded \text{ } to \text{ } 1,102 \text{ (Rule 3)}$$
$$1,102 \times 1.05 = 1,157.10 \text{ } rounded \text{ } to \text{ } 1,157 \text{ (Rule 1)}$$
$$1,157 \times 1.05 = 1,214.85 \text{ } rounded \text{ } to \text{ } 1,215 \text{ (Rule 2)}.$$

Calculations

Throughout the text, illustrative calculations made in project analysis are given (within parentheses or brackets) after the explanation of how they are derived. Most of these calculations are done by simple arithmetic. (For the sake of completeness, there are many calculations presented in this manner that are very simple; I hope the reader will be patient with such obvious examples.) More elaborate formulas are displayed on the page.

Units of Measurement and Currency

Metric units are used for all measurements unless otherwise specified—thus, "tons" refers to metric tons, not "long" or "short" tons.

Special units—for example, "animal units" or "work days"—are defined in the text and in the glossary-index (see "Supporting Materials," below).

To emphasize the worldwide scope of agricultural development efforts, examples of project accounts give money amounts in the currency of the country in which the project is located. The standard symbols for these currencies are identified in the text and tables; when appropriate, generic "currency units" are also used.

Notation

An explanation of the conventions used for notation in this book may help in reading the tables, mathematical formulations, and the six-decimal discount factors.

Tables

In the tables in this book a zero indicates "none" or "no amount," and a dash (—) indicates "not applicable." In chapters 4, 5, and 6, and in tables 9-7 and 9-8 where financial accounts are discussed, the accounting convention of indicating negative numbers by parentheses has been adopted. In all other tables, negative numbers are indicated by a minus sign ($-$).

The tables in this book are of several general kinds: tables that lay out methods of calculation (for example, tables 3-3 and 7-2); "pattern account" tables that lay out a recommended format for project accounts for either financial analysis (the tables in chapter 4) or economic analysis (the tables in chapter 7); and the usual sort of table that simply presents project data.

In some of the pattern account tables additional information for understanding (for example, the financial or economic rate of return) is given after the main rows of entries. The reader is reminded that, to arrive at the total values in the tables of chapters 9 and 10 that include entries for multiyear spans, annual amounts must be included for the number of years involved.

In tables that illustrate financial accounts, the reader should note that in some cases intervening years have been omitted (see, for example, table 5-1).

To aid computation, portions of *Compounding and Discounting Tables for Project Evaluation* (Gittinger 1973) have been reproduced in the seven compounding and discounting tables that appear in this book.

Mathematics

As noted above, standard arithmetical notation has been used throughout the book. When division is indicated in a line of figures, a division sign ($\div$) is used rather than a slash (/).

In the section in chapter 10 entitled "Calculator Applications in Project Analysis" the operations that are indicated on the keys of the simple electronic calculator used are shown in the text in **boldface** type.

Six-decimal discount factors

When six-decimal discount factors are used in the text or in tables, a notation of inserting a space between the third and fourth decimal places has been followed to make the factors easier to read.

Technical Terms

Specialized financial, accounting, economic, and project terms (and the few acronyms and abbreviations used in the book) have been compiled and defined in the glossary-index (see "Supporting Materials," below). The most important of these, of course, are also defined in the text where they apply.

As a guide to understanding the format of project accounts, the principal headings of the pattern account tables—categories that are likely to appear in most agricultural project analyses—have been listed in *italic* type in the text of chapters 4, 5, 6, and 8.

Supporting Materials

The reader may find supporting materials that are included in this book, or available from the sources indicated, helpful for further study of project analysis.

Appendixes

Chapter appendixes supplement the discussion of topics in chapters 4, 8, and 9. Appendixes to the book provide general guidelines for preparing an agricultural project analysis report (appendix A); give summary discounting tables for common discount rates and the formulas for computing discount factors directly using an electronic calculator (appendix B); and discuss the bilateral and multilateral sources of specialized assistance for the preparation of complex agricultural projects (appendix C). The assistance discussed in appendix C is negotiated and undertaken at the institutional level by the agencies and governments involved.

Bibliographic sources

Primary sources have been identified in the text by the author's surname and the publication date of the material cited. These sources, and additional references, are listed and annotated in the bibliography.

Sources of some individual tables and figures are not listed in the bibliography but are cited in full in the appropriate table or figure legend. Some of these source materials have restricted circulation and are unavailable to the general public.

I could not have written this book without access to the experience of the Economic Development Institute (EDI) and its parent institution, the World Bank. The record of this experience is predominantly in the public domain. Information about how to obtain publications of the EDI and of the World Bank will be found on the last page of this book.

Glossary-Index

As an aid to the reader, the index has been enhanced by incorporating glossary entries that define the principal technical terms used in this book. Because interpretation of some of these terms varies among the specialists involved in preparing agricultural project analyses (these professionals are an inquisitive lot—they have to be—and the field is a dynamic and changing one), the definitions given cannot be "definitive"—they reflect the use of these terms in this book.

Project examples

Data from actual agricultural project investments assisted by the World Bank or other international development agencies or financed by governments have been used to illustrate the analytical methodology presented here. The adaptation and interpretation of these data are my own. The use of project information in this book is purely illustrative; it does not represent a judgment by the funding agency or borrowing government about any particular project.

PART ONE

The Project Concept

1

Projects,
The Cutting Edge
of Development

PROJECTS ARE THE CUTTING EDGE OF DEVELOPMENT. Perhaps the most difficult single problem confronting agricultural administrators in developing countries is implementing development programs. Much of this can be traced to poor project preparation.

Project preparation is clearly not the only aspect of agricultural development or planning. Identifying national agricultural development objectives, selecting priority areas for investment, designing effective price policies, and mobilizing resources are all critical. But for most agricultural development activities, careful project preparation in advance of expenditure is, if not absolutely essential, at least the best available means to ensure efficient, economic use of capital funds and to increase the chances of implementation on schedule. Unless projects are carefully prepared in substantial detail, inefficient or even wasteful expenditure is almost sure to result—a tragic loss in nations short of capital.

Yet in many countries the capacity to prepare and analyze projects lags. Administrators, even those in important planning positions, continually underestimate the time and effort needed to prepare suitable projects. So much attention is paid to policy formulation and planning of a much broader scope that administrators often overlook the specific

Facing page: Plowing a field in Rajasthan, India.

projects on which to spend available money and on which much development depends. Ill-conceived, hastily planned projects, virtually improvised on the spot, are too often the result.

What Is a Project?

In this book we will discuss how to compare the stream of investment and production costs of an agricultural undertaking with the flow of benefits it will produce. The whole complex of activities in the undertaking that uses resources to gain benefits constitutes the agricultural project. If this definition seems broad, it is intentionally so. As we shall see, the project format can accommodate diverse agricultural endeavors. An enormous variety of agricultural activities may usefully be cast in project form. The World Bank itself lends for agricultural projects as different as irrigation, livestock, rural credit, land settlement, tree crops, agricultural machinery, and agricultural education, as well as for multisectoral rural development projects with a major agricultural component. In agricultural project planning, form should follow analytical content.

We generally think of an agricultural project as an investment activity in which financial resources are expended to create capital assets that produce benefits over an extended period of time. In some projects, however, costs are incurred for production expenses or maintenance from which benefits can normally be expected quickly, usually within about a year. The techniques discussed in this book are equally applicable to estimating the returns from increased current expenditure in both kinds of projects.

Indeed, the dividing line between an "investment" and a "production" expenditure in an agricultural project is not all that clear. Fertilizers, pesticides, and the like are generally thought of as production expenses used up within a single crop season or, in any event, within a year. A dam, a tractor, a building, or a breeding herd is generally thought of as an investment from which a return will be realized over several years. But the same kind of activity may be considered a production expense in one project and an investment in another. Transplanting rice is a production expense. Planting rubber trees is an investment. But from the standpoint of agronomics and economics they are not different kinds of activities at all. In both cases young plants grown in a nursery are set out in the fields, and from them a benefit is expected when they mature. The only difference is the time span during which the plants grow.

Often projects form a clear and distinct portion of a larger, less precisely identified program. The whole program might possibly be analyzed as a single project, but by and large it is better to keep projects rather small, close to the minimum size that is economically, technically, and administratively feasible. Similarly, it is generally better in planning projects to analyze successive increments or distinct phases of activity; in this way the return to each relatively small increment can be judged separately. If a project approaches program size, there is a danger that high returns from one part of it will mask low returns from another. A 100,000-hectare land settlement program may well be better analyzed as five 20,000-hectare projects if the soils and slopes in some parts are markedly different from those in others. Analyzing the whole project may hide the fact that it is economically unwise to develop some parts of the 100,000-hectare area instead of moving on to an entirely different region. When arranging for external financing or planning the administrative structure, it is sometimes convenient for planners to group several closely related projects into a single, larger "package." In these instances it may still be preferable to retain the separate analyses of individual components, in a composite of the whole, rather than to aggregate them into a single, overall analysis.

Again, all we can say in general about a project is that it is an activity for which money will be spent in expectation of returns and which logically seems to lend itself to planning, financing, and implementing as a unit. It is the smallest operational element prepared and implemented as a separate entity in a national plan or program of agricultural development. It is a specific activity, with a specific starting point and a specific ending point, intended to accomplish specific objectives. Usually it is a unique activity noticeably different from preceding, similar investments, and it is likely to be different from succeeding ones, not a routine segment of an ongoing program.

It will have a well-defined sequence of investment and production activities, and a specific group of benefits, that we can identify, quantify, and, usually in agricultural projects, determine a money value for.

If development can be pictured as a progression with many dimensions—temporal, spatial, sociocultural, financial, economic—projects can be seen as the temporal and spatial units, each with a financial and economic value and a social impact, that make up the continuum. A project is an undertaking an observer can draw a boundary around—at least a conceptual boundary—and say "this is the project." As well as its time sequence of investments, production, and benefits, the project normally will have a specific geographic location or a rather clearly understood geographic area of concentration. Probably there will also be a specific clientele in the region whom the project is intended to reach and whose traditional social pattern the project will affect.

Given the usefulness of the project format in the development process, the project has increasingly been used as a "time slice" of a long-term program for a region, a commodity, or a function such as agricultural extension. Although such projects normally have a definite beginning and end, the importance of these starting and finishing points is reduced. Such a use of the project format also makes quantification of benefits more difficult because some benefits may not be realized until subsequent phases of the program that are not included in the project. Often a project will have a partially or wholly independent administrative structure and set of accounts and will be funded through a specifically defined financial package. I hope that, after following the methodology presented here, readers will also subject their projects to an analysis of financial results and economic justification. People are sometimes concerned that they do not have an academic definition of what a project is. There is no need to be; in practice, the definition works itself out. There are much more important aspects of project analysis to grapple with than an academic formulation of a project definition.

Plans and Projects

Virtually every developing country has a systematically elaborated national plan to hasten economic growth and further a range of social objectives. Projects provide an important means by which investment and other development expenditures foreseen in plans can be clarified and realized. Sound development plans require good projects, just as good projects require sound planning. The two are interdependent.

Sound planning rests on the availability of a wide range of information about existing and potential investments and their likely effects on growth and other national objectives. It is project analysis that provides this information, and those projects selected for implementation then become the vehicle for using resources to create new income. Realistic planning involves knowing the amount that can be spent on development activities each year and the resources that will be required for particular kinds of investment.

Project selection must always be based in part on numerical indicators of the value of costs and returns. These can often be measured through valuation at the market prices—the prices at which goods or services are actually traded. Unfortunately, however, market prices may be misleading indicators of the use and return of real resources, so governments need to look at other aspects of potential investments to judge the real effects the investments will have. For this, good project analysis is a tremendous asset, since the investment proposal can be valued to reflect the true scarcity of resources when market prices do not. (Note that by market prices we refer to the actual prices at which goods and services are traded in a generalized system of exchange, not to the particular place at which the exchange takes place. To talk of a village "market" or a wholesale "market" is to use the word in a slightly different sense. This may seem an obvious distinction, but in project analysis it does make a difference whether the "market price" is collected in the appropriate "market," and we will return to this issue later.)

Well-analyzed projects often become the vehicle for obtaining outside assistance when both the country and the external financing agency agree on a specific project activity and know the amount of resources involved, the timing of loan disbursements, and the benefits likely to be realized. But project analysis should not be confined to only those investments for which external financing will be sought. The more investments there are that can be analyzed as projects, the more likely it is that the total use of resources for development will be efficient and effective. To concentrate a high proportion of available analytical skills on preparing projects for external assistance, and to leave investment of local resources basically unplanned, is a wasteful allocation of talent. If carefully designed and high-yielding projects are offset by essentially unplanned investments, then the net contribution to national objectives is substantially undermined.

Sound planning requires good projects, but effective project preparation and analysis must be set in the framework of a broader development plan. Projects are a part of an overall development strategy and a broader planning process; as such, they must fit appropriately. Governments must allocate their available financial and administrative resources among many sectors and many competing programs. Project analysis can help improve this allocation, but it alone cannot be relied upon to achieve the optimal balance of objectives. Within the broad strategy, analysts must identify potential projects that address the policy or production targets and priorities. Further, to make a realistic estimate about the course of a project, some idea must be gained of what other development activities will be taking place and what policies are likely to be pursued. Will employment growth make labor relatively more productive and thus more expensive to use in the project? Will input supplies be available at the time the project needs them? Will quotas be relaxed? Will food grain prices be allowed to rise? Integration of plans and projects becomes all the more important as the size of the project grows larger relative to the total economy. If the project alone is likely to have a significant effect on the availability of resources and on prices in the economy as a whole, then it must be very carefully planned in coordination with other investments and within an appropriate policy framework included in the national plan.

For the project itself, some elements used in agricultural project analysis should not be worked out in isolation by the individual analyst. All the projects being prepared and analyzed should use a consistent set of assumptions about such things as the relative scarcity of investment funds, foreign exchange, and labor. All project analyses should use the same assumptions about the social policies and objectives to be reflected in such decisions as the location of the project, the size of the landholding to be established, the amount of social services to be included, and the like.

Advantages of the Project Format

Projects carefully prepared, within the framework of broader development plans, both advance and assess the larger development effort. The project format itself is an analytical tool. The advantage of casting proposed investment decisions in the project format lies in establishing the framework for analyzing information from a wide range of sources. Because no plan can be better than the data and assumptions about the future on which it is based, the reality of the analysis to a large degree depends on information from various sources and the considered judgments of various specialists in different areas. The project format facilitates gathering the information and laying it out so that many people can participate in providing information, defining the assumptions on which it is based, and evaluating how accurate it is.

The project format gives us an idea of costs year by year so that those responsible for providing the necessary resources can do their own planning. Project analysis tells us something about the effects of a proposed investment on the participants in the project, whether they are farmers, small firms, government enterprises, or the society as a whole. Looking at the effects on individual participants, we can assess the possible incentives a proposed project has and judge if farmers and others may successfully be induced to participate.

Casting a proposed investment in project form enables a better judgment about the administrative and organizational problems that will be encountered. It enables a strengthening of administrative arrangements if these appear to be weak and tells something of the sensitivity of the return to the investment if managerial problems arise. Careful project planning should make it more likely that the project will be manageable and that the inherent managerial difficulties will be minimal. The project format gives both managers and planners better criteria for monitoring the progress of implementation.

The project format encourages conscious and systematic examination of alternatives. The effects of a proposed project on national income and other objectives can conveniently be compared with the effects of projects in other sectors, of other projects in the same sector, or—very important—of alternative formulations of virtually the same project. One alternative can be the effects of no project at all.

Another advantage of the project format is that it helps contain the data problem. In many developing countries, national data are unavailable or are, to a substantial degree, unreliable. It is true that a project must be seen in a national context, but in many instances the direction that a country's development effort should take is well known, even if precise figures are not available. Most countries know they must increase food production even if they cannot cite reliable figures about total production or recent growth rates. By channeling much of the development effort into projects; the lack of reliable national data can be mitigated. Once the project area or clientele has been determined—once a conceptual boundary has been drawn—local information on which to base the analysis can be efficiently gathered, field trials can be undertaken, and a judgment can be made about social and cultural institutions that might influence the choice of project design and its pace of implementation. Investment can then proceed with confidence.

Because of the advantages of the project format in development planning, I would recommend that its use be extended to as many kinds of investment analysis as possible, even when this stretches the form. For projects of the production type—with clear-cut investments and easily valued costs and benefits, as is so often the case in agriculture—the project format is of course well suited. But many kinds of activities that might otherwise be thought of as programs can also be effectively cast in project form. Rural credit activities and even agricultural education, agricultural extension, and agricultural research can be put in project form to good effect, although the benefits from these kinds of projects may be impossible to value. In these instances, the orientation of the analysis may simply be changed to that of least-cost comparisons, and the other advantages of the project format will continue to be realized. These include systematic contributions to the preparation and review of the project by a wide range of specialists, carefully specified objectives, systematic consideration of alternatives, year-by-year estimates of cost, and the opportunity to examine carefully the organizational and managerial implications.

Limitations of the Project Format

Although the project format has many advantages, the results of project analysis must be interpreted with caution. Obviously, the quality of project analysis depends on the quality of the data used and of the forecasts of costs and benefits made. Here the GIGO principle—"garbage in, garbage out"—works with a vengeance. Unrealistic assumptions about yields, acceptance by farmers, response to incentives by entrepreneurs, the trend of future prices and the relative effect of inflation upon them, market shares, or the quality of project management can make garbage out of the project analysis.

To begin with, projects will exist in a changing technical environment. For some projects the possibility of technological obsolescence will affect judgments about the attractiveness of the investment. Fortunately, in agriculture this is not often a serious problem, although in other sectors it can be.

Because future circumstances will change, we must judge the risk and uncertainty surrounding a project, and here techniques of project analysis offer only limited help. It is impossible to quantify completely the risks of a project. We can, however, note that different kinds of projects or different formulations of essentially the same project may involve different degrees of risk. These differences will affect the choice of project design. We can also test a project for sensitivity to changes in some specific element, see how the benefit produced by the project will be affected, and then judge how likely it is that such changes will occur and whether the changes in benefits will alter our willingness to proceed. We could do such "sensitivity analysis," for example, by assuming that future yields will be less than our best estimate or that future prices will be lower than the level of our most likely projection, and then decide how probable such shortfalls will be and whether we still wish to continue with the project. Sensitivity analyses that simply assume "all costs increased by 10 percent" or "all benefits lowered by 10 percent," which are easy to perform if machine computation is used, are generally of little usefulness; tests for specific changes that can lead to decisions on project design are far superior. Techniques have been developed for more formal analysis of risk, but they have not been widely applied to agricultural projects. They rest on assigning probabilities to a range of alternative assumptions. These techniques are complex and generally require machine computation.

Project analysis is a species of what economists call "partial analysis." Normally we assume that the projects themselves are too small in relation to the whole economy to have a significant effect on prices. In many instances, however, a proposed project is relatively large in relation to a national or regional economy. In this event we must adjust our assumptions about future price levels to take account of the impact of the project itself. At best, such adjustments are approximate and may severely limit the usefulness of the measures of project worth that will be discussed in chapter 9. Much more elaborate analytical procedures than those discussed here must then be called into play—generally some form of a programming model. Such techniques were used by the World Bank to analyze development of the Indus Basin in India and Pakistan, for instance (Lieftinck, Sadove, and Creyke 1968), and have been applied to regional agricultural development programs in Mexico (Norton and Solis 1982) and Brazil (Kutcher and Scandizzo 1981), among other countries. Even in those instances, however, the partiality of the assumptions means that the results must be interpreted with care.

The greater the differences among alternative projects, the more difficult it is to use formal analytical techniques to compare them. Financial and economic analyses of the sort discussed in this book are quite good for comparing such close alternatives as two versions of an irrigation project, or even an irrigation project and a land settlement project. They are relatively good for comparing alternative projects having costs and benefits that can be valued reasonably well—for instance, a project for a food processing plant and another for irrigation. But when we wish to compare projects whose benefits can be valued rather well (such as projects to increase agricultural output, or light manufacturing projects) with projects whose benefits cannot be valued (such as education or rural domestic water supply projects), then the formal techniques can hardly be used to determine the best alternative. In such instances, the allocation between different projects must be done more subjectively and as part of an overall development plan. The usefulness of the project format in these instances is not so much in facilitating comparison between two projects as in ensuring that both projects are planned so that they can be carried out efficiently.

By and large, project analysis is more useful when it is applied to unique investment activities. Ongoing services such as police and fire protection, extension services, export promotion, and even normal education services are probably better treated as part of a program than as individual projects. The project form works best where there is a rather clear investment-return cycle and a rather clear definition of geographical area or clientele.

Another limitation of the project format is an underlying conceptual problem about valuation based on the price system. The relative value of items in a price system depends on the relative weights that individuals participating in the system attach to the satisfaction they can obtain with their incomes. They choose among alternatives, and thus the prices of goods and services balance with the values attached to these goods and services by all who participate in the market. Such a system, however, reflects the distribution of income among its participants; in the end, values trace back to existing income distribution. Project analysis takes as a premise that inequities of income distribution can be corrected by suitable policies implemented over a period of time. If such a premise is not accepted, then the whole basis of the valuation system in project analysis (and of the underlying price system upon which it rests) is called into question.

Although project analysis must consciously be placed in a broader political and social environment, in general the effects of a project on this environment can be assessed only subjectively. Often economists refer to "externalities" or side effects, such as skill creation and the development of managerial abilities, that are by-products of a project. Projects may also be undertaken to further many objectives—such as regional integration, job creation, or improving rural living conditions—beyond economic growth alone. The less subject to valuing these objectives are, the less formal are the project analysis techniques that can be used to compare them, although the project format can still be effectively used to encourage careful planning and efficiency.

Furthermore, projects are not the only development initiatives that governments may undertake. The development process calls for such measures as good price policies, carefully designed tariff policies, and participation in discussions to obtain wider market access, and none of these lends itself easily to being cast in project form.

Projects are planned and implemented in a political environment. This is as it must be, since it is the political process that enables societies to balance many, often conflicting, objectives. But questions inevitably arise about the political overtones of project analysis. Is the "national" interest the same as the "social" interest? In project planning and analysis how do we adequately incorporate such considerations as national integrity, nation building, or national defense? One objective may be to benefit disadvantaged groups or regions, but projects in which these objectives are important may not always be the most remunerative. Political leaders must respond to all sorts of pressures, and the way they weigh various tradeoffs may not lead to the same conclusions a project analyst would reach.

All this is to say that, even though the analytical methods we will discuss can be of great help in identifying which projects will increase national income most rapidly, they will not make the actual decision of project investment. That decision is one on which many, many factors other than quantitative or even purely economic considerations must be brought to bear. A settlement project and a plantation project may have roughly similar economic benefits, but the settlement alternative may be chosen because it promises better income distribution benefits. Or, the analysis may reveal that the plantation project is more profitable and may give an idea of just how much so. Is the social benefit of the lower-paying project worth forgoing the probable future income from the higher-paying project? In the final analysis, any national investment decision must be a political act that embodies the best judgment of those responsible. The function of project analysis is not to replace this judgment. Rather, it is to provide one more tool (a very effective one, we hope) by which judgment can be sharpened and the likelihood of error reduced.

Aspects of Project Preparation and Analysis

To design and analyze effective projects, those responsible must consider many aspects that together determine how remunerative a proposed investment will be. All these aspects are related. Each touches on the others, and a judgment about one aspect affects judgments about all the others. All must be considered and reconsidered at every stage in the project planning and implementation cycle. A major responsibility of the project analyst is to keep questioning all the technical specialists who are contributing to a project plan to ensure that all relevant aspects have been explicitly considered and allowed for. Here we will divide project preparation and analysis into six aspects: technical, institutional-organizational-managerial, social, commercial, financial, and economic. These categories derive from those suggested by Ripman (1964), but alternative groupings would be equally valid for purposes of discussion.

Technical aspects

The technical analysis concerns the project's inputs (supplies) and outputs (production) of real goods and services. It is extremely important, and the project framework must be defined clearly enough to permit the technical analysis to be thorough and precise. The other aspects of project analysis can only proceed in light of the technical analysis, although the technical assumptions of a project plan will most likely need to be revised as the other aspects are examined in detail. Good technical staff are essential for this work; they may be drawn from consulting firms or technical assistance agencies abroad. They will be more effective if they have a good understanding of the various aspects of project analysis, but technical staff, no matter how competent, cannot work effectively if they are not given adequate time or if they do not have the sympathetic cooperation and informed supervision of planning officials.

The technical analysis will examine the possible technical relations in a proposed agricultural project: the soils in the region of the project and their potential for agricultural development; the availability of water, both natural (rainfall, and its distribution) and supplied (the possibilities for developing irrigation, with its associated drainage works); the crop varieties and livestock species suited to the area; the production supplies and their availability; the potential and desirability of mechanization; and pests endemic in the area and the kinds of control that will be needed. On the basis of these and similar considerations, the technical analysis will determine the potential yields in the project area, the coefficients of production, potential cropping patterns, and the possibilities for multiple cropping. The technical analysis will also examine the marketing and storage facilities required for the successful operation of the project, and the processing systems that will be needed.

The technical analysis may identify gaps in information that must be filled either before project planning or in the early stages of implementation (if allowance is made for the project to be modified as more information becomes available). There may need to be soil surveys, groundwater surveys, or collection of hydrological data. More may need to be known about the farmers in the project, their current farming methods, and their social values to ensure realistic choices about technology. Field trials may be needed to verify yields and other information locally.

As the technical analysis proceeds, the project analyst must continue to make sure that the technical work is thorough and appropriate, that the technical estimates and projections relate to realistic conditions, and that farmers using the proposed technology on their own fields can realize the results projected.

Institutional-organizational-managerial aspects

A whole range of issues in project preparation revolves around the overlapping institutional, organizational, and managerial aspects of projects, which clearly have an important effect on project implementation.

One group of questions asks whether the institutional setting of the project is appropriate. The sociocultural patterns and institutions of those the project will serve must be considered. Does the project design take into account the customs and culture of the farmers who will participate? Will the project involve disruption of the ways in which farmers are accustomed to working? If it does, what provisions are made to help them shift to new patterns? What communication systems exist to bring farmers new information and teach them new skills? Changing customary procedures is usually slow. Has enough time been allowed for farmers to accept the new procedures, or is the project plan overly optimistic about rates of acceptance?

To have a chance of being carried out, a project must relate properly to the institutional structure of the country and region. What will be the arrangements for land tenure? What size holding will be encouraged? Does the project incorporate local institutions and use them to further the project? How will the administrative organization of the project relate to existing agencies? Is there to be a separate project authority? What will be its links to the relevant operating ministries? Will the staff be able to work with existing agencies or will there be institutional jealousies? Too often a project's organization simply builds up opposition within other agencies; at the very least, the project analyst must be sure such friction is minimized. He should arrange for all agencies concerned to have an opportunity to comment on the proposed organization of the project and ensure that their views enter in the deliberation to the fullest extent possible.

The organizational proposals should be examined to see that the project is manageable. Is the organization such that lines of authority will be clear? Are authority and responsibility properly linked? Does the organizational design encourage delegation of authority, or do too many people report directly to the project director? Does the proposed organization take proper account of the customs and organizational procedures common in the country and region? Or, alternatively, does it introduce enough change in organizational structure to break out of ineffective traditional organizational forms? Are ample provisions included for managers and government supervisors to obtain up-to-date information on the progress of the project? Is a special monitoring group needed? What about training arrangements? Does the project have sufficient authority to keep its accounts in order and to make disbursements promptly?

Managerial issues are crucial to good project design and implementation. The analyst must examine the ability of available staff to judge whether they can administer such large-scale public sector activities as a complex water project, an extension service, or a credit agency. If such skills are scarce or absent, should this be reflected in a less complex project organization? Perhaps the technical analysis of the project should be consulted and the project design concentrate on fewer or less complex technological innovations. When managerial skills are limited, provision may have to be made for training, especially of middle-level personnel. In some cases expatriate managers may have to be hired, and this may raise other problems, such as the acceptance of the project manager by the local people and the loss of the experience the expatriate manager gained while working on the project when the manager leaves the country. In many instances it would be preferable if possible to design the organization of the project to avoid the need for management services of expatriates.

In agricultural projects the analyst will also want to consider the managerial skills of the farmers who will participate. A project design that assumes new and complex managerial skills on the part of participating farmers has obvious implications for the rate of implementation. If farmers with past experience limited to crop production are to become dairy farmers, enough time must be allotted for them to gain their new skills; the project design cannot assume that they will be able to make the shift overnight. There must be extension agents who can help farmers learn the new skills, and provision must be made for these agents in the organizational design and in the administrative costs of the project.

In considering the managerial and administrative aspects of project design, not only are we concerned that managerial and administrative problems will eventually be overcome, but that a realistic assessment is made of how fast they will be resolved. The contribution an investment makes to creating new income is very sensitive to delays in project implementation.

Social aspects

We have mentioned the need for analysts to consider the social patterns and practices of the clientele a project will serve. More and more frequently, project analysts are also expected to examine carefully the broader social implications of proposed investments. We have noted proposals to include weights for income distribution in the formal analytical framework so that projects benefiting lower-income groups will be favored. In the analytical system outlined in this book, such weights are not incorporated, so it is all the more important in the project design that explicit attention be paid to income distribution.

Other social considerations should also be carefully considered to determine if a proposed project is as responsive to national objectives as it can be. There is a question about creating employment opportunities that is closely linked to, though not quite the same as, the question of income distribution. For social reasons, many governments want to emphasize growth in particular regions and want projects that can be implemented in these regions. The project analyst will want to consider carefully the adverse effects a project may have on particular groups in particular regions. In the past, the introduction of high-yielding seed varieties and fertilizers, coupled with the easy availability of tractors, has led to displacement of tenant farmers and has forced them into the ranks of the urban unemployed. Can the project be designed to minimize such effects, or be accompanied by policy changes that will? Changes in technology or cropping patterns may change the kind of work done by men and women. In some areas the introduction of mechanical equipment or of cash crops has deprived women of work they needed to support their children. Will a proposed project have such an adverse effect on the income of working women and their families?

There are also considerations concerning the quality of life that should be a part of any project design. A rural development project may well include provisions for improved rural health services, for better domestic water supplies, or for increased educational opportunities for rural children. Project analysts will want to consider the contribution of alternative projects or other designs of essentially the same project in furthering these objectives.

Those designing or reviewing projects will also want to consider the issue of adverse environmental impact (Wall 1979; Lee 1982). Irrigation development may reduce fish catches or increase the incidence of schistosomiasis in regions where this snail-transmitted disease is endemic, and waste from industrial plants may pollute water. Project sites may be selected with an eye to preserving notable scenic attractions or to preserving unique wildlife habitats. It is far better to ensure preservation of the environment by appropriate project design than to incur the expense of retrofitting technology or reclaiming land after an environmentally unsound project has been implemented.

Commercial aspects

The commercial aspects of a project include the arrangements for marketing the output produced by the project and the arrangements for the supply of inputs needed to build and operate the project.

On the output side, careful analysis of the proposed market for the project's production is essential to ensure that there will be an effective demand at a remunerative price. Where will the products be sold? Is the market large enough to absorb the new production without affecting the price? If the price is likely to be affected, by how much? Will the project still be financially viable at the new price? What share of the total market will the proposed project supply? Are there suitable facilities for handling the new production? Perhaps provision should be included in the project for processing, or maybe a separate marketing project for processing and distribution is in order (Austin 1981). Is the product for domestic consumption or for export? Does the proposed project produce the grade or quality that the market demands? What financing arrangements will be necessary to market the output, and what special provisions need to be made in the project to finance marketing? Since the product must be sold at market prices, a judgment about future government price supports or subsidies may be in order.

On the input side, appropriate arrangements must be made for farmers to secure the supplies of fertilizers, pesticides, and high-yielding seeds they need to adopt new technology or cropping patterns. Do market channels for inputs exist, and do they have enough capacity to supply new inputs on time? What about financing for the suppliers of inputs and credit for the farmers to purchase these supplies? Should new channels be established by the project or should special arrangements be made to provide marketing channels for new inputs?

Commercial aspects of a project also include arrangements for the procurement of equipment and supplies. Are the procurement procedures such that undue delays can be avoided? Are there procedures for competitive bidding to ensure fair prices? Who will draw up the specifications for procurement?

Finally, there are the two aspects of project analysis that are the primary concerns of this book, the financial and the economic.

Financial aspects

The financial aspects of project preparation and analysis encompass the financial effects of a proposed project on each of its various participants. In agricultural projects the participants include farmers, private sector firms, public corporations, project agencies, and perhaps the national treasury. For each of these, separate budgets must be prepared, along lines suggested in chapters 4 through 6. On the basis of these budgets, judgments are formed about the project's financial efficiency, incentives, creditworthiness, and liquidity.

A major objective of the financial analysis of farms is to judge how much farm families participating in the project will have to live on. The analyst will need budget projections that estimate year by year future gross receipts and expenditures, including the costs associated with production and the credit repayments farm families must make, to determine what remains to compensate the family for its own labor, management skills, and capital. Part of the income the family will receive may be in food that is consumed directly in the household, so a judgment must be made about this quantity and its value. Even if a family realizes a considerable increase in income or "net incremental benefit" by participating in the project—as a result, say, of borrowing to purchase fertilizers to increase rice production—its absolute income may still be so low that nearly all of the incremental production is consumed in the household. Financial analysis must judge whether the family will then have sufficient cash to repay the production credit for fertilizer. If not, the analyst may have to make a policy judgment about how much to subsidize families with very low incomes.

The farm budget becomes the basis for shaping the credit terms to be made available. The analyst must judge whether farmers will need loans to finance on-farm investment (and if so, what proportion the farmers should invest from their own resources) or to meet some production costs, and whether seasonal short-term credit should be provided for working capital to finance inputs and pay for hired labor. In tree-crop projects with long development periods, such as those for oil palm or citrus, the analyst must judge whether farmers will have adequate income to live on during the period before the trees begin to bear, or whether special financing arrangements must be made to sustain them. The objective of all these judgments is to shape credit terms that will be generous enough to encourage farmers to participate in the project, yet be stiff enough that the society as a whole can capture fairly promptly a share of the benefit from the increased production. This benefit can, in turn, be used to hasten growth by relending it to other farmers or by reinvesting it elsewhere in the economy.

The analysis of farm income will also permit assessment of the incentives for farmers to participate in the project. What will be the probable change in farm income? What will be the timing of this change? How likely are price changes or fluctuations that could affect farm income severely enough that farmers will refuse to run the risk of participating in the project? What will be the effect of subsidy arrangements on farm income, and what changes in government policy might affect the income earned by farmers? Will new subsidies be needed to provide sufficient incentive for the project to proceed?

A similar group of considerations applies to the financial analysis of private firms involved in the project. Will they have capital for expanding facilities? Will they have the working capital needed to carry inventories of farm supplies or stocks of processed goods awaiting sale? What return will the firms realize on their capital investment, and is this sufficiently attractive?

An analysis of the financial aspects of the project's administration will also be needed. What investment funds will the project need and when? What will be the operating expenses when the project is under way? Will these expenses depend on budget allocations or will the project produce sufficient revenue to cover its administrative costs? Will changes in government policy be needed to finance the project, such as water charges levied in a new irrigation project? What about salary scales for project personnel? How will replacement of equipment be financed?

Finally, the fiscal impact of some projects will need to be considered. Will the increased output yield significant new tax revenues, perhaps from an export tax? Will new subsidies be needed to encourage farmers to participate, and how much will subsidies have to grow as project implementation proceeds? If the administrative costs of the project are not to be met from revenues, how will this affect the national budget in the future? If the project investment is to be financed by a grant or by borrowing from abroad, while the operation and maintenance cost is to be financed from domestic resources, how will this affect the treasury?

The methodology of discounted cash flow discussed in chapters 9 and 10 shows the way in which this financial analysis customarily is set up and the usual elements included in the cost and benefit streams. The methodology enables an estimate of the return to the equity capital of each of the various project participants, public or private. It is then a policy decision whether to change that return by income taxes, special lending terms, price subsidies, or any of the other tools open to society.

Economic aspects

The economic aspects of project preparation and analysis require a determination of the likelihood that a proposed project will contribute significantly to the development of the total economy and that its contribution will be great enough to justify using the scarce resources it will need. The point of view taken in the economic analysis is that of the society as a whole.

The financial and economic analyses are thus complementary—the financial analysis takes the viewpoint of the individual participants and the economic analysis that of the society. But, because the same discounted cash flow measures (discussed in chapter 9) are applied in the financial analysis to estimate returns to a project participant and in the economic analysis to estimate returns to society, confusion between the two analyses easily arises. There are three very important distinctions between the two that must be kept in mind. These qualifications are summarized here and are taken up in greater detail later.

First, in economic analysis taxes and subsidies are treated as transfer payments. The new income generated by a project includes any taxes the project can bear during production and any sales taxes buyers are willing to pay when they purchase the project's product. These taxes, which are part of the total project benefit, are transferred to the government, which acts on behalf of the society as a whole, and are not treated as costs. Conversely, a government subsidy to the project is a cost to the society, since the subsidy is an expenditure of resources that the economy incurs to operate the project. In financial analysis such adjustments are normally unnecessary; taxes are usually treated as a cost and subsidies as a return.

Second, in financial analysis market prices are normally used. These take into account taxes and subsidies. From these prices come the data used in the economic analysis. In economic analysis, however, some market prices may be changed so that they more accurately reflect social or economic values. These adjusted prices are called "shadow" or "accounting" prices and in the analytical system recommended here are efficiency prices, as noted earlier. In both financial and economic analysis projected prices are used, so both rely to a substantial extent on what are, in effect, hypothetical prices.

Third, in economic analysis interest on capital is never separated and deducted from the gross return because it is part of the total return to the capital available to the society as a whole and because it is that total return, including interest, that economic analysis is designed to estimate. In financial analysis, interest paid to external suppliers of money may be deducted to derive the benefit stream available to the owners of capital. But interest imputed or "paid" to the entity from whose point of view the financial analysis is being done is not treated as a cost because the interest is part of the total return to the equity capital contributed by the entity. Hence, it is a part of the financial return that entity receives.

The methodology of comparing costs and benefits discussed in chapters 9 and 10 is the same for either an economic or a financial measurement of project worth, but what is defined as a cost and what is considered a benefit are different. For the moment, it is enough to recognize that there is a difference between economic and financial analysis; we will discuss the differences in detail later.

Policymakers must be concerned about the investment of scarce capital resources that will best further national objectives. This is true whether the resources committed are being invested by the government directly or by individuals within the economy. The techniques of economic analysis presented here help identify those projects that make the greatest contribution to national income. The economic analysis in general allows for remuneration to labor and other inputs either at market prices or at shadow prices that are intended in the system recommended here to better approximate efficiency prices or "opportunity costs"—the amount we must give up if we transfer a resource from its present use to the project. The remainder is then compared with the capital stream necessary for the project. Those projects with the best return to capital, given the total resources available, are then selected for implementation. Inherent in this approach is the assumption that capital is the most important limit to faster economic growth. What is not implicit in the approach is that capital alone causes economic growth. All the productive factors combined in a project contribute to the new income created, but the methods we will be discussing do not address themselves to the question of what the proportionate contribution of each factor is.

We will apply the methods discussed here in economic (but not financial) analysis in such a way that the economic analysis does not itself address the issue of income distribution. Although the analysis will determine the amount of the income stream generated over and above the costs of labor and other inputs, it does not specify who actually receives it. Part of a project's benefit is usually taken through taxes for purposes outside the project. Part is generally made available to compensate capital owners (including governments) for the use of their money. Part may become the basis of an indirect transfer of income, as is the case if farmers benefiting from a land settlement project are charged less than the full cost of establishing their holdings. The economic analysis applied in this book is silent about such distribution. Once the analyst knows what the more economically remunerative alternatives are likely to be, however, he can choose those that have better effects on income distribution or other social objectives. Although the formal economic analysis will not decide issues of income distribution, the final decision on project investment will be an informed one that is then made in accord with views about income distribution.

Many economists prefer analytical systems that explicitly include income distribution weights. They note that the system outlined here accepts in its formal structure the income distribution as it exists in a society and does not distinguish projects that have the most desirable effects on income distribution. They argue that simply choosing projects subjectively from among the higher-yielding alternatives is not enough. Systems using income distribution weights are used infrequently, however, and most project investment decisions follow the general practice recommended here. Even economists who prefer using income distribution weights often recommend applying them only to that small fraction of projects in which there is reason to believe the weights might change an investment decision. Readers wishing to consult a fuller treatment of income distribution weights in project analysis may turn to Little and Mirrlees (1974) and Squire and van der Tak (1975).

Because economic analysis of a project as applied here tells us nothing about income distribution, it also tells us nothing about capital ownership. The value of a capital asset arises from the right to receive the future income the asset generates. Since our method of economic analysis does not specify who in the economy is to receive the income that a project earns, it does not address the question of who owns the capital. Economic measures of project worth reached by means of the analytical system outlined here help determine the most attractive alternative from the society's standpoint when the objective of the analysis is to increase national income. In this analytical frame, projects are equally valid whether the capital is to come from public revenue or private sources, whether there are income taxes or not, and whether the project is to be operated by public agencies or by individuals on their own behalf. In a manner analogous to the approach taken for income distribution, governments may then choose from economically remunerative projects those that lead to higher reinvestment and, hence, faster growth.

Some economists, however, take economic growth generated by investment, not income regardless of whether it is consumed or invested, as contituting at least part of their formal objective. If that is the case, then the source of the capital for a project makes a difference, as does who receives the benefits. A project financed by private sources that will consume all of the benefits will be less economically valuable than one in which all benefits accrue to a private individual who reinvests everything. Also, both will have values different from that of an identical project in which the benefit accrues to the government. As with income distribution weights, systems that weight capital sources or the investment use of benefits become quite complex. Again, the reader may refer to Little and Mirrlees (1974) and Squire and van der Tak (1975).

The Project Cycle

There tends to be a natural sequence in the way projects are planned and carried out, and this sequence is often called the "project cycle." As was the case with aspects of project analysis, there are many ways—all equally valid—in which this cycle may be divided. Here we will divide it into identification, preparation and analysis, appraisal, implementation, and evaluation. The sequence is adapted from an article by Baum (1978).

Identification

The first stage in the cycle is to find potential projects. There are many, many sources from which suggestions may come. The most common will be well-informed technical specialists and local leaders. While performing their professional duties, technical specialists will have identified many areas where they feel new investment might be profitable. Local leaders will generally have a number of suggestions about where investment might be carried out. Ideas for new projects also come from proposals to extend existing programs. A program to develop water resources will probably lead to suggestions of additional areas for irrigation. An existing land settlement program will probably generate suggestions of new areas for settlement.

Suggestions for new projects usually arise because some agricultural products are in short supply—or will be in a few years if production is not expanded or imports increased. The analysis may be based on general knowledge or upon a more systematic examination of market trends and import statistics. In addition, many countries have development banks intended to encourage growth of domestic industry. Often local firms will come to these banks with food processing proposals for which they are seeking finance.

Such project-by-project approaches may overlook important potential initiatives in agricultural development. Most developing countries have an economic development plan of some formality that identifies sectors to be given priority and areas where investment is needed. These generalized areas for priority are too vague to become the basis of investment themselves, but they lead to specific projects in crop or livestock production, land settlement, irrigation, food processing, expansion of export crop production, and the like. In the process of preparing an economic development plan, specific suggestions for projects usually will have come from the operating agencies responsible for project implementation, and these agencies may be encouraged to proceed with detailed project preparation.

Frequently, a separate sector survey of the current situation in agriculture will indicate what initiatives are needed. Such surveys may be undertaken with the help of an international agency or some agency for bilateral assistance. The sector survey will examine the current status of agriculture, project future needs for agricultural products over the next decade or so, and consider programs to improve the quality of rural life. It will examine prospects for expanding agricultural exports by considering potential increases in production and the outlook for marketing possibilities, and it will identify the gaps in existing plans and programs. The survey will probably generate suggestions about new areas for investment and the relative priority to be given different initiatives. It may even identify specific projects, especially larger ones, that merit consideration for future investment.

Occasionally one hears that there is a lack of projects available for investment in developing countries. Usually there is no shortage of proposals for projects that have been identified. But there may be a shortage of projects prepared in sufficient detail to permit implementation.

Preparation and analysis

Once projects have been identified, there begins a process of progressively more detailed preparation and analysis of project plans. This process includes all the work necessary to bring the project to the point at which a careful review or appraisal can be undertaken, and, if it is determined to be a good project, implementation can begin. In the preparation and analysis of projects, consideration will be given to each of the aspects discussed earlier.

The usual first step in project preparation and analysis is to undertake a feasibility study that will provide enough information for deciding whether to begin more advanced planning. The detail of the feasibility study will depend on the complexity of the project and on how much is already known about the proposal. Quite often a succession of increasingly detailed feasibility studies will be needed. The feasibility study should define the objectives of the project clearly. It should explicitly address the question of whether alternative ways to achieve the same objectives may be preferable, and it will enable project planners to exclude poor alternatives. The feasibility study will provide the opportunity to shape the project to fit its physical and social environment and to ensure that it will be high yielding.

Even at this early stage, the kind of financial and economic analyses discussed in this book should be brought into play. As projects are planned in greater and greater detail, the investment of time and money becomes more and more substantial, and the expectations of vested interests continue to grow. Being faced only at a late stage in the planning process with the decision to accept or reject a project on financial or economic grounds is obviously an uncomfortable position to be in. Far better that the financial and economic analyses enter early in the planning process, so that the feasibility studies introduce these aspects in the project plan.

The staff needed to work on feasibility studies will depend on how complex the studies are. To start, a single staff member may make a preliminary estimate in a relatively short time. Later the services of a small team, or perhaps outside consultants, may be engaged.

Once the feasibility studies have indicated which proposed project will likely be worthwhile, detailed planning and analysis may begin. By this time the less promising alternatives will have been eliminated, but even at this point the selected project will continue to be redefined and shaped as more and more becomes known. This is the stage at which detailed studies will commence—the carefully done soil surveys, the detailed hydrological analyses, the thorough examination of cropping patterns, the month-by-month estimates of labor requirements, the detailed farm budgets, and so forth. Again, all the aspects of analysis noted in the last section must be considered and correlated so that realistic estimates can be made of how the project might be implemented and of its likely income-generating capacity.

Detailed planning takes time, often a year or two or longer for complex agricultural projects. It may also be quite expensive. In agriculture, preparing the detailed project plan may well cost 7 to 10 percent of the total project investment. Yet thorough preparation increases a project's efficiency and helps ensure its smooth implementation in the future, so that the additional time and money required will probably be returned many times over by the increased return from the investment. Hastily prepared, superficial analyses will very likely yield projects that fall behind schedule, have lower returns, and waste scarce resources.

Preparation of the plan should itself be planned so that delays can be avoided and resources conserved. The timing of special studies needs to be considered, and the services of outside consultants should be scheduled so they will be available when needed—but not before the consultants' specialized knowledge can be used. The project may be prepared by a special team assembled for the purpose and given sufficient time and resources, or it may be prepared by a consulting firm or a technical assistance agency such as the Investment Centre of the Food and Agriculture Organization (FAO).

Appraisal

After a project has been prepared, it is generally appropriate for a critical review or an independent appraisal to be conducted. This provides an opportunity to reexamine every aspect of the project plan to assess whether the proposal is appropriate and sound before large sums are committed. The appraisal process builds on the project plan, but it may involve new information if the specialists on the appraisal team feel that some of the data are questionable or some of the assumptions faulty. If the appraisal team concludes that the project plan is sound, the investment may proceed. But if the appraisal team finds serious flaws, it may be necessary for the analyst to alter the project plan or to develop a new plan altogether.

If a project is to be financed by an international lending institution such as the World Bank or by a bilateral assistance agency, such an external lender will probably want a rather careful appraisal even if it has been closely associated with earlier steps in the project cycle. The World Bank, for example, routinely sends a separate mission to appraise proposed projects for which one of its member governments intends to borrow.

Implementation

The objective of any effort in project planning and analysis clearly is to have a project that can be implemented to the benefit of the society. Thus, implementation is perhaps the most important part of the project cycle. It is also clear, however, that considerations of implementation and project management are far too extensive for discussion here. Yet there are some aspects of implementation that are of particular relevance to project planning and analysis. The first, obviously, is that the better and more realistic a project plan is, the more likely it is that the plan can be carried out and the expected benefit realized. This emphasizes once again the need for careful attention to each aspect of project planning and analysis.

Second, project implementation must be flexible. Circumstances will change, and project managers must be able to respond intelligently to these changes. Technical changes are almost inevitable as the project progresses and more is known about soils, their response to nitrogen applications, susceptibility to waterlogging, and the like. Price changes may necessitate different cropping patterns or adjustments in inputs. Other changes in the project's economic or political environment will alter the way in which it should be implemented. The greater the uncertainty of various aspects of the project, or the more innovative and novel the project is, the greater the likelihood that changes will have to be made. Even as project implementation is under way, project managers will need to reshape and replan parts of the project, or perhaps the entire project. All of the general considerations we have discussed, as well as the analytical tools we will take up in detail in the following chapters, must be brought into play once again. Implementation is a process of refinement, of learning from experience—in effect, it is a kind of "mini-cycle" within the larger project cycle we have outlined.

Project analysts generally divide the implementation phase into three different time periods. The first is the investment period, when the major project investments are undertaken. In agricultural projects this usually extends three to five years from the start of the project. If the project is to be financed with the assistance of a loan from an external financing agency, the investment period may coincide with the agency's period for loan disbursements. Then, as its production builds up, the project is spoken of as being in the development period. This often takes an additional three to five years, but it may be extended if the project involves cattle herds, tree crops, or other investments with long gestation. The duration of the development period reflects not only physical factors but also the rate of adoption at which farmers take up new techniques. Once full development is reached, it continues for the life of the project. Usually the project life is keyed to the normal life of the major asset, although for practical reasons a project life rarely exceeds twenty-five to thirty years. Both the financial and economic analyses of the project relate to this time horizon.

Evaluation

The final phase in the project cycle is evaluation. The analyst looks systematically at the elements of success and failure in the project experience to learn how better to plan for the future. Evaluation is not limited only to completed projects. It is a most important managerial tool in ongoing projects, and rather formalized evaluation may take place at several times in the life of a project. Evaluation may be undertaken when the project is in trouble, as the first step in a replanning effort. It may be appropriate when a major capital investment such as a dam is in place and operating, even though the full implementation of the plan to utilize the water and power is still under way. Careful evaluation should precede any effort to plan follow-up projects. And, finally, evaluation should be undertaken when a project is terminated or is well into routine operation.

Evaluation may be done by many different people. Project management will be continuously evaluating its experience as implementation proceeds. The sponsoring agency—perhaps the operating ministry, the planning agency, or an external assistance agency—may undertake evaluation. In large and innovative projects, the project's administrative structure may provide a separate evaluation unit responsible for monitoring the project's implementation and for bringing problems to the attention of the project's management. Often the evaluation unit will include persons with planning skills who enable the unit to take part in any necessary replanning. The evaluation unit may also be responsible for planning follow-up projects.

In many instances, the project's management or the sponsoring agency will want to turn to outside evaluators. University staff may be well suited to undertake the task. Whoever does the evaluation will want to read the relevant documents carefully and then have extensive conversations with those who have had a part in the project—planners, project managers, operating staff, farmers participating in the project, or local people affected by the project.

The extent to which the objectives of a project are being realized provides the primary criterion for an evaluation. The objectives cannot be accepted uncritically, however; the inquiry should consider whether the objectives themselves were appropriate and suitable. The evaluators will want to know if these goals were made clear to the planners and to project management.

The project plan should be reviewed to see if it was an appropriate one in light of the objectives set forth. Each objective should be examined to determine whether it was considered carefully and whether appropriate provision for it was made in the project plan. Was the technology proposed appropriate? Were the institutional, organizational, and managerial arrangements suited to the conditions? Were the commercial aspects properly considered? Were the financial aspects carefully worked out on the basis of realistic assumptions, and were the economic implications properly explored? How did the project in practice compare with each aspect of the project analysis?

The evaluation should consider the response of project management and the sponsoring agencies to changing circumstances. Did management respond quickly enough to changes? Was its response carefully considered and appropriate? Did the institutional and organizational structure in the project permit a flexible response? How could the project's structure be altered to make the response to change more flexible and appropriate in the future?

From the evaluation should come carefully considered recommendations about how to improve the appropriateness of each aspect of the project design so that plans for project implementation can be revised if the project is ongoing and so that future projects can be better planned if the project evaluated has been completed.

Accuracy of Agricultural Project Analyses

Since agricultural project analyses are intended to become the basis for investment decisions, just how accurately do they foretell project results?

The World Bank systematically reviews the performance of projects for which it lends and publishes the results annually. These reviews generally are undertaken at the end of the implementation phase of the project. The most recent report, from which this section draws extensively, reviewed thirty-two agricultural projects for which performance audits were completed in 1980 (World Bank 1981a). Although the particular projects reviewed by no means constitute a random sample, the results of the review confirm earlier trends and may be taken as generally indicative of all agricultural projects the World Bank finances. The projects included those for credit, irrigation, tree crops, fisheries, food crop production, livestock, storage, drought relief, and technical assistance.

Economic effects

Economic rates of return had been calculated at the time of appraisal for twenty-four of the projects included in the 1981 review and were reestimated at the time of the performance audit. (The other eight projects were either canceled before implementation or were of a nature—such as drought relief—that no rate of return was calculated.) The reestimates, of course, were done at the end of the implementation phase and so still included projections for the balance of the project life. Fourteen had rates of return that were within 2 percent of the rate estimated at appraisal or were greater than the appraisal estimate, and ten fell more than 2 percent below the rate of return estimated at appraisal. Of the twenty-four projects, nineteen had reestimated rates of return at the time of the review at or above 10 percent, a minimum acceptable rate in most developing countries. The rates of return alone, however, can be somewhat misleading. Several projects varied substantially from what was anticipated at the time of appraisal, but the variations were offsetting. One project that had an acceptable rate of return when reestimated at the time of the performance audit, for example, increased food grain output only about half as much as anticipated, but increases in grain prices offset the production shortfall and gave the project an acceptable rate of return.

For all projects taken together, the weighted reestimated return was 20 percent, well in line with the estimates of earlier years. Credit projects performed the best. They had an average rate of return of 26 percent, the lowest cost overruns and lower than average time overruns, and a clear advantage in reaching poor farmers. The largest subgroup, irrigation projects, had an average rate of return of 22 percent. In line with the results of previous surveys, "decentralized, small-scale groundwater and lift irrigation projects where each farmer develops his own potential were relatively smoothly implemented, resulted in lower costs per hectare, and proved extremely profitable. On the other hand, larger, centralized projects supported by detailed studies and designs and implemented by specialized agencies were beset with problems, were completed late and at much higher costs, resulted in high costs per hectare developed, and proved modestly profitable" (World Bank 1980, p. 29). The tree-crop projects had reestimated returns of 17 percent, substantially in line with the consistently good performance noted for this kind of project in earlier years. In the five projects that had unacceptable rates of return, the failure could generally be traced to a combination of inappropriate technology and poor management.

Effect on incomes of rural poor

The World Bank has been particularly pleased that performance reviews of the projects it finances demonstrate that agricultural projects focusing on small farmers and the rural poor perform as well as other projects in the sector. The 1980 review showed that rural development projects—those specifically designed to reach large numbers of small farmers and the rural poor—had an average return of 17 percent compared with the average of 20 percent for all other kinds of agricultural projects. "They have also reached ten times as many farmers per project, at a fraction of the cost of serving medium and larger farmers. Although the absolute amount of the income increases obtained through small farmer projects were a fraction of those received by medium and larger farmers, they were larger in relative terms . . ." Because they were received by so many farmers, "they had a substantial impact on income distribution" (World Bank 1980, p. 18).

Implementation experience

Of the thirty-two projects reviewed in 1981, only five were completed without delay or with delays of 10 percent or less. (This is much below the experience reported in earlier years, when about a third of the projects were completed on time.) Of the twenty-seven projects experiencing serious delays, fourteen were completed within 50 percent more time, six were completed in from 50 to 100 percent more time, and seven took more than twice as long to complete as scheduled at appraisal.

The experience of cost increases paralleled that of time delays. The average cost increase was 29 percent. Of the thirty-two projects, only twelve were completed with cost increases of 10 percent or less, five were within the range of 10 to 59 percent cost overrun, six were in the range of 50 to 100 percent overrun, and five cost twice or more the appraisal estimate.

The major reason for delay, which affected eight projects, was poor performance by executing agencies or contractors. The second most common cause, which affected six projects, was delay caused by bidding and procurement procedures. The third most common cause was delay due to unanticipated technical problems. As had been the experience in earlier reviews, the most common reasons for cost increases were general price inflation and underestimation of unit costs at appraisal, but other reasons included increases in the scope of a project and in the total number of input units required. Delays in project implementation aggravated the effects of inflation.

Among subsector averages for timing of completion, tree-crop projects on the whole were completed on time or with very little delay, followed by credit projects, with an average time overrun of 31 percent, and livestock and irrigation projects, with an average delay of about 50 percent. The most serious delays were encountered in emergency rehabilitation projects, which took about twice as long as anticipated, and in technical assistance projects, which took 78 percent longer on the average than planned. No regional concentration of implementation delays was apparent.

The incidence of cost increases by subsector showed that the largest increases were in irrigation projects, which had an average cost overrun of 71 percent, an experience in line with that of earlier reviews. Time and cost overruns were thus both substantial in irrigation. Agricultural credit, area development, emergency relief and rehabilitation, and technical assistance projects were completed without, or with minor, cost increases; livestock projects had moderate increases; and tree-crop projects had substantial cost increases, on average 57 percent.

Of the thirty-two projects reviewed, twenty-seven were changed, formally or informally, during implementation. The most important causes were poor or incomplete original design, which affected fifteen cases; changes in government policies and strategies, which affected eleven cases; beneficiary preferences different from those anticipated, which affected seven cases; and impending cost overruns, which affected seven cases. Most projects were affected by a combination of these factors.

Shortcomings in design appear to have been a result of projects' being approved without sufficient preparation. Not all project changes during implementation, however, are undesirable or avoidable. Some projects are designed to be of a pilot nature, and in other projects changes in the price environment lead logically to changes in the mix of products. As the review noted, "project design should be sufficiently well developed to allow for immediate and straightforward project implementation but flexible enough to allow for adaptation without causing undue delay, wasted expenditures, or cost increases, all of which might reduce" the benefit of a project (World Bank 1981*a*, p. 34).

Why Agricultural Project Analyses Prove Wrong

When an agricultural project analysis proves to be a poor predictor of the actual outcome of a project, it may be that the project design or implementation is at fault, or it may be that the project analyst has done a poor job of incorporating a good project design in an analytical framework.

Problems of project design and implementation

The same World Bank performance audits used in the previous section to judge the accuracy of agricultural project analyses in estimating economic returns also examine the reasons for poor performance (World Bank 1980 and 1981*a*). In the most recent of these reviews and in an earlier summary of project experience prepared by Olivares (1978), the most common reasons agricultural projects run into problems of implementation may be grouped into five major categories: (1) inappropriate technology; (2) inadequate support systems and infrastructure; (3) failure to appreciate the social environment; (4) administrative problems, including those of the project itself and of the overall administration within the country; and (5) the policy environment, of which the most important aspect is producer price policy.

INAPPROPRIATE TECHNOLOGY. Given the use and availability of land in most developing countries, increased crop production generally must depend on greater crop yields rather than on area extension. Thus, improved technology is a key element in most agricultural projects. Among the thirty-two projects in the 1981 review, as many as twenty-two depended on technological packages substantially new to the farmers in the project area. The introduction of new technology was concentrated in irrigation, tree-crop, rural development, and fisheries projects.

New technologies included a range of innovations. For irrigation projects, a farm input package with water as the main input was followed by improved seeds and further complemented by fertilizers and sometimes other inputs and improved cultural practices. For tree-crop projects, innovations took the form of improved cultural practices and equipment, early-maturing and high-yielding hybrids, and chemical instead of manual weed control. Rural development projects introduced farm input packages similar to those for irrigation; livestock projects emphasized pasture improvement; fisheries projects introduced improved fishing techniques and boats and equipment; and the storage project provided for modernized grain storage, pest control, and transport.

In fifteen of the projects reviewed, information was available about the effect of the technological innovation. In general, new technology was successful; eleven projects achieved or surpassed target yields. The major success factors appear to have been the appropriateness of the technology proposed for the given local conditions, the complementarity of recommended inputs, and the strength of the support systems (including research and extension to adapt the offered technologies to suit changing circumstances; see the section on infrastructure and support systems, below). In other projects, poor performance could be traced to inappropriate technology. In one project that failed to achieve the target yield, the failure of small farmers to apply more fertilizer was attributed to their desire to minimize risk by maximizing the return on a given investment rather than the return per hectare. In another project, farmers were ready to apply selected low-risk, productivity-raising inputs but not the entire package of recommended cultivation techniques. High density and early sowing, in particular, were largely rejected. Farmers preferred to avoid risk by staggering sowing dates and planting a larger number of low-density plots. The review concluded that "new technologies for dry farming should be more risk-reducing than those for irrigated farming where assured water supply eliminates much of the usual risk" (World Bank 1981*a*, p. 26).

INFRASTRUCTURE AND SUPPORT SYSTEMS. Of the thirty-two projects reviewed in 1981, twenty-eight could be viewed as part of an essential chain of support systems and infrastructure. The links in the chain include the relevant research, extension services, credit availability, input supply, and product markets; the importance of the chain lies in the introduction of technical packages, an essential element in most agricultural projects. These packages must first be developed and tested through research, adapted to the ecological conditions found in the project, and then delivered to the farmers through an adequately staffed, qualified, and motivated extension service that can then provide feedback for further research. In most cases, farmers do not have sufficient funds to purchase the recommended packages, and credit has to be made available. The input supply has to be organized, and this includes introduction of improved high-yielding varieties, provision of better livestock breeds, and the strategic location of stores where fertilizers, pesticides, and machinery such as pumps and their spare parts are available. Finally, the marketing of farm produce has to be organized in a manner that provides sufficient incentives to producers and avoids costly losses.

As may be expected, the content and detail of the support systems and infrastructure vary widely from project to project. In the projects reviewed, marketing systems received the most frequent attention (twenty out of twenty-eight projects), research support was given significant emphasis (seventeen projects), and credit and extension support received equal treatment (about one-half of the twenty-eight projects). Input supply systems received the least attention (one-third of the projects).

Deficiencies in the back-up research component were noted at appraisal in eight projects; in all cases a research component was included in the project, or arrangements were made for supporting research to be undertaken by an appropriate research group. In six of the eight projects, the research arrangements proved effective. In two cases, the projects suffered from lack of specific research, although both of these had included a research component in the original project design.

A major problem in agricultural and rural development projects is organizing farmers efficiently to provide them services, especially in their adapting new technology. The appropriate organization of farmers into self-help schemes is especially difficult, and the record of cooperatives has not been good. There are no easy solutions to these problems. A critical factor is to recognize at the project design stage that the small farmer will not take risks that could involve losing his livelihood and that some form of organizing farmers into self-help groups is essential to economical provision of government service.

Extension services were to be provided by the project unit in nine projects included in the 1981 review; in all but one of these the national extension service was judged to be inadequate. In general, these extension efforts were effective, but in two projects the extension effort failed to reach a minimum level of performance. In one project centered on grain production, output increased by only half the amount projected at appraisal. In the other, poor administration, including a failure to provide adequate extension, combined with poor design and unfavorable government policies to produce a negative return.

Credit was the major instrument for development in thirteen of the twenty-eight projects. It was used to promote a technical package in eight projects and other investment expenditures in the remaining five. The balance of the projects, with one exception, were clearly judged not to require credit.

Only a single input was supplied through the project in a number of cases, the full complement being provided in others. For the most part, inputs were supplied by the project units in estate projects where production was under full control of the project unit, or where small growers received credit in kind and were expected to follow specified production practices. In other projects that had an input supply component, the private sector met the needs.

Lack of marketing facilities is among the most difficult factors to provide for or change through projects directed mainly toward production. The principal marketing component in the projects was for the project unit to purchase the output of small producers. One project provided credit to market centers and cooperatives so that they could in turn provide advances to farmers for production and living expenses. One fisheries project provided cold storage facilities to improve marketing. Of the twenty-eight projects where infrastructure and support systems were central, only two were judged at audit to have been affected by lack of marketing facilities.

FAILURE TO APPRECIATE THE SOCIAL ENVIRONMENT. Sometimes the technical aspects of a project may be fairly well foreseen, but the social effects inadequately assessed. In one West African rice intensification project, progress was initially much slower than anticipated. A study revealed that in this area rice was produced by women, but that the credit needed for new inputs was channeled through institutions of which only men were members—and the men were not about to borrow for a woman's crop. When the national credit agency set up credit channels that could lend directly to women, implementation accelerated markedly.

In another African project, in an area of traditional extended family groupings a limit was established on individual loans for crop intensification. As a result, instead of the head of the family, who was responsible for allocating land to be cultivated, being able to borrow on behalf of the whole family, individual cultivators had to seek credit. Borrowing directly for production on their own account gave the cultivators a new, independent income. The impact of this change—whether good or bad—on the social structure of the area was not even considered by the analyst when the project was formulated (Olivares 1978).

ADMINISTRATIVE PROBLEMS. The experience of the projects reported in the 1981 review reinforced conclusions about administrative structures reached in earlier reviews. Among the projects in the 1981 review, the performance level was high in ten of the twenty-two completed projects in which special efforts had been made to strengthen administrative and technical capabilities; partial success was achieved in another six; and the results were negligible in four. In line with the experience of previous years, there was frequently a close association between institutional and project performance. On the one hand, the three worst performers included in the 1981 review—all with negative rates of return—shared a pattern of weak management that was not corrected as implementation proceeded. On the other hand, nine of the best-performing projects reviewed in 1981 were implemented by agencies that were noted for good administration or that made special efforts to improve their administrative effectiveness during the implementation period. In at least one instance, an effort to improve the effectiveness of implementation paid dividends by enabling the agency to overcome initial administrative and design difficulties.

Past project performance reviews have led to the conclusion that "specially created project implementation units [have] an isolated and precarious existence, usually [run] into difficulties, and should, as far as possible, be avoided as a temporary device to by-pass institutional weaknesses and to insulate . . . projects from the larger institutional environment" (World Bank 1981a, p. 27).

Staffing is a major problem in almost all development projects. Difficulties can be institutional—for example, restrictive governmental salary policies, civil service procedures, and promotion regulations—or can take the form of shortages of certain kinds of skilled people. One solution is often the use of consultants. Yet there frequently are difficulties between local project personnel and external consultants. Other common personnel problems include incompetent staff, ineffective training, high turnover, and poor matching of specific individuals with specific jobs.

Seven of the projects in the 1981 review made use of coordinating committees as an institutional instrument. As had been the case in earlier reviews, the experience was less than satisfactory. On the basis of this experience, the review concluded that "(1) high-level coordinating committees are generally not effective; (2) if formal coordination is needed, it should be established at the required technical or administrative level; and (3) a project unit within an existing organization may usefully undertake coordinating administrative functions" (World Bank 1981a, p. 28).

Delays in procurement will result in shortages of material, especially of foreign equipment. Sometimes delay is due to inadequate foresight and forward planning and sometimes (particularly in rural development projects) to unfamiliarity with procurement practices. The importance of timely procurement must be emphasized from the first stages of the project cycle and should be prominently included in the detailed implementation schedules.

Government administrative and managerial practices are at least as important to project implementation as the skills of project managers. If the central or local administrative processes are inadequate, the projects will encounter delays and, almost always, consequent cost increases. Common problems include slow and cumbersome decisionmaking, poor systems to authorize disbursement of project funds, ill-defined organizational arrangements, inadequate coordination among different agencies involved with a project, and, sometimes, government structures that deny appropriate authority to the project manager.

POLICY ENVIRONMENT. Every project must be implemented within a framework of policies set by the government. If these are such that farmers' incentives are destroyed or other serious impediments are put in the way of project implementation, then the project cannot be expected to achieve satisfactory results.

The overriding importance of producer prices in affecting producer income, production levels, and economic efficiency was confirmed in the 1981 review. Prices contributed to expansion of production by encouraging farmers to participate in the project, to expand areas devoted to the project crops, and to use more inputs and thereby increase yields. The 1981 review analyzed project performance in relation to prices in eighteen projects. Eleven out of thirteen projects implemented under favorable prices achieved or surpassed their production objectives; all five under unfavorable prices failed to do so. Projects implemented under favorable prices offered an average rate of return at reestimate of 22 percent, whereas those under unfavorable prices averaged 10 percent.

The issue of producer prices was developed in more detail in the 1980 review (World Bank 1980). Producer price information was available from twenty-seven projects. Of those in which producer prices were judged unfavorable, 33 percent reflected low world market prices about which the individual country could do little, 25 percent had producer prices much below world market levels because of government decisions about price policy, and in the remaining 42 percent there was no direct link between the producer prices and the world market.

Depressed world market prices for dairy produce affected one agricultural credit project in a North African country. Local milk production had to compete with reconstituted milk, which was imported at very low prices. This hampered the dairy farm component of the project because farmers were unwilling to invest in uncompetitive dairy enterprises. In a large irrigation project in Latin America, about 70 percent of the cropped project area was originally planted with cotton when the project began operation in 1967 because farmers were encouraged by very high prices and readily available credit. As international prices declined, the area planted in cotton dropped to 40,000 hectares in 1973 and climbed back to 62,000 hectares in 1978 when the prices recovered again, but the area remained substantially below the 100,000 hectares projected at appraisal.

Government policy to tax farmers producing groundnuts and cotton kept the producer prices much below world market levels in two projects in one East African country, and the area under these crops fell 40 to 50 percent short of appraisal estimates. Another example comes from a tobacco project in another country in the same region. Producer prices for tobacco in the country increased 26 percent during the 1972–78 period, while world market prices went up 75 percent and the price of maize, a competing crop, by 226 percent. Government policies to tax export crops and equalize average returns on labor for all crops caused the farmer's share in the selling price of processed tobacco to decline from 66 percent in 1965–66 to 37 percent in 1977–78. As a result, tobacco production stagnated, and the project itself became economically viable only because farmers switched to higher-valued maize production.

Other projects suffering from low producer prices not directly linked to world market prices included: a commercial farming project in a third East African country in which poor handling of tobacco resulted in low quality and low prices; a project with a vegetable component in West Africa in which the project authority limited tomato production by paying low prices to farmers; and a Central American livestock project in which the freezing of milk prices caused most of the specialized dairy farms around the capital city to close down permanently.

In contrast, profitable producer prices—prevalent in only about 30 percent of the projects included in the 1980 review—had strong positive effects. In one livestock project, for instance, milk production after four years was already 50 percent of the target for full development after eight years, mainly because of the government's pricing policy for milk relative to beef. A West African cotton project similarly benefited from higher-than-expected world cotton prices. Although production targets were not met, farm income objectives were achieved, and cotton export earnings and targets for economic return were exceeded.

Such experiences, repeated over and over, emphasize the importance of taking price policies into account as a factor when designing and implementing agricultural projects.

Problems of poor project analysis

When a project analysis has failed to anticipate the outcome of a project investment, a common reason appears to have been simply poor preparation of the analysis. A number of such cases were analyzed in a review prepared by Olivares (1978), from which this section draws heavily.

Underestimated costs were common, either as a result of the analyst's being systematically optimistic about cost or making an especially poor estimate about the cost of particular components. Sometimes a component necessary for proper functioning of the project or an activity critical to the project was omitted from the cost estimates, even though in the same analysis it was noted that it would be essential to proper execution of the project. In the projects reviewed, components commonly omitted from the cost estimates (although not necessarily from the project and closely associated activities planned by the technicians) included agricultural extension to help farmers adopt new practices, training programs for project technicians, agronomic and livestock trials, complementary infrastructure such as roads or market facilities, and the expansion of the credit availability critical to the farmers' ability to adopt new techniques based on purchased inputs.

Excessively optimistic projections frequently were made during project preparation. In the projects reviewed, overestimates were common in projecting areas to be brought under cultivation, yields, rates of increase in livestock herds, and total production in the project area. The most common of these overestimates proved to be in cultivation intensity in irrigation projects and in the calving rate in cattle production projects. Project analyses frequently were too optimistic about the rate at which new cultivation practices would be adopted with irrigation, about the rate at which new areas would be brought under methods of improved cultivation, and about the rate at which the new technology could be applied under farm conditions.

When analyses of crop or livestock projects in rainfed areas did not predict the outcome well, the reason was often a failure to consider explicitly the variability of the climate and thus to overestimate returns. The analysis for one project undertaken in the Sahel region of Africa made no allowance for the variability of the climate, although the same analysis noted the likelihood of one or two dry years about once every five to seven years. The drought of 1973–75 paralyzed the project and forced planners to reevaluate and completely redesign the project. One livestock project in a Mediterranean country assumed that the weather during the project life would be "normal," despite the fact that in this region almost no year approaches this statistical computation. Nearly every particular year in the region is either too dry or too rainy, with the rains coming either too early or too late, and so forth. Naturally, making no allowance for this variability led to an overestimate of the project's yield and its attractiveness to the farmers involved.

Project evaluations commonly assumed too optimistic a calendar for project implementation. The analyses often did not test the effect on the project return of delays in getting the project under way—almost a normal situation in agricultural projects in general—or of delays in project execution at a later stage.

The return from investment in the agricultural projects examined was found to have been overestimated sometimes because the analysis failed to account for an adverse effect of the investment on production, either in the project area or elsewhere. In one project in Latin America, the main canals were lined to prevent water loss and to increase water delivery to the field. The analyst failed, however, to account for the irrigation of adjacent areas by wells recharged by seepage from the canals. The reduced output from these adjacent areas once the project was under way was not deducted from the benefits in the analysis. Of course, this led to an overestimate of the benefit from the irrigation project. Several irrigation projects in Asia were found to have reduced the spawning grounds of commercially important fish. The result was that much of the benefit from expanded irrigation was offset by a fall in fish production and reduced income for thousands of fishermen.

Project analysts often made errors when translating technical assumptions into projections of project performance. In one project it was assumed that 80 percent of the projected increase in area to be cultivated using more intensive technology would be reached in the first year, with the remaining 20 percent realized over the succeeding four years. In another project, expansion of the irrigated area was assumed to take place before the basic irrigation construction was to have been completed. In yet another case, the analyst assumed that fruit trees would reach full production the year they were planted. Such obvious errors could have been avoided just by cross-checking with the technical specialists as the analysis proceeded.

Steps in Project Analysis

Preparing a project analysis is anything but a neat, continuous process with well-defined steps, each of which is completed before the next and never retraced. Instead, the whole process is iterative; that is, the analyst must continuously go back and adjust earlier decisions in the light of what is learned from later analysis. In general, the process begins with an idea about the broad nature and objectives of a proposed project that has been supplied by the political or planning process. We will know, for example, that we are expected to prepare an irrigation project in a particular area, or a marketing project to reduce seasonal fluctuations in the price of an agricultural product, or an extension of an existing land settlement project. The next step is to examine carefully the pertinent technical relations on which to base the technical planning. We then begin to price these technical requirements and to develop some projections of inputs and outputs as the basis for the financial analysis. These financial prices are then adjusted to give economic values on which to base the economic analysis and to judge the project's contribution to the national income. At each step we must consider the institutional, organizational, and managerial aspects and the social effects. And, of course, at each step we may want to go back and revise earlier parts of the plan. The flow chart in figure 1-1 depicts this process schematically.

The sequence of topics in this book generally follows the order of the analytical process in preparing a financial, and then an economic, analysis of an agricultural project. We will not consider in detail the technical, institutional-organizational-managerial, social, or commercial aspects of preparing a project. Instead, we will assume that such preparations are already well in hand and that specialists knowledgeable in these matters can be easily consulted in the course of the analytical process.

We will turn first to what constitute costs and benefits in agricultural projects (chapter 2). Then we will proceed to how one can find market prices on which to base the project analysis (chapter 3). From these topics

Figure 1-1. *Formulation and Analysis of Agricultural Projects*

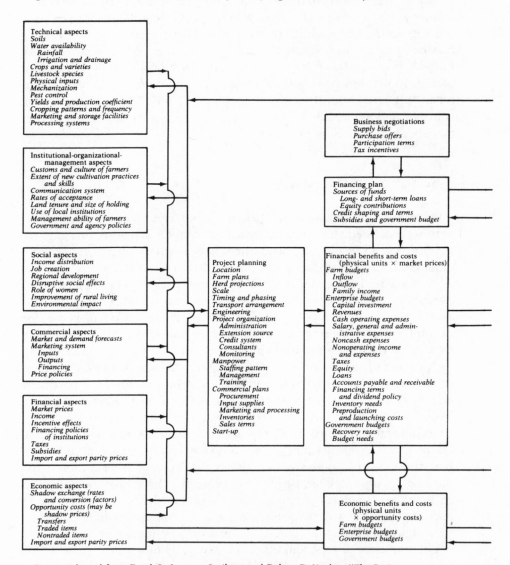

Source: Adapted from Frank L. Lamson-Scribner and Robert B. Youker, "The Project Cycle and the Project Appraisal Process," training material of the Economic Development Institute (EDI), CN-419 (Washington, D.C.: World Bank, 1975), exhibit 5.

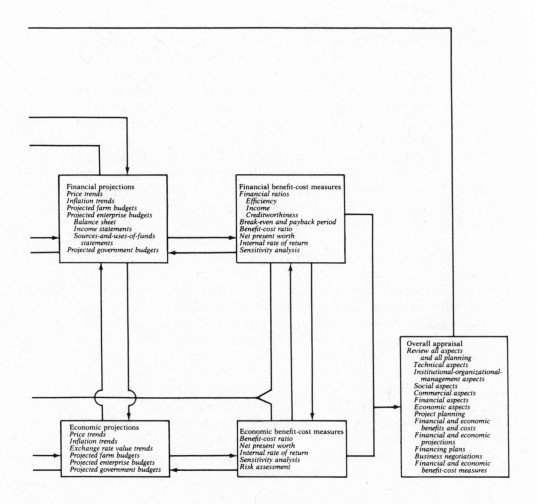

we will move on to discuss how these market prices can be transformed into accounts, which become the basis for the financial analysis, first by laying out and projecting model farm budgets (chapter 4). These projected farm budgets form the basis of an idea about how much a farm family participating in a project will have to live on as the project proceeds. This amount with the project, compared with what would be the amount without the project, yields an estimate about the incremental income that will accrue to the farm family. On the basis of this estimate, a judgment can be formed about the incentive effect of a proposed project on farmers who might participate. One can also estimate the rate of return to the farmer's own capital investment and to all capital invested on the farm.

By preparing and projecting budgets for agricultural processing industries such as sugar mills or cotton gins that may be included in a project (chapter 5), one can make similar judgments about the incremental net benefit arising from investment in these firms, whether they are in the public or the private sector, and about the incentives for participation by the private sector if this is to be the vehicle for investment. A separate set of accounts for government agencies (chapter 6) will permit an estimate of the effect of the project on government revenue.

With these budgets in hand, the various market prices used in each are adjusted, if need be, to reflect economic values from the standpoint of the society as a whole (chapter 7). These economic values are then totaled or "aggregated," as it is more often termed (chapter 8). This is done for the incremental farm production from the project (either by aggregating according to model types for the total number of farms in the project or by aggregating the total area devoted to the various crops in the project), for all the revenue-earning entities, and for the various government agencies. The aggregation gives the total incremental net benefit the society will realize from the project. From this and from earlier budgets, we can estimate the return that individuals and the society will realize from their investment in the project (chapters 9 and 10). Of course, at each stage in this sequence we will want to review our earlier work and revise it in light of later analysis.

The book concludes with a set of generalized guidelines for preparing reports of agricultural and rural development project analyses (appendix A), two discounting tables (appendix B), and a brief discussion about institutional sources of assistance for the preparation of agricultural projects (appendix C). An annotated bibliography and a glossary-index are included as references for the reader.

2

Identifying
Project Costs
and Benefits

WE UNDERTAKE ECONOMIC ANALYSES of agricultural projects to compare costs with benefits and determine which among alternative projects have an acceptable return. The costs and benefits of a proposed project therefore must be identified. Furthermore, once costs and benefits are known, they must be priced, and their economic values determined. All of this is obvious enough, but frequently it is tricky business.

What costs and benefits in agricultural projects are, and how we can define them in a consistent manner, are the topics of this chapter. In chapter 3 we will examine how we can obtain market prices. After the financial analyses are discussed in chapters 4–6, the economic analysis is addressed in chapter 7 with a discussion of how to adjust market prices to reflect the real resource flows.

Objectives, Costs, and Benefits

In project analysis, the objectives of the analysis provide the standard against which costs and benefits are defined. Simply put, a cost is anything that reduces an objective, and a benefit is anything that contributes to an objective.

Facing page: Harvesting rice in the Alto Turi region, northeast Brazil.

The problem with such simplicity, however, is that each participant in a project has many objectives. For a farmer, a major objective of participating is to maximize the amount his family has to live on. But this is only one of the farmer's interests. He may also want his children to be educated; as a result, they may not be available to work full time in the fields. He may also value his time away from the fields: a farmer will not adopt a cropping pattern, however remunerative, that requires him to work ten hours a day 365 days a year. Taste preference may lead a farmer to continue to grow a traditional variety of rice for home consumption even though a new, high-yielding variety might increase his family income more. A farmer may wish to avoid risk, and so may plan his cropping pattern to limit the risk of crop failure to an acceptable level or to reduce the risk of his depending solely on the market for the food grains his family will consume. As a result, although he may be able to increase his income over time if he grows cotton instead of wheat or maize, he would rather continue growing food grains to forestall the possibility that in any one year the cotton crop might fail or that food grains might be available for purchase in the market only at a very high price. All these considerations affect a farmer's choice of cropping pattern and thus the income-generating capacity of the project. Yet all are sensible decisions in the farmer's view. In the analytical system presented here, we will try to identify the cropping pattern that we think the farmer will most probably select, and then we will judge the effects of that pattern on his incremental income and, thus, on the new income generated by the project.

For private business firms or government corporations, a major objective is to maximize net income, yet both have significant objectives other than simply making the highest profit possible. Both will want to diversify their activities to reduce risk. The private store owner may have a preference for leisure, which leads him to hire a manager to help operate his store, especially during late hours. This reduces the income—since the manager must be paid a salary—but it is a sensible choice. For policy reasons, a public bus corporation may decide to maintain services even in less densely populated areas or at off-peak hours and thereby reduce its net income. In the analytical system here, we first identify the operating pattern that the firms in the project will most likely follow and then build the accounts to assess the effects of that pattern on the income-generating capacity of the project.

A society as a whole will have as a major objective increased national income, but it clearly will have many significant, additional objectives. One of the most important of these is income distribution. Another is simply to increase the number of productive job opportunities so that unemployment may be reduced—which may be different from the objective of income distribution itself. Yet another objective may be to increase the proportion of savings in any given period so there will be more to invest, faster growth, and, hence, more income in the future. Or, there may be issues to address broader than narrow economic considerations—such as the desire to increase regional integration, to upgrade the general level of education, to improve rural health, or to safeguard national security. Any of these objectives might lead to the choice of a project (or a form of a project) that is not the alternative that would contribute most to national income narrowly defined.

No formal analytical system for project analysis could possibly take into account all the various objectives of every participant in a project. Some selection will have to be made. In the analytical system here, we will take as formal criteria very straightforward objectives of income maximization and accommodate other objectives at other points in the process of project selection. The justification for this is that in most developing countries increased income is probably the single most important objective of individual economic effort, and increased national income is probably the most important objective of national economic policy.

For farms, we will take as the objective maximizing the incremental net benefit—the increased amount the farm family has to live on as a result of participating in the project—derived as outlined in chapter 4. For a private business firm or corporation in the public sector, we will take as the objective maximizing the incremental net income, to which we will return in chapter 5. And for the economic analysis conducted from the standpoint of the society as a whole, we will take as the objective maximizing the contribution the project makes to the national income— the value of all final goods and services produced during a particular period, generally a year. This is virtually the same objective, except for minor formal variations in definition, as maximizing gross domestic product (GDP). It is important to emphasize that taking the income a project will contribute to a society as the formal analytical criterion in economic analysis does not downgrade other objectives or preclude our considering them. Rather, we will simply treat consideration of other objectives as separate decisions. Using our analytical system, we can judge which among alternative projects or alternative forms of a particular project will make an acceptable contribution to national income. This will enable us to recommend to those who must make the investment decision a project that has a high income-generating potential and also will make a significant contribution to other social objectives. For example, from among those projects that make generally the same contribution to increased income, we can choose the one that has the most favorable effects on income distribution, or the one that creates the most jobs, or the one that is the most attractive among those in a disadvantaged region.

Thus, in the system of economic analysis discussed here, anything that reduces national income is a cost and anything that increases national income is a benefit. Since our objective is to increase the sum of all final goods and services, anything that directly reduces the total final goods and services is obviously a cost, and anything that directly increases them is clearly a benefit. But recall, also, the intricate workings of the economic system. When the project analyzed uses some intermediate good or service—something that is used to produce something else—by a chain of events it eventually reduces the total final goods and services available elsewhere in the economy. On the one hand, if we divert an orange that can be used for direct consumption—and thus is a final good—to the production of orange juice, also a final good, we are reducing the total available final goods and services, or national income, by the value of the orange and increasing it by the value of the orange juice. On the other hand, if we use cement to line an irrigation canal, we are not directly reducing the final goods and services available; instead, we are simply reducing the availability of an intermediate good. But the consequence of using the cement in the irrigation project is to shift the cement away from some other use in the economy. This, in turn, reduces production of some other good, and so on through the chain of events until, finally, the production of final goods and services, the national income, is reduced. Thus, using cement in the project is a cost to the economy. How much the national income will be reduced by using the cement for the project is part of what we must estimate when we turn, in chapter 7, to deriving economic values. On the benefit side, we have a similar pattern. Lining a canal increases available water that, in turn, may increase wheat production, and so on through a chain of events until in the end the total amount of bread is increased. By this mechanism, the project leads to an increase in the total amount of final goods and services, which is to say it increases the national income. Again, part of the analyst's task in the economic analysis is to estimate the amount of this increase in national income available to the society; that is, to determine whether, and by how much, the benefits exceed the costs in terms of national income.

If this rather simple definition of economic costs and benefits is kept in mind, possible confusion will be avoided when shadow prices are used to value resource flows, a matter taken up in chapter 7.

Note that, by defining our objective for economic analysis in terms of change in national income, we are defining it in real terms. (Real terms, as opposed to money terms, refer to the physical, tangible characteristics of goods and services.) To an important degree, economic analysis, in contrast to financial analysis, consists in tracing the real resource flows induced by an investment rather than the investment's monetary effects.

With these objectives defined, we may then say that in financial analysis our numeraire—the common measurement used as the unit of account—is a unit of currency, generally domestic currency, whereas in economic analysis our numeraire is a unit of national income, generally also expressed in domestic currency. We will return to this topic in our discussion of determining economic values in chapter 7.

In the economic analysis we will assume that all financing for a project comes from domestic sources and that all returns from the project go to domestic residents. [This is one reason why we identify our social objective with the gross *domestic* product (GDP) instead of the more familiar gross *national* product (GNP).] This convention—almost universally accepted by project analysts—separates the decision of how good a project is in its income-generating potential from the decision of how to finance it. The actual terms of financing available for a particular project will not influence the evaluation. Instead, we will assume that the proposed project is the best investment possible and that financing will then be sought for it at the best terms obtainable. This convention serves well whenever financing can be used for a range of projects or even versions of roughly the same project. The only case in which it does not hold well is the rather extreme case in which foreign financing is very narrowly tied to a particular project and will be lost if the project is not implemented. Then the analyst may be faced with the decision of implementing a lower-yielding project with foreign financing or choosing a higher-yielding alternative but losing the foreign loan.

"With" and "Without" Comparisons

Project analysis tries to identify and value the costs and benefits that will arise *with* the proposed project and to compare them with the situation as it would be *without* the project. The difference is the incremental net benefit arising from the project investment. This approach is not the same as comparing the situation "before" and "after" the project. The before-and-after comparison fails to account for changes in production that would occur without the project and thus leads to an erroneous statement of the benefit attributable to the project investment.

A change in output without the project can take place in two kinds of situations. The most common is when production in the area is already growing, if only slowly, and will probably continue to grow during the life of the project. The objective of the project is to increase growth by intensifying production. In Syria at the time the First Livestock Development Project was appraised, for example, production in the national sheep flock was projected to grow at about 1 percent a year without the project. The project was to increase and stabilize sheep production and the incomes of seminomadic flock owners and sheep fatteners by stabilizing the availability of feed and improving veterinary services. With the project, national flock production was projected to grow at the rate of 3 percent a year. In this case, if the project analyst had simply compared the output before and after the project, he would have erroneously attributed the total increase in sheep production to the project investment. Actually, what can be attributed to the project investment is only the 2 percent incremental increase in production in excess of the 1 percent that would have occurred anyway (see figure 2-1).

A change in output can also occur without the project if production would actually fall in the absence of new investment. In Guyana, on the north coast of South America, rice and sugarcane are produced on a strip of clay and silt soil edging the sea. The coast was subject to erosion from wave action. Under the Sea Defense Project, the government of Guyana has built seawalls to prevent the erosion. The benefit from this project, then, is not increased production but avoiding the loss of agricultural

Figure 2-1. *National Sheep Flock, First Livestock Development Project, Syria*

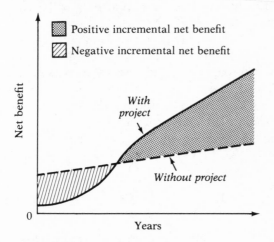

output and sites for housing. A simple before-and-after comparison would fail to identify this benefit (figure 2-2).

In some cases, an investment to avoid a loss might also lead to an increase in production, so that the total benefit would arise partly from the loss avoided and partly from increased production. In Pakistan, many areas are subject to progressive salinization as a result of heavy irrigation and the waterlogging that is in part attributable to seepage from irrigation canals. Capillary action brings the water to the surface where evaporation occurs, leaving the salt on the soil. If nothing is done to halt the process, crop production will fall. A project is proposed to line some of the canals, thus to reduce the seepage and permit better drainage

Figure 2-2. *Sea Defense Project, Guyana*

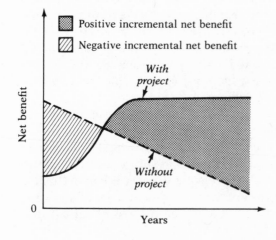

Figure 2-3. *Canal-lining Project, Pakistan*

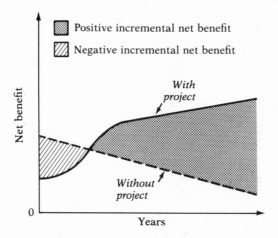

between irrigations. The proposed project is expected to arrest saliniza-tion, to save for profitable use the irrigation water otherwise lost to seepage, and to help farmers increase their use of modern inputs. The combination of measures would not only avoid a loss but also lead to an increase in production. Again, a simple before-and-after comparison would fail to identify the benefit realized by avoiding the loss (figure 2-3).

Of course, if no change in output is expected in the project area without the project, then the distinction between the before-and-after compari-son and the with-and-without comparison is less crucial. In some proj-ects the prospects for increasing production without new investment are minimal. In the Kemubu Irrigation Project in northeastern Malaysia, a pump irrigation scheme was built that permitted farmers to produce a second rice crop during the dry season. Without the project, most of the area was used for grazing, and with the help of residual moisture or small pumps some was used to produce tobacco and other cash crops. Produc-tion was not likely to increase because of the limited amount of water available. With the project now in operation, rice is grown in the dry season. Of course, the value of the second rice crop could not be taken as the total benefit from the project. From this value must be deducted the value forgone from the grazing and the production of cash crops. Only the incremental value could be attributed to the new investment in pumps and canals (figure 2-4).

Another instance where there may be no change in output without the project is the obvious one found in some settlement projects. Without the project there may be no economic use of the area at all. In the Alto Turi Land Settlement Project in northeastern Brazil, settlers established their holdings by clearing the forest, planting upland rice, and then estab-lishing pasture for production of beef cattle. At the time the settlers took up their holdings the forest had not been economically exploited—nor was it likely to be, at least for many years, in the absence of the project. In

Figure 2-4. *Kemubu Irrigation Project, Malaysia*

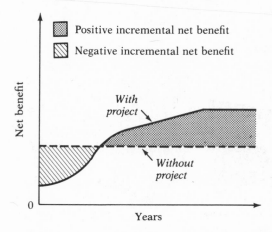

this case, the output without the project would be the same as the output before the project (figure 2-5).

Direct Transfer Payments

Some entries in financial accounts really represent shifts in claims to goods and services from one entity in the society to another and do not reflect changes in national income. These are the so-called direct transfer payments, which are much easier to identify if our definition of costs and benefits is kept in mind. In agricultural project analysis four kinds of direct transfer payments are common: taxes, subsidies, loans, and debt service (the payment of interest and repayment of principal).

Figure 2-5. *Alto Turi Land Settlement Project, Brazil*

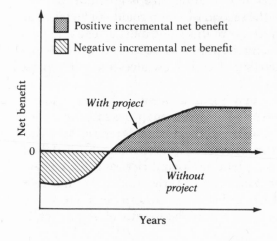

Take taxes, for example. In financial analysis a tax payment is clearly a cost. When a farmer pays a tax, his net benefit is reduced. But the farmer's payment of tax does not reduce the national income. Rather, it transfers income from the farmer to the government so that this income can be used for social purposes presumed to be more important to the society than the increased individual consumption (or investment) had the farmer retained the amount of the tax. Because payment of tax does not reduce national income, it is not a cost from the standpoint of the society as a whole. Thus, in economic analysis we would not treat the payment of taxes as a cost in project accounts. Taxes remain a part of the overall benefit stream of the project that contributes to the increase in national income.

Of course, no matter what form a tax takes, it is still a transfer payment—whether a direct tax on income or an indirect tax such as a sales tax, an excise tax, or a tariff or duty on an imported input for production. But some caution is advisable here. Taxes that are treated as a direct transfer payment are those representing a diversion of net benefit to the society. Quite often, however, government charges for goods supplied or services rendered may be called taxes. Water rates, for example, may be considered a tax by the farmer, but from the standpoint of the society as a whole they are a payment by the farmer to the irrigation authority in exchange for water supplied. Since building the irrigation system reduces national income, the farmer's payment for the water is part of the cost of producing the crop, the same as any other payment for a production input. Other payments called taxes may also be payments for goods and services rendered rather than transfers to the government. A stevedoring charge at the port is not a tax but a payment for services and so would not be treated as a duty would be. Whether a tax should be treated as a transfer payment or as a payment for goods and services depends on whether the payment is a compensation for goods and services needed to carry out the project or merely a transfer, to be used for general social purposes, of some part of the benefit from the project to the society as a whole.

Subsidies are simply direct transfer payments that flow in the opposite direction from taxes. If a farmer is able to purchase fertilizer at a subsidized price, that will reduce his costs and thereby increase his net benefit, but the cost of the fertilizer in the use of the society's real resources remains the same. The resources needed to produce the fertilizer (or import it from abroad) reduce the national income available to the society. Hence, for economic analysis of a project we must enter the full cost of the fertilizer.

Again, it makes no difference what form the subsidy takes. One form is that which lowers the selling price of inputs below what otherwise would be their market price. But a subsidy can also operate to increase the amount the farmer receives for what he sells in the market, as in the case of a direct subsidy paid by the government that is added to what the farmer receives in the market. A more common means to achieve the same result does not involve direct subsidy. The market price may be maintained at a level higher than it otherwise would be by, say, levying an import duty on competing imports or forbidding competing imports altogether. Although it is not a direct subsidy, the difference between the higher controlled price set by such measures and the lower price for competing imports that would prevail without such measures does represent an indirect transfer from the consumer to the farmer.

Credit transactions are the other major form of direct transfer payment in agricultural projects. From the standpoint of the farmer, receipt of a loan increases the production resources he has available; payment of interest and repayment of principal reduce them. But from the standpoint of the economy, things look different. Does the loan reduce the national income available? No, it merely *transfers* the control over resources from the lender to the borrower. Perhaps one farmer makes the loan to his neighbor. The lending farmer cannot use the money he lends to buy fertilizer, but the borrowing farmer can. The use of the fertilizer, of course, is a cost to the society because it uses up resources and thus reduces the national income. But the loan transaction does not itself reduce the national income; it is, rather, a direct transfer payment. In reverse, the same thing happens when the farmer repays his loan. The farmer who borrowed cannot buy fertilizer with the money he uses to repay the loan his neighbor made, but his neighbor can. Thus, the repayment is also a direct transfer payment.

Some people find the concept of transfer payments easier to understand if it is stated in terms of real resource flows. Taking this approach in economic analysis, we see that a tax does not represent a real resource flow; it represents only the transfer of a claim to real resource flows. The same holds true for a direct subsidy that represents the transfer of a claim to real resources from, say, an urban consumer to a farmer. This line of reasoning also applies to credit transactions. A loan represents the transfer of a claim to real resources from the lender to the borrower. When the borrower pays interest or repays the principal, he is transferring the claim to the real resources back to the lender—but neither the loan nor the repayment represents, in itself, *use* of the resources.

Costs of Agricultural Projects

In almost all project analyses, costs are easier to identify (and value) than benefits. In every instance of examining costs, we will be asking ourselves if the item reduces the net benefit of a farm or the net income of a firm (our objectives in financial analysis), or the national income (our objective in economic analysis).

Physical goods

Rarely will physical goods used in an agricultural project be difficult to identify. For such goods as concrete for irrigation canals, fertilizer and pesticides for increasing production, or materials for the construction of homes in land settlement projects, it is not the identification that is difficult but the technical problems in planning and design associated with finding out how much will be needed and when.

Labor

Neither will the labor component of agricultural projects be difficult to identify. From the highly skilled project manager to the farmer maintaining his orchard while it is coming into production, the labor inputs raise less a question of what than of how much and when. Labor may, however, raise special valuation problems that call for the use of a shadow price. Confusion may also arise on occasion in valuing family labor. Valuing family labor will be discussed with farm budgets in chapter 4, and the overall question of valuing unskilled labor will be taken up in chapter 7.

Land

By the same reasoning, the land to be used for an agricultural project will not be difficult to identify. It generally is not difficult to determine where the land necessary for the project will be located and how much will be used. Yet problems may arise in valuing land because of the very special kind of market conditions that exist when land is transferred from one owner to another. These valuation problems will also be considered with farm budgets in chapter 4 and with determining economic values in chapter 7.

Contingency allowances

In projects that involve a significant initial investment in civil works, the construction costs are generally estimated on the initial assumption that there will be no modifications in design that would necessitate changes in the physical work; no exceptional conditions such as unanticipated geological formations; and no adverse phenomena such as floods, landslides, or unusually bad weather. In general, project cost estimates also assume that there will be no relative changes in domestic or international prices and no inflation during the investment period. It would clearly be unrealistic to rest project cost estimates only on these assumptions of perfect knowledge and complete price stability. Sound project planning requires that provision be made in advance for possible adverse changes in physical conditions or prices that would add to the baseline costs. Contingency allowances are thus included as a regular part of the project cost estimates.

Contingency allowances may be divided into those that provide for physical contingencies and those for price contingencies. In turn, price contingency allowances comprise two categories, those for relative changes in price and those for general inflation. Physical contingencies and price contingencies that provide for increases in relative costs underlie our expectation that physical changes and relative price changes are likely to occur, even though we cannot forecast with confidence just how their influence will be felt. The increase in the use of real goods and services represented by the physical contingency allowance is a real cost and will reduce the final goods and services available for other purposes; that is, it will reduce the national income and, hence, is a cost to the society. Similarly, a rise in the relative cost of an item implies that its productivity elsewhere in the society has increased; that is, its potential contribution to national income has risen. A greater value is forgone by using the item for our project; hence, there is a larger reduction in national income. Physical contingency allowances and price contingency allowances for relative changes in price, then, are expected—if unallocated—project costs, and they properly form part of the cost base when measures of project worth are calculated.

General inflation, however, poses a different problem. As we will note in chapter 3 in discussing future prices, in project analysis the most common means of dealing with inflation is to work in constant prices, on the assumption that all prices will be affected equally by any rise in the general price level. This permits valid comparisons among alternative projects. If inflation is expected to be significant, however, provision for its effects on project costs needs to be made in the project financing plan so that an adequate budget is obtained. Contingency allowances for inflation would not, however, be included among the costs in project accounts other than the financing plan.

Taxes

Recall that the payment of taxes, including duties and tariffs, is customarily treated as a cost in financial analysis but as a transfer payment in economic analysis (since such payment does not reduce the national income). The amount that would be deducted for taxes in the financial accounts remains in the economic accounts as part of the incremental net benefit and, thus, part of the new income generated by the project.

Debt service

The same approach applies to debt service—the payment of interest and the repayment of capital. Both are treated as an outflow in financial analysis. In economic analysis, however, they are considered transfer payments and are omitted from the economic accounts.

Treatment of interest during construction can give rise to confusion. Lending institutions sometimes add the value of interest during construction to the principal of the loan and do not require any interest payment until the project begins to operate and its revenues are flowing. This process is known as "capitalizing" interest. The amount added to the principal as a result of capitalizing interest during construction is similar to an additional loan. Capitalizing interest defers interest cost, but when the interest payments are actually due, they will, of course, be larger because the amount of the loan has been increased. From the standpoint of economic analysis, the treatment of interest during construction is clear. It is a direct transfer payment the same as any other interest payment, and it should be omitted from the economic accounts. Often interest during construction is simply added to the capital cost of the project. To obtain the economic value of the capital cost, the amount of the interest during construction must be subtracted from the capital cost and omitted from the economic account.

In economic analysis, debt service is treated as a transfer within the economy even if the project will actually be financed by a foreign loan and debt service will be paid abroad. This is because of the convention of assuming that all financing for a project will come from domestic sources and all returns from the project will go to domestic residents. This convention, as noted earlier, separates the decision of how good a project is from the decision of how to finance it. Hence, even if it were expected that a project would be financed, say, by a World Bank loan, the debt service on that loan would not appear as a cost in the economic accounts of the project analysis.

Sunk costs

Sunk costs are those costs incurred in the past upon which a proposed new investment will be based. Such costs cannot be avoided, however poorly advised they may have been. When we analyze a proposed investment, we consider only future returns to future costs; expenditures in the past, or sunk costs, do not appear in our accounts.

In practice, if a considerable amount has already been spent on a project, the future returns to the future costs of completing the project would probably be quite attractive even if it is clear in retrospect that the project should never have been begun. The ridiculous extreme is when only one dollar is needed to complete a project, even a rather poor one, and when no benefit can be realized until the project is completed. The "return" to that last dollar may well be extremely high, and it would be clearly worthwhile to spend it. But the argument that because much has already been spent on a project it therefore must be continued is not a valid criterion for decision. There are cases in which it would be preferable simply to stop a project midway or to draw it to an early conclusion so that future resources might be freed for higher-yielding alternatives.

For evaluating past investment decisions, it is often desirable to do an economic and financial analysis of a completed project. Here, of course, the analyst would compare the return from all expenditures over the past life of the project with all returns. But this kind of analysis is useful only for determining the yield of past projects in the hope that judgments about future projects may be better informed. It does not help us decide what to do in the present. Money spent in the past is already gone; we do not have as one of our alternatives not to implement a completed project.

Tangible Benefits of Agricultural Projects

Tangible benefits of agricultural projects can arise either from an increased value of production or from reduced costs. The specific forms in which tangible benefits appear, however, are not always obvious, and valuing them may be quite difficult.

Increased production

Increased physical production is the most common benefit of agricultural projects. An irrigation project permits better water control so that farmers can obtain higher yields. Young trees are planted on cleared jungle land to increase the area devoted to growing oil palm. A credit project makes resources available for farmers to increase both their operating expenditures for current production—for fertilizers, seeds, or pesticides—and their investment—for a tubewell or a power thresher. The benefit is the increased production from the farm.

In a large proportion of agricultural projects the increased production will be marketed through commercial channels. In that case identifying the benefit and finding a market price will probably not prove too difficult, although there may be a problem in determining the correct value to use in the economic analysis.

In many agricultural projects, however, the benefits may well include increased production consumed by the farm family itself. Such is the case in irrigation rehabilitation projects along the north coast of Java. The home-consumed production from the projects increased the farm families' net benefit and the national income just as much as if it had been sold in the market. Indeed, we could think of the hypothetical case of a farmer selling his output and then buying it back. Since home-consumed production contributes to project objectives in the same way as marketed production, it is clearly part of the project benefits in both financial and economic analysis. Omitting home-consumed production will tend to make projects that produce commercial crops seem relatively high-yielding, and it could lead to a poor choice among alternative projects. Failure to include home-consumed production will also mean underestimating the return to agricultural investments relative to investments in other sectors of the economy.

When home-consumed crops will figure prominently in a project, the importance of careful financial analysis is increased. In this case, it is necessary to estimate not only the incremental net benefit—including the value of home-consumed production and money from off-farm sales—but also the cash available to the farmer. From the analysis of cash income and costs, one can determine if farmers will have the cash in hand to purchase modern inputs or to pay their credit obligations. It is possible to have a project in which home-consumed output increases enough for the return to the economy as a whole to be quite attractive, but in which so little of the increased production is sold that farmers will not have the cash to repay their loans.

Quality improvement

In some instances, the benefit from an agricultural project may take the form of an improvement in the quality of the product. For example, the analysis for the Livestock Development Project in Ecuador, which was to extend loans to producers of beef cattle, assumed that ranchers would be able not only to increase their cattle production but also to improve the quality of their animals so that the average live price of steers per kilogram would rise from S/5.20 to S/6.40 in constant value terms over the twelve-year development period. (The symbol for Ecuadorian sucres is S/.) Loans to small dairy farmers in the Rajasthan Smallholder Dairy Improvement Project in India are intended to enable farmers not only to increase output but also to improve the quality of their product. Instead of selling their milk to make ghee (cooking oil from clarified butter), farmers will be able to sell it for a higher price in the Jaipur fluid milk market. As in these examples, both increased production and quality improvement are most often expected in agricultural projects, although both may not always be expected. One word of warning: both the rate and the extent of the benefit from quality improvement can easily be overestimated.

Change in time of sale

In some agricultural projects, benefits will arise from improved marketing facilities that allow the product to be sold at a time when prices are more favorable. A grain storage project may make it possible to hold grain from the harvest period, when the price is at its seasonal low, until later in the year when the price has risen. The benefit of the storage investment arises out of this change in "temporal value."

Change in location of sale

Other projects may include investment in trucks and other transport equipment to carry products from the local area where prices are low to distant markets where prices are higher. For example, the Fruit and Vegetable Export Project in Turkey included provision for trucks and ferries to transport fresh produce from southeastern Turkey to outlets in the European Common Market. The benefits of such projects arise from the change in "locational value."

In most cases the increased value arising from marketing projects will be split between farmers and marketing firms as the forces of supply and demand increase the price at which the farmer can sell in the harvest season and reduce the monopolistic power of the marketing firm or agency. Many projects are structured to ensure that farmers receive a larger part of the benefit by making it possible for them to build storage facilities on their farms or to band together into cooperatives, but an agricultural project could also involve a private marketing firm or a government agency, in which case much of the benefit could accrue to someone other than farmers.

Changes in product form (grading and processing)

Projects involving agricultural processing industries expect benefits to arise from a change in the form of the agricultural product. Farmers sell paddy rice to millers who, in turn, sell polished rice. The benefit to the millers arises from the change in form. Canners preserve fruit, changing its form and making it possible at a lower cost to change its time or location of sale. Even a simple processing facility such as a grading shed gives rise to a benefit through changing the form of the product from run-of-the-orchard to sorted fruit. In the Himachal Pradesh Apple Marketing Project in northern India, the value of the apples farmers produce is increased by sorting; the best fruit is sold for fresh consumption while fruit of poorer quality is used to make a soft drink concentrate. In the process, the total value of the apples is increased.

Cost reduction through mechanization

The classic example of a benefit arising from cost reduction in agricultural projects is that gained by investment in agricultural machinery to reduce labor costs. Examples are tubewells substituting for hand-drawn or animal-drawn water, pedal threshers replacing hand threshing, or (that favorite example) tractors replacing draft animals. Total production may not increase, but a benefit arises because the costs have been trimmed (provided, of course, that the gain is not offset by displaced labor that cannot be productively employed elsewhere).

Reduced transport costs

Cost reduction is a common source of benefit wherever transport is a factor. Better feeder roads or highways may reduce the cost of moving produce from the farm to the consumer. The benefit realized may be distributed among farmers, truckers, and consumers.

Losses avoided

In discussing with-and-without comparisons in project analyses earlier in this chapter, we noted that in some projects the benefit may arise not from increased production but from a loss avoided. This kind of benefit stream is not always obvious, but it is one that the with-and-without test tends to point out clearly. In Jamaica, lethal yellowing is attacking the Jamaica Tall variety of coconut. The government has undertaken a large investment to enable farmers to plant Malayan Dwarf coconuts, which are resistant to the disease. Total production will change very little as a result of the investment, yet both the farmers and the economy will realize a real benefit because the new investment prevents loss of income. The Lower Egypt Drainage Project involves the largest single tile drainage system in the world. The benefit will arise not from increasing production in the already highly productive Nile delta, but from avoiding losses due to the waterlogging caused by year-round irrigation from the Aswan High Dam.

Sometimes a project increases output through avoiding loss—a kind of double classification, but one that in practice causes no problem. Proposals to eradicate foot-and-mouth disease in Latin America envision projects by which the poor physical condition or outright death of animals will be avoided. At the same time, of course, beef production would be increased.

Other kinds of tangible benefits

Although we have touched on the most common kinds of benefits from agricultural projects, those concerned with agricultural development will find other kinds of tangible, direct benefits most often in sectors other than agriculture. Transport projects are often very important for agricultural development. Benefits may arise not only from cost reduction, as noted earlier, but also from time savings, accident reduction, or development activities in areas newly accessible to markets. If new housing for farmers has been included among the costs of a project, as is often the case in land settlement and irrigation projects, then among the benefits will be an allowance for the rental value of the housing. Since this is an imputed value, there are valuation problems that will be noted later.

Secondary Costs and Benefits

Projects can lead to benefits created or costs incurred outside the project itself. Economic analysis must take account of these external, or secondary, costs and benefits so they can be properly attributed to the project investment. (Of course, this applies only in economic analysis; the problem does not arise in financial analysis.)

When market prices are used in economic analysis, as has been the custom in the United States for water resource and other public works projects, it is necessary to estimate the secondary costs and benefits and then add them to the direct costs and benefits. This is a theoretically difficult process, and one easily subject to abuse. There is an extensive and complex literature on secondary costs and benefits that specifically addresses this analytical approach. For those who would like to review this literature, a good place to begin is the article by Prest and Turvey (1966), which outlines the historical development of the discussion. A highly technical review of the arguments can be found in Mishan (1971).

Instead of adding on secondary costs and benefits, one can either adjust the values used in economic analysis or incorporate the secondary costs and benefits in the analysis, thereby in effect converting them to direct costs and benefits. This is the approach taken in most project analyses carried out by international agencies, in the systems based on shadow prices proposed in more recent literature on project analysis, and in the analytical system presented here.

Incorporating secondary costs or benefits in project analysis can be viewed as an analytical device to account for the value added that arises outside the project but is a result of the project investment. In the analytical system here, as will be explained in more detail in chapter 7, every item is valued either at its opportunity cost or at a value determined by a consumer's willingness to pay for the item. The effect is to eliminate all transfers—both the direct transfers discussed earlier in this chapter and the indirect transfers that arise because prices differ from opportunity costs. By this means we attribute to the project investment all the value added that arises from it anywhere in the society. Hence, it is not necessary to add on the secondary costs and benefits separately; to do so would constitute double counting.

One qualification must be made. If a project has a substantial effect on the quantity other producers are able to sell in imperfect markets—and most markets are imperfect—there may be gains or losses not accurately accounted for. Squire and van der Tak (1975, p. 23) cite the example of an improved road that diverts traffic from a railway that charges rates below marginal cost. This diversion entails a social gain from reduced rail traffic (in avoiding the social losses previously incurred on this traffic) in addition to the benefits to the road users measured directly. In agricultural projects, this is a rather infrequent case because prices generally are more flexible than in other sectors of the economy. In any event, in the practice of contemporary project analysis the size of these gains or losses is generally assumed to be insignificant, and no provision is made for them in the analysis.

Although using shadow prices based on opportunity costs or willingness to pay greatly reduces the difficulty of dealing with secondary costs and benefits, there still remain many valuation problems related to goods and services not commonly traded in competitive markets. One way to avoid some of these problems is to treat a group of closely related investments as a single project. For example, it is common to consider the output of irrigation projects as the increased farm production, since valuing irrigation water is difficult. Another example is found in development roads built into inaccessible areas. It is argued that the production arising from the induced investment activities of otherwise unemployed new settlers should be considered a secondary benefit of the road investment. One way of avoiding the problem is to view this case as a land settlement project in which the road is a component. New production is then properly included among the direct benefits of the project and can be included in the project accounts at market or shadow prices, and no attempt need be made to allocate the benefits between road investment and the other kinds of investment that must be made by settlers and government if settlement is to succeed.

Another group of secondary costs and benefits has been called "technological spillover" or "technological externalities." Adverse ecological effects are a common example, and the side effects of irrigation development are often cited as an illustration. A dam may reduce river flow and lead to increased costs for dredging downstream. New tubewell development may have adverse effects on the flow of existing wells. Irrigation development may reduce the catch of fish or may lead to the spread of schistosomiasis. When these technological externalities are significant and can be identified and valued, they should be treated as a direct cost of the project (as might be the case for reduced fish catches), or the cost of avoiding them should be included among the project costs (as would be the case for increased dredging or for investment to avoid pollution).

It is sometimes suggested that project investments may give rise to secondary benefits through a "multiplier effect." The concept of the multiplier is generally thought of in connection with economies having excess capacity. If excess capacity exists, an initial investment might cause additional increases in income as successive rounds of spending reduce excess capacity. In developing countries, however, it is shortage of capacity that is characteristic. Thus, there is little likelihood of excess capacity giving rise to additional benefits through the multiplier. In any event, most of the multiplier effect is accounted for if we shadow-price at opportunity cost. Since the opportunity cost of using excess capacity is only the cost of the raw materials and labor involved, only variable costs will enter the project accounts until existing excess capacity is used up.

It is also sometimes suggested that there is a "consumption multiplier effect" as project benefits are received by consumers. Consumption multipliers are very difficult to identify and value. In any case, they presumably would be much the same for alternative investments, so omitting them from a project analysis would not affect the relative ranking of projects.

Intangible Costs and Benefits

Almost every agricultural project has costs and benefits that are intangible. These may include creation of new job opportunities, better health and reduced infant mortality as a result of more rural clinics, better nutrition, reduced incidence of waterborne disease as a result of improved rural water supplies, national integration, or even national defense. Such intangible benefits are real and reflect true values. They do not, however, lend themselves to valuation. How does one derive a figure for the long-term value of a child's life saved, or for the increased comfort of a population spared preventable, debilitating disease? Benefits of this kind may require a modification of the normal benefit-cost analysis to a least-cost type of analysis, a topic we will take up when we discuss valuation. Because intangible benefits are a factor in project selection, it is important that they be carefully identified and, where at all possible, quantified, even though valuation is impossible. For example, how many children will enroll in new schools? How many homes will benefit from a better system of water supply? How many infants will be saved because of more rural clinics?

In most cases of intangible benefits arising from an agricultural project, the costs are tangible enough: construction costs for schools, salaries for nurses in a public health system, pipes for rural water supplies, and the like. Intangible costs, however, do exist in projects. Such costs might be incurred if new projects disrupt traditional patterns of family life, if development leads to increased pollution, if the ecological balance is upset, or if scenic values are lost. Again, although valuation is impossible, intangible costs should be carefully identified and if possible quantified. In the end, every project decision will have to take intangible factors into account through a subjective evaluation because intangible costs can be significant and because intangible benefits can make an important contribution to many of the objectives of rural development.

PART TWO

Financial Aspects
of Project Analysis

3

Pricing
Project Costs
and Benefits

ONCE COSTS AND BENEFITS have been identified, if they are to be compared they must be valued. Since the only practical way to compare differing goods and services directly is to give each a money value, we must find the proper prices for the costs and benefits in our analysis.

Prices Reflect Value

Underlying all financial and economic analysis is an assumption that prices reflect value—or can be adjusted to do so. In this chapter we will discuss how to find these prices. Before proceeding, however, it is necessary to define two economic concepts crucial to project analysis: marginal value product and opportunity cost.

Consider a Filipino farmer who applies nitrogenous fertilizer to his rice. In the 1979–80 season this fertilizer cost him ₱3.98 per kilogram of elemental nitrogen (N), and he received ₱1.050 for every kilogram of paddy rice he sold. (The symbol for Philippine pesos is ₱.) Table 3-1 shows the responsiveness of his rice to fertilizer. At low levels of application, fertilizer has a great effect on rice yield. Increasing the application from no fertilizer to 10 kilograms of elemental nitrogen increased the farmer's

---

Facing page: Crossing an irrigation canal in Sudan.

Table 3-1. *Crop Response to Nitrogen Fertilizer in the Philippines*

| Nitrogen[a] (kilograms per hectare) | Paddy rice | | | Shelled maize | | |
	Yield (kilograms per hectare)	Value[b] (₱)	Marginal value product[c] (₱)	Yield (kilograms per hectare)	Value[d] (₱)	Marginal value product (₱)
0	3,442	3,614	29.50	2,600	2,688	23.80
10	3,723	3,909	26.10	2,830	2,926	21.70
20	3,971	4,170	22.60	3,040	3,143	19.70
30	4,187	4,396	19.20	3,230	3,340	17.60
40	4,370	4,588	15.80	3,400	3,516	15.50
50	4,520	4,746	12.30	3,550	3,671	13.40
60	4,637	4,869	8.80	3,680	3,805	11.40
70	4,721	4,957	5.40	3,790	3,919	9.30
80	4,772	5,011	2.00	3,880	4,012	7.20
90	4,791	5,031	−1.50	3,950	4,084	5.20
100	4,777	5,016	e	4,000	4,136	3.10
110				4,030	4,167	1.00
120				4,040	4,177	−1.00
130				4,030	4,167	

₱ Philippine pesos.

Source: Personal communication from Pedro R. Sandoval, University of the Philippines at Los Baños, September 1980. Rice responses are based on *Changes in Rice Farming in Selected Areas of Asia* (Manila: International Rice Research Institute, 1978), p. 61. Maize responses are based on University of the Philippines at Los Baños Experiment Station records. Prices are from the Bureau of Agricultural Economics, Ministry of Agriculture, Republic of the Philippines.

a. The farm-gate price of elemental nitrogen (N) in 1979–80 was ₱3.98 per kilogram.

b. The farm-gate price of paddy rice in 1979–80 was ₱1.050 per kilogram.

c. The marginal value product is the extra revenue that comes from increasing the quantity of an input used by one unit, all other quantities remaining constant. In this instance, the marginal value product is the increased value of paddy rice or shelled maize from using 1 additional kilogram of elemental nitrogen. Note that in this table the interval between levels of elemental nitrogen is 10 kilograms. Thus, the marginal value product of elemental nitrogen applied to rice between the 60- and 70-kilogram levels of application is the difference in value of output between the two levels divided by 10, or ₱8.80 [(4,957 − 4,869) ÷ 10 = 8.80].

d. The farm-gate price of shelled yellow maize in 1979–80 was ₱1.034 per kilogram.

e. Beyond application of 100 kilograms of elemental nitrogen, all marginal value products for paddy rice are negative; therefore, figures for these applications of nitrogen to rice are not reported.

yield from 3,442 kilograms to 3,723 kilograms per hectare and increased the value of his output by ₱295, from ₱3,614 to ₱3,909. Thus, for every additional kilogram of elemental nitrogen the farmer applied at this level, he received ₱29.50 in return [(3,909 − 3,614) ÷ 10 = 29.50]. The extra revenue from increasing the quantity of an input used, all other quantities remaining constant, is the marginal value product of the input. In this case, then, the marginal value product of a kilogram of fertilizer is ₱29.50.

If the farmer could buy fertilizer for ₱3.98 a kilogram and use it to increase output by ₱29.50, it obviously would have paid him to apply more. But as the intensity of application increases, each additional kilogram of fertilizer has less and less effect on production. If the farmer had increased his application from 80 to 90 kilograms per hectare, he would have increased the value of his production by only ₱20, from ₱5,011 to ₱5,031, and the marginal value product of a kilogram of fertilizer would have fallen to only ₱2.00 [(5,031 − 5,011) ÷ 10 = 2.00]. Since he would have had to pay ₱3.98 per kilogram, it clearly would not have been worthwhile to apply fertilizer at this rate. In fact, it would only have paid the farmer to apply fertilizer up to the rate at which the marginal value product just equaled the price. For this Filipino farmer, it would have paid him to apply approximately 80 kilograms of nitrogen: between 70 and 80 kilograms the marginal value product of each additional kilogram was some ₱5.40, whereas between 80 and 90 kilograms it fell to ₱2.00. Thus, the farmer would have expanded his fertilizer use until he reduced the marginal value product of the fertilizer to its market price, and the market price, therefore, is an estimate of the marginal value product of the fertilizer.

The optimal amount of fertilizer to use will change, of course, when the price of fertilizer changes relative to the price of rice. If the relative price of fertilizer were to rise, the farmer would respond by reducing the amount of fertilizer he applies, increasing the marginal value product of the fertilizer (but reducing the total amount and value of production) until the marginal value product of the fertilizer again just equals its price. Suppose fertilizer were to double in price to ₱8.00 per kilogram of elemental nitrogen, and rice prices remained unchanged. Then, table 3-1 indicates the farmer should reduce the amount of fertilizer applied to a hectare from 80 kilograms to 70 kilograms, since between 60 and 70 kilograms the marginal value product was some ₱8.80 but between 70 and 80 kilograms it was only some ₱5.40.

In practice, because of risk and limited resources, the farmer would probably not have applied the amounts indicated here. We may consider that the farmer reduces his expected return by some "risk discount." Even so, the principle we are illustrating remains the same: the farmer equates the expected marginal value product less some risk discount to the price of fertilizer.

If this farmer also grew maize, for which in 1979–80 he would have received ₱1.034 per kilogram of shelled grain, table 3-1 indicates it would have paid him (in the absence of risk) to apply some 100 kilograms of elemental nitrogen to each hectare, because between 90 and 100 kilograms the marginal value product of a kilogram of nitrogen applied to maize was ₱5.20, whereas between 100 and 110 kilograms the marginal value product fell to ₱3.10, below the price of fertilizer.

Now, suppose the farmer had limited resources and could not obtain sufficient credit to increase his fertilizer application on both rice and maize to where the marginal value product equaled the price. Suppose the farmer had only 2 hectares, 1 planted in rice and 1 in maize, and resources sufficient to purchase just 80 kilograms of nitrogen. How should he have used it? Should he have put it all on rice and none on maize? If he did, he would have applied fertilizer to his rice at the level where the marginal value product was just about equal to its market price. But suppose he had shifted some fertilizer, instead, to maize. If he had shifted 10 kilograms, he would have reduced the value of his rice production by ₱54—from ₱5,011 to ₱4,957, or by ₱5.40 for each kilogram shifted—but he could have obtained some ₱238 for the 10 kilograms applied to maize, since the marginal value product between 0 and 10 kilograms was some ₱23.80 per kilogram. In other words, at these levels each kilogram of nitrogen shifted would reduce the rice value by ₱5.40 but increase the value of maize output by some ₱23.80. In the language of economics, the opportunity cost of fertilizer shifted from rice to maize was ₱5.40. Opportunity cost, thus, is the benefit forgone by using a scarce resource for one purpose—in this case applying fertilizer to maize—instead of for its best alternative use—in this case using the fertilizer to produce rice. Said another way, the opportunity cost is the return a resource can bring in its next best alternative use. What would be the opportunity cost if the farmer were to move a kilogram of fertilizer in the other direction, back from maize to rice? He would have given up ₱23.80 to gain only ₱5.40—not a very attractive proposition—and the opportunity cost, obviously, would be some ₱23.80.

Given his limited resources, it would pay the farmer to shift fertilizer from rice to maize until the marginal value product of fertilizer applied to both crops is the same. In the case of the Filipino farmer who could buy only 80 kilograms of fertilizer, if on the one hand he were to move 40 kilograms to maize, reducing his application on rice from 80 kilograms to 40 kilograms, he would have increased the marginal value product of the fertilizer on his rice to some ₱15. On the other hand, the 40 kilograms shifted away from rice and put on maize would have decreased the marginal value product of nitrogen applied to maize also to about ₱15. At these levels, there would be no advantage in shifting fertilizer between the two crops—the opportunity cost of shifting more fertilizer from rice to maize would be about ₱15, but the gain would also be only about ₱15—and the farmer would have reached the optimal level of application to both crops.

Note, however, that if the farmer could somehow have bought as much fertilizer as he wanted at the market price of ₱3.98 per kilogram—perhaps through a credit program—then the market price of fertilizer would have become its opportunity cost, and (in the absence of a risk discount) he should have increased his application to 80 kilograms on rice and 100 kilograms on maize.

From a single farmer to the economy as a whole, the same principles apply. In a "perfect" market—one that is highly competitive, with many buyers and sellers, all of whom have perfect knowledge about the market—every economic commodity would be priced at its marginal value product, since every farmer will have expanded his fertilizer use to where its marginal value product equals its price, and the same will have happened for every other item in the economy. That is, the price of every good and service would exactly equal the value that the last unit utilized contributes to production, or the value in use of the item for consumption would exactly balance the value it could contribute to additional production. If a unit of goods or services could produce more or bring greater satisfaction in some activity other than its present use, someone would have been willing to bid up its price, and it would have been attracted to the new use. When this price system is in "equilibrium," the marginal value product, the opportunity cost, and the price will all be equal. Resources will then have been allocated through the price mechanism so that the last unit of every good and service in the economy is in its most productive use or best consumption use. No transfer of resources could result in greater output or more satisfaction.

Without moving further into price theory, we can consider some direct implications for agricultural projects of the assumption that prices reflect value.

First, as everyone knows, markets are not perfect and are never in complete equilibrium. Hence, prices may reflect values only imperfectly. Even so, there is a great deal of truth in this price theory based on the model of perfect markets. In general, the best approximation of the "true value" of a good or service that is fairly widely bought and sold is its market price. Somebody in the economy is willing to pay this price. One can presume that this buyer will use the item to increase output by at least as much as its price, or that he is willing to exchange something of value equal to the price to gain the satisfaction of consuming the item. Hence, the market price of an item is normally the best estimate of its marginal value product and of its opportunity cost, and most often it will be the best price to use in valuing either a cost or a benefit. In financial analysis, as we have noted, the market price is always used. But in economic analysis some other price—a "shadow price"—may be a better indicator of the value of a good or service; that is, a better estimate of its true opportunity cost to the economy. When prices other than market prices are used in economic analysis, however, the burden of proof is on the analyst.

Finding Market Prices

Project analyses characteristically are built first by identifying the technical inputs and outputs for a proposed investment, then by valuing the inputs and outputs at market prices to construct the financial accounts, and finally by adjusting the financial prices so they better reflect economic values. Thus, the first step in valuing costs and benefits is finding the market prices for the inputs and outputs, often a difficult task for the economist.

To find prices, the analyst must go into the market. He must inquire about actual prices in recent transactions and consult many sources— farmers, small merchants, importers and exporters, extension officers, technical service personnel, government market specialists and statisticians, and published or privately held statistics about prices for both national and international markets. From these sources the analyst must come up with a figure that adequately reflects the going price for each input or output in the project.

Point of first sale and farm-gate price

In project analysis, a good rule for determining a market price for agricultural commodities produced in the project is to seek the price at the "point of first sale." If the point of first sale is in a relatively competitive market, then the price at which the commodity is sold in this market is probably a relatively good estimate of its value in economic as well as financial terms. If the market is not reasonably competitive, in economic analysis the financial price may have to be adjusted better to reflect the opportunity cost or value in use of the commodity.

For many agricultural projects in which the objective is increased production of a commodity, the best point of first sale to use is generally the boundary of the farm. We are after what the farmer receives when he sells his product—the "farm-gate" price. The increased value added of the product as it is processed and delivered to a market arises as a payment for marketing services. This value added is not properly attributed to the investment to produce the commodity. Rather, it arises from the labor and capital engaged in the marketing service. Usually the price at point of first sale can be accepted as the farm-gate price; even if this point is in a nearby village market, the farmer sells his output there and thus earns for himself any fee that might be involved in transporting the commodity from the farm to the point of first sale. But if any new equipment is necessary to enable the farmer to do this—say, a new bullock cart or a new truck—then that new equipment must be shown as a cost incurred to realize the marketing benefit in the project.

In projects producing commodities for well-organized markets, the farm-gate price may not be too difficult to determine. This would be true for most food grains traded domestically in substantial quantities. One may think of wheat in most countries of the Middle East and South Asia, of rice in South and Southeast Asia, and of maize in much of Latin America. It would also be true of farm products for which the processor is generally the first buyer (such as fresh fruit bunches for palm oil in Malaysia or milk in Jamaica), where the price quoted to the farmer is the price on his farm, and the firm responsible for the marketing comes to the farm to pick up the product.

In many cases, however, the prices in a reasonably competitive market or in the price records kept by the government statistical service will include services not properly attributable to the investment in the project itself. This may happen, for instance, when the only price series available for a product records the prices at which it has been sold in a central market—such as the price for eggs in Madras, for melons in Tehran, or for vegetables in Bogota. In that case, the project analyst will have to dig deeper to find out how to value the marketing services. Then he can adjust the central market price to reduce it to the farm-gate price.

The farm-gate price is generally the best price at which to value home-consumed production. In some cases it may be extremely difficult to determine just what a realistic farm-gate price is for a crop produced primarily for home consumption because so little of the crop appears on markets. This is the case, for example, for manioc and cocoyam in Africa. On the one hand, some argue that the true value of the crop is overstated if the market price is used as a basis for valuation because such a small proportion of the product is actually sold. On the other hand, the same crop in different situations may not be so difficult to value. Manioc is sold extensively in Nigeria to make *gari* flour, and it is commonly traded in local markets in tropical Latin America and the Caribbean.

The farm-gate price may be a poor indicator of the true opportunity cost we want to use in economic analysis. In Ghana the Marketing Board takes some proportion of the cocoa price as a tax for development purposes. In Thailand, a rice "premium"—that is, a tax on rice exports—effectively keeps the domestic price well below what the international market would pay. In these cases, when the commodity is traded its economic value would have to be considered higher than the actual farm-gate price, and this price distortion will have to be corrected in the economic analysis. In other cases, just the opposite happens. In Mexico the price of maize is maintained at a high level to transfer income to *ejidatarios*, the small farmers. In Malaysia, the price of rice is supported above world market levels to encourage local production and to reduce imports. In these cases, part of the price does not really reflect the economic value of the product—its cost if it could be imported—but rather an indirect income transfer to small farmers. Again, this price distortion will have to be corrected in the economic analysis.

Pricing intermediate goods

By emphasizing the point of first sale as a starting point for valuing the output of our projects, we are also implying that imputed prices should be avoided for intermediate goods in our analysis. An intermediate good is an item produced primarily as an input in the production of another good. If an intermediate good is not freely traded in a competitive market, we cannot expect to obtain a price established by a range of competitive transactions. Fodder produced on a farm and then fed to the dairy animals on the farm is an example of such an intermediate product. If increased fodder production is an element in the proposed agricultural project, the analyst would avoid valuing it. Instead, the analyst would treat the whole farm as a unit and value the milk produced at its point of first sale or value the calves sold as feeder cattle. Treatment of intermediate products will vary from project to project depending on the particular marketing structures. In some countries it would hardly make sense in an egg production project to value the pullets produced in a pullet production enterprise and then "sell" these pullets to the egg production enterprise on the same farm. But in other countries there might be an active market in pullets, which would mean that we could expect to find a reasonably competitive price to use in the economic analysis. To avoid most of the problems that might be introduced by trying to impute values for intermediate products, the financial accounts in agricultural projects are based on budgets for the whole farm instead of on budgets for individual activities on the farm; that is, on the budget for the egg farm as a whole rather than on the budget for a pullet production activity.

A frequently encountered intermediate good in agricultural projects is irrigation water. The "product" of an irrigation system—water—is, of course, really intended to produce agricultural commodities. The price farmers are charged for the water is generally determined administratively, not by any play of competitive market forces. If the analyst were to try to separate the irrigation system from the production it makes possible, he would be faced with a nearly impossible task of determining the value of irrigation water. Hence, it is not surprising that the economic analyses of most irrigation projects take as the basis for the benefit stream the value of the agricultural products that *are* offered in a relatively free market at the point of first sale.

Other problems in finding market prices

Considerable confusion often arises in determining the values for two important inputs in agricultural projects, land and labor. This happens primarily when the analysis moves from the financial project accounts to the economic analysis (to which we will turn in chapter 7). In the accounts prepared for the financial analysis, the treatment of prices for land and labor is quite straightforward: the price used is the price actually paid. Thus, if the farmers in a settlement project are expected to pay the project authority a price for the land they acquire, perhaps through a series of installments, then the actual price in the year it is paid is entered in the project accounts. In the *financial* analysis, we do not question whether this is a "good" price in economic terms. Similarly, if land must be bought for the right-of-way for canals in an irrigation project, the actual price to be paid is entered in the project accounts in the financial analysis. Or, if the project includes tenant farmers who will receive help in increasing wheat production, then in the financial accounts for these tenant farmers the analyst will enter the rent paid each year at the amount actually paid, or at the farm-gate value of the wheat delivered to the landowner if the tenants pay rent in kind.

If farm accounts are laid out on a with-and-without basis following the format suggested in chapter 4, in those instances where the project involves only changing the cropping pattern (say, a shift from pasture to irrigated sorghum), the cost of the land (in this instance an opportunity cost) need not be separately entered because of the form of the account. When the net benefit without the project is subtracted from the net benefit with the project, the contribution of the land to the old cropping pattern is also subtracted and only the incremental value remains.

In valuing labor for the financial analysis accounts, again, the problems arise when the financial accounts are adjusted to reflect economic values. For financial analysis, the analyst enters the amounts actually paid to hired labor, either in wages or in kind, in the farm budgets or project accounts. Family labor is treated differently. It is not entered as a cost; instead, the "wages" for the family become a part of the net benefit. Thus, if our project increases the net benefit, it also in effect increases the family's income or "wages" for its labor. Again, if we follow the format suggested in chapter 4, the account will automatically value the family labor at its opportunity cost, and the incremental net benefit will reflect any increased return the family may receive for its labor.

Prices for agricultural commodities generally are subject to substantial seasonal fluctuation. If this is the case, some decision must be made about the point in the seasonal cycle at which to choose the price to be used for the analysis. A good starting point is the farm-gate price at the peak of the harvest season. This is probably close to the lowest price in the cycle. The line of reasoning here is that as prices rise during the cycle at least some part of that rise is a result not of the production activities of the farmer but of the marketing services embodied in storing the crop until consumers want it. But, markets being what they are, there may be an element of imperfection in the harvest price level. Market channels may become so glutted that merchants try actively to discourage farmers from immediately bringing their crop to the market by offering a price that even the merchants themselves would admit is too low. Even so, the need to sell immediately to meet debt obligations may force farmers to offer their crops despite these artificially low, penalty prices. In some cases, therefore, a price higher than the farm-gate price in the harvest season may be selected. But there is an obligation here to justify the price chosen as more valid than the lowest seasonal price. One way to resolve this problem may be to include an element of credit in the project design. This would permit farmers to withhold their product from the market until prices have had a chance to rise from their seasonal lows but at the same time to have enough money to meet their cash obligations and family living expenses. The credit element may also include credit for building on-farm storage so that farmers will have a safe place to store their production until they decide to market it at a better price.

Prices vary among grades of product, of course, and picking the proper price for project analysis may involve making some decisions about quality of the product. In general, it can be assumed that farmers will produce in the future much the same quality as they have in the past and will market their product ungraded. In many agricultural projects, however, one objective is to upgrade the quality of production as well as to increase the total output. Small dairy farmers, for instance, may be able with the help of the project investment to meet the sanitation standards of the fluid milk market and to command a higher price; or reduced time for delivery may hold down sucrose inversion in sugarcane; or better pruning will increase the average size of the oranges Moroccan farmers can offer European buyers. In such cases, the proper price to select is the average price expected for the quality to be produced.

A special problem occurs in pricing housing. If project investment includes housing construction, as would be the case for a settlement project, then one benefit arising from the investment is the rental value of the house. Since the rental value will usually be an imputed value rather than a real market price, care must be exercised in determining it. No more should be allowed for the rental value than would normally be paid by a prospective tenant family. Nor should more rental value be allowed than the family would be expected to pay for a comparable house in the vicinity or in a similar area elsewhere (if the new settlement is in a distant locale). In particular, the temptation should be avoided to take as a rental value some arbitrary proportion of the housing cost. Otherwise, overly elaborated housing construction might be justified simply by assigning it an unrealistically high imputed value.

Project boundary price

Prices used in analyzing agricultural projects are not necessarily farm-gate prices. The concept of a farm-gate price may be expanded to a "project boundary" price if a project has a marketing component or if it is a purely marketing project. Many projects have a marketing component, perhaps because there is no competitive channel reaching down to the farm-gate level for the unprocessed product. Of concern in these projects are both the farm-gate price (on which to base the estimates of the net benefit to the farmer) and the price at which the processed product is sold in the market (after being handled in the facilities financed by the project). Such a case is found in the Rahad project in the Sudan. There the Roseires dam on the Blue Nile will provide irrigation water for the production of cotton, which will be ginned in new facilities financed by the project. The analyst, of course, is interested in the price of cotton paid to the farmers so that their incomes can be estimated. But, since this price is set administratively, it could not be used directly in the economic analysis of the project. The analyst is also interested in the price of ginned cotton because that is the first product the project will actually sell in a reasonably competitive market. In this case, the point of first sale is f.o.b. (free on board) Port Sudan, and the price there becomes the basis for the benefit stream.

Predicting Future Prices

Since project analysis is about judging future returns from future investment, as analysts we are immediately involved in judging just what future prices may be. This is a matter of judgment, not mechanics. No esoteric mathematical model exists to come to the aid of the project analyst; like everyone else he must take into consideration all the facts he can find, seek judgments from those he respects, and then come to a conclusion himself. It tends to be a rather unsettling process. The only consolation is that careful, considered judgment about the course of future prices is better than giving the matter no thought at all and wasting scarce resources on incompletely planned projects.

We have been discussing how to find market prices, and it is from these current prices that we begin. The best initial guess about future prices is that they will retain the present relationships, or perhaps the average relationship they have borne to each other over the past few years. We must consider, however, whether these average relationships will change in the future and how we will deal with a general increase in the level of prices owing to inflation.

Changes in relative prices

We may first raise the question of whether *relative* prices will change. Will some inputs become more expensive over time in relation to other commodities? Will some prices fall relatively as supplies become more plentiful? Not easy questions to deal with, but some approaches to answers can be made. In financial analysis, of course, a change in a relative price means a change in the market price structure that producers face either for inputs or for outputs. A change in a relative price, then, is reflected directly in the project's financial accounts. A rise in the relative price of fertilizer reduces the incremental net benefit—the amount the farm family has to live on. It is thus clearly a cost in the farm account. The same line of reasoning can be applied in the financial analysis for any other group participating in the project.

A change in the relative price of an item implies a change in its marginal productivity—that is, a change in its marginal value product—or a change in the satisfaction it contributes when it is consumed. In economic analysis, where maximizing national income is the objective, a change in the relative price of an input implies a change in the amount that must be forgone by using the item in the project instead of elsewhere in the economy; it is therefore a change in the contribution the output of the project makes to the national income. Thus, changes in relative prices have a real effect on the project objective and must be reflected in project accounts in the years when such changes are expected.

There are several kinds of commodities subject to future changes in relative prices. Most agricultural project analysts would probably agree that the relative price of energy-intensive agricultural inputs is likely to continue to rise over the next several years, just as it has done over the past few years. Thus, on the input side the project accounts might show an annual increase, at least for the first decade or so, in the cost of fuel for tractors, for transporting the harvested crop, for drying grain, and for such petroleum-based inputs as fertilizers and chemical pesticides. On the output side, there may be some commodities that will probably continue to be in short supply and whose prices will rise as incomes increase—one might think of mutton from fat-tailed sheep in Iran, or, for that matter, of most meat products worldwide. How much will prices increase relative to those of other products? Certainly a difficult question, but one the project analyst must confront. For a range of products—from industrial crops such as fibers or oilseeds to food grains and vegetables—judgments will have to be made on the best possible basis.

In some countries, relative wages of rural labor may rise as economic development proceeds during the life of a project. This will have implications not only for the prices assumed for hired labor, but also for the incentive effect exerted by a given change in net benefit and for the technology assumed as a basis for projections in the farm budgets and project accounts.

Inflation

In the past few years, virtually every country has experienced inflation, and the only realistic assessment is that this will continue. No project analyst can escape deciding how to deal with inflation in his analysis.

The approach most often taken is to work the project analysis in constant prices. That is, the analyst assumes that the current price level (or some future price level—say, for the first year of project implementation) will continue to apply. It is assumed that inflation will affect most prices to the same extent so that prices retain their same general relations. The analyst then need only adjust future price estimates for anticipated relative changes, not for any change in the general price level. By comparing these estimates of costs and benefits with the constant prices, he is able to judge the effects of the project on the incomes of participants and its income-generating potential for the society as a whole. Although the absolute (or money) values of the costs and benefits in both the financial and the economic analyses will be incorrect, the general relations will remain valid, and so the measures of project worth discussed in chapter 9 may be applied directly. Working in constant prices is simpler and involves less calculation than working in current prices; for the latter, every entry has to be adjusted for anticipated changes in the general price level.

It is quite possible, however, to work the whole project analysis in current prices. This has the advantage that all costs and benefits shown would be estimates of what the real prices will be in each year of the project. Furthermore, estimates of investment costs will be in current terms for the year in which they are expected to occur, so that the finance ministry can more easily anticipate these needs and budget the amounts necessary to finance the project on schedule. The problem in this approach is that it involves predicting inflation rates. For items to be imported, some help is available in the World Bank report on *Price Prospects for Major Primary Commodities* (1982a), which is published biennially and updated in six-month intervals and includes an estimate of inflation in developed countries. For domestic inflation rates in developing countries, other sources will have to be consulted, but obtaining an estimate in which one can place even minimal confidence will be difficult, to say the least. Even casting the project analysis in current terms may raise problems for the project analyst. Many governments have policy goals that call for greatly reduced inflation, and they cannot permit the circulation of official documents that assume rapid inflation will continue.

The mere mechanics of using current prices presents no analytical problem in project analysis, although it does complicate the computations. When we consider measures of project worth, some means of deflating future prices must be adopted for comparing future cost and benefit streams in terms that are free from the effects of general price increases. We will illustrate the methodology in chapter 10 in the section "Calculating Measures of Project Worth Using Current Prices."

Even when constant prices are used in the more conventional approach to project analysis, a table estimating the budgetary effects of the project in current terms that will prevail at least during the investment phase should be included either in the analysis or as a separate memorandum. It would list in current prices domestic currency needs, foreign exchange requirements, and subsidies. The finance ministry would then have better estimates to work with, and delays because of budgetary shortfalls could more easily be avoided.

Prices for Internationally Traded Commodities

For commodities that enter significantly in international trade, whether inputs or outputs, project analysts usually obtain price information from various groups of specialists who follow price trends and make projections about relative prices in the future. In many countries where agricultural exports are important, there are groups in the agriculture ministry or the finance ministry whose help may be sought.

There are also several international organizations and trade groups to which the analyst may turn. The World Bank, for instance, publishes its projections under the title *Price Prospects for Major Primary Commodities*. The Food and Agriculture Organization (FAO) sponsors intergovernmental groups that publish price information on rice; grains (other than rice); citrus; hard fibers; fibers (other than hard fibers); oilseeds, oils and fats; bananas; wine and wine products; tea; meat; and cocoa. Information may be obtained from the secretary of the relevant intergovernmental group at the FAO headquarters in Rome or from the FAO representative in individual countries.

Several international commodity organizations keep detailed price information for the products of their interest. These include the International Tea Committee, the International Cocoa Organization, the International Wool Secretariat, the International Coffee Organization, the International Association of Seed Crushers, the International Rubber Study Group, and the International Sugar Organization, all with headquarters in London; the International Olive Oil Council in Madrid; and the International Cotton Advisory Committee in Washington.

Some individual nations systematically collect production and price information for crops and livestock products of interest to them, and they often are willing to share this information with analysts in other countries without charge or restriction. The United States Department of Agriculture—probably the most important of these—publishes detailed studies about most major crops traded in international markets. Information may be obtained from agricultural attaches in American embassies, or directly from the department's Foreign Agriculture Service. The Commonwealth Secretariat in London publishes information about price trends for commodities of interest to its member nations. A detailed list of "Sources of Information on World Prices" is available from the World Bank (Woo 1982).

Financial Export and Import Parity Prices

In projects that produce a commodity significant in international trade, the price estimates are often based on projections of prices at some distant foreign point. The analyst must then calculate the appropriate price to use in the project accounts, either at the farm gate or at the project boundary.

If the farm-gate or project boundary prices for the internationally traded commodities in the project are already known, and the prices in the particular country tend to follow world market prices, the farm-gate prices may be adjusted by the same relative amount as indicated, say, by the medium trend projected in the future relative prices supplied by one or another international organization. Also, in financial analysis, if the farm-gate price is set administratively and is not allowed to adjust freely to world prices, the relevant price to use is the administratively set price.

Simply adjusting domestic prices by the same relative amount as foreign prices often arrives at figures too rough for project analysis. The approach ignores the fact that marketing margins in commodity trade tend to be less flexible than the commodity prices themselves. There are also many instances in estimating the economic value of a traded commodity that involve deriving a shadow price based on international prices. In such instances it is necessary to calculate export or import parity prices. (See chapter 7, the subsection "Economic export and import parity values.") These are the estimated prices at the farm gate or project boundary, which are derived by adjusting the c.i.f. (cost, insurance, and freight) or f.o.b. prices by all the relevant charges between the farm gate and the project boundary and the point where the c.i.f. or f.o.b. price is quoted. The elements commonly included in c.i.f. and f.o.b. are given in table 3-2.

One common case for which an export parity price has to be calculated is that of a commodity produced for a foreign market. Table 3-3 gives an example based on the Rahad project in the Sudan. It shows the generalized elements for calculating export parity prices so that the same methodology can be applied in other cases. As noted earlier, the Rahad project included cotton gins. Since the gins produce lint and cottonseed for export and scarto, a by-product of very short fibers not suitable for

Table 3-2. *Elements of C.i.f. (Cost, Insurance, Freight)*
and F.o.b. (Free on Board)

Item	Element
C.i.f.	*Includes*:
	F.o.b. cost at point of export
	Freight charges to point of import
	Insurance charges
	Unloading from ship to pier at port
	Excludes:
	Import duties and subsidies
	Port charges at port of entry for taxes, handling, storage, agents' fees, and the like
F.o.b.	*Includes*:
	All costs to get goods on board—but still in harbor of exporting country:
	Local marketing and transport costs
	Local port charges including taxes, storage, loading, fumigation, agents' fees, and the like
	Export taxes and subsidies
	Project boundary price
	Farm-gate price

Source: William A. Ward, "Calculating Import and Export Parity Prices," training material of the Economic Development Institute, CN-3 (Washington, D.C.: World Bank, 1977), p. 8.

export and sold locally, the analyst needed three prices. For the lint and seed estimates, he began with forecasts of the 1980 c.i.f. prices in current terms at Liverpool, which were available from World Bank publications. From these c.i.f. prices, he then deducted insurance, ocean freight, export duties, port handling costs, and rail freight from the cotton gin at the project site to Port Sudan, thus obtaining the export parity prices at the project boundary: £Sd178.650 for lint and £Sd18.097 for seed. (The symbol for Sudanese pounds is £Sd.) The price for scarto, which was not exported, was based on the prevailing domestic price.

To illustrate, we may continue to calculate the export parity price at the farm gate, although in the Rahad example, where the farm-gate price was set administratively, this calculation was not made. The computations are laid out in the part of table 3-3 that continues from the entry for "*Equals* export parity price at project boundary." Here a new issue arises. The three products that the gin produces—lint, seed, and scarto—must be converted into their seed cotton equivalents, since it is seed cotton that the farmer sells. Similar conversions have to be made in many other instances—for example, rice milling or groundnut decortication. For the Rahad project, a weighted price of £Sd83.239 for the seed cotton was calculated using a ginning outturn of 40 percent lint, 59 percent seed, and 1 percent scarto. From this weighted price were deducted the ginning, baling, and storage charges and the costs of collection and transport from the farm gate to the gin, thus arriving at the farm-gate export parity price of £Sd66.946.

A parallel computation leads to the import parity price. Here the issue is the price at which an import substitute can be sold domestically if it must compete with imports. Table 3-4 illustrates this issue with the example of maize production in Nigeria. The same example is presented diagrammatically in figure 3-1. Nigeria is a net maize importer, and the project is to produce maize for domestic consumption to replace imported maize. We begin with the f.o.b. price at the point of export—in this case U.S. ports on the Gulf of Mexico—derived from World Bank commodity estimates. To this we add freight and insurance to obtain the c.i.f. price at either Lagos or Apapa, the two Nigerian ports concerned. Then we would add any tariffs and subsidies (in this case there are none); add

Table 3-3. *Financial Export Parity Price for Cotton, Rahad Irrigation Project, Sudan*
(1980 forecast prices)

Step in the calculation	Relevant step in the Sudanese example	Value per ton		
		Lint	Seed	Scarto[a]
C.i.f. at point of import	C.i.f. Liverpool (taken as estimate for all European ports)	US$639.33	US$103.39	—
Deduct unloading at point of import				
Deduct freight to point of import	Freight and insurance	– 39.63	– 24.73	—
Deduct insurance				
Equals f.o.b. at point of export	F.o.b. Port Sudan	US$599.70	US$78.66	—
Convert foreign currency to domestic currency at official exchange rate	Converted at official exchange rate of £Sd1.000 = US$2.872	£Sd208.809	£Sd27.389	—
Deduct tariffs	Export duties	– 17.813	– 1.000	—
Add subsidies	(None)			
Deduct local port charges	Port handling cost Lint: £Sd5.564 per ton Seed: £Sd1.510 per ton	– 5.564	– 1.510	—
Deduct local transport and marketing costs from project to point of export (if not part of project cost)	Freight to Port Sudan at £Sd6.782 per ton	– 6.782	– 6.782	—
Equals export parity price at project boundary	Export parity price at gin at project site	£Sd178.650	£Sd18.097	—

Table 3-3 (*continued*)

Step in the calculation	Relevant step in the Sudanese example	Value per ton		
		Lint	Seed	Scarto[a]
Conversion allowance if necessary	Convert to seed cotton (£Sd178.650 × 0.4 + £Sd18.097 × 0.59 + £Sd110.200 × 0.01)[b]	71.460	10.677	1.102
		£Sd83.239		
Deduct local storage, transport, and marketing costs (if not part of project cost)	Ginning, baling, and storage (£Sd15.229 per ton)		− 15.229	
	Collection and internal transfer (£Sd1.064 per ton)		− 1.064	
Equals export parity price at farm gate	Export parity price at farm gate	£Sd66.946		

£Sd Sudanese pounds. US$ U.S. dollars.

Source: Adapted from World Bank, "Appraisal of the Rahad Irrigation Project," PA-139b (Washington, D.C., 1973; restricted circulation), annex 16, table 6. The format of the table is adapted from Ward, "Calculating Import and Export Parity Prices," p. 9.

a. Scarto is a by-product of very short, soiled fibers not suitable for export and is sold locally at a price of £Sd110.200 per ton.

b. Seed cotton is converted into lint, seed, and scarto assuming 1 ton of seed cotton yields 400 kilograms lint, 590 kilograms seed, and 10 kilograms scarto.

local port charges for harbor dues, fumigation, handling, and the like; and add local transport to the relevant inland market. The result is the wholesale price of imported maize. It is this wholesale price of maize in the inland market that is the focal point of our calculation. The alternative to project production is not to import the maize and transport it to the project area. Rather, the alternative is to import it and market it directly on the inland market. Thus the price the farmer can expect to receive in the absence of tariffs, subsidies, or an import ban is the wholesale price less the cost of moving his maize to the market. If the project had included processing facilities, then the relevant project boundary price would have been this wholesale price less handling costs from the processing facility to the wholesale market. In the Nigerian project, no processing facilities were included, so the relevant import parity price is the farm-gate price. As we move back from the wholesale market to the farm gate, we would have to provide for any conversion allowance. In this case none is necessary, since it is assumed that the farmer will sell shelled maize. From the wholesale price, then, we deduct local marketing costs including assembly, bags, and intermediary mar-

Table 3-4. *Financial Import Parity Price of Early-crop Maize,*
Central Agricultural Development Projects, Nigeria
(1985 forecast prices in 1976 constant terms)

Steps in the calculation	Relevant steps in the Nigerian example	Value per ton
F.o.b. at point of export	F.o.b. U.S. Gulf ports No. 2 U.S. yellow corn in bulk[a]	US$116
Add freight to point of import	Freight and insurance	31
Add unloading at point of import	(Included in freight estimate)	
Add insurance		
Equals c.i.f. at point of import	C.i.f. Lagos or Apapa	US$147
Convert foreign currency to domestic currency at official exchange rate	Converted at official exchange rate of ₦1 = US$1.62	₦91
Add tariffs	(None)	
Deduct subsidies	(None)	
Add local port charges	Landing and port charges (including cost of bags)	22
Add local transport and marketing costs to relevant market	Transport (based on a 350-kilometer average)	18
Equals price at market	Wholesale price	₦131
Conversion allowance if necessary	(Not necessary)	
Deduct transport and marketing costs to relevant market	Primary marketing (includes assembly, cost of bags, and intermediary margins)	− 14
	Transport (based on a 350-kilometer average)	− 18
Deduct local storage, transport, and marketing costs (if not part of project cost)	Storage loss (10 percent of harvested weight)	− 9
Equals import parity price at farm gate	Import parity price at farm gate	₦90

₦ Nigerian naira.
Source: Adapted from World Bank, "Supplementary Annexes to Central Agricultural Development Projects," 1370-UNI (Washington, D.C., 1976; restricted circulation), supplement 11, appendix 2, table 4. The format of the table is adapted from Ward, "Calculating Import and Export Parity Prices," p. 10.
a. Forecast from World Bank, *Price Prospects for Major Primary Commodities*, 814/76 (Washington, D.C., 1976), annex 1, p. 12.

gins, transport from the farm to the market, and storage losses, thus obtaining the import parity price at the farm gate of ₦90. (The symbol for Nigerian naira is ₦.) This is the maximum price the farmer could expect to receive, again in the absence of tariffs, subsidies, or an import ban.

Figure 3-1. *Diagrammatic Derivation of Import Parity Price
of Early-crop Maize, Central Agricultural Development Projects, Nigeria*
(1985 forecast prices in 1976 constant terms)

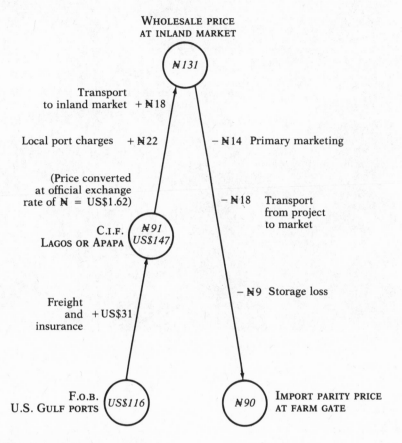

WHOLESALE PRICE
AT INLAND MARKET

₦131

Transport
to inland market + ₦18

Local port charges   + ₦22   − ₦14 Primary marketing

(Price converted
at official exchange
rate of ₦ = US$1.62)   − ₦18   Transport
                                               from project
                                               to market

C.I.F.   ₦91
LAGOS OR APAPA US$147

                                       − ₦9 Storage loss

Freight
and + US$31
insurance

F.O.B.   US$116   ₦90   IMPORT PARITY PRICE
U.S. GULF PORTS   AT FARM GATE

₦ Nigerian naira.
US$ U.S. dollars.
Source: Same as table 3-4.

4

Farm Investment Analysis

ONCE MARKET PRICES have been determined for those items that enter the cost and benefit streams, this information must be arranged in "pattern" accounts to begin the assessment of the effects a proposed project will have on the farmers, public and private enterprises, and government agencies that will participate in project implementation. These accounts are central to the financial analysis of agricultural projects; they are always based on market prices.

Although we will touch on the essential elements of financial analysis, much more could be taken up here. Just how elaborate the financial analysis must be for a particular project will depend on the complexity of the project. Most agricultural projects will call for a financial projection based on at least one pattern farm plan that is assumed for participating farmers. This pattern (or model) farm plan projects resource use and income flows for a group of similar farms participating in the project. The financial projections for the private and public firms or project entities may be quite summary in nature for a simply organized project, but a project in which several different firms and project entities are concerned or one that poses special financial problems may involve a much more complex analysis. The major accounts needed will be outlined in this chapter and in chapters 5 and 6, and pattern formats

Facing page: Setting out for the field in Paraguay.

suggested. This will enable the project analyst to proceed with the confidence that he is preparing an acceptable financial analysis. For more
complex projects, especially those projects involving more complex public or private firms with specialized cost, revenue, or financing situations,
the project analyst will have to move beyond what is discussed here.
Agricultural project analysts may want to turn for more technical help to
financial analysts or accountants, just as they would turn to agriculturalists or livestock technicians for their particular expertise. Many financial
analysts and accountants, however, will not be familiar with methodologies of agricultural project analysis or with the particular analytical
needs of the financial aspects of these projects, so even financial analysts
and accountants may find that the following discussion may help them
respond to a request for assistance.

Objectives of Financial Analysis

Six major objectives for financial analysis occur in analyzing agricultural projects.

Assessment of financial impact

The most important objective of financial analysis is to assess the
financial effects the project will have on farmers, public and private
firms, government operating agencies, and any others who may be participating in it. This assessment is based on an analysis of each participant's current financial status and on a projection of his future financial
performance as the project is implemented. Detailed financial projections are needed for this analysis.

Judgment of efficient resource use

The overall return of the project and the repayment of loans extended
to individual enterprises are important indicators of the efficiency of
resource use. For management especially, overall return is important
because managers must work within the market price framework they
face. Farm investment analysis and financial ratio analysis provide the
tools for this review. Project analysts and others concerned with decisions on policies for national economic growth and development will
have to look beyond the financial analysis—at market prices—and form a
judgment about the effects of the project on real resources for the economy as a whole. In chapter 7 we take up this issue in the discussion of how
to determine economic values.

Assessment of incentives

The financial analysis is of critical importance in assessing the incentives for farmers, managers, and owners (including governments) who

will participate in the project. Will farm families have an incremental income large enough to compensate them for the additional effort and risk they will incur? Will private sector firms earn a sufficient return on their equity investment and borrowed resources to justify making the investment the project requires? For semipublic enterprises, will the return be sufficient for the enterprises to maintain a self-financing capability and to meet the financial objectives set out by the society?

Provision of a sound financing plan

A principal objective of the financial analysis is to work out a plan that projects the financial situation and sources of funds of the various project participants and of the project itself. The financial plan provides a basis for determining the amount and timing of investment by farmers and for setting repayment terms and conditions for the credit extended to support the investment. It provides the same basis for an assessment of the investment plans and debt repayment capacities of public and private firms participating in the project. Finally, for the project as a whole, the financial plan is the basis for determining the amount and timing of outside financing—whether from the national treasury or from international sources—and for establishing how rapidly the borrowed resources should be repaid. The estimated effect of inflation on both revenues and costs should be taken into account in making this assessment.

Coordination of financial contributions

The financial plan allows the coordination of the financial contributions of the various project participants. The coordination is made on the basis of an overall financial projection for the project as a whole. It addresses itself to such questions as whether the availability of resources from the treasury or international agency is matched with farmers' investment capacities and available funds for investment and operating expenses as well as with the timing of expenditures for project investments such as feeder roads and irrigation structures and for working capital needed for stocks in processing industries and the like.

Assessment of financial management competence

On the basis of a projection of the pattern financial accounts, especially for the larger firms and project entities, the analyst can form a judgment about the complexity of the financial management the project will require and about the capability of those who will manage the project's implementation. And from this assessment, the analyst can then judge what changes in organization and management may be necessary if the project is to proceed on schedule and what specialized training may be advisable.

Table 4-1. *Differences between Farm Income Analysis, Funds Flow Analysis, and Farm Investment Analysis*

Item	Farm income analysis	Funds flow analysis[a]	Farm investment analysis[b]
General objective	Check current performance of farm	Check farmer's liquidity	Check attractiveness of additional investment
Period usually analyzed	Individual years	Loan repayment period	Useful life of investment
Prices used	Current prices	Current prices	Constant prices
Treatment of capital	Annual depreciation charge	Cash purchases and sales	Initial investment, residual value
Off-farm income	Excluded	Cash portion included	Cash and noncash included
Home-consumed farm production	Included	Excluded	Included
Performance criteria	Return to capital and labor engaged on farm	Cash available to farm family	Return to additional resources engaged
Time value	Undiscounted	Undiscounted	Discounted
Performance indicators	Profit as a percentage of net worth, family income	Cash surplus or deficit	Net present worth, internal rate of return, benefit-cost ratio, net benefit-investment ratio, net benefit increase

Source: Schaefer-Kehnert (1980).
a. Also called sources-and-uses-of-funds analysis.
b. Benefit-cost analysis of on-farm investments.

Preparing the Farm Investment Analysis

The starting point for both the financial and the economic analysis of an agricultural project is generally a group of investment analyses of pattern or model farms, based on budgets for individual pattern farms. These pattern farm budgets compare the situation with the project to that anticipated without the project for the duration of the project. They enable the analyst to form a sound judgment about the likely benefit to farmers of participating in an agricultural project and about the incentives for farmers to do so.

Farm investment analysis is the topic of this chapter. This analysis is similar to, and sometimes confused with, farm management analyses done by agricultural economists, which may be distinguished as farm income analysis and funds flow analysis. The differences are summarized in table 4-1.

Farm income analysis is generally used to evaluate the performance of a farm in a particular year. Its objective is to help improve the management of the farm. Current prices are used, and a depreciation allowance is included to account for that portion of longer-term capital investment used up in the year being considered. Noncash items such as home-consumed production and payments in kind are included. Off-farm income and expenditure are excluded because the analysis is intended to evaluate the performance only of the farm itself. The analysis provides an estimate of the return to capital invested and to the farmer's labor, and this may then be compared with the return to alternative cropping patterns or to off-farm opportunities.

Funds flow analysis, also called sources-and-uses-of-funds analysis, is used to determine a farmer's liquidity in an analysis of his credit situation. Only cash items, including purchase and sale of capital goods, enter the analysis. Off-farm cash income and expenditure are included, but home-consumed production is not. The analysis shows the cash available to the family over a period of time.

Farm investment analysis, in contrast, is undertaken to determine the attractiveness of a proposed investment to farmers and to other participants, including the society as a whole. It projects the effect on farm income of a particular investment and estimates the return to the capital engaged. It follows the principles of discounted cash flow analysis (discussed in detail in chapters 9 and 10). The analysis is projected over the useful life of the investment. The initial investment is shown at the beginning of the projection, and a residual value at the end. In general, the analysis is cast in constant prices, although allowance may have to be made for inflation. Off-farm income is included. Even though we use the term "cash flow," noncash elements enter the projection, including home-consumed production and payments and receipts in kind. (The term was first applied to industrial investments, in which noncash elements are less common.) When doing farm investment analysis, some elements of funds flow analysis are often incorporated to enable the analyst to assess the farmer's liquidity and his credit use. Those who wish to pursue farm income analysis or funds flow analysis in relation to project analysis may refer to standard farm management texts such as Harsh, Connor, and Schwab (1981) and Kay (1981). Those who want more detail about the application of farm budgets to project analysis may consult Brown (1979).

Pattern farm investment analysis that includes farm budgets should be prepared for almost every agricultural project. Although agricultural project analyses that do not have farm budgets are used, it is increasingly accepted that farm budgets are an extremely desirable, if not essential, part of project analysis. The benefit stream of an agricultural project may be built up simply by multiplying the total area to be planted by the expected yield, essentially treating the whole area as one undifferentiated farm. If this is all that is done, it may hide crucial information about the effects of the project on individual farmers and obscure underlying unrealistic assumptions. Even when the project involves only a public sector undertaking, a farm budget is likely to be necessary to test the feasibility of the cropping pattern and the financial viability of the enterprise.

The purpose in preparing farm investment analyses for a project is not to take a sample of the farms in the project area. Rather, it is to select major farm types expected to participate and to look at the impact of the project on them. These farm investment analyses are usually projections for the life of the project, often twenty to twenty-five years, not for just a single year. The analyst will want to examine the cropping pattern and perhaps to diagram it; to determine the labor that will be required if farmers are to participate in the project and perhaps to prepare a month-by-month labor budget showing requirements and the availability of family labor; to look at production and inputs; and, finally, to prepare a farm budget in the detail needed for understanding and evaluating the effects of the project on the income of participating farmers. From these, the analyst can assess the financial effect of the proposed project on typical farms—both to judge incentives for participation and to determine whether national policies on minimum incomes for project participants are being met.

Farm investment analyses and farm budgets can of course be prepared for farms of any size. The problems of analyses for smaller farms are the focus here, since many, if not most, agricultural projects in developing countries will be directed toward smallholders whose families consume a large part of the food they produce.

Large commercial farms and plantations, however, whether publicly or privately held, are more like other business enterprises than they are like small, family-operated farms. Projected accounts for these large agricultural undertakings are probably more appropriately cast in formal financial statements such as those of the agricultural processing industries discussed in chapter 5.

In considering small farms, the analyst will be particularly concerned with the effect of the project on the total income of the farm family. The aspects of the small farm as a family unit and as a business firm must be clearly understood and appreciated. These will differ from society to society, and the project analyst should either know the society well enough to anticipate the farmers' response or be advised by others who do. One must assess the attitude of the family to proposed cropping patterns that involve more days of labor, to patterns that increase cash crop output and reduce food crop production below household requirements, to patterns that change the work responsibilities of men and women, and to patterns that require the family to run a considerable market risk. Farmers *are* price responsive, of course; the extensive research has amply confirmed this (Krishna 1967). But farmers live in a particular cultural and risk environment, and project analysts must take this environment into account when they project their pattern farm investment analyses.

Backed by this understanding of the particular cultural environment, the analyst will prepare the farm investment analyses as realistically as possible to determine what the family gains by participating in the project. The projection must be based on a specific package of technological innovation. The effectiveness of the proposed new technology on small farms must be realistically assessed, and the technological assumptions must be checked to ensure that they reflect on-farm conditions and not those of an experiment station. The analyst must form a judgment about how rapidly farmers will be willing to adopt new practices. The farm investment analysis should confirm that adoption of a new technology will really be financially worthwhile, for farmers can respond to financial incentives only when it is truly remunerative for them to do so. The analyst must determine how much credit will stimulate farmers to adopt new practices and must assess how risky a new technology is and how variable the farm income may be under the project. The analyst will want to test the effect of risk on family income by determining what happens if yields fall below expectations or if prices are lower than anticipated and by undertaking similar sensitivity tests. Through such tests a margin to allow for bad years can be built into the farm plan.

Although in agricultural projects the analyst generally looks at budgets for entire farms, partial budgeting techniques can be used for undertakings that involve only a relatively minor change in the farm organization. To do this, one looks at the marginal cost (including opportunity cost) of adding a production activity and compares it with the marginal increase in benefit that the new activity will bring. Partial budgets are an effective tool for helping to search out the best combination of production activities. Brown (1979) discusses their use in some detail. In most projects, however, we expect rather substantial changes over a prolonged period, and under these circumstances it is better to project whole farm budgets. Then the total effect of the project on family income can be better assessed.

The information on which the project analyst will base his farm investment analysis will come from many sources. Project analysts will have to rely heavily on their professional colleagues to determine a sensible cropping pattern and livestock activity for a proposed project, the output that may be expected, the inputs that will be required, and the relevant prices for products. The project analyst will want to pay particular attention to the realism of the estimates provided by the agriculturalists and livestock specialists he consults. Unrealistic assumptions about yields, input levels, or rates of farmer acceptance and, hence, of buildup in project benefits will negate the best of project analyses.

The analyst will certainly want to visit the site of the proposed project and typical farms that will be included. Nothing substitutes for the firsthand knowledge that being there brings.

A crucial source of information in every agricultural project is the farmers themselves. Only through interviews with farmers can a project analyst reach a valid conclusion about the realism of his farm investment analysis. The project analyst will want to interview farmers about their present cropping patterns, labor requirements, use of inputs, and the market prices actually received and paid. He will want to gain a sense about the farmers' willingness to participate in the project were it to proceed. In a project area or on a similar site some farmers often are already using a proposed new technology. It is most important that these farmers be interviewed to tap their experience. The analyst will want to know the yields the farmers actually have realized with the new technology, the inputs they actually must employ, and their general comments on the new technology and cropping pattern proposed for the project. The analyst will want to assess the labor requirements farmers have found necessary to use the new technology.

Interviewing farmers is an art in itself, and only a few comments can be made here. The information farmers give will usually be contradictory, but out of a group of interviews the project analyst can gain a sense of feasible technological and financial relations. Farmers will have to be interviewed in the field, not in the office. The analyst will have to know the local measurements and not expect everything to be reported neatly on a unit basis. The analyst or one of his staff should probably conduct the interviews alone or with very few other people around. Great care should be taken to establish a good atmosphere in the interview so that farmers are not overawed by the analyst's presence; farmers should also know that the information they give will not be used for tax purposes. A formal questionnaire may be helpful, especially if much information is to be collected by assistants, but any questionnaire should be carefully pretested in the field before use. It may be better for the analyst or his assistants to fill in the questionnaire only after the interview is complete and the interviewer has left the farmer. In any event, before the interviews the analyst should have formed a clear idea about the information he needs, perhaps in the form of a list of questions, so that critical information will not be overlooked. Questions put to farmers should be as specific as possible. Most information gathered should relate to actual experience, perhaps in the last cropping season. Questions about hypothetical situations should be avoided to the extent possible. The

very nature of seeking information about a proposed project will, however, of necessity involve many "what if" kinds of questions.

Cropping patterns are usually based on the judgment of the agriculturalists and livestock specialists working with the project analyst. Their
judgment, in turn, will be based on their familiarity with the agriculture
of the area, on research results and the results of pilot projects—perhaps
undertaken especially as part of the project preparation—and on their
knowledge of the farmers who will participate in the project. In most
instances, experienced technicians can propose realistic patterns close to
the optimum, but sometimes linear programming may be used as a more
formal methodology to optimize cropping patterns. Linear programming has been applied in preparing agricultural project analyses but is
not regularly used either in national planning agencies or in international lending agencies. It is a complex methodology that requires
more formal input-output data than does simple budgeting, and in practice it requires computers. There are serious methodological limitations
to the use of linear programming for agricultural project analysis: problems of dealing with risk, farmers' cultural traditions, variability of soils
within farms, water availability in different areas of a farm, and other
farm-level variations. Even so, when preparing a project for an area
where there is inadequate experience to rely on in forming subjectively
determined cropping patterns or when dealing with very complex patterns, the project analyst may want to consult specialists in linear programming for assistance. In these cases, the project preparation takes on
some of the character of a research effort. Because it is a well-known
methodology widely used in farm management research, many agricultural colleges have staff familiar with linear programming.

In most agricultural projects, about half a dozen or so pattern farm
investment analyses will suffice, but generalization about this is danger-
ous. The number of pattern farm analyses depends entirely on the complexity of the project. The analyst will want a pattern farm investment
analysis for each major group of soil and water conditions in the project
area and for each major difference in the size of holdings. Of course, each
major cropping pattern or livestock activity will require a separate farm
investment analysis. Remember that the objective is an indication of the
effect of the project, not some kind of rigorously drawn, random sample.
In practice, the number of farm budgets prepared for any given project
analysis is a tradeoff between the complexity of the proposed project and
the availability of staff to prepare the investment analyses.

Each farm investment analysis will be the result of careful consultation with technical specialists and interviews with farmers. Just as it is
not possible to generalize about how many pattern farm budgets will be
necessary, neither is it possible to generalize about how many interviews
with farmers will be needed. Thorough preparation of a complex project
may require twenty-five to fifty or even more interviews to provide the
information for each farm analysis. But a simpler project that will use a
better-known technology may require only half a dozen to a dozen inter-

views for each pattern farm budget. A group doing an appraisal of a proposed project would probably interview fewer farmers than was necessary in the initial project preparation. Each situation will have to be judged by itself in the light of how confident the analyst needs to be about the project analysis, how complex the project is, how well known the technology is, and how available are staff for project preparation.

Similar considerations apply in deciding the level of detail necessary in a farm investment analysis. Any farm investment analysis is intended to improve the decisionmaking for a project. It is, of necessity, an abstraction. This imprecision is forced on us by the very fact that we must predict future events, but it also arises from the question of just how much detail is necessary. In every farm investment analysis, the project analyst will reach a point at which further elaboration or further detail would make such a marginal contribution to the investment decision that it is not worth the time. Just when that point is reached will vary from project to project according to the circumstances of the project and the circumstances of the decisionmaking process.

It is easy to conceive of a set of pattern farm investment analyses that would be so enormously detailed and have so many different budgets that the process would quickly become bogged down in detail. Because of staff limitations and because of the approximate nature of the underlying data, it is better to hold both the number of pattern farms and the level of detail to the minimum that will serve to lay out clearly the major points about the project.

The project analyst will have to determine how best to present his information so that those who must review his work and make decisions about the project can work efficiently and yet have the information they need. The major entries, the level of detail, and the like will vary from project to project. Some of the elements given in separate tables in the illustrative examples in this chapter may be better combined in the tables that present a particular project. In many project reports, only a summary of background information, plus a detailed farm budget, will be needed. Other, more detailed tables can be included in annexes or in a separate volume of background information reproduced in limited quantities and circulated only to those most interested in the project. This kind of additional data can even be kept in a separate project information file that can be made available to anyone seriously interested. (In the Paraguay report used as an example in this chapter, the analyst presented his farm investment analysis in four annex tables and collected the supporting information in a separate project information file.)

What we will present here is a pattern format that includes the features most commonly of significance in agricultural project analysis. This pattern format uses a terminology generally accepted by both farm management specialists and accountants. In using the format, the analyst will have to determine for himself, for each project in his charge, exactly how much detail is necessary to support the analysis and exactly how this detail is best reported to facilitate decisions about the particular project.

Elements of Farm Investment Analysis

The principal elements of farm investment analysis are outlined in this subsection and are listed in table 4-2. A flow chart for preparing the analysis is given in figure 4-1. Not every element will be necessary in every analysis, and the means of presenting the elements will vary from project to project according to circumstances.

The most important elements of a farm investment analysis can be illustrated by an example adapted from the Paraguay Livestock and Agricultural Development Project. (Tables that illustrate particular elements of the analysis are noted in table 4-2.) The project is to increase agricultural production, productivity, and income on some 940 livestock farms and some 3,000 mixed farms, mostly small, through on-farm investments supported by credit, technical assistance, feeder roads, and market improvement. Most of the important aspects of preparing a farm investment analysis are touched on in this example, but it is clear that no single example can cover every possibility. Each project analyst will want to build on the illustrative tables that outline this one example for the purposes of his own project analysis. As in all accounts, the objectives of the farm investment account determine its content and format.

Accounting convention for farm investment analysis

Because farm investment analysis follows the principles of discounted cash flow, it is convenient to adopt an accounting convention that is congruent with those principles. [This convention has been called "time-adjusted" by Schaefer-Kehnert (1980), who has elaborated its use.] The discounting process used in discounted cash flow analysis implicitly assumes that every transaction falls at the end of the accounting period. It is desirable that the farm investment analysis match this assumption. This is simply accomplished if we consider the initial investment to take place at the end of year 1 of the project, regardless of whether it will actually take a full year or only a few weeks. Year 2, then, is the first accounting period in which increases in operating cost and incremental benefits occur. Thus, the dividing line between the end of the initial investment period and the beginning of the incremental production operations coincides exactly with the dividing line between years 1 and 2 of the project. (Some analysts accomplish much the same result by considering investment to fall in year 0, but this gives rise to problems when cash flows are aggregated.) Considering that preparing a farm plan, making a loan, constructing or purchasing investment items, and purchasing new inputs can take at least several months to a year, reserving year 1 for investment is not unrealistic. Doing so, however, is not dictated by real events but by the accounting convention.

If all transactions are considered to fall at the end of the accounting period, then we must allow for the availability of the needed operating

Table 4-2. *Principal Elements of Farm Investment Analysis*

Element	Illustrative table
Farm resource use	
Land use	4-4
(Land use calendar)	(Figure 4-2)
Labor use	
Annual labor requirement by crop operation, by crop for 1 hectare	4-5
Labor distribution by crop and month, per hectare	4-6
(Labor use diagram)	(Figure 4-3)
Labor requirement by crop and month	4-7
Hired labor by crop and month	4-8
Off-farm labor	Not illustrated
Farm production	
Crops and pasture	
Yield and carrying capacity	4-9
Crop and pasture production	4-10
Livestock	
Herd projection	4-27
Herd composition, purchases, sales	4-11
Herd productivity	4-28
Feeding period and daily ration	4-29
Feed requirement and production	4-30
Yield per animal	Not illustrated
Valuation	
Farm-gate prices	4-12
Value of production	
Crops	
Livestock	4-13
Incremental residual value	4-14
Farm inputs	
Investment	
Physical	4-15
Foreign exchange component	Not illustrated
Value of investment	4-15
Operating expenditure	
Crop	
Livestock	4-16
Incremental working capital	4-17
Farm budget	
Without project	4-18
With project	
Net benefit before financing	4-19
Debt service	4-24
Net benefit after financing	
Cash position	4-19

Figure 4-1. *Flow Chart for Farm Investment Analysis*

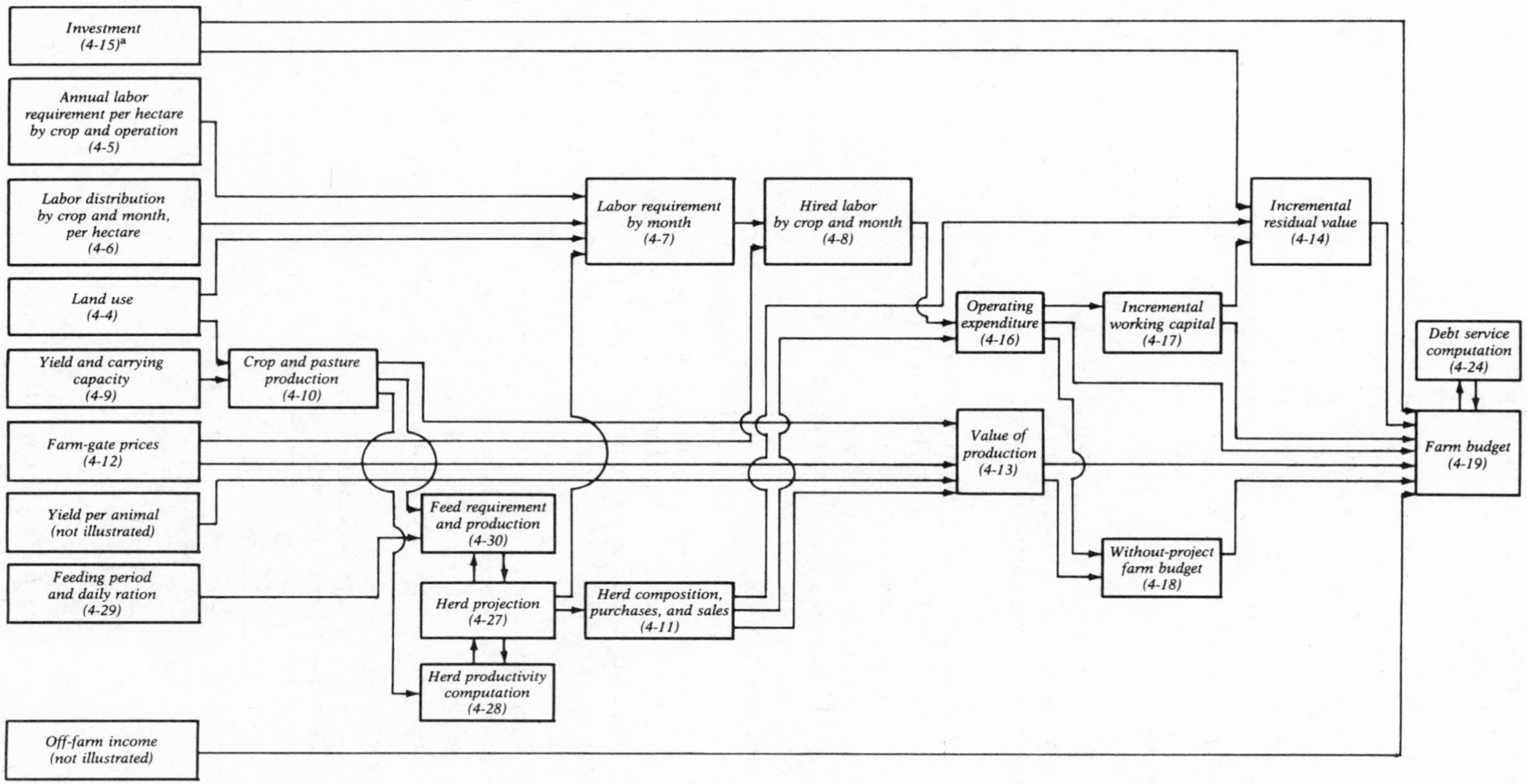

a. Numbers in parentheses refer to the illustrative tables in this chapter.

expenditure at the beginning of the cropping season. This is accomplished by incorporating in the analysis an entry for incremental work-ing capital at the end of the preceding year. The amount of the working capital needed is related to the farming system being analyzed. If a single annual crop is produced, then nearly all the operating expenditure will be needed at the beginning of the crop year. But if two crops are to be produced in succession, only the operating expenditure for the first crop need be on hand at the beginning of the crop year, since there will be a harvest during the year that will provide proceeds to replace the input supplies needed before the second crop is harvested. Thus, only half the total annual operating expenditure need be on hand at the beginning of the year. The *incremental* working capital needed (either an increase or a decrease) at the beginning of the year, then, is entered at the end of the year *preceding* the year when it will be expended for production. A set of recommended adjustments in incremental operating expenditure to obtain incremental working capital is given in table 4-3. Introducing an incremental working capital stream reflects real resource use. When an investment is undertaken, short-term inputs such as seed, fertilizer, feed, and the like must be on hand. They are replaced from the proceeds of the harvest or livestock sales during the year and are again on hand for production in the following year. If operations are to expand the next year, then stocks of inputs for production must be increased, and this will be reflected in another incremental working capital entry. Since the incremental working capital is entered separately, it will easily be in-cluded in the total investment shown when the farm budget is prepared and will not be inadvertently overlooked. At the end of the project, the incremental working capital for each year is added together algebra-ically and taken out of the project as part of the residual value. Thus, including incremental working capital in the accounts does not result in double counting.

One practical outcome of this accounting convention is that operating expenditures and benefits in year 1 generally remain the same as they were without the project. In some cases new investment might require an increase in operating expenditure in year 1, even though production

Table 4-3. *Incremental Working Capital as a Percentage of Incremental Operating Expenditure*

Item	Percent
Tree crops (slowly maturing, one harvest season)	100
Annual crops	
One season	80–100
Two seasons	40–60
Continuous cropping and continuously producing livestock enterprises	20–40

Source: Schaefer-Kehnert (1980).

would not be affected until year 2. In other instances, both operating expenditures and production might actually decrease—as might happen if new irrigation canals were to be constructed, disrupting farming operations. In laying out the farm investment analysis, however, it is usually considered that working capital is not freed as a result of the investment so that the layout of the farm budget can be simplified. If this were not done, both data for the case without the project and data for a "preproject" year or "year 1" would be needed to accommodate the decision rule that working capital be a proportion of the increase or decrease in the operating expenditure for the following year.

Showing working capital as a separate entry facilitates determining how much short-term credit may be needed by the farmer. A judgment may be made about whether the farmer will have savings from which to finance increased working capital or whether some proportion or all will have to be covered by extending the farmer a short-term loan, which then can be incorporated into the financing section of the farm budget.

The accounting convention adopted here is not much different from that most commonly used by project analysts. The most important difference is the rule of reserving year 1 for investment only and assuming the investment to fall at the end of the year. It is more common to include investment in year 1 but to assume that it will occur at the *beginning* of the year, even though the discounting process assumes it falls at the end of the year. Production is then assumed to be increased in year 1, an assumption that leads to an overestimate of the rate of return on the capital used. It also leads to a considerable overestimate of the farmer's income in the early years of the project and, hence, to an underestimate of his need for both long-term and short-term credit. The other difference between the accounting convention adopted here and that most commonly used by project analysts is only a matter of completeness. It is easy inadvertently to omit or underestimate working capital unless such capital is included in the convention. This convention for working capital leaves the crop year intact and therefore facilitates the supporting technical projections.

Farm resource use

Once the agronomists, livestock technicians, and other technical specialists have determined the components of a proposed farming system for a pattern farm, the analyst may proceed to prepare the farm investment analysis.

LAND USE. The first step is to determine what the land use on the farm will be. The land use for the Paraguay project is given in table 4-4. Note that the crop year is taken to extend from July of one calendar year to June of the next, since this arrangement makes the break in the year come during the Paraguayan winter season, when there are the fewest crops in the ground. The total farm area is 20.0 hectares, divided into *cultivated area, pasture, forest,* and a *house plot.* (Throughout the text of this chapter,

Table 4-4. *Land Use, 20-Hectare Mixed Farm, Livestock and Agricultural Development Project Model IV, Paraguay*
(hectares)

Type of use and crop[a]	Without project	With project					
		Year 1	2	3	4	5	6–20
Cultivated area							
Maize[b]	0.5	0.5	0.5	0.5	0.5	0.5	0.5
Manioc[b]	1.0	1.0	1.0	1.0	0.5	0.5	0.5
Beans	0.5	0.5	0.5	0.5	0.5	0.5	0.0
Cotton	2.0	2.0	2.0	2.0	2.2	2.5	3.0
Soybeans	0.0	0.0	1.0	1.0	2.2	2.5	3.0
Sunflower[c]	0.0	0.0	2.0	2.0	2.2	2.5	3.0
Total	4.0	4.0	7.0	7.0	8.1	9.0	10.0
Total cropland[d]	4.0	4.0	5.0	5.0	5.9	6.5	7.0
Cropping intensity[e]	1.0	1.0	1.4	1.4	1.4	1.4	1.4
Pasture							
Natural	10.5	7.0	3.5	0.0	0.0	0.0	0.0
Improved	0.0	3.5	7.0	10.5	10.5	10.5	10.5
Total	10.5	10.5	10.5	10.5	10.5	10.5	10.5
Forest	5.0	5.0	4.0	4.0	3.1	2.5	2.0
House plot	0.5	0.5	0.5	0.5	0.5	0.5	0.5
Total farm area	20.0	20.0	20.0	20.0	20.0	20.0	20.0

Source: Adapted from World Bank, "Staff Appraisal Report: Paraguay—Livestock and Agricultural Development Project," 2272–PA (Washington, D.C., 1979; restricted circulation), annex 1, table 17.

a. Operated by one family with six members and a work potential of 70 work days a month. A work day is the time (generally eight hours) devoted by one person during one day.

b. Maize and manioc are intercropped.

c. Double-cropped after cotton or soybeans. The area given is the area planted in the year shown.

d. Does not include second crop area, in this case the area planted in sunflower.

e. Cropping intensity is determined by dividing the total cultivated area by the total cropland.

the most common or generalized categories from the pattern tables will be shown in *italic* type. These items would be considered in any farm investment analysis. In all tables the generalized analytical framework applies, but in some the categories are all specific to the project analyzed.)

The land use, in accord with the accounting convention adopted, would remain unchanged in year 1, except for establishment of improved pasture that is part of the investment. In year 2, in which the proposed cropping pattern calls for sunflower to be introduced and to be double-cropped after either cotton or soybeans (depending on the year), both the total cultivated area and the total *cropland* are shown. The total culti-vated area is the total area planted in crops, whereas the total cropland is the area available to cultivate. When the total cultivated area is divided by the total cropland, the *cropping intensity* is obtained. In year 2, for example, the cropping intensity is 1.4 (7.0 ÷ 5.0 = 1.4). Many analysts prefer to report cropping intensity in percentages, so this would be reported as 140 percent. One check of the feasibility of the cropping pattern is the intensity. The analyst should be cautious about accepting a cropping pattern that has a very high cropping intensity or one that is markedly different from the pattern existing in the area. Farmers may well have good reasons for not driving up the intensity.

Many analysts also like to devise a cropping diagram, such as that given in figure 4-2, and this should be subdivided to indicate any existing farm plots. Such a diagram is usually drawn up only for the full-development situation. The diagram indicates the area to be devoted to each category of land use and each crop. In the case of our example, it extends over two years to show that the seasonal timing of the cotton-sunflower-soybean rotation occurs on one plot in one year and on another in the next. Checking vertically at any one time, we can be sure the cropping pattern does not call for more area than the farm has. Checking horizontally, we can determine when each crop must be planted and whether enough land will be available at the proper season. The left and right sides of the boxes showing the area to be planted in each crop are slanted to indicate the planting and harvest time necessary for each crop. Examining the cropping diagram can help determine if there will be adequate time between crops to prepare the land.

Figure 4-2. *Land Use Calendar for Project Years 6–20, 20-Hectare Mixed Farm, Livestock and Agricultural Development Project, Paraguay*

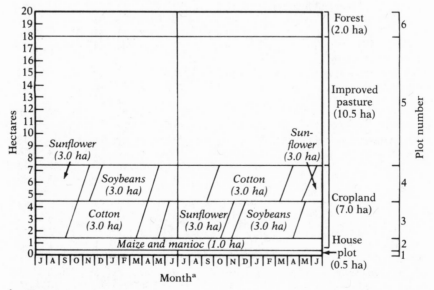

ha Hectares.
Source: Table 4-4.
a. Crop year is from July to June.

LABOR USE. A second aspect of the farm resource use is labor. To determine the labor the farm will require, we need to know the labor used to cultivate a hectare of each crop in each project year. It is desirable to be able to see this in two forms, by operation and by month. Table 4-5 shows the annual labor requirements for 1 hectare by crop and operation for the Paraguay project example. It includes the labor required not only for the various crops to be produced, but also for the pasture. The labor unit is a work day, the time (generally eight hours) devoted by one person during one day. The labor requirement for crops drops sharply between years 1 and 2 because of the introduction of draft animal power. In the case of pasture, the labor requirement for fencing and seeding is included in years 1 through 3. In the Paraguay model, other activities of pasture establishment are to be undertaken by a contractor, so there will be no call for labor from the farmer. If, however, labor for establishing some other kind of improvement were expected, such as farmers' digging their own tertiary canals in an irrigation project, then this should be included in the labor requirement.

Table 4-5. *Annual Labor Requirement per Hectare by Crop and Operation, 20-Hectare Mixed Farm, Paraguay Project* (work days)

Crop and operation	Without project	With project						
		Year 1	2	3	4	5	6	7–20
Crops								
Maize								
Land preparation and planting	22	22	11	11	11	11	11	11
Cultivation[a]	9	9	2	2	2	2	2	2
Harvesting	28	28	28	31	31	33	33	36
Total	59	59	41	44	44	46	46	49
Manioc								
Land preparation and planting	14	14	10	10	10	10	10	10
Cultivation[a]	27	27	15	15	15	15	15	15
Harvesting	19	19	19	21	21	23	23	25
Total	60	60	44	46	46	48	48	50
Beans								
Land preparation and planting	24	24	19	19	19	19	19	19
Cultivation	10	10	4	4	4	4	4	4
Harvesting	20	20	20	22	22	22	22	22
Total	54	54	43	45	45	45	45	45
Cotton								
Clearing	⎫	⎫	8	8	8	8	8	8
Plowing	⎬ 18	⎬ 18	3	3	3	3	3	3
Harrowing (2 times)	⎭	⎭	2	2	2	2	2	2
Seeding	4	4	1	1	1	1	1	1
Thinning	6	6	6	6	6	6	6	6
Cultivation (3 times)	30	30	3	3	3	3	3	3
Spraying (5 times)	10	10	10	10	10	10	10	10
Harvesting	37	37	43	43	46	46	49	49
Drying, packing, marketing	4	4	4	4	4	4	4	4
Total	109	109	80	80	83	83	86	86

Table 4-5 (*continued*)

Crop and operation	Without project	With project Year 1	2	3	4	5	6	7–20
Soybeans								
Clearing	—	—	8	8	8	8	8	8
Plowing	—	—	3	3	3	3	3	3
Harrowing (2 times)	—	—	2	2	2	2	2	2
Seeding	—	—	1	1	1	1	1	1
Thinning	—	—	6	6	6	6	6	6
Cultivation (2 times)	—	—	2	2	2	2	2	2
Spraying (2 times)	—	—	4	4	4	4	4	4
Harvesting	—	—	18	18	20	20	22	22
Transport	—	—	3	3	3	3	4	4
Total	—	—	47	47	49	49	52	52
Sunflower								
Clearing	—	—	6	6	6	6	6	6
Plowing	—	—	3	3	3	3	3	3
Harrowing (2 times)	—	—	2	2	2	2	2	2
Sowing	—	—	1	1	1	1	1	1
Thinning	—	—	6	6	6	6	6	6
Cultivation (2 times)	—	—	2	2	2	2	2	2
Spraying (2 times)	—	—	4	4	4	4	4	4
Harvesting	—	—	13	14	14	15	15	15
Drying, packing, marketing	—	—	4	4	4	5	5	5
Total	—	—	41	42	42	44	44	44
Pasture								
Improved establishment								
Fencing	—	7	7	7	0	0	0	0
Seeding	—	2	2	2	0	0	0	0
Maintenance	—	—	3	3	3	3	3	3

Note: For the area in various crops, see table 4-4.

Source: Adapted from A. O. Ballantyne, "Paraguay—Small Farmer Credit Component, Livestock and Agricultural Development Project," working papers on file (Washington, D.C.: World Bank, 1978; restricted circulation).

a. Maize and manioc are intercropped. Hence, during the period when both are growing, the allocation of cultivation time between the two crops has an arbitrary element.

The total labor requirement per hectare for each crop is distributed by month in table 4-6. The monthly distribution is most important because we must determine not only the total annual labor requirement on the farm but also its timing to assess whether sufficient family labor will be available and, if there is not enough, how much hired labor will be needed. Although some farm management analysts break down the labor requirement by week or fortnight, for purposes of project analysis the monthly distribution is sufficient.

On a mixed farm, livestock will also require labor. This may be calculated by determining how much time will be needed per animal unit in the livestock herd. An animal unit is a measurement of feed demand by a particular class of animal. (This is discussed in more detail in the appendix to this chapter. The total animal units for each year are reported in table 4-11. They are given in that table for the livestock herd that could exist on 100 model farms to avoid the problem of divisibility that arises when the increase in large livestock on a small farm is projected. Thus, to obtain the animal units on one farm, the total reported in table 4-11 must be divided by 100. We will return to a discussion of this convention in the next subsection, when we discuss the herd composition.) In the Paraguay example, it is assumed that each animal unit will require five minutes of care a day and that the requirement will be the same each month throughout the year. The labor requirement is determined on the basis of the animal units at the beginning of the year. Using animal units rather

Table 4-6. *Labor Distribution by Crop and Month,*
20-Hectare Mixed Farm, Paraguay Project
(work days per hectare)

Crop	Jul	Aug	Sept	Oct	Nov	Dec	Jan	Feb	Mar	Apr	May	Jun	Total
Maize[a]													
Without project, year 1	14	8	0	5	4	28	0	0	0	0	0	0	59
Year 2	9	2	0	1	1	28	0	0	0	0	0	0	41
Years 3–4	9	2	0	1	1	31	0	0	0	0	0	0	44
Years 5–6	9	2	0	1	1	33	0	0	0	0	0	0	46
Years 7–20	9	2	0	1	1	36	0	0	0	0	0	0	49
Manioc[a]													
Without project, year 1	0	0	14	3	3	3	4	3	5	3	3	19	60
Year 2	0	0	10	2	2	1	2	2	2	2	2	19	44
Years 3–4	0	0	10	2	2	1	2	2	2	2	2	21	46
Years 5–6	0	0	10	2	2	1	2	2	2	2	2	23	48
Years 7–20	0	0	10	2	2	1	2	2	2	2	2	25	50
Beans													
Without project, year 1	0	0	0	0	24	5	5	20	0	0	0	0	54
Year 2	0	0	0	0	19	2	2	20	0	0	0	0	43
Years 3–5	0	0	0	0	19	2	2	22	0	0	0	0	45
Cotton													
Without project, year 1	0	0	8	14	8	19	19	7	20	14	0	0	109
Years 2–3	0	0	8	6	8	6	5	8	25	14	0	0	80
Years 4–5	0	0	8	6	8	6	5	8	27	15	0	0	83
Years 6–20	0	0	8	6	8	6	5	9	28	16	0	0	86
Soybeans													
Years 2–3	0	0	0	0	13	8	3	2	10	8	3	0	47
Years 4–5	0	0	0	0	13	8	3	2	10	10	3	0	49
Years 6–20	0	0	0	0	13	8	3	2	11	11	4	0	52
Sunflower[b]													
Year 2	2	9	3	13	4	0	0	0	0	0	6	4	41
Years 3–4	2	9	3	14	4	0	0	0	0	0	6	4	42
Years 5–20	2	9	3	15	5	0	0	0	0	0	6	4	44
Pasture													
Improved establishment													
Fencing	2	5	0	0	0	0	0	0	0	0	0	0	7
Seeding	0	0	0	0	2	0	0	0	0	0	0	0	2
Maintenance	0	0	0	0	0	0	0	1	0	0	1	1	3

Note: Same as table 4-5.
Source: Same as table 4-5.
a. See note a, table 4-5.
b. Labor requirements for sunflower apply to the year of planting. Thus, in year 2 the labor requirement is for the crop planted in May of year 2 and harvested in October of year 3.

than each individual class of animal as the basis for estimating the labor requirement considerably simplifies the computation and is not un-realistic. In the convention recommended here, for example, closing livestock figures do not include heifers two to three years old or steers sold during the year, in this case steers three to four years old. Opening livestock figures, however, omit calves. In reality, closing and opening figures tend to balance each other, since heifers will be transferred to the breeding herd throughout the year and surplus heifers and steers will be sold throughout the year, whereas calves will be born throughout the year. Attempting a more precise estimate would only lead to superficial precision because the error in estimating the daily requirement for labor considerably exceeds any gain in accuracy.

Having determined the labor requirement for each crop or animal unit by month, we proceed to calculate the labor requirement for the pattern farm. This is given for the Paraguay example in table 4-7. Here the labor required for each crop during each project year is given. The total by month and the amount to be provided by *family labor* and by *hired labor* are determined. In the Paraguay example, it is assumed that the family on the pattern farm will have available 70 work days of labor a month and that any labor requirement in excess of this amount will be supplied by hired labor. This is a very mechanistic assumption, of course. Not only will families vary widely in the labor they have available—even on farms of quite comparable size and cropping pattern—but families will also tend to work longer hours in busy seasons and rest in the off-season. For purposes of the farm investment analysis, however, this approximation is quite sufficient, given the wide margin of error in the estimates of the labor requirement in general. In the Paraguay example, table 4-7 shows that hired labor will be needed on the farm from year 4 onward. By year 7, in the peak month of March, about 44 percent of the total labor required for cotton and soybeans will have to be hired.

When a labor budget shows a need for hired labor, as this example does, the project analyst must consider carefully whether the labor will be available in the project area. Totaling the hired labor requirement for the project as a whole is one of the real advantages of including the labor budget in the farm investment analysis, since the analyst must then consider the realism of the proposed pattern in light of the added hired labor that can reasonably be expected to be available in the project area. Postulating 56 additional work days of hired labor in March is one thing; whether such additional labor would be available for an entire proposed project is another. It may be that a proposed cropping pattern will prove unrealistic in its requirements of additional hired labor, and a less labor-intensive cropping pattern must be proposed. Furthermore, if the project will call for substantial amounts of additional hired labor in relation to the supply available in the region, this may have implications about the sources from which the labor must be drawn and, hence, about the opportunity cost of the hired labor. In turn, this opportunity cost will have to be considered when making the estimates of the economic value of the labor (see chapter 7).

Table 4-7. *Labor Requirement by Crop and Month, 20-Hectare Mixed Farm, Paraguay Project*
(work days)

Year and crop or activity	Unit	Jul	Aug	Sept	Oct	Nov	Dec	Jan	Feb	Mar	Apr	May	Jun	Total
Without project														
Maize	0.5 ha	7	4	0	2	2	14	0	0	0	0	0	0	29
Manioc	1.0 ha	0	0	14	3	3	3	4	3	5	3	3	19	60
Beans	0.5 ha	0	0	0	0	12	2	2	10	0	0	0	0	26
Cotton	2.0 ha	0	0	16	28	16	38	38	14	40	28	0	0	218
Livestock[a]	13.6 a.u.	4	4	4	4	4	4	4	4	4	4	4	4	48
Total		11	8	34	37	37	61	48	31	49	35	7	23	381
Family labor[b]		11	8	34	37	37	61	48	31	49	35	7	23	381
Hired labor		0	0	0	0	0	0	0	0	0	0	0	0	0
Year 1														
Maize	0.5 ha	7	4	0	2	2	14	0	0	0	0	0	0	29
Manioc	1.0 ha	0	0	14	3	3	3	4	3	5	3	3	19	60
Beans	0.5 ha	0	0	0	0	12	2	2	10	0	0	0	0	26
Cotton	2.0 ha	0	0	16	28	16	38	38	14	40	28	0	0	218
Livestock	13.6 a.u.	4	4	4	4	4	4	4	4	4	4	4	4	48
Improved pasture														
Fencing and seeding	3.5 ha	7	18	0	0	7	0	0	0	0	0	0	0	32
Total		18	26	34	37	44	61	48	31	49	35	7	23	413
Family labor		18	26	34	37	44	61	48	31	49	35	7	23	413
Hired labor		0	0	0	0	0	0	0	0	0	0	0	0	0

Item	Area													Total
Year 2														
Maize	0.5 ha	4	1	0	0	0	14	0	0	0	0	0	0	19
Manioc	1.0 ha	0	0	10	2	2	1	2	2	2	2	2	19	44
Beans	0.5 ha	0	0	0	0	10	1	1	10	0	0	0	0	22
Cotton	2.0 ha	0	0	16	12	16	12	10	16	50	28	0	0	160
Soybeans	1.0 ha	0	0	0	0	13	8	3	2	10	8	3	0	47
Sunflower[c]	2.0 ha	0	0	0	0	0	0	0	0	0	0	12	8	20
Livestock	17.2 a.u.	5	5	5	5	5	5	5	5	5	5	5	5	60
Improved pasture														
Fencing and seeding	3.5 ha	7	18	0	0	7	0	0	0	0	0	0	0	32
Maintenance[d]	3.5 ha	0	0	0	0	0	0	0	4	0	0	4	4	12
Total		16	24	31	19	53	41	21	39	67	43	26	36	416
Family labor		16	24	31	19	53	41	21	39	67	43	26	36	416
Hired labor		0	0	0	0	0	0	0	0	0	0	0	0	0
Year 3														
Maize	0.5 ha	4	1	0	0	0	16	0	0	0	0	0	0	21
Manioc	1.0 ha	0	0	10	2	2	1	2	2	2	2	2	21	46
Beans	0.5 ha	0	0	0	0	10	1	1	11	0	0	0	0	23
Cotton	2.0 ha	0	0	16	12	16	12	10	16	50	28	0	0	160
Soybeans	1.0 ha	0	0	0	0	13	8	3	2	10	8	3	0	47
Sunflower	2.0 ha	0	0	0	0	0	0	0	18	20	24	12	8	82
Livestock	19.9 a.u.	6	6	6	6	6	6	6	6	6	6	6	6	72
Improved pasture														
Fencing and seeding	3.5 ha	7	18	0	0	7	0	0	0	0	0	0	0	32
Maintenance	7.0 ha	0	0	0	0	0	0	0	7	0	0	7	7	21
Total		17	25	32	20	54	44	22	62	88	68	30	42	504
Family labor		17	25	32	20	54	44	22	62	88	68	30	42	504
Hired labor		0	0	0	0	0	0	0	0	0	0	0	0	0

(Table continues on following pages.)

Table 4-7 (continued)

Year and crop or activity	Unit	Jul	Aug	Sept	Oct	Nov	Dec	Jan	Feb	Mar	Apr	May	Jun	Total
Year 4														
Maize	0.5 ha	4	1	0	0	0	16	0	0	0	0	0	0	21
Manioc	0.5 ha	0	0	5	1	1	0	1	1	1	1	1	10	22
Beans	0.5 ha	0	0	0	0	10	1	1	11	0	0	0	0	23
Cotton	2.2 ha	0	0	18	13	18	13	11	18	59	33	0	0	183
Soybeans	2.2 ha	0	18	0	0	29	18	7	4	22	22	7	0	109
Sunflower	2.2 ha	4	18	6	28	8	0	0	0	0	0	13	9	86
Livestock	22.7 a.u.	7	7	7	7	7	7	7	7	7	7	7	7	84
Improved pasture Maintenance	10.5 ha	0	0	0	0	0	0	0	10	0	0	10	10	30
Total		15	26	36	49	73	55	27	51	89	63	38	36	558
Family labor		15	26	36	49	70	55	27	51	70	63	38	36	536
Hired labor		0	0	0	0	3	0	0	0	19	0	0	0	22
Year 5														
Maize	0.5 ha	4	1	0	0	0	16	0	0	0	0	0	0	21
Manioc	0.5 ha	0	0	5	1	1	0	1	1	1	1	1	12	24
Beans	0.5 ha	0	0	0	0	10	1	1	11	0	0	0	0	23
Cotton	2.5 ha	0	0	20	15	20	15	12	20	68	38	0	0	208
Soybeans	2.5 ha	0	0	0	0	32	20	8	5	25	25	8	0	123
Sunflower	2.5 ha	4	20	7	31	9	0	0	0	0	0	15	10	96
Livestock	24.6 a.u.	8	8	8	8	8	8	8	8	8	8	8	8	96
Improved pasture Maintenance	10.5 ha	0	0	0	0	0	0	0	10	0	0	10	10	30
Total		16	29	40	55	80	60	30	55	102	72	42	40	621
Family labor		16	29	40	55	70	60	30	55	70	70	42	40	577
Hired labor		0	0	0	0	10	0	0	0	32	2	0	0	44

Year 6

Item													Total
Maize	0.5 ha	4	1	0	0	0	0	0	16	0	0	0	21
Manioc	0.5 ha	0	0	5	1	1	1	1	0	1	1	12	24
Cotton	3.0 ha	0	0	24	18	24	48	84	18	15	27	0	258
Soybeans	3.0 ha	0	0	0	38	39	33	33	24	9	6	12	156
Sunflower	3.0 ha	5	22	8	8	12	18	0	0	0	0	18	115
Livestock	25.1 a.u.	8	8	8	8	8	8	8	8	8	8	8	96
Improved pasture Maintenance	10.5 ha	0	0	10	10	0	0	0	0	10	10	10	30
Total		17	31	65	84	66	33	52	126	49	90	49	700
Family labor		17	31	65	70	66	33	52	70	49	70	42	610
Hired labor		0	0	0	14	0	0	0	56	0	20	0	90

Years 7–20

Item													Total
Maize	0.5 ha	4	1	0	0	0	0	0	18	0	0	0	23
Manioc	0.5 ha	0	0	5	1	1	1	1	0	1	1	12	24
Cotton	3.0 ha	0	0	24	18	24	48	84	18	15	27	0	258
Soybeans	3.0 ha	0	0	0	45	39	0	33	24	15	0	12	156
Sunflower	3.0 ha	6	27	9	9	15	24	0	0	0	0	18	132
Livestock	25.0 a.u.	8	8	8	8	8	8	8	8	8	8	8	96
Improved pasture Maintenance	10.5 ha	0	0	10	10	0	0	0	0	10	10	10	30
Total		18	36	46	87	68	33	52	126	49	90	49	719
Family labor		18	36	46	70	70	33	52	70	49	70	42	624
Hired labor		0	0	0	17	0	0	0	56	0	20	0	95

ha Hectares; a.u. animal units.

Source: Calculated from tables 4-4 and 4-6.

a. Assumes five minutes a day per animal unit, eight hours a day, and thirty days a month. The labor requirement is based on the animal units at the beginning of the year (as given in table 4-11) divided by 100 to give the labor requirement for a single farm. See text (the subsection "Farm production. Livestock") for a discussion of this convention.

b. Assumes 70 work days per month of available family labor.

c. Area and labor requirement for sunflower apply to the year of planting. Thus, the area assumed in the first five months of project year 5 is the 2.2 hectares planted in May of project year 4.

d. Calculated on the basis of improved pasture established in previous years (as shown in table 4-4). Thus, in year 2 it is based on 3.5 hectares and in year 3 on 7.0 hectares.

Some analysts like to work out a labor use diagram such as the one shown in figure 4-3. This usually is done only for the full-development situation. The graphic presentation makes the problem of peak labor requirements readily apparent.

Once the total hired labor has been determined, it must be allocated among the various crops so that it may be included in the proper category of operating expenditure. This is done in table 4-8. In the Paraguay example the allocation is made in proportion to the total work days

Figure 4-3. *Labor Use Diagram for Project Years 7–20, 20-Hectare Mixed Farm, Paraguay Project*

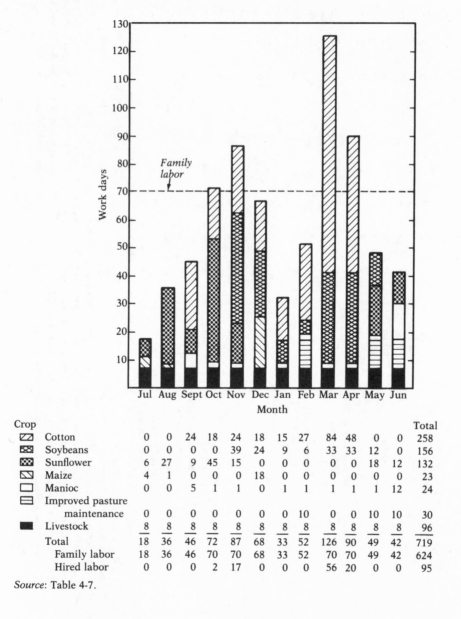

Crop	Jul	Aug	Sept	Oct	Nov	Dec	Jan	Feb	Mar	Apr	May	Jun	Total
Cotton	0	0	24	18	24	18	15	27	84	48	0	0	258
Soybeans	0	0	0	0	39	24	9	6	33	33	12	0	156
Sunflower	6	27	9	45	15	0	0	0	0	0	18	12	132
Maize	4	1	0	0	0	18	0	0	0	0	0	0	23
Manioc	0	0	5	1	1	0	1	1	1	1	1	12	24
Improved pasture maintenance	0	0	0	0	0	0	0	10	0	0	10	10	30
Livestock	8	8	8	8	8	8	8	8	8	8	8	8	96
Total	18	36	46	72	87	68	33	52	126	90	49	42	719
Family labor	18	36	46	70	70	68	33	52	70	70	49	42	624
Hired labor	0	0	0	2	17	0	0	0	56	20	0	0	95

Source: Table 4-7.

required for each cash crop in each month for which hired labor would be needed. In other circumstances, such a mechanistic allocation would be inappropriate. In many areas, certain crop operations are done by hired labor and not by family labor, even if family labor is available. Thus, in Southeast Asia, transplanting rice is done in many areas entirely by hired labor; the only family labor engaged is that of the farmer himself, who supervises the work. Both the amount of hired labor and its allocation among crops should be closely related to the expected cultural practices of people in the project area.

Farm production

Having determined the use of land and labor resources for the pattern farm, the analyst next assesses the projected farm production. The investment analysis of crop and pasture and livestock production is discussed in this subsection, and issues of valuation (both of farm production and incremental residual value on the farm) are addressed.

Table 4-8. *Hired Labor by Crop and Month,*
20-Hectare Mixed Farm, Paraguay Project
(work days)

Year and crop[a]	Jul	Aug	Sept	Oct	Nov	Dec	Jan	Feb	Mar	Apr	May	Jun	Total
Year 4													
Cotton	0	0	0	0	1	0	0	0	14	0	0	0	15
Soybeans	0	0	0	0	2	0	0	0	5	0	0	0	7
Total	0	0	0	0	3	0	0	0	19	0	0	0	22
Year 5													
Cotton	0	0	0	0	3	0	0	0	23	1	0	0	27
Soybeans	0	0	0	0	5	0	0	0	9	1	0	0	15
Sunflower	0	0	0	0	1	0	0	0	0	0	0	0	1
Total	0	0	0	0	9[b]	0	0	0	32	2	0	0	43[b]
Year 6													
Cotton	0	0	0	0	4	0	0	0	40	12	0	0	56
Soybeans	0	0	0	0	7	0	0	0	16	8	0	0	31
Sunflower	0	0	0	0	2	0	0	0	0	0	0	0	2
Total	0	0	0	0	13[b]	0	0	0	56	20	0	0	89[b]
Years 7–20													
Cotton	0	0	0	1	5	0	0	0	40	12	0	0	58
Soybeans	0	0	0	0	8	0	0	0	16	8	0	0	32
Sunflower	0	0	0	1	3	0	0	0	0	0	0	0	4
Total	0	0	0	2	16[b]	0	0	0	56	20	0	0	94[b]

Source: Calculated from table 4-7.

a. Hired labor is allocated to cash crops—cotton, soybeans, and sunflower—in proportion to their total labor requirements in that month. In November of year 4, for example, 55 work days are required for cash crops, of which 3 work days are to be hired. Eighteen work days are required for cotton. To determine the hired labor for cotton, the proportion of total labor required for cash crops that is to be applied to cotton is multiplied by the total hired labor requirement for the month; this gives the hired labor to be applied to cotton, or 1 work day $\{[18 \div (18 + 29 + 8)] \times 3 = 1\}$.

b. Does not equal the total in table 4-7 because of rounding.

CROPS AND PASTURE. For *crops* and *pasture*, the yield and carrying capacity are tabulated as illustrated in table 4-9. In the table, yields are shown only for crops and pasture actually in the cropping pattern in the year reported. Thus, no without-project yield is reported for soybeans, whereas for sunflower, which will be planted following cotton in year 2, yield is reported only beginning in year 3 since the first crop is not harvested until that time.

Multiplying the production per hectare by the number of hectares of each of the *crops* and of *pasture* in the land use pattern shown in table 4-4, we obtain the crop and pasture production illustrated in table 4-10. Again, since sunflower is first planted in year 2 but first harvested in year 3, the production from the first planting of 1.8 tons is shown in year 3. Similarly, sunflower planted each year produces in the following year.

Because all the feed for the livestock to be produced on the pattern farm in the Paraguay project is assumed to come from pasture, no deduction is made in table 4-10 for crops to be used for feed. Should the production pattern of a model farm call for the use of crops and crop by-products for feed, table 4-10 would then be adjusted to show that use. *Total production* of crops would be shown and expanded to include crop by-products if these were to be fed or if they have a sale value. From this total would be deducted the *feed consumption* taken from an estimate of feed requirement and production such as that illustrated in table 4-30. The result would be the *net production available for sale or household consumption.*

LIVESTOCK. *Herd composition, purchases, and sales* are given in table 4-11. Projecting the herd (or flock) composition, purchases, and sales in a farm investment analysis that involves livestock introduces a computational process that can become quite complex.

Table 4-9. *Yield and Carrying Capacity,*
20-Hectare Mixed Farm, Paraguay Project

Product	Without project	With project						
		Year 1	2	3	4	5	6	7–20
Crops								
(tons per hectare)								
Maize	1.1	1.1	1.1	1.2	1.2	1.3	1.3	1.4
Manioc	18.0	18.0	18.0	20.0	20.0	22.0	22.0	24.0
Beans	0.9	0.9	0.9	1.0	1.0	1.0	—	—
Cotton	1.3	1.3	1.5	1.5	1.6	1.6	1.7	1.7
Soybeans	—	—	1.4	1.4	1.6	1.6	1.8	1.8
Sunflower	—	—	—	0.9	1.0	1.1	1.2	1.2
Pasture								
(animal units per hectare)								
Natural	1.2	1.2	1.2	1.2	1.2	1.2	1.2	1.2
Improved	—	2.5	2.5	2.5	2.5	2.5	2.5	2.5

Source: Same as table 4-4.

Table 4-10. *Crop and Pasture Production,*
20-Hectare Mixed Farm, Paraguay Project
(tons)

Product	Without project	With project						
		Year 1	2	3	4	5	6	7–20
Crops								
Total production								
Maize	0.6	0.6	0.6	0.6	0.6	0.6	0.6	0.7
Manioc	18.0	18.0	18.0	20.0	10.0	11.0	11.0	12.0
Beans	0.4	0.4	0.4	0.5	0.5	0.5	—	—
Cotton	2.6	2.6	3.0	3.0	3.5	4.0	5.1	5.1
Soybeans	—	—	1.4	1.4	3.5	`4.0	5.4	5.4
Sunflower[a]	—	—	—	1.8	2.0	2.4	3.0	3.6
Feed consumption[b]								
Maize	—	—	—	—	—	—	—	—
Manioc	—	—	—	—	—	—	—	—
Soybeans	—	—	—	—	—	—	—	—
Sunflower	—	—	—	—	—	—	—	—
Net production available for sale or house-hold consumption								
Maize	0.6	0.6	0.6	0.6	0.6	0.6	0.6	0.7
Manioc	18.0	18.0	18.0	20.0	10.0	11.0	11.0	12.0
Beans	0.4	0.4	0.4	0.5	0.5	0.5	—	—
Cotton	2.6	2.6	3.0	3.0	3.5	4.0	5.1	5.1
Soybeans	—	—	1.4	1.4	3.5	4.0	5.4	5.4
Sunflower	—	—	—	1.8	2.0	2.4	3.0	3.6
Pasture								
Carrying capacity (animal units)	12.6	17.2	21.7	26.2	26.2	26.2	26.2	26.2

Source: Calculated from tables 4-4 and 4-9.

a. Sunflower is harvested in the year following planting. Thus, the production in year 2 is zero, and in year 3 it is 1.8 tons, which is determined by multiplying the 2.0 hectares planted in year 2 by the yield of 0.9 tons per hectare harvested in year 3 (2.0 × 0.9 = 1.8).

b. If there were a substantial livestock production activity on the farm that used crops for feed, the amounts would be estimated in a feed requirement and production table such as table 4-30 and tabulated here. The table would be expanded to include crop by-products used for feed. As indicated, the use of crops for feed would be deducted from the total production, and the result would be the net production available for sale or household consumption.

Herd projections are done to forecast use of future facilities, pasture, or feed by applying *technical coefficients*, such as those shown at the bottom of table 4-11, to trace the changes in the size and composition of the herd.

For poultry, stall feeding, or feedlot projections, it is usually assumed that enough young animals can be purchased in a given year to bring the numbers up to the level of feed availability or of proposed production facilities. Brown (1979, pp. 76–85) gives a methodology for broiler and egg production. For pigs, a projection is made applying the technical coefficients; since the gestation period of swine is short, the projection is simplified and uncomplicated.

Table 4-11. *Herd Composition, Purchases, and Sales,*
100 20-Hectare Mixed Farms, Paraguay Project
(head)

Item	Without project	With project Year 1	2	3	4	5	6	7–20
Herd composition at beginning of year								
Bulls	100	100	100	100	100	100	100	100
Breeding cows	500	500	655	800	800	800	800	800
Heifers 1–2 years	157	157	157	221	294	285	285	285
Heifers 2–3 years	152	152	152	152	217	288	279	279
Steers 1–2 years	157	157	157	221	294	285	285	285
Steers 2–3 years	152	152	152	152	217	288	279	279
Steers 3–4 years	147	147	147	147	149	213	282	273
Work oxen	—	0	200	200	200	200	200	200
Total	1,365	1,365	1,720	1,993	2,271	2,459	2,510	2,501
Animal units	1,365	1,365	1,720	1,993	2,271	2,459	2,510	2,501
Carrying capacity (beginning of year)[a]	1,260	1,260	1,720	2,170	2,620	2,620	2,620	2,620
Purchases								
Bulls	18	33	20	20	20	20	20	20
Heifers 2–3 years	0	91	131	2	0	0	0	0
Steers 1–2 years	0	0	0	0	0	0	0	0
Work oxen	0	200	38	36	36	36	36	36
Total	18	324	189	58	56	56	56	56
Sales (including culls)								
Culled bulls	15	30	17	18	18	18	18	18
Culled cows	60	60	98	120	112	112	112	112
Culled heifers	8	8	15	15	22	29	28	28
Surplus heifers 2–3 years	64	0	0	0	63	125	117	117
Steers 1–2 years	0	0	0	0	0	0	0	0
Steers 3–4 years	143	143	143	144	146	209	276	268
Culled work oxen	—	0	32	32	32	32	32	32
Total	290	241	305	329	393	525	583	575
Herd productivity (percent)[b]	20							23
Technical coefficients (percent)								
Calving rate	70	70	75[c]	80[c]	75	75	75	75
Calf mortality	10	10	10	8	5	5	5	5
Adult mortality	3	3	3	2	2	2	2	2
Culling rate (bulls)	15	30	17	18	18	18	18	18
Culling rate (cows)	12	12	15	15	14	14	14	14
Culling rate (heifers)	5	5	10	10	10	10	10	10
Culling rate (work oxen)	—	0	16	16	16	16	16	16
Bulls/breeding females[d]	—	—	—	—	—	—	—	—
Carrying capacity (per hectare; end of year)[a]	1.2	1.6	2.1	2.5	2.5	2.5	2.5	2.5

Source: Same as table 4-4 (annex 1, table 18). See computations in table 4-27.

a. In animal units. The carrying capacity at the beginning of the year is determined by multiplying the animal units per farm at the end of the previous year (given in table 4-10) by the 100 farms in the model. The carrying capacity per hectare at the end of the year is determined by dividing the animal units per farm by the 10.5 hectares of pasture on each farm; it is thus a weighted average of natural and improved pasture.

(Notes continue on the following page.)

The projection can become computationally quite complicated, however, for larger animals fed mainly pasture, such as sheep or cattle used for dairy or beef production. The project analyst often relies on the livestock technician for these projections and simply incorporates them into his farm investment analysis. But livestock technicians themselves may be unfamiliar with the details of how to make these computations—and especially with how to make them so they conform to the accounting convention adopted here for the farm investment analysis. For this reason, the computation for the herd projection in the Paraguay example is discussed in considerable detail in the appendix to this chapter (where definitions of the specialized livestock terms may also be found). This methodology can be adapted, with only minor variations, to projections for dairy animals. As in the treatment here, the details of the projection need not form part of the main body of most project reports; only a summary need be given (as in table 4-11 from the Paraguay example), with the details laid out in an annex or in the project file.

Projecting the herd composition on a small farm when larger animals are to be produced introduces the difficult problems of divisibility. As noted, herd projections for animals that are mainly grazed on pasture are based on the estimated feed availability. Technical coefficients, such as mortality and calving rates, are often directly influenced by the amount of available feed, but in cattle production changes do not happen immediately. For example, an increase in feed availability in one season will improve the calving rate and decrease calf losses only during the next season.

The projected coefficients are applied to the herd at the beginning of the project. The result begins to appear in the herd composition at the beginning of year 2. Often, the projected coefficients indicate that the herd's composition and its overall size will not change fast enough to utilize the increased feed available. As a solution, in-calf heifers can be purchased to increase the reproductive component of the herd, or feeder steers can be purchased for fattening until the herd can utilize the forage resources.

This use of technical coefficients raises few problems of interpretation for larger farms or ranches with herds of 100 or more animals. For small farms, however, the technical coefficients lead to many "fractional animals." In the Paraguay example, for instance, at full development from years 7 through 20 the farm is expected to have eight breeding cows. The adult mortality is expected to be 2 percent, so do we report that 0.16 cows die each year ($8 \times 0.02 = 0.16$)? Such nonsensical results have led project

---

b. Herd productivity is the sum of the off-take rate and the herd growth rate. Only the values for a stable herd are given.

c. Represents a weighted average between the calving rate of breeding cows in the existing herd, which is 70 percent, and that of purchased in-calf heifers, which is nearly 100 percent.

d. Note that in this project a minimum of one bull per farm is assumed, or a minimum of 100 bulls on 100 farms. Normally the number of bulls per 100 breeding females would be three or four for all years.

analysts to seek means to overcome the divisibility problem. Some have simply ignored technical coefficients, such as mortality, that result in very small, fractional animal figures. This omission, however, considerably distorts the pattern farm investment analysis. To avoid such distortion, other analysts have devised systems that carry fractional animals in the computation until the fractions add up to a whole animal, which is then reported. In the Paraguay example, for instance, the calving rate at full development is 75 percent. Thus, six calves are born, of which half may be expected to be female. Calf mortality is 5 percent, and this gives a figure of 2.8 to be carried over to the next year as heifers 1–2 years old [8 × 0.75 ÷ 2 − (8 × 0.75 ÷ 2 × 0.05) = 2.8]. Of these, 2 percent are reported and 0.8 is carried over to the following year, which then will show a figure of 3.6 (0.8 + 2.8 = 3.6). Of these, 3 are reported and 0.6 is carried forward, and so forth.

Mortality may sometimes be treated by incorporating a more formal probability assumption. Such systems become quite complex and in the end do not satisfactorily project an individual small herd. Another approach that is increasingly used—and that is adopted and recommended here—is to do the herd projection for a number of farms, say 100, that will contain or eliminate the divisibility problem. Purchases and sales are then valued, and only the values are entered in the farm investment analysis for a single pattern farm. In effect, this says that *on the average* a farm will have a certain level of purchases and sales. This, too, is not a fully satisfactory convention. Its results do not state, for example, how many animals are actually on the farm at any given time. It does have the virtue, however, of being simpler than other systems—even if it is still quite complex—and of generating somewhat less distortion.

Project designers may want to introduce an insurance scheme to protect project participants from, say, the loss of a bull. Then, in effect, the values in the farm investment analysis for a single farm for the purchase of bulls include an insurance premium that insures that the farmer will be reimbursed in the event of the death of a bull. Such insurance schemes are found in developing countries, but they give rise to possibilities of abuse and to difficult administrative problems, and they often are not very effective.

In the Paraguay example summarized in table 4-11, the *herd composition* is given for each major class of animals without the project and for each project year. (The table is drawn from the worksheet reproduced in table 4-27.) Note that the analyst assumed that each farm would have a bull, so that the number of bulls remains 100, many more than would be needed if the analysis were, indeed, for a single herd rather than for 100 small farms. Note, also, the purchase of draft animals at the end of the first year. It is assumed that each farm will purchase two work oxen. The total *animal units* for the herd are shown, and for convenience this figure is compared with the *carrying capacity*. As noted in the appendix to this chapter, the number of breeding cows has been rounded to an even multiple of the number of farms in the model so that each farm has five breeding cows without the project and increases its herd to eight breeding cows at full development. As a result, the total of animal units does not very closely approximate the carrying capacity. Since estimates of carrying capacity are quite approximate, however, overstocking of up to 10 percent would probably be acceptable.

Purchases of each class of animal are treated next in the investment analysis; these will form the basis for the investment and operating expenditure for the livestock aspect of the 20-hectare mixed farm. The *sales* give the basis for the inflow for the farm. The *herd productivity*, a measure of the efficiency of the herd, is also given; it relates the number of head sold plus the increase in herd size to the number of head carried at the beginning of the year. Only the figures for the stable herd without the project and at full development are given. The dynamics of herd growth tend to distort the measure during the period when the herd is increasing in size. (The details of the computation are given in table 4-28.) Finally, the *technical coefficients* for the herd are given. These are crucial parameters of the herd growth and are indicators of management effectiveness, animal health care, and feed availability.

When feed concentrates are important in the farm production pattern, it may be desirable to project the feed requirements the livestock activity will involve. (An illustrative example is included in tables 4-29 and 4-30 in the appendix to this chapter in connection with the discussion of herd projections.)

In some instances it may be desirable to report yield per animal if the valuation system is based, say, on kilograms. In the Paraguay example the prices are based on individual animals without regard to weight, so yield per animal is not needed and is therefore not illustrated.

VALUATION. To begin the valuation of the farm production, the farm-gate prices for items entering the farm investment analysis are listed as shown in table 4-12. (The symbol for Paraguayan guaranis is ₲.) If a farm-gate price is used in only one table of the investment analysis, it may not be included in the farm-gate price table but may appear in the appropriate table. (Such is the case, for example, of the prices for land improvement, which are included in table 4-15, devoted to investment, and not in the table of farm-gate prices.) Some farm-gate prices were collected and projected by the project analyst on the basis of field observation. Other prices were collected in the field but forecast using the projections of the World Bank. Prices and their derivation were discussed in more detail in chapter 3.

The value of production for the farm is given in table 4-13. For *crops*, values are determined by multiplying the production in table 4-10 by the price per ton in table 4-12. For *livestock*, the value is obtained by multiplying sales from table 4-11 by the price per animal given in table 4-12. The product is then divided by 100 to give the value for a single farm, in line with the convention recommended to avoid the divisibility problem.

INCREMENTAL RESIDUAL VALUE. In the last year of the farm investment analysis, the incremental residual (or terminal) value on the farm is

Table 4-12. *Farm-Gate Prices, 20-Hectare Mixed Farm,*
Paraguay Project
(thousands of ₲)

	Project year			
Item[a]	*1*	*2*	*3–5*	*6–20*
Farm labor (per work day)	0.3	0.3	0.3	0.3
Crops (per ton)				
Maize	12.0	12.0	12.0	12.0
Manioc	3.0	3.0	3.0	3.0
Beans	28.0	28.0	28.0	28.0
Cotton	44.4	45.1	45.1	44.9
Soybeans	23.6	20.9	26.2	28.9
Sunflower	20.0	20.0	20.0	20.0
Livestock (per head)				
Bulls	30.0	30.0	32.4	33.6
Culled bulls	23.0	23.0	24.8	25.8
Breeding cows	18.7	18.7	20.2	20.9
Culled cows	17.0	17.0	18.4	19.0
Heifers 1–2 years	12.5	12.5	13.5	14.0
Heifers 2–3 years	18.7	18.7	20.2	20.9
Culled heifers 2–3 years	17.0	17.0	18.4	19.0
Steers 1–2 years	12.5	12.5	13.5	14.0
Steers 2–3 years	18.7	18.7	20.2	20.9
Steers 3–4 years	23.0	23.0	24.8	25.8
Work oxen	35.0	35.0	37.8	39.2
Culled work oxen	23.0	23.0	24.8	25.8

₲ Paraguayan guaranis.
Source: Same as table 4-4.
a. Prices of maize, soybeans, and livestock are adjusted for the real price changes
projected by the Commodities and Export Projections division of the World Bank. Other
prices are assumed to remain constant in real terms.

included among the inflows in the farm budget and "credited" to the
project investment. This is done because not all the utility of an investment may be exhausted in the course of a project. Note that it is the
incremental value that is sought, not the total value. In some instances
there is no distinction, since the value of an item such as construction
may be entirely incremental. But for items such as land, livestock, and
working capital, there may have been values existing at the beginning of
the project, and only the incremental residual value may properly be
credited to the project investment. Since the incremental residual value
enters the farm investment analysis in the final year, it bears relatively
little weight in the discounting process. As a result, rather broad estimates of residual values are acceptable in project analysis.

Three kinds of residual value may be noted. The first is the salvage
value of capital assets that have been largely consumed by the end of the
project and that, for the most part, can only be salvaged for their scrap
value or have only a short portion of their normal life expectancy remaining at the end of the project period. Buildings and other construction or
machinery such as irrigation pumps or tractors are common examples. A
second kind of residual value is the working capital. This is automati-

cally allowed for under the accounting convention we have adopted for the farm investment analysis. The third kind of residual value is the value of items that have a substantial useful life remaining at the end of the project and may even have increased in value as a result of the project investment; land with associated improvements and a livestock herd are examples.

All three kinds of residual value are illustrated for the Paraguay example in table 4-14. In a land improvement project such as this one, there usually would be an entry for the incremental value of *land*, although in this instance the analyst chose not to include it because the site in Paraguay is a frontier area and the land market is not very active. In more crowded societies where a project involves land improvement such as better irrigation and drainage, the incremental value of the land might be quite substantial. Next for consideration would be the incremental residual value of *construction*. In the Paraguay example, the construction is all incremental, so the incremental residual value is quite simply obtained by taking a proportion of the initial construction, in this case 10 percent. The incremental residual value of *equipment* is assumed to be negligible, although that would not necessarily be the case in other projects. Then the analyst considers the incremental value of *livestock*. In this case, care must be taken to distinguish between the total residual value of the livestock herd and the incremental residual value. There was, of course, a livestock herd at the beginning of the project, so only the increased value of the herd at the end of the project can be attributed to the project investment itself. Hence, each class of animals is valued at the beginning of the project and at the end of the project, and only the difference—or increment—is carried forward as the incremental residual value. Finally, there is the total incremental *working capital*. The reader will recall that, in the discussion of the accounting convention for farm investment analysis, considerable attention was devoted to estimating the incremental working capital year by year. Once this is done, all that is needed to obtain the total incremental working capital is simply to add the incremental working capital for each year algebraically—that is, adding the increases and subtracting decreases—to obtain the incremental residual value entered in the final year.

Farm inputs

When the estimates of production are complete, the estimates of the necessary inputs may be prepared. Inputs comprise the investment, operating expenditure, and incremental working capital for the project.

INVESTMENT. Investment for the project is a crucial element. The investment contemplated for the Paraguay pattern farm is given in table 4-15. It is convenient to show the unit and unit cost in the investment table; for convenience, items appearing only in the investment table may be omitted from the farm-gate price table. As in this presentation, the total physical investment may be incorporated in the investment cost

Table 4-13. *Value of Production, 20-Hectare Mixed Farm, Paraguay Project*
(thousands of ₲)

Item	Without project				With project						
	Year 1	2	3–5	6–20	1	2	3	4	5	6	7–20
Crops[a]											
Maize	7.2	7.2	7.2	7.2	7.2	7.2	7.2	7.2	7.2	7.2	8.4
Manioc	54.0	54.0	54.0	54.0	54.0	54.0	60.0	30.0	33.0	33.0	36.0
Beans	11.2	11.2	11.2	11.2	11.2	11.2	14.0	14.0	14.0	—	—
Cotton	115.4	117.3	117.3	116.7	115.4	135.3	135.3	157.8	180.4	229.0	229.0
Soybeans	—	—	—	—	—	29.3	36.7	91.7	104.8	156.1	156.1
Sunflower	—	—	—	—	—	—	36.0	40.0	48.0	60.0	72.0
Total	187.8	189.7	189.7	189.1	187.8	237.0	289.2	340.7	387.4	485.3	501.5
Livestock[b]											
Culled bulls	3.4	3.4	3.7	3.9	6.9	3.9	4.5	4.5	4.5	4.6	4.6
Culled cows	10.2	10.2	11.0	11.4	10.2	16.7	22.1	20.6	20.6	21.3	21.3
Culled heifers	1.4	1.4	1.5	1.5	1.4	2.6	2.8	4.0	5.3	5.3	5.3
Surplus heifers	12.0	12.0	12.9	13.4	0	0	0	12.7	25.2	24.5	24.5
Steers 3–4 years	32.9	32.9	35.5	36.9	32.9	32.9	35.7	36.2	51.8	71.2	69.1
Culled work oxen	—	—	—	—	—	7.4	7.9	7.9	7.9	8.3	8.3
Total	59.9	59.9	64.6	67.1	51.4	63.5	73.0	85.9	115.3	135.2	133.1
Total value	247.7	249.6	254.3	256.2	239.2	300.5	362.2	426.6	502.7	620.5	634.6

Source: Calculated from tables 4-10, 4-11, and 4-12.
a. Production from table 4-10 multiplied by the price per ton from table 4-12. For year 2 without the project, for example, the value of cotton is the without-project production from table 4-10 times the price in year 2 in table 4-12.
b. Sales from table 4-11 multiplied by the price per animal from table 4-12; product is then divided by 100 to give the value for a single farm. See text for a discussion of this convention.

Table 4-14. *Incremental Residual Value,*
20-Hectare Mixed Farm, Paraguay Project
(thousands of ₲)

	Value		
Item	*At beginning of project*	*At end of project*	*Incremental*
Land	a	a	a
Construction[b]	0	18.0	18.0
Equipment[c]	0	0	0
Livestock[d]			
Bulls	30.0	33.6	
Breeding cows	93.5	167.2	
Heifers 1–2 years	19.6	39.9	
Heifers 2–3 years	28.4	58.3	
Steers 1–2 years	19.6	39.9	
Steers 2–3 years	28.4	58.3	
Steers 3–4 years	33.8	70.4	
Work oxen	—	78.4	
Total	253.3	546.0	292.7
Working capital[e]	—	—	119.9
Total			430.6

Source: Calculated from other tables as noted.

a. In the Paraguay example, the analyst chose not to include an incremental value of land improvements in his computation of residual value. This amount usually is included if there has been substantial land improvement.

b. The residual value of construction is taken as 10 percent of the total construction investment given in table 4-15.

c. The residual value of equipment is assumed to be negligible. Only equipment purchased for the project is included in the computation, not the equipment existing on the farm at the beginning of the project.

d. The value of the livestock at the beginning of the project is calculated from the herd composition at the beginning of the year in table 4-11 multiplied by the year-1 prices in table 4-12. The value of the livestock at the end of the project is calculated from the year-20 herd composition in table 4-11 multiplied by the year-20 prices in table 4-12.

e. From table 4-17.

table; in other instances, a separate table may be needed. Although it is not shown for the Paraguay example, including the foreign exchange component of the investment cost is often desirable. It is important that an agricultural project report detail the foreign exchange needed for the project because the availability of foreign exchange may be a major constraint.

Investment for the Paraguay example is divided into *land improvement, construction, equipment,* and *livestock,* the major categories likely to be found in an agricultural project. Within each category the major items are noted, and the investment for them is tabulated by project year. The total investment by year and for the pattern as a whole is given. Note how the analyst accommodated the existing equipment found on project farms in this pattern by listing equipment totaling ₲206 thousand, but then subtracting ₲50 thousand as an average of existing equipment.

For livestock, it is assumed that all heifer purchases and culling in excess of that normally done without the project are an investment.

Table 4-15. *Investment, 20-Hectare Mixed Farm, Paraguay Project*
(thousands of ₲)

Item[a]	Unit cost	Project year			Total
		1	2	3	
Land improvement (per hectare)					
Clear, cut and burn forest[b]	15.0	52.5	52.5	52.5	157.5
Destumping[c]	20.0	100.0	0	40.0	140.0
Pasture establishment[d]	1.0	3.5	3.5	3.5	10.5
Total		156.0	56.0	96.0	308.0
Construction (per single unit)					
Storage	40.0	40.0	0	0	40.0
Well[e]	50.0	50.0	0	0	50.0
Fencing wire (for 1 ha)	8.6	30.1	30.1	30.1	90.3
Total		120.1	30.1	30.1	180.3
Equipment (per single unit)					
Plow	18.0	18.0	0	0	18.0
Disc harrow	65.0	65.0	0	0	65.0
Seeder	30.0	30.0	0	0	30.0
Cultivator	17.0	17.0	0	0	17.0
Ox cart	50.0	50.0	0	0	50.0
Sprayer	11.0	11.0	0	0	11.0
Hand tools	15.0	15.0	0	0	15.0
Subtotal		206.0	0	0	206.0
Less existing equipment[f]		(50.0)	0	0	(50.0)
Total		156.0	0	0	156.0
Livestock (per head)[g]					
Heifers 2–3 years[h]	—	17.0	24.5	0.4	41.9
Bulls[i]	30.0	4.5	0	0	4.5
Work oxen[j]	35.0	70.0	0	0	70.0
Total		91.5	24.5	0.4	116.4
Total investment		523.6	110.6	126.5	760.7

Note: Parentheses indicate negative numbers.

Source: Same as table 4-4 (annex 1, table 16).

a. Family labor is valued at its opportunity cost (see the discussion of the farm budget). The number of work days required is given in table 4-7.

b. Clearing is done by a contractor. It is assumed that forest will be cleared to establish improved pasture and that clearing proceeds at the pace given for incremental improved pasture in table 4-4.

c. Destumping is done by a contractor. Following the land use given in table 4-4, it is assumed that 5 hectares, consisting of the 4 hectares of existing cropland plus the additional hectare to be cultivated in year 2, will be destumped in year 1 and the remaining 2 hectares in year 3.

d. The cost of pasture establishment includes only the purchase of colonial variety grass (*Panicum maximum*).

e. An open well of 20 meters at ₲2.5 thousand a meter.

f. It is assumed that, of the equipment listed, farmers will already own items of a total value amounting to ₲50 thousand (in parentheses).

g. From the purchases in table 4-11 multiplied by the prices in table 4-12, the product then divided by 100 to give the value for a single farm. See text for a discussion of this convention. Normal replacement of death loss and culls is considered an operating cost.

h. All heifer purchases are considered investment. The prices are taken from table 4-12.

i. The excess over normal death loss and without-project culling for bulls in year 1 is considered investment. For the 100-farm herd, table 4-27 shows 33 replacement bulls will

Thus, the heifers purchased are included in the investment tabulation, as are the excess bulls culled in year 1. The work oxen purchased in year 1 are clearly an investment. In years 2 through 20, oxen purchased are to replace animals lost through death and culling; thus, these purchases are considered as operating expenditure. The amounts for the livestock investment are obtained by taking the numbers of animals given in table 4-11, multiplying by the prices in table 4-12, and then dividing by 100 to obtain the amount from a single farm. This is in line with the convention recommended in the discussion of the herd composition, purchases, and sales. (The sale of replaced livestock, such as indigenous cows sold because improved cows are purchased, is better treated as a "negative investment" and not as a benefit.)

In the investment cost tabulation, allowance would be made for any hired labor used for investment purposes. In the Paraguay example, none is used because the clearing and destumping are assumed to be done by contractors. No allowance is made for family labor devoted to investment. This is because the farm family is the recipient of the incremental net benefit as shown in the farm budget. Thus, the family remuneration is the net income stream. Including it under investment cost would constitute double counting. Note, however, that the family does contribute some investment in the Paraguayan example. The fencing and pasture establishment, for instance, are done by family labor. The demand for family labor for investment is accounted for under the labor requirement in tables 4-6 and 4-7.

OPERATING EXPENDITURE. The operating expenditure is given for *crops*, *livestock*, and *equipment* for the Paraguay pattern farm in table 4-16. (The term "expenditure," rather than the more common "cost," is used here because operating cost implies an element of depreciation not included when the farm investment analysis is laid out in accord with the principles of discounted cash flow analysis.) Although unit expenditure per hectare is given in the table, it could have been tabulated instead from the farm-gate prices in table 4-12 on a price-per-unit basis, with the amounts needed for a hectare listed in the table for operating expenditure. This would have been less convenient but more revealing.

For livestock, replacement of normal death loss and without-project culling are considered operating expenditures. As with the investment cost, they are obtained by taking the purchases from table 4-11, multiplying by the farm-gate prices in table 4-12, then dividing by 100 to obtain the value for a single farm. The operating expenditure for minerals, vaccines, and the like is based on the animal units in the herd at the beginning of the year. The cost of pasture maintenance is estimated on

be purchased in year 1. Of these, 3 are to replace death loss, and 15 represent the normal culling as practiced without the project. The additional 15 bulls culled in year 1 are considered investment. Their value is divided by 100 to give the value for a single farm of ₲4.5 thousand {[(33 − 3 − 15) × 30] ÷ 100= 4.5}.

j. Work oxen purchased in year 1 are considered investment.

Table 4-16. *Operating Expenditure, 20-Hectare Mixed Farm, Paraguay Project*
(thousands of ₲)

Product and operation[a]	Expenditure per hectare	Without project			With project						
		Year 1–2	3–5	6–20	1	2	3	4	5	6	7–20
Crops											
Maize[b]	0	0	0	0	0	0	0	0	0	0	0
Manioc[b]	0	0	0	0	0	0	0	0	0	0	0
Beans[b]	0	0	0	0	0	0	0	0	0	0	0
Cotton											
Hired labor[c]	—	0	0	0	0	0	0	4.5	8.1	16.8	17.4
Seed[d]	0.8	1.6	1.6	1.6	1.6	1.6	1.6	1.8	2.0	2.4	2.4
Pesticides[d]	4.6	9.2	9.2	9.2	9.2	9.2	9.2	10.1	11.5	13.8	13.8
Total cotton		10.8	10.8	10.8	10.8	10.8	10.8	16.4	21.6	33.0	33.6
Soybeans											
Hired labor[c]	—	—	—	—	—	0	0	2.1	4.5	9.3	9.6
Seed[d]	2.8	—	—	—	—	2.8	2.8	6.2	7.0	8.4	8.4
Pesticides[d]	1.5	—	—	—	—	1.5	1.5	3.3	3.8	4.5	4.5
Fertilizer[d]	8.0	—	—	—	—	8.0	8.0	17.6	20.0	24.0	24.0
Threshing[e]	—	—	—	—	—	2.8	2.8	7.0	8.0	10.8	10.8
Total soybeans		—	—	—	—	15.1	15.1	36.2	43.3	57.0	57.3
Sunflower											
Hired labor[c]	—	—	—	—	—	0	0	0	0.3	0.6	1.2
Seed[d]	0.6	—	—	—	—	1.2	1.2	1.3	1.5	1.8	1.8
Pesticides[d]	1.2	—	—	—	—	2.4	2.4	2.6	3.0	3.6	3.6
Threshing[e]	—	—	—	—	—	0	3.6	4.0	4.8	6.0	7.2
Total sunflower		—	—	—	—	3.6	7.2	7.9	9.6	12.0	13.8
Total crops		10.8	10.8	10.8	10.8	29.5	33.1	60.5	74.5	102.0	104.7

Livestock											
Minerals, vaccines, etc.[f]	—	6.8	6.8	6.8	6.8	8.6	10.0	11.4	12.3	12.6	12.5
Improved pasture[g]	1.0	—	—	—	0	3.5	7.0	10.5	10.5	10.5	10.5
Replacement purchases[h]											
Bulls[i]	—	5.8	6.0	5.4	5.4	6.0	6.5	6.5	6.5	6.7	6.7
Work oxen[j]	—	—	—	—	0	13.3	13.6	13.6	13.6	14.1	14.1
Total livestock	12.2	12.6	12.8	12.2	12.2	31.4	37.1	42.0	42.9	43.9	43.8
Equipment											
Operation and maintenance[k]	2.5	2.5	2.5	2.5	2.5	10.3	10.3	10.3	10.3	10.3	10.3
Total equipment	2.5	2.5	2.5	2.5	2.5	10.3	10.3	10.3	10.3	10.3	10.3
Total operating expenditure	25.5	25.5	25.9	26.1	25.5	71.2	80.5	112.8	127.7	156.2	158.8

Source: Calculated from other tables as noted.

a. Family labor is valued at its opportunity cost (see the discussion of the farm budget). The number of work days required is given in table 4-7.

b. Assumes no cash expenditure needed for production.

c. From table 4-8 multiplied by the ₡300 a day shown in table 4-12. For sunflower, table 4-8 allocates labor according to the labor requirement in table 4-7 for the year of planting. See note c in table 4-7.

d. From the areas in table 4-4 times the unit cost given. For sunflower, seed and pesticide costs are based on the year of planting.

e. From production in table 4-10 multiplied by a threshing cost of ₡2 thousand per ton.

f. At ₡500 an animal unit multiplied by the animal units of herd pasture requirement in table 4-11 at the beginning of the year, the product then divided by 100 to give the value for a single farm.

g. Maintenance; calculated on the basis of improved pasture established in previous years as shown in table 4-4.

h. From the purchases in table 4-11 multiplied by the prices in table 4-12, the product then divided by 100 to give the value for a single farm. See text for a discussion of this convention. Normal replacement of death loss and culls is considered an operating cost.

i. The normal death loss and without-project culling for bulls in year 1 is considered operating expenditure. For the 100-farm herd, table 4-27 shows that 33 replacement bulls will be purchased in year 1. Of these, 3 are to replace death loss, and 15 represent the normal culling as practiced without the project, so all may be considered an operating expenditure. The value of the 18 replacement animals is divided by 100 to give the value for a single farm of ₡5.4 thousand (18 × 30 ÷ 100 = 5.4). The additional 15 bulls culled in year 1 are considered investment. For years 2 through 20, all bull purchases are considered replacements and thus operating expenditure.

j. Work oxen purchased to replace death loss and culls from years 2 through 20 are considered operating expenditure. Work oxen purchased in year 1 are considered investment.

k. Operation and maintenance cost of equipment is taken to be 5 percent of the investment cost beginning the year after acquisition. It is assumed that without the project the farm has ₡50 thousand of equipment and thus an annual equipment, operation, and maintenance expense of ₡2.5 thousand (50 × 0.05 = 2.5). With the project, this expense continues, plus the maintenance of the incremental ₡156 thousand worth of equipment purchased in year 1 as shown in table 4-15, giving a total of ₡10.3 thousand [2.5 + (156 × 0.05) = 10.3].

the basis of improved pasture established as of the end of the previous year.

Expenditure for operation and maintenance of equipment is taken to be 5 percent of the initial investment cost beginning the year after acquisition. Expenditure for operation and maintenance of equipment, such as that for pumps, is often included in the operating expenditure of the crop for which the equipment is used. When it is not, as in this example, then it must be shown separately.

The operating expenditure does not include a separate entry for family labor or for land. Rather, these are valued at their opportunity cost by the approach taken in designing the farm budget. (Opportunity cost was defined early in chapter 3, in the section "Prices Reflect Value.") We will return to a discussion of how this is accomplished after we have discussed the farm budget, below.

INCREMENTAL WORKING CAPITAL. The *incremental working capital* for the Paraguay pattern farm is given in table 4-17. As noted in the discussion of the accounting convention adopted for farm investment analysis and in table 4-3, the incremental working capital is derived from the information on *total operating expenditure* in table 4-16 by taking some proportion of the *incremental operating expenditure* for the following year. To simplify the calculation, it is assumed that the Paraguay pattern farm is predominantly a one-season, annual crop farm. Referring to table 4-3, we note the incremental working capital as a percentage of incremental operating expenditure for one season annual crops ranges between 80 and 100 percent. The incremental working capital needed, then, may be taken at the midpoint of the range, or 90 percent of the incremental operating expenditure in the following year. In year 2, for example, the

Table 4-17. *Incremental Working Capital,*
20-Hectare Mixed Farm, Paraguay Project
(thousands of ₲)

Item	Project year								
	1	*2*	*3*	*4*	*5*	*6*	*7*	*8–20*	*Total*
Total operating expenditure[a]	25.5	71.2	80.5	112.8	127.7	156.2	158.8	158.8	—
Incremental operating expenditure	—	45.7	9.3	32.3	14.9	28.5	2.6	0	133.3
Incremental working capital[b]	41.1	8.4	29.1	13.4	25.6	2.3	0	0	119.9

Source: Calculated from tables 4-3 and 4-16.

a. From table 4-16.

b. Taken to be 90 percent of the incremental operating expenditure in the following year. For year 1, for example, this comes to ₲41.1 thousand [(71 − 25.2) × 0.9 = 41.1]. This is based on the recommendation that incremental working capital be a percentage of incremental operating expenditure as given in table 4-3. For purposes of this calculation, it is taken that the model farm is dominantly a one-season, annual crop farm, even though there is a second crop of sunflower and there is a livestock enterprise. Accepting this assumption somewhat overstates the incremental working capital needed.

incremental operating expenditure is ₲45.7 thousand (71.2 − 25.5 = 45.7) and the incremental working capital in year 1, which is 90 percent of the incremental operating expenditure in the following year, is thus ₲41.1 thousand (45.7 × 0.9 = 41.1). This simplification somewhat overstates the working capital needed. Note that by totaling the incremental working capital year by year we obtain the ₲119.9 thousand residual incremental working capital shown in table 4-14.

Had we wished to make a more precise estimate of the incremental working capital, we could have calculated the amount needed for each category of operating expenditure as given in table 4-16. For crops, we could have taken from table 4-3 the same 90 percent estimate we accepted in our simplification. Taking year 5 as an illustration, the incremental working capital for crops would have been ₲24.8 thousand [(102.0 − 74.5) × 0.9 = 24.8]. For livestock, we might have accepted 30 percent from the recommended range of 20 to 40 percent in table 4-3. Since the without-project working capital will also increase during the life of the project, the computation of the incremental working capital is somewhat more complicated for livestock than for crops. The without-project incremental operating expenditure must be subtracted from the with-project incremental operating expenditure. This is a minor adjustment and might have been ignored. Taking year 5 as an illustration again, the incremental working capital for livestock would be ₲0.2 thousand {[(43.9 − 42.9) − (12.8 − 12.6)] × 0.3 = 0.2}. For equipment, we would have taken the full incremental operating expenditure; this, however, does not increase between years 5 and 6 and so is zero (10.3 − 10.3 = 0). Adding the combined incremental working capital for all three categories, we reach an incremental working capital for the farm in year 5 of ₲25.0 thousand (24.8 + 0.2 + 0 = 25.0). This compares with the estimate of incremental working capital of ₲25.6 thousand that our simplified calculation in table 4-17 gave us for year 5.

Farm budget

With the pattern farm resource use, production, and inputs known, the analyst may proceed to draw up the farm budget.

When a farm budget for project analysis is prepared, the objective is an estimate of the incremental net benefit arising on the farm as a result of the project. Clear layout of the incremental net benefit is the main reason for the particular format adopted here and illustrated in tables 4-18 through 4-20 for the farm budget of the Paraguay project.

The analyst first calculates the net benefit without the project as shown in table 4-18. The overall format of the pattern farm budget can be seen in the with-project farm budget shown in table 4-19. If we take the *inflow* received on the farm year by year and subtract the *outflow*, we have the stream for *net benefit before financing*. This entry tells what the farm will earn without consideration of any effects of financing. It includes both the value of the crop and livestock production sold off the farm and the value of home-consumed production. Next we subtract the without-

Table 4-18. *Without-Project Farm Budget,*
20-Hectare Mixed Farm, Paraguay Project
(thousands of ₲)

	Project year			
Item	*1*	*2*	*3–5*	*6–20*
Inflow				
Gross value of production[a]	247.7	249.6	254.3	256.2
Total	247.7	249.6	254.3	256.2
Outflow				
Operating expenditure[b]	25.5	25.5	25.9	26.1
Other				
Tax on cattle sale[c]	2.3	2.3	2.3	2.3
Total	27.8	27.8	28.2	28.4
Net benefit before financing[d]	219.9	221.8	226.1	227.8

Source: Calculated from other tables as noted.
a. From table 4-13.
b. From table 4-16.
c. A tax of ₲800 is paid on each animal sold. The amount is calculated by multiplying the total sales given in table 4-11 by the tax and dividing the result by 100 to obtain the amount for each farm.
d. No financing would be received without the project.

project net benefit (table 4-18) to obtain the incremental net benefit before financing. In many projects, the without-project incremental net benefit is assumed to remain constant throughout the life of the project, and a without-project column is inserted before the columns for the project years. This constant without-project amount is then subtracted from the net benefit before financing in each project year to obtain the incremental net benefit before financing. In the Paraguay example, the without-project net benefit before financing changes during the life of the project, so this approach cannot be used. Instead, a separate figure for without-project net benefit before financing is calculated as shown in table 4-18; this figure has been entered in the with-project farm budget in table 4-19.

Note that in the early years of the with-project farm budget the incremental net benefit before financing will generally be negative as investment is undertaken. Later, when the stream turns positive, it is a measurement of the additional amount that the farm will produce as a result of the project. The stream of the incremental net benefit before financing is the cash flow as defined in chapter 9. When it is discounted, again as discussed in chapter 9, it becomes the basis for such measurements of project worth as the *net present worth of all resources engaged*, the *financial rate of return to all resources engaged*, or the *net benefit-investment ratio of all resources engaged*. Deriving measurements of project worth based on all resources engaged, whether the resources come from the farmer's own contribution or a lending institution, is commonly done to judge the financial viability of the investment on the farm. It is especially favored by analysts who have accounting experience.

If we eliminate transfer payments and value entries at efficiency prices as discussed in chapter 7, the incremental net benefit before financing is the incremental contribution to the national income. Aggregated to the project level, it becomes the basis for the benefit stream for the project and for calculating the net present worth, the economic rate of return, or the net benefit-investment ratio for the project—that is, the return which the project contributes to the economy as a whole.

If we proceed to look at the *financing* available with the project—after we allow for *loan receipts* and *debt service* including interest payments and repayment of principal, which together give the *net financing*—we reach the *net benefit after financing*. This is also called the farm family net benefit, since it is the amount that the family has to live on for the year. Maximizing the net benefit after financing is taken to be the objective of the farm family; it is thus defined consistently with the objectives laid out in chapter 2. This is a most important estimate because, obviously, it directly affects the incentive to the farm family to participate in the project.

The difference between what the family would receive without the project and the net benefit after financing is the *incremental net benefit after financing*. This is the additional amount the family would receive by participating in the proposed project over and above what it would receive without the project. Note that, as in the Paraguayan example, the incremental net benefit generally will be negative in the first few years if the farmer must invest some of his own resources to participate in the project. The incremental net benefit (or incremental farm family net benefit) is, in effect, the direct incentive to the family to participate in the project. It is the cash flow seen from the point of view of the farmer, as defined in chapter 9. Discounted, it will give the *financial rate of return to the farmer's own resources* if he has invested any of his own capital in the project. Discounting the net benefit after financing and dividing by the discounted net benefit after financing without the project yields the *net benefit increase*, a measure of farmer incentive discussed in more detail in the section devoted to that topic later in this chapter.

It is extremely convenient to separate the financing transactions in the farm budget, as is illustrated in the Paraguay example. By leaving financing to a later part of the table, we can concentrate on what the farm will produce in arriving at the incremental net benefit before financing. This gives a direct estimate of how much total investment will be needed from all sources for the pattern farm. The incremental net benefit before financing is derived directly, and this makes it convenient to calculate the measures of project worth based on all resources engaged. This format directly provides a basis for aggregation and is also the starting point for the economic analysis discussed in chapter 7. Grouping the financing transactions is convenient if there is a credit element in the project, as there so often is, because it permits looking at the credit

Table 4-19. *Farm Budget, 20-Hectare Mixed Farm, Paraguay Project*
(thousands of G̶)

Item	\	\	\	\	\	\	Project year	\	\	\	\	\
	1	2	3	4	5	6	7	8–11	12	13	14–19	20
Inflow												
Gross value of production[a]												
Crops	187.8	237.0	289.2	340.7	387.4	485.3	501.5	501.5	501.5	501.5	501.5	501.5
Livestock	51.4	63.5	73.0	85.9	115.3	135.2	133.1	133.1	133.1	133.1	133.1	133.1
Off-farm income	—	—	—	—	—	—	—	—	—	—	—	—
Incremental residual value[b]	—	—	—	—	—	—	—	—	—	—	—	430.6
Total inflow	239.2	300.5	362.2	426.6	502.7	620.5	634.6	634.6	634.6	634.6	634.6	1,065.2
Outflow												
Investment[c]	523.6	110.6	126.5	0	0	0	0	0	0	0	0	0
Incremental working capital[d]	41.1	8.4	29.1	13.4	25.6	2.3	0	0	0	0	0	0
Operating expenditure[e]	25.5	71.2	80.5	112.8	127.7	156.2	158.8	158.8	158.8	158.8	158.8	158.8
Other												
Tax on cattle sale[f]	1.9	2.4	2.6	3.1	4.2	4.7	4.6	4.6	4.6	4.6	4.6	4.6
Total outflow	592.1	192.6	238.7	129.3	157.5	163.2	163.4	163.4	163.4	163.4	163.4	163.4
Net benefit before financing												
Total	(352.9)	107.9	123.5	297.3	345.2	457.3	471.2	471.2	471.2	471.2	471.2	901.8
Without project[g]	219.9	221.8	226.1	226.1	226.1	227.8	227.8	227.8	227.8	227.8	227.8	227.8
Incremental	(572.8)	(113.9)	(102.6)	71.2	119.1	229.5	243.4	243.4	243.4	243.4	243.4	674.0
Financing[h]												
Loan receipts	508.2	107.1	140.0	0	0	0	0	0	0	0	0	0
Debt service	—	66.1	80.0	98.2	98.2	159.2	172.1	188.9	61.8	35.0	0	0
Net financing	508.2	41.0	60.0	(98.2)	(98.2)	(159.2)	(172.1)	(188.9)	(61.8)	(35.0)	0	0

Net benefit after financing

Total	155.3	148.9	183.5	199.1	247.0	298.1	299.1	282.3	409.4	436.2	471.2	901.8
Without project[g]	219.9	221.8	226.1	226.1	226.1	227.8	227.8	227.8	227.8	227.8	227.8	227.8
Incremental	(64.6)	(72.9)	(42.6)	(27.0)	20.9	70.3	71.3	54.5	181.6	208.4	243.4	674.0

Cash position

Net benefit after financing	155.3	148.9	183.5	199.1	247.0	298.1	299.1	282.3	409.4	436.2	471.2	901.8
Less home-consumed production[i]	50.0	50.0	50.0	50.0	50.0	40.2	44.4	44.4	44.4	44.4	44.4	44.4
Cash surplus (or deficit)	105.3	98.9	133.5	149.1	197.0	257.9	254.7	237.9	365.0	391.8	426.8	857.4

Net present worth at 12 percent of all resources engaged = ₲416 thousand[i]

Financial rate of return to all resources engaged = 18 percent[j]

Net benefit-investment ratio at 12 percent of all resources engaged = ₲1,091.6 ÷ ₲675.4 = 1.62[j]

Financial rate of return to the farmer's own resources = 26 percent[k]

Net benefit increase = (₲385.0 ÷ ₲1,686.4 × 100) = 23 percent[l]

Source: Calculated from other tables as noted.

a. From table 4-13.

b. From table 4-14.

c. From table 4-15.

d. From table 4-17.

e. From table 4-16. If labor had been hired and paid in kind and this had not been included in the operating expenditure table, it would be shown here under operating expenditure as a separate line.

f. A tax of ₲800 is paid on each animal sold. The amount is calculated by multiplying the total sales given in table 4-11 by the tax and dividing the result by 100 to obtain the amount for each farm.

g. From table 4-18. No financing would be received without the project.

h. The farmer receives a loan from the Paraguayan National Development Bank for 90 percent of the investment cost and for 90 percent of the incremental working capital during the investment period, which is years 1 through 3. The loan is for a ten-year period, with a four-year grace period during which interest is paid. The loan received each year is treated as a separate transaction. Thus, for the loan received at the end of year 1, the grace period is for years 2 through 5 and the principal of the loan is repaid during years 6 through 11. The interest rate is 13 percent. See table 4-24 for details of the computation.

i. Assumes that the family would eat all of the maize and beans and part of the manioc in years 1 through 5. From year 6 onward it is assumed that the family will consume all of the maize and manioc.

j. Calculated on the basis of the incremental net benefit before financing. For details about the method of computation, see chapter 9.

k. Calculated on the basis of the incremental net benefit after financing.

l. The net benefit increase is the present worth of the incremental net benefit after financing with the project divided by the present worth of the net benefit after financing without the project; expressed in percentage. See text for a discussion of this measure. For details about the method of the present worth computation, see chapter 9.

131

transaction separately. The timing of the loan receipts, the timing of the debt service, and the net financing can all be determined easily by simple inspection. Then, by examining the incremental net benefit after financing, an assessment can be made about the amount of credit a farmer will need to participate and when he should repay it. With the incremental net benefit after financing now available, it is a simple matter to discount it to determine the *financial rate of return to the farmer's own resources*.

Of the individual entries included under the *inflow* in table 4-19, the first is the *gross value of production*, which is derived directly from table 4-13. This entry includes only that production available for use off the farm or by the farm family itself; it does not include any production used as an intermediate product on the farm. In particular, it does not include feed produced and fed to animals on the farm. Note the gross value of production includes any production consumed at home; it is not, therefore, the gross *sales*. In the Paraguayan example, the family will consume most of the maize, manioc, and beans it produces, as noted in the last section of the farm budget. If we fail to include the value of home-consumed production as part of the gross value of production, we will understate the attractiveness to the farmer of participating in the project. Furthermore, when we recast the budget to reflect economic values we will understate the true contribution of the project to the national income. In turn, this will make the measures of project worth of those projects in which a high proportion of the incremental production is to be consumed by the farm family look relatively less attractive than those of projects in which a high proportion of the incremental production is to be sold. We may thus penalize many of the very projects that provide the greatest benefit to the most disadvantaged farmers.

It is important that any *off-farm income* the farmer may earn be included in the budget. Hence, a dummy line has been included in table 4-19 even though there is no off-farm income involved in the Paraguay example. As we will discuss in detail in the next section, by including off-farm income in the budget we are automatically able to value family labor at its opportunity cost. This avoids trying to impute separately an appropriate wage for family labor.

Two other items may enter under the inflow that were not needed in the Paraguay example. The first is direct *grants* received by the farmer. Subsidies that benefit the farmer by lowering the cost of an input or by increasing the price he receives for his production would not be entered here. Instead, they would be accounted for by entering the subsidized market price in the account. Later, in the economic analysis, these items would have to be revalued to reflect the subsidy.

A second entry that might appear as an inflow in a farm budget but that is not needed in the Paraguay example is the *rental value of the farm house*. In most projects, no investment in housing is made, and the rental value remains unchanged with or without the project. As a result, the rental value has no effect on the incremental net benefit and so is generally omitted. If, however, the cost of the project has included housing, as might be the case in a settlement project, then the rental value of that housing is a benefit for which allowance must be made. In most instances the rental value will be imputed and—as with all imputed values—great care must be exercised in determining it.

The last of the inflow items in table 4-19 is the *incremental residual value*. This is derived for the Paraguayan example from table 4-14.

First among the elements of the *outflow* is the on-farm *investment*. Note that the total on-farm investment is included here, not just that proportion the farmer is expected to pay from his own funds. The investment the farmer must make himself as of the end of the year will appear as a negative *incremental net benefit after financing* at the bottom of the table. For most farm investment analyses, the major items of investment would be detailed in a supporting table such as table 4-15, since the focus so often is upon some on-farm investment. In projects where the major investment is made off the farm, as might be the case in irrigation, there may be no substantial on-farm investment.

The next outflow is the *incremental working capital*, taken from table 4-17. As noted earlier in this chapter in the discussion of the accounting convention, the incremental working capital is calculated as some proportion of the increase or decrease in operating expenditure the following year. It reflects, of course, the need to have on hand at the beginning of the season sufficient funds to finance inputs for crop and livestock production.

The next entry for outflow is the *operating expenditure*, taken from table 4-16. If hired labor paid in kind were omitted from table 4-16 (which some analysts prefer to treat as a list of cash expenditures), then a separate entry would have to be included under the *operating expenditure*.

Finally, an entry is made for *other* outflows. In the Paraguayan pattern farm budget, the only other outflow is for a tax on cattle sales. A tax on land, however, might also be found under this entry, as might general overhead, a betterment levy, or a capital recovery charge for an irrigation project. An income tax would usually not be shown here; it is uncommon for a small farmer to have to pay income tax, and, in any event, it is generally considered that income tax is levied against the farmer as an individual rather than against the farm as such. (This, of course, is in contrast to corporate income taxes, which would be shown if levied; see chapter 5 for a discussion of accounts for agricultural processing industries.) In general, indirect taxes such as sales taxes or tariffs on imported items will be included in the price of inputs; this works well for financial analysis, but it may lead to complications when the economic values are being estimated. The total inflow less the total outflow gives the *net benefit before financing*.

The section of table 4-19 devoted to *financing* begins with the projection of the *loan receipts* the farmer may expect if he participates in the project. Loan receipts are commonly divided into short-term and medium- or long-term. In the Paraguay example, only medium-term loans are to be received. Loans are entered in the year they are to be received.

Debt service—the payment of interest and repayment of principal— follows. Usually it, too, will be disaggregated by the length of the loan maturity. Interest and principal repayments are often shown as a single entry, although sometimes interest payments and the principal repayment are shown separately. The details of how to calculate interest payments and principal repayments are discussed in the section "Computing Debt Service" later in this chapter.

The debt service is subtracted from the loan receipts to reach the *net financing*, which is shown with an indication of whether it is positive or negative. In the Paraguay example, in years 1 through 3 the loan receipts exceed the debt service, so the net financing is positive; in years 4 through 13, however, debt service exceeds the loan receipts, and so the net financing is negative.

The net financing subtracted from (or added to, as appropriate) the net benefit before financing gives the *net benefit after financing*, also called the farm family net benefit. As noted, this is the amount the family has to live on with the project and is most important for judging incentive effects of the project. It is probably an estimate of this amount that most farmers make when they decide whether to participate in a project, although no doubt they arrive at it by a less formal means.

If we subtract the net benefit after financing without the project from the net benefit after financing for each project year, we arrive at the *incremental net benefit after financing*, or incremental farm family net benefit. This is the same incremental net benefit or cash flow defined in chapter 9. It represents an undifferentiated return of and to the farmer's capital; discounted, it gives the financial rate of return to the farmer's own resources. The incremental net benefit after financing also provides us with another basis for a judgment about incentive effects. Would a farmer be willing to shoulder the additional risk and effort needed to participate in the project if he can expect this kind of incremental income?

Because home-consumed production is included in the farm budget, if any high proportion of the incremental production is expected to be consumed in the farm household, it is desirable to have a section on the *cash position* to determine whether the farmer will have the cash he needs to purchase modern inputs and to meet his credit obligations. (This is the point at which a bit of funds flow analysis is mixed in with the farm investment analysis.) One means is to calculate a separate cash budget as Brown suggests (1979, pp. 25–30). Another means is shown at the bottom of table 4-19. Here, a line is added to subtract the value of *home-consumed production* from the *net benefit after financing*. The remainder is the *cash surplus (or deficit)*. If there is a deficit, it must be made up from family savings or other sources if the farmer is not to fall behind in his investment plan or to default on his credit obligations. Alternatively, we may wish to adjust the amount of short-term credit extended or alter the conditions of long-term credit to avoid the cash deficit.

The farm budget presented in table 4-19 assumes that the real burden of debt service will continue throughout the life of the loan the farmer receives. As in most countries, in the Paraguay project the lending terms to farmers call for repayment in nominal—that is, money—terms. Interest is stated at a given rate, and the nominal amount of principal repayment is agreed upon. If, however, a country experiences inflation that reduces the real value of money over time, the result is that farmers whose debt service payments are fixed in money terms have a declining real burden of debt service. Some countries try to adjust for this by indexing loans so that the nominal amount a farmer pays changes to maintain the same real burden of debt service, but most do not.

If Paraguay were expected to experience inflation, then the farm budget would be a more realistic indicator of income and incentive if it reflected the declining real burden of debt service. Predicting future inflation rates is difficult at the very least (and may lead to political complications for analysts in public agencies if the government has adopted a strong anti-inflation program). Past experience is some indication of what future inflation may be. In 1977 the wholesale price index in Paraguay rose by 8 percent, so that rate might be accepted as an estimate of future inflation. If we assume constant inflation of 8 percent during the life of the loan, then the debt service each year will be reduced by dividing it by 1 plus the rate of inflation stated in decimal terms to reflect the declining real burden. The farm budget for the Paraguay example is recast in table 4-20 to incorporate this assumption. The table projects that the real value of the loan receipts in years 2 and 3 will remain the same—which is to say that their nominal value will increase by the amount of inflation. This is perhaps an unrealistic assumption in many countries. If so, not only the debt service but the real value of the loan receipts might be reduced by the amount of the inflation, and the farmer would have to invest more of his own resources to keep his investment program on schedule. (The details about how the loan receipts and debt service were calculated are given in the section "Computing Debt Service" and in table 4-26, below.)

The recast farm budget in table 4-20 begins with the net benefit before financing, which is the same as that in table 4-19 since table 4-19 is cast in constant terms and the relative prices are correct. (The reader will recall that the prices in table 4-12, which formed one of the bases for table 4-19, were varied to allow for changing relative values.) Since all prices in both tables 4-19 and 4-20 maintain the same relation to each other or have been changed to reflect changing relations, the tables are, in effect, cast in terms of the value of the guarani in project year 1. The terms of the loan to the farmer from the Paraguayan National Development Bank are the same as those outlined in table 4-19 and are set in nominal terms. Comparing the debt service line in tables 4-19 and 4-20 shows the effect of assuming a declining real burden of debt service, as does a comparison between the two lines for the incremental net benefit after financing.

Recasting the farm budget to reflect the declining real burden of debt service shows that the real return to the farmer for his own resources would rise from the 26 percent estimated in table 4-19 to 34 percent. The net benefit increase (discussed later in this chapter) would rise from 23 percent to 35 percent. Both increases, of course, reflect the declining real burden of the debt service.

Casting the farm budget to reflect the declining real burden of debt service that occurs in inflationary circumstances certainly is more realistic than assuming a constant burden. It probably also will lead to a better

Table 4-20. *Farm Budget Assuming Declining Real Burden of Debt Service, 20-Hectare Mixed Farm, Paraguay Project* (thousands of ₲)

Item	Project year														
	1	2	3	4	5	6	7	8	9	10	11	12	13	14–19	20
Net benefit before financing[a]	(359.2)	107.9	123.5	297.3	345.2	457.3	471.2	471.2	471.2	471.2	471.2	471.2	471.2	471.2	901.8
Financing[b]															
Loan receipts[a]	508.2	107.1	140.0	0	0	0	0	0	0	0	0	0	0	0	0
Debt service[c]	—	61.2	69.6	81.3	75.2	111.1	111.6	114.9	106.3	98.4	91.1	29.8	16.2	0	0
Net financing	508.2	45.9	70.4	(81.3)	(75.2)	(111.1)	(111.6)	(114.9)	(106.3)	(98.4)	(91.1)	(29.8)	(16.2)	0	0
Net benefit after financing															
Total	149.0	153.8	193.9	216.0	270.0	346.2	359.6	356.3	364.9	372.8	380.1	441.4	455.0	471.2	901.8
Without project[a]	219.9	221.8	226.1	226.1	226.1	227.8	227.8	227.8	227.8	227.8	227.8	227.8	227.8	227.8	227.8
Incremental	(70.9)	(68.0)	(32.2)	(10.1)	43.9	118.4	131.8	128.5	137.1	145.0	152.3	213.6	227.2	243.4	674.0

Cash position														
Net benefit after financing	149.0	153.8	193.9	216.0	270.0	346.2	359.6	356.3	364.9	372.8	380.1	441.4	455.0	471.2	901.8
Less home-consumed production[a]	50.0	50.0	50.0	50.0	50.0	40.2	44.4	44.4	44.4	44.4	44.4	44.4	44.4	44.4	44.4
Cash surplus (or deficit)	99.0	103.8	143.9	166.0	220.0	306.0	315.2	311.9	320.5	328.4	335.7	397.0	410.6	426.8	857.4

Net present worth at 12 percent of all resources engaged = ₲416 thousand[d]

Financial rate of return to all resources engaged = 18 percent[d]

Net benefit-investment ratio at 12 percent of all resources engaged = ₲1,091.6 ÷ ₲675.4 = 1.62[d]

Financial rate of return to the farmer's own resources = 34 percent[e]

Net benefit increase = ((₲595.8 ÷ ₲1,686.4 × 100) = 35 percent[f]

Source: Calculated from other tables as noted.

a. From table 4-19.

b. The terms and conditions of the financing are assumed to be the same as those in table 4-19, note h. It is assumed that there will be a constant inflation of 8 percent during the term of the loans. The table is stated in real terms in constant guaranis of project year 1 (except for the nominal terms for the loan receipts). Since debt service is denominated in nominal (money) terms, the real burden declines each year by the amount of inflation. Loan receipts are stated in real terms under the entry for loan receipts, and the nominal amounts for the second and third-year loans are given. The nominal amount is increased by the amount of inflation.

c. For details of the computation, see the section "Computing Debt Service" and table 4-26 later in this chapter.

d. Calculated on the basis of the incremental net benefit before financing. (Note that this is the same value as in table 4-19.) For details about the method of computation, see chapter 9.

e. Calculated on the basis of the incremental net benefit after financing.

f. The net benefit increase is the present worth of the incremental net benefit after financing with the project divided by the present worth of the net benefit after financing without the project expressed in percentage. See text for a discussion of this measurement. For details about the method of computing the present worth, see chapter 9.

estimate of the real attractiveness of a project to farmers, since most farmers will have some sense of the effect of inflation on nominal values. Except for the additional computations needed to project the farm budget, such an approach creates no analytical complications. Project aggregations can simply be based on the farm budgets that assume a declining real burden of debt service, just as they would be if the budget assumed that the burden of the debt service would remain constant and that the loan would be indexed. Of course, allowing for a declining real burden of debt service in the farm budget would not change the economic rate of return of a project, since that is based on the net benefit before financing valued in economic terms (discussed in chapter 7).

COST OF FAMILY LABOR. A common conceptual problem met when preparing farm investment analyses is how to determine the cost of family labor. The general principle, as with most questions of valuation, is to value family labor at its opportunity cost; that is, the benefit the family must forgo to participate in the project. This is done simply and more or less automatically if the farm budget format recommended here is followed.

This method has the tremendous practical advantage that the cost of family labor need not be estimated directly. Rather, the cost of family labor is taken to be what the family could earn in its next most remunerative alternative without the project. To accomplish this, the farm budget must compare the with-project situation with the without-project situation, and the off-farm labor income must be included in the budget—at least if there is to be any change in the amount earned from off-farm labor. The cost of the family labor needed to adopt the with-project cropping pattern, then, is the labor income in the without-project situation that must be given up. If the number of days of off-farm work must be reduced for the farm family to participate in the project, to that extent the cost of incremental family labor is the off-farm wage. If the with-project cropping pattern calls for a shift of family labor from one production activity on the farm to another, the cost of the labor shifted is implicitly set at the labor income forgone in the without-project activity. Finally, if more total family labor is called for in the with-project cropping pattern than in the pattern without the project, as is the case in the Paraguay example, this additional labor is implicitly priced at an opportunity cost of zero, since no income must be forgone to use the labor in the with-project cropping pattern. This assumes, in effect, that the family would have worked more days of the year in the without-project situation had there been suitable opportunities available either through additional farm work or off the farm. Any incremental labor needed in the with-project cropping pattern compared with the without-project cropping pattern plus off-farm employment is assumed to be taken from undesired leisure given up. (Later, when the analyst converts from financial prices to economic values, the off-farm earning would be valued at the appropriate shadow wage.)

If the family would not, in fact, give up leisure for the amount it could earn from additional farm labor by participating in the project, then the proposed cropping pattern is unrealistic and should not be used. Such a situation could easily arise. In many societies, the period just after harvest is a time of family festivals. A proposed cropping pattern calling for substantial family labor during this time would in all likelihood be unacceptable to the farmers. In effect, we are saying that the family has a "reservation price" for leisure—the price at which the family is willing to give up leisure for additional work—that is greater than the return the family would receive for working the additional work days. Note that we do not attempt in this process to determine any value for leisure time. All we are saying is that the reservation price for leisure is greater than the return the family can earn from the proposed project's cropping pattern.

Of course, the reservation price for leisure will vary widely with the circumstances. For substantially unemployed rural labor, the reservation price may be quite low. But if every adult family member is already engaged some 200 days a year, then the reservation price for labor just after the harvest season may be rather high, for continued labor at this time may mean missing treasured family occasions. As the number of days of labor approaches the physical maximum, the reservation price will rise until almost no return is great enough to elicit additional labor.

If we lay out the pattern farm budgets as suggested here, and family labor is valued at its opportunity cost, there is no need to have a separate entry for the value of family labor. To have such an entry amounts to double counting. Even so, because many analysts are uncomfortable presenting a budget with no directly identified allowance for family labor, a separate value for family labor is commonly found to be included erroneously in agricultural project analyses.

COST OF LAND. A parallel approach to that suggested for the opportunity cost of family labor may be taken to determine the cost of land. This is especially convenient whenever the project does not contemplate a change in ownership but rather a change only in land use. If farmers shift from rainfed sorghum to irrigated rice without changing the land ownership, as has happened in several agricultural projects along the major rivers of West Africa, the cost of the land is its contribution to the value of the sorghum production that the farmers must forgo to use the land for rice. This is automatically provided for when we lay out the farm budget to show the difference with and without the project. Therefore, a separate entry for the cost of land is not needed, either in the financial or in the economic accounts.

When there is a separate rent paid by the farm family for the use of the land, then the rent is properly shown as a cost in the financial analysis—in both the without-project and the with-project situations—since it reduces the net benefit available to the family. However, when we convert this budget to efficiency prices for the economic analysis, as discussed in chapter 7, simply casting the economic account on a with and without basis without entering the rent separately would be the simplest way to allow for the opportunity cost of land.

If the land is to be purchased, the purchase price would properly be shown as a cost in the financial accounts. Again, however, in converting to efficiency prices for the economic analysis the opportunity cost would be taken as the economic value. As before, simply comparing the situations with and without the project in the economic accounts is generally the most convenient approach and will correctly value the land at its opportunity cost. Sometimes, however, different approaches may be taken in the economic accounts, a topic to which we will return in chapter 7 in the subsection "Step 3. Adjustment for price distortions in non-traded items."

Net Benefit Increase

We should note that, although the farm budgets given in this chapter place a fair amount of stress on determining the net present worth, the financial rate of return, and the net benefit-investment ratio to the farmer's own resources, these measures of project worth are in fact not very important to the farmer. Far more important to farmers is the actual amount of additional income they expect to receive. It is probably fair to say that for most small farmers the concept of capital return hardly plays any part in their decision. Indeed, in many farm budgets these measures of project worth are almost meaningless. For example, in the Third Agricultural Credit Project in Kenya, for the model ii smallholder in farm zone B, the return to the farmer's own capital resources is extremely high. This is so because it is proposed to lend to the farmer most of the cost of the incremental investment for a new dairy enterprise, and the incremental return from the new enterprise from year 2 onward is sufficient to make the incremental net benefit after financing positive. Thus, the farmer really needs very little in the way of his own capital resources to participate in the project, although he will still have to bear most of the risk. Despite the high rate of return, since the farmer's own capital contribution is small, the absolute amount of his return is also small. Indeed, the whole incremental net benefit after financing, or incremental farm family net benefit, is not all that great. Hence, no one would worry about the apparently very high windfall return the farmer would receive on his own capital resources engaged in the project.

Farmers probably pay more attention to the potential increase in their incremental net benefit after financing, so it is convenient to have a measure that succinctly describes what that is. Schaefer-Kehnert (1980) has proposed the net benefit increase for this purpose. This is the present worth of the incremental net benefit after financing with the project, divided by the present worth of the net benefit after financing without the project, expressed in percentage terms. (The mechanics of determining the present worth are discussed in chapter 9.) In the farm budget for the Paraguay project pattern farm given in table 4-19, for example, at a 12 percent discount rate the present worth of the incremental net benefit after financing with the project is G385.0 thousand, and the present worth of the net benefit after financing without the project is G1,686.4 thousand. The net benefit increase, thus, is 23 percent (385.0 ÷ 1,686.4 × 100 = 23). The net benefit increase may be interpreted as the weighted average incremental increase in income the farmer will receive over the life of the project if he participates. The net benefit increase provides a basis for determining whether the increased income will be sufficient to attract farmers' participation in a project and for comparing easily the relative attractiveness to farmers of alternative project possibilities.

Unit Activity Budgets

We have discussed in considerable detail preparation of whole farm budgets for farm investment analysis. This generally is the preferable analytical approach in agricultural project analysis. An alternative approach, however, is to prepare a "unit activity budget"; that is, a budget which applies only to some particular investment activity—say, a hectare of fruit trees or a broiler chicken production unit. This approach is related to the "partial" budgeting commonly used by farm management specialists in that it examines the return to a single activity on the farm rather than to the farm as a whole, with that one activity incorporated in the cropping pattern. Brown discusses partial budgets for agricultural project analysis (1979, pp. 25–30).

Unit activity budgets are particularly convenient when a project focuses on a single crop or livestock activity. Often these activities are considered as additions to existing farm activities that will encourage increased output of the commodity in question and will increase farm incomes. Usually it is thought that the activity can be added to the ongoing farm cropping pattern without disruption and without seriously reducing the resources available for other activities on the farm. Rather than develop a range of pattern whole farm budgets incorporating the new activity, many analysts choose simply to do a unit activity budget showing the cost and return per unit to the individual farmer who adopts the innovation and then to aggregate by multiplying the results by the number of hectares or of livestock production units to be included in the project. Unit activity budgets are used to good advantage where specification of opportunity costs for land or labor is not crucial. They may be used when estimating the area is difficult or inappropriate and where it is considered that the labor involved will not be seriously competitive with other farm activities. They have been used, for example, as the basis for agricultural project analysis where the objective was to encourage small-scale planting of grapes for raisin production in Afghanistan, to encourage stall feeding of cattle in Kenya, and to encourage the addition of a small dairy enterprise to existing farms in India. Unit activity budgets have the advantage of generally being easier to prepare, since it is not necessary to collect and analyze information on any farm production activity other than the one to be encouraged in the project.

There are, however, significant limitations in unit activity budgets. The most important is that they fail to assess the effect of undertaking a new activity on the resource use of the farm and on overall farm income. In the absence of whole farm budgets, the analyst may give too little attention to the place of a proposed innovation in the cropping pattern of the entire farm and thus make an erroneous judgment about incentive effects. It may be overlooked that incorporating a particular crop or innovation in the farm as a whole may cause labor shortages arising either from competition for family labor or for the total labor supply in the area. The analyst may fail to appreciate the competition for land of a new crop with other crops grown on the farm. Using unit activity budgets instead of whole farm budgets also reduces the analyst's ability to assess the farmer's credit need and repayment capacity, which are influenced not only by the incremental income from a particular production innovation but also by the financial position of the farm as a whole.

A major problem with unit activity budgets is that it is easy to overlook opportunity costs or to value them erroneously. One substantial advantage of laying out whole farm budgets in the manner suggested in this chapter is that this method correctly allows for the opportunity cost of land and labor—including, most importantly, family labor. Unit activity budgets generally are done directly on an incremental basis, rather than cast in a with-and-without form. This means that all opportunity costs must be estimated directly to obtain the incremental net benefit, and great care must be taken to see that they are correctly estimated. Conceptually, of course, if the opportunity costs are correctly stated, there will be no difference in the estimated incremental net benefit, either to the individual farmer or to the society as a whole, whether the basis is a whole farm budget or a unit activity budget. In practice, however, the situation is quite different. Both the opportunity cost of the land to be used for the new crop or livestock undertaking and the opportunity cost of family labor must be imputed rather than derived from established market prices. Such estimates are difficult to make correctly; they are frequently in error and will give results that will differ from those that would be obtained by using whole farm budgets. (The full "partial" budgeting technique developed by farm management specialists can also be used for estimating the opportunity cost of land and labor, but the full approach is not often used in practice for agricultural project analysis.)

We may illustrate a unit activity budget with an example drawn from the Indian Cashewnut Project. The project is to help finance a cashew production program in four Indian states; the project includes 35,000 hectares to be developed by smallholders. The project analyst chose to use the unit activity approach because most cashews in India are grown by smallholders in small clumps, in hedgerows, or as backyard trees. Preparing pattern whole farm budgets that reasonably represented the range of possible combinations of farm sizes and cashew production activities would entail a large number of examples. Instead, six unit activity budgets for a hectare of cashews each were prepared for new plantings and two for rehabilitation of existing plantings. The incremental net benefit from each unit activity budget was then multiplied by the area foreseen in the project for each pattern to obtain the contribution to the total project benefit of increased cashew production by smallholders.

The relevant background information to the Indian project is given in table 4-21. This gives the *value of production* and the *investment and operating expenditure*. (The symbol for Indian rupees is Rs.) In the budget as prepared by the analyst, no distinction was made between investment and operating expense; instead, both were simply defined as "production" cost, a conceptually correct approach. To keep this presentation parallel to that for the Paraguay whole farm budget discussed earlier in this chapter, however, all expenditure before the trees begin to bear is rather arbitrarily considered investment, whereas that incurred after bearing begins is considered operating expenditure. The advantage of this treatment is that it makes it analytically convenient to calculate the incremental working capital needed. In the summary reproduced here, the details about the amounts and unit prices of the materials needed, which were included in the original project analysis, have been omitted to conserve space.

The background information points up some of the problems of using the unit activity approach to budgeting. Among the investment and operating expenditures, the analyst has indeed included all the opportunity costs. Both the opportunity cost for land and for labor were estimated directly. In the Indian Cashewnut Project, the trees are assumed to be planted in areas otherwise put to no economic use; the opportunity cost of the land can thus be appropriately taken as zero. In other instances, however, the opportunity cost of the land might be positive, and the points we have made earlier in the "Farm budget" subsection about estimating the opportunity cost of land would have to be considered. It might be appropriate, for instance, to use rent as an estimate of the contribution of land to the value of production forgone to undertake the new activity. In still other instances, the purchase price of the land might appropriately account for its opportunity cost, even though purchase price is generally a poor estimate. This might be the case in a livestock-fattening project, for instance, where the area involved is small and the opportunity cost of the land is minor in relation to overall costs, so that using the purchase price would not lead to a significant error in the investment decision. Finally, in some instances it may prove necessary to estimate the contribution of the land to the forgone production directly, say, by assigning the residual after deducting all other costs from the value of production to land. This might be the case if farmers are expected to shift some of the land they already crop to another production activity.

Another problem with the unit activity budget approach is pointed up

Table 4-21. *Value of Production, Investment, and Operating Expenditure,*
1-Hectare Planting Model, Cashewnut Project, Smallholder Component, Karnataka, India

Item	Project year										
	1	2	3	4	5	6	7	8	9	10	11–40
Value of production											
Yield (kg/ha)	0	0	0	50	150	400	600	700	800	900	900
Price[a] (Rs/kg)	—	—	—	4.1	4.2	4.3	4.4	4.6	4.8	4.9	5.1
Gross value of production (Rs)	0	0	0	205	630	1,720	2,640	3,220	3,840	4,410	4,590
Investment and operating expenditure[b]											
Land											
Rent (opportunity cost) (Rs)[c]	0	0	0	0	0	0	0	0	0	0	0
Total land (Rs)	0	0	0	0	0	0	0	0	0	0	0
Labor (work days)											
Land clearing, development	70	0	0	0	0	0	0	0	0	0	0
Pit digging	15	0	0	0	0	0	0	0	0	0	0
Planting seedlings	6	0	0	0	0	0	0	0	0	0	0
Crescent bunding	0	25	25	0	0	0	0	0	0	0	0
Ringweeding	0	20	15	0	0	0	0	0	0	0	0
Gap filling	0	1	0	0	0	0	0	0	0	0	0
Bund maintenance	0	0	0	4	5	5	5	5	5	5	5

Mulching, weeding, watering	10	0	10	20	15	12	10	10	10	10
Fertilizer application	4	5	5	5	5	5	5	5	5	5
Plant protection	2	2	4	5	9	10	10	10	10	10
Harvesting	0	0	0	3	10	16	24	28	32	36
Miscellaneous	3	3	3	3	5	5	5	5	5	5
Total labor	110	56	62	40	49	53	59	63	67	71
Wage (Rs/day)	8	8	8	8	8	8	8	8	8	8
Labor cost (Rs)	880	448	496	320	392	424	472	504	536	568
Materials[d] (Rs)										
Plant materials	50	10	0	0	0	0	0	0	0	0
Fertilizer	150	250	350	400	400	400	400	400	400	400
Plant protection	40	80	120	150	175	175	175	175	175	175
Miscellaneous	20	20	20	20	20	20	20	20	20	20
Total materials	260	360	490	570	595	595	595	595	595	595
Total investment	1,140	808	986	0	0	0	0	0	0	0
Total operating expenditure	0	0	0	890	987	1,019	1,067	1,099	1,131	1,163

Rs Indian rupees; kg. kilograms.

Source: Adapted from World Bank, "India, Cashewnut Project, Staff Appraisal Report," 2437-IN (Washington, D.C., 1980; restricted circulation), annex 4, table 1.

a. Based on projected f.o.b. price adjusted to give the export parity value at the farm gate. Details given in the original project report, from which this example is drawn, are not reproduced here.

b. The analyst of the project did not distinguish between investment and operating expenditure, preferring instead to treat both simply as "production" cost. Production cost in years 1 to 3 before the trees bear is taken to be investment, in years 4 to 40 to be operating expenditure.

c. Trees are assumed to be planted in areas that otherwise would be put to no economic use.

d. Details of application rates and prices given in the original project report are not reproduced here.

145

by the background information. Labor represents a high proportion of the operating expenditure, characteristically on the order of half. Labor has been valued at a daily wage of Rs8, and this in turn was shadow-priced in the economic analysis at 70 percent of the market rate to allow for rural unemployment along the lines discussed in chapter 7. But, since most of the smallholder plantings will be in very small areas, even backyards, it is likely that family members will do most of the work. And they will probably do this at odd times, when they otherwise do not have opportunities for productive employment either on their own holdings or as hired labor. Thus, the opportunity cost to the family may be close to zero and the incremental net benefit correspondingly larger, making the project that much more attractive to farmers and reducing the need for credit. Similarly, when converting the financial prices to economic values along the lines discussed in chapter 7, if much of the labor is supplied by the family at times when there are no other opportunities for productive employment, then the economic value of the labor may also be close to zero—and the economic attractiveness of the smallholder component of the project that much more attractive from the standpoint of the economy as a whole.

The unit activity budget is given in table 4-22. Its format follows that adopted for the whole farm budget. From the *inflow* (including a subsidy for planting) is subtracted the *outflow* to obtain the *incremental net benefit before financing*. Discounted, this will give the net present worth, financial rate of return, or net benefit-investment ratio to all resources engaged. Changing the financial prices to economic values and omitting transfer payments (see chapter 7) will give the incremental net benefit in economic terms. This may then be aggregated by multiplying by the number of units expected in the project to give the total incremental net benefit contributed to the project by the on-farm production.

Proceeding to the *financing, loan receipts* less *debt service* give the *net financing*. The terms and conditions of the loans are given in the notes to the table. (A detailed exposition of how the debt service was calculated is given, in the subsection on computing debt service, using "equal installments with interest capitalized," later in this chapter.) The computation is made more complex because the interest is capitalized during the investment period. Also, the interest rate for the loan is 10.5 percent, and many discounting tables do not give factors for high fractional interest rates. The relevant factors, however, may easily be calculated on a simple hand calculator (as discussed in chapter 10 under "Calculator Applications in Project Analysis"). These credit estimates again raise the problem of estimating opportunity costs. The amount of credit is calculated assuming that the farmer will pay Rs8 per day for all the labor engaged. But if family labor were used for which the opportunity cost were lower, perhaps even zero, then the farmer would not need so much credit to undertake the new activity. Were credit extended on the basis of the unit activity budget, there might be more lent than necessary to further the project, and there would be significant "leakage." This could be avoided by a credit agency if its staff made separate analyses for each borrower based on the borrower's real costs rather than simply applying a rule of thumb derived from the unit activity budget.

Finally, we reach the entry for *incremental net benefit after financing*. Discounted, this will give the *financial rate of return to the farmer's own resources*, assuming that the farmer invested his own capital in the project as indicated in the budget and that all costs have been correctly estimated.

Computing Debt Service

In many farm budgets there will be a credit element, and the analyst will have to calculate the amount of the debt service. In this section, we will briefly review how to compute the amount of interest due and the amount of the principal repayment for four different repayment terms. We will also consider how to adjust for the declining real burden of debt service when there is inflation. Computations will be carried to the nearest whole currency unit or to some other convenient rounding aggregate, since that is the common practice in most farm budgets used in project analysis. Credit agencies, of course, will have to work to the nearest unit in common use for commercial transactions: cents, paise, nguawa, or whatever.

In the examples given here, where the term of the loan is a year or longer we will follow the accounting convention adopted—that loans are to be received at the end of a project year and that debt service is to begin in the following year. Often in project accounts, however, the analyst will choose to assume that the loan is made at the beginning of the accounting period and that debt service is paid at the end. As noted, this leads to the anomaly that for a loan of a year or longer both the loan receipt and the first interest payment, and perhaps even the first principal repayment, are shown within the same project year. It can also lead to an understatement of the short-term credit the farmer will need and to an overstatement of his financial rate of return.

Simple interest

The easiest term to calculate, of course, is common simple interest such as that found in short-term credit lent for seasonal expenses. In the Kenya Third Agricultural Credit Project, for example, the farmer receives a loan in year 1 of KSh1,374, which he is to repay twelve months later at 11 percent interest. (The symbol for Kenyan shillings is KSh.) Thus, the interest is KSh151 ($1,374 \times 0.11 = 151$). The total amount to be repaid by the Kenyan farmer is the principal borrowed plus the interest, or KSh1,525 ($1,374 + 151 = 1,525$). If we are concerned only about the total amount to be repaid and do not need to separate interest and principal, as is often the case in preparing farm budgets, then it is simpler to calculate the total repayment in one step by multiplying the principal

Table 4-22. *Unit Activity Budget, 1-Hectare Planting, India Cashewnut Project* (Rs)

Item	Project year												
	1	2	3	4	5	6	7	8	9	10	11–13	14–39	40
Inflow													
Gross value of production[a]	0	0	0	205	630	1,720	2,640	3,220	3,840	4,410	4,590	4,590	4,590
Subsidy[b]	300	300	300	0	0	0	0	0	0	0	0	0	0
Incremental residual value[c]	—	—	—	—	—	—	—	—	—	—	—	—	1,163
Total	300	300	300	205	630	1,720	2,640	3,220	3,840	4,410	4,590	4,590	5,753
Outflow													
Investment[a]	1,140	808	986	0	0	0	0	0	0	0	0	0	0
Incremental working capital[d]	—	—	890	97	32	48	32	32	32	0	0	0	0
Operating expenditure[a]	—	—	—	890	987	1,019	1,067	1,099	1,131	1,163	1,163	1,163	1,163
Other	0	0	0	0	0	0	0	0	0	0	0	0	0
Total	1,140	808	1,876	987	1,019	1,067	1,099	1,131	1,163	1,163	1,163	1,163	1,163
Incremental net benefit before financing	(840)	(508)	(1,576)	(782)	(389)	653	1,541	2,089	2,677	3,247	3,427	3,427	4,590

Financing[e]												
Loan receipts	783	468	1,482	733	338	0	0	0	0	0	—	—	—
Debt service	0	0	0	0	0	499	499	1,108	1,108	1,108	—	—	—
Net financing	783	468	1,482	733	338	(499)	(499)	(1,108)	(1,108)	(1,108)	—	—	—
Incremental net benefit after financing	(57)	(40)	(94)	(49)	(51)	154	1,042	981	1,569	2,139	2,319	3,427	4,590

Net present worth at 12 percent of all resources engaged = Rs 9,324[f]
Financial rate of return to all resources engaged = 29 percent[f]
Net benefit-investment ratio at 12 percent of all resources engaged = 12,318 ÷ 2,994 = 4.11[f]
Financial rate of return to the farmer's own resources = >50 percent[g]

Source: Same as table 4-21.

a. From table 4-21.

b. Participating smallholders receive a 25 percent subsidy of the cost of new planting or Rs900 per hectare, whichever is less.

c. The incremental residual value consists entirely of the working capital. It is assumed the trees have no residual value at the end of the project.

d. The incremental working capital is calculated on the assumption that all operating expenditure should be taken as the basis for the calculation. For each year 100 percent of the incremental operating expenditure is taken as recommended in table 4-3. This makes the implicit assumption that the labor cost represents an accurate estimate of the opportunity cost of the family labor used. See text for discussion.

e. Participating smallholders may borrow 95 percent of investment, incremental working capital, and operating expenditure less the amount of subsidy received and less the gross value of production in years when the net benefit before financing is negative. In year 4, for example, the amount of the loan is 95 percent of the incremental working capital plus the operating expenditure less the gross value of production $\{[0.95(97 + 890)] - 205 = 733\}$. Loans extend for twelve years, including a six-year grace period beginning with the year after the first loan is made. That is, repayment of all loans begins in year 8 after termination of the six-year grace period from years 2 through 7. Interest is capitalized during the period of disbursement; interest only is paid in years 6 and 7; and equal installments of debt service are made from years 8 through 13. See the section "Computing Debt Service," and table 4-25 for an explanation of how the calculations are made.

f. Calculated on the basis of the incremental net benefit before financing. For details about the method of computation, see chapter 9.

g. Calculated on the basis of the incremental net benefit after financing.

by 1 plus the interest rate stated in decimal terms to reach the total amount to be repaid of KSh1,525 (1,374 × 1.11 = 1,525).

Often, short-term credit is extended for a period less than a full year. In the Ceara Rural Development Project in northeast Brazil, for example, a farmer is assumed to receive short-term credit amounting to Cr$3,056 at an annual interest of 7 percent. (The symbol for Brazilian cruzeiros is Cr$.) He is to repay the loan at the end of six months, so he need pay interest for only that period. The amount of interest due is only six-twelfths, or half the annual amount, so the analyst simply divided the annual amount by two to obtain the interest payment of Cr$107 (3,056 × 0.07 ÷ 2 = 107). The total repayment, therefore, is the amount of principal plus interest, or Cr$3,163 (3,056 + 107 = 3,163). It would have been an easier computation to have done the calculation in one step by first dividing the interest rate in decimal form by 2, then adding 1 and multiplying the amount of the principal by that sum {3,056 × [1 + (0.07 ÷ 2)] = 3,163}.

Of course, fractional interest rates present no problem in these calculations because discounting tables are not used. In Morocco, for example, farmers participating in the Doukkala II Irrigation Project receive short-term credit through the Moroccan Regional Agricultural Development Office at an annual interest rate of 9.5 percent. In the farm budget prepared for the project analysis, a farmer on a 4-hectare farm is assumed to receive a short-term loan of DH4,395 to be repaid in six months. (The symbol for Moroccan dirhams is DH.) His repayment of principal and interest, thus, is DH4,604 {4,395 × [1 + (0.095 ÷ 2)] = 4,604}.

Repayment of equal amounts of principal

When loans extend beyond one year, interest must be paid on any outstanding balance, and the way in which the principal will be repaid must be determined. The simplest way to calculate this term is to assume that the principal will be repaid in equal annual installments, with interest paid on the remaining outstanding balance. On long-term loans the first repayment of principal often will not be due for several years so that the farmer can build up his production before beginning to repay the amount he has borrowed. This grace period begins at the time the loan is extended and continues for over a year or more after. Thus, a four-year grace period for a loan received at the end of project year 1 would mean that the grace period would be project years 2 through 5, and the first repayment of principal would be due at the end of project year 6. (If the accounting convention for farm investment analysis we have adopted were not used, and the loan were assumed to be made at the beginning of the project year, then the four-year grace period would be years 1 through 4, and the first repayment of principal would be at the end of project year 5.) Interest on the outstanding balance is usually paid during the grace period, although it may be forgiven or capitalized as discussed below.

The example in table 4-23 from the Honduras Agricultural Credit

Project, taken from a pattern farm budget for a 50-hectare beef-fattening unit, illustrates the debt service computation on a loan for which the principal is to be paid in equal amounts and interest is to be paid on the outstanding balance. The computation when the budget assumes our accounting convention for farm investment analysis is shown in the first part of the table. The farmer is to be loaned a total of L12,699 in three installments during the first three years of the project. (The symbol for Honduran lempiras is L.) For the first installment he is allowed a three-year grace period, for the second a two-year grace period, and for the third a one-year grace period. Then he is to repay his loan over a three-year period from years 5 through 7. The principal is to be repaid in three equal installments of L4,233 (12,699 ÷ 3 = 4,233). (In the actual project, the analyst chose to change the principal repayments slightly to make the loan balance a round figure.) The interest rate is 11 percent a year. The interest paid in year 3, for instance, is computed on the basis of the loan of L3,123 received at the end of year 2 plus the loan of L7,767 received at the end of the first year that is still outstanding, or a total principal on which interest is to be paid of L10,890. The interest due is L1,198 [(7,767 + 3,123) × 0.11 = 1,198]. As the principal is repaid, interest is due only on the remaining outstanding balance. We assume that the loan repayment is made at the end of the year, so interest is due on the full amount of the principal outstanding at the end of the previous year. Thus, in year 4 interest must be paid on the total amount of the loan received, L12,699, and amounts to L1,397 (12,699 × 0.11 = 1,397). In year 5 a repayment of L4,233 is made, so that the outstanding balance at the end of the year is L8,466 (12,699 − 4,233 = 8,466). It is assumed, however, that the principal repayment is made at the end of the year, and thus interest must be paid for the full year on the L12,699 outstanding at the end of the previous year, or another interest payment of L1,397. For year 6 the outstanding balance at the end of the previous year has been reduced by the principal repayment of L4,233 made at the end of year 5, so the interest is calculated on the outstanding balance of L8,466 and amounts to L931 (8,466 × 0.11 = 931).

In the second part of table 4-23, the Honduras example is recast assuming that the loan is made at the beginning of the accounting year and the first interest payment is due at the end of the same year. The computations remain the same; only the years in which the figures appear in the budget vary. In the first year a loan of L7,767 is received at the beginning of the year, and interest is paid on this amount at the end of the year, so an interest payment of L854 appears in year 1 (7,767 × 0.11 = 854). The three-year grace period for the first loan begins in the year of the loan, so it extends from year 1 through year 3. Repayment of principal begins in year 4 with a payment of L4,233. Interest is also paid at the end of year 4 for the amount of the loan outstanding during the year, which is L12,699, shown at the end of year 3; the interest amounts, of course, to L1,397 (12,699 × 0.11 = 1,397). Note that the effect of assuming the loan to be made at the beginning of the year is simply to bring forward every interest payment and loan repayment by one accounting period.

Table 4-23. *Debt Service Computation Assuming Repayment of Equal Amounts of Principal, Beef-Fattening Unit, Agricultural Credit Project, Honduras*
(Honduran Ls)

Item	Project year						
	1	2	3	4	5	6	7
Loan receipts beginning in year 1, debt service beginning in year 2							
Loan receipts and balances							
Loan receipts	7,767	3,123	1,809	0	0	0	0
Outstanding balance at end of year	7,767	10,890	12,699	12,699	8,466	4,233	0
Debt Service							
Interest	—	854	1,198	1,397	1,397	931	466
Repayment of principal	—	—	—	—	4,233	4,233	4,233
Total	—	854	1,198	1,397	5,630	5,164	4,699
Net financing	7,767	2,269	611	(1,397)	(5,630)	(5,164)	(4,699)
Internal rate of return to net financing flow = 11 percent[a]							
Loan receipts beginning in year 1, debt service beginning in year 1							
Loan receipts and balances							
Loan receipts	7,767	3,123	1,809	0	0	0	—
Outstanding balance at end of year	7,767	10,890	12,699	8,466	4,233	0	—
Debt service							
Interest	854	1,198	1,397	1,397	931	466	—
Repayment of principal	—	—	—	4,233	4,233	4,233	—
Total	854	1,198	1,397	5,630	5,164	4,699	—
Net financing	6,913	1,925	412	(5,630)	(5,164)	(4,699)	—
Internal rate of return to net financing flow = 15 percent[a]							

L Honduran lempiras.
Source: Adapted from World Bank, "Appraisal of an Agricultural Credit Project—Honduras," 1044a-HO (Washington, D.C., 1976; restricted circulation), annex 4, table 7. See text for a discussion of how the figures in this table were derived.
a. For details about the method of computation, see chapter 9.

An advantage of our accounting convention for farm investment analysis becomes evident at this point. If we discount the net financing flow when the farm budget is cast assuming the loan to be received at the beginning of the accounting period, we find the internal rate of return to be 15 percent; but we know it should be 11 percent because the interest rate on the loan is 11 percent. (The internal rate of return is the weighted average return to all resources while they are still engaged. The method of computation is discussed in the section devoted to the topic in chapter 9.) The error is introduced by the assumption that the loan is made at the beginning of the first year and that the first interest payment will be made at the end of the first year. In contrast, when the farm budget uses our accounting convention, which assumes the loan to be received at the end of the accounting period and the interest payment to be made at the end of the following period, the internal rate of return to the net financing flow is exactly 11 percent, which we know to be correct from the assumption about the terms of the loan.

Equal installments

Farmers would usually prefer to pay the same amount every year on a long-term loan rather than to make the varying payments when principal is repaid in equal annual amounts. Thus, it is common practice in most long-term transactions to arrange for the debt service to be paid in a series of equal annual installments, also called level payments or an equated annuity.

The calculation of these equal installments can be illustrated by returning to the Paraguay pattern farm budget of table 4-19, for which the financing is calculated in table 4-24. In this project, the farmer receives a loan from the Paraguayan National Development Bank for 90 percent of the investment expenditure and for 90 percent of the incremental working capital during the investment period, which is years 1 through 3. The loan is for ten years with a four-year grace period during which interest is paid. The loan is repaid in six equal annual installments. The loan received each year is treated as a separate transaction. Thus, for the loan received at the end of year 1, the grace period is years 2 through 5, and the loan is repaid during years 6 through 11. The interest rate is 13 percent.

During the four-year grace period, the interest is calculated at 13 percent on the outstanding balance at the end of the previous year. For the first-year loan of ₲508.2 thousand, for example, the interest due at the end of year 2 is ₲66.1 thousand (508.2 × 0.13 = 66.1). After the grace period, the principal is to be repaid, together with interest on the outstanding balance, in six equal installments. To calculate the amount of each annual installment, we will need to have the capital recovery factor for 13 percent for 6 years. Usually, this may conveniently be obtained from a set of standard tables such as *Compounding and Discounting Tables for Project Evaluation* (Gittinger 1973). When a fractional interest rate is involved, however, it may be difficult to find a set of tables that gives the capital recovery factor at a specific fractional rate, although many give factors for the more common fractional rates. If no table is readily available, the capital recovery factor may be easily computed using a simple hand calculator. (The computation is illustrated in the last section of chapter 10, "Calculator Applications in Project Analysis.") Consulting the tables [the relevant portion is reproduced from Gittinger (1973) in compounding and discounting table 1 on page 156], we turn to the page for 13 percent interest and follow down the column for the capital recovery factor to find the factor opposite the sixth year, which is 0.250 153. Now, we simply multiply the amount of the outstanding balance of ₲508.2 thousand (due on the first-year loan at the end of the grace period in year 5) by the capital recovery factor to obtain the annual installment of ₲127.1 thousand (508.2 × 0.250 153 = 127.1).

Table 4-24. *Debt Service Computation Assuming Equal Installments, 20-Hectare Mixed Farm, Paraguay Project*
(thousands of ₲)

Item	Project year												
	1	2	3	4	5	6	7	8	9	10	11	12	13
Investment and working capital[a]													
Investment	523.6	110.6	126.5	0	0	0	0	0	0	0	0	0	0
Incremental working capital	41.1	8.4	29.1	13.4	25.6	2.3	0	0	0	0	0	0	0
Total	564.7	119.0	155.6	13.4	25.6	2.3	0	0	0	0	0	0	0
Loan receipts and balances													
Loan receipts	508.2	107.1	140.0	0	0	0	0	0	0	0	0	0	0
Outstanding balance at end of year													
First-year loan	508.2	508.2	508.2	508.2	508.2	447.2	378.2	300.3	212.2	112.7	0[b]	0	0
Second-year loan		107.1	107.1	107.1	107.1	107.1	94.2	79.6	63.1	44.5	23.5	0[b]	0
Third-year loan	—	140.0	140.0	140.0	140.0	140.0	140.0	123.2	104.2	82.7	58.5	31.1	0[b]
Total	508.2	615.3	755.3	755.3	755.3	694.3	612.4	503.1	379.5	239.9	82.0	31.1	0

154

Debt service											
First-year loan											
Interest	66.1	66.1	66.1	66.1	58.1	49.2	39.0	27.6	14.7	—	—
Repayment of principal	0	0	0	61.0	69.0	77.9	88.1	99.5	112.4	—	—
Subtotal	66.1	66.1	66.1	127.1	127.1	127.1	127.1	127.1	127.1	—	—
Second-year loan											
Interest	—	13.9	13.9	13.9	13.9	12.2	10.3	8.2	5.8	3.1	—
Repayment of principal	—	0	0	0	12.9	14.6	16.5	18.6	21.0	23.7	—
Subtotal	—	13.9	13.9	13.9	26.8	26.8	26.8	26.8	26.8	26.8	—
Third-year loan											
Interest	—	—	18.2	18.2	18.2	18.2	16.0	13.5	10.8	7.6	4.0
Repayment of principal	—	—	0	0	0	16.8	19.0	21.5	24.2	27.4	31.0
Subtotal	—	—	18.2	18.2	18.2	35.0	35.0	35.0	35.0	35.0	35.0
Total	66.1	80.0	98.2	159.2	172.1	188.9	188.9	188.9	188.9	61.8	35.0
Net financing	508.2	41.0	60.0	(159.2)	(172.1)	(188.9)	(188.9)	(188.9)	(188.9)	(61.8)	(35.0)

Source: Calculated from table 4-19. See text for a discussion of how the calculations were made.

a. From table 4-19.

b. The total repayments of principal do not exactly equal the loan receipts because of rounding. The outstanding balance, however, is shown as zero.

COMPOUNDING AND DISCOUNTING TABLES
1. *Capital Recovery Factor, 13 Percent Interest*

RATE
13%

**CAPITAL RECOVERY
FACTOR**
Annual payment that will
repay a $1 loan in X years
with compound interest
on the unpaid balance

Capital Recovery Factor	Year
1.130 000	1
.599 484	2
.423 522	3
.336 194	4
.284 315	5
.250 153	6
.226 111	7
.208 387	8
.194 869	9
.184 290	10
.175 841	11
.168 986	12

Source: Gittinger (1973), p. 27.

Each annual installment consists of varying proportions of interest and principal. By inspection, we do not know how much of any given installment is interest and how much is repayment of principal. The amounts can, of course, be calculated, and one method is illustrated in table 4-24. The interest due on the outstanding balance is subtracted from the annual installment, and the remainder is taken to be the principal repayment. Thus, for the first-year loan for year 6 the interest is ₡66.1 thousand, and the repayment of the principal is ₡61.0 thousand (127.1 − 66.1 = 61.0). Subtracting the principal repayment from the outstanding balance of the loan at the end of year 5 of ₡508.2 thousand means that at the end of year 6 we have an outstanding balance due of only ₡447.2 thousand (508.2 − 61.0 = 447.2). Now, in year 7, the farmer must pay interest of ₡58.1 thousand on that outstanding balance (447.2 × 0.13 = 58.1). The annual installment in year 7, of course, remains ₡127.1 thousand, so that when we subtract the interest payment from the installment we have a principal repayment of ₡69.0 thousand (127.1 − 58.1 = 69.0), and this reduces the outstanding balance at the end of year 7 to ₡378.2 thousand (447.2 − 69.0 = 378.2). The same process continues to the end of the loan period in year 11. In this instance, the total principal payment shown is ₡0.3 thousand less than the loan received because of rounding. Calculating the interest and repayment of

Table 4-25. *Debt Service Computation Assuming*
Equal Installments with Interest Capitalized,
1-Hectare Planting, India Cashewnut Project
(Rs)

Year of loan	Amount of loan	Compounding factor for 1 (10.5 percent)		Principal and interest due at end of fifth year
1	783	1.490	902	1,167
2	468	1.349	233	631
3	1,482	1.221	025	1,810
4	733	1.105	000	810
5	338	1.000	000	338
Total	3,804			4,756

Interest during sixth and seventh years = Rs4,756 × 0.105 = 499
Combined annual installment of interest and principal repayment
due from eighth through thirteenth years =
4,756 × 0.232   982 = 1,108

Source: Same as table 4-21. See text for a discussion of how the calculations were made.

principal year by year as done here is generally unnecessary; simply
calculating the equal annual installment using the capital recovery factor ordinarily will suffice.

Equal installments with interest capitalized

In some loan transactions, the lender will agree to "capitalize" the
interest due during the grace period. This means that the borrower need
not pay any interest during the grace period; the interest due is, in effect,
added to the principal of the loan (hence the term "capitalize"). When the
repayment of principal begins, the amount borrowed plus the interest
added to the principal during the grace period is then repaid in a series of
equal installments.

We may illustrate how to calculate the interest payment and the
repayment of principal by an example adapted from the Indian Cashewnut Project (discussed earlier in connection with unit activity budgets).
The credit computation for the India project is laid out in table 4-25. A
farmer is to be loaned Rs3,804, disbursed over five years, to establish a
stand of cashewnut trees. The loan term is for twelve years at 10.5 percent
interest with a six-year grace period. Interest due during the disbursement period in years 1 through 5 is added to the principal—that is,
capitalized. Interest on the capitalized amount is to be paid in years 6
and 7. Repayment of the principal plus capitalized interest is to be made
in six equal annual installments beginning at the end of the eighth year
and ending at the completion of the thirteenth year.

For each year that the loan is being disbursed, the amount of the
disbursement is multiplied by the compounding factor for 1 for the

remaining length of the disbursement period to determine the amount of principal and interest due on that disbursement at the end of the disbursement period. The compounding factor for 1 may be obtained from Gittinger (1973) or from a similar source, or it can be calculated using a simple electronic hand calculator (see chapter 10, the section "Calculator Applications in Project Analysis"). For the disbursement made in year 1, for example, the amount of principal and capitalized interest due by the end of the fifth year is calculated by multiplying the principal received, Rs783, by 1.490 902, which is the compounding factor for 1 at 10.5 percent interest for the number of years after the loan is disbursed until the end of the fifth year—in this case, four years. The result is a total due of Rs1,167 (783 × 1.490 902 = 1,167). The amounts of principal and interest due on each disbursement at the end of the fifth year are then totaled to determine the total principal and interest due at the end of that year. Interest is paid on that capitalized interest in years 6 and 7 in the amount of Rs499 (4,756 × 0.105 = 499). The annual installment necessary to pay the interest due and to repay the principal in six equal payments is determined by taking the total value of Rs4,756, the loan outstanding at the end of the fifth year including capitalized interest, and multiplying it by 0.232 982, the capital recovery factor for six years at 10.5 percent interest, to obtain the annual installment of Rs1,108 thousand (4,756 × 0.232 982 = 1,108). (The capital recovery factor for six years at 10.5 percent interest was calculated by taking the reciprocal of the present worth of an annuity factor for six years at 10.5 percent. See chapter 10, the section "Calculator Applications in Project Analysis," for a discussion of how to make the computation using a simple calculator.

Declining real burden of debt service

The examples of debt service calculation to this point have assumed that debt service will be constant in real terms. Yet in most countries lending terms to farmers call for repayment in nominal—that is, money—terms. Interest is stated at a given rate, and the nominal amount of principal repayment is agreed upon. If there were to be inflation, which would reduce the real value of money over time, the result would be that farmers would have a declining real burden of debt service over the life of the loan. If a farmer agrees to make a series of fixed annual installments to repay his loan, the real burden of that fixed installment is reduced by the extent the value of money declines. (Some countries index loans so that the nominal amount the farmer pays increases with inflation to maintain the farmer's real debt burden.)

We have noted that it is common practice in project analysis to deal with inflation by assuming that all prices will move by the same proportion. Thus, relative prices remain the same—or the analyst changes the price he uses to reflect the change in relative value. Our calculations, then, are done at constant prices. This convention generally is appropriate for farm investment analysis, with one important exception—repayment of credit in fixed money terms. When there is inflation, if our farm budget shows the same amount of debt service to repay a loan each year, we in effect are assuming that the loan is indexed and that its real burden will remain the same relative to all other prices. The opposite, however, is often true—inflation raises the nominal prices of the goods and services the farmer buys and sells, but the nominal amount of the debt burden remains the same. Thus the real burden falls, and if our project accounts are cast in constant terms the debt service should be reduced to reflect the changing value of the debt service payment relative to other prices. Such adjustments have been infrequent in project analysis to date, but with continuing high inflation in many countries it is a reasonable expectation that they will become more common.

An illustration of a farm budget that assumes a declining real burden of debt service, based on the farm budget for the Paraguay project used in table 4-19, was given in table 4-20. The debt service under this assumption is worked out on the basis of equal nominal annual installments in table 4-26. It is assumed that there will be constant inflation of 8 percent during the period of the financing. The terms and conditions of the financing are the same as those used in the example of equal annual installments in table 4-24—the loan is for ten years at 13 percent interest, with a four-year grace during which interest is paid and with six equal annual installments of interest and repayment of principal thereafter.

The loan receipts in real terms are taken from table 4-24. They are, in fact, stated in constant terms in guaranis of project year 1. It is assumed that the farmer will continue the real investment program laid out in the farm budget in constant terms of table 4-18, so that in nominal terms the second- and third-year loans will increase by the amount of the inflation. To calculate the nominal amounts, the real value is multiplied by the compounding factor for 1 for the number of years *after* project year 1, which is the base year for the computation. [The compounding factor for 1 may be obtained from Gittinger (1973) or some similar source.] The nominal amount of the second-year loan, then, would be its real value of ₲107.1 thousand multiplied by 1.080 000, the compounding factor for 1 for 8 percent (the assumed inflation rate) for one year, and this gives the result of ₲115.7 thousand (107.1 × 1.080 000 = 115.7). The nominal amount of the third-year loan is the real value of ₲140.0 multiplied by 1.166 400, the compounding factor for 1 for two years, and this gives the result of ₲163.3 thousand (140.0 × 1.166 400 = 163.3). For this and all other calculations where the compounding factor for 1 is used, repeated multiplications or divisions may be used (140.0 × 1.08 × 1.08 = 163.3). If a calculator is available that computes powers directly, the nominal value of the third-year loan may be simply determined by raising 1 plus the rate of inflation to the power of the number of years after the base date (140.0 × 1.08^2 = 163.3).

The calculation of the debt service in nominal terms is given for comparison with the nominal calculation in table 4-24 and with the calculation in real terms later in table 4-26. The nominal debt service is

Table 4-26. *Debt Service Computation Assuming Equal Installments and Declining Real Burden of Debt Service, 20-Hectare Mixed Farm, Paraguay Project*
(thousands of ₲)

Item	1	2	3	4	5	6	7	8	9	10	11	12	13
						Project year							
Loan receipts													
Real terms[a]	508.2	107.1	140.0	0	0	0	0	0	0	0	0	0	0
Nominal terms	508.2	115.7	163.3	0	0	0	0	0	0	0	0	0	0
Debt service													
Nominal terms													
First-year loan	—	66.1	66.1	66.1	66.1	127.1	127.1	127.1	127.1	127.1	127.1	—	—
Second-year loan	—	—	15.0	15.0	15.0	15.0	28.9	28.9	28.9	28.9	28.9	28.9	—
Third-year loan	—	—	—	21.2	21.2	21.2	21.2	40.8	40.8	40.8	40.8	40.8	40.8
Total	—	66.1	81.1	102.3	102.3	163.3	177.2	196.8	196.8	196.8	196.8	69.7	40.8
Net financing	508.2	49.6	82.2	(102.3)	(102.3)	(163.3)	(177.2)	(196.8)	(196.8)	(196.8)	(196.8)	(69.7)	(40.8)
Real terms[b]													
First-year loan	—	61.2	56.7[c]	52.5[c]	48.6	86.5	80.1	74.2	68.7	63.6	58.9	—	—
Second-year loan	—	—	12.9	11.9	11.0[c]	10.2	18.2	16.9	15.6	14.4[c]	13.3[c]	12.3[c]	—
Third-year loan	—	—	—	16.9	15.6	14.4	13.3[c]	23.8	22.0[c]	20.4	18.9	17.5	16.2
Total	—	61.2	69.6	81.3	75.2	111.1	111.6	114.9	106.3	98.4	91.1	29.8	16.2
Net financing	508.2	45.9	70.4	(81.3)	(75.2)	(111.1)	(111.6)	(114.9)	(106.3)	(98.4)	(91.1)	(29.8)	(16.2)

Source: Calculated from tables 4-19 and 4-24. See text for a discussion of how the calculations were made.

a. From table 4-24.

b. Calculated by dividing each entry in the line, except for the first interest installment and the first installment of combined interest and principal repayment, by 1.08. These exceptions are determined by multiplying the nominal amount of the loan by the interest rate or the capital recovery factor and then dividing by the compounding factor for 1 for 8 percent (or 1.08ⁿ) for the number of years after the first year of the project. Thus, for the first interest payment for the second-year loan, the nominal amount of the loan of ₲115.7 thousand is multiplied by the interest of 13 percent and then divided by the compounding factor for 1 for two years, 1.166, to obtain the interest payment of ₲12.9 thousand (115.7 × 0.13 ÷ 1.166 = 12.9). For the first annual installment of combined interest and principal repayment for the second-year loan, the nominal amount of the loan of ₲115.7 thousand is multiplied by the capital recovery factor for six years at 13 percent, 0.250 153, and then divided by the compounding factor for 1 for six years, 1.587, to obtain the payment of ₲18.2 thousand (115.7 × 0.250 153 ÷ 1.587 = 18.2).

c. Calculated as explained in note b; this calculation introduces a slight rounding error. Direct calculation using the formulas in the text obtains a slightly different result.

calculated in the same manner as the computations in table 4-24 but is based on the nominal amounts of the loan receipts. Thus, for the second-year loan the nominal interest during the grace period would be the nominal value of the loan receipt of ₲115.7 thousand multiplied by the interest rate of 13 percent, and this gives an interest payment of ₲15.0 thousand (115.7 × 0.13 = 15.0). The equal annual installment would be the nominal value of the loan of ₲115.7 thousand multiplied by 0.250 153, the capital recovery factor for six years at 13 percent, and this gives an installment of ₲28.9 (115.7 × 0.250 153 = 28.9).

To calculate the debt service in real terms, the nominal amounts must be reduced by the extent of inflation since the loan was made. To do this, the nominal amount is divided by the compounding factor for 1 for the number of years involved. For the first-year loan, the receipt is ₲508.2 thousand, and the nominal payment due at the end of year 2 at a 13 percent interest rate is ₲66.1 thousand (508.2 × 0.13 = 66.1). Since inflation is assumed to be 8 percent, the real burden is reduced between the loan receipt at the end of year 1 and the first interest payment at the end of year 2; this reduction makes the real burden of the first interest payment in guaranis of project year 1 only ₲61.2 thousand (66.1 ÷ 1.08 = 61.2). In year 3, the interest in real terms is again reduced by the amount of the inflation, to ₲56.7 thousand (61.2 ÷ 1.08 = 56.7). The interest in years 4 and 5 is calculated in a similar manner.

Repayment of principal combined with interest on the remaining outstanding balance begins in year 6. The equal annual installment in nominal terms that the farmer would pay from years 6 through 11 is determined by multiplying the amount of the loan received, ₲508.2 thousand, by the capital recovery factor for six years at 13 percent, 0.250 153. The result is a nominal payment of ₲127.1 thousand (508.2 × 0.250 153 = 127.1). Since this is in nominal terms, the real burden is reduced by five years of inflation between the end of year 1, when the loan is received, and the end of year 6, when the first annual installment of interest and principal repayment is made. To do this, the nominal payment of ₲127.1 thousand is divided by the compounding factor for 1 for 8 percent for five years to obtain the real burden of the payment at the end of year 6, ₲86.5 thousand (127.1 ÷ 1.469 328 = 86.5). In year 7 the real burden is again reduced by the amount of the inflation, and this gives a real burden of ₲80.1 thousand (86.5 ÷ 1.08 = 80.1). The same process is continued through the remaining life of the loan.

For the second-year loan, the debt service is again calculated on the basis of the nominal value of the loan, ₲115.7 thousand. The nominal interest due during the four-year grace period at the rate of 13 percent, therefore, is ₲15.0 thousand (115.7 × 0.13 = 15.0). This payment is due, however, in year 3, or two years after the base of the constant value, which is stated in year-1 guaranis. Hence, the nominal value of the interest payment must be reduced by the amount of inflation in both years 2 and 3 by dividing it by the compounding factor for 1 for two years to obtain the real value at the end of year 3, which is ₲12.9 thousand

(15.0 ÷ 1.166 400 = 12.9). The real value of the interest payment in year 4 may be obtained by dividing the interest payment made in year 3 by 1 plus the inflation rate stated in decimal terms, and this gives ₡11.9 thousand (12.9 ÷ 1.08 = 11.9). The nominal value of the equal annual installment from years 7 through 12 is obtained by multiplying the nominal value of the second-year loan of ₡115.7 thousand by 0.250 153, the capital recovery factor for six years at 13 percent; the result is ₡28.9 thousand. Since this amount is due at the end of the seventh project year, or six years after the base in project year 1, it is divided by the compounding factor for 1 for six years to obtain the real value of ₡18.2 (115.7 × 0.250 153 ÷ 1.586 874 = 18.2). The real burden of the next installment in year 8 is obtained by dividing the year 7 payment of ₡18.2 thousand by 1.08; this yields ₡16.9 thousand (18.2 ÷ 1.08 = 16.9). The same process is continued through the life of the loan.

Determining the real burden of each payment is more rapidly and accurately accomplished if an algebraic formula is used instead of the iterative process outlined here. The interest during the grace period may be determined as:

$$R_m = \frac{L(1 + f)^{n-1} r}{(1 + f)^{m-1}};$$

the real burden of the annual installment of combined interest and principal may be determined as:

$$R^*_m = \frac{L(1 + f)^{n-1} F}{(1 + f)^{m-1}};$$

in both equations,

R_m = real burden of debt service in project year m during grace period

R^*_m = real burden of debt service in project year m during period of annual installment of combined interest and repayment of principal

n = project year in which loan is received
m = project year in which debt service is made
L = real value of loan receipt
F = capital recovery factor
r = rate of interest paid on loan
f = rate of inflation.

If a calculator that determines powers directly is not available, the compounding factor for 1 for the appropriate rate and number of years may be used in place of the expressions $(1 + f)^{n-1}$ and $(1 + f)^{m-1}$.

Although we have by no means given examples of all possible loan terms in this section, the debt service for most other loan terms may be readily calculated following these illustrations.

Appendix. Herd Projections

A basic element in the analysis of agricultural projects that involve a livestock component is a projection of the number of animals. For small animals with a generation interval within the accounting period—for example, poultry—the projections can be done simply by estimating the number of animals that can be maintained with the feed and facilities available. This usually is also the approach for hogs. But for larger animals that take more than one accounting period to mature—including dairy and beef cattle, sheep, and goats—the projections are usually based on herd buildups that reflect the number of breeding animals, the number of animals born, mortality, and sales. A pattern herd projection is given in table 4-27; it is based on the Paraguay example and is compatible with the accounting convention recommended for farm budgets in this book. A herd productivity computation is given in table 4-28. Whether estimated directly or through the use of a more elaborate herd projection, the number of animals forecast is then priced and the value incorporated in the farm budget as was illustrated in the Paraguay example. [This appendix draws heavily from materials especially prepared by Meyn, Gittinger, and Schaefer-Kehnert (1980) and Schaefer-Kehnert (1981*a*)].

In the text of this chapter (the subsection "Farm Production. Livestock"), we noted that the purpose of a herd projection is to apply to a herd at the beginning of a project technical coefficients that are estimates of the improvements in management, animal health, and nutrition the project investment will make possible. The herd projection allows estimates of future feed requirements, handling facilities, investments, and the productivity of the herd. The herd development is continued until—through natural increase, purchases, or reduced sales—the herd has reached a level at which it can make best use of the available resources.

In the same subsection of the text we also noted that, for small farms involving dairy or beef cattle (and to some extent sheep and goats), the problem of divisibility (the reporting of fractional animals) must be resolved. The most satisfactory method of doing this is to take a group of farms—often 100—and to project the herd for all the farms in the group. All calculations in the projections can then be rounded to the nearest whole animal. This avoids having fractional animals in the herd projection, which happens when the technical coefficients are applied to the number of animals in a small herd. The values for purchases and sales for the full 100-farm group are then divided by 100 and entered in the farm budget for the individual farm. In effect, this assumes that on the average a farm will have a given level of purchases and sales. Although this convention is not fully satisfactory, it is better than trying to project herds on the basis of probability or carrying fractional animals in the projection until they aggregate to a whole animal.

Herd projections generally are done by someone with a considerable knowledge of livestock production because these projections depend on judgments about feed availability, management improvement, and the like. Thus, most agricultural project analysts would turn to a livestock specialist for assistance with a herd projection, just as they would turn to other agricultural specialists for assistance with such things as crop yields or irrigation construction costs.

We will illustrate the methodology of herd projections with the example of the Paraguay project we have been following in this chapter. This is for a beef production activity on a 20-hectare mixed farm, but with rather minor adaptations it can be used for a dairy herd or, with somewhat more adaptation, for sheep and goats.

Terminology and definitions

Livestock specialists use a group of special terms that may not be familiar to all agricultural project analysts. A breeding cow is, of course, the mature female of the species that has borne at least one calf; the male is the bull. A calf (plural, calves) is the young animal; its age in these projections is one year and less. Heifers are young females that are older than calves but younger than a predetermined age (in this case, three years) and that have not yet borne calves. Steers are castrated male animals. Culled animals are those taken from the herd because they do not meet performance standards.

Carrying capacity refers to the ability of an area of pasture to support animals; it is generally expressed in terms of animal units, a standard measurement of feed. By expressing carrying capacity in animal units, a single measurement for the pasture requirements of the herd is obtained. The standard animal, or one animal unit, in herd projections for cattle is usually a cow of average size in the reference area.

Computational conventions

A group of simplifying conventions makes calculation of the herd projection less complex and allows it to fit with the accounting convention used for the rest of the farm investment analysis. Analysts vary in the details of the conventions they apply, but the ones we will discuss here, which are used in tables 4-11 and 4-27, are fairly representative, are consistent, and are amenable to computation by hand with a simple calculator.

All calculations are rounded to the nearest whole animal. Stock taking for the analysis occurs at the end of the year. Purchases enter the herd at the end of the accounting year, and sales from the herd also occur at the end of the accounting year. Adult mortality is calculated on the basis of the number of animals present at the beginning of the year. For calves, mortality is deducted from the number of calves born during the course of the year. Internal transfers of young animals are accomplished by carrying forward the end-of-year closing stock figure to the opening stock figure of the next higher age category at the beginning of the next year. Transfers of heifers 2–3 years old are added to the number of breeding cows at the end of the year, the sum being the closing stock of breeding cows for that year. For bulls and work oxen, the previous end-of-year figures serve as beginning-of-year figures in the following year. The number of bulls in the Paraguay example is taken to be one for each farm, or 100 bulls in the 100-farm herd. The number of bulls required, however, would usually be a function of the number of breeding cows in the herd at the beginning of the year. Additional bulls needed, including those needed for purchased heifers brought into the herd, are assumed to be purchased at the end of the year. There would usually be three to four bulls for 100 breeding cows. For the purpose of the projection, male and female calves are accounted for separately, and the numbers of each are determined by multiplying the number of breeding cows at the beginning of the year by half the calving rate. Treating male and female calves separately permits the analyst to apply different technical coefficients to male and female calves, if that reflects reality (the case for calf mortality in East Africa, for example), or to make assumptions that male and female calves will be treated differently (the case in dairy operations where male calves may be sold soon after birth). Culling rates are applied to the number of animals at the beginning of the year.

Since herd projection computations can become quite complex, it is important to have good worksheets. A pattern herd projection worksheet that uses data from the Paraguay example is shown in table 4-27. This pattern can rather easily be adapted to the conditions and assumptions of different projects, which vary so widely as to make it impractical to have a standardized worksheet. As these adaptations are made, several principles should be kept in mind so that the worksheet will remain compatible with the accounting convention recommended for farm budgets. Year 1 is reserved for investment (which may extend over more than one year). Production in year 1 may be reduced by the investment— by plowing grassland to establish improved pasture, for example. In-cremental production begins no earlier than the beginning of year 2; it may begin later if investment takes longer. All purchases and sales, as well as transfers of animals to another category, take place at the end of each year. Thus, purchases that are part of the investment take place at the end of year 1. The first sales generated through incremental produc-tion can occur no earlier than the end of year 2. Heifers retained as breeding cows are transferred at the end of each year. Using brackets to insert the technical coefficients, and boxes to indicate the elements of the preliminary closing stock, are format devices that greatly reduce the likelihood of error when using the worksheets.

Technical coefficients

The herd projection is built up by applying the technical coefficients to the initial herd until a herd size is reached that just consumes the increased feed to be made available or until some other predetermined limit, such as the size of handling facilities and the like, is reached. The technical coefficients come from field observation and statistics collected by government services as the project is being prepared.

For the Paraguay example, the technical coefficients without the project were determined to be those given in the last part of table 4-27. In general, these improve over the life of the project, in reflection of the analyst's assumption about the effects on the number of animals of project investment and improved management by the farmer. In a herd projection, particular attention to the underlying biological facts must be paid. For example, assume that 30 percent of the bulls in a herd will be replaced with bulls of an improved breed at the end of year 1. Suppose in addition that the age of first calving for heifers in the herd is three to four years. Not until year 5 can introducing better bulls have any effect on herd production. At that time, 30 percent of the steers three to four years old will be heavier, and 30 percent of the heifers giving birth to calves will produce more milk. Very often these facts are neglected; the result is an overoptimistic projection that field results cannot meet.

CALVING RATE. The calving rate is the proportion of breeding cows that bear live calves during the year. It is applied to the number of breeding cows in the herd at the beginning of the year. In the pattern worksheet, the number of male and female calves is determined separately by dividing the calving rate in half. In the Paraguay example the calving rate is expected to improve from 70 percent at the beginning of the project to 75 percent as a result of improved management. The calving rate of 80 percent during year 3 is the result of purchasing in-calf heifers, which increases the calving rate. Calving rates range from about 50 percent or even less in pastoral herds in areas with one long dry season a year to about 90 percent in well-managed herds in areas with high potential.

CALF MORTALITY. The calf mortality is the proportion of live calves born during the year that do not survive to the end of the year. It applies to the number of calves born during the year. In the Paraguay example, it is assumed that improved management will reduce the calf mortality from 10 percent without the project to 5 percent by project year 4. Calf mortality ranges from 40 percent in cattle herds kept under extreme nutritional and climatic stress to less than 3 percent in well-managed beef herds in a favorable environment. Calf losses of 10 percent are common even in well-managed dairy herds.

ADULT MORTALITY. The adult mortality is the proportion of animals older than one year that are lost during the year. It is applied to the number of adult animals in each class at the beginning of the year. It is customary to apply the adult mortality rate to all animals above one year old, although losses somewhat higher than average may be expected among first-calf heifers and older cows. In the Paraguay project, adult mortality is already low at 3 percent at the beginning of the project and declines only slightly to 2 percent from year 3 of the project because of better husbandry. Adult mortality ranges from 10 percent to about 2 percent under practical conditions in developing countries.

CULLING RATE—BULLS. The culling rate for bulls is the proportion of bulls removed from the herd each year because they fail to meet the performance standards or reach a predetermined culling age. It is applied to the number of bulls in the herd at the beginning of the year. In the Paraguay project, the culling rate for bulls would increase slightly from 15 percent to 18 percent. This reflects a decrease in the productive life of the bulls from about 5.6 years assuming a 3 percent mortality rate [1 ÷ (0.15 + 0.03) = 5.6] to about 5.0 years assuming a 2 percent mortality rate [1 ÷ (0.18 + 0.02) = 5.0]. The productive life of a breeding bull cannot be much longer than six years; usually it is two to eight years for temperate-zone cattle and three to nine years for zebu cattle. When genetic improvement is an important part of the management system, farmers will change bulls more frequently than required by the biological utility of the bull.

CULLING RATE—COWS. The culling rate for cows is the proportion of breeding cows removed from the herd each year because they do not meet the performance standards. It is applied to the total number of breeding cows at the beginning of the year. In the Paraguay example, the culling rate rises from 12 percent at the beginning of the project to 15 percent in years 2 and 3, a result of an attempt to improve the performance standard of the breeding cows. It then drops slightly to 14 percent. At a 14 percent culling rate and a 2 percent mortality rate, the average productive life of a breeding cow would be about 6.2 years [1 ÷ (0.14 + 0.02) = 6.2]. If the age of first calving is taken to be 4 years, this implies that the cows would normally leave the herd at about 10.2 years of age (6.2 + 4 = 10.2). The productive life of cows in a breeding herd ranges from three years in intensive dairy herds to about eight years in beef herds, equivalent to a culling rate of 33 percent and 12 percent respectively, excluding mortality.

CULLING RATE—HEIFERS. The culling rate for heifers is the proportion of heifers that are unsuitable for breeding. It is applied to the number of heifers ready for service at the beginning of the year. In the Paraguay example, heifers two to three years old are considered ready for service, but heifers of one to two years are assumed not to be ready and so are not culled. In this example, the culling rate for heifers rises from 5 percent without the project to 10 percent beginning in year 2. The higher culling reflects tighter performance standards for breeding cows. In most breeding herds, from 5 to 10 percent of the heifers would be expected to be unsuitable for breeding.

CULLING RATE—WORK OXEN. The culling rate for oxen is the proportion of the oxen removed each year because they do not meet the performance standards. In the Paraguay project, the culling rate is assumed to be 16 percent, reflecting an average working life of some 6.2 years for oxen, about average in most parts of the world (1 ÷ 0.16 = 6.2).

RATIO OF BULLS TO BREEDING FEMALES. The percentage of bulls in relation to breeding cows is applied to the number of breeding cows in the herd at the beginning of the year. If in-calf heifers are purchased, addi-

(*Text resumes on p. 174.*)

Table 4-27. *Herd Projection Worksheet, 100 20-Hectare Mixed Farms, Paraguay Project*
(head)

	Without development			Development year					
Item	Stable 1,000-cow herd		100-farm herd		1		2		3	
Breeding bulls			*Livestock class*							
Opening stock	100		100		100		100		100	
− Deaths [%][a]	− 3	[3]	− 3	[3]	− 3	[3]	− 3	[3]	− 2	[2]
− Culls [%][b]	− 15	[15]	− 15	[15]	− 30	[30]	− 17	[17]	− 18	[18]
+ Purchases for existing herd	+ 18		+ 18		+ 33		+ 20		+ 20	
Subtotal [%][c]	= 100	[—]	= 100	[—]	= 100	[—]	= 100	[—]	= 100	[—]
+ Purchases for purchased heifers	+ 0		+ 0		+ 0		+ 0		+ 0	
Closing stock	= 100		= 100		= 100		= 100		= 100	
Breeding cows										
Opening stock	1,000		500		500		655		800	
− Deaths [%][a]	− 30	[3]	− 15	[3]	− 15	[3]	− 20	[3]	− 16	[2]
− Culls [%][d]	− 120	[12]	− 60	[12]	− 60	[12]	− 98	[15]	− 120	[15]
Subtotal	= 850		= 425		= 425		= 537		= 664	
+ Heifer transfers	+ 150		+ 75		+ 230		+ 263		+ 136	
Closing stock	= 1,000		= 500		= 655		= 800		= 800	
Female calves										
Births [%][e]	350	[35]	175	[35]	175	[35]	246	[37.5]	320	[40]
− Deaths [%][f]	− 35	[10]	− 18	[10]	− 18	[10]	− 25	[10]	− 26	[8]
Closing stock	= 315		= 157		= 157		= 221		= 294	
Heifers 1–2 years										
Opening stock	315		157		157		157		221	
− Deaths [%][a]	− 9	[3]	− 5	[3]	− 5	[3]	− 5	[3]	− 4	[2]
Closing stock	= 306		= 152		= 152		= 152		= 217	
Heifers 2–3 years										
Opening stock	306		152		152		152		152	
− Deaths [%][a]	− 9	[3]	− 5	[3]	− 5	[3]	− 5	[3]	− 3	[2]
− Culls [%][g]	− 15	[5]	− 8	[5]	− 8	[5]	− 15	[10]	− 15	[10]
Subtotal	= 282		= 139		= 139		= 132		= 134	
− Sales	− 132		− 64		− 0		− 0		− 0	
+ Purchases	+ 0		+ 0		+ 91		+ 131		+ 2	
Transfer to cows	= 150		= 75		= 230		= 263		= 136	
Male calves										
Births [%][e]	350	[35]	175	[35]	175	[35]	246	[37.5]	320	[40]
− Deaths [%]	− 35	[10]	− 18	[10]	− 18	[10]	− 25	[10]	− 26	[8]
Closing stock	= 315		= 157		= 157		= 221		= 294	
Steers 1–2 years										
Opening stock	315		157		157		157		221	
− Deaths [%][a]	− 9	[3]	− 5	[3]	− 5	[3]	− 5	[3]	− 4	[2]
Subtotal	= 306		= 152		= 152		= 152		= 217	
+ Purchases	+ 0		+ 0		+ 0		+ 0		+ 0	
Closing stock	= 306		= 152		= 152		= 152		= 217	

	Development year			Full development	
4	5	6		Years 7–20	Stable 1,000-cow herd
		Livestock class			
100	100	100		100	100
− 2 [2]	− 2 [2]	− 2 [2]	− [2]	− 2 [2]	− 2 [2]
− 18 [18]	− 18 [18]	− 18 [18]	− [18]	− 18 [18]	− 18 [18]
+ 20	+ 20	+ 20	+	+ 20	+ 20
= 100 [—]	= 100 [—]	= 100 [—]	= [—]	= 100 [—]	= 100 [—]
+ 0	+ 0	+ 0	+	+ —	+ —
= 100	= 100	= 100	=	= 100	= 100
800	800	800		800	1,000
− 16 [2]	− 16 [2]	− 16 [2]	− [2]	− 16 [2]	− 20 [2]
− 112 [14]	− 112 [14]	− 112 [14]	− [14]	− 112 [14]	− 140 [14]
= 672	= 672	= 672	=	= 672	= 840
+ 128	+ 128	+ 128	+	+ 128	+ 160
= 800	= 800	= 800	=	= 800	= 1,000
300 [37.5]	300 [37.5]	300 [37.5]	[37.5]	300 [37.5]	375 [37.5]
− 15 [5]	− 15 [5]	− 15 [5]	− [5]	− 15 [5]	− 19 [5]
= 285	= 285	= 285	=	= 285	= 356
294	285	285		285	356
− 6 [2]	− 6 [2]	− 6 [2]	− [2]	− 6 [2]	− 7 [2]
= 288	= 279	= 279	=	= 279	= 349
217	288	279		279	349
− 4 [2]	− 6 [2]	− 6 [2]	− [2]	− 6 [2]	− 7 [2]
− 22 [10]	− 29 [10]	− 28 [10]	− [10]	− 28 [10]	− 35 [10]
= 191	= 253	= 245	=	= 245	= 307
− 63	− 125	− 117	−	− 117	− 147
+ 0	+ 0	+ 0	+	+ 0	+ —
= 128	= 128	= 128	=	= 128	= 160
300 [37.5]	300 [37.5]	300 [37.5]	[37.5]	300 [37.5]	375 [37.5]
− 15 [5]	− 15 [5]	− 15 [5]	− [5]	− 15 [5]	− 19 [5]
= 285	= 285	= 285	=	= 285	= 356
294	285	285		285	356
− 6 [2]	− 6 [2]	− 6 [2]	− [2]	− 6 [2]	− 7 [2]
= 288	= 279	= 279	=	= 279	= 349
+ 0	+ 0	+ 0	+	+ 0	+ —
= 288	= 279	= 279	=	= 279	= 349

(Table continues on the following pages.)

Table 4-27 (continued)

	Without development		Development year		
Item	Stable 1,000-cow herd	100-farm herd	1	2	3

Livestock class

Steers 2–3 years					
Opening stock	306	152	152	152	152
− Deaths [%][a]	− 9 [3]	− 5 [3]	− 5 [3]	− 5 [3]	− 3 [2]
Closing stock	= 297	= 147	= 147	= 147	= 149
Steers 3–4 years					
Opening stock	297	147	147	147	147
− Deaths [%][a]	− 9 [3]	− 4 [3]	− 4 [3]	− 4 [3]	− 3 [2]
Sales	= 288	= 143	= 143	= 143	= 144
Work oxen					
Opening stock	—	0	0	200	200
− Deaths [%][a]	− — [3]	− 0 [3]	− 0 [3]	− 6 [3]	− 4 [2]
− Culls [%][h]	− — [—]	− 0 [—]	− 0 [0]	− 32 [16]	− 32 [16]
+ Purchases for existing herd	+ —	+ 0	+ 200	+ 38	+ 36
Closing stock	= —	= 0	= 200	= 200	= 200

Herd totals

Total herd stock					
Opening	2,639	1,365	1,365	1,720	1,993
Prelim. closing	2,771	1,429	1,629	1,862	2,269
Over(under)-stocking	—	169	(91)	(308)	(351)
Balancing sales					
Heifers 2–3 years	− 132	− 64	− 0	− 0	− 0
Balancing purchases					
Heifers 2–3 years	+ 0	+ 0	+ 91	+ 131	+ 2
Bulls for above	+ —	+ 0	+ 0	+ 0	+ 0
Steers 1–2 years	+ 0	+ 0	+ 0	+ 0	+ 0
Actual closing	= 2,639	= 1,365	= 1,720	= 1,993	= 2,271
Carrying capacity (end of year)[i]		1,260	1,720	2,170	2,620

Herd growth

Herd composition (opening stock)					
Bulls		100	100	100	100
Breeding cows		500	500	655	800
Heifers 1–2 years		157	157	157	221
Heifers 2–3 years		152	152	152	152
Steers 1–2 years		157	157	157	221
Steers 2–3 years		152	152	152	152
Steers 3–4 years		147	147	147	147
Work oxen		—	0	200	200
Total (animal units)		1,365	1,365	1,720	1,993
Carrying capacity (beginning of year)[i]		1,260	1,260	1,720	2,170
Purchases					
Bulls		18	33	20	20
Heifers 2–3 years		0	91	131	2
Steers 1–2 years		0	0	0	0
Work oxen		0	200	38	36
Total		18	324	189	58

	Development year				Full development	
	4	5	6		Years 7–20	Stable 1,000-cow herd

Livestock class

4	5	6		Years 7–20	Stable 1,000-cow herd
217 − 4 [2] = 273	288 − 6 [2] = 282	279 − 6 [2] = 273	 − [2] =	279 − 6 [2] = 273	349 − 7 [2] = 342
149 − 3 [2] = 146	213 − 4 [2] = 209	282 − 6 [2] = 276	 − [2] =	273 − 5 [2] = 268	342 − 7 [2] = 335
200 − 4 [2] − 32 [16] + 36 = 200	200 − 4 [2] − 32 [16] + 36 = 200	200 − 4 [2] − 32 [16] + 36 = 200	 − [2] − [16] + =	200 − 4 [2] − 32 [16] + 36 = 200	200 − 4 [2] − 32 [16] + 36 = 200

Herd totals

4	5	6		Years 7–20	Stable 1,000-cow herd
2,271	2,459	2,510		2,501	3,052
2,522	2,635	2,618		2,618	3,199
(98)	15	(2)		(2)	—
− 63	− 125	− 117	−	− 117	− 147
+ 0	+ 0	+ 0	+	+ 0	+ 0
+ 0	+ 0	+ 0	+	+ 0	+ 0
+ 0	+ 0	+ 0	+	+ 0	+ 0
= 2,459	= 2,510	= 2,501	=	= 2,501	= 3,052
2,620	2,620	2,620		2,620	

Herd growth

4	5	6		Years 7–20	Stable 1,000-cow herd
100	100	100		100	
800	800	800		800	
294	285	285		285	
217	288	279		279	
294	285	285		285	
217	288	279		279	
149	213	282		273	
200	200	200		200	
2,271	2,459	2,510		2,501	
2,620	2,620	2,620		2,620	
20	20	20		20	
0	0	0		0	
0	0	0		0	
36	36	36		36	
56	56	56		56	

(Table continues on the following pages.)

Table 4-27 (continued)

| Item | Without development | | Development year | | |
	Stable 1,000-cow herd	100-farm herd	1	2	3
		Herd Growth			
Sales					
Culled bulls	--------	15	30	17	18
Culled cows	--------	60	60	98	120
Culled heifers	--------	8	8	15	15
Surplus heifers 2–3 years	--------	64	0	0	0
Steers 1–2 years	--------	0	0	0	0
Steers 3–4 years	--------	143	143	143	144
Culled work oxen	--------	—	0	32	32
Total	--------	290	241	305	329
		Technical coefficients (percent)			
Calving rate	--------	70	70	75[j]	80[j]
Calf mortality	--------	10	10	10	8
Adult mortality	--------	3	3	3	2
Culling rate, bulls	--------	15	30	17	18
Culling rate, cows	--------	12	12	15	15
Culling rate, heifers	--------	5	5	10	10
Culling rate, work oxen	--------	—	0	16	16
Bulls/breeding females[k]	--------	—	—	—	—
Carrying capacity (per hectare, end of year)[i]	--------	1.2	1.6	2.1	2.5

$$\frac{\text{Without-development area carrying capacity}}{\text{Without-development pasture requirement of stable 1,000-cow herd + followers}} = \frac{1,260 - 100}{2,639 - 100} = \frac{1,160}{2,539} = 0.457$$

Note: Brackets indicate technical coefficients; parentheses indicate negative numbers; boxes indicate elements of preliminary closing stock. The blank column before the columns under the heading "full development" is included because the analyst will not know in advance just how many years it will take to achieve full development. The worksheet should include a generous number of columns under the heading "development year" even though at the end of the herd computation some of these will be unused.

Source: Same as table 4-11.

a. Adult mortality rate.
b. Culling rate of bulls.
c. Bulls/breeding females rate.
d. Culling rate of cows.

e. One-half of calving rate.
f. Calf mortality rate.
g. Culling rate of heifers.
h. Culling rate for work oxen.

	Development year			Full development	
4	*5*	*6*		*Years 7–20*	*Stable 1,000-cow herd*
		Herd Growth			
18	18	18	--------	18	--------
112	112	112	--------	112	--------
22	29	28	--------	28	--------
63	125	117	--------	117	--------
0	0	0	--------	0	--------
146	209	276	--------	268	--------
32	32	32	--------	32	--------
393	525	583	--------	575	--------
		Technical coefficients (percent)			
75	75	75	75	75	--------
5	5	5	5	5	--------
2	2	2	2	2	--------
18	18	18	18	18	--------
14	14	14	14	14	--------
10	10	10	10	10	--------
16	16	16	16	16	--------
—	—	—	—	—	--------
2.5	2.5	2.5	2.5	2.5	--------

$$\frac{\text{With-development area carrying capacity}}{\begin{array}{c}\text{With-development pasture}\\ \text{requirement of stable}\\ \text{1,000-cow herd + followers}\end{array}} = \frac{2,620 - 100 - 200}{3,052 - 100 - 200} = \frac{2,320}{2,752} = 0.843$$

i. In animal units. The carrying capacity at the beginning of the year is determined by multiplying the animal units per farm at the end of the previous year given in table 4-10 by the 100 farms in the model. Similarly, the carrying capacity at the end of the year is determined by multiplying the animal units per farm at the end of the year given in table 4-10 by the 100 farms in the model. The carrying capacity per hectare at the end of the year is determined by dividing the animal units per farm by the 10.5 hectares of pasture on each farm; it is thus a weighted average of natural and improved pasture.

j. Represents a weighted average between the calving rate of breeding cows in the existing herd, which is 70 percent, and that of purchased bred heifers, which is nearly 100 percent.

k. Note that in this project a minimum of one bull per farm is assumed, or a minimum of 100 bulls on 100 farms. The number of bulls per 100 breeding females would usually be three to four for all years.

tional bulls will be needed; the number is determined by multiplying the number of heifers by the bulls/breeding females percentage. In the Paraguay example, there is an exceptionally high number of bulls in the herd because it is assumed that each farm will keep one bull for breeding. The biological requirement for the proportion of bulls in relation to breeding cows would be on the order of 3 to 4 percent in ranch herds and 2 to 3 percent in more intensive operations. In a smallholder district it would make sense for farmers to form groups or cooperatives to share the use of bulls, especially in dairy herds where detection of cows in heat is relatively easy. In the long term, dairy herds would be expected to be given access to an artificial insemination service, and then no bulls would be required on the individual farms.

Animal units

The size of a beef or dairy herd should be related to the feed available. This availability is denominated in animal units, a standardized measurement that permits comparison between herds and between the herd size and feed availability. When the major source of feed is to be pasture, as is the case in the Paraguay example, the total feed consumption of the herd can then be fitted to the grazing anticipated to be available. By converting grazing animals into animal units, a better measurement for feed requirements is obtained than is possible by using the total number of animals alone. The variation in feed consumption between age and sex groups makes this conversion desirable. It is also possible to permit aggregation with other animal species using the same grazing resource.

Use of animal units is not uniform in contemporary practice among livestock specialists. Rather, it is common to take a breeding cow, generally without a calf, as the unit and to relate other animals to that base. Thus, the basic animal unit in most developing countries would probably be something on the order of a 250-kilogram breeding cow. In areas where the average breeding cow is heavier, the animal unit used in computation might be the heavier cow.

For a beef herd fed mainly on pasture, estimates of carrying capacity are very approximate, and so a short-cut computation of animal units is used. This has been incorporated in the Paraguay herd projection in table 4-27. The total of animal units is taken to be the number of adult animals in the herd (that is, the total number of animals less the calves). Although this introduces some distortion into the estimate of the animal units, it is well within the margin of error of estimating carrying capacity and greatly facilitates the herd projection. Many analysts, however, prefer to assign different animal unit weights to different classes of animals according to the different consumption of each class. Breeding cows remain the basic unit. A set of conversion factors commonly employed assigns 1.2 animal units to bulls, 1.0 animal units to breeding cows, 0.3 animal units to calves of zero to one year, 0.6 animal units to cattle of one to two years, 0.8 animal units to cattle of two to three years, 1.0 animal units to cattle over three years, and 1.2 animal units to work oxen.

For projections of sheep and goat herds, the reference animal may be assumed to be equivalent to one-sixth, or 0.17, of an animal unit. (Recall that the animal unit is based on the average breeding cow in the area. The relation between body weight and animal units is not proportional between animals of different weights because smaller animals consume proportionately more feed per unit of body weight. The factor is also influenced by the different grazing habits of sheep and goats in contrast with those of cattle.) Thus, ewes or does would be 0.17 animal units; lambs and kids between birth and six months, 0.09 animal units; sheep and goats over six months, 0.17 animal units; and rams or billy goats, 0.20 animal units. Camel cows may be converted to 1.5 animal units and buffalo cows to 1.8 animal units, with the different age groups bearing the same proportionate number of animal units as they would in a cattle herd.

Because of the low accuracy of carrying capacity estimates, an over- or understocking of 10 percent is permissible in herd projections, although as the herd buildup proceeds the stocking rate would be held within a narrower range until the number of breeding females in the stable herd with the project has been reached.

Determining the stable herd

Before turning to the computation of the herd projection itself, there are several ground rules to note. In making the projection, we will round the number of breeding cows without the project and at full development to a multiple of the number of farms in the model. This makes it possible to speak of a single farm as having a whole number of breeding cows. Thus, we can tell from table 4-27 that the 20-hectare mixed farm has five breeding cows without the project, and this increases to eight at full development of the project. Also, as the herd buildup proceeds, we will not allow the number of breeding cows in any year to exceed the number at full development. Thus, at the end of year 2, which is the beginning of year 3, the number of breeding cows is not allowed to exceed 800—the number at full development—even though there would be some additional carrying capacity available. Finally, in following the Paraguay example, we will conform to the analyst's assumption that no feeder steers—steers purchased from outside the herd, to be fattened for sale—would be available. In other beef herd projections, however, purchases of feeder steers might be used to utilize any excess carrying capacity.

To begin our herd projection, we prepare a worksheet similar to that shown in table 4-27 and insert the relevant technical coefficients within the brackets. By using this format, there is less danger of applying erroneous technical coefficients. Note the boxes for some numbers; this device also facilitates the computation and should be included in the worksheet prepared. Since it is not known in advance just how many years it will take for the herd to stabilize at the full development configuration, the worksheet should contain a generous number of columns even though at the end of the computation there will be unused columns (such as the last, blank column under the heading "development year" in table 4-27).

The first task in preparing the herd buildup is to determine the size of the stable herd without the project and at full project development. First we will determine what would be a stable herd for 1,000 breeding cows and the number of animal units such a stable herd would consume. We will then take the ratio between the 1,000-cow herd consumption and the carrying capacity of 100 farms in the project and adjust the 1,000-cow herd to that capacity. (In some instances, the herd will not be stable at the beginning of the project. In that case, the technical coefficients observed in the field will be applied to the 1,000-cow herd at the beginning of the project.)

This process of determining the stable herd can be illustrated by following the computation for the stable herd at full development. We begin by working through the last column of the herd projection worksheet in table 4-27. We calculate the deaths and culls for 100 bulls by multiplying the opening stock by the relevant technical coefficients (transferred to the brackets from the bottom of the table). For the 100 bulls there would be a 2 percent mortality and an 18 percent culling rate, so that 80 bulls would remain after applying the coefficients $[100 - (100 \times 0.02) - (100 \times 0.18) = 80]$. To bring the total number of bulls back to the opening stock position of 100, we thus would need to purchase 20 bulls $(100 - 80 = 20)$. The opening stock position of 100 bulls, then, is entered on the subtotal box. Since the herd is stable, no heifers would be purchased, and the closing stock number of 100 may be entered directly. (Were this not a model for smallholders but for one large 1,000-cow herd, the number of bulls in the opening and closing stock would be determined by multiplying the number of breeding cows at the beginning of the year by the bulls/breeding cows percentage.)

Turning to the breeding cows, we subtract the 20 deaths and the 140 culls from the opening stock of 1,000 cows to obtain the 840 breeding cows entered in the subtotal box $[1,000 - (1,000 \times 0.02) - (1,000 \times 0.14) = 840]$. That means we will have to transfer 160 heifers to the breeding cow herd at the end of the year to bring the closing stock back up to 1,000 $(1,000 - 840 = 160)$.

Proceeding to the female calves, we multiply the 1,000 cows in the herd at the beginning of the year by 37.5 percent, which is one half the calving rate of 75 percent $(75 \div 2 = 37.5)$, to obtain the 375 births $(1,000 \times 0.375 = 375)$. Now we multiply 375 by the calf mortality rate of 5 percent to obtain the loss of female calves, which is 19. This is subtracted from 375 to reach the closing stock number of 356 $[375 - (375 \times 0.05) = 356]$.

We enter the 356 closing stock female calves as the opening stock number for heifers one to two years old. We multiply 356 by the adult mortality rate of 2 percent and subtract the result from the opening stock figure, 356, to obtain 349 [356 − (356 × 0.02) = 349].

We enter the closing stock number of 349 heifers of one to two years as the opening stock number for heifers of two to three years, then multiply it by the adult mortality rate of 2 percent and the culling rate for heifers of 10 percent. The results are then subtracted from the opening stock number to obtain the subtotal for heifers of two to three years of 307 [349 − (349 × 0.02) − (349 × 0.10) = 307]. We enter the 160 end-of-year transfers that will be needed to bring the closing stock of breeding cows to 1,000 (as we calculated at the top of the column) and subtract this from the 307 subtotal of heifers two to three years old to obtain the sales of 147 animals (307 − 160 = 147).

For male calves, we multiply the opening stock of 1,000 cows in the herd at the beginning of the year by 37.5 percent, which is one half the calving rate of 75 percent (75 ÷ 2 = 37.5), to obtain the 375 births (1,000 × 0.375 = 375). Applying the calf mortality of 5 percent we obtain the loss of 19 calves (375 × 0.05 = 19), which is subtracted from the births to obtain the closing stock entry of 356 [375 − 19 = 356].

The closing stock of male calves becomes the opening stock of steers one to two years old, of which 2 percent are lost through mortality, for a closing stock of 349 [356 − (356 × 0.02) = 349].

The closing stock number of 349 steers one to two years old becomes the opening stock number for steers two to three years old. We multiply 349 by the 2 percent adult mortality rate and subtract the result, 7, to obtain the closing stock figure of 342 [349 − (349 × 0.02) = 342].

The closing stock of steers two to three years old becomes the opening stock number for steers three to four years old. This number is, in turn, reduced by the 2 percent adult mortality rate; the remainder becomes the 335 steers three to four years old that are sold [342 − (342 × 0.02) = 335].

In the Paraguay example, we know the closing stock of oxen will be 200. We enter this closing stock figure as the opening stock figure. We multiply the opening stock figure of 200 oxen by the adult mortality rate of 2 percent and the culling rate of 16 percent to obtain the number of oxen that will be taken from the herd. In this case, that number is 36; 36 oxen must be purchased to bring the closing stock back to 200 [(200 × 0.02) + (200 × 0.16) = 36; 200 − 36 + 36 = 200].

Proceeding to the herd totals, we sum the opening stock figures (recall that calves are not part of the opening stock—they are born during the year) to obtain the opening stock of 3,052. Our preliminary closing stock figure of 3,199 is obtained by adding all the figures in the boxes. The difference is 147, which is the number of heifers sold, so that figure may be entered under balancing sales to bring the actual closing stock down to 3,052 animals.

The number of animal units that the stable 1,000-cow herd will consume is estimated by taking the number of adult animals, which, conveniently, is also the opening stock of 3,052.

We know from the pasture production given in table 4-10 that at full development each farm will have a carrying capacity of 26.2 animal units, so the total carrying capacity of 100 farms will be 2,620 animal units. Now, in order to obtain the number of breeding cows that would be needed in a stable herd that consumes 2,620 animal units, we simply determine the ratio of available carrying capacity to the animal units needed by the 1,000-cow herd and apply that ratio to 1,000 to obtain the number of breeding cows in the stable herd at full development that will consume 2,620 animal units. Recall that there will be 100 bulls and 200 oxen in both the stable 1,000-cow herd and the full-development herd, so we must subtract the consumption of those animals before determining the ratio. Now we obtain the ratio as shown in table 4-27 and determine that it is 0.843 [(2,620 − 100 − 200) ÷ (3,052 − 100 − 200) = 0.843]. Multiplying the 1,000-cow herd by this ratio gives us 843 breeding cows (1,000 × 0.843 = 843). Most analysts would prefer to round this to the nearest multiple of the number of farms in the model so that fractional animals are not reported for the individual farm, at least if the result of rounding to the nearest multiple keeps the total animal units within ± 10 percent of the carrying capacity. In the Paraguay example, the rounded number would be 800 breeding cows.

Now, to determine the stable full-development herd we start with 800 breeding cows and work out the stable herd in exactly the same manner as we did for the 1,000-cow herd. The result, tabulated in table 4-27, gives a total herd of 2,501 animals at the beginning of each year, which has a total animal unit consumption of 2,501 using our short-cut calculation. This results in an understocking of 5 percent, but that is sufficiently within the ±10 percent margin that good practice allows.

Exactly the same procedure would be followed to determine the stable herd without development; we thus would have a stable herd for 100 farms at the beginning of the project and at full development. The next step is to calculate the growth of the herd from the without-project stable herd to the full-development stable herd.

The procedure we have suggested for determining a stable herd can also be done algebraically in one step. A formula can be set up in which the unknown is the number of breeding cows, since the number of all other classes of animals (except bulls and oxen) derive from it. Only those classes of animals in the herd at the beginning of the year are included in the formula. There would be breeding cows, animals one to two years old, animals two to three years old, steers three to four years old, bulls, and oxen. (Of course, all calves would have become animals of one to two years at the beginning of the year.) In most instances, the number of bulls would be dependent upon the number of breeding cows, but in the Paraguay example the number is fixed at 100. Similarly, the number of oxen is fixed at 200. The formula would then look as follows:

Breeding			
cows	*1–2-year animals*	*2–3-year animals*	
x	$+$ $(0.75)(0.95)x$	$+$ $(0.75)(0.95)(0.98)x$	

	3–4-year steers	*Bulls*	*Oxen*
$+$	$(0.75)(0.5)(0.95)(0.98)(0.98)x$	$+$ 100	$+$ 200

$$\begin{array}{rl}
& \textit{Carrying} \\
& \textit{capacity} \\
= & 2{,}620.
\end{array}$$

In the formula, x is the unknown number of breeding cows. The first element in each expression where the unknown appears is the calving rate. For steers three to four years old, the next element is the 50 percent of the calves born that are male. The remaining elements represent the survival rate; that is, 1 less the mortality rate for each year of age. For steers three to four years old, for example, the survival rate of calves in year 1 is 0.95 $(1 - 0.05 = 0.95)$, and in years 2 and 3 it is 0.98 $(1 - 0.02 = 0.98)$. For bulls and oxen the number is fixed, so we enter the number of animals in the herd at the beginning of the year. The carrying capacity, of course, comes from the full-development carrying capacity of a 20-hectare mixed farm multiplied by 100. When we solve the formula, we obtain 843 breeding cows—exactly the same number we determined by the ratio method described earlier. This would be rounded to 800 animals, and the result put in the subtotal for breeding cows in the herd projection worksheet (table 4-27). The stable full-development herd would then be calculated by applying the technical coefficients as we have discussed. If the herd turns out not to be stable when this is done, there is an error in formulating or in solving the formula. (If different classes of animals were to be assigned weights, in contrast with the short-cut of assigning one animal unit to each adult animal, then each expression in the formula would be multiplied by the appropriate animal unit weight.)

Tracing the herd growth

Once the stable herd at the beginning of the project and the stable herd at full development have been determined, the herd growth can be traced from the beginning of the project to the state of full development.

To do this, we may continue to use the pattern worksheet laid out in table 4-27. First, we transfer all closing stock numbers of the without-project stable herd to the appropriate blanks in year 1. The closing stock of 100 bulls in the 100-farm stable herd without the project becomes the opening stock of bulls in year 1; the closing stock of 500 breeding cows becomes the opening stock of breeding cows in year 1; the 157 female calves becomes the opening stock of heifers one to two years old; the closing stock of 147 end-of-year steers two to three years old becomes the opening stock of steers three to four years old; and so forth. Then we trace the effect of the various technical coefficients that act on the herd by the same procedure used in determining the stable herd for the bulls, breeding cows, heifers, steers, and oxen. For heifers two to three years old, we work down only to the subtotal box, since purchases and sales of these animals are balancing transactions. If we were determining the number of bulls on the basis of the bulls/breeding females percentage, we would work only to the subtotal box for bulls. Since the number of bulls is fixed at well above the bulls/breeding females percentage in the Paraguay example, the subtotal directly becomes the closing stock number. Similarly, if the plan for the herd growth called for purchase and sale of feeder steers, we would work only to the subtotal box for the steers. In the Paraguay project, since there is no purchase or sale of feeder steers, the subtotal in all years becomes the closing stock figure. In year 1, 200 oxen will be purchased and added to the 100-farm herd, so they show as purchases. Because all purchases are assumed to occur at the end of the year, there are no deaths or culls, and all 200 oxen remain at the end of the year. Losses and culls will, of course, be calculated from year 2 onward.

Next we total the opening stock (which, of course, includes no calves), which comes to 1,365 animals, and enter that in the herd total. Then we add all the figures in the boxes to arrive at the preliminary closing stock of 1,629. Comparing that with the carrying capacity at the end of the year of 1,720 animal units, we find we are understocked by 91 animal units. That permits us to purchase 91 heifers of two to three years to make our actual closing stock 1,720 adult animals and thus exactly match the carrying capacity. Then we may enter the 91 heifers in the table as purchases and complete the column by calculating the transfers to cows of 230 animals.

Now we can complete the herd summary for year 1, totaling the opening stock herd composition, the purchases, and the sales, and noting the carrying capacity.

This same procedure is then repeated for each year until the herd reaches the stable full-development configuration. In the Paraguay project, this occurs in year 7.

Note the effect of the decision rule of not allowing the number of breeding cows to exceed the full-development number of 800. This means that after year 3 there are no more purchases of heifers two to three years old, and excess heifers two to three years old are sold beginning in year 4.

For example, we may trace through the calculations in detail for year 3.

The opening stock of bulls is 100 (the closing stock in year 2), of which 2 percent are lost to mortality and 18 percent are culled. Eighty therefore remain, and 20 must be purchased to bring the subtotal back to 100, which then directly becomes the closing stock $[100 - (100 \times 0.02) - (100 \times 0.18) + 20 = 100]$.

The opening stock of breeding cows is 800, a figure that was reached during year 2 and that our decision rule prevents us from exceeding. Of these, 2 percent are lost to mortality and 15 percent are culled, for an entry in the subtotal box of 664 $[800 - (800 \times 0.02) - (800 \times 0.15) = 664]$.

To bring the closing stock back to 800, we need 136 heifer transfers (800 − 664 = 136).

There are 320 female calves born, determined by applying half the calving rate of 80 percent to the opening stock of breeding cows (800 × 0.80 ÷ 2 = 320). Of these, 8 percent die, leaving a closing stock of 294 [320 − (320 × 0.08) = 294].

The 221 opening stock of heifers one to two years old was the closing stock in year 2 of female calves. Two percent are lost to mortality, leaving 217 as the closing stock [221 − (221 × 0.02) = 217].

The 152 heifers two to three years old are the closing stock of heifers one to two years old in year 2. Mortality is 2 percent, or 3 animals, and culling is 10 percent, or 15 animals, leaving 134 heifers to be entered as the subtotal [152 − (152 × 0.02) − (152 × 0.10) = 134]. We skip heifer purchases and sales for the moment but will return to them after we know the situation of the balancing transactions.

The 320 male calves born represent half the calving rate of 80 percent applied to the 800 breeding cattle in the opening stock (800 × 0.8 ÷ 2 = 320). Applying the 8 percent calf mortality rate reduces these by 26 animals, to 294 [320 − (320 × 0.08) = 294].

The 221 opening stock of steers one to two years old transferred from the closing stock of male calves in year 2 is reduced by the 2 percent mortality rate to give a subtotal of 217 animals; this is also the closing stock, since we are assuming there will be no steers one to two years old available for purchase as a balancing transaction [221 − (221 × 0.02) = 217].

Similarly, the opening stock of 152 steers two to three years old (which is the closing stock in year 2 of steers one to two years old) is reduced by the 2 percent adult mortality rate to a closing stock figure of 149 [152 − (152 × 0.02) = 149].

The 147 opening stock of steers three to four years old transferred from the year-2 closing stock of steers two to three years old is also reduced by the 2 percent mortality, leaving 144 steers three to four years old for sale [147 − (147 × 0.02) = 144].

The work oxen open with 200 animals; 2 percent, or 4 animals, are lost to mortality, and 16 percent, or 32 animals, are culled. This leaves 164 work animals, so 36 must be purchased to bring the closing stock up to 200 again (200 − 4 − 32 + 36 = 200).

Turning to the herd totals, the opening stock is 1,993 animals, the same as the closing stock in year 2. Adding the numbers in the boxes, we reach the preliminary closing stock of 2,269. When we compare this with the carrying capacity at the end of year 3 which is 2,620 animal units, we find an understocking of 351 animal units. This means we would have the pasture resources to permit feeding as many as 351 purchased animals. But we only need 2 animals to bring the number of heifer transfers up to the 136 needed to restore the number of breeding cows to the maximum allowable of 800, and 136 can thus be put in the entry for transfer to breeding cows under heifers two to three years old. Since we cannot purchase feeder steers to utilize the remaining available carrying capac-

Table 4-28. *Computation of Herd Productivity, 100 20-Hectare Mixed Farms, Paraguay Project*
(animal units)

Item	Without development	Development year						Full development (years 7–20)
		1	2	3	4	5	6	
Opening stock[a]	1,365	1,365	1,520	1,793	2,071	2,259	2,310	2,310
Off-take								
Sales[a]	290	241	273	297	361	493	551	543
+ Home consumption[b]	+ 0	+ 0	+ 0	+ 0	+ 0	+ 0	+ 0	+ 0
– Purchases[a]	– 18	– 124	– 151	– 22	– 20	– 20	– 20	– 20
Total	272	117	122	275	341	473	531	523
Rate (%)	20	9	8	15	16	21	23	23
Herd growth								
Following-year opening stock[a]	1,365	1,520	1,793	2,071	2,259	2,310	2,310	2,310
Growth	0	155	273	278	188	51	0	0
Rate (%)	0	11	18	16	9	2	0	0
Herd productivity[c]								
Rate (%)	20	20	26	31	25	23	23	23

Source: Calculated from table 4-24.
a. Work oxen are omitted to give a better estimate of the productivity of the beef herd.
b. In the Paraguay example, no home consumption is assumed because the computation is done for 100 farms and the values carried to the individual model farm budgets. Were the accounts structured to note home consumption separately, it would have to be included in the productivity computation.
c. The sum of the off-take rate plus the herd growth rate.

ity, the closing stock for the total herd of 2,271 remains well below the carrying capacity of 2,620. The results of our calculations can now be transferred to the summary table.

Once we have the worksheets completed, the results are summarized in the herd composition, purchases, and sales table along the lines of table 4-11. The herd composition at the beginning of the year, the purchases, the sales including culls, and the technical coefficients are transferred from the worksheet to the table. The details of the computation need not be reported in a project report. Rather, the worksheets can be made available to anyone who wishes to review the computation.

It is convenient to have a summary measure of herd productivity. Table 4-28 shows one such measure. It is the sum of the off-take rate and the herd growth rate. It shows that the herd productivity grows from 20 percent without the project to 23 percent with the project. These two figures are transferred to the herd computation, purchases, and sales summary in table 4-11. The interim figures during the development period are tabulated in table 4-28, but they may be misleading because of distortions arising from the dynamics of the herd growth, and so are better not transferred to the summary.

Machine computation

Calculations of herd projection, clearly, become very complex and tedious and are easily subject to arithmetic errors. As a result, some analysts have turned to machines for help. Espadas (1977) has prepared a program for a programmable calculator, and several programs are available for a full computer [see that of Powers (1975)]. Using machines for herd projections has the advantage not only of increasing accuracy but of making it possible to do sensitivity analyses easily by changing basic assumptions and technical coefficients—something that is almost never done in practice, when the analyst must rely on computation by hand.

Feed budget

In projects where the major feed supply is to be pasture—as in the Paraguay Livestock and Agricultural Development Project we have been following in this chapter—the farm feed requirement and production are appropriately dealt with by estimating the carrying capacity and thus the total animal units that will be available from the pasture, always keeping in mind the rather low accuracy of those estimates. But in projects where more intensive livestock production is planned—such as poultry, pigs, dairy cattle, and feedlot beef—a more accurate feed budget for each pattern farm should be prepared. This will compare the feed requirement with the on-farm production and estimate the quantities the farmer must purchase or can sell. The feed requirement and production estimate is also needed to assess how farm production patterns may be changed to produce sufficient feed or to utilize excess feed. These estimates will require a considerable knowledge of livestock production,

Table 4-29. Feeding Period and Daily Ration, 20-Hectare Mixed Farm, Paraguay Project

	Feeding period			Number of animals	Number of feeding days	Daily ration								
Livestock class	From	To	Days			Whole milk (liters)	Maize (kg)	Soy-beans (kg)	Sun-flower (kg)	Chick mash (kg)	Protein concentrate (kg)	Manioc tubers (kg)	Maize stover (kg)	Soy hay (kg)
Cattle														
Dairy cows	1 May.	30 Sept	152	8	1,216	—	1.0	1.0	—	—	—	—	5.0	3.0
Calves, rearing 1[a]	—	—	84	3	252	3.0	—	—	—	—	—	—	—	—
Calves, rearing 2[b]	—	—	160	3	480	—	0.5	0.5	—	—	—	—	—	1.0
Steers	—	—	—	—	—	—	—	—	—	—	—	—	—	—
Heifers	—	—	—	—	- -	—	—	—	—	—	—	—	—	—
Bulls	1 May	30 Sept	152	1	152	—	1.0	1.0	—	—	—	—	6.0	3.0
Work oxen	1 Sept	30 Nov	90	2	180	—	1.0	1.0	—	—	—	—	6.0	3.0
Pigs														
Dry sows	—	—	100	5	500	—	0.5	0.5	0.5	—	—	3.0	—	—
Suckling sows	—	—	265	5	1,325	—	2.0	1.0	0.5	—	—	2.0	—	—
Boars	1 Jan	31 Dec	365	1	365	—	1.0	0.5	0.5	—	—	3.0	—	—
Piglets[c]	—	—	56	72	4,032	—	0.3	0.2	—	—	0.1	—	—	—
Fattening pigs	—	—	150	70	10,500	—	0.5	0.5	—	—	0.5	6.0	—	—
Poultry														
Chicks[d]	—	—	56	20	1,120	—	—	—	—	0.036	—	—	—	—
Growers[d]	—	—	112	20	2,240	—	—	—	—	0.080	—	—	—	—
Layers[e]	1 Jan	31 Dec	365	20	7,300	—	0.06	—	—	—	0.06	—	—	—

Source: Calculated from assumptions based on tables 4-4, 4-10, and 4-11.
a. Rearing period with milk twelve weeks; individual dates vary. Three liters a day whole milk during first twelve weeks.
b. Rearing period on concentrates 160 days starting after three weeks.
c. Rearing period on concentrates fifty-six days starting after four days.
d. Rearing period twenty-four weeks, consumption per head 2 kilograms chick mash and 9 kilograms grower mash.
e. Home-prepared ration.

and the project analyst probably will wish to consult livestock specialists when he prepares estimates of feed supply and use.

Preparation of a feed requirement and production estimate can be illustrated by adapting the Paraguay example. We will work only with the full-development period, years 7–20. Note, however, that the estimate was not part of the original project analysis because it was assumed that farmers would depend primarily upon pasture for feed. As a result, the example for feed requirement and production only partially articulates with the other illustrations in this chapter that fully interlink with one another and were drawn directly from the Paraguay project.

FEEDING PERIOD AND DAILY RATION.   To prepare a feed requirement and production estimate, we may begin by estimating the feeding period and daily ration for each class of livestock on the farm, as shown in table 4-29. For purposes of illustration, we may assume that the 20-hectare mixed farm in the Paraguay example will produce beef and dairy cattle, pigs, and poultry (this, of course, was not in fact the case in the project from which this example was drawn). We enter each class of livestock on the farm that receives supplementary feeding in addition to grazing for part or all of the year. Steers and heifers that are fed entirely from pasture are included in the illustration for the sake of completeness. The feeding period for a constant ration for each group that is to receive supplementary feed is shown along with the number of animals in the class. When there are two quite different kinds of ration that are to be fed a class of livestock, they are shown separately, as is the case for calves. Multiplying the number of days each animal is to be fed by the number of animals gives the number of "feeding days" for each class. For dairy cows, for example, this comes to 1,216 days ($152 \times 8 = 1,216$). The composition of each daily ration is shown. The order of the major components of the ration is considered to be a good one: milk, cereals, oilseeds, milling and agroindustrial by-products, concentrates, tubers, and roughage.

FEED REQUIREMENT AND PRODUCTION.   From the estimates for the feeding period and the daily ration, the annual *feed requirement* for each class of animals may be determined as shown in table 4-30. (As in the main text of the chapter, principal categories from the pattern table are shown in *italic* type.) For dairy cows, for example, we know from table 4-29 that each animal is to receive 5.0 kilograms daily of maize stover (chopped stalks and cobs), and there are 1,216 feeding days each year. As a result, the annual need for stover for dairy cattle can be estimated at 6.08 tons ($1,216 \times 5 \div 1,000 = 6.08$). Adding the requirement for each class gives the *total requirement*. The *on-farm feed production* would be taken from the crop and pasture production given in table 4-10. (Since crop by-products such as maize stover and soy hay are not included in table 4-10, they are calculated as indicated in the notes to table 4-30.) This can now be compared with the total requirement to estimate the *feed purchase and sale*. For example, the total requirement for sunflower is 1.09 tons, where-

Table 4-30. *Feed Requirement and Production, 20-Hectare Mixed Farm, Paraguay Project*
(tons)

Item	Whole milk	Maize	Soy-beans	Sun-flower	Chick/grower mash	Protein concen-trate	Manioc tubers	Maize stover	Soy hay
Feed requirement									
Cattle									
Dairy cows	—	1.22	1.22	—	—	—	—	6.08	3.65
Calves, rearing 1 (liters)	756	—	—	—	—	—	—	—	—
Calves, rearing 2	—	0.24	0.24	—	—	—	—	—	0.48
Steers	—	—	—	—	—	—	—	—	—
Heifers	—	—	—	—	—	—	—	—	—
Bulls	—	0.15	0.15	—	—	—	—	0.91	0.46
Work oxen	—	0.18	0.18	—	—	—	—	1.08	0.54
Pigs									
Dry sows	—	0.25	0.25	0.25	—	—	1.50	—	—
Suckling sows	—	2.65	1.32	0.66	—	—	2.65	—	—
Boars	—	0.36	0.18	0.18	—	—	1.10	—	—
Piglets	—	1.21	0.81	—	—	0.40	—	—	—
Fattening pigs	—	5.25	5.25	—	—	5.25	63.00	—	—
Poultry									
Chicks	—	—	—	—	0.04	—	—	—	—
Growers	—	—	—	—	0.18	—	—	—	—
Layers	—	0.44	—	—	—	0.44	—	—	—
Total requirement	756	11.95	9.60	1.09	0.22	6.09	68.25	8.07	5.13
On-farm feed production[a]	—	0.70	5.40	3.60	—	—	12.00	1.00[b]	5.40[c]
Feed purchase and sale									
Surplus for sale	—	—	—	2.51	—	—	—	—	0.27
Quantity to be purchased	—	11.25	4.20	—	0.22	6.09	56.25	7.07	—

Source: Calculated from tables 4-10 and 4-29.
a. From table 4-10.

b. Assumes 2 tons of maize stover production per hectare from 0.5 hectares.
c. Assumes 1.8 tons of soy hay production per hectare from 3.0 hectares.

as the total production is estimated to be 3.60 tons; there is therefore a *surplus for sale* of 2.51 tons (3.60 − 1.09 = 2.51). But 11.95 tons of maize are estimated to be required, and only 0.7 ton will be produced; the *quantity to be purchased* of maize is therefore 11.25 tons (11.95 − 0.70 = 11.25). The estimated surplus or purchase valued at farm-gate prices would then be carried through to the farm budget.

5

Financial Analysis of Processing Industries

AGRICULTURAL PROJECTS frequently include processing facilities such as packing sheds, preserving and canning plants, oil extraction mills, rice mills, sugar refineries, and the like. For these agriculturally based industries (or "agroindustries"), we must project and analyze financial statements to judge efficiency, incentive, creditworthiness, and liquidity and to determine the costs and benefits that are to be included in the overall project. Whether such enterprises are publicly or privately owned, there is the same need to analyze their financial structure.

Analyzing and projecting financial statements for these enterprises requires a considerable, specialized expertise that those responsible for agricultural project analysis often do not possess. The purpose of this chapter is thus twofold. First, for those who do not consider themselves experts in financial analysis, it provides an analytical pattern to apply to less complex agricultural industries included in their projects. Second, for an accountant or financial analyst, it indicates the kinds of financial information needed for agricultural projects. Then, when a project analyst turns to these specialists for their help, they can adapt the pattern formats in this chapter to develop appropriate financial statements for a particular agricultural project.

Facing page: Harvesting coffee in the Kenya highlands.

The treatment here of these issues is necessarily brief; project analysts may want to consult Upper (1979), a collection of teaching materials that expands many of the elements only summarized here. Much of the following discussion is drawn directly from these materials. Those interested in more detail may also wish to consult a standard accounting textbook such as Niswonger and Fess (1977), which uses the U.S. accounting conventions, or Bigg and Perrins (1971), which uses the British conventions. In the discussion here, we will generally follow the accounting conventions of U.S. practice and note some of the important ways that it differs from British practice. Both conventions, however, are essentially identical; differences are almost entirely limited to conventions of presentation and to a few specialized terms used for accounting concepts.

We will illustrate the kinds of accounts that are appropriate for the financial analysis of a processing enterprise that is a part of an agricultural project with examples adapted from the sugar mill included in the South Nyanza Sugar Project in Kenya. We will reproduce the figures for selected years; the original accounts were projected for sixteen years.

The overall South Nyanza project included establishment of a nucleus sugarcane plantation; development of a network of small farmers, or outgrowers, who would supply additional cane; and a processing component—a sugar mill initially capable of crushing 60,000 tons of cane a year, 90,000 tons of cane after later expansion. The accounts presented contain all the elements necessary for analysis of much simpler enterprises but are also complex enough to be useful as a pattern to be adapted by those with specialized knowledge of financial analysis.

For an agriculturally based industry included in a project, three basic financial statements should be prepared: balance sheets, income statements, and sources-and-uses-of-funds statements. If the project represents an expansion of an existing facility, then these accounts should include historical information for, say, about five years previous to the beginning of the project. Both for enterprises that are to be expanded and new enterprises, these statements would be projected over the life of the project.

The balance sheets give a view of the assets and liabilities of the processing enterprise at the end of each accounting period, which is usually a year—a kind of still photograph of the financial state of the enterprise at a given moment. The income statements summarize the revenues and expenses of the enterprise during each accounting period and give a kind of cinematic picture of activities over time. The sources-and-uses-of-funds statements are a summary of the financial transactions taking place during each accounting period. In essence, they convert the income statement to a cash (or funds) basis. They highlight large transactions, such as the purchase of assets and creation of new obligations (both debt and equity), that appear as changes in the balance sheets for the opening and closing of each period.

On the basis of these financial statements, the project analyst can form a judgment about the efficiency of current operations and about how efficient proposed new facilities are likely to be. He can assess the returns to investors if the project is to be financed by private funds or by account-able public enterprises. The statements may reveal losses that will have to be made up through a subsidy if the enterprise is to remain financially solvent; from them the analyst can examine the creditworthiness and liquidity of the enterprise during the project life as a basis for arranging its financing. In general, the project analyst will make use of three sets of ratios, which are derived from the financial statements and which give him insight to help form his financial judgments—efficiency ratios, in-come ratios, and creditworthiness ratios.

The financial data essential to analyze any new project are, of course, based on incremental expenses and revenues. The South Nyanza exam-ple for our discussion was a new project, and virtually the whole sugar mill was incremental. (There were a few existing assets.) Many projects, however, will entail expansion of existing facilities. In these instances, the analysis centers on incremental growth in the parent enterprise, the situation with and without the expansion that the parent enterprise will carry out. Costs and revenues that would be realized by the parent enterprise whether or not a particular project is undertaken are not considered in the estimate of the incremental contribution. On the one hand, the potential future effects of a proposed project must be isolated from the overall accounts of the parent enterprise. On the other hand, the project analyst will be concerned not only with the financial dimensions of a proposed expansion alone. He must also be satisfied that the parent enterprise is financially able to carry out the expansion, and that may require projecting financial statements for the enterprise as a whole, including the expansion envisioned by the project.

Accounts are kept for operating entities rather than for the persons who own, manage, or are otherwise employed by them. The enterprise represents a group of resources subject to common control. In financial analysis, it is the operating entity that is viewed as controlling the resources and receiving the income. The entity is, in turn, owned by its proprietors or shareholders. The management of the enterprise acts on behalf of the owners, whether private or government.

Accounts for operating enterprises are kept on an accrual basis. That is, revenues are recorded in financial statements for the period in which they are earned, and expenses are recorded in the period incurred, re-gardless of when the corresponding cash transactions took place. In contrast, cash accounting shows transactions only when cash payments are actually made. Governments generally keep their accounts on a cash basis, as do some small businesses. Public sector enterprises, however, normally follow the accrual principle because it is more useful for man-agerial decisionmaking.

The most common and generalized categories of items included in the accounts of the South Nyanza project appear in *italic* type in the text of this chapter. If the analyst takes the italicized items and the illustrative tables as a general pattern and adapts them to the particular project he is working on, he will arrive at a satisfactory account for most simple processing enterprises. Conceptual errors would probably be limited and have little effect on the overall project investment decision, although the analyst may wish to verify his projected financial statements by consulting an accountant. Consultation with a financial analyst early in project preparation will probably be necessary when the financial statements for the processing plant become more complex.

Balance Sheet

The most well-known financial statement is the balance sheet. It is a snapshot of an enterprise at a particular point of time. In the South Nyanza example in table 5-1, the *assets* of the sugar mill are listed above and its *liabilities and equity* below. Assets and liabilities are listed according to the U.S. convention of showing the most liquid, or current, first and then progressing through less and less liquid forms to end with fixed assets and long-term liabilities. British usage shows the least liquid first,

Table 5-1. *Balance Sheets, Factory Capacity of 90,000 Tons, South Nyanza Sugar Company, South Nyanza Sugar Project, Kenya*
(thousands of KSh, constant 1977 prices)

Item	Project year			
	1	9	10	11
Assets				
Current assets				
Cash and bank balance	3,323	17,241	69,559	106,234
Accounts receivable—outgrowers[a]	2,952	47,202	48,047	48,471
Inventories				
Nucleus estate standing crop[b]	3,428	25,546	24,181	22,174
Other inventories[c]	1,525	7,000	7,000	7,000
Total current assets	11,228	96,989	148,787	183,879
Fixed assets				
Buildings and equipment at cost	34,549	469,736	472,094	479,923
Less accumulated depreciation	(2,872)	(207,498)	(241,560)	(275,741)
Construction in progress	84,437	—	—	—
Net fixed assets	116,114	262,238	230,534	204,182
Other assets	—	—	—	—
Total assets	127,342	359,227	379,321	388,061
Liabilities and equity				
Liabilities—current				
Accounts payable	—	—	—	—
Short-term loans	—	—	—	—
Long-term loans—current portion				
World Bank	—	6,563	6,563	6,563
European Investment Bank	—	10,956	10,956	10,956
East African Development Bank	—	2,846	2,846	2,844

Table 5-1 (*continued*)

Item	Project year 1	9	10	11
Suppliers' credits—current portion				
Suppliers' credit—Germany	—	7,050	7,050	—
Suppliers' credit—India	—	6,381	6,331	—
Taxes payable	—	—	—	—
Total current liabilities	—	33,796	33,746	20,363
Liabilities—long-term				
Long-term loans				
World Bank	—	98,435	91,872	85,309
European Investment Bank	33,400	54,780	43,824	32,868
U.S. Export-Import (Exim) Bank	7,900	—	—	—
East African Development Bank	6,070	5,690	2,844	—
Suppliers' credits				
Suppliers' credit—Germany	17,200	7,050	—	—
Suppliers' credit—India	15,500	6,331	—	—
Total long-term liabilities	80,070	172,286	138,540	118,177
Total liabilities	80,070	206,082	172,286	138,540
Equity				
Share capital	57,000	196,500	196,500	196,500
Retained earnings	(9,728)	(43,355)	10,535	53,021
Total equity	47,272	153,145	207,035	249,521
Total liabilities and equity	127,342	359,227	379,321	388,061

KSh Kenyan shillings.
Note: Parentheses indicate negative numbers.
Source: Adapted from World Bank, "Kenya: Appraisal of the South Nyanza Sugar Project," 1418-KE (Washington, D.C., 1977; restricted circulation), annex 20, table 12.
   a. Represents the net value of services and inputs provided to outgrowers (small farmers), including company overhead cost allocated to outgrowers.
   b. Includes investment in sugarcane (current value less production cost of sugarcane; excludes value of land).
   c. Includes spare parts, tools, and operating materials.

working through to the most current. (Also, if assets and liabilities are listed in parallel columns instead of at the top and bottom of a page, U.S. custom is to show assets on the left-hand side, whereas British usage is to put the liabilities on the left.) Assets and liabilities plus equity are defined so that they must always be equal. Thus we have the identity: assets ≡ liabilities + owners' equity. Assets must be owned by the enterprise and be of measurable value. There are three principal kinds of assets: current, fixed, and other. *Current assets* consist of *cash*, including checking accounts in a bank; *accounts receivable*, which are amounts owed to the firm by customers and are expected to be converted into cash in the reasonably near future, usually in less than a year; and *inventories* intended for rather prompt sale. In the South Nyanza example, the standing crop of sugarcane on the nucleus plantation is treated as an inventory. *Fixed assets* include durable goods of relatively long life to be used by the enterprise in production of goods and services rather than to be held for sale. Property, plant and equipment, and land are the most common fixed assets. Often, as in the South Nyanza example, *buildings*

Table 5-2. *Income Statements, Factory Capacity of 90,000 Tons, South Nyanza Sugar Company*
(thousands of KSh, constant 1977 prices)

Item	Project year 1	Project year 9	Project year 10	Project year 11
Revenue				
Sale of sugar[a]	—	227,378	244,351	265,487
Sale of molasses[b]	—	9,194	9,880	10,734
Total revenue	—	236,572	254,231	276,221
Cash operating expenses				
Nucleus estate sugarcane production[c]	—	11,173	9,657	10,241
Outgrowers' sugarcane purchase[d]	—	72,296	80,532	85,404
Molasses—transport and excise tax[e]	—	5,412	5,815	6,318
Factory variable cost	—	15,133	16,263	17,670
Factory overhead	—	10,714	10,714	10,714
Total cost of goods sold	—	114,728	122,981	130,347
Gross income (profit)	—	121,844	131,250	145,847
Selling, general, and administrative expenses				
General administration	646	7,843	7,843	7,843
Training	37	267	267	267
Research	477	627	627	627
Management fee—nonvariable	1,121	1,210	1,210	1,210
Management fee—variable	—	3,890	4,225	4,886
Total selling, general, and administrative expenses	2,281	13,837	14,172	14,833
Funds from operations (operating income before depreciation)	(2,281)	108,007	117,078	131,041
Noncash operating expenses				
Depreciation				
Factory, general administration, research and housing assets	748	24,172	24,172	24,172
Nucleus estate and outgrowers' assets	2,124	15,628	18,160	20,125
Other	—	—	—	—
Total noncash operating expenses	2,872	39,800	42,332	44,297
Total operating expenses	5,153	168,365	179,485	189,477
Operating income (profit)	(5,153)	68,207	74,746	86,744
Nonoperating income and expenses				
Interest received	(—)	(4,245)	(4,770)	(5,048)
Interest paid	4,575	19,738	17,008	14,545
Duties and indirect taxes	—	—	—	—
Subsidies	(—)	(—)	(—)	(—)
Total nonoperating expenses	4,575	15,493	12,238	9,497
Income (profit) before income taxes	(9,728)	52,714	62,508	77,247
Income taxes	—	—	8,618	34,761
Net income (profit) after taxes	(9,728)	52,714	53,890	42,486

Source: Same as table 5-1 (annex 20, table 11).

a. Valued at KSh3,050 per ton.

b. Valued at KSh350 per ton f.o.b. Mombasa.

c. Represents total cost of production of sugarcane on the nucleus estate.

d. Value of sugarcane purchased from outgrowers at KSh155 per ton.

e. Includes excise tax of KSh6 per ton and transport charges of KSh10 per ton from factory to dockside in Mombasa.

and equipment at cost are shown at their original cost, and then the *accumulated depreciation* allowances are deducted. Land, by convention, is never depreciated. In the South Nyanza example, construction in progress is shown separately as a fixed asset. A third kind of asset, called simply *other assets*, is not needed in the South Nyanza balance sheet. This category would include investments in other companies or long-term securities; deferred expenses, such as start-up expenses for a new project, to be charged over several accounting periods; intangible assets such as patents and trademarks that have no physical existence but are of value to the enterprise; and miscellaneous additional assets peculiar to particular types of enterprises.

Liabilities are the claims against the assets of the enterprise that creditors hold—in other words, the outstanding debts of the enterprise. There are two principal kinds. *Current liabilities* comprise debts falling due within a year, such as *accounts payable, short-term loans*, and the *current portion* of *long-term loans* and *suppliers' credits* that must be paid within the coming accounting period. *Taxes payable* but not yet paid are also a current liability. *Long-term liabilities* are the debts that become payable after one year from the date of the balance sheet. They may consist of *medium-* and *long-term loans* and *suppliers' credits*.

Owners' *equity* consists of claims against the assets of the enterprise by its owners—in other words, what is left after all liabilities have been deducted from total assets. In the case of public sector enterprises, the owner is generally the government, although some public sector firms may have nongovernment shareholders. Owner's equity generally takes the form of *share capital* paid in by owners of the enterprise and *retained earnings* ("reserves" in British usage). Various other kinds of reserves may also appear under equity that do not fit precisely into the description of capital and retained earnings.

Income Statement

The income statement is a financial report that summarizes the revenues and expenses of an enterprise during the accounting period. It is thus a statement that shows the results of the operation of the enterprise during the period. Net income, or profit, is what is left after expenses incurred in production of the goods and services delivered have been deducted from the revenues earned on the sale of these goods and services. In other words, income (profit) = revenues − expenses. Thus, in the South Nyanza example in table 5-2, the net income is the sales revenue less all expenses.

Revenue in most processing enterprises will come from sales of goods and services—in the South Nyanza example, sugar and molasses. Sales are shown net of sales discounts, returned goods, and sales taxes.

The *cash operating expenses* list all the cash expenditures incurred to produce the output. Important among these are expenditures for labor (which in the South Nyanza example is included in factory variable cost) and for raw materials, in this case largely sugarcane purchased from outgrowers. Subtracting these direct costs incurred in the production of the goods sold from the revenue gives the *gross income* (or *gross profit*).

Selling, general, and administrative expenses are shown next. These include a number of overhead items—in the South Nyanza example, general administration, training, research, and the management fee to be paid the firm that will operate the sugar mill. Maintenance costs are often included as a separate entry in this category.

We now reach the *funds from operations*, also called the *operating income before depreciation*. This is the net benefit or cash flow of the enterprise that arises from operations. If the account is built on an incremental basis, it is the incremental net benefit from operations. (It is *not* the incremental net benefit or cash flow for the enterprise as a whole during each year over the life of the project, since we must deduct the investment costs that come from the sources-and-uses-of-funds statement discussed in the next section. This expense is shown as depreciation in the income statement. See the last section of this chapter, on financial rate of return.) Funds from operations are sometimes also called the internally generated funds. *Funds from operations* becomes the first element in the sources-and-uses-of-funds statement and is also the basis for transferring the net benefits of the enterprise to the summary project accounts from which the estimated economic return of the project is derived. Before this is done, however, any element in the revenues, cash operating expenses, and selling, general, and administrative expenses that is a direct transfer payment or that has an economic value different from its market price must be omitted or revalued along the lines given in chapter 7.

Next we list the *noncash operating expenses*, of which the primary element is *depreciation*. In accounting, depreciation refers to the process of allocating a portion of the original cost of a fixed asset to each accounting period so that the value is gradually used up, or written off, during the course of the useful life of the asset. Allowance may be made for the resale value of the fixed asset—its residual value—at the end of its useful life to the enterprise. The most common depreciation method is "straight-line depreciation," which allocates an equal portion of the value of the fixed asset to each accounting period; in contrast, various methods of accelerated depreciation allocate more of the depreciation to earlier accounting periods than to later. The principal *other* noncash operating expense is amortization, the gradual writing off of intangible assets such as royalties or patents.

Deducting the noncash operating expenses gives us *operating income* (or *operating profit*), also called the profit before interest and taxes.

Nonoperating income and expense are subtracted next. When an enterprise will receive interest payments, as is the case of the South Nyanza example, it is convenient to include *interest received* at this point, so that all interest transactions will appear at one point in the income statement. Interest received is thus shown as a "negative expense." In most enterprises, *interest paid* is among the most important nonoperating income and expense items. *Duties and indirect taxes* are also included among the nonoperating income and expenses unless they have been allowed for elsewhere. Duties, for instance, may appropriately be included among the expenses. In the South Nyanza example, duties on imported machinery were included in the purchase price of the machinery and thus were not shown separately under this entry. Indirect taxes also may not appear separately in income statements. In the South Nyanza example, we noted earlier that sales taxes were deducted before entering the sale revenues in accord with normal practice. In effect, the enterprise is simply acting on behalf of the government when it collects a sales tax, and the amount of the tax does not enter the income statement. In the South Nyanza example, the excise tax on molasses also was not shown separately but is properly included as part of the expenses. Among the indirect taxes that might be shown are franchise taxes and a value added tax—a tax levied as a proportion of the increased value generated at each stage in the processing and handling of a product up to the final sale. Finally appear *subsidies*. Again, subsidies may not appear at this point in the income statement. They may be incorporated elsewhere (for example, in the price that an enterprise pays for a subsidized input), or they may be shown as a revenue (as in the case of export incentive payments).

Thus we reach *income (profit) before income taxes*. Now, deducting the *income taxes*, we obtain the final entry, the *net income (profit) after taxes*. This is the return to the owners of the enterprise and is available either for distribution to them or for reinvestment in the enterprise.

Financial accounts must be linked to all other accounts. As the accountants put it, accounts must be "articulated." We noted that the *funds from operations* in the income statement becomes the first element in the sources-and-uses-of-funds statement. The income statement is also a bridge between successive balance sheets. The net income, after payment of dividends to shareholders, is transferred to the balance sheet as retained earnings and thereby increases the owners' equity. To trace this transaction, a reconciliation statement, such as a retained earnings statement, would be required to show any distribution of earnings as dividends before the retained earnings are added to the owners' equity in the balance sheet. In the South Nyanza example, it was assumed that all earnings would be retained by the enterprise throughout the sixteen years for which the projected accounts were prepared. Looking at years 9 and 10 reproduced in tables 5-1 and 5-2, we can see the articulation between the balance sheet and the income statement. The net income in year 10 given in the income statement in table 5-2 is KSh53,890 thousand. Adding this amount to the retained earnings at the end of year 9, shown in the projected balance sheets in table 5-1 to be − KSh43,355 thousand, gives a retained earnings in year 10 of KSh10,535 thousand (− 43,355 + 53,890 = 10,535). Table 5-3 shows projected retained earnings statements for the South Nyanza example. Reconciliation accounts

Table 5-3. *Retained Earnings Statements, Factory Capacity of 90,000 Tons, South Nyanza Sugar Company*
(thousands of KSh, constant 1977 prices)

	Project year			
Item	1	9	10	11
Net income	(9,728)	52,714	53,890	42,486
Dividends	—	—	—	—
Increase in retained earnings	(9,728)	52,714	53,890	42,486
Accumulated retained earnings	(9,728)	(43,355)	10,535	53,021

Source: Same as table 5-2.

are uncommon for government-owned operating entities that retain all earnings in the enterprise.

Sources-and-Uses-of-Funds Statement

The sources-and-uses-of-funds statement highlights the movements of investment funds over the life of the project. It is a vehicle for measuring the total flow of financial resources into and out of an enterprise during an accounting period and for projecting this total flow into the future. The sources-and-uses-of-funds statement is also called the sources-and-applications-of-funds statement, the funds statement, the statement of change in working capital, or sometimes simply the cash flow, since the flow of funds is reflected in the final analysis by changes in the cash position of an enterprise. This accounting definition of cash flow, however, differs from that used in project analysis to measure the return on the resources engaged in the project.

The most common *sources* of funds are outlined in the first part of table 5-4. The first of these is *funds from operations* (or the *operating income before depreciation*). When the accounts are laid out following the pattern given here, this can be taken directly from the income statement as illustrated in the South Nyanza example. Often, however, the funds from operations does not show as a separate item in a set of accounts and will have to be constructed by adding depreciation and other noncash charges back to the operating income.

To the funds from operations are added the *increase in equity*, the *long-term loans received*, and the *increase (decrease) in short-term loans*. In the South Nyanza example, equity and loans come from a wide variety of sources. The government of Kenya contributes part of the equity financing that, in turn, it is to obtain from the proceeds of a World Bank loan, and part of the equity comes from a private firm. Long-term loans come from a variety of international financing institutions and from suppliers' credits. The capital structure of the firm is such that it does not need short-term loans in the years we have chosen as illustrative examples, but in many agricultural processing enterprises short-term loans would be needed to enable the enterprise to carry inventories of raw materials purchased at harvest time and stocks of processed goods that will be sold during the year.

Interest received is the next source of funds; in the South Nyanza example, it comes from short-term loans made to outgrowers. The *increase (decrease) in accounts payable and other short-term liabilities (except current portion of long-term loans received)* follows. An enterprise might obtain part of its funds by increasing the amounts purchased on terms from its suppliers or by postponing payment to its suppliers. If it reduces the amount purchased on terms or the average time it takes to pay its suppliers from one year to the next, this would cause a decrease in accounts payable and a reduction of the funds available. Because we are looking, in general, at an expanding firm that will be increasing its accounts payable in the normal course of widening the scope of operations under the project, an increase in accounts payable will usually be found in the sources-and-uses-of-funds statement. When a decrease occurs, however, it is convenient to enter it as a "negative source" in the accounts rather than as an additional line among the uses of funds. In some agricultural projects, the processing enterprise may be expected to operate at a loss to increase the income of farmers. If so, the firm may expect direct *subsidies* to be one source of its funds.

Among the major *uses* of funds (second part of table 5-4) in the projected sources-and-uses-of-funds statements for a project with an expanding processing enterprise will likely be the *increase (decrease) in gross fixed assets*. This item shows the investment in fixed assets during each year; in the South Nyanza example, this is principally investment in new milling capacity. In other cases an enterprise may decrease fixed assets by selling them. If this transaction exceeds the purchase of fixed assets, the net result would most easily be shown as a "negative use" among the uses of funds rather than as a separate entry for the proceeds from the sales of fixed assets among the sources of funds.

A major item in the projected sources-and-uses-of-funds statements for an enterprise included in an agricultural project will most likely be *repayment of long-term loans*. (Recall that among the sources of funds shown is the increase or decrease in short-term loans. Since this is shown on a net basis, there is no need for a separate entry among the uses of funds for repayment of short-term loans.) Only the principal repayment is included under the repayment of long-term loans. *Interest payments on long-term loans* and *interest payments on short-term loans* are segregated and shown separately. (In the South Nyanza example, the analyst assumed that the repayment of the short-term loans, shown as a decrease in short-term loans among the sources of funds, would be made at the very beginning of the accounting period; hence, there is no short-term interest shown in the account for year 9.) An enterprise that has borrowed for expansion, such as the South Nyanza Sugar Company, may have to pay *loan commitment fees* for undisbursed amounts of loans that have been made to it.

The *increase (decrease) in inventories* shows the change in the inventory position of the enterprise. Because most projected accounts are for expanding enterprises, it is likely that this entry will reflect an increase in inventories; the entry is therefore included among the uses of funds. Sometimes, however, there may be a decrease in inventories. Rather than have an additional line under sources of funds, it is convenient to treat a reduction in inventory as a negative use. In the South Nyanza example, the major inventory is the standing cane crop on the nucleus

Table 5-4. *Sources-and-Uses-of-Funds Statements,*
Factory Capacity of 90,000 Tons,
South Nyanza Sugar Company
(thousands of KSh, constant 1977 prices)

Item	Project year			
	1	9	10	11
Sources				
Funds from operations (operating income before depreciation)	(2,281)	108,007	117,078	131,041
Increase in equity				
Government	54,150	—	—	—
Mehta Group	2,850	—	—	—
Total increase in equity	57,000	—	—	—
Long-term loans received				
World Bank	—	—	—	—
Suppliers' credit	32,700	—	—	—
European Investment Bank	33,400	—	—	—
Exim Bank	7,900	—	—	—
East African Development Bank	6,070	—	—	—
Total long-term loans received	80,070	—	—	—
Increase (decrease) in short-term loans	—	(19,000)	—	—
Total increase (decrease) in short-term loans	—	(19,000)	—	—
Interest received	—	4,245	4,770	5,048
Increase (decrease) in accounts payable and other short-term liabilities (except current portion of long-term loans received)	—	—	—	—
Subsidies	—	—	—	—
Total sources	134,789	93,252	121,848	136,089
Uses				
Increase (decrease) in gross fixed assets[a]	118,986	22,445	10,628	18,064
Repayment of long-term loans				
World Bank	—	6,563	6,563	6,563
Suppliers' credit	—	13,431	13,431	13,381
European Investment Bank	—	10,956	10,956	10,956
Exim Bank	—	—	—	—
East African Development Bank	—	2,846	2,846	2,846
Total repayment of long-term loans	—	33,796	33,796	33,746

Table 5-4 (*continued*)

Item	Project year 1	9	10	11
Interest payments on long-term loans				
World Bank	—	11,370	10,681	9,992
Suppliers' credit	—	3,482	2,411	1,607
European Investment Bank	2,004	3,946	3,289	2,632
Exim Bank	711	—	—	—
East African Development Bank	668	940	627	314
Interest payments on short-term loans	—	—	—	—
Total interest payments	3,383	19,738	17,008	14,545
Loan commitment fees				
World Bank	984	—	—	—
Exim Bank	69	—	—	—
East African Development Bank	139	—	—	—
Total loan commitment fees	1,192	—	—	—
Total debt service	4,575	53,534	50,804	48,291
Increase (decrease) in inventories				
Standing cane crop	3,428	(827)	(1,365)	(2,007)
Other inventories[b]	1,525	—	—	—
Total change in inventories	4,953	(827)	(1,365)	(2,007)
Increase (decrease) in accounts receivable	2,952	2,295	845	424
Increase (decrease) in other short-term assets except cash	—	—	—	—
Income taxes paid	—	—	8,618	34,761
Dividends paid	—	—	—	—
Adjustments for items not covered above	—	—	—	—
Total uses	131,466	77,447	69,530	99,533
Net funds flow				
Current surplus (deficit)	3,323	15,805	52,318	36,556
Opening cash balance	—	1,436	17,241	69,559
Cumulative surplus (deficit)	3,323	17,241	69,559	106,115

Source: Same as table 5-1 (annex 20, table 13).

a. Includes investment in the factory, agriculture, administration, housing, and company-related research.

b. Includes spare parts, tools, and operating materials.

plantation. As indicated in table 5-4, this inventory does decrease during years 9 through 11—thus it is shown as a negative entry in the account.

The *increase (decrease) in accounts receivable* appears next. If a firm is expanding, it will likely be extending credit to an increasing number of customers, and its accounts receivable will expand. But if it is able to reduce the average length between delivery and payment or be more restrictive in extending credit, its accounts receivable may decrease during the year and be shown as a negative use. The *increase (decrease) in other short-term assets except cash* would allow for changes in holdings of such short-term assets as notes, certificates of deposit, or treasury bills.

Income taxes paid are an obvious use of funds for an enterprise, and there may be *dividends paid* by the enterprise to its equity owners.

Finally, an entry for *adjustments for items not covered above* comprises those items that for various reasons do not fit well into one of the pattern categories. Any items of substance in this entry should be fully disclosed in footnotes to the accounts.

What remains is the *net funds flow*, of which the first element is the *current surplus (deficit)*. Adding the *opening cash balance* to the surplus or deficit gives the *cumulative surplus (deficit)*. If the projected accounts indicate a cumulative cash deficit—a deficiency of funds—then some arrangements will have to be made to sustain the enterprise during this period. It may be necessary to reduce planned dividends, arrange for additional loans or equity, or in some other way plan to provide the necessary funds.

Projecting the sources-and-uses-of-funds statements enables the analyst to be certain that the available financing for the enterprise will be sufficient to cover the investment program—including increases in inventories, other permanent working capital, and all cash expenditures for operations—and to cover obligations of interest and the principal repayment on all outstanding loans. Projecting the sources-and-uses-of-funds statements year by year makes it possible to check the timing of inflows from various sources to be certain that these inflows will be available as the need arises. Credit agencies can assess the total flow of funds from operations before debt service to determine how adequately the debt service is covered. Owners will be looking at the projected flow of funds after debt service to judge what their returns will be. For private investors, the funds generated after debt service and the projected dividends will be important elements in their decisions about whether to participate in the project.

Financial Ratios

From the projected financial statements for an enterprise, the financial analyst is able to calculate financial ratios that allow him to form a judgment about the efficiency of the enterprise, its return on key aggregates, and its creditworthiness. We will discuss several of the most significant of these ratios, but there are many others that financial analysts use and that are particularly appropriate for specific kinds of enterprises. For each ratio we will discuss, the means of computation is summarized in table 5-5. Two examples of the application of the ratios are given in the table, based on years 10 and 11 of the South Nyanza Sugar Company accounts reproduced in tables 5-1, 5-2, and 5-4.

In general, it is not possible to give ranges within which financial ratios should fall. Instead, the analyst will have to form a judgment about whether the ratio indicates an acceptable situation for the kind of enterprise that is the subject of the projected accounts. For more information about the use of financial ratios, the project analyst may consult a standard accounting text or Upper (1979), from which this discussion draws heavily.

The ratios given here have all been computed using the figures at the end of each year. This weights the analysis toward the last months of operations; as long as clarity and consistency are maintained, this usually poses no problem. If the activities of an enterprise are highly seasonal, as is often the case in agricultural projects, calculating the ratios on a year-end basis could easily be misleading. In that instance, the analyst may want to examine the pattern of seasonal fluctuations within the accounting period and make a judgment about whether the seasonal variation would affect his conclusions about the efficiency, return, or creditworthiness of the proposed enterprise.

Efficiency ratios

The first group of ratios (first part of table 5-5) enables the analyst to form a judgment about the efficiency of the proposed enterprise. They provide measurements of asset use and expense control.

Inventory turnover measures the number of times that an enterprise turns over its stock each year and indicates the amount of inventory required to support a given level of sales. The ratio can be computed in several ways. In the form given here, the cost of goods sold is divided by the inventory. In the South Nyanza example in table 5-5, for year 10 this amounts to 3.94 times a year. In agricultural processing industries, this ratio may be low compared with that of many manufacturing enterprises; this lower ratio reflects the highly seasonal nature of agricultural processing. The inventory turnover can also relate to the average length of time a firm keeps its inventory on hand. In the South Nyanza example, the firm has about ninety-three days of inventory on hand at the end of year 10. We determine this by dividing the days in the year by the inventory turnover ratio ($365 \div 3.94 = 93$). We could also state this in months—the firm has about three months of inventory on hand—by dividing the months of the year by the inventory turnover ratio ($12 \div 3.94 = 3$). A low turnover ratio may mean that a company with large stocks on hand may find it difficult to sell its product, and this may be an indicator that the management is not able to control its inventory effectively. A low turnover ratio may, however, also mean that large stocks must be held to ensure that production schedules are met. A low ratio means a sizeable amount of funds are tied up. A high turnover ratio may mean that the enterprise is able to recover its inventory investment rapidly and that there is a good demand for its products. On the one hand, when the ratio is much higher than the industry average, it may mean that the enterprise is very efficient in managing its inventories. On the other hand, it may mean that the enterprise is starved of funds and cannot afford to maintain a sufficient inventory; as a result, it may be forced to forgo sales opportunities.

The *operating ratio* is obtained by dividing the operating expenses by

Table 5-5. *Financial Ratios, Factory Capacity of 90,000 Tons, South Nyanza Sugar Company*

Ratio	Project year	
	10	11
Efficiency ratios		
Inventory turnover = $\dfrac{\text{Cost of goods sold}}{\text{Inventory}}$	$\dfrac{122,981}{24,181 + 7,000} = 3.94$	$\dfrac{130,347}{22,174 + 7,000} = 4.47$
Operating ratio (percent) = $\dfrac{\text{Operating expenses}}{\text{Revenue}}$	$\dfrac{179,485}{254,231} \times 100 = 71$	$\dfrac{189,477}{276,221} \times 100 = 69$
Income ratios		
Return on sales (percent) = $\dfrac{\text{Net income}}{\text{Revenue}}$	$\dfrac{53,890}{254,231} \times 100 = 21$	$\dfrac{42,486}{276,221} \times 100 = 15$
Return on equity (percent) = $\dfrac{\text{Net income}}{\text{Equity}}$	$\dfrac{53,890}{207,035} \times 100 = 26$	$\dfrac{42,486}{249,521} \times 100 = 17$
Return on assets (percent) = $\dfrac{\text{Operating income}}{\text{Assets}}$	$\dfrac{74,746}{379,321} \times 100 = 20$	$\dfrac{86,744}{388,061} \times 100 = 22$

Creditworthiness ratios

Current ratio =

$$\frac{\text{Current assets}}{\text{Current liabilities}} \qquad \frac{148,787}{33,746} = 4.41 \qquad \frac{183,879}{20,363} = 9.03$$

Debt-equity ratio =

$$\frac{\text{Long-term liabilities}}{\text{Long-term liabilities} + \text{equity}} \qquad \frac{138,540}{138,540 + 207,035} = 0.40 \qquad \frac{118,177}{118,177 + 249,521} = 0.32$$

and

$$\frac{\text{Equity}}{\text{Long-term liabilities} + \text{equity}} \qquad \frac{207,035}{138,540 + 207,035} = 0.60 \qquad \frac{249,521}{118,177 + 249,521} = 0.68$$

therefore

Debt-equity ratio = 40:60 \qquad 32:68

Debt service coverage ratio =

$$\frac{\text{Net income} + \text{depreciation} + \text{interest paid}}{\text{Interest paid} + \text{repayment of long-term loans}} \qquad \frac{53,890 + 24,172 + 18,160 + 17,008}{17,008 + 33,796} = 2.23 \qquad \frac{42,486 + 24,172 + 20,125 + 14,545}{14,545 + 33,746} = 2.10$$

Source: Tables 5-1, 5-2, and 5-4.

the revenue. In the South Nyanza example, for year 10 the operating ratio is 71 percent. The operating ratio is an indicator of the ability of the management to control operating costs, including administrative expenses. This ratio is most useful when operations of the same enterprise are compared year by year or when the enterprise is compared with similar industries. If the ratio is increasing, it may mean that the cost of raw materials is increasing, that the management is having problems controlling labor costs, that there is waste in the production process, or, when sales decline, that expenses have not been trimmed proportionately. It may also mean that there is substantial competition and that it is necessary to reduce prices. If there is uncertainty about whether the increase in the ratio is due to increasing costs or decreasing sales prices, the answer can usually be found by taking the operating expenses and dividing that by the company sales volume on a unit basis (for instance, the number of tons of refined sugar sold in the South Nyanza example). In general, the larger the capital investment is relative to sales volume, the lower will be the operating ratio. If a company has made a large investment, it must be able to recover it with a high cash flow, which can only be accomplished generally through a low operating ratio. If an enterprise has a high operating ratio, say in the neighborhood of 90 percent, it may have difficulty making an adequate return. If it is abnormally low, say 50 percent, then some costs have likely been omitted or underestimated.

Income ratios

The long-term financial viability of an enterprise depends on the funds it can generate for reinvestment and growth and on its ability to provide a satisfactory return on investment. We will look at three ratios (second part of table 5-5) that can be used to judge net income or profitability—*return on sales*, *return on equity*, and *return on assets*. Because of their importance in project analysis and because they are somewhat more difficult to calculate, we will defer to the next section consideration of three other income measures—the rate of return on all resources engaged, the rate of return on equity before income taxes, and the rate of return on equity after taxes.

Income ratios are calculated on a year-to-year basis and may be noted in the projected statements for an enterprise. That will provide some idea of the changing income ratios over the life of the project. If a company is granted a tax holiday for the first years of its operations, it is necessary to forecast its accounts through the end of the tax holiday period to determine the full effect of taxes on the company.

The return on sales shows how large an operating margin the enterprise has on its sales. This is determined by dividing the net income by the revenue. In the South Nyanza example, the return on sales in year 10 is 21 percent. The lower the return on sales—hence, the operating margin—the greater the sales that must be made to make an adequate return on investment. The ratio is most useful when comparing companies in the same sector or industry or when analyzing the results of past operations and comparing projections for future expansions. Comparisons among industries may have little meaning because of the widely varying structure of different industries.

One of the most important ratios is the return on equity. It is obtained by dividing the net income after taxes by the equity. In the South Nyanza example, for year 10 this is 26 percent. This ratio is frequently used because it is one of the main criteria by which owners are guided in their investment decisions. It can also be used to weigh incentives for individual owners if the enterprise is to be in the private sector.

The earning power of the assets of an enterprise is vital to its success. A principal means of judging this is to determine the return on assets, which is the operating income divided by the assets. In the South Nyanza example for year 10, this is 20 percent. The return on assets is the financial ratio that comes closest to the rate of return on all resources engaged (for more detail, see the next section). A crude rule of thumb is that, once the enterprise is operating at normal capacity, the return on assets should exceed the cost of capital in the society as measured by, say, the bank lending rate to industries—provided that there is no interest subsidy. Public sector enterprises usually should also be able to realize a return of this order, since if they do not, it is evidence that public funds would be better employed in other enterprises.

Creditworthiness ratios

The purpose of creditworthiness ratios (final part of table 5-5) is to enable a judgment about the degree of financial risk inherent in the enterprise before undertaking a project. They are also a basis for the project analyst to estimate what financing an enterprise will need and what will be suitable terms. Some firms, especially those in the private sector, attempt to finance their projects with as much debt as possible so they may realize maximum return on their own equity contribution. This can be risky, especially in an unstable industry or in an economy subject to substantial business cycles. An enterprise should be financed in such a way that it is able to survive adverse circumstances without emergency measures.

The *current ratio* is the current assets divided by the current liabilities. In the South Nyanza example, for year 10 the ratio is 4.41. From the standpoint of the credit agency, the current ratio is an indication of the margin that the enterprise has for its current assets to shrink in value before it faces difficulty in meeting its current obligations. In the South Nyanza example, in year 10—even if the current assets are worth only one-fourth the value given in the accounts—the sugar mill could still pay its creditors from these assets.

A rule of thumb sometimes applied to the current ratio is that it should be around 2. As with all rules of thumb, this figure should be used with caution. If the company has a rapid inventory turnover and can easily collect its receivables, the current ratio can be lower. If the ratio drops to near 1, then the enterprise will be in a potentially unstable position. If the ratio is low, it may mean that the enterprise is undercapitalized, and consideration will have to be given to providing more capital, either through increased equity or more long-term debt. Faced with a low current ratio, an enterprise will have to exist on a day-to-day basis, and thus it may have to adopt uneconomic practices. Its products may have to be sold at lower prices to receive payment in cash, or it may lose sales to competitors that can offer better credit terms. It may not be able to carry sufficient inventories to meet its sales needs. Inventories of raw material may be so low that its production efficiency is impaired. It may have to buy from importers in high-cost, small lots instead of buying large, low-priced shipments of inputs direct from overseas suppliers, and it may be forced to buy on credit instead of being able to take advantage of cash discounts. With a low current ratio, an enterprise may be forced to defer preventive maintenance, and this drives up costs later.

An important financial ratio for credit agencies is the *debt-equity ratio*. The amount of equity in an enterprise can be described as a "cushion" by which a company can absorb initial losses or weather bad times. Because debt carries a fixed rate of interest and fixed repayment of principal, too much debt may saddle a company with obligations it cannot meet when conditions are unfavorable. (A better measure of the cushion is the *debt service coverage ratio*, discussed below.)

The debt-equity ratio is calculated by dividing long-term liabilities by the sum of long-term liabilities plus equity to obtain the proportion that long-term liabilities are to total debt and equity, and then by dividing equity by the sum of the long-term liabilities plus equity to obtain the proportion that equity is of the total debt and equity. These are then compared in the form of a ratio. In the case of the South Nyanza example, for year 10 the long-term liabilities divided by the sum of the long-term liabilities plus the equity is 0.40. The equity divided by the sum of the long-term liabilities plus equity is 0.60. The debt-equity ratio, therefore, is 40 to 60. This may be interpreted as saying that, of the total capitalization in the enterprise, 40 percent is debt and 60 percent is equity. There is no good rule of thumb for the debt-equity ratio. In newly established enterprises, equity ideally should exceed the debt, but in many developing countries equity capital may be scarce, and such a conservative rule may not be sensible given the national objectives. If the enterprise is in the public sector, with a high proportion of the debt held by public sector agencies, the debt-equity ratio may lose some of its importance because of the presumption that, if the company falls on hard times, it will be possible to renegotiate some portion of the debt held by public agencies. In agricultural projects, enterprises are likely to need a strong equity base because they process or sell commodities that may sharply fluctuate in price and that are subject to adverse weather conditions or a fall in crop or livestock production.

The most comprehensive ratio of creditworthiness is the *debt service coverage ratio*. This is the net income plus depreciation plus interest paid divided by interest paid plus repayment of long-term loans. In the case of the South Nyanza example, for year 10 the debt service coverage ratio is 2.23.

The debt service coverage ratio could also be calculated on a before-tax basis, in which case it is simply the funds from operations divided by the interest plus repayment of long-term loans. In the case of the South Nyanza example, for year 10 (not shown in table 5-5) this would be 2.30 [117,078 ÷ (17,008 + 33,796) = 2.30]. Financial analysts who use the after-tax basis argue that taxation is a routine and unavoidable aspect of doing business. But analysts who prefer the before-tax basis argue that debt service coverage should be seen as the ability of funds from operations to satisfy debt obligations before such tax shields as depreciation and other noncash charges are applied to reduce taxable profits. The viewpoint of the analyst will be affected by whether the company is in the public or private sector.

Again, it is hard to give a rule of thumb for the debt service coverage ratio. One way of looking at it is that, in the case of the South Nyanza Sugar Company in year 10, the net income plus depreciation plus interest paid could drop by half and the enterprise could still meet its debt obligations. The analyst would have to look at each of the elements making up the ratio and form a judgment about how likely it is that any element could vary from the projected amount. A declining trend in the debt service coverage ratio in a projected account might indicate overly ambitious expansion. A persistently low debt service coverage ratio might indicate that consideration should be given to changing the credit terms to lengthen the repayment period.

The debt service coverage ratio interpreted alone can be misleading. There are many requirements that a successful enterprise must satisfy in addition to simply covering its debt service obligations. A full analysis of the sources and uses of funds for the enterprise is needed. The true buffer for debt service is only the pool of funds remaining after meeting all requirements for maintenance and improvement of current operations and orderly expansion.

Financial Rate of Return

A useful financial measure that is very important in project analysis is the financial rate of return. We will discuss three variations that differ only in the standpoint from which the calculations are made—the financial rate of return to all resources engaged, the financial rate of return to equity, and the financial rate of return to equity after taxes.

Calculations of rates of return are based on an incremental net benefit flow. This is the "cash flow" that is meant by references to discounted cash flow measures of project worth such as the net present worth, the internal rate of return, or the net benefit-investment ratio (all are discussed in detail in chapters 9 and 10). In this section we will discuss only derivation of the incremental net benefit; the discussion of discounting and of the measures based on incremental net benefit flows will be found in chapter 9.

In rate of return calculations we want to determine the actual cash inflows and outflows of the project each year and incorporate them in the incremental net benefit. Noncash receipts and expenditures are omitted (except for items in kind such as those we discussed in chapter 4 in connection with the farm budgets). Thus, the year an investment is made it reduces the net benefit for that year; when a revenue is realized, it too is reflected in the same year it is received. Because we are preparing the projected accounts over the life of the project, it is unnecessary to include depreciation (which is the major noncash expenditure in most accounts) to allow on an annual basis for the capital value consumed during the year.

From the projected income statements and sources-and-uses-of-funds statements for an enterprise as we have laid them out, we can determine the incremental net benefit streams we need to calculate the financial rate of return. The general format is given in table 5-6 and is illustrated by the South Nyanza Sugar Project accounts examined in tables 5-2 and 5-4. All the relevant entries are included in table 5-6 for illustrative purposes, even if the South Nyanza example did not use a particular entry. The entries appear in the order they are found when consulting

Table 5-6. *Derivation of Incremental Net Benefit,*
Factory Capacity of 90,000 Tons,
South Nyanza Sugar Company
(thousands of KSh, constant 1977 prices)

Item	Without project	Project year			
		1	*9*	*10*	*11*
Inflow					
Revenue	—	—	236,572	254,231	276,221
Subsidies	—	—	—	—	—
Total inflow	—	—	236,572	254,231	276,221
Outflow					
Cash operating expenses	—	—	114,728	122,981	130,347
Selling, general, and administrative expenses	—	2,281	13,837	14,172	14,833
[Funds from operations]	—	[(2,281)	108,007	117,078	131,041]
Duties and indirect taxes	—	—	—	—	—
Increase (decrease) in gross fixed assets	—	118,986	22,445	10,628	18,064
Increase (decrease) in inventories	—	4,953	(827)	(1,365)	(2,007)
Total outflow	—	126,220	150,183	146,416	161,237
Net benefit before financing					
Total	—	(126,220)	86,389	107,815	114,984
Incremental	—	(126,220)	86,389	107,815	114,984

Table 5-6 (*continued*)

Item	Without project	Project year			
		1	*9*	*10*	*11*
Financing					
Long-term loans received	—	80,070	—	—	—
Increase (decrease) in short-term loans	—	—	(19,000)	—	—
Interest received	—	—	4,245	4,770	5,048
Increase (decrease) in accounts payable and other short-term liabilities	—	—	—	—	—
Repayment of long-term loans	—	—	(33,796)	(33,796)	(33,746)
Interest payments	—	(3,383)	(19,738)	(17,008)	(14,545)
Loan commitment fees	—	(1,192)	—	—	—
Decrease (increase) in accounts receivable	—	(2,952)	(2,295)	(845)	(424)
Decrease (increase) in other short-term assets except cash	—	—	—	—	—
Net financing	—	72,543	(70,584)	(46,879)	(43,667)
Net benefit after financing					
Total	—	(53,677)	15,805	60,936	71,317
Incremental	—	(53,677)	15,805	60,936	71,317
Income taxation					
Income taxes paid	—	—	—	8,618	34,761
Net benefit after financing and taxes					
Total	—	(53,677)	15,805	52,318	36,556
Incremental	—	(53,677)	15,805	52,318	36,556

Financial rate of return to all resources engaged = 14 percent[a]
Financial rate of return to equity before income taxes = 16 percent[b]
Financial rate of return to equity after taxes = 13 percent[c]

Source: Tables 5-2 and 5-4.

a. Calculated from the incremental net benefit before financing. For details about the methodology of the computation, see chapter 9.

b. Calculated from the incremental net benefit after financing.

c. Calculated from the incremental net benefit after financing and taxes.

first the income statements and then the sources-and-uses-of-funds statements. Only the rate of return is usually reported. Were the table itself to be used in a project report, it might be desirable to group the entries so that related items are not separated.

The first financial rate of return to be determined is the *financial rate of return to all resources engaged*, which is a measurement of the financial viability of an enterprise. It is based on the *incremental net benefit before financing*. In the South Nyanza example, the rate of return to all resources engaged, assuming a thirty-year life for the project, is 14 percent. When all the elements that enter into the derivation of the incremental net benefit before financing are revalued to reflect economic values (as discussed in chapter 7) and any transfer payments are taken out, the incremental net benefit before financing becomes the basis for aggregating the net economic benefit from the enterprise and carrying it into the economic accounts for the project.

To obtain the incremental net benefit before financing, we begin with the *revenue* and direct *subsidies* received; these are taken from the income statements, which total to give the *total inflow*. The first two entries among the outflows are the *cash operating expenses* and the *selling, general, and administrative expenses*, also taken from the income statements. (At this point, if there were no direct subsidies, we would have the *funds from operations*; an alternative calculation of financial rates of return would therefore be to begin with the funds from operations, add any direct subsidies, and deduct any of the other elements of the outflow that are relevant.) Continuing with the outflow entries, we add *duties and indirect taxes* as shown in the income statements and add or subtract, as appropriate, the *increase (decrease) in gross fixed assets* and the *increase (decrease) in inventories* as shown in the sources-and-uses-of-funds statements. The result is the *total outflow*. Subtracting the total outflow from the total inflow provides the *total net benefit before financing*. Subtracting what would be the net benefit without the project (which, in the South Nyanza example, is nothing), we now reach the incremental net benefit before financing.

The *financial rate of return to equity before income taxes* will be an important consideration to any potential private investors. It is also of concern if the enterprise is to be a financially responsible public sector enterprise that must demonstrate the good use it makes of resources put at its disposal. The return to equity before income taxes will help the project analyst judge the attractiveness of the proposed enterprise to potential investors and to determine if the financing plan will give rise to undue windfall profits. It may also help in deciding what special tax holiday or other exemption may be justified. For the South Nyanza example, the return on equity before income taxes is 16 percent. To determine the return to equity before income taxes, we need to calculate the *incremental net benefit after financing*, and to reach this we add or subtract the financing elements shown in the sources-and-uses-of-funds statements, indicating the sign in the account as we proceed. Note the inclusion of *accounts payable* and *accounts receivable* as part of the financing. Because a decrease in accounts receivable increases the funds available to the enterprise, it is decreases that are added to obtain the net financing. The heading on these entries has been reversed from that in the sources-and-uses-of-funds statements to indicate that decreases are to be added and increases subtracted. Finding the algebraic total gives the *net financing*, and subtracting that from the net benefit before financing gives the *total net benefit after financing*. Subtracting the without-project net benefit after financing (in this case, nothing), we reach the incremental net benefit after financing.

Finally, we determine the *financial rate of return to equity after taxes*, which is based on the *incremental net benefit after financing and taxes*. For the South Nyanza example, it is 13 percent. To determine the incremental net benefit after financing and taxes, we deduct income taxes from the net benefit after financing and subtract the without-project amount (in this case, nothing). This is the flow that will accrue to the equity owners after the enterprise has met its tax obligation. It is, of course, this flow that is of most concern to potential investors, and so the rate of return to equity after taxes is an important measure on which to base judgments about the incentives to invest in an enterprise.

6

Analyzing Project Effects on Government Receipts and Expenditures

IMPLEMENTING AN AGRICULTURAL PROJECT has obvious implications for government receipts and expenditures. The amount and timing of additional government receipts generated by a project and the effect of the project on government expenditures should be traced by the analyst. This will permit the government to plan for the capital investment in the project and to ensure that sufficient government funds will be available to meet the recurrent cost of the project. By tracing the foreign exchange flow generated by the project, the analyst can estimate the effect of the project on the balance of payments. The proportion of the cost and the proportion of the new benefit to be recovered by the government from the project beneficiaries should be estimated. It may be desirable, too, to determine how the cost of the project could equitably be allocated among the various groups that will benefit from it.

The primary issue analysis of government receipts and expenditures addresses is whether the project will generate sufficient funds to reimburse the government for the resources expended on the project. The analysis should treat the government as a distinct financial entity and should focus on inflows and outflows to and from governmental budgetary and extrabudgetary accounts to anticipate the amount and timing of project needs from government sources. Such an analysis permits

---

Facing page: Preparing land for swamp rice in Senegal.

careful consideration of the implications a project has for government finance to meet not only the initial investment needs of the project but also its recurrent cost. Too often inadequate attention is paid to recurrent cost, and then budgetary stringencies starve a project for funds—greatly reducing its efficiency, leading to a waste of resources, and dashing the expectations of farmers and others who participate.

It is common in agricultural projects that user charges or benefit taxes assessed on the project beneficiaries are insufficient both to recover the capital investment in the project and to pay all the operation and mainte- nance costs of the project. This might be the case in an irrigation project, for example, in which water charges are less than the amount the govern- ment incurs for capital repayment and operating the system or in which a program to increase production makes no charge for the services of agricultural extension agents. Sometimes other revenues arising from the project will be sufficient to reimburse the government for its costs. Such might be the case if the project increased agricultural production that is destined for export and is subject to an export tax. In many instances, however, not enough of the benefit from the project will be captured through charges or by the workings of the fiscal system to reimburse the government fully. In these instances, the difference will have to come from taxes levied elsewhere in the economy or through inflation. Whether this is to be the practice or not is a policy decision; one consideration may be that poor farmers are entitled to some income transfer through an agricultural project. The point of the analysis is not to say that the project beneficiaries must pay enough to cover all the costs of the project, both capital and recurrent. It is to say that the fiscal effects of the project need to be traced so that a conscious decision can be made about reimbursement of cost incurred by the government.

Because of problems associated with budgetary stringencies, in many projects in which not all the costs are to be recovered from charges levied on project beneficiaries, the beneficiaries may still be charged enough to pay the recurrent cost of the project. This frees the project from depen- dence on year-to-year budget appropriations that may be subject to sudden cuts and decrease the efficiency of project implementation.

The importance of anticipating future recurrent expenditure goes much beyond the individual project analysis, of course. Any one proj- ect—unless it is very large relative to the government budget—would not impose a serious burden for recurrent expenditure. All development investments together, however, may well lead to significant recurrent government expenditure. As a general rule of thumb, in developing countries capital expenditures tend to give rise to between 10 and 15 percent of their value in recurrent costs. Moreover, as the nature of development programs in many developing countries has tended to shift more and more toward projects that do not generate revenues sufficient to reimburse the government for recurrent cost, these expenditures have tended to grow rapidly. One result has been a persistent tendency to underestimate the burden of recurrent cost.

The elements of the flows that affect government receipts and expenditures vary from project to project, and some may not always be obvious. They can, however, conveniently be cast in the form of a government cash flow account valued at market prices. Inflows will include user charges levied on project beneficiaries, new tax revenues generated as a result of the project investment, debt service for loans made to project participants, the surplus or profit made on sales of the project or on services provided, and receipts from foreign loans made to help finance the project. Expenditures will include the initial capital expenditure on the project, including direct expenditure on such items as dams and canals; loans to project participants; equity positions taken in a processing industry; recurrent costs of the project in whatever guise they occur, whether operation and maintenance, general administration, or some other form; and debt service, including commitment fees on any foreign loans received to support the project. The analysis includes among the government expenditures related costs needed to make the project effective (such as the costs of new roads or other infrastructure facilities) because, although these may not be the responsibility of the project management, they are costs incurred for the project and would appear in the project accounts when they are aggregated as discussed in chapter 8.

Many agricultural projects will have an effect on the balance of payments, so it may be desirable to do a separate analysis of the project's foreign exchange effects in a foreign exchange flow account.

Analysis of project effects on government receipts and expenditures can be illustrated by an example drawn from the South Nyanza Sugar Project, the same project used in the last chapter to illustrate the financial analysis of processing industries. As before, the general headings that might be expected to appear in most analyses of this kind will appear in *italic* type in the text.

Government Cash Flow

The government cash flow account for the South Nyanza Sugar Project is excerpted in table 6-1.

There is a problem about whether to make government cash flow projections in constant or current terms. For financial planning by the treasury and other government agencies, a current projection is much preferred, even though this involves projecting the inflation rate both domestically and worldwide. [A projection of worldwide inflation for capital goods is available in *Price Prospects for Major Primary Commodities* (World Bank 1982*a*).] But projecting inflation is difficult at best, and when done for more than just a few years it is of very little usefulness. In the South Nyanza project, therefore, the analyst chose a useful compromise: he projected the government cash flow in current terms for the five years of the investment phase during which the sugar factory was to be built. Then, from year 6 onward, he projected the cash flow in constant

Table 6-1. *Government Cash Flow,*
South Nyanza Sugar Project, Kenya
(thousands of KSh)

	Project year				
Item	1	2	6	7	16
Inflow					
Loan receipt[a]					
World Bank	19,480	35,280	—	—	—
African Development Bank	3,540	13,710	—	—	—
Total loan receipt	23,020	48,990	—	—	—
Taxes					
Sugar excise[b]	—	—	63,771	79,043	127,260
Molasses excise[b]	—	—	142	176	277
SNSC income[c]	—	—	—	—	54,853
Other duties and taxes[d]	15,462	27,625	15,675	13,775	17,069
Debt service receipt					
Interest payment	—	270	13,437	12,748	6,547
Loan commitment fee	984	965	—	—	—
Repayment of principal	—	—	6,563	6,563	6,563
Dividends[e]	—	—	—	—	63,691
Total inflow	39,466	77,850	99,588	112,305	276,260
Outflow					
Equity in SNSC	54,150	71,250	—	—	—
Loans to SNSC[f]	—	2,570	—	—	—
Financing of Kenya Sugar Authority and training[g]	1,828	5,555	5,563	5,726	5,451
Grant to National Sugar Research Institute[h]	297	3,393	2,371	2,470	2,371
Road construction and maintenance[i]	4,430	17,294	4,996	4,996	4,996
Subtotal	60,705	100,062	12,930	13,192	12,818
Debt service payment					
Interest					
World Bank	1,751	4,930	49,750	48,505	37,300
African Development Bank	283	1,380	3,287	2,922	—
Loan commitment fee					
World Bank	1,411	1,145	—	—	—
African Development Bank	316	213	—	—	—
Repayment of principal					
World Bank	—	—	13,833	13,833	13,833
African Development Bank	—	—	4,565	4,565	—
Total debt service payment	3,761	7,668	71,435	69,825	51,133
Total outflow	64,466	107,730	84,365	83,017	63,951
Net cash flow					
Current surplus (deficit)	(25,000)	(29,880)	15,223	29,288	212,309
Cumulative surplus (deficit)	(25,000)	(54,880)	(13,582)	15,706	1,313,167

KSh Kenyan shillings.

Note: In current prices for years 1 through 5 (1977–81); thereafter, in year-5 (1981) constant prices. Parentheses indicate negative numbers.

Source: Adapted from World Bank, "Kenya: Appraisal of the South Nyanza Sugar Project," 1418-KE (Washington, D.C., 1977; restricted circulation), annex 20, table 17.

a. The disbursement of the German and Indian suppliers' credit and loans from the European Investment Bank, East African Development Bank, and the U.S. Export-Import (Exim) Bank have been assumed to be directly to the South Nyanza Sugar Company (SNSC) and not through the government.

b. The excise tax per ton is in constant 1976 prices and is assumed at KSh1,000 for sugar and KSh6 for molasses for years 1 through 5, adjusted to current terms by using a factor of terms at year-5 prices. This avoided making a long-term projection of inflation. (Note that this would not be a suitable format if the cash flow were to be discounted as discussed in chapter 9.) The analyst also chose to include in his cash flow table a total column after year 5 for the first five years (not reproduced in the excerpt in table 6-1). The government cash flow is projected for sixteen years, long enough to trace the effect of all the financial transactions except the repayment of the World Bank loan.

The government cash flow account is divided into cash *inflow* and cash *outflow*. The first inflow is the *loan receipt* obtained from abroad to support the project. In the case of the South Nyanza project, the government of Kenya received loans from the World Bank and the African Development Bank for the project. Other loans were made by suppliers and by other international lending agencies that dealt directly with the South Nyanza Sugar Company. The flows from these loan transactions, since they did not go through the government, do not show in the government cash flow. Next in the table are the *taxes*. The South Nyanza project is expected to generate new tax revenues from the sugar excise tax collected at the factory gate and a similar excise tax on molasses; company income tax; and other taxes that include import duties on materials, machinery, vehicles and equipment, excise duty on capital and current inputs, and income taxes on staff salaries. Next comes the *debt service receipt* from the South Nyanza Sugar Company for the loan it has received from the government. The debt service is broken down into the *interest payment, loan commitment fee*, and *repayment of principal*. Finally, there is the transfer of company profit that is made to the government in lieu of *dividends*. Some proportion of this profit would by agreement customarily be reinvested in company expansion. Had there been any *user charges*, these, too, would have been included in the cash inflow.

The first entry in the cash outflow is the *equity* participation the government contributed to the South Nyanza Sugar Company, followed by *loans* to the company. These, in effect, constitute the capital cost contributed from the government budget to the company operation. Two other outflows are the financing for the Kenya Sugar Authority for training not directly administered by the company, including overseas university education in business management and sugar technology and participation in international symposia and conventions, and a grant to the

---

32.2 percent in year 4 (1980) and 41.4 percent in year 5 (1981) and thereafter.

c. Values are in constant 1976 prices adjusted by 41.4 percent to year-5 (1981) constant prices.

d. Includes import duties on materials, machinery, vehicles, and equipment; excise taxes on capital and current input; and income tax on staff salaries. The values are in constant 1976 prices adjusted by 41.4 percent to year-5 (1981) constant prices.

e. It is assumed that SNSC dividends to the government will be 95 percent of SNSC net profits after tax, expressed in year-5 (1981) constant prices.

f. The on-lending margin to SNSC has been assumed to be 1.5 percent.

g. Includes the incremental cost to the Kenya Sugar Authority arising from the project and the cost of training and conference participation not included in the SNSC accounts.

h. Incremental cost to the National Sugar Research Institute arising from the project.

i. Includes the cost of roads needed for the project not included in SNSC nucleus estate.

National Sugar Research Institute to reimburse it for incremental expenses arising from the project. This is followed by road construction that is a part of the project cost to be paid directly by the government and not channeled through the company.

Then comes the *debt service payment* the government must make as a result of the project. This includes *interest, loan commitment fee,* and *repayment of principal* to the World Bank and the African Development Bank.

The difference between the cash inflow and the cash outflow gives the cash *current surplus (deficit)*, which in the South Nyanza case is negative through project year 3 and positive thereafter. The *cumulative surplus (deficit)* indicates how long it will be before the government recovers its net expenditure on the project in undiscounted terms—six years in the South Nyanza example. In other projects, of course, both the current and the cumulative surplus (deficit) might remain negative throughout the life of the project.

Foreign Exchange Flow

The foreign exchange flow generated by the South Nyanza project is calculated in table 6-2.

Table 6-2. *Foreign Exchange Flow, South Nyanza Sugar Project*
(thousands of KSh)

Item	Project year				
	1	*2*	*6*	*7*	*16*
	Inflow				
Loan receipt					
Suppliers' credit—Germany	17,200	27,400	—	—	—
Suppliers' credit—India	15,500	24,750	—	—	—
World Bank	19,480	35,280	—	—	—
European Investment Bank	33,400	53,200	—	—	—
African Development Bank	3,540	13,710	—	—	—
East African Development Bank	6,070	9,670	—	—	—
Exim Bank	7,900	10,380	—	—	—
Total loan receipt	103,090	174,390	—	—	—
Foreign exchange value of sugar production[a]	—	—	248,501	308,009	495,000
Export of molasses[b]	—	—	8,261	10,235	16,114
Total inflow	103,090	174,390	256,762	318,244	511,114
	Outflow				
Foreign exchange component of:					
Agriculture	15,674	15,096	30,304	51,132	45,522
Sugar factory	68,832	107,162	51,982	14,275	19,325
General management and administration	2,251	2,814	5,442	5,311	5,442
Road construction and maintenance	3,532	13,676	3,612	3,612	3,612
Housing and social amenities	4,223	4,735	—	—	—
Research	655	2,470	1,622	2,469	1,622
Training	120	294	648	648	648

Table 6-2 (*continued*)

Item	Project year				
	1	2	6	7	16
Kenya Sugar Authority	617	1,825	1,634	1,814	1,572
Management fee	—	—	2,410	3,240	6,940
Total foreign exchange component	95,904	148,072	97,654	82,501	84,683
Debt service payment					
Interest					
Suppliers' credit—Germany	—	—	3,509	2,946	—
Suppliers' credit—India	—	—	3,190	2,678	—
World Bank	1,751	4,930	49,750	48,505	37,300
European Investment Bank	2,004	5,196	5,917	5,260	—
African Development Bank	283	1,380	3,287	2,922	—
East African Development Bank	668	1,732	1,879	1,566	—
Exim Bank	771	1,645	780	388	—
Total interest payment	5,477	14,883	68,312	64,265	37,300
Loan commitment fee					
World Bank	1,411	1,145	—	—	—
African Development Bank	316	213	—	—	—
Exim Bank	69	17	—	—	—
Total commitment fee	1,796	1,375	—	—	—
Repayment of principal					
Suppliers' credit—Germany	—	—	7,050	7,050	—
Suppliers' credit—India	—	—	6,381	6,381	—
World Bank	—	—	13,833	13,833	13,833
European Investment Bank	—	—	10,956	10,956	—
African Development Bank	—	—	4,565	4,565	—
East African Development Bank	—	—	2,846	2,846	—
Exim Bank	—	—	4,354	4,354	—
Total repayment of principal	—	—	49,985	49,985	13,833
Total outflow	103,177	164,330	215,951	196,751	135,816
Net foreign exchange flow					
Current surplus (deficit)	(87)	10,060	40,811	121,493	375,298
Cumulative surplus (deficit)	(87)	9,973	258,251	379,744	3,080,980

Note: In current prices for years 1 through 5 (1977–81); thereafter in year-5 (1981) constant prices.

Source: Same as table 6-1.

a. Based on the foreign exchange element of the import substitution price of KSh3,897 per ton in constant March 1977 prices adjusted for inflation to KSh5,152 per ton in year 4 and KSh5,510 per ton from year 5 onward.

b. Based on molasses price f.o.b. Mombasa of KSh463 per ton in year 4 and KSh495 per ton from year 5 onward.

As in the case of the government cash flow, the question arises of whether to calculate the foreign exchange flow in constant or current terms. Matching his choice for the government cash flow, the analyst chose to project the foreign exchange flow in current terms for the five years of the implementation phase of the project while the sugar factory was to be built and then, from year 6 onward, in constant terms at year-5 prices. As before, this provided the treasury and other planning agencies with a current projection of the foreign exchange effects of the project for the first few years of its implementation but avoided a long-term projection of inflation. Again, the analyst chose to carry out his calculations for sixteen years, long enough to trace all the financial transactions except repayment of the World Bank loan.

The foreign exchange flow is derived by tabulating the *inflow*, deducting the *outflow*, and obtaining the *net foreign exchange flow*. The first inflow is the *loan receipt* in support of the project. Note that the suppliers' credit and loans from several international agencies were received directly by the South Nyanza Sugar Company, so they do not show in the government cash flow examined in the previous section but do appear here. Then comes the foreign exchange value of the sugar production. This is the foreign exchange saved as a result of substituting domestically produced sugar for imported sugar. The last inflow listed is the foreign exchange earned from the export of molasses.

Foreign exchange outflows include the *foreign exchange component* of the various aspects of project implementation, including equipment and materials purchased from abroad and management fees. The other major component of the foreign exchange outflow is the *debt service payment* for loans received from abroad. This includes *interest*, any *loan commitment fee*, and *repayment of principal* to the suppliers of equipment and the international agencies that lent to support the project.

Subtracting the *total outflow* from the *total inflow* gives the net foreign exchange flow, which is reported in two variations: the *current surplus (deficit)* and the *cumulative surplus (deficit)*. In part because of the financing available, the foreign exchange effect of the South Nyanza project is positive every year except the first.

Cost Recovery

When governments invest in projects that increase the incomes of individual farmers, the question arises about how much of the government expenditure should be recovered from the project beneficiaries. Only through appropriate cost recovery policies can governments recoup the money expended on a project for investment in other projects that will benefit other members of the society. To the extent that the cost of a project is not recovered, some part of the project benefit individuals receive represents a subsidy paid by others in the society who did not benefit from the project.

There are two important issues to be addressed in formulating cost recovery policy. One is the proportion of the cost expended on a project to be repaid. The other is the proportion of the benefit received by individuals (which may be far higher than the cost) to be recovered through direct charges and such indirect means as increased tax revenue. Project analysis, however, clearly cannot make the policy decision. Moreover, attempts to determine the proportion of government expenditure and individual benefit to be recovered under various alternative policies very quickly run into great practical difficulties. These involve estimating values, often imputed values, and more theoretical economic issues, so that in the end cost recovery computations are of necessity more indicative than precise. Even so, cost recovery estimates based on sound economic principles can greatly improve understanding of the issues and improve the efficiency and equity of cost recovery policies.

Some aspects of cost recovery have little to do with the specifics of computation. Many countries have well-established policies about such things as water charges or taxes, policies that may not be politically possible to change all at once. Other considerations have to do with the project itself. Those projects which provide reliable service to farmers are more likely to have a better record on cost recovery than projects in which farmers feel services are poor and unreliable and, to that extent, not worth paying for.

In the final analysis, any cost recovery policy must be a political decision; it cannot be divorced from the broader sectoral and social setting. Any approach to cost recovery must be flexible and based on a recognition that what might be a good policy decision at one place or at one time is not necessarily the best decision at another place or time.

Problems of cost recovery in agricultural projects tend to be prominent in irrigation projects because these projects often are very expensive and bring proportionally large increases in income to the farmers who benefit. Much of the discussion of cost recovery, therefore, has centered around water resource projects, and the examples used in this section to illustrate methods of computation will be drawn from an irrigation project in India. The discussion here must necessarily be very general; more detailed information can be found in "Irrigation Water Charges, Benefit Taxes, and Cost Recovery Policies" (World Bank 1982b).

Objectives of cost recovery

Three basic objectives are involved in considerations of cost recovery issues: (1) economic efficiency, (2) income distribution, and (3) public saving.

ECONOMIC EFFICIENCY. The first objective concerns the level and structure of the prices to be charged—in irrigation projects, the price for water. The objective is to minimize waste and to allocate water optimally to maximize the net benefit from the project to the economy. The best way to do this would be through a price that would be equal to the contribution the water would make to increased output—an "efficiency price." This theoretical ideal is very rarely, if ever, met. It would require sale of water on a volumetric basis, which would lead to difficult problems in practice and would require estimating the contribution of water. But even a nominal price for water, perhaps one based on an acceptable if less than perfect measurement technique, would offer users an incentive to eliminate at least some of the conspicuous waste and overwatering that occur when farmers treat water as a free good. This, in turn, could reduce drainage and salinization problems.

Even if it were possible to charge farmers an optimal economic price, this might not be compatible with objectives of income distribution and public saving and investment. Hence, other criteria of assessing charges will have to be considered to ensure an equitable income effect from the project and an adequate recovery of project costs by charges that prospective beneficiaries can afford to pay and that still leave them adequate incentive to participate. Some recovery of benefits and costs will usually come from existing general taxes, such as an export tax or an income tax. But this recovery method is not geared to the circumstances of the particular project and is often unsatisfactory from the point of view of either income distribution or public savings. Moreover, capturing a larger part of the benefits and recovering more of the costs of a project through an increase in general taxation also affects those who do not directly benefit from the project. Hence, any measure to recover costs and benefits in addition to water pricing and existing general taxes should be selective and affect, to the greatest extent possible, only the project beneficiaries. These measures are usually called "benefit taxes." The most common form is a betterment levy assessed against the land benefited and perhaps varied according to the different crops grown.

INCOME DISTRIBUTION. The second objective of a cost recovery policy is to collect charges equitably and in line with national policy for income distribution. It may be desired to charge small farmers proportionately less than large farmers in the same project. Thus, specific taxes designed to capture part of the benefit of a project should take into account differences in income level and in the ability of beneficiaries to pay. Benefit taxes should allow for the quite different amounts of net benefit a project generates on farms quite similar in size and other characteristics. The taxes will have to be set taking into account disincentives, tax evasion, and the cost of collection. In irrigation projects, in practice only the broadest income distribution measures are implemented. A ceiling may be set on the total area an individual family may irrigate, for example, and an effort is usually made to ensure that small farmers at least do not pay a higher proportion of their benefit from the project than do larger farmers.

PUBLIC SAVING. Most governments in developing countries are short of financial resources for development. Consequently, it may be desirable for the government to collect more resources than would be generated solely from efficiency pricing (which, in any case, is generally impractical) or from recovering only the cost of the project and no part of the net benefit. Not only would this make the projects financially self-supporting, but it would also enable governments to undertake additional rural development projects that would reach other members of the society. But farmers participating in a project may be poor. To recover more than the cost of the project may therefore be unacceptable, and it may be desirable to recover less.

Setting the level of water charges and benefit taxes

As the discussion to this point has indicated, the level at which to set water charges and benefit taxes will depend on a broad range of considerations. First, some estimate must be made of the net benefit received from the project by various participants. Then a system of charges and taxes must be established that captures an acceptable proportion of the benefit generated by the project while still meeting criteria of efficiency, income distribution, and equity. The level of charges and taxes must take into account similar levies in other areas and the political feasibility of charging a different amount in the project area, the disincentive effects of a benefit tax, and the administrative problems of tax collection. Benefit taxes should be designed to minimize the adverse effects these taxes may have on the production and consumption decisions of the farmers and others in the economy. It might be possible in some cases, for example, to recover costs by selling farm inputs to project beneficiaries at prices higher than those paid by others, or to purchase the output from beneficiaries at prices lower than otherwise would be paid—that is, to establish a monopolistic marketing margin. Such discriminatory taxes may induce choice of the wrong crops by farmers, although these taxes may be impossible to avoid completely. Volumetric sale in some form acceptable to farmers and project-specific betterment levies are generally better options.

The extent and manner of cost recovery directly affects the financial cash flows of the farmer, the project organization, and usually more than one government agency. Cost recovery can also affect the contribution an irrigation project will make to increasing national income. If cost recovery plans impose too heavy a burden on the farmers, the farmers may have insufficient incentive to participate fully in the project, and the anticipated output of the project will not be realized. In contrast, if cost recovery levels are set too low, the project organization may have too small an operation and maintenance budget—whether it is financed by water charges paid by farmers or by a government subsidy—so that water deliveries to farmers may be insufficient and unreliable, and production again could suffer.

The total benefit arising from the project sets a theoretical upper limit to the amount of revenue that can be collected from water charges and benefit taxes, but the actual amount collected will always be less—and usually much less—than the total benefit arising from the project. This is true simply because it is necessary to allow for errors of measurement and for the desire to increase the income of the poorest farmers. The lower limit of charges to be collected cannot be stated arbitrarily. A rule of thumb followed by many governments, however, is to attempt to establish water charges and benefit taxes that will at least recover the operation and maintenance cost. This will avoid an outright drain on current government revenues by the project. It will also reduce the likelihood of problems arising from delays in receiving operation and maintenance funds caused by budget stringencies. There is another advantage. Where systems receive their operation and maintenance funds from the project beneficiaries, and the beneficiaries have a significant influence on the operation of the system (often through an appropriate local farmers' organization), the systems generally are fairly well managed and maintained. Past experience in World Bank projects suggests that cost recovery as a percentage of incremental net cash income rarely exceeds 30 to 35 percent.

Once established, cost recovery charges—whether water charges or benefit taxes—should be indexed so they can change in response to changing costs and to inflation. Because in new projects it is likely that farmers will need several seasons to learn to use new water efficiently, a grace period is probably appropriate during which the full water charges and benefit taxes can be phased in.

Measuring cost and rent recovery

Two measures are usually calculated to help form judgments about cost recovery. They are the cost recovery index, which gives an idea of what proportion of public expenditure on a project will be recovered directly from the beneficiaries and through taxes collected off the farm, and the rent recovery index, which gives an idea of what proportion of the total benefit will be recovered from the project beneficiaries and from other sources. These ratios are descriptive only—they should only supplement, not substitute for, an analysis of proposed water charges as they bear on efficiency, income distribution, public sector savings, and such factors as tax disincentives, costs of tax collection, broader sectoral considerations, and the political implications of any charge or tax. Furthermore, both measures depend on several values that are impossible to establish with precision, so that decisions based upon them must be treated with great caution.

COST RECOVERY INDEX. The first measure of cost recovery is the cost recovery index. It is:

$$\frac{\text{Present worth of incremental water charges} + \text{present worth of incremental benefit taxes}}{\text{Present worth of incremental public sector outlays}}.$$

The cost recovery index is calculated using constant market prices. The appropriate discount rate is the economic opportunity cost of capital.

An example of how to calculate the cost recovery index is given in table 6-3, which is drawn from the Maharashtra II Irrigation Project in India. The first element is an estimate of the *present worth of capital cost* (per hectare of net cultivable "command area"—the area that can be irrigated by a particular group of irrigation works). This is based on the same cost estimates for the project as are used for other parts of the

Table 6-3. *Total Cost Recovery Index, Bhima Irrigation Scheme,*
Maharashtra II Irrigation Project, India
(Rs per hectare, constant 1979 prices)

Item	Amount
Present worth of capital cost (per hectare of net cultivable command area)[a]	
Irrigation infrastructure	18,550
Supporting works	1,850
Total	20,400
Annual financial equivalent (per hectare of net cultivable command area)	
Irrigation infrastructure[b]	1,871
Supporting works[c]	301
Operation and maintenance	100
Total	2,272
Cost recovery (under existing charges)	
Direct	
Incremental water charge	258
Incremental benefit tax[d]	306
Indirect receipts[e]	95
Total	659
Total cost recovery index (percent)[f]	29

Rs Indian rupees.

Source: Adapted from World Bank, "India, Staff Appraisal Report, Maharashtra Irrigation II Project," vol. I, "Main Report," 2529a-IN (Washington, D.C., 1979; restricted circulation), pp. 83–84.

a. For the method of calculating present worth, see chapter 9.

b. Annuity for recovery over fifty years at 10 percent interest rate. Calculated by multiplying the present worth of the capital cost of the irrigation infrastructure by the capital recovery factor for fifty years at 10 percent, which is 0.100 859, to give Rs1,871 (18,550 × 0.100 859 = 1,871).

c. Annuity for recovery over ten years at 10 percent interest rate. Calculated by multiplying the present worth of the capital cost of the supporting works by the capital recovery factor for ten years at 10 percent, which is 0.162 745, to give Rs301 (1,850 × 0.162 745 = 301).

d. Incremental benefit taxes include a tax to recover the capital cost of the supporting works, amounting to Rs301 per hectare (see note c above), and an incremental land revenue assessment of Rs5 per hectare, or a total of Rs306 (301 + 5 = 306).

e. Indirect cost recovery receipts average Rs40 per hectare for the purchase tax on sugarcane and Rs55 per hectare for the sales tax on cotton and oilseeds, or Rs95 per hectare (40 + 55 = 95).

f. Total cost recovery under existing charges divided by annual financial equivalent per hectare of net cultivable command area multiplied by 100 (659 ÷ 2,272 × 100 = 29).

project analysis. Next, the *annual financial equivalent* (per hectare of net cultivable command area) is determined. For capital items—in this instance, the irrigation infrastructure and the supporting irrigation works—this value is calculated by multiplying the present worth of the capital cost by the capital recovery factor for the appropriate period and discount rate. [For capital recovery factors, see Gittinger (1973) or a similar set of compounding and discounting tables.] In this Maharashtra example, the irrigation infrastructure was assumed to have a life of fifty years, and the opportunity cost of capital was taken to be 10 percent, so the capital recovery factor for fifty years at 10 percent, or 0.100 859, was applied to the present worth of the irrigation infrastructure. The supporting works were taken to have a life of only ten years, so the capital recovery factor for ten years at 10 percent, or 0.162 745, was applied to them. The *operation and maintenance* charge, of course, is an annual charge, so it may be taken directly. Next the *cost recovery* is determined, in this case calculated assuming that existing charges will continue. The Maharashtra project is typical of many irrigation projects in that part of the cost recovery will come directly through water charges and a benefit tax, and part of the cost recovery will come from an indirect charge in the form of an excise tax on incremental sugarcane production and incremental sales tax revenues from marketing cotton and oilseeds. The *total cost recovery index*, then, is simply the *total cost recovery* divided by the *total annual financial equivalent* and multiplied by 100, which in this instance gives 29 percent (659 ÷ 2,272 × 100 = 29).

There are variations that may be calculated, depending on the need for information on which to base cost recovery charges and benefit taxes. In the case of the Maharashtra project, for example, table 6-3 illustrates computation of the total cost recovery index, which includes as part of the cost recovery both the direct recovery through water charges and benefit taxes and the indirect recovery through excise and sales taxes. An alternative would be to calculate the direct cost recovery; that is, the amount recovered directly from the farmers themselves. In this instance the direct water charges and benefit taxes come to Rs564 per hectare (258 + 306 = 564), which would be divided by the total annual financial equivalent of Rs2,272 per hectare and multiplied by 100, so that the direct cost recovery index would be 25 percent (564 ÷ 2,272 × 100 = 25). (The symbol for Indian rupees is Rs.)

The cost recovery index in various forms may then be used as a basis for conclusions about cost recovery policy. The effect of various levels of water charges and benefit taxes can be tested until a decision is reached about a suitable level and combination of these given such other public policy considerations as equity and the amounts charged elsewhere in the country.

RENT RECOVERY INDEX. The other cost recovery measure commonly calculated is the rent recovery index. It is based on projected farm budgets that are similar to those developed in chapter 4 but that have significant differences in that they include imputed values for labor, management, return to capital, and risk. In the illustrative calculation that follows, the rent recovery index for beneficiaries will be used to estimate the proportion of the benefit received by project beneficiaries that is recovered by the public authorities. The rent recovery index is:

$$\frac{\text{Incremental revenue from water sales} + \text{incremental benefit taxes}}{\text{Incremental economic rent accruing to project beneficiaries}}.$$

Since the rent recovery index is generally computed to be used in forming a judgment about the amount of water charges and benefit taxes, it is not a discounted measure; rather, it is done for one year at the full development period. It is based on market prices.

In a general sense, the rent recovery index may be thought of as being based on the farmer's "ability to pay," his "capacity to pay," or his "repayment capacity." To calculate the rent recovery index, however, the more formal concept of "economic rent" is used. Economic rent is the surplus remaining after beneficiaries receive the rewards necessary to attract physical inputs, labor, entrepreneurship, and the willingness to bear risk. Economic rent is allied to the more familiar concept of rent as a payment for use of a capital item, but it is quite distinct from this more common use of the term "rent" and should not be confused with it.

In the case of an irrigation project, to calculate the economic rent accruing to a beneficiary, one starts with the incremental gross value of farm production, from which is deducted all incremental cash payments, incremental depreciation of farm assets, the imputed value of family labor and of management, a return on the family's own incremental capital, incremental general taxes, and an allowance for additional risk and uncertainty. Incremental water charges and incremental benefit taxes related to the project are not deducted. It will immediately be seen that estimating economic rent is not easy and is subject to a large margin of error. The various noncash and imputed values of costs cannot be determined with precision; they inevitably involve substantial judgment. It is necessary to make some estimate of this sort, however, to judge whether a sufficient proportion of the benefits received by farmers in the project is being recovered because these same elements must be considered however benefits may be measured.

An example of the computation of the rent recovery index is found in table 6-4, which is drawn from the same Maharashtra irrigation project used as an example in the previous subsection. The computation starts with the *gross value of farm production at farm-gate prices without sales taxes*. Of this, *sales* without the project amount to half, but as the family's income rises the proportion of sales rises sharply. From the gross value of farm production is deducted the *cash production cost*, and this gives the *net benefit*. This is consistent with the net benefit as defined in chapter 4 and as illustrated by the farm budget in tables 4-18 and 4-19, except for any off-farm income the family may receive. The *net cash income* is determined by subtracting the cash production cost from the sales. The net cash income can be compared later with any incremental water charge or benefit tax levied.

Next a group of imputed values are deducted. The first of these is *depreciation*. Since the rent recovery index is computed on the basis of one year at full development, depreciation must be deducted as a cost. Then an estimate of the *imputed value of family labor* is deducted. This is an estimate of the wage necessary to induce the family to operate its farm. In practice, it is suggested that the analyst take the weighted average of the seasonal market wage as a proxy. Next comes an estimate

Table 6-4. *Rent Recovery Index, Full Development, 5-Hectare Farm,*
Light Soils, Bhima Scheme, Maharashtra Project
(Rs, constant 1979 prices)

	Amount		
Item	*Without project*	*With project*	*Incremental*
Gross value of farm production at farm-gate prices			
without sales taxes	7,500	33,380	25,880
Sales	3,750	28,380	24,630
Cash production cost[a]	(2,690)	(11,690)	(9,000)
Gross value *less* cash production cost			
equals net benefit	4,810	21,690	16,880
Sales *less* cash production cost			
equals net cash income	1,060	16,690	15,630
Net benefit *less*			
Depreciation[b]	0	0	0
Imputed value of family labor	(720)	(1,350)	(630)
Imputed value of management services[c]	(70)	(1,030)	(960)
Imputed return on own capital[d]	0	0	0
Allowance for risk and uncertainty[e]	(3,380)	(10,010)	(6,630)
General taxes[f]	0	0	0
Equals economic rent (surplus)	640	9,300	8,660
Economic rent as a percentage of net benefit[g]	13	43	51
Incremental water charges[h]	—	—	1,290
Incremental benefit taxes[i]	—	—	1,530
Total incremental direct charges and benefit taxes[j]	—	—	2,820
Rent recovery index (percent)[k]	—	—	33

Source: Same as table 6-3.

a. May include some payment in kind for labor.

b. Since the farmer has few physical assets other than land, no depreciation was assumed.

c. An imputed value of management services equivalent to 10 percent of the net benefit less the imputed value of family labor and the allowance for risk and uncertainty rounded to the nearest Rs10. For the with-project situation, this amounts to Rs1,030 rounded to the nearest Rs10 {0.1[21,690 − (1,350 + 10,010)] = 1,033}.

d. Since the family has few physical assets, no imputed return to the family's own capital was assumed.

e. Some studies of farmers' behavior show that a simple approach can be adopted to take account of the farmer's risk aversion. An allowance for risk and uncertainty is estimated based on the coefficient of variation of the gross value of farm production—the standard deviation divided by the mean—and a measure of farmers' risk aversion. The formula used is

$$RA = EV \times n \times v,$$

where RA is the risk allowance, EV is the expected value, v is the coefficient of variation, and n is a factor that expresses farmers' risk aversion. The studies indicate that the farmers' choice of cropping patterns and production can be predicted for values of n in the interval between 1 and 2 and that n decreases when the farm size increases. For this analysis, it is assumed that $n = 1.5$ for 5-hectare farms. For the project area, the coefficient of variation of gross returns under rainfed conditions is roughly 30 percent of the average value. It has been assumed that under the with-project conditions, the gross returns would vary within 20 percent of the net returns. The results were rounded to the nearest Rs10. Following this approach, the allowance for risk and uncertainty in the with-project situation was estimated to be Rs10,010 rounded to the nearest Rs10 (33,380 × 1.5 × 0.2 = 10,014).

of the *imputed value of management services*. This is a very difficult estimate to reach. In practice, project analysts take an arbitrary amount. A common estimate is 5 to 10 percent of the net benefit. In the Maharashtra project, however, the analyst took 10 percent of the net benefit less the imputed value of family labor and the allowance for risk and uncertainty. The *imputed return on own capital* is an estimate based on the incremental net value of assets financed by farmers out of their own savings and should reflect the rate of return that their funds could earn elsewhere. In the Maharashtra project, no imputed return on own capital was assumed because the family had relatively few physical assets. Other analysts, however, might at least have imputed a return to the family's own capital invested in land.

The next imputed value deducted is the *allowance for risk and uncertainty*. This is extremely difficult to formulate conceptually and notoriously difficult to estimate with confidence. Again, most project economists use a rule of thumb—a common one is 10 percent of the gross value of farm production in the first line of the table. The project analyst in the Maharashtra project used a more sophisticated approach. He based his estimate on the standard deviation of farm production in the project area and on an estimated factor that expresses the farmers' risk aversion. (The details of this computation are given in note e of table 6-4.) Most project analysts probably will have some sense of the variability of farm production in the project area for which they are preparing the analysis, and they may even have some more formal estimate such as the standard deviation. This will provide a basis for estimating the allowance for risk and uncertainty, but it will have to be substantially modified in light of the analyst's judgment about the accuracy of the estimate of variability and the willingness of farmers in the project area to accept risk. The last imputed value deducted is an estimate of the *general taxes* the farmer pays. These are taxes that are not specific to the project as a benefit tax would be. General taxes might include, for example, income taxes or a land tax to raise general revenue that is not linked to the project nor to improvements arising from the project investment.

When all these values have been deducted, the remainder is an estimate of the *economic rent (surplus)* accruing to the farmer. It is thus an estimate of the surplus remaining for the farmer after paying the rewards necessary to attract the physical inputs, labor, entrepreneurship, and willingness to bear risk necessary to operate the farm—the definition of

---

f. No general taxes are expected to be levied.

g. Economic rent divided by net benefit multiplied by 100. For the incremental net benefit this amounts to 51 percent ($8,660 \div 16,880 \times 100 = 51$).

h. Incremental direct water charges are Rs258 per hectare of net cultivable area, or Rs1,290 for the 5-hectare farm ($258 \times 5 = 1,290$).

i. Incremental benefit taxes include a tax of Rs301 per hectare to recover the capital cost of the supporting works and an incremental land revenue assessment of Rs5 per hectare, or Rs1,530 for the 5-hectare farm [$(301 + 5) \times 5 = 1,530$].

j. Incremental water charges plus incremental benefit taxes.

k. Total incremental direct charges and benefit taxes divided by economic rent multiplied by 100 ($2,820 \div 8,660 \times 100 = 33$).

economic rent above. The *economic rent as a percentage of net benefit*, the next entry in the table, relates economic rent to the net benefit received by the farmer, which for the incremental net benefit amounts to 51 percent ($8,660 \div 16,880 \times 100 = 51$).

Next are entered the proposed *incremental water charges* and *incremental benefit taxes* that the farmer is expected to pay. Dividing the total of these by the economic rent gives the *rent recovery index*. This is an estimate of the proportion of the surplus the farmer receives over and above the minimum necessary to induce him to participate in the project that will be recaptured by the public authorities. In the case of the Maharashtra project, this recovery amounts to 33 percent of the economic rent [$(1,290 + 1,530) \div 8,660 \times 100 = 33$].

This discussion of the rent recovery index has highlighted the many elements of the estimate that can be approximate at best. Hence, the rent recovery index, although very useful as an aid for setting cost recovery policy, must be used with caution.

As with the cost recovery index, there are variations of the rent recovery index that give insight into other questions about a project. A common variation is to estimate the rent recovery index for the project (as opposed to that for the beneficiaries, as illustrated in table 6-4). For this the project rent must be estimated. Essentially the same elements are used as discussed above, except that the concept of the incremental benefit tax is expanded to include not only benefit taxes collected directly from the beneficiary but also taxes arising from the incremental output due to the project but collected off the farm. These include, in the case of the Maharashtra project, the excise tax on sugarcane and the sales tax on cotton and oilseeds. In other cases they might include an export tax or the net increase in a marketing board margin (technically, in the monopolistic marketing margin) arising from handling incremental production from the project area. In general, estimates of project rent are made for each major farm pattern, and the results are aggregated to the project level. Since the incremental benefit taxes include taxes and marketing margins arising off the farm, the project rent recovery index will be higher than the weighted average of the beneficiary economic rent received by the individual farmers. In the case of the Maharashtra project, for instance, the rent recovery index for the individual farm pattern analyzed in table 6-4—33 percent—rises to 40 percent for the Bhima scheme as a whole (including pattern farms other than the one represented in table 6-4) because the additional taxes are included.

Another variation of the rent recovery index is to calculate it, for either beneficiaries or the project, on a discounted basis. This provides a means to estimate on the basis of present worth the proportion of the benefit of a project captured by the public authorities. This is useful from a public policy standpoint, but is not a suitable basis on which to determine the level of water charges and benefit taxes at full development. From a public policy standpoint, one can then test varying assumptions about water charges and benefit taxes until a rent recovery index is reached that is considered to be equitable given the income of the farmers in the project and the charges levied elsewhere in the country.

Joint Cost Allocation

When a government undertakes to implement a multipurpose project, a problem arises about how to allocate the cost of the project among the various beneficiaries. The complication arises, of course, because there are joint costs in a multipurpose project, costs that cannot clearly be attributed to one purpose or another. A technique often used to allocate joint cost—especially in multipurpose water development projects, but by no means limited only to them—is that known as the "separable costs–remaining benefits" method.

We will discuss joint cost allocation using market prices and as a financial problem, since this is by far the most common practice. The same techniques we will outline, however, can be applied to economic values, and in some cases this may be more appropriate. In the Senegal River Development Program we will use as an example for joint cost allocation, the prices for agricultural commodities were indeed taken not as the internal administered prices actually paid farmers but as the border prices at world market values—already a step away from strict financial analysis and toward economic values and the use of shadow prices. This was done because the major objective of the analysis was to determine a fair cost allocation among the participating nations, not to determine equitable financial charges to levy on benefiting farmers.

General principles of cost allocation

There are several general principles or guidelines of joint cost allocation that underlie the rationale of the separable costs–remaining benefits method.

In general, no project purpose should be assigned a cost that is in excess of the value of its benefit nor be supported by the benefit of another purpose. Thus, the charge for irrigation water should not be greater than the contribution of that water to the benefit of the project. Similarly, in general we feel that no purpose should be subsidized by another purpose. Power users in most cases should not be charged high rates to make irrigation water available at low cost to farmers.

All the cost incurred for one purpose only should be allocated wholly to that purpose. The cost of canals is wholly allocated to the irrigation purpose, and the cost of the transmission lines wholly to the power purpose. Each "separable cost" is the minimum that can be charged for the respective purpose. If the cost of the canals alone exceeds the benefit from the irrigation water, then clearly the project should not include an irrigation component.

No purpose, however, should be assigned a cost that is any greater than would be incurred if that function were to be supplied by the most economic alternative single-purpose project. The alternative single-purpose project establishes the maximum that can be charged for any one purpose. It is not equitable to allocate to the power component of a multipurpose water development project a cost more than that of the alternative thermal plant that could provide the same electrical service, nor is it equitable to charge the irrigation component more than the cost of an alternative single-purpose pumping scheme.

Separable costs–remaining benefits method

The application of the separable costs–remaining benefits method is illustrated by the Senegal River Development Program cost allocation in table 6-5. The three West African states of Mali, Mauritania, and Senegal have formed the Senegal River Development Organization (known by the initials of its French name, omvs) to plan and develop a multipurpose project on the Senegal River. In the configuration for which the joint cost allocation is outlined as an example, the project would consist of the multipurpose Manantali Dam on the Bafing River, a major tributary of the Senegal River, to provide a regulated flow; the Diama Dam close to the mouth of the river to prevent upstream intrusion of salty ocean water; a power generation station with associated distribution network at the Manantali Dam; and navigation improvements to permit year-round service to Mali. The benefits of the project are (1) increased production of agricultural crops because of double cropping in the dry season and better water regulation in the wet season, (2) power, and (3) reduced transport costs because of the navigation improvements. [This example is adapted from Riley and others (1978).]

We will follow the analysis line by line. The first part of table 6-5 summarizes the *basic information* about the project that will be needed to allocate cost. The technical information would be supplied by the engineers and the other technicians; the cost and benefit would be estimated by the technical staff working with the economists.

We begin with the *project cost to be allocated* (line 1.1). This is the total cost for the project as a whole that is to be allocated among the three purposes. Included are both the *construction* cost (line 1.1.1), stated at its present worth as of the beginning of the project, and the *annual operation and maintenance cost* (often abbreviated in project accounts as o&m; line 1.1.2) necessary to operate the project.

The *annual project benefit* for each purpose is listed and the total of these is entered (line 1.2). In the Senegal River case, the power benefit was assumed to be the amount for which the power could be sold. In most instances, however, the power benefit would be assumed to be the annual cost of providing the same amount of electricity by means of the most economic single-purpose alternative project—always assuming that consumers would purchase electricity at that price. This simplification avoids the problems associated with valuing electricity. It implies that the real benefit of power—whatever that might be—is greater than the cost of the single-purpose alternative. The effect of this assumption is to set the maximum that can be charged for power to equal the benefit of the most economic alternative single-purpose project, which is what the analytical technique would do in any case.

Next is listed the *alternative cost* for each purpose (line 1.3), both for *construction*, stated at its present worth (line 1.3.1), and for the *annual operation and maintenance* charge (line 1.3.2). As noted, an alternative cost is the cost of the most economic single-purpose project that could provide one of the same benefits provided by the multipurpose project. An alternative does not have to be located at the multipurpose site, but it should be capable of producing its benefit in essentially the same geographic area as the one in which the benefit from the multipurpose project is to be utilized. The alternative project may be of an entirely different physical nature, as would be the case if the alternatives to a multipurpose river development were pump irrigation and a thermal generating plant. Of course, the most economic single-purpose alternative might cost more than the benefit it would generate; even the most economic alternative might not be justified as a separate project.

Next is the *separable cost* (line 1.4) given by purpose, both for construction at present worth (line 1.4.1) and for the annual operation and maintenance charge (line 1.4.2). Separable cost is expenditure that could be avoided if one purpose were excluded from the project. It is possible to find that no portion of the joint cost is solely and clearly traceable to a particular purpose. In measuring the separable cost, each purpose should be treated as if it were the last increment added to a project that serves all the other multiple purposes; in this way favoring one purpose over another may be avoided.

In many projects, the annual figures such as those for the operation and maintenance cost and annual benefit in the Senegal River example would not be constant during the life of the project. In these instances, the present worth of the cost or benefit stream would be substituted because that is what is called for in the joint cost allocation in the second part of table 6-5. Indeed, Riley and his colleagues (1978) do treat both operation and maintenance cost and annual benefit in this manner in the report from which this example is drawn.

The *discount rate* (line 1.5) is either the financing cost of the project if the project is to be constructed using loan funds or the government borrowing rate if the project is to be financed from allocations in the current government budget.

The *project life* (line 1.6) and the length of the *construction period* (line 1.7) are part of the technical data supplied by those responsible for designing the project. Carrying out the analysis for a very long period, however, has little meaning because of the very small present worth of values assumed in the distant future. In the Senegal River project, for example, the physical facilities would probably last much longer than the thirty-year period chosen for analysis, but extending the period of analysis would hardly affect the joint cost allocation.

The last part of tabulating the basic information for the joint cost allocation is to derive the factors for converting between annual values and present worth. The *factor to convert annual cost or benefit to present worth* (the present worth of an annuity factor; line 1.8) is computed for the discount rate as indicated. (The method of deriving the present worth of an annuity factor for a period beginning in the future is discussed in chapter 9, under "The Time Value of Money. Present worth of a stream of future income.") The *factor to convert present worth of cost or benefit to annual cost* (capital recovery factor) for a period beginning some time in the future (line 1.9) cannot be computed directly from the capital recovery factors given in standard tables in a manner similar to the computation of the present worth of an annuity factor. This problem may be avoided, however, by taking advantage of the fact that the capital recovery factor for any period is the reciprocal of the present worth of an annuity factor for that period. Thus, we find that the capital recovery factor for the tenth through the thirtieth year at 10 percent is 0.272 636 $(1 \div 3.667\ 890 = 0.272\ 636)$.

Table 6-5. *Joint Cost Allocation,*
Senegal River Development Program, West Africa
(millions of CFAF)

Line and item	Purpose			
	Irriga-tion	Power	Naviga-tion	Total
1. Basic information				
1.1. Project cost to be allocated				
1.1.1 Construction (at present worth)				41,464
1.1.2 Annual o&m[a]				449
1.2. Annual project benefit	25,707	14,035	21,820	61,652
1.3. Alternative cost				
1.3.1 Construction (at present worth)	16,120	5,233	23,980	45,333
1.3.2 Annual o&m	152	3,060	223	3,435
1.4. Separable cost				
1.4.1 Construction (at present worth)	5,494	5,424	7,867	18,785
1.4.2 Annual o&m	55	109	75	239
1.5. Discount rate: 10 percent				
1.6. Project life: 30 years				
1.7. Construction period: 9 years				
1.8. Factor to convert annual cost or benefit to present worth (present worth of an annuity factor):				
Present worth of an annuity factor for 30 years at 10 percent				9.426 914
Less present worth of an annuity factor for 9 years at 10 percent				−5.759 024
Present worth of an annuity factor for 10th through 30th years at 10 percent				3.667 890
1.9. Factor to convert present worth of cost of benefit to annual cost (capital recovery factor):				

$$\begin{matrix} \text{Capital recovery factor} \\ \text{for 10th through 30th years} \\ \text{at 10 percent} \end{matrix} = \begin{matrix} \text{Reciprocal} \\ \text{of present} \\ \text{worth factor} \end{matrix} = \frac{1}{3.667\ 890} = 0.272\ 636$$

2. Joint cost allocation				
(All values at present worth except distribution percentage)				
2.1. Cost to be allocated				
2.1.1 Construction (1.1.1)				41,464
2.1.2 o&m [(1.1.2) × 3.667 890]				1,647
Total [(2.1.1) + (2.1.2)]				43,111
2.2. Benefit [(1.2) × 3.667 890]	94,290	51,479	80,033	225,802

Table 6-5 (*continued*)

	Purpose			
Line and item	Irriga-tion	Power	Naviga-tion	Total
2.3. Alternative cost				
2.3.1 Construction (1.3.1)	16,120	5,233	23,980	45,333
2.3.2 O&M [(1.3.2) × 3.667 890]	558	11,224	818	12,600
Total [(2.3.1) + (2.3.2)]	16,678	16,457	24,798	57,933
2.4. Justifiable expenditure [lesser of (2.2) or (2.3)]	16,678	16,457	24,798	57,933
2.5. Separable cost				
2.5.1 Construction (1.4.1)	5,494	5,424	7,867	18,785
2.5.2 O&M [(1.4.2) × 3.667 890]	202	400	275	877
Total [(2.5.1) + (2.5.2)]	5,696	5,824	8,142	19,662
2.6. Remaining justifiable expenditure [(2.4) − (2.5)]	10,982	10,633	16,656	38,271
2.7. Percentage distribution of (2.6)	28.70	27.78	43.52	100.00
2.8. Remaining joint cost [total from lines indicated allocated according to (2.7)]				
2.8.1 Remaining construction cost [(2.1.1) − (2.5.1)]	6,509	6,300	9,870	22,679
2.8.2 Remaining O&M [(2.1.2) − (2.5.2)]	221	214	335	770
Total [(2.8.1) + (2.8.2)]	6,730	6,514	10,205	23,449
2.9. Total allocated cost				
2.9.1 Construction cost [(2.5.1) + (2.8.1)]	12,003	11,724	17,737	41,464
2.9.2 O&M [(2.5.2) + (2.8.2)]	423	614	610	1,647
Total [(2.9.1) + (2.9.2)]	12,426	12,338	18,347	43,111
3. Annual costs				
3.1. Annual cost				
3.1.1 Construction [(2.9.1) × 0.272 636]	3,272	3,196	4,836	11,304[b]
3.1.2 O&M [(2.9.2) × 0.272 636]	115	167	166	448[b]
Total [(3.1.1) + (3.1.2)]	3,387[b]	3,363[b]	5,002	11,752[b]

CFAF African Financial Community francs.

Source: Adapted from Riley and others (1978).

a. O&M Operation and maintenance cost.

b. The annual cost does not exactly equal the allocated cost times the capital recovery factor because of rounding.

The second part of table 6-5 lays out the computation of the *joint cost allocation*. Note that all values (except the distribution percentages) are stated in their present worth equivalents.

The *cost to be allocated* (line 2.1) is the *total* cost of the project, obtained by adding the construction cost at present worth (line 2.1.1), taken from line 1.1.1, and the present worth of the operation and maintenance cost for the project (line 2.1.2), computed by taking the value of CFAF449 million supplied in line 1.1.2 and multiplying it by the present worth of an annuity factor for the tenth through the thirtieth years, which gives CFAF1,647 million (449 × 3.667 890 = 1,647). (The symbol for African

Financial Community francs is CFAF.) It is this cost that is to be allocated among the various purposes.

The *benefit* (line 2.2) is the annual project benefit given in line 1.2 multiplied by the present worth of an annuity factor for the tenth through the thirtieth years. Thus, the present worth of the irrigation benefit stream over the life of the project is CFAF94,290 million (25,707 × 3.667 890 = 94,290).

The *alternative cost* (line 2.3) lists the *total* costs for the most economic alternative single-purpose projects with the same benefit as the appropriate components of the multipurpose project. The subentries that are added for the total are taken from the first part of the table: the alternative *construction* cost (line 2.3.1) is given in line 1.3.1; the operation and maintenance cost for the alternative single-purpose projects (line 2.3.2) is taken from the annual operation and maintenance cost in line 1.3.2 and is converted to present worth using the present worth of an annuity factor.

The *justifiable expenditure* for each purpose (line 2.4) is either the benefit on line 2.2 or the total alternative cost on line 2.3, whichever is less. The sum of the justifiable expenditure for the various purposes is the total justifiable expenditure for the multipurpose project; this amount is entered in the total column of line 2.4. We noted this earlier: the amount to be allocated to a particular purpose is limited on the one hand by the benefit it will produce and on the other hand by the cost of the most economic single-purpose alternative.

The separable cost (line 2.5) is taken from the first part of the table. The separable construction cost for each purpose (line 2.5.1) comes from line 1.4.1. The present worth of the separable annual operation and maintenance cost (line 2.5.2) is derived by multiplying the value in line 1.4.2 by the present worth of an annuity factor. The separable cost is then totaled. In general, the total separable cost for each purpose will be the minimum allocation that will be charged to that purpose.

To determine the *remaining justifiable expenditure* (line 2.6) for each purpose and for the project as a whole, the separable cost of each purpose given in line 2.5 is deducted from the justifiable expenditure given in line 2.4. In the case of the irrigation purpose, for example, the separable cost of CFAF5,696 million is subtracted from the justifiable expenditure of CFAF16,678 million, and this leaves a remaining justifiable expenditure of CFAF10,982 million (16,678 − 5,696 = 10,982). Of course, if the value for any purpose is negative, it means that the present worth of the benefit at the discount rate being used is less than the present worth of the cost. If one purpose is not to subsidize another, then any purpose with a negative justifiable expenditure should be omitted from the project.

The *percentage distribution* of the remaining justifiable expenditure in line 2.6 is calculated and entered in line 2.7.

Now we must calculate the *remaining joint cost* for each purpose (line 2.8). This is done by allocating the joint cost of the project to each purpose in proportion to the excess over the separable cost that we would be justified in spending to realize the benefit from each purpose. We begin by determining the total *remaining* (joint) *construction cost* in the last column of line 2.8.1. To do this, the total separable construction cost for the entire project in the last column of line 2.5.1 is subtracted from the total construction cost for the entire project in line 2.1.1 to give the total remaining joint construction cost of CFAF22,679 million, which then is entered in the last column of line 2.8.1 (41,464 − 18,785 = 22,679).

Similarly, the total *remaining* (joint) *operation and maintenance cost* in the last column of line 2.8.2 is determined by subtracting the separable operation and maintenance cost in line 2.5.2 from the total operation and maintenance cost in line 2.1.2. This gives a value of CFAF770 (1,647 − 877 = 770). These totals are then allocated to the various purposes according to the percentage distribution of the remaining justifiable expenditure in line 2.7. Thus, the remaining construction cost for irrigation is 28.70 percent of CFAF22,679, or CFAF6,509 (22,679 × 0.2870 = 6,509), and the remaining operation and maintenance cost for power is 27.78 percent of CFAF770, or CFAF214 (770 × 0.2778 = 214). The total of the remaining joint cost for each purpose is the sum of the remaining joint cost for construction (line 2.8.1) and operation and maintenance cost (line 2.8.2).

The *total allocated cost* (line 2.9) may now be determined. The *total allocated construction cost* (line 2.9.1) for each purpose is determined by adding the separable construction cost for that purpose in line 2.5.1 to the remaining joint construction cost in line 2.8.1. Thus, the total allocated construction cost for the irrigation component is CFAF12,003 million (5,494 + 6,509 = 12,003). Similarly, the *total allocated operation and maintenance cost* for each purpose (line 2.9.2) is the sum of the separable *operation and maintenance cost* for that purpose in line 2.5.2 and the remaining joint *operation and maintenance cost* in line 2.8.2. Hence, the total allocated operation and maintenance cost for the irrigation purpose is CFAF423 million (202 + 221 = 423). The sum of the total allocated construction cost for each purpose and the total allocated operation and maintenance cost for each purpose is the total allocated cost for each purpose. Of course, the total allocated cost in the last column of line 2.9 must equal the total cost to be allocated in the last column of line 2.1, and this provides an internal check on the calculations.

The third part of table 6-5 gives the *annual costs*. The *annual cost* (line 3.1) for each purpose is determined by multiplying the total allocated cost in line 2.9 by the capital recovery factor for the tenth through the thirtieth year at 10 percent as computed in the first part of the table. Thus, the annual cost for navigation is determined by multiplying the total allocated cost by the capital recovery factor to obtain the annual cost of CFAF5,002 million (18,347 × 0.272 636 = 5,002). Because of rounding, the annual costs for irrigation and power do not quite check when calculated in this manner. In table 6-5 the total annual cost (line 3.1) is shown as the total of the annual construction and annual operation and maintenance costs. The *annual construction cost* (line 3.1.1) and the *annual operation and maintenance cost* (line 3.1.2) may be determined separately as explained above. Thus, the annual construction cost for irrigation is CFAF3,272 million (12,003 × 0.272 636 =

3,272), and the annual operation and maintenance cost chargeable to irrigation is CFAF115 million ($423 \times 0.272\ 636 = 115$). An equitable annual charge for the use of irrigation water in the project would thus be CFAF3,387 million, of which CFAF3,272 million would go toward the construction cost and CFAF115 million would be for operation and maintenance cost ($3,272 + 115 = 3,387$). If it were determined that the governments were to bear the capital cost of irrigation and the farmers to pay only the operation and maintenance cost, the farmers would have to pay only the CFAF115 million annual operation and maintenance charge. (In the Senegal River project, there would be additional cost to bring the water from the river to the fields, but this falls outside the project cost as such.)

Note that the separable costs–remaining benefits method when calculated using market prices only specifies what would be an equitable financial charge using as a sole criterion the cost incurred for each purpose and the benefit generated by each purpose. What the beneficiaries actually will be charged depends on many other considerations, as noted in the previous section on cost recovery. Sometimes, for example, the capital cost for irrigation will be assumed by the treasury and be paid from general tax revenues, but farmers will be assessed enough to pay for the operation and maintenance cost. Other services may also not be charged precisely the amounts the separable costs–remaining benefits method indicates as equitable. Often, for example, no charge is levied for flood control benefits that are paid for from the general revenue, and it is likely that power users will be charged the prevailing rate for the area served by the multipurpose project and not the rate determined by the annual cost of the project power component.

We have covered the primary elements of joint cost allocation in this discussion. Readers who wish to go further might consult the report prepared by Riley and his group (1978) from which the Senegal River example is drawn; the report includes variations on the allocation method outlined here as well as interesting discussions of valuing benefit and allocating cost equitably between countries. A more extensive discussion of joint cost allocation will be found in James and Lee (1970), and Loughlin (1977) proposes a modification of the separable costs–remaining benefits methodology to increase the equity by applying weights for the relative amounts of the separable cost assigned to each purpose.

PART THREE

Economic Aspects
of Project Analysis

7

Determining Economic Values

Once financial prices for costs and benefits have been determined and entered in the project accounts, the analyst estimates the economic value of a proposed project to the nation as a whole. The financial prices are the starting point for the economic analysis; they are adjusted as needed to reflect the value to the society as a whole of both the inputs and outputs of the project.

When the market price of any good or service is changed to make it more closely represent the opportunity cost (the value of a good or service in its next best alternative use) to the society, the new value assigned becomes the "shadow price" (sometimes referred to as an "accounting price"). In the strictest sense, a shadow price is any price that is not a market price, but the term usually also carries the connotation that it is an estimate of the economic value of the good or service in question, perhaps weighted to reflect income distribution and savings objectives.

In chapter 2, for purposes of project analysis, we took the objective of a farm to be to maximize the farm family's incremental net benefit, the objective of the firm to maximize its incremental net income, and the objective of the society to maximize the contribution a project makes to the national income—the value of all final goods and services produced in the country during a particular period. These objectives, and the

---

Facing page: Examining a farmer's poultry during an extension visit in Nigeria.

analysis to test their realization, were seen in financial terms for farms and firms. But economic analysis of a project moves beyond financial accounting. Strictly speaking, we may say that in financial analysis our numeraire—the common yardstick of account—is the real income change of the entity being analyzed valued in domestic market prices and in general expressed in domestic currency. But in economic analysis, since market prices do not always reflect scarcity values, our numeraire becomes the real, net national income change valued in opportunity cost. As we will note below, one methodology expresses these economic values in domestic currency and uses a shadow price of foreign exchange; the shadow price increases the value of traded goods to allow for the premium on foreign exchange arising from distortions caused by trade policies. Another method in use expresses the opportunity cost value of real national income change in domestic currency converted from foreign exchange at the official exchange rate and applies a conversion factor to the opportunity cost or value in use of nontraded goods expressed in domestic currency; the conversion factor reduces the value of nontraded goods relative to traded goods to allow for the foreign exchange premium.

Before a detailed discussion of adjusting financial accounts to reflect economic values commences, an important practical consideration must be emphasized. Many of the adjustments to the financial accounts can become quite complex. Not every point made in this chapter will apply to every agricultural project, nor will all points have the same importance in those projects where they do apply. The complexity of some calculations and the relative importance of some adjustments recall the reason for undertaking an economic analysis of a project: to improve the investment decision. Some adjustments will make a considerable difference to the economic attractiveness of a proposed project; others will be of minor importance, and no reasonable adjustment would change the investment decision. What we need to do here is to adopt an accounting practice—the doctrine of materiality. The analyst must focus his attention on those adjustments to the financial accounts that are likely to make a difference in the project investment decision. He should use rough approximations or ignore trivial adjustments that will not make any difference in the decision. There is an important balance to be struck between analytical elegance and getting on with the job.

In this chapter we will adjust the financial prices of tangible items to reflect economic values in three successive steps: (1) adjustment for direct transfer payments, (2) adjustment for price distortions in traded items, and (3) adjustment for price distortions in nontraded items. Before embarking on this series of adjustments, we will examine the problem of determining the appropriate premium for foreign exchange. After completing the adjustments, we will summarize the main points in a "decision tree" for determining economic values.

The series of successive adjustments to the financial accounts will lead to a set of economic accounts in which all values are stated in "efficiency prices," that is, in prices that reflect real resource use or consumption satisfaction and that are adjusted to eliminate direct and indirect transfers. These values will be market prices when market prices are good estimates of economic value or they will be shadow prices when market prices have had to be adjusted for distortions. When we adjust financial prices to reflect economic values better, in the vast majority of cases we will use the opportunity cost of the good or service as the criterion. We will use opportunity costs to value all inputs and outputs that are intermediate products used in the production of some other good or service. For some final goods and services, however, the concept of opportunity cost is not applicable because it is consumption value that sets the economic value, not value in some alternative use. In these instances, we will adopt the criterion of "willingness to pay" (also called "value in use"). We need to do this, however, only when the good or service in question is nontraded (perhaps as a result of government regulation) during some part of the life of the project—a point to which we will return later in our discussion. Because the ultimate objective of all economic activity is to satisfy consumption wants, all opportunity costs are derived from consumption values, and thus from willingness to pay.

An example may clarify our use of willingness to pay and opportunity cost. Suppose a country that is a rather inefficient producer of sugar has a policy to forbid sugar imports to protect its local industry. The price of sugar may then rise well above what it would be if sugar were imported. Even at these higher prices, most consumers will still buy some sugar for direct consumption—say, in coffee or tea—even though they may use less sugar than if the price were lower. The domestic price of sugar will be above the world market price and will represent the value of the sugar by the criterion of willingness to pay. If we were now to consider the economic value of sugar from the standpoint of its use in making fruit preserves, its value would become the opportunity cost of diverting the sugar from direct consumption, where willingness to pay is the criterion and has set the economic value.

Economic analysis, then, will state the cost and benefit to the society of the proposed project investment either in opportunity cost or in values determined by the willingness to pay. The costs or values will be determined in part by both the resource constraints and the policy constraints faced by the project. The difference between the benefit and the cost—the incremental net benefit stream—will be an accurate reflection of the project's income-generating capacity—that is, its net contribution to real national income.

The system outlined here will make no adjustment for the income distribution effects of a proposed project nor for its effect on the amount of the benefit generated that will be invested to accelerate future growth. Rather, the economic project analysis, stated in efficiency prices, will judge the capacity of the project to generate national income. The analyst can then choose from those alternative projects (or alternative formulations of roughly the same project) the high-yielding alternative that in his subjective judgment also makes the most effective contribution to objectives other than maximizing national income—objectives such as income distribution, savings generated, number of jobs produced, regional development, national security, or whatever. The choice about the *kind* of project will of course be made rather early in the project cycle. Thus, it may be determined early on that for reasons of social policy a project will be preferred that encourages smallholder agriculture rather than plantations. Then, the choices will likely be several projects or variants of projects that encourage smallholders; the analytical technique presented here can determine from among the projects that will further the desired social objective the ones that are more economically efficient.

Although the system outlined here makes no adjustment for income distribution effects or for saving versus consumption, it is compatible with other analytical systems that do. In particular, Squire and van der Tak (1975) recommend evaluating proposed projects first by using essentially the same efficiency prices that will be estimated here and then by further adjusting these prices to weight them for income distribution effects and for potential effects on further investment of the benefits generated. The systems in Little and Mirrlees (1974) and the UNIDO *Guidelines for Project Evaluation* (1972a), with minor departures, also propose evaluating the project by first establishing its economic accounts in efficiency prices and then by adjusting these accounts to weight them for income distribution and savings effects. Making allowances for income distribution and savings effects involves somewhat more complex adjustments than those necessary to estimate efficiency prices; it also unavoidably incorporates some element of subjective judgment. Although these systems have attracted widespread interest among economists, their application has been only partial or on a limited scale. The system of economic analysis using efficiency prices that is outlined here is essentially the one currently used for all but a few World Bank projects and also the one used for most analyses of projects funded by other international organizations.

The economic analysis follows on the financial analysis presented in the preceding chapters; it will be based on projected farm budgets similar to those in chapter 4, on projected accounts for commercial firms such as those in chapter 5, and on projected government cash flows such as those in chapter 6. Since these accounts are projected for the life of the project, there will be no separate allowance for depreciation. Instead, as noted earlier, the costs will have been entered in the years they are incurred and the returns in the year they are realized.

In the economic analysis, we will want to work with accounts cast on a constant basis; thus we will want to be sure that any inflation contingency allowances have been taken out. As noted in chapter 2, however, physical contingency allowances and contingency allowances intended to allow for *relative* price changes are properly incorporated in the economic accounts, even when the accounts are in constant prices. Of course, any of the items included among the contingencies may be revalued, if necessary, to adjust them from their market prices to economic values. The projected financial accounts will usually not have any entry for cash. Instead, they will show separately the cash position of the farmer or note a cumulative cash surplus or deficit. It is possible, however, that some accounts may have a cash balance included in an entry for working capital or the like. If such an entry exists, it must be removed from the economic analysis; since we will be working on a real basis in the economic accounts, we will show real costs when they occur and real benefits when they are realized.

Determining the Premium on Foreign Exchange

Adjusting the financial accounts of a project to reflect economic values involves determining the proper premium to attach to foreign exchange. That determination quickly involves issues of obtaining proper values and of economic theory. Fortunately for most agricultural project analysts, the answer to the question about how to determine the foreign exchange premium is simple (and simplistic): ask the central planning agency. The point is that if various alternative investment opportunities open to a nation are to be compared, the same foreign exchange premium must be used in the economic analysis of each alternative. Otherwise we will be mixing apples and oranges and cannot use our analysis reliably to choose among alternatives. Sometimes, however, the analyst will be forced to make his own estimate of the foreign exchange premium. A practical approach, along with some of the theoretical and applied problems of the computation, is given by Ward (1976). Little and Mirrlees (1974), Squire and van der Tak (1975), and the UNIDO *Guidelines* (1972*a*) also outline in considerable detail how to make the conversion between foreign exchange and domestic currency when their analytical systems are used.

The need to determine the foreign exchange premium arises because in many countries, as a result of national trade policies (including tariffs on imported goods and subsidies on exports), people pay a premium on traded goods over what they pay for nontraded goods. This premium is not adequately reflected when the prices of traded goods are converted to the domestic currency equivalent at the official exchange rate. The premium represents the additional amount that users of traded goods, on an average and throughout the economy, are willing to pay to obtain one more unit of traded goods. Since all costs and benefits in economic analysis are valued on the basis of opportunity cost or willingness to pay, it is the relation between willingness to pay for traded as opposed to nontraded goods that establishes their relative value.

The premium people are willing to pay for traded goods, then, represents the amount that, on the average, traded goods are mispriced in relation to nontraded items when the official exchange rate is used to convert foreign exchange prices into domestic values. By applying the premium to traded goods, we are able to compare the values of traded and nontraded goods by the criterion of opportunity cost or willingness to pay. Although this premium is commonly referred to as the foreign exchange premium, it should be recognized that the premium is actually a premium for traded goods; foreign exchange itself has no intrinsic value. The premium for traded goods is a premium on the particular "basket" of traded goods that the present and projected trade pattern implies. Of course, future patterns of trade could change the exact composition of the basket, and thus the premium would change; to estimate these changes involves a knowledge of elasticities—the way demand and supply of goods and services vary when prices change—that is generally not available. Where such elasticities are known, it is possible for a well-trained economist to provide the project analyst with a more accurate estimate of the expected premium on foreign exchange.

If traded items were to be taken into the project analysis at an economic value obtained by simply multiplying the border price by the official exchange rate without adjusting for the foreign exchange premium, imported items would appear too cheap and domestic items too dear. This would encourage overinvestment in projects that use imports. For example, if combine harvesters look cheap because no allowance is made for the premium on traded goods, then imported combines might displace local harvest labor, even though the local labor might have no other opportunities for employment.

There are two equivalent ways of incorporating the premium on foreign exchange in our economic analysis. The first is to multiply the official exchange rate by the foreign exchange premium, which yields a shadow foreign exchange rate. [Note that this derivation of the shadow exchange rate is appropriate for efficiency analysis of projects and thus has a discrete definition. Other definitions of the shadow exchange rate are appropriate depending on the uses to which the rate will be put. Bacha and Taylor (1972) discuss some of these alternatives.] The shadow exchange rate is then used to convert the foreign exchange price of traded items into domestic currency. The effect of using the shadow exchange rate is to make traded items relatively more expensive in domestic currency by the amount of the foreign exchange premium. (An alternative arithmetic formulation is to convert the foreign exchange price into domestic currency at the official exchange rate and then multiply by 1 plus the foreign exchange premium stated in decimal terms.) The shadow exchange rate approach has been used in the past in most World Bank projects when adjustments have been made to allow for the foreign exchange premium on traded goods, and it is also used in the UNIDO *Guidelines* (1972a).

An alternative way to allow for the foreign exchange premium on traded items that is increasingly coming into use is to reduce the domestic currency values for nontraded items by an amount sufficient to reflect the premium. This is sometimes called the "conversion factor" approach. In its simplest form, based on straightforward efficiency prices, a single conversion factor—the "standard conversion factor" of Squire and van der Tak—is derived by taking the ratio of the value of all exports and imports at border prices to their value at domestic prices (Squire and van der Tak 1975, p. 93). In this form, the standard conversion factor bears a close relation to our shadow exchange rate; indeed, the standard conversion factor may be determined by dividing the official exchange rate by the shadow exchange rate or by taking the reciprocal of 1 plus the foreign exchange premium stated in decimal terms. Market prices or shadow prices of nontraded items are then multiplied by this standard conversion factor, and this reduces them to their appropriate economic value. Little and Mirrlees and Squire and van der Tak both adopt the conversion factor approach. In addition, both pairs of authors recommend deriving specific conversion factors for particular groups of products that will allow for any difference between market prices and opportunity costs and for the foreign exchange premium on traded items. As a result, their specific conversion factors may always be applied directly to domestic market prices. These authors also recommend that their conversion factors be calculated in social prices by including distribution weights.

In the valuation system followed here, all items are valued at efficiency prices without allowance for distribution weights (the issue of selecting projects to achieve distributional objectives is treated as a subsequent decision). This being the case, consideration of the distribution-weighted conversion factors proposed by Little and Mirrlees and Squire and van der Tak may be left aside, and we may focus our discussion on the Squire and van der Tak standard conversion factor as it relates to efficiency prices.

The relation between the official exchange rate (in the equations below, OER), the foreign exchange premium (FX premium), the shadow exchange rate (SER), and the standard conversion factor (SCF) is perhaps easier to understand in equation form:

$$\text{OER} \times (1 + \text{FX premium}) = \text{SER and,} \quad \frac{1}{(1 + \text{FX premium})} = \text{SCF},$$

so that, as Squire and van der Tak note (1975, p. 93),

$$\text{SER} = \frac{\text{OER}}{\text{SCF}} \quad \text{and} \quad \text{SCF} = \frac{\text{OER}}{\text{SER}}.$$

We may illustrate these relations by an example taken from the Agricultural Minimum Package Project in Ethiopia. At the time the project was appraised, the analyst knew that the official exchange rate of Eth\$2.07 = US\$1 failed to account for a foreign exchange premium of at least 10 percent. (The symbol for the Ethiopian dollar is Eth\$; since this project was appraised the name of the currency unit has been changed to birr.) Thus, the analyst multiplied the official exchange rate by 1 plus a 10 percent foreign exchange premium to obtain a shadow exchange rate of Eth\$2.28 = US\$1 (2.07 × 1.1 = 2.28) that he rounded up to Eth\$2.30 = US\$1. The shadow exchange rate was then applied to all traded items in the financial accounts, thereby increasing their relative value.

If the domestic currency is worth more per unit than the foreign exchange, the arithmetic is somewhat different. At the time the Nucleus

Estate/Smallholder Oil Palm Project in Rivers State, Nigeria, was appraised, the official exchange rate was ₦1 = US$1.54. (The symbol for Nigerian naira is ₦.) The project analysts were given a shadow exchange rate of ₦1 = US$1.27 to use in their economic evaluation. If, however, they had simply been informed that the foreign exchange premium was 21 percent, they could have determined the shadow exchange rate by dividing the dollar value by 1 plus the premium stated in decimal terms (1.54 ÷ 1.21 = 1.27).

Of course, the effect of applying the shadow exchange rate to the traded items in the Ethiopian project was to make all nontraded items 10 percent less expensive in relation to the traded items in the economic accounts as opposed to the financial accounts. Now, instead of increasing the relative value of traded items, we could reduce the value of all nontraded items appearing in the financial accounts so that in the economic account they are relatively 10 percent less expensive. To do this we calculate the standard conversion factor, which is 1 divided by 1 plus the amount of the foreign exchange premium stated in decimal terms. In this case, the result is a factor of 0.909 (1 ÷ 1.1 = 0.909). To obtain the economic values, we would then multiply all financial prices for nontraded items by this factor if these market prices have been judged good estimates of opportunity cost or good estimates of economic value on grounds of willingness to pay. For nontraded items such as wage rates for unskilled labor for which it is felt that the market price has overstated the economic values, we would first determine a good estimate of the economic value in domestic currency and then multiply that by the standard conversion factor. Financial prices for traded items, whether imports or exports, would be left unchanged in the economic accounts except that any transfer payment included in these prices would be taken out. To get all values into the same currency, we would convert all foreign currency prices to domestic currency values using the official exchange rate.

When we turn to determining measures of project worth in chapter 9, we will find that the absolute value of the net present worth differs depending on which approach we use, shadow exchange rate or conversion factor, but that the relative net present worths of different projects analyzed by the same approach will not change. Whichever approach is used, the internal rate of return, the benefit-cost ratio, and the net benefit-investment ratio do not change. (Using a number of disaggregated conversion factors, rather than a standard conversion factor, can give different values for the measures of project worth. Hence, for projects at the margin of acceptability, using specific conversion factors rather than a standard conversion factor or a shadow exchange rate may result in a different decision on whether to accept or reject, but such cases are infrequent.)

Adjusting Financial Prices to Economic Values

Let us now proceed with the adjustments necessary to convert financial prices to economic values. We will divide these into three steps: (1)

adjustment for direct transfer payments, (2) adjustment for price distortions in traded items, and (3) adjustment for price distortions in nontraded items. We will then note that, for what are termed "indirectly traded" items (locally produced items that use a high proportion of traded inputs, such as locally assembled tractors, or construction that uses imported materials), steps 2 and 3 must be done at the same time.

Step 1. Adjustment for direct transfer payments

The first step in adjusting financial prices to economic values is to eliminate direct transfer payments.

Direct transfer payments (see chapter 2) are payments that represent not the use of real resources but only the transfer of claims to real resources from one person in the society to another. In agricultural projects, the most common transfer payments are taxes, direct subsidies, and credit transactions that include loans, receipts, repayment of principal, and interest payments. Two credit transactions that might escape notice are accounts payable and accounts receivable. All these entries should be taken out before the financial accounts are adjusted to reflect economic values.

Many important subsidies in agriculture operate not by means of direct payments but through mechanisms that change market prices. These subsidies are not direct subsidies treated as direct transfer payments but rather are indirect subsidies. The financial price of an item for which the price has been changed because of an indirect subsidy is converted to an economic value according to the procedures outlined below for traded items in step 2 and, as appropriate, for nontraded items in step 3.

Step 2. Adjustment for price distortions in traded items

The second step in adjusting financial prices to economic values is the adjustment for distortions in market prices of traded items.

Traded items are those for which, if exports,

$$\text{f.o.b. price} > \text{domestic cost of production,}$$

or the items may be exported through government intervention by use of export subsidies and the like, and, if imports,

$$\text{domestic cost of production} > \text{c.i.f. price.}$$

Conceptually—and usually in practice, too—prices for traded items in project analysis are more easily dealt with than those for nontraded items. We begin the valuation by determining the "border price." For imports, this normally will be the c.i.f. price and, for exports, normally the f.o.b. price. The border price is then adjusted to allow for domestic transport and marketing costs between the point of import or export and the project site; the result is the efficiency price to be used in the project account (see the subsection on "Economic export and import parity values," below).

If the proposed project produces something that can be used in place of imported goods—that is, if it produces an "import substitute"—the value to the society is the foreign exchange saved by using the domestic product valued at the border price, in this case the c.i.f. price. But if the project uses items that might otherwise have been exported—that is, if it uses "diverted exports"—then the opportunity cost to the society of these items is the foreign exchange lost on the exports forgone valued at the border price, this time the f.o.b. price.

If we are using conversion factors to allow for the foreign exchange premium, the economic value of a traded item would be obtained by converting the foreign exchange price to its domestic currency equivalent using the official exchange rate.

If we are using the shadow exchange rate to allow for the foreign exchange premium, the economic value of a traded item would be obtained by converting the foreign exchange price to its domestic currency equivalent using the shadow exchange rate.

To illustrate how these computations are made, we may take as an example an imported item such as a combine harvester for which the c.i.f. price is US$45,000. In the financial accounts, we will convert this price to domestic currency using the official exchange rate of, say, Rs10 = US$1, obtaining a c.i.f. price in domestic currency of Rs450,000 (45,000 × 10 = 450,000). To this would be added any import duty, say 10 percent, or Rs45,000 (450,000 × 0.10 = 45,000); the price of the combine in our financial accounts would therefore be Rs495,000 (450,000 + 45,000 = 495,000). (The costs of moving the harvester to the project site would also be added; see the subsection on "Economic export and import parity values," below.) If we are using the conversion factor approach to allow for the foreign exchange premium in our economic accounts, we would enter the combine in the accounts at the c.i.f. price expressed in domestic currency converted at the official exchange rate, or Rs450,000 (45,000 × 10 = 450,000). There would be no allowance for the duty because that is a transfer payment. If we are using the shadow exchange rate approach to allow for the foreign exchange premium, however, we would increase the price of the imported items to reflect the premium. Suppose we assume the foreign exchange premium to be 20 percent; our shadow exchange rate thus becomes Rs12 = US$1 (10 × 1.2 = 12). Now the Rs495,000 item in our financial accounts becomes Rs540,000 in our economic account (45,000 × 12 = 540,000). We could have accomplished the same thing, of course, by multiplying our domestic financial price (net of transfer payments) by 1 plus the foreign exchange premium (450,000 × 1.2 = 540,000). The effect of our computation, obviously, is to make imported items more expensive in our economic analysis.

The same logic works in reverse for exports. The ton of wheat that is worth $176 a ton f.o.b. at the port of export will be entered in the financial accounts by converting the foreign exchange price to its domestic currency equivalent using the official exchange rate. This gives a value of Rs1,760 (176 × 10 = 1,760), assuming that there is no export subsidy. The same rupee value would be entered in the economic accounts if we are using the conversion factor approach to allow for the foreign exchange premium. If we are using the shadow exchange rate approach to allow for the foreign exchange premium, we multiply the foreign exchange border price of the wheat by the shadow exchange rate instead of the official exchange rate to calculate the economic value expressed in domestic currency. This increases the relative value of the wheat, which now will be valued at Rs2,112 (176 × 12 = 2,112). We could have accomplished the same thing, of course, by multiplying our financial domestic price by 1 plus the foreign exchange premium stated in decimal terms (1,760 × 1.2 = 2,112). Now the ton of wheat, like other exported goods, is valued at its opportunity cost and is seen to be relatively much more valuable.

Diverted exports and import substitutes are valued by the same line of reasoning, except that for a diverted export we would take the f.o.b. price as the basis for valuation and for import substitutes we would take the c.i.f. price. In the examples of the previous paragraphs, if the country exported combines but diverted them to a domestic project, the opportunity cost would be based on the f.o.b. price instead of the c.i.f. price we assumed for imported combines. Similarly, if the wheat produced were to substitute for imports, we would base its value on the c.i.f. price of wheat rather than on the f.o.b. price we assumed for the case of exports.

In practice, values for most traded items are determined by taking the border price as we have been using it and then either subtracting or adding the domestic handling costs to obtain an economic value at the farm gate or project boundary—the economic export or import parity value (see the subsection on "Economic export and import parity values," below). Also, many items that are locally produced incorporate a significant proportion of imported components and may be considered indirectly imported items (see the section on "Indirectly Traded Items," below). To determine either parity values or values for indirectly traded items involves valuing separately not only the traded component but the nontraded component as well, so we will defer detailed discussion of these values until we have discussed valuing nontraded items.

Step 3. Adjustment for price distortions in nontraded items

The third step in adjusting financial prices to economic values is the adjustment for distortions in market prices of nontraded items.

Nontraded items are those for which

$$\text{c.i.f. price} > \text{domestic cost of production} > \text{f.o.b. price,}$$

or the items are nontraded because of government intervention by means of import bans, quotas, and the like.

Often, nontraded items will be bulky goods such as straw or bricks, which by their very nature tend to be cheaper to produce domestically than to import but for which the export price is lower than the domestic cost of production. In other instances, nontraded items are highly perishable goods such as fresh vegetables or fluid milk for direct consumption.

In general, these are produced under relatively competitive conditions—
they are produced either by many small farmers or by a few industrial
producers for whom entry into the market is relatively easy; thus prices
cannot rise too far out of line before new competition appears.

If we are using the shadow exchange rate approach to allow for the
foreign exchange premium, and if the market price of a nontraded item is
a good estimate of the opportunity cost, or willingness to pay is the
criterion, we will accept the market price directly as our economic value.
Otherwise, we will adjust the market price to eliminate distortions by the
methods outlined in this section and then use the estimate of the opportunity cost we obtain as the shadow price to be entered in the economic
accounts.

If we are using the conversion factor approach to allow for the foreign
exchange premium, an additional step is necessary. All prices for nontraded items are reduced by multiplying them by the appropriate conversion factor. When willingness to pay is the criterion or when the
market price is considered to be a good estimate of opportunity cost, the
market price is accepted as the basis for valuation and then reduced by
multiplying it by the conversion factor to obtain the economic value. But
if we are using the standard conversion factor and the market price must
be adjusted to obtain a better estimate of the opportunity cost, then the
opportunity cost must, in turn, be multiplied by the standard conversion
factor. (If specific conversion factors have been developed, as Little and
Mirrlees and Squire and van der Tak suggest in their systems, then these
factors incorporate the adjustments for nontraded goods distortions,
opportunity costs, and distribution weights; the market price need only
be multiplied by the specific conversion factor to reach the economic
value.) Whether we use a shadow exchange rate or a standard conversion
factor to allow for the foreign exchange premium, the adjustments we
make to allow for distortions in market prices of nontraded items are
essentially the same; only the step of multiplying the market price or the
opportunity cost by the standard conversion factor differs.

As we said earlier in the chapter, prices for traded items are more easily
adjusted to economic values than are prices for nontraded items. The
following subsections treat some of the difficulties encountered in determining economic values for various nontraded items.

MARKET PRICES AS ESTIMATES OF ECONOMIC VALUE. In a perfectly competitive market, the opportunity cost of an item would be its price, and this
price would also be equal to the marginal value product of the item (see
chapter 3). If a nontraded item is bought and sold in a relatively competitive market, the market price is the measure of the willingness to pay and
is generally the best estimate of an opportunity cost. Most agricultural
projects are expected to meet a growing demand for food or fiber and are
small relative to the total agricultural production of the nation. If that is
the case, in general we can accept the market price directly as our
estimate of the economic value of a nontraded item. Also, if we are
valuing a domestically produced project input that is produced by a

supply industry operating near full capacity, we can generally accept the market price of the input as its economic value.

In some instances more common in industrial and transport projects than in agricultural, the output of the project is large relative to the market. The output from the project may therefore cause the price to fall. But the economic value of the new production, despite the fall in price, is not lower to the *old* users of the product; to them, it is still worth what the price was without the project. Yet to *new* users, the project output is not worth what the old price was; otherwise, the price would not have fallen. Under these circumstances, the economic value of the new output is neither the old price nor the new; rather, it is estimated by some weighted average of the old and new values. In technical economic terms, the total value of the new output is measured by the additional area under the demand curve as project output is increased, and the marginal value in use for each new buyer is measured by the demand curve at the point the buyer enters the market. The problem is that the precise shape of the demand curve is rarely known. As a result most project economists, when dealing with a project whose output is large relative to the market, adopt a simplifying rule of thumb—they assume that the demand curve is linear and downward sloping at 45 degrees. They then take the new estimate of the average value in use or opportunity cost—hence, of economic value—to be the average of the price without the project and the lower price with the project.

Sometimes a project will be proposed that does not meet new demand but replaces other goods or services in the market. Again, this is more common in industrial and transport projects than it is in agricultural. In such situations, if the project accounts are cast on a with-and-without basis, the economic value of the incremental net benefit stream would reflect only the saving from the new project compared with the old. This is because one of the costs of the new project would be the benefit forgone from the old production no longer realized and because one of the benefits would be the cost avoided for the old production. Such a case might arise, for instance, if an inefficient food processing plant were to be replaced by a more modern and efficient one, or if a high-cost railway branch line were to be replaced by bus and truck transport along an existing highway. Occasionally, however, a project will be proposed for a new plant that will replace existing output, and the analyst fails to recognize the with-and-without situation. Instead, he values the output from the new plant as if it were meeting new demand and forgets to charge as a cost to the project the benefit forgone from the production of the old plant that is to be displaced. If the project is not to be cast on a with-and-without basis, then the analyst must take as his gross benefit only the economic value of the resources saved by replacing the old plant, not the economic value of the output from the new plant.

Note that some nontraded items may involve using significant amounts of imported raw materials. These will be considered below, in the discussion of indirectly traded items. Such items might include machinery assembled domestically from imported components or electricity that is generally nontraded but that may require imported generating equipment and traded fuels for production.

One nontraded item that can sometimes lead to confusion is insurance. At first glance, insurance might look like a transfer payment and thus would not be included in the economic accounts of the project. We may, however, look upon insurance as a kind of sharing of the risk of real economic loss. This would be the case for fire insurance if project buildings were to be pooled with many other buildings in the society. In the event of a fire, there is a real economic cost. The resources used to replace a burned building, or the output forgone because a building no longer is available, reduce the amount of final goods and services available to the society and thus create a real reduction of the national income. Therefore, to the extent an insurance cost represents sharing of risk, it represents a proportionate sharing of real economic cost and should be included in the economic accounts. The insurance rate is usually based on the probability of a real loss and the value of the item insured.

Although the market price can frequently be accepted as a good estimate of the economic value of a nontraded item, for institutional reasons of one kind or another the market price can vary significantly from the opportunity cost of the item to the society. Two such nontraded items are important in most agricultural projects: land and labor.

VALUING LAND. The opportunity cost of land is the net value of production forgone when the use of the land is changed from its without-project use to its with-project use.

The simplest case to value is one in which land changes use but not management control, either because an owner-operator is farming the land or because the same tenant continues to farm it. This is a common case in agricultural projects in which farmers are simply encouraged to adopt a more productive technology. If the analyst has laid out the financial accounts to show the situations with and without the project for farm budgets as suggested in chapter 4, then the incremental net benefit (that is, the incremental cash flow) of the project, when financial prices have been converted to economic values and the accounts aggregated as suggested in chapter 8, will include an allowance for the net value of production forgone by changing the land use. Take, for example, the Kemubu Irrigation Project in Malaysia in which new irrigation water permitted changing the land use in the dry season from rather unproductive pasture to second-crop paddy rice production. The contribution of the land to the value of the pasture—hence, its opportunity cost—would be properly accounted for when the value of the weight gain of the livestock pastured on the land without the project is subtracted from the value of the paddy rice produced on the land with the project. Converting project financial prices to economic values—say, changing the market price of the weight gain of the animals on the pasture and the market price of paddy rice to their economic equivalents if these are seen to be different from the market prices—automatically revalues the opportunity cost of the change in land use from financial to economic terms.

In other instances, however, the financial accounts must show a cost for purchasing land or the right to use it. Here problems arise because in many countries agricultural land is hardly sold at all, and, when it is, considerations of investment security and prestige may push its price well above what the land could reasonably be expected to contribute to agricultural production. In these instances, we will not want to accept the market purchase price as a good estimate of the economic opportunity cost of the land and must search for an alternative. Many times that alternative will be to take the rental value of the land. In a number of countries, although land is infrequently sold, there is a fairly widespread and competitive rental market. This may be true if there is considerable tenancy in the country, of course, but it may also hold true if the dominant form of land tenure is the owner-occupied farm. Older farmers may not wish to cultivate all of their holdings themselves and will be willing to rent a field to a younger neighboring farmer; widows may not wish to operate their holdings themselves; or a farmer suffering from an illness may wish to rent part of his farm for a season while he recovers. When such a rental market exists, it probably provides a fairly good indication of the net value of production of the land and, hence, of the opportunity cost if the land use is changed. A renter is not likely to pay any premium for prestige or investment security and thus will not pay a rent higher than the contribution the land can make to the crop he proposes to grow. That rental value may then be entered in the project's financial account year by year as a cost. Alternatively, it may be capitalized by dividing the rent by an appropriate rate of interest stated in decimal terms; the capitalized value is then entered in the first year of the project's financial accounts. The appropriate rate of interest actually would be the economic rate of return (see chapter 9), but this may well involve repetitive computations. Some analysts prefer to use the opportunity cost of capital (also discussed in chapter 9). If this rate were, say, 12 percent and the going rental rate were Rs525 a hectare, then the capital value of a hectare would be Rs4,375 ($525 \div 0.12 = 4,375$). If we were using the conversion factor approach to allow for the foreign exchange premium, this capitalized value would be, in turn, multiplied by a conversion factor. If the standard conversion factor were 0.909, for instance, the land would then have an economic value of Rs3,977 ($4,375 \times 0.909 = 3,977$). At the end of the project, the same value of the land could be credited to the project as a residual value.

Inevitably, however, there will be instances in which neither the purchase price nor the rental value is a good estimate; we then will have to make a direct estimate of the productive capability of the land. Such a direct estimate is not difficult if idle land is to be used for a settlement project. In the projects financed by the World Bank in the Amazon basin at Alto Bene in Brazil and in the Caqueta region of Colombia, the land without the project would in effect have produced no economically valuable output at all. Hence, the net value of production forgone was clearly zero, and no value for the land was entered in the project economic accounts. If settlers were required to pay the government a purchase price, either all at once or in installments, the farm budgets at market prices in the financial analysis would have to show those payments as a cost. When these financial farm budgets were converted to economic values, however, there would be no cost entered for the land because there was no reduction in national income as a result of shifting its use from jungle to farmland. (Of course, the cost of clearing jungle land should be reflected somewhere in the project costs.)

In other cases it will not be so simple. The analyst will have to make a direct estimate of the net value of production forgone for bringing the land into the project. A straightforward approach is to take the gross value of the land's output at market prices and deduct from that all the costs of production—including allowances for hired and family labor and for the interest on the capital engaged, again all at market prices. The analyst can assign the residual as the contribution of the land to the production of the output and take that as the opportunity cost of the land in financial terms. This set of computations can then be converted to economic terms by using economic values for each of the input and output entries. For those familiar with the technique, estimating a production function would provide a much more accurate estimate of the contribution of the land to the value of the output than the direct method described here and thus is a preferable approach.

VALUING LABOR. Wage rates for labor in many developing countries may not accurately reflect the opportunity cost of shifting labor from its without-project occupation to its with-project use.

The price of labor in a perfectly competitive market, like other prices in that impossible place, would be determined by its marginal value product. That is, the wage would be equal to the value of the additional product that one additional laborer could produce. It would pay a farmer to hire an additional laborer—for harvesting, for example—so long as that extra worker increased total output by a value more than the wage the farmer had to pay him.

Even in labor-abundant societies, there are probably peak seasons at planting and harvesting when most rural workers can find employment. At those seasons, the market wage paid rural labor is probably a pretty good estimate of its opportunity cost and its marginal value product; therefore, we could accept the market wage as the economic value of the rural labor.

The problem of course is that, except for the peak seasons, in many crowded countries the addition of one more laborer may add very little to the total production—in an extreme instance, nothing at all. That is, if there is a surplus of agricultural workers, there may be very little or virtually no productive outlet for their energies in the off-season. In technical language, we may say that the marginal value product of such labor—the amount such labor adds to the national income—is very close to zero. Because the marginal value product of labor is also the opportunity cost of labor in the economic accounts, we may make another statement: if we take a laborer away from a farm community where he is producing very little or nothing and put him to work productively in an agricultural project that produces something of value, we do not have to forgo very much to use this labor to realize new production. This being the case, we can consider the cost of the laborer to be very low—some economists would say even zero. By this line of reasoning, the proper value to enter in the economic (not financial) account as the cost of labor would be very small, perhaps only a fraction of the going market wage. If the opportunity cost of labor in an agricultural project is properly priced at a very small amount, then it is likely that the rate of return on the project will look very favorable in comparison, say, with a capital-intensive alternative project that uses labor-saving tractors or expensive imported harvesting machinery.

Note that the validity of this reasoning is not changed by the fact that agricultural labor is, in fact, paid a wage well above its opportunity cost. A common example of a "wage" paid, even though little productive work is available on the margin, is found in the case of family labor. Older children and the farmer's wife will be entitled to a share of the family income even if the family farm is too small to give them an opportunity to be productive. In this instance, if an older son were to find productive employment elsewhere, the total production on the farm might be reduced by very little or none at all. Yet, because the older son is entitled to a share of the total family income, he would accept new employment far away from his home only if he were offered a wage in excess of his share—and that might be well above what his marginal value product would be and the reduction in farm output that would occur if he were to leave.

Rural wages may be above the marginal value product because of a traditional concept of a "proper" wage or because of social pressure on the more prosperous farmers in a community to share their wealth with their less fortunate neighbors. In parts of Java, for example, social custom prevents even quite small farmers from harvesting their own rice. Instead, they permit landless laborers to do the work, even though the farmer himself may well have the time to do it. This is explicitly seen by the community as a means of providing at least something for the poorest agricultural laborers. Unfortunately, increasing economic pressures on small farmers and continued population growth are leading to a breakdown of this system.

Virtually all economists now agree that the marginal value product of agricultural labor on an annual basis worldwide is more than zero, so that in every instance our opportunity cost of labor, at least in some season or another, will be positive—even though it may still be very low. [A more detailed discussion of the marginal value product of agricultural labor can be found in McDiarmid (1977) and in Barnum and Squire (1979).]

To begin our discussion of how actually to determine an economic value for labor, we can take the easiest case. In most instances, skilled labor in developing countries is considered to be in rather short supply and would most likely be fully employed even without the project being considered. Hence, the wages paid workers such as mechanics, foremen, or project managers are in general assumed to represent the true marginal value product of these workers, and the wages are entered at their market values in the economic accounts. The rationale here is that, if those skills are in such scarce supply that they would be worth more than the going wage, then someone in the society would be prepared to pay more, and the skilled worker would then move to where he could earn that higher wage, thus establishing a new equilibrium. This convention of accepting market wages as good estimates of economic value may substantially undervalue skilled labor or the management skills of such top civil servants as extension specialists and project managers—or project analysts!

Note too that, as we consider the opportunity cost of labor and how to estimate it, if we set the financial accounts so they correctly show the situations with and without the project, then the opportunity cost of family labor will be appropriately priced in financial terms. Suppose that, in the dry season without the project, a farmer along the north coast of Java could find essentially no gainful employment. With the advent of the Jatiluhur Irrigation Project he now is able to produce a second crop of rice, and his net benefit rises accordingly. When we subtract his without-project net benefit (which would be essentially only what the family could earn for a rainy-season rice crop) from the with-project net benefit (which will include earnings from two crops), the incremental net benefit will correctly show the labor return the family had to give up during the dry season (essentially nothing) to participate in the project and produce a second crop of rice. Shifting the financial prices in the farm budget to economic values also automatically converts the opportunity cost of family labor to economic values.

To make our farm budgets work this way, we must remember to include any off-farm earnings in the accounts. Suppose we assume that the farmer from the north coast of Java goes to Jakarta and finds employment in the construction industry during the dry season, as many such farmers do. The without-project net benefit will thus be increased by the amount of the farmer's off-farm earnings. If he wishes to use Jatiluhur irrigation water to produce a second crop of rice, he must now give up the construction wages he could otherwise have earned in the dry season. In turn, when we subtract the without-project net benefit from the with-project net benefit, which includes the returns from two crops of rice, the incremental net benefit will be smaller by the amount of the opportunity cost of labor at the market wage, that is, by the amount of construction earnings the farmer must forgo. We may proceed to convert these financial accounts to economic terms by revaluing the appropriate entries at their shadow prices. In doing so, however, we must remember that one shadow price will be the shadow wage rate for the construction earnings the farmer had to forgo. It is to estimating this shadow wage rate that we now may turn.

In most discussions of the marginal value product of labor—hence, of its economic opportunity cost—the standard is the productivity of the marginal agricultural laborer. This is true not only for agricultural projects but also for projects in other sectors, since it is assumed that additional manufacturing employment, for example, will tend to reduce the number of unemployed agricultural laborers. This would be true even if it is urban workers drawn from some other urban occupation who actually take the new factory jobs, since it is assumed the jobs they vacate will, in turn, be filled by workers drawn from agriculture.

Cast in this form, our estimate of the shadow wage rate must now focus on how to estimate the marginal value product of agricultural labor without the project. We can begin by noting that in most agricultural communities there is usually a season when virtually everyone who wants work can find it. Even unemployed urban laborers may return to their home villages in these peak seasons to help their families or to work as hired laborers. This happens at harvest time in Java, and may happen at the peak planting time in other areas where transplanted rice is grown. Thus, we may reasonably assume that this peak season labor market is a relatively competitive one, that labor is in relatively short supply at this period, and that the daily wage at this period is a good indicator of the daily marginal value product of the labor engaged.

With this accepted, a good estimate of the annual shadow wage for agricultural labor is the number of days in the year when most rural labor can expect to find employment, multiplied by the daily wage rate at such times, and reduced by a conversion factor if appropriate. If an agricultural worker's daily wage at harvest were Rs7.50, and during harvest and other peak seasons most people in the rural work force could find employment for 90 days, then his annual shadow wage might be Rs675 if we are using the shadow exchange rate approach to allow for the foreign exchange premium (7.50 × 90 = 675), or Rs614 if we are using the conversion factor approach and the factor is 0.909 (7.50 × 90 × 0.909 = 614). Now if we wanted to hire an agricultural laborer to work in our project for 250 days a year, all the society would give up in production— the opportunity cost—would be Rs675 if we are using the shadow exchange rate approach, or Rs614 if we are using the conversion factor approach. This opportunity cost is the economic value of the annual earnings of the laborer without the project. Note that we surely would have to expect to pay a wage much greater than this amount, and thus our financial accounts at market prices would have quite a different cost for this same agricultural laborer. It is possible, for instance, that the hired laborer would expect a wage of Rs7.50 a day for all 250 days he worked during the year, or an annual wage of Rs1,875 (7.50 × 250 = 1,875). More probably, he would be willing to work for rather less a day outside the harvest season—say, Rs5.00 a day. Thus, his annual wage might be something more on the order of Rs675 for 90 days and Rs5.00 a day for the remaining 160 days, or an annual total wage of Rs1,475 [(7.50 × 90) + (5.00 × 160) = 1,475]. The project analyst would clearly have to form a judgment of the shadow wage of hired labor on the best basis he could, just as he must for every other price estimate he makes.

Of course, in many agricultural projects labor is not engaged on a year-round basis. Rather, the work is quite seasonal, and we must consider in which particular season hired labor would be engaged. If our new cropping pattern calls for work to be done during the peak season, then we will have to consider that the peak season market wage is probably a good estimate of the marginal value product, and we could not justify using a lower wage as the basis for our shadow wage rate, even though there might be considerable unemployment in the off-season. In Egypt, for example, a common rotation calls for both rice and cotton to be harvested in October. If we were to propose a project incorporating these crops—or another crop requiring hired labor at this period—then the going wage (in 1975 about E£0.30 a day; the symbol for Egyptian pounds is E£) would be paid. Since even in a country as populous as Egypt most rural labor can find employment at this peak season, the use of a shadow wage rate derived from a basis less than the market wage would be unjustified. But suppose our project called for growing maize, which is planted in May when there is little other agricultural work available and harvested in August before the peak harvest season for rice and cotton. Then we might find that, on the margin, many agricultural laborers were either unemployed or not very productively engaged at that season and that to draw them into maize planting might entail an opportunity cost considerably less than the going wage, although it would perhaps not be zero. Thus, we might estimate that at this season the combination of being able to work only two or three days a week on the average, and then at jobs of rather low productivity, would justify taking a shadow wage rate based on half the going market rate. This would mean the equivalent of E£0.15 in 1975 if we are using the shadow foreign exchange rate approach (0.30 ÷ 2 = 0.15), or E£0.14 if we are using the conversion factor approach and the conversion factor is 0.909 (0.30 ÷ 2 × 0.909 = 0.14), even though our farm budget at market prices would continue to show a wage for hired labor of E£0.30.

All of these considerations will have to be adapted to fit the circumstances of any given project. For example, in India nationwide we might expect a shadow wage rate for agricultural labor rather less than the going wage rate. But using a nationwide shadow wage rate in particular projects might underestimate the true opportunity cost of the labor actually engaged in a project. The peak season in the Punjab, for instance, finds virtually all agricultural labor fully engaged, but in the neighboring state of Haryana the marginal labor in agriculture is not fully engaged. While many laborers from Haryana do migrate in search of peak season employment in the Punjab, not enough do so to meet the demand for labor completely. Using a very low shadow wage rate for a project in the Punjab might be unjustified because at the peak season the project would have to bid labor away from harvesting. Thus, although the shadow wage rate might not be as high as the harvest wage (but it might), neither would it be as low as conditions in neighboring Haryana might otherwise indicate.

This discussion of how to value labor applies whether labor is to be paid a money wage or is to be compensated in kind. The discussion so far has emphasized that it is the opportunity cost that determines the value of labor in the system of economic analysis we have adopted. The value of the payment actually made to labor—whether in money or in kind—is not the issue. If we shadow-price labor, we already are acknowledging that the wage the labor receives is different from the benefit forgone by using that labor in the project instead of in its next best alternative use without the project. It is the opportunity cost of the labor, not the form of payment, that sets the economic value of labor. Hence, it is irrelevant in a determination of the economic value of labor whether labor is paid a money wage or is compensated in kind—for example, in food grain, even though the food grain may be a tradable commodity and even though the food grain itself might need to be shadow-priced if it is to be valued.

EXCESS CAPACITY. In some projects, a domestically produced input may come from a plant that is not operating at its full capacity. If that is the case, then the opportunity cost of using the input in a new project is only the marginal variable cost of producing the input, and no allowance need be made for the fixed capital cost of the plant itself. If the national cement industry is operating at less than its full capacity and it is proposed to line irrigation canals with cement, then the cost of the cement for the canals would be only the marginal variable cost of producing the cement. This would be less than the average cost of cement production, which would include some allowance for fixed costs of production.

Situations such as these are more common in industrial projects than in agricultural projects. When they do occur, however, they may influence the timing of projects. A canal-lining project might be quite attractive if it is begun soon, while there is excess cement-manufacturing capacity, but much less attractive later, when demand has caught up with the cement industry's capacity. To supply cement for canal lining later, after demand has picked up, would entail constructing an additional cement plant. At that time, new fixed as well as variable costs would be incurred, and the analyst would include all costs, both fixed and variable, plus an estimate of the "normal" profit in calculating the cost of cement.

TRADABLE BUT NONTRADED ITEMS. In the system of project analysis presented here, we lay out the economic accounts as best we can to reflect the real resource costs and benefits of the proposed project. The project will be carried out within a framework of economic policies set by the government. The project analyst must make the best judgment about what those policies are and *will* be, not just what they ought to be, and work the economic analysis accordingly. This can lead to difficult choices when the analyst must evaluate the real effects on resources of a project that involves items that could be traded but probably will not be because of government regulation. These items, which are "tradable but nontraded" across national boundaries, are valued as nontraded.

Such items would usually be imported were it not for an import quota or an outright ban that is enforced against them. Their domestic price may well rise high above the prevailing price on the world market. The import restriction might be enforced to protect domestic industries, even though the imported item may be preferred by consumers. Import of foreign engines for tubewells, for example, may be forbidden so that domestic manufacture might be encouraged. Yet, the domestic equivalent may not be as efficient or as durable as the imported engine and may cost more to produce. The domestic engine clearly could not compete on the world market, and it would therefore be a nontraded item. For those few imported engines allowed to enter the country, the price may rise quite high. This indicates that to some buyer the imported item is worth more than its domestic equivalent. If our project will use one of these engines, the economic value is *not* a price based on the world market as if the engines could be relatively freely traded. Rather, it is the higher domestic market price of the imported engine, which indicates its high opportunity cost. Upon reexamination, of course, we might consider changing the project design to use the domestic engine—for example, we might do so if we find the domestic engine to be less costly when valued at shadow prices.

For the domestic equivalent of an imported item, the market price usually will closely approximate the real resource use that went into producing it. But if there is a shortage and the price is bid up, in the absence of additional imports the market price will rise above the cost of production. In this case, the opportunity cost of the item will not be determined by the resources used to produce it but by its marginal value product in its best alternative use. If the price is higher than is justified by the resources used to produce the item, it may well be because to *someone* that high price for the domestic engine is worth it—for this buyer's purposes, the marginal value product of the scarce engine at least equals the market price. If we wish to bid that engine away for use in our project, we are denying its use to the other potential buyer. If we use the engine in our project, the economy must forgo the productive contribution of the engine in the alternative use the other potential buyer had in mind—our standard concept of opportunity cost. Again, in this instance the opportunity cost is most likely well estimated by the market price; if it were not, other buyers would not have bid the price up so high for the limited number of engines available.

If there is an import ban on an imported final good or service, then we will base the economic valuation on the criterion of willingness to pay and accept the market price as a good indicator of the economic value of the product—provided that we expect the trade ban to remain in force throughout the life of the project. Earlier we cited the example of a ban on sugar imports that would force the domestic price of sugar above its border price. If the ban on imports will continue, then the higher price of sugar indicates a willingness to pay that, in turn, is an indicator of the economic value set on sugar by the consumers. In the project analysis, we would accept this market price as the economic value, not a border price as if the sugar were being traded.

For both kinds of import substitutes we have cited, the analyst may want to prepare an analysis that will indicate the effect on the proposed project of lifting the import ban. We will discuss this topic further below, in the section on using economic analysis to signal alternative trade policies.

Note that, when we refer to items that are nontraded because of government regulation, we are really referring to those items that are nontraded on the margin. In other words, if there is a rigidly enforced quota on an imported item that restricts imports well below the quantity that otherwise would be imported, and if our project represents an additional demand for the imported item, then the item must be considered nontraded for the purpose of our project analysis.

It is not only imports that may be nontraded items because of government regulation, although imports are probably the most common examples. Export bans may drive the price of a product below what the price would be if the product were traded. Several years ago, egg producers in Pakistan had developed a brisk trade with the Persian Gulf states, and Pakistani egg production was expanding to fill the demand. Production could not, however, expand fast enough to prevent domestic egg prices from rising. Egg prices were, in fact, reflecting the world market price. To protect lower-income urban consumers, the government imposed an export ban on eggs. The domestic market was immediately oversupplied, and the price fell well below the export price. The willingness to pay for the additional production was reflected in the low price. Domestic consumers were willing to purchase the additional eggs only if the prices were quite attractive. If we had been contemplating an egg production project at that time, and we judged that the government regulation forbidding export would continue in force, then the value of eggs taken for our analysis would have been the low domestic market price arising from the willingness to pay, not some price derived as if the eggs were traded.

By valuing tradable but nontraded goods as nontraded, our system incorporates less of a free trade bias than if we assumed that all tradable items could and should be traded. Policies forbidding export or import of tradable items, however, will lead to a less than optimal allocation of resources in the economy, at least in the short run and, thus, to economic inefficiencies. We will return to this below when we discuss trade policy signals from project analysis.

Indirectly traded items

Some nontraded items in fact involve a substantial import content and are thus indirectly traded. When this is the case, it is good practice to value these items by valuing the domestic content as a nontraded item but the imported component as a traded item. Indirectly traded items in agricultural projects might be locally assembled tractors or construction that uses materials with a high import content.

Indirectly traded items offer no conceptual problem. In the financial analysis, as usual we accept the actual market price. In the economic analysis, however, we must "decompose" the indirectly imported item into its imported component and its domestically produced component and value each separately. Take locally assembled tractors, for example. We may be told that the market price of Rs65,000 includes a 30 percent local component (in other words, 30 percent of the market price represents domestic value added) and that 70 percent of the market price represents the imported component, which includes a 15 percent tariff. Thus, the local component will amount to Rs19,500 (65,000 × 0.3 = 19,500), and the imported component including the tariff will amount to Rs45,500 (65,000 × 0.7 = 45,500). The domestic value added will most likely arise from sources such as wages paid domestic skilled labor and domestically manufactured items that use mainly domestic raw materials. If so, we probably can accept the market price as a good indicator of the opportunity cost to the economy of these items.

To determine the economic value of the imported component of the tractor, the tariff must first be eliminated. This may be done by dividing the value of the imported component including the tariff by 1 plus the percentage of the tariff stated in decimal terms; this calculation gives a value for the imported component without the tariff of Rs39,565 (45,500 ÷ 1.15 = 39,565). This is, of course, the c.i.f. price converted to its domestic equivalent at the official exchange rate.

Now, if we are using the shadow exchange rate to allow for the foreign exchange premium, we will want to revalue the imported component of the indirect import (after the tariff has been eliminated) to reflect the distortion in the prices of traded goods. To do this, we can take the c.i.f. price converted at the official exchange rate and multiply it by 1 plus the foreign exchange premium stated in decimal terms. If the official exchange rate is Rs10 = US$1 and the foreign exchange premium is 20 percent, then for the imported component of the tractor we derive a value of Rs47,478 (39,565 × 1.2 = 47,478). (We could, of course, have taken the c.i.f. price in foreign exchange and converted it to its domestic equivalent by the shadow exchange rate; this would have given the identical result.) The shadow price of the tractor is now the market price of the domestic component, which we calculated to be Rs19,500, plus the shadow-priced value of the imported component of Rs47,478—or a total economic value of Rs66,978 (19,500 + 47,478 = 66,978).

If we are using the conversion factor to allow for the foreign exchange premium, the economic value of the imported component will be the c.i.f. price converted to the domestic currency equivalent at the official exchange rate after eliminating the tariff, or Rs39,565. To obtain the economic value of the domestic component we will need to multiply it by the conversion factor. For efficiency prices, we would use the standard conversion factor of 1 divided by 1 plus the foreign exchange premium stated in decimal terms. In this instance, the foreign exchange premium is 20 percent, so the standard conversion factor becomes 0.833 (1 ÷ 1.2 = 0.833). Applying this to the domestic component of the tractor, estimated to be Rs19,500 at market prices, gives us an economic value of Rs16,244 (19,500 × 0.833 = 16,244). The shadow price of the tractor now becomes the sum of the imported component valued at c.i.f. converted at the official exchange rate and the shadow price for the domestic component, or Rs55,809 (39,565 + 16,244) = 55,809).

In some agricultural projects, electricity is an important cost that may raise valuation problems. Electricity is usually thought of as a nontraded commodity. In reality, part of the value of electricity in most developing countries arises from the imported generating and transmission equipment and, perhaps, from imported fuel. Thus, in our system of project analysis, electricity might be an indirectly traded item. The first difficulty is that the price charged for electricity is not competitively set, since there is no competition in electricity. Rather, electricity rates are administered prices, and electricity prices thus may bear little relation to marginal value product or to opportunity cost. No easy means exists to resolve this problem. Some average rate, or perhaps some weighted average rate, will probably have to suffice as an estimate of opportunity cost at market prices. Once a rate is accepted, an estimate will have to be made of the domestic and imported components, and the components revalued using the shadow exchange rate or a conversion factor as appropriate, just as for any other indirectly imported item (and as we illustrated earlier by the example of tractors assembled from imported components). These calculations would usually not be undertaken by agricultural project analysts. The planning office should estimate a shadow price for electricity and other utilities to be used in all project analyses.

For some agricultural projects, new generating facilities will be required. In the simplest case, we might think of a project remote from the electric grid, such as a settlement project, in which a diesel generating unit might be included as a cost of the project. In that instance, there would be no particular problem of valuation. When new generating facilities would be needed to meet the demand on the power grid arising from an irrigation project, however, the problem would not be so simple. Here, the best approach would probably be to ask the electricity authority for an estimate of the additional cost the authority would incur for this particular project, and then to treat that cost—properly shadow-priced to allow for the imported component—as the opportunity cost. The cost of the additional facilities needed for the project will probably have to be reduced to a kilowatt-hour basis (using, perhaps, the capital recovery factor to estimate the annual charge for the new facilities).

We have contrasted use of a shadow exchange rate and a conversion factor to correct for price distortions caused by import and export tariffs and subsidies, and we have noted that the same correction can be realized whichever approach is used. This is illustrated in table 7-1, in which an economic account for a hypothetical project is drawn up using both a shadow exchange rate and a standard conversion factor.

When indirectly traded items will be used repeatedly in projects, it may be convenient to have specific conversion factors that, once they are derived, can be directly applied to the same class of indirectly traded items. This is the approach both Little and Mirrlees (1974) and Squire

Table 7-1. *Use of Shadow Exchange Rate and Standard Conversion Factor Compared*

| Item | Financial value[a] | | Economic value (Rs)[b] | | Remarks |
	Rs	US$	Using shadow exchange rate[c]	Using standard conversion factor[d]	
Inflow					
Gross value of wheat produced	1,750	175	2,100	1,750	Traded item
Total	1,750	175	2,100	1,750	
Outflow					
Unskilled labor (shadow wage rate = 50% market wage)	600	60	300	250	Nontraded item
Imported fertilizer	200	20	240	200	Traded item
Tractor services					Indirectly traded item
75% imported component	90 ⎱	9 ⎱	108 ⎱	90 ⎱	
25% domestic component	30 ⎰ 120	3 ⎰ 12	30 ⎰ 138	25 ⎰ 115	
Total	920	92	678	565	
Net benefit	830	83	1,422	1,185	
Ratio of inflow to outflow	1.90	1.90	3.10	3.10	

Rs Indian rupees. US$ U.S. dollars.

a. The official exchange rate is assumed to be Rs10 = US$1. Financial prices are converted by this official exchange rate.

b. The foreign exchange premium is assumed to be 20 percent. As in note a, the official exchange rate is assumed to be Rs10 = US$1.

c. The shadow exchange rate is the official exchange rate of Rs10 multiplied by 1 plus the percentage of the foreign exchange premium stated in decimal terms, or Rs12 (10 × 1.2 = 12), so that Rs12 = US$1. Foreign exchange prices are converted into domestic currency values by multiplying the foreign currency price by Rs12.

d. The standard conversion factor is the reciprocal of 1 plus the foreign exchange premium stated in decimal terms, or 0.833 (1 ÷ 1.2 = 0.833). Foreign currency prices are converted into decimal currency values at the official exchange rate. Domestic currency prices are multiplied by the standard conversion factor of 0.833.

and van der Tak (1975) suggest, and both sets of authors recommend that some central agency prepare specific conversion factors for project analysts to use. It is possible in a parallel manner to derive "specific shadow exchange rates" that may then be applied repeatedly, although in practice this has rarely been done. Instead, when the shadow exchange rate approach is followed, nontraded items are decomposed into their traded and nontraded elements and each is valued separately. Use of a specific conversion factor can be illustrated by referring to table 7-1. Suppose we planned a number of projects in which tractor services would be important and we wanted a specific conversion factor for tractor services. Once we had the conversion factor in hand, we could multiply the domestic market price of items in each project by the same specific conversion factor to obtain the various economic values. In table 7-1, in the column illustrating use of the standard conversion factor, we have a value for the imported component of the tractor services of Rs90, which was converted at the official exchange rate. The domestic component was multiplied by the standard conversion factor to obtain an economic value of Rs25. If we accept this as a good estimate of the value of the domestic component, then by adding the two we reach an economic value for the tractor services of Rs115. If we divide this economic value by the domestic price, we obtain a specific conversion factor of 0.958 (115 ÷ 120 = 0.958). In the future, we can simply multiply the market price of tractor services by the specific conversion factor to obtain the economic value directly.

Economic export and import parity values

The economic value of a traded item—either an export or an import—at the farm gate or project boundary is its export or import parity value. These values are derived by adjusting the c.i.f. (cost, insurance, and freight) or f.o.b. (free-on-board) prices (converted to economic values) by all the relevant charges (again converted to economic values) between the farm gate or project boundary and the point where the c.i.f. or f.o.b. price is quoted. The general method of calculating export and import parity prices was discussed in the last section of chapter 3. When these financial prices are adjusted to derive their economic equivalent, both traded and nontraded elements must be valued simultaneously.

The methods for deriving import and export parity values are parallel. Thus, it is unnecessary to discuss the method for both; instead, we will discuss only derivation of the import parity price as an example because import parity values tend to be a bit more complicated to derive.

We may return to the example of the imported combine harvester used earlier in the chapter to illustrate economic valuation of a traded item. In our financial accounts, the c.i.f. price of US$45,000 was converted to its domestic currency equivalent at the official exchange rate of Rs10 = US$1, to which we would add, say, a 10 percent duty, Rs1,500 in domestic handling and marketing charges, and Rs2,250 in internal transport costs to the project site—for an import parity price at the farm gate of Rs498,750 [(45,000 × 10) + (45,000 × 10 × 0.10) + 1,500 + 2,250 = 498,750].

To obtain the economic import parity value at the farm gate or project boundary when using the shadow exchange rate to allow for the foreign exchange premium, we would make the same computations except that we would use the shadow exchange rate and omit the tariff, which is a transfer payment. In the illustration of valuing traded items, we assumed that the foreign exchange premium on the imported combine was 20 percent, and so we assumed a shadow exchange rate of Rs12 = US$1 (10 × 1.2 = 12). Now, to obtain the import parity value of the harvester, we would convert the c.i.f. price to its domestic equivalent using the shadow exchange rate, omit the tariff, and then add the value of the nontraded domestic items. To simplify matters, we will assume that all costs of moving the combine to the project site reflect only nontraded items— although that might not be acceptable if, say, the transport costs included significant amounts of petroleum fuel. We now reach an economic import parity value of Rs543,750 [(45,000 × 12) + 1,500 + 2,250 = 543,750].

If we are using the conversion factor to allow for the foreign exchange premium, the foreign exchange would be converted to its domestic currency equivalent in the economic accounts by using the official exchange rate, and every nontraded item would be reduced by the conversion factor. Recalling that the standard conversion factor is 1 divided by 1 plus the foreign exchange premium stated in decimal terms, we obtain a standard conversion factor of 0.833 (1 ÷ 1.2 = 0.833). Now, to obtain the economic import parity value of the harvester at the farm gate or project boundary, we convert all foreign exchange costs to domestic currency at the official exchange rate and reduce all prices of nontraded items by applying the standard conversion factor. Again, we will assume that the transport costs are predominantly made up of nontraded items. As before, we will omit the tariff because it is a transfer payment. The economic import parity price thus becomes Rs453,124 [(45,000 × 10) + (1,500 × 0.833) + (2,250 × 0.833) = 453,124].

In certain instances, the value in local currency of an imported item at the project site will be known, as will the rate of tariff and local transport charges from the point of import to the project site. If this is the case, to determine the economic value it is necessary to determine the c.i.f. price, take out the tariff, and allow for the cost of domestic transport. Using our previous values, we may know, for example, that a combine harvester delivered to the project site costs Rs498,750, that the tariff on imported harvesters is 10 percent, and that local transport and domestic handling from the point of import to the project site costs Rs3,750. We know that the official exchange rate is Rs10 = US$1 and that the foreign exchange premium is 20 percent, so the shadow exchange rate would be Rs12 = US$1 (10 × 1.2 = 12) and the standard conversion factor 0.833 (1 ÷ 1.2 = 0.833). We deduct the cost of local transport to obtain a financial value of Rs495,000 at the point of entry, which includes the c.i.f. price plus the duty (498,750 − 3,750 = 495,000). To take out the duty, we divide by 1 plus the percentage of the duty stated in decimal terms to obtain

Rs450,000 (495,000 ÷ 1.1 = 450,000). This is the c.i.f. value at the official exchange rate. We can then divide by the official exchange rate to obtain the c.i.f. value in foreign exchange of US$45,000 (450,000 ÷ 10 = 45,000). If we are using the shadow exchange rate to allow for the foreign exchange premium, we can obtain our c.i.f. economic value by multiplying by the shadow exchange rate of Rs12 = US$1 to obtain a value of Rs540,000 (45,000 × 12 = 540,000). Then, to obtain the economic value at the project site, we would add the cost of transport from the point of entry to the project site; this yields an economic import parity value for the harvester at the farm gate or project boundary of Rs543,750 (540,000 + 3,750 = 543,750). If we are using the conversion factor to allow for the foreign exchange premium, the economic value of the combine at the port will be the c.i.f. foreign exchange price converted at the official exchange rate, or Rs450,000 (45,000 × 10 = 450,000). To obtain the economic import parity value at the farm gate or project boundary, we would add to this c.i.f. value the cost of domestic transport and domestic handling, reduced by the standard conversion factor, to obtain an economic import parity value of Rs453,124 [450,000 + (3,750 × 0.833) = 453,124].

It is clear that to derive the import and export parity values in the economic analysis we must omit transfer payments, allow for the foreign exchange premium, and use shadow prices for those domestic goods and services for which prices are inaccurate indicators of opportunity cost. The same examples from the Sudanese and Nigerian projects used to illustrate the discussion of import and export parity prices in chapter 3 (tables 3-3 and 3-4) are used again in tables 7-2 and 7-3 to show economic parity values using both the shadow exchange rate and the conversion factor to allow for the foreign exchange premium.

Trade Policy Signals from Project Analysis

Up to this point, we have been discussing an analytical system that estimates the contribution of a proposed project to national income within a policy framework that the project analyst considers will exist during the life of the project. We have assumed that the project analyst has very little influence on trade policies, for this is true in the agriculture sector in most countries. Questions often arise, however, about the effects on a proposed project if trade policies were to change, and about whether changes in trade policies should be recommended. Unfortunately, when assessing the effects on a project of policies that would lift or impose a ban on trade, the analytical issues become very complex, and the analysis of a single project is of limited usefulness. The limitations of project analysis in influencing policy arise from the partial nature of project analysis and from the assumption that the project investment does not significantly change price relations in the economy as a whole.

Two important cases involving trade policy often arise that cause soul-searching among project analysts. The first is when a quota or prohibitive tariff prevents entry of a crucial input—perhaps fertilizer—

Table 7-2. *Economic Export Parity Value of Cotton, Rahad Irrigation Project, Sudan*
(1980 forecast prices)

Steps in the calculation	Relevant steps in the Sudanese example	Value per ton		
		Lint	*Seed*	*Scarto*[a]
C.i.f. at point of entry	*Using shadow exchange rate* C.i.f. Liverpool taken as estimate for all European ports)	US$639.33	US$103.39	—
Deduct unloading at point of import *Deduct* freight to point of import *Deduct* insurance	Freight and insurance	— 39.63	— 24.73	—
Equals f.o.b. at point of export	F.o.b. Port Sudan	US$599.70	US$78.66	—
Convert foreign currency to domestic currency at shadow exchange rate	Converted at shadow exchange rate of £Sd1.000 = US$2.611[b]	£Sd229.682	£Sd30.126	—
Deduct local port charges	Port handling cost Lint: £Sd5.564 per ton Seed: £Sd1.510 per ton	5.564	1.510	—
Deduct local transport and marketing costs from project to point of export (if not part of project cost)	Freight to Port Sudan at £Sd6.782 per ton	6.782	6.782	—
Equals export parity value at project boundary	Export parity value at gin at project site	£Sd217.336	£Sd21.834	—

Conversion allowance if necessary	Convert to seed cotton (£Sd217.336 × 0.4 + £Sd21.834 × 0.59 + £Sd110.200 × 0.01)[c]	86.934 12.882 1.102	£Sd100.918	
Deduct local storage, transport, and marketing costs (if not part of project cost)	Ginning, baling, and storage (£Sd15.229 per ton)		− 15.229	
	Collection and internal transfer (£Sd1.064 per ton)		− 1.064	
Equals export parity value at farm gate	Export parity value at farm gate		£Sd84.625	
	Using conversion factors			
C.i.f. at point of entry	C.i.f. Liverpool (taken as estimate for all European ports)	US$639.33	US$103.39	
Deduct unloading at point of import / *Deduct* freight to point of import / *Deduct* insurance	Freight and insurance	− 39.63	− 24.73	
Equals f.o.b. at point of export	F.o.b. Port Sudan	US$599.70	US$78.66	
Convert foreign currency to domestic currency at official exchange rate	Converted at official exchange rate of £Sd1.000 = US$2.872[b]	£Sd208.809	£Sd27.389	

(Table continues on the following pages.)

Table 7-2 (continued)

Steps in the calculation	Relevant steps in the Sudanese example	Value per ton		
		Lint	Seed	Scarto[a]
Convert nontraded goods to equivalent domestic value using conversion factors	Converted using standard conversion factor of 0.909[b]			—
Deduct local port charges	Port handling cost Lint: £Sd5.564 per ton Seed: £Sd1.510 per ton	— 5.058	— 1.373	—
Deduct local transport and marketing costs from project to point of export (if not part of project cost)	Freight to Port Sudan at £Sd6.782 per ton	— 6.165	— 6.165	—
Equals export parity value at project boundary	Export parity value at gin at project site	£Sd197.586	£Sd19.851	—
Conversion allowance if necessary	Convert to seed cotton (£Sd197.586 × 0.4 + £Sd19.851 × 0.59 + £Sd110.200 × 0.909 × 0.01)[c]	79.034	11.712	1.002
			£Sd91.748	

Deduct local storage, transport, and marketing costs (if not part of project cost)	Ginning, baling, and storage (£Sd15.229 per ton)	− 13.843
	Collection and internal transfer (£Sd1.064 per ton)	− 0.967
Equals export parity value at farm gate	Export parity value at farm gate	£Sd76.938

£Sd Sudanese pounds.

Source: Adapted from World Bank, "Appraisal of the Rahad Irrigation Project," PA-139b (Washington, D.C., 1973; restricted circulation), annex 16, table 6. The format of the table is adapted from William A. Ward, "Calculating Import and Export Parity Prices," training material of the Economic Development Institute, CN-3 (Washington, D.C.: World Bank, 1977), p. 9.

a. Scarto is a by-product of very short, soiled fibers not suitable for export and is sold locally at a price of £Sd110.200 per ton.

b. For purposes of illustration, there is assumed to be a foreign exchange premium of 10 percent. Thus, the dollar value of the Sudanese pound at the official exchange rate of £Sd1.000 = US$2.872 has been divided by 1.1 to give an assumed shadow exchange rate of £Sd1.000 = US$2.611 (2.872 ÷ 1.1 = 2.611), whereas the standard conversion factor is divided by 1 plus the foreign exchange premium, or 0.909 (1 ÷ 1.1 = 0.909). In the appraisal report that is the source of this table, no foreign exchange premium was assumed.

c. Seed cotton is converted to lint, seed, and scarto assuming that a ton of seed cotton yields 400 kilograms lint, 590 kilograms seed, and 10 kilograms scarto.

and this forces use of a more costly domestic alternative and thus greatly reduces the contribution of the project to national income. The second is when an import quota imposed on products that compete with the project's output makes the contribution of the project investment to national income high, even though the cost of production per unit of output from the project is higher than the cost of competing imports.

When the domestic cost of an important project input is higher than the world market price because of a quota or prohibitive tariff, the potential contribution of the proposed investment to national income

Table 7-3. *Economic Import Parity Value of Early Crop Maize, Central Agricultural Development Projects, Nigeria*
(1985 forecast prices in 1976 constant terms)

Steps in the calculation	Relevant steps in the Nigerian example	Value per ton
Using shadow exchange rate		
F.o.b. at point of export	F.o.b. U.S. Gulf ports No. 2 U.S. yellow corn in bulk[a]	US$116
Add freight to point of import	Freight and insurance	31
Add unloading at point of import	(Included in freight estimate)	
Add insurance		
Equals c.i.f. at point of import	C.i.f. Lagos or Apapa	US$147
Convert foreign currency to domestic currency at shadow exchange rate	Converted at an assumed shadow exchange rate of ₦1 = US$1.47[b]	₦100
Add local port charges	Landing and port charges (including cost of bags)	22
Add local transport and marketing costs to relevant market	Transport (based on a 350-kilometer average)[c]	10
Equals value at market	Wholesale value	₦132
Conversion allowance if necessary	(Not necessary)	
Deduct transport and marketing costs to relevant market	Primary marketing (includes assembly, cost of bags, and intermediary margins)[c]	− 12
	Transport (based on a 350-kilometer average)[c]	− 10
Deduct local storage, transport, and marketing costs (if not part of project cost)	Storage loss (10 percent of harvested weight)	− 9
Equals import parity value at farm gate	Import parity value at farm gate	₦101
Using conversion factors		
F.o.b. at point of export	F.o.b. U.S. Gulf ports No. 2 U.S. yellow corn in bulk[a]	US$116
Add freight to point of import	Freight and insurance	31
Add unloading at point of import	(Included in freight estimate)	
Add insurance		
Equals c.i.f. at point of import	C.i.f. Lagos or Apapa	US$147
Convert foreign currency to domestic currency at official exchange rate	Converted at official exchange rate of ₦1 = US$1.62[b]	₦91

Table 7-3 *(continued)*

Steps in the calculation	Relevant steps in the Nigerian example	Value per ton
Convert nontraded goods to equivalent domestic value using conversion factors	Converted using standard conversion factor of 0.909[b]	
Add local port charges	Landing and port charges (including cost of bags, ₦22)	20
Add local transport and marketing costs to relevant market	Transport (based on a 350-kilometer average, ₦10)[c]	9
Equals value at market	Wholesale value	₦120
Conversion allowance if necessary	(Not necessary)	
Deduct transport and marketing costs to relevant market	Primary marketing (includes assembly, cost of bags, and intermediary margins, ₦12)[c] –	11
	Transport (based on a 350-kilometer average, ₦10)[c] –	9
Deduct local storage, transport, and marketing costs (if not part of project cost)	Storage loss (10 percent of harvested weight) –	8
Equals import parity value at farm gate	Import parity value at farm gate	₦92

₦ Nigerian naira.

Source: Adapted from World Bank, "Supplementary Annexes to Central Agricultural Development Projects," 1370-UNI (Washington, D.C., 1976; restricted circulation), supplement 11, appendix 2, table 4. The format of the table is adapted from Ward, "Calculating Import and Export Parity Prices," p. 10.

a. Forecast from *Price Prospects for Major Primary Commodities* (1976, annex 1, p. 12; see World Bank 1982a).

b. For purposes of illustration, there is assumed to be a foreign exchange premium of 10 percent. Thus, the dollar value of the naira at the official exchange rate of ₦1 = US$1.62 has been divided by 1.1 to give an assumed shadow exchange rate of ₦1 = US$1.47 (1.62 ÷ 1.1 = 1.47), whereas the standard conversion factor is 1 divided by 1 plus the foreign exchange premium, or 0.909 (1 ÷ 1.1 = 0.909). In the appraisal report that is the source of this table, no foreign exchange premium was assumed.

c. Shadow prices were assumed for transport and for primary marketing because in the financial analysis the market wage overvalued the opportunity cost of unskilled labor. The value given is the opportunity cost in naira (before applying the standard conversion factor).

will be reduced by the tariff or quota. *Given the policy prevailing*, the project analysis will be an accurate indicator of the project's worth. Take fertilizer, for instance. If it is expensive to produce domestically, this is an indication that fertilizer production uses a large amount of scarce domestic resources relative to the resources necessary to produce some other product that could be exported to earn the foreign exchange needed to import the fertilizer from a foreign supplier. But if the domestic fertilizer must, in fact, be used for the project to move forward, then it will take a lot of domestic resources to produce the project's agricultural output, and the project will not, accordingly, make as much of a contribution to the national income as it could were imported fertilizer available. If the quota or prohibitive tariff against the input were removed, then the project investment would look quite different. A change in trade policy, however, will have implications ranging far beyond the boundary of the project itself, implications for both efficiencies in the economy and for noneconomic objectives. A change in trade policy may bring a wide range of changes in other prices in the economy as well as in the price of fertilizer used on nonproject farms, and to be valid an investment analysis would have to be run with the new price relations and include nonproject farms. Predicting these changes could be very difficult if the change in trade policy were significant. At best, the project analyst could run his analysis again using a c.i.f. price for fertilizer and making a broad guess about what the changes might be in the rest of the economy both within and outside agriculture. He could then turn to those responsible for trade policy and say that his project analysis signaled a need to consider with care removing the quota against fertilizer. But note that the project analysis is only a signal, not a criterion for decision; much, much more must go into a reevaluation of trade policy than the analysis of one project.

The other important case in which a change in a quota proves very difficult for the project analyst is that of a quota against imports that would compete with the output of a proposed project. If the imports are prohibited, the output of the project will sell for more in the protected market, and what otherwise might not be a very attractive project may now make sufficient contribution to national income to be justified. Again, *if policies are not going to be changed*, this is an accurate indicator of the contribution to the national income. But if the domestic cost per unit of project output—say, apples—valued at shadow prices is greater than the c.i.f. cost of imported apples, then this is an indication that it would be more efficient from the standpoint of the economy as a whole for the project to produce something else, export it to earn foreign exchange, and then use the foreign exchange to import apples. Under the circumstances, the project analyst may want to run his analysis again using an import parity price and perhaps also adjusting some of the other price relations in the direction he thinks might prevail under a change in trade policy. He may find that domestic production would not make enough of a contribution to national income at these prices to justify the investment required. He might also want to determine the domestic resource cost of the import substitute along the lines discussed in the section of chapter 10 devoted to that topic; this will show that it costs more to save a unit of foreign exchange by producing apples domestically than the shadow exchange rate indicates the foreign exchange to be worth. His analysis has now signaled that trade policies should perhaps be reviewed. Again, it is only a signal; the analysis of this one project does not itself provide a complete decision criterion. The trade policy change will have many other effects that will be felt far beyond the boundary of the project itself.

Valuing Intangible Costs and Benefits

The methodology outlined for converting financial prices to economic values is one that is most appropriate for tangible costs and benefits. When intangible costs or benefits enter into investment considerations, they raise difficult issues of valuation.

Intangible factors have come up frequently in earlier discussions of identifying costs and benefits and of valuing them. They comprise a whole range of considerations—economic considerations such as income distribution, number of jobs created, or regional development; national considerations such as national integration or national security; and environmental considerations that can be both ecological and aesthetic, such as the preservation of productive ecosystems, recreation benefits, or famous spots of scenic beauty. [Lee (1982) discusses ecological considerations to be kept in mind when designing agricultural projects for tropical regions.]

The question of how to treat intangible factors most often arises when we are considering the benefits of a project. Many development projects are undertaken primarily to secure intangible benefits—education projects, domestic water supply projects, and health projects are a few common ones. Intangible benefits are usually not the major concern in agricultural projects, although many agricultural and rural development projects include components such as education or rural water supply from which intangible benefits are expected. Whether in agricultural projects or in other kinds of projects, intangible benefits, even though universally agreed to be valuable, are nevertheless virtually impossible to value satisfactorily in monetary terms. Yet costs for these projects are in general tangible enough, and the considerations of financial and economic valuation we have discussed earlier apply unambiguously.

Intangible costs are not uncommon, however, and prove just as difficult to bring within a valuation system as benefits. Often costs are merely the inverse of the benefits that are sought: illiteracy, disease, unemployment, or the loss of a productive environment or treasured scenic beauty.

Some costs in agricultural projects, while tangible, are very difficult to quantify and to value. Siltation, waterlogging, salinization, and soil loss are examples. These costs should not be ignored, and if they are likely to be substantial they should be treated in the project analysis in a manner analogous to intangible costs.

When considering projects in which intangible benefits or costs are important, the least the project analyst can do is to identify them: lives that will be saved, jobs created, kind of education provided, region to be developed, location of a park, ecosystem or kind of scenery to be preserved.

Very often, the analyst can also quantify intangibles: number of lives saved, number of jobs created, number of students to be enrolled, number of people expected to use a park. Even such simple quantification is often a substantial help in making an investment decision.

Economists have tried repeatedly to find means to value intangibles and thus bring them within the compass of their valuation system. The benefits of education have been valued by comparing the earnings of an educated man with those of one who is uneducated. Health and sanitation benefits have been valued in the number of hours of lost work avoided by decreasing the incidence of disease. Nutrition benefits have been valued in terms of increased productivity. Population projects have been valued by attaching a value to the births avoided. Although work in these areas continues—especially with regard to environmental impact—few applied project analyses in developing countries currently attempt to use such approaches to valuing intangible costs and benefits. For one thing, such efforts generally greatly underestimate the value of the intangibles. The value of an education is much more than just the increase in income—ask any mullah, monk, or priest. Good health is a blessing far in excess of merely being able to work more hours. Good nutrition is desirable for more reasons than just increased productivity. Moreover, the methodological approaches used to value intangibles turn out to be unreliable and open to serious question. Finally, there may be moral issues involved—many who support population programs do so out of considerations that extend far beyond any benefit-cost calculation.

In contemporary practice of project analysis in developing countries, the only method used to any extent to deal with intangible benefits is to determine on a present worth basis the least expensive alternative combination of tangible costs that will realize essentially the same intangible benefit. This is often referred to as "least-cost combination" or "cost effectiveness" (for an application of the method to sanitation projects, see Kalbermatten, Julius, and Gunnerson 1982, chapter 3). If the same education benefits can be provided by centralized schools that realize economies of scale but require buses or by more expensive smaller schools to which students can walk, which schools are cheaper? Can the same health benefits be provided at less cost by constructing fewer large hospitals but more clinics manned by paramedical personnel? By constructing a waterborne sewerage system or by installing low-cost household sanitation facilities that do not require sewers? Can the same number of lives be saved more cheaply by buying up all the property rights in a flood plain and moving people out than by constructing dykes and levees? Given two park sites that would give similar recreation benefits—perhaps one that would require buying warehouse sites and another that would require extensive filling and flood control along a river—which would be cheaper? Once it is determined that the least expensive alternative has been identified and its costs valued, then the subjective question can be more readily addressed: is it worth it?

Interestingly enough, electricity projects are customarily analyzed using least-cost combination. The marginal value product of electricity is in general considered greatly understated by the administered price charged; in any event, much electricity is used for home lighting that is very difficult to value. In practice, most power projects simply compare alternative means of producing the same amount of power: steam generating stations versus a hydroelectric dam; a large generator with transmission costs and several years of idle capacity versus a series of smaller stations close to the demand centers.

A variation of the least-cost combination method can be used to deal with intangibles in multipurpose projects. From the total cost of the project are deducted all those costs that can be directly attributed to tangible benefits—flood damage avoided, irrigation, navigation, and the like. These costs are compared with their associated benefits to determine if the purpose is worthwhile at all. Is the flood damage avoided worth the direct costs incurred? Finally, the residual costs for the project are compared with the residual, intangible benefits. Is the number of lives saved by the project worth the residual cost that must be incurred? (A method of allocating residuals was outlined in the section on joint cost allocation in chapter 6.)

The problems with valuing intangibles are more common and more difficult to deal with in sectors other than agriculture. In agricultural projects, most of the benefits usually are tangible and can be valued. The costs and benefits can be compared directly to choose the highest-yielding alternative. There are, however, several aspects of intangible benefits that are frequently encountered in agricultural projects. Agricultural extension services, for example, are sometimes considered to give an intangible benefit in greater farmer education. For the most part, it is best to treat such costs that may give rise partly to intangible benefits—or, at least, the incremental amount of such costs—as necessary within a project if the total, tangible benefits are to be realized. If a dairy production project requires helping farmers to learn better sanitation procedures, then the extension agents who teach the procedures are essential to the success of the project, and the benefit of their effort is the tangible one of more and better milk.

In rural development projects, there are often components that are hardly essential to the main production objectives and that produce generally intangible benefits. This is the case when village schools, rural water supplies, rural clinics, or even agricultural research costs are included in a project. If these components are relatively small in comparison with total project costs, as they often are, then the problem of valuing the benefits may be ignored. But if such components form a significant part of total project cost, they probably should be separated out and treated on a least-cost combination basis. This procedure was followed in the analysis for the Korea Rural Infrastructure Project. The project included irrigation, feeder roads, community fuelwood plots, rural domestic water supply, and rural electrification. The irrigation, feeder roads, and community fuelwood components were analyzed by

Figure 7-1, part A. *Decision Tree for Determining Economic Values: Major Steps*

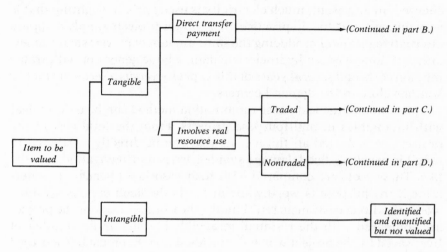

Figure 7-1, part B. *Decision Tree for Determining Economic Values: Direct Transfer Payments*

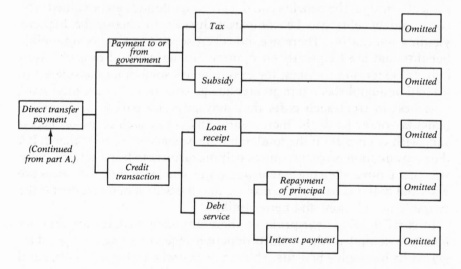

Figure 7-1, part C. *Decision Tree for Determining Economic Values: Traded Items*

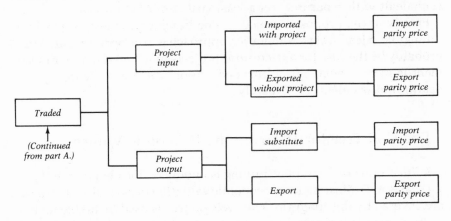

Figure 7-1, part D. *Decision Tree for Determining Economic Values: Nontraded Items*

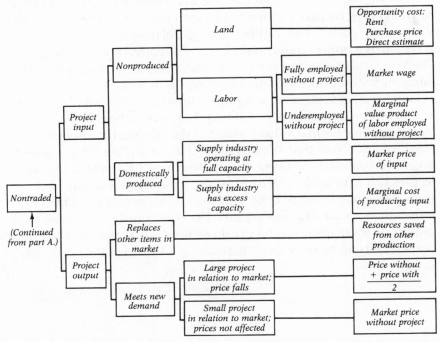

Source: Adapted from William A. Ward, "Economic Valuation Decision Tree," training material of the Economic Development Institute (EDI), CN-61 (Washington, D.C.: World Bank, 1978).

comparing their tangible costs with their tangible benefits, but the components for rural domestic water supply and rural electrification were each dealt with separately on a least-cost combination basis.

Finally, if the proposed project is one in which the output is wholly intangible, a least-cost combination approach is appropriate. This would probably be the case for agricultural projects in which the major investment is in extension, agricultural education, rural water supply, rural health improvement, or research.

Decision Tree for Determining Economic Values

A "decision tree" for determining economic values is given in figure 7-1, parts A–D. Most issues of economic valuation in agricultural projects are covered by this diagram. The decision tree is used by taking an item to be valued in an agricultural project and tracing through the tree, following each alternative as it applies to the item until the end of the tree is reached, where a suggestion about how to value the item will be found.

To illustrate, we may trace through a few common elements in agricultural projects. Take fertilizer to be used in an irrigation project that will produce cotton. The fertilizer is tangible, involves real resource use, is traded, is a project input, and would be imported without the project. Therefore, it is valued at the import parity price. Or take agricultural labor to be used to apply the fertilizer. It is tangible, involves real resource use, is nontraded, is a project input, is nonproduced, is labor, and would be underemployed without the project. Therefore, it is valued by taking the marginal value product of the labor in its without-project employment. (Note that labor is defined as a tangible item, a possible source of confusion in using the decision tree.) Or take a tax on the fertilizer. It is tangible, is a direct transfer payment, is a payment to or from government, and is a tax. Therefore, it is omitted from the project economic account. Or, finally, take the cotton to be produced in the project. It is tangible, involves real resource use, is traded, is a project output, and will be an export. Therefore, it is valued at the export parity price.

8

Aggregating Project Accounts

To ESTIMATE THE CONTRIBUTION a project makes to national income, the analyst first recasts the financial accounts—the farm budgets, the accounts for the processing industries, and the budgets for the government agencies—from financial prices to economic values. Then these values are aggregated to reach the economic incremental net benefit of the project, generally called the economic cash flow.

Aggregating Farm Budgets

Benefits and costs realized on individual farms in an agricultural project are aggregated to obtain the values for the project as a whole. In agricultural projects, it is most common for analysts to work with whole farm budgets. They will make a judgment about how many of each pattern farm will be included in the project and about the phasing of participation in the project. Then they will revalue each pattern farm budget to economic terms and aggregate by taking separately the benefit and cost from each pattern farm multiplied by the number of farms to reach summary on-farm benefit and cost figures for the whole project.

An alternative path is to revalue the pattern whole farm budgets in economic terms and then to multiply the incremental net benefit before

---

Facing page: Burning pearl millet stubble to permit plowing in Ghana.

financing for the pattern farm by the number of farms of that pattern, add the results for all the patterns, and thereby reach a summary incremental net benefit figure for all farms in the project. If farm budgets have been laid out on a whole farm basis along the lines of chapter 4, this is a simple means to aggregate.

Other analysts aggregate on the basis of unit activity crop budgets similar to those discussed in chapter 4. An estimate of the total area under each crop is made and a judgment about phasing formed. Then the benefits and costs in the crop budgets are converted to economic values, totaled separately, and entered in the summary account for the project.

Which is the better approach for aggregation, unit activity crop budgets or whole farm budgets? Each has its use, and the same analyst may use one approach or the other as circumstances demand. The unit activity approach is especially convenient when the focus of the project is on a particular crop that will simply be added to existing farms without causing major reorganization. This approach was taken, for instance, in the Nucleus Estate/Smallholder Oil Palm Project in Rivers State, Nigeria, where the typical smallholder farm budget was a 1-hectare model that was aggregated by multiplying by the 10,000 hectares proposed for planting by smallholders in the project. Costs and benefits were then aggregated separately into a summary economic account.

A problem with unit activity crop budgets is that they are infrequently done on a with-and-without basis; rather, in general they are simply cast incrementally, beginning in project year 1. This means that the opportunity cost of land and family labor must be estimated directly. If whole farm budgets are used, however, the with-and-without format automatically values correctly the opportunity cost of land and labor, as noted in chapter 4.

Whole farm budgets provide a much better picture of the effects that a proposed project has on the participating farmers' family income; therefore they give a much better idea about incentives and such considerations of project design as debt service timing. Of course, whole farm budgets can be used even when the focus of the project is on a particular crop, and they are almost essential if there will be a considerable reorganization of the farm or if new farms are to be established.

A problem with using whole farm budgets is that they may lead either to awkwardly sized units or to peculiar total areas. If a 10,000-hectare area is anticipated in the project and the pattern farm is 6 hectares, then 1,667 farmers must be anticipated in the project; the odd figure gives a spurious indication of accuracy. Alternatively, if the number of participating farmers is rounded to 1,700, then the pattern farm becomes 5.88 hectares, again a spurious indication of accuracy. If we instead take 1,700 farmers each with a 6-hectare holding, then the result is a project area of 10,200 hectares, itself a peculiar figure. Such anomalies are not easy to avoid. In practice, the most common approach is to use round figures for the number of farms and size of holding and to reach the area figure on this basis, even if the resultant total area is a bit awkward.

Some analysts have used both unit activity budgets and whole farm budgets for the same area in a project. They use the unit activity approach to estimate the incremental net benefit stream. Then they do a series of whole farm budgets to test the effect of the project on certain kinds of farmers who would not be average but toward the extremes of the distribution. What will be the effect on a very small farmer if he participates? When the sensitivity tests are run, do they show that the smallest farmers have a disproportionate risk? If so, that may have implications for the participation of small farmers and for the project design. Yet, if large farmers participate, will they stand to gain windfall advantage? Whole farm budgets are well suited to analyze these questions. By using whole farm budgets in addition to a basic unit activity budget, the analyst avoids focusing only on average farms; he also avoids the anomalies in pattern farm size or total area that occur when whole farm budgets are the sole basis of aggregation.

In general, despite the problem of fitting together the pattern farm and the total areas, whole farm budgets are preferable as a basis for preparing agricultural project analyses. This is because whole budgets emphasize the farm family and its income as a whole and because they avoid the problem of estimating directly the opportunity cost of land and labor.

Whatever aggregation path is followed, the analyst will need to allow for the phasing of participation in the project. Not all farmers may be ready to participate in a project during its first year of operation—nor is the project administration likely to be ready in the first year to include all the farmers who will eventually take part in the project. Some judgment will have to be formed both about the willingness of farmers to participate and about the number of farmers the project administration will be able to handle effectively. In the Drought-Prone Areas Project in India, for example, some 225,000 farmers were expected to be reached over a seven-year period, phased so that 5 percent of the expected total would participate in the first year, an additional 7.5 percent in the second year, another 12.5 percent in the third year, and so forth. Such a long phasing period is unusual, however; most projects would be expected to reach the full number of farmers within three or four years.

Other Aggregation Issues

A process similar to that for farm budgets is followed for the budgets of processing industries. The accounts are first converted from financial prices to economic values. The benefits and costs are usually then carried forward separately to a summary project account. Alternatively, the incremental net benefit before financing may be carried forward.

Finally, the net benefits from various government agencies are added and carried to the summary account. Since government agencies normally have a net expenditure, this is often shown in the summary account as a project administrative cost or some similar entry. But if a user fee is to be charged, as might be the case for water charges and benefit taxes in an irrigation project, the project administration may actually run a surplus, which would then be shown as a project benefit or, perhaps, as a "negative cost" under the summary cost entry.

Table 8-1, adapted from the Ghana Upper Region Agricultural Development Project, is a summary account of a general form frequently

Table 8-1. *Economic Measures of Project Worth,*
Upper Region Agricultural Development Project, Ghana
(thousands of ₵)

Item	Project year			
	1	2	3	10–20
Inflow				
Incremental crop benefit	1,829	7,071	14,217	36,822
Incremental livestock benefit	763	1,065	2,542	9,482
Total inflow	2,592	8,136	16,759	46,304
Outflow				
On-farm production cost				
Incremental crop input	2,635	5,836	9,464	18,724
Incremental livestock input	299	477	385	234
Total on-farm cost	2,934	6,313	9,849	18,958
Project administrative and processing cost				
Crops				
Buildings	4,709	3,476	1,895	0
Plant, vehicles, and equipment	6,249	1,505	240	383
Salaries and allowances	1,487	1,730	1,840	482
Plant and vehicle operation	446	1,254	1,335	967
General administration	65	(43)	25	0
Physical contingencies	648	396	267	92
Total crop administrative and processing cost	13,604	8,318	5,602	1,924
Livestock				
Buildings	942	662	0	0
Plant, vehicles, and equipment	245	65	0	57
Salaries and allowances	264	275	275	215
Plant and vehicle operation	71	82	82	82
Physical contingencies	76	54	18	18
Total livestock administrative and processing cost	1,598	1,138	375	372
Total outflow	18,136	15,769	15,826	21,254
Incremental net benefit (cash flow)	(15,544)	(7,633)	933	25,050

Net present worth at 12 percent opportunity cost of capital = ₵85,274[a]
Economic rate of return = 40 percent[a]
Net benefit-investment ratio at 12 percent opportunity cost
of capital = ₵104,759/₵19,485 = 5.38[a]

₵ Ghanaian cedis.

Source: Adapted from World Bank, "Appraisal of Upper Region Agricultural Development Project, Ghana," 1061a-GH (Washington, D.C., 1976; restricted circulation), annex 11, table 18.

a. Calculated from the incremental net benefit (cash flow). For details about the methodology of the computation, see chapter 9.

found. As in earlier chapters, the general categories of items included in the account appear in the text in *italic* type. The analyst chose to work entirely on an incremental basis instead of on a with-and-without basis. The table is divided into incremental *inflow* and incremental *outflow*. The difference between the two is the *incremental net benefit (cash flow)*.

The inflow is taken to be the incremental value of production from the project. The basic farm accounts for the crop benefit were unit activity crop budgets for several crops cast on a hectare basis. The unit activity crop budgets were revalued to economic terms and multiplied by the number of hectares expected to be included in the project, properly phased. For crops that required processing such as cotton and ground-nuts, the economic value was based on the economic export parity value at the project boundary, since the cost of processing is included in the outflow. The basic farm accounts for the livestock benefit were the pattern whole farm budgets for the ranches to be established. Thus, the analyst used both aggregation paths in one project—the unit activity budget for crops and the whole farm budget for the livestock ranches—according to his needs.

In the outflow, the first element was the on-farm production cost for crops and livestock, which was calculated along lines parallel to those discussed for the benefits. To this was added the project administrative and processing cost, again separated into the crop production component and the livestock production component. The analyst chose to carry forward the various categories of cost for each of the units to be established under the program. Thus, there was one entry for buildings; another for plant, vehicle, and equipment operating cost; and a third for salaries and allowances. Had it suited his purpose better, the analyst could have chosen to list cost by the kind of administrative unit; he could have shown, for example, the Upper Region Project Management Unit—perhaps broken down by major subunits—the Ghana Broadcasting Corporation, the Farmers Service Company, the Agricultural Development Bank, the Cotton Development Board, and the like.

Subtracting the outflow from the inflow gives the incremental net benefit, or cash flow, for the project as a whole. As expected, this is negative in the early years of the project, but it becomes positive in later years. This flow would then be discounted, as discussed in chapter 9, to give the *net present worth, economic rate of return*, and the *net benefit-investment ratio* for the project as a whole. (The symbol for Ghanaian cedis is ₵.)

A flow chart for aggregating project economic accounts is given in figure 8-1.

Appendix. A Diagrammatic Project Model

Some of the relations among farm budgets, processing industry accounts, government agency budgets, and the contribution a project makes to national income can perhaps be more easily visualized by

Figure 8-1. *Aggregating Project Accounts*

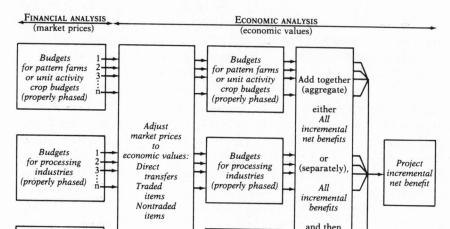

means of a simple diagrammatic model of a project. (This model originally was developed by George B. Baldwin of the World Bank.)

Measures of national income

National income is usually measured either by the gross domestic
product (abbreviated GDP) or by the gross national product (abbreviated
GNP). Most national plans define the economic objective of development
as growth of one or the other measure.

The gross domestic product is defined as the value of the gross output of
goods and services produced in the country less the value of the intermediate goods and services—that is, those used to produce other
goods or services. Gross national product is the same as gross domestic
product except that it includes income earned abroad and excludes
income transferred out of the country by foreign owners.

The gross domestic product can be measured in three ways, all of
which are equivalent and give the same result: (1) the value of all expenditure on final goods and services produced (plus an allowance for home-
consumed production), less imports; (2) the sum of all factor income
payments, including capital consumption allowances, and (for a market
price measure) all indirect taxes net of subsidies; and (3) the sum of the
value added from every producing unit.

Although the first measure is the most frequently used because the data
are most readily available, the third is of most interest to us because it is
through the value added that we link project analysis theory with national income theory.

Value added

The value added of any enterprise is the market price of the goods and services produced less the cost of materials and services purchased from others—the difference between gross output and the value of intermediate consumption. Value added may be gross or net. Gross value added includes payment for taxes, interest, rent, profits, reserves for depreciation, and compensation to management and other employees, including social security. Net value added excludes depreciation. For our present purposes we are interested in gross value added because it is the gross value added by all the productive enterprises in the economy that adds up to the gross domestic product.

Project model

Starting from this view of national income as the sum of the value added of all the productive enterprises (including, of course, projects), we may lay out a schematic picture, or diagrammatic model, of a project. (The way we will present the model is most directly applicable to the criterion of the economic rate of return discussed in chapter 9. With minor modifications, the model is equally applicable to the criteria of net present worth, benefit-cost ratio, or net benefit-investment ratio.)

We can picture a project in its simplified form as in figure 8-2, the general model of a project showing real resource flows. Here, we see that the difference between what the external inputs are worth and what the final output is worth is the value added created by the project.

How does the project create this value added? Obviously, through the use of its own internal resources. We may conveniently divide these internal resources into two major categories, labor and capital, as indicated in figure 8-2. The arrow represents the flow of output from a project—say, rice from a new irrigation scheme. The broken lines of the rectangle indicate the project boundary. The total output is made up of the contributions to the stream of output generated directly by the external inputs (say, fertilizer, pesticides, and so forth) and the contribution of the project's own internal inputs of labor and capital. The value added is that amount of the total output stream which is attributable only to the contribution of the internal inputs of labor and capital.

So far, we have been talking of "real" resource flows. That is, of rice or coconuts or wheat or beef cattle (or, moving outside agriculture, automobiles or gasoline or consumer services).

Flowing in the other direction is the value stream—the money actually paid for each of the real goods or services, or the value of each stated at shadow prices if market prices do not estimate the opportunity cost well. The project receives payment from its customers and, in turn, pays its suppliers for the external inputs it uses. What is left over is available to remunerate the internal factors of production. This more complicated

Figure 8-2. *General Model of a Project:*
Real Resource Flows

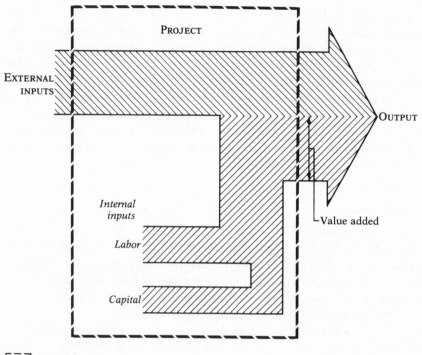

[⁻ ⁻] Project boundary.

[\\\\] Contribution of external
inputs to output.

[///] Contribution of internal
inputs to output.

pattern is indicated in figure 8-3, the general model of a project showing
economic value flows.

In figure 8-3, within the broken lines of the rectangle, the project
boundary, we represent the value flows that are the remuneration to
internal factors of production. Note that the value added is identical to
the total remuneration to all internal factors of production. The value
added amounts, of course, to the difference between the value of goods
and services provided by outside suppliers and the value of what is
supplied by the project to consumers plus the value of unsold output,
including home-consumed production. The value added, in turn, is divided between remuneration to labor and remuneration to capital.

Labor payments include all kinds of remuneration for all kinds of
labor—wages, salaries, bonuses, payments in kind, home-consumed production, consultants' fees, and social security contributions.

There is a conceptual difficulty in the treatment of the manager's
remuneration. Is an entrepreneur's compensation a return for his management skill or a return to his capital? We resolve this, sometimes
rather arbitrarily, by assuming that the manager's salary is whatever we

Figure 8-3. *General Model of a Project:*
Economic Value Flows

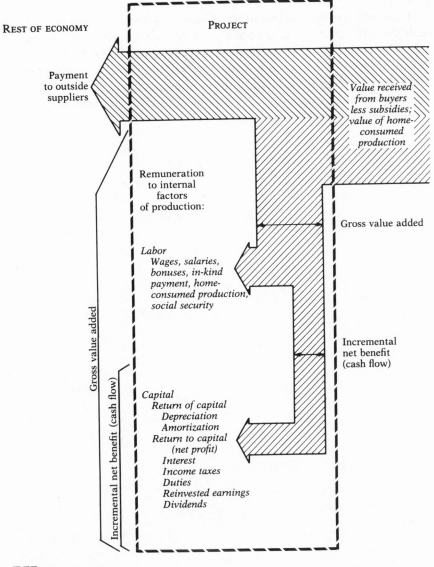

REST OF ECONOMY   PROJECT

Payment
to outside
suppliers

Value received
from buyers
less subsidies;
value of home-
consumed
production

Remuneration
to internal
factors
of production:

Gross value added

Labor
Wages, salaries,
bonuses, in-kind
payment, home-
consumed production,
social security

Gross value added

Incremental
net benefit
(cash flow)

Incremental net benefit (cash flow)

Capital
Return of capital
Depreciation
Amortization
Return to capital
(net profit)
Interest
Income taxes
Duties
Reinvested earnings
Dividends

Project boundary.

Payment to outside suppliers.

Remuneration to internal
factors of production.

would have to pay to attract a manager of equal competence who contributes none of the capital. In agricultural project analyses, we are
inclined to simplify even further. In the case of farmers who own their
farms and supply most of both the labor and management skills, we are
likely to attribute to the farmer only the equivalent of his wage as a
laborer and nothing at all for his management skill. Anything over the
farmer's wage is considered return to capital.

Since we value labor at its going wage or at its marginal value product—its shadow price—it receives the same remuneration per unit regardless of its use.

The residual is the incremental net benefit, which we generally call the cash flow. If we can now choose the project alternative that will maximize the cash flow relative to the capital resources used, then we will know that we are at the same time maximizing the value added and, in turn, maximizing the contribution of the capital to national income. That is our macroeconomic investment objective, and that is what our project analysis enables us to do.

PART FOUR

Measures of Project Worth

9

Comparing Project Costs
and Benefits

WHEN COSTS AND BENEFITS have been identified, priced, and valued, the analyst is ready to determine which among various projects to accept, which to reject.

The analyst immediately confronts two problems. He must find some way to evaluate projects that will last several years and that have differently shaped future cost and benefit streams. He must also be able to evaluate projects of varying size. The usual method of addressing these two problems is through discounting. We will concentrate on four discounted measures suitable for application to agricultural projects: net present worth (often abbreviated NPW), internal rate of return (often abbreviated IRR), benefit-cost (often abbreviated B/C) ratio, and net benefit-investment (often abbreviated N/K) ratio. The arithmetic of these discounted measures, and the way we interpret the measures and their limitations, is exactly the same whether we are using them for financial analysis or for economic analysis. The difference is only whether we apply the techniques to financial prices or to economic values.

There is an extensive and occasionally esoteric literature devoted to discounted measures of project worth. A review of that literature, or any attempt to deal with all the issues it raises, is beyond the scope of this volume. Rather, I would like to point out a few practical considerations

Facing page: Digging field channels in central Luzon, Philippines.

about using discounted measures to evaluate the worth of agriculture projects and to touch upon some of the more common criticisms of the four discounted measures. If the reader wishes to proceed from this discussion, a good place to begin is with the review articles by Prest and Turvey (1966) and the texts by Merrett and Sykes (1973), Bierman and Smidt (1980), and Irvin (1978).

At the beginning, let me make clear two critical points. First, there is no one best technique for estimating project worth (although some are better than others, and some are especially deficient). Second, don't forget that these financial and economic measures of investment worth are only tools of decisionmaking. There are many nonquantitative and noneconomic criteria for making project decisions. The usefulness of the analytical techniques we will discuss is to improve the decisionmaking process (and to give some idea of the economic cost of noneconomic decisions), not to substitute for judgment.

Undiscounted Measures of Project Worth

The merits of discounting can be illustrated by an example that shows how some common undiscounted measures of project worth can be misleading. [This section owes much to Bierman and Smidt (1980).]

The analyst has before him four hypothetical projects, each calling for an investment in an irrigation pump. All may be thought of as being more or less alternatives for each other, but if there were sufficient funds, all could be accepted. Since these projects are only illustrative, we will be making some highly unrealistic assumptions about irrigation in the hope of illustrating more clearly and quickly some points about project analysis. Later we will try to make the analysis as realistic as is worthwhile in practice.

For these irrigation investments, we have invented a new kind of pump: one that is completely used up (or, perhaps to say it more technically, has no residual value) after two to three years of operation. We might say that in the project area the water is so sandy that the pump wears out in two to three years. We will assume for convenience that there is no uncertainty about either the costs or returns of the projects.

To emphasize that what is generally called "operation and maintenance cost" and what is generally considered to be "production cost" must both be included in estimating project worth, each has been given a separate column. For illustrative purposes, of course, we could just as well have combined these into one cost column called "operation, maintenance, and production cost." Table 9-1 gives details about the four alternative projects for pump irrigation.

Ranking by inspection

In some cases, we can tell by simply looking at the investment cost and the "shape" of the stream for the net value of incremental production

Table 9-1. *Four Hypothetical Pump Irrigation Projects*
(thousands of currency units)

Year	Capital items	Incremental cost — Operation and maintenance	Produc- tion	Gross	Value of incremental production (gross benefit)	Net value of incremental production[a]
Project I						
1	30,000	—	—	30,000	—	—
2	—	2,000	3,000	5,000	20,000	15,000
3	—	2,000	3,000	5,000	20,000	15,000
4	—	—	—	—	—	—
Total	30,000	4,000	6,000	40,000	40,000	30,000
Project II						
1	30,000	—	—	30,000	—	—
2	—	2,000	3,000	5,000	20,000	15,000
3	—	2,000	3,000	5,000	20,000	15,000
4	—	2,000	3,000	5,000	9,100	4,100
Total	30,000	6,000	9,000	45,000	49,100	34,100
Project III						
1	30,000	—	—	30,000	—	—
2	—	2,000	3,000	5,000	7,000	2,000
3	—	2,000	3,000	5,000	19,000	14,000
4	—	2,000	3,000	5,000	31,000	26,000
Total	30,000	6,000	9,000	45,000	57,000	42,000
Project IV						
1	30,000	—	—	30,000	—	—
2	—	2,000	3,000	5,000	7,000	2,000
3	—	2,000	3,000	5,000	31,000	26,000
4	—	2,000	3,000	5,000	19,000	14,000
Total	30,000	6,000	9,000	45,000	57,000	42,000

a. The net value of incremental production is the value of incremental production less the operation and maintenance cost and the production cost.

that one project should be accepted over another if we must choose. (The shape of a stream of values refers to the times when the values occur. Use of the term derives from graphing values over time in a manner similar to that in the graph in the bottom part of table 9-12.) In general, there are two such instances: (1) with the same investment, two projects produce the same net value of incremental production for a period, but one continues to earn longer than the other (in the examples of table 9-1, we would choose project II rather than project I); (2) in other instances, for the same investment, the total net value of incremental production may be the same, but one project has more of the flow earlier in the time sequence (thus, in table 9-1 we would choose project IV rather than project III; we cannot tell by inspection, however, if project IV would be preferred to project II—more elaborate analysis is necessary).

In many cases, projects can indeed be examined and rejected on the basis of inspection. A clear-cut case might be two alternative investments in irrigation, one of which will cost more but yield no more return. Most people would probably not even consider such a choice project analysis; they would simply look for the cheapest means to realize a given end.

Payback period

The payback period is the length of time from the beginning of the project until the net value of the incremental production stream reaches the total amount of the capital investment. The payback period for the four pump irrigation alternatives is shown in table 9-2.

The payback period is a common, rough means of choosing among investments in business enterprises, especially when the choice entails a high degree of risk. In agricultural projects, however, it is not often used.

As a measure of investment worth, the payback period has two important weaknesses. First, it fails to consider earnings after the payback period. Both project I and project II have the same payback period of three years, but we know by inspection that project II will continue to return benefits in the third year, whereas project I will not. Hence, the payback period is an inadequate criterion for choice between these two alternatives, one of which we know by inspection to be better than the other.

The second weakness of the payback period as a measure of investment worth is that it does not adequately take into consideration the timing of proceeds. Suppose we modify projects III and IV so that each has a capital cost of $42,000. Now each has a payback period of four years, and they have equal rank or order of preference for undertaking alternative investments. Yet we know by inspection that we would choose project IV over project III because more of the returns to project IV are realized earlier. This is obviously desirable, since the earlier a benefit is received, the earlier it can be reinvested (or consumed)—hence, the more valuable it is.

Proceeds per unit of outlay

Investments are sometimes ranked by the proceeds per unit of outlay, which is the total net value of incremental production divided by the total amount of the investment as shown in table 9-3.

By this criterion, we find that projects I and II are correctly ranked. But projects III and IV receive equal rank, although we know by simple inspection that we would choose project IV because its returns are received earlier. Here, again, the criterion of proceeds per unit of outlay fails to consider timing; money to be received in the future weighs as heavily as money in hand today.

Table 9-2. *Payback Period, Four Hypothetical Pump Irrigation Projects*

Project	Payback period (years)	Rank
I	3.0	1
II	3.0	1
III	3.5	4
IV	3.1	3

Table 9-3. *Proceeds per Unit of Outlay, Four Hypothetical Pump Irrigation Projects*
(thousands of currency units)

Project	Incremental cost Capital items	Total net value of incremental production	Proceeds per unit of outlay	Rank
I	30,000	30,000	1.00	4
II	30,000	34,100	1.14	3
III	30,000	42,000	1.40	1
IV	30,000	42,000	1.40	1

Average annual proceeds per unit of outlay

Another criterion for investment choice is the average annual proceeds per unit of outlay, which is obviously related to proceeds per unit of outlay. To calculate this measure, the total of the net value of incremental production is first divided by the number of years it will be realized and then this average of the annual proceeds is divided by the original outlay for capital items. Table 9-4 illustrates the measure.

This investment criterion has a very serious flaw. By failing to take into consideration the length of time of the benefit stream, it automatically introduces a serious bias toward short-lived investments with high cash proceeds. We can see how this operates: project I ranks much better than project II, although we know by simple inspection that project II is the project we would choose. Similarly, the criterion cannot choose between projects III and IV, although, again by inspection, we know we would prefer project IV because it returns its benefits earlier. This criterion is misleading because it seems to allow for time by introducing "annual" into the terminology.

Average income on book value of the investment

A final undiscounted measure of investment worth is the average income on the book value of the investment. This is the ratio of average income to the book value of the assets (that is, the value after subtracting

Table 9-4. *Average Annual Proceeds per Unit of Outlay, Four Hypothetical Pump Irrigation Projects*
(thousands of currency units)

Project	Incremental cost Capital items	Net value of incremental production	Average net value of incremental production	Average annual proceeds per unit of outlay	Rank
I	30,000	30,000	15,000	0.50	1
II	30,000	34,100	11,367	0.38	4
III	30,000	42,000	14,000	0.47	2
IV	30,000	42,000	14,000	0.47	2

depreciation) stated in percentage terms. This measure is a useful and commonly used way of assessing the performance of an individual firm. Because it is widely known as a measure of performance, it is also sometimes used as an investment criterion.

For purposes of illustration, we will assume straight-line depreciation of our irrigation projects and thus will compute the average book value by dividing the investment by two. Table 9-5 shows this measure.

Although this procedure correctly chooses between projects I and II, it fails to choose between projects III and IV because it does not take adequate account of the timing of the benefit stream.

We can see that all these measures of investment worth share a common weakness: they fail to take into account adequately the timing of the benefit stream. In the case of ordinary inspection, there was no way of choosing between projects II and IV; in any event, if the projects were much more complex than these oversimplified examples, the projects would be too complicated to rank by inspection. As for the other measures, they all founder on the problem of timing.

The Time Value of Money

> *A bird in hand is worth two in the bush.*
> *Mas vale pajaro en mano que cien volando.*
> *Un tiens vaut mieux que deux tu l'auras.*
> عصفــور فى اليــد خيــر من عشــرة على الشجــرة

As the folk wisdom of people through the ages has recognized, present values are better than the same values in the future, and earlier returns are better than later. We can use the principle of these proverbs to overcome the weaknesses of the undiscounted measures of project worth we have considered and include a time dimension in our evaluation through the use of discounting. Discounting is essentially a technique by which one can "reduce" future benefit and cost streams to their "present worth." Then we may consider the differences between these present worths (the net present worth), determine what discount rate would be

Table 9-5. *Average Income on Book Value, Four Hypothetical Pump Irrigation Projects*
(thousands of currency units)

Project	Average net value of incremental production (proceeds)	Annual depreciation	Average income (proceeds less depreciation)	Average book value	Average income on book value (percent)	Rank
I	15,000	15,000	0	15,000	0	4
II	11,367	10,000	1,367	15,000	9	3
III	14,000	10,000	4,000	15,000	27	1
IV	14,000	10,000	4,000	15,000	27	1

necessary to make the net present worth equal to zero (a measure of the interest-paying capacity of the project known as the internal rate of return), derive a ratio of the present worths of the benefit stream and the cost stream (the benefit-cost ratio), or compare the present worth of the net benefits with the present worth of the investment (the net benefit-investment ratio). At first glance discounting may seem complicated and abstract. In practice it is not.

Interest

If we lend our money to someone to use, we usually can expect to be paid interest for the use of that money. In the same manner, banks, cooperatives, and credit unions will pay interest on savings deposits. How much interest will be paid varies from time to time and also with anticipated inflation and the chances that the borrowed money may not be repaid either on time or at all. The principle, however, is well known and simple.

Economists generally explain interest as arising for one of two reasons, although many others are sometimes suggested. The simplest explanation is that, if we lend money to someone else, we are deferring until the future the possibility of using that money for our own present pleasures. If we do this we are entitled to a reward—and interest is that reward. Another explanation, similar but rather better, is that interest is related to current income forgone. If a farmer lends money to his neighbor, on the one hand the farmer is passing up the opportunity to use that money for some productive purpose of his own—say, to increase his use of fertilizer. On the other hand, his neighbor is gaining the use of the money to put to another productive purpose—say, to increase the amount of fertilizer he applies to his crops. It is only reasonable that the lender be compensated for the income he has forgone and that the borrower pay something for his use of the lender's money.

Compounding

Consider a case in which the going interest rate is 5 percent a year and a one-year loan of J$1,000 is made on December 31. (The symbol for Jamaican dollars is J$.) The following December 31 the borrower will owe J$50 interest $(1,000 \times 0.05 = 50)$. Since the borrower must also repay the amount of the principal, he must pay a total of J$1,050 $(1,000 + 50 = 1,050)$. (As we noted in chapter 4 in connection with debt service, in interest computations it is easier to calculate the total of both principal and interest at one time by multiplying the principal by 1 plus the interest rate stated in decimal form. The "1" then covers the principal repayment, and the decimal statement of the interest rate covers the interest repayment. We would then calculate the repayment in this instance as $1,000 \times 1.05 = 1,050$.)

Suppose the borrower wants to keep the money for two years. He must pay 5 percent for the use of the money for the first year; for the second year he must pay an additional 5 percent. In addition, of course, he must pay interest on the amount he would have paid the lender at the end of the first year—that is, he must pay "compound" interest. Thus:

	Amount at beginning of year (J$)		One plus interest rate		Amount at end of year (J$)
1990					1,000
1991	1,000	×	1.05	=	1,050
1992	1,050	×	1.05	=	1,102
1993	1,102	×	1.05	=	1,157
1994	1,157	×	1.05	=	1,215
1995	1,215	×	1.05	=	1,276

Let us note two accounting conventions. The first is that interest is generally stated on an annual basis. Hence, if we say a loan is made at 5 percent, it is implied that we mean 5 percent a year. Interest is sometimes compounded monthly or quarterly or even continuously, but in project analysis we generally assume that the period we are talking about is a year. The second accounting convention is that the money is borrowed at the end of a period (say, midnight December 31, 1990—which is, of course, the same as the first instant of January 1, 1991) and is returned on the last day of a period (say, December 31, 1995).

Another widely used accounting convention is followed in this book, although it is not as universal as the conventions for the period for which interest is paid and the assumed dates. That is, the present (or the day just before the beginning of the project period) will be noted as t_0 and the end of the first year noted as t_1, so that money is lent today, or t_0, and interest is paid at the end of the first year, or t_1. (This causes some difficulty later, when we talk about investment, but is clear enough for the present.)

Let us take another series for illustration. Suppose we were to lend out J$817 for five project years (t_0 through t_5), at 8 percent interest:

	Calendar year	Amount at beginning of year (J$)		One plus interest rate		Amount at end of year (J$)
t_0						817
t_1	1991	817	×	1.08	=	882
t_2	1992	882	×	1.08	=	953
t_3	1993	953	×	1.08	=	1,029
t_4	1994	1,029	×	1.08	=	1,111
t_5	1995	1,111	×	1.08	=	1,200

Hence, if we were to lend out J$817 for five years at 8 percent annual interest, compounded, at the end of the fifth year the total of J$1,200 would be due to be repaid.

In practice, it is cumbersome to calculate compound interest in the manner we have been using here. A "compounding table" is usually used to simplify the computation. A convenient set is Compounding and Discounting Tables for Project Evaluation (Gittinger 1973), but there are many other, equivalent sets of tables available. Compounding may also be done by using a simple electronic calculator as discussed in chapter 10, the section "Calculator Applications in Project Analysis."

To illustrate how the compounding tables are used, we may consider the table for 8 percent from Compounding and Discounting Tables for

Project Evaluation [the relevant portion is reproduced from Gittinger (1973) in compounding and discounting table 2]. For our purposes, each line refers to a year, but it can also be interpreted as referring to any other compounding period. At the head of each column is stated what that column indicates. We are interested in the first column on the left-hand page entitled "Compounding Factor for 1—What an initial amount becomes when growing at compound interest." This is often called the compound interest factor. Now, if we want to know what will be due when we lend J$817 for five years at 8 percent interest, we look down the first column opposite the fifth period to find the compounding factor, which is 1.469 rounded to three decimals. To find out how much is due, we multiply the amount of the initial loan by the compounding factor for the proper number of years to obtain J$1,200 (817 × 1.469 = 1,200).

For most project purposes, given the nature of the underlying data, it will be accurate enough to carry out factors to no more than three decimal places.

Note that the factors in compounding and discounting tables are computed assuming they fall on the last day of the period for which they are computed. Thus the column in a table reading "year" or "period" really is for the *"end* of year" or *"end* of period."

COMPOUNDING AND DISCOUNTING TABLES
2. *Compounding Factor for 1, 8 Percent Interest*

RATE
8%

COMPOUNDING FACTOR
FOR 1
What an initial
amount becomes
when growing at
compound interest

Year	
1	1.080 000
2	1.166 400
3	1.259 712
4	1.360 489
5	1.469 328
6	1.586 874
7	1.713 824
8	1.850 930
9	1.999 005
10	2.158 925
11	2.331 639
12	2.518 170
13	2.719 624
14	2.937 194
15	3.172 169
16	3.425 943
17	3.700 018

Source: Gittinger (1973), p. 16.

The shortcut of using tables is obviously a great convenience. If, for instance, we want to lend the same J$817 at 8 percent interest for 15 years, we can find out very quickly that J$2,592 will be due at the end of that period of time (817 × 3.172 = 2,592).

Discounting (present worth)

Now suppose we ask a somewhat different question. If a borrower promises to pay us J$1,200 at the end of five years and an interest rate of 8 percent is assumed, how much is that promise worth to us today? Put another way, what is the present worth of J$1,200 five years in the future if the interest rate is assumed to be 8 percent? To answer the question, we must divide the amount due by 1.08 for each project year, as follows:

	Calendar year	Amount at end of year (J$)		One plus interest rate		Amount at beginning of year (J$)
t_5	1995	1,200	÷	1.08	=	1,111
t_4	1994	1,111	÷	1.08	=	1,029
t_3	1993	1,029	÷	1.08	=	953
t_2	1992	953	÷	1.08	=	882
t_1	1991	882	÷	1.08	=	817
t_0	1990	817				

Or, the present worth of J$1,200 five years in the future is J$817.

Note that the calculation we have laboriously gone through is exactly upside down from what we had done earlier for compound interest. Then we asked what would be the amount to be repaid five years in the future if we loaned J$817 today at 8 percent compound interest, and we found that the amount repayable would be J$1,200. Turning the question upside down, we asked what would be the present worth of J$1,200 paid five years in the future assuming an interest rate of 8 percent; we computed that value to be J$817.

This process of finding the present worth of a future value is called "discounting." The interest rate assumed for discounting is the "discount rate." The only variation is the point of view. The interest rate used for compounding assumes a viewpoint from here to the future, whereas discounting looks backward from the future to the present.

Again, it is laborious to calculate this in the manner illustrated, so "discounting tables" normally are used, or factors are calculated using a simple electronic calculator as noted in chapter 10 (the section "Calculator Applications in Project Analysis"). If one turns to the table for 8 percent in *Compounding and Discounting Tables for Project Evaluation*, on the right-hand page one finds the column entitled "Discount factor— How much 1 at a future date is worth today" at an 8 percent discount rate (which is the same as saying an 8 percent interest rate). The relevant portion is reproduced in compounding and discounting table 3. This column gives the discount factor for 8 percent. This is often called the present worth factor. Opposite the fifth year we find the value of 0.681 (rounded to three decimals). To find the present worth to us of J$1,200

COMPOUNDING AND DISCOUNTING TABLES
3. *Discount Factor, 8 Percent Interest*

RATE
8%

DISCOUNT FACTOR
How much 1 at
a future date
is worth today

Discount factor	Year
.925 926	1
.857 339	2
.793 832	3
.735 030	4
.680 583	5
.630 170	6
.583 490	7
.540 269	8
.500 249	9
.463 193	10
.428 883	11
.397 114	12
.367 698	13
.340 461	14
.315 242	15

Source: Gittinger (1973), p. 17.

---

received five years in the future, we multiply the amount due in the future by the discount factor for the fifth year to obtain J$817 (1,200 × 0.681 = 817).

The same discounting series, rounded to three decimals, is reproduced in the summary discount factor table (compounding and discounting table 6) in appendix B. The intervals are chosen to be convenient for project analysis, and for most project purposes these three-place tables are sufficient and may be more convenient. We may use these summary tables to illustrate again how to compute present worth. What is the present worth to us of M$6,438 received nine years in the future if the discount rate is 15 percent? (The symbol for Malaysian ringgats is M$.) The relevant portion is reproduced in compounding and discounting table 4. We search out the column for 15 percent, and opposite the ninth period we find 0.284. Now we multiply the future amount by the discount factor to obtain the present worth of M$1,828 (6,438 × 0.284 = 1,828).

Present worth of a stream of future income

Instead of someone promising to pay a single amount in some future year, suppose we receive a stream of income for a period of years. What would be the present worth to us today of that stream of future income?

COMPOUNDING AND DISCOUNTING TABLES
4. *Discount Factor, Various Rates*

DISCOUNT FACTOR—How much 1 at a future date is worth today.

Year	1%	3%	5%	6%	8%	10%	12%	14%	15%	16%	18%
1	.990	.971	.952	.943	.926	.909	.893	.877	.870	.862	.847
2	.980	.943	.907	.890	.857	.826	.797	.769	.756	.743	.718
3	.971	.915	.864	.840	.794	.751	.712	.675	.658	.641	.609
4	.961	.888	.823	.792	.735	.683	.636	.592	.572	.552	.516
5	.951	.863	.784	.747	.681	.621	.567	.519	.497	.476	.437
6	.942	.837	.746	.705	.630	.564	.507	.456	.432	.410	.370
7	.933	.813	.711	.665	.583	.513	.452	.400	.376	.354	.314
8	.923	.789	.677	.627	.540	.467	.404	.351	.327	.305	.266
9	.914	.766	.645	.592	.500	.424	.361	.308	.284	.263	.225
10	.905	.744	.614	.558	.463	.386	.322	.270	.247	.227	.191

Source: Gittinger (1973), p. 102.

This is a common question. An agricultural project often will return the same benefit in each of several years, and we need to know the present worth of that future income stream to know how much we are justified in investing today to receive that income stream. To resolve this question, we will again need to know the interest rate, the period of time we are talking about, and, of course, the amount of the income stream.

Suppose we take the M\$6,438 noted above and assume we are to receive that amount at the end of each year for nine project years (t_1 through t_9). We can discount that income stream back to the present for each year using the discount factors from the column for 15 percent in compounding and discounting table 4:

	Calendar year	Amount to be received (M\$)		Discount factor (present worth factor) at 15 percent		Present worth (M\$)
t_1	1991	6,438	×	0.870	=	5,601
t_2	1992	6,438	×	0.756	=	4,867
t_3	1993	6,438	×	0.658	=	4,236
t_4	1994	6,438	×	0.572	=	3,683
t_5	1995	6,438	×	0.497	=	3,200
t_6	1996	6,438	×	0.432	=	2,781
t_7	1997	6,438	×	0.376	=	2,421
t_8	1998	6,438	×	0.327	=	2,105
t_9	1999	6,438	×	0.284	=	1,828
Total		57,942		4.772		30,722

Thus, the present worth of M\$6,438 received yearly for nine years at a discount rate (which is, of course, a rate of interest) assumed to be 15 percent is M\$30,722. That is, the present worth is the sum of all the present worths for all the years together. (Note that, although the total undiscounted money value of the income stream is M\$57,942, the present worth is *not* that amount. Clearly, M\$6,438 received nine years in the future is not worth M\$6,438 to us today; that is what discounting is all about.)

Working out the present worth of a future income stream by this means is a little awkward and time consuming. It is faster if we just take the sum of the discount factors (that is, present worth factors) and multiply by the annual income to be received, to obtain the present worth of M$30,722 (6,438 × 4.772 = 30,722).

We can use discounting tables directly to find the present worth of a future income stream. In the 15 percent tables in *Compounding and Discounting Tables for Project Evaluation*, the second column on the right-hand page is entitled "Present worth of an annuity—How much 1 received or paid annually for X years is worth today." (An annuity is an amount payable yearly or at other regular intervals.) This column gives us the present worth of a future income stream of 1 currency unit a year. The same series, rounded to three decimals, is reproduced in the summary present worth of an annuity factor table (compounding and discounting table 7) in appendix B and is reproduced in part in compounding and discounting table 5. Note that the present worth of an annuity is simply the running subtotal of the discount factors. Thus, in the first year the present worth of an annuity factor and the discount factor for 15 percent both are 0.870. In the second year, however, the discount factor is 0.756. If we received the same income in both the first year and the second year, the present worth of the two-year income stream would be the annual amount received multiplied by the sum of the two present worth factors, 1.626 (0.870 + 0.756 = 1.626). If we look now at the value in compounding and discounting table 5 for the present worth of an annuity for 15 percent for two years, we will find that it is 1.626, and we have saved ourselves the trouble of adding up the discount factor column as we go along.

We can try another example. What is the present worth of ₱12,869 received annually for 14 years if the discount rate is 8 percent? (The

---

COMPOUNDING AND DISCOUNTING TABLES

5. *Annuity Factor, Various Rates*

PRESENT WORTH OF AN ANNUITY FACTOR—
How much 1 received or paid annually for X years is worth today.

Year	1%	3%	5%	6%	8%	10%	12%	14%	15%	16%	18%
1	.990	.971	.952	.943	.926	.909	.893	.877	.870	.862	.847
2	1.970	1.913	1.859	1.833	1.783	1.736	1.690	1.647	1.626	1.605	1.566
3	2.941	2.829	2.723	2.673	2.577	2.487	2.402	2.322	2.283	2.246	2.174
4	3.902	3.717	3.546	3.465	3.312	3.170	3.037	2.914	2.855	2.798	2.690
5	4.853	4.580	4.329	4.212	3.993	3.791	3.605	3.433	3.352	3.274	3.127
6	5.795	5.417	5.076	4.917	4.623	4.355	4.111	3.889	3.784	3.685	3.498
7	6.728	6.230	5.786	5.582	5.206	4.868	4.564	4.288	4.160	4.039	3.812
8	7.652	7.020	6.463	6.210	5.747	5.335	4.968	4.639	4.487	4.344	4.078
9	8.566	7.786	7.108	6.802	6.247	5.759	5.328	4.946	4.772	4.607	4.303
10	9.471	8.530	7.722	7.360	6.710	6.145	5.650	5.216	5.019	4.833	4.494
11	10.368	9.253	8.306	7.887	7.139	6.495	5.938	5.453	5.234	5.029	4.656
12	11.255	9.954	8.863	8.384	7.536	6.814	6.194	5.660	5.421	5.197	4.793
13	12.134	10.635	9.394	8.853	7.904	7.103	6.424	5.842	5.583	5.342	4.910
14	13.004	11.296	9.899	9.295	8.244	7.367	6.628	6.002	5.724	5.468	5.008
15	13.865	11.938	10.380	9.712	8.559	7.606	6.811	6.142	5.847	5.575	5.092

Source: Gittinger (1973), p. 104.

symbol for Philippine pesos is ₱.) In the table for 8 percent in *Compounding and Discounting Tables for Project Evaluation*, or in the 8 percent column in compounding and discounting table 5, opposite the fourteenth year we find a value of 8.244.

Multiplying the amount to be received annually of ₱12,869 by the present worth of an annuity factor at a discount rate of 8 percent for fourteen years, we find the present worth of the stream to be ₱106,092 (12,869 × 8.244 = 106,092). Put another way, if the going rate of interest is 8 percent, then we could afford to invest ₱106,092 in an enterprise that would yield us an annual return of ₱12,869 for each of fourteen years.

Many investments, of course, do not begin to repay us the first year. Suppose we are thinking of oil palm, which begins to bear about the fifth year and continues to produce commercially for about twenty years. In this case, we are concerned only with the present worth of a future income stream beginning with the fifth year and continuing through the twenty-fourth year.

To illustrate how we may determine the present worth of this future income stream, let us return to the example in Malaysian ringgats given above. Suppose our hypothetical investment, instead of paying us M\$6,438 each project year from the first through the ninth year, would only repay M\$6,438 each year beginning with the fifth project year and continuing through the ninth (t_5 through t_9). What would be the present worth of that income stream assuming the same 15 percent discount rate?

	Calendar year	Amount to be received (M\$)		Discount factor (present worth factor) at 15 percent		Present worth (M\$)
t_5	1995	6,438	×	0.497	=	3,200
t_6	1996	6,438	×	0.432	=	2,781
t_7	1997	6,438	×	0.376	=	2,421
t_8	1998	6,438	×	0.327	=	2,105
t_9	1999	6,438	×	0.284	=	1,828
Total		32,190		1.916		12,335

Thus, an income stream of M\$6,438 received from the fifth through the ninth project years at a discount rate of 15 percent has a present worth to us of M\$12,335 today.

Note that we could have calculated the present worth of our income stream by multiplying the M\$6,438 received annually by the sum of the discount factors for the fifth through the ninth years (6,438 × 1.916 = 12,335).

For just five years, it is easy enough to add the discount factors, but when we are working with longer periods, it is easier to use a shortcut. From the present worth of an annuity factor for an income stream received for the whole period we simply subtract the present worth of an annuity factor for the income stream for the period before the future income begins. Referring to the present worth of an annuity column in the table for 15 percent in *Compounding and Discounting Tables for Project Evaluation*, to compounding and discounting table 5, or to the summary present worth of an annuity factor table in appendix B, the present worth of an annuity factor for nine years at 15 percent is 4.772 and, for four years at 15 percent, 2.855. Now we subtract:

Present worth of an annuity factor for nine years at 15 percent	4.772
Less present worth of an annuity factor for four years at 15 percent	−2.855
Equals present worth of an annuity factor for fifth through ninth years at 15 percent	1.917

In this case, we would have been off by one point because of rounding.

Do not overlook that, if we want values for the fifth through the ninth project years, we subtract the figure for the *fourth* (not the fifth) year from the figure for the ninth year, since we want a factor that represents the years from five through nine *inclusive*.

If the discount factors are always totaled when the computation is laid out, this provides an internal check that they have been correctly listed without an error in computation or an error in subtracting the wrong year. When the discount factors are totaled, the sum will equal the present worth of an annuity factor for the number of years in the computation. It is uncommon for rounding errors to be greater than 0.001.

Discounted Measures of Project Worth

The technique of discounting permits us to determine whether to accept for implementation projects that have variously shaped time streams—that is, patterns of when costs and benefits fall during the life of the project that differ from one another—and that are of different durations. The most common means of doing this is to subtract year-by-year the costs from the benefits to arrive at the incremental net benefit stream—the so-called cash flow—and then to discount that. This approach will give one of three discounted cash flow measures of project worth: the net present worth, the internal rate of return, or the net benefit-investment ratio. Another discounted measure of project worth is to find the present worths of the cost and benefit streams separately and then to divide the present worth of the benefit stream by the present worth of the cost stream to obtain the benefit-cost ratio. Because the benefit and cost streams are discounted, the benefit-cost ratio is a discounted measure of project worth. But because the benefit and cost streams are discounted separately rather than subtracted from one another year-by-year, the benefit-cost ratio is not a discounted *cash flow* technique.

Choosing the discount rate

To be able to use discounted measures of project worth, we must decide upon the discount rate to be used for calculating the net present worth, the benefit-cost ratio, the net benefit-investment ratio, or the rate below which it will be unacceptable for the internal rate of return to fall—the so-called "cut-off rate."

For financial analysis, the discount or cut-off rate is usually the marginal cost of money to the farm or firm for which the analysis is being done. This often will be the rate at which the enterprise is able to borrow money. If the incremental capital to be obtained is a mixture of equity and borrowed capital, the discount rate will have to be weighted to take account of the return necessary to attract equity capital on the one hand and the borrowing rate on the other [(equity capital × return needed to attract equity capital ÷ total capital) + (borrowed capital × borrowing rate ÷ total capital) = discount rate].

For economic analysis using efficiency prices, there are two rates that might be chosen and a third that is sometimes proposed. Probably the best discount or cut-off rate to use is the "opportunity cost of capital." This is the rate that will result in utilization of all capital in the economy if all possible investments are undertaken that yield that much or more return. It would be the return on the last or marginal investment made that uses up the last of the available capital. If set perfectly, the rate would reflect the choice made by the society as a whole between present and future returns, and, hence, the amount of total income the society is willing to save. Although good as a theoretical definition, this is difficult to apply as a practical working tool. No one knows what the opportunity cost of capital really is. In most developing countries, it is assumed to be somewhere between 8 and 15 percent in real terms. A common choice is 12 percent, and we will use that rate in the illustrative examples in this chapter.

A second discount rate that might be chosen for economic analysis is the borrowing rate the nation must pay to finance the project. This is most commonly proposed when the country expects to borrow abroad for investment projects. Using the borrowing rate, however, has the undesirable result that the selection of projects will be influenced by the financial terms available and will not be based solely on the relative contribution of projects to national income. It is best to break the link between choosing projects and financing them—to choose the best selection of projects given the resources available and the ability to prepare them and then to set out to obtain the best terms possible for external financing.

A third rate sometimes proposed is the "social time preference rate." It is suggested that the discount attached to future returns by the society as a whole is different from the discount individuals would use. It is usually felt that the society has a longer time horizon, so that its discount rate would be lower. This implies that a different (generally lower) discount rate would be used for public projects than for private projects, and this gives rise to some awkward problems of allocation both in theory and in application. The social time preference rate would differ from the opportunity cost of capital in that the opportunity cost of capital derives from both public and private investment activities and gives the same weight to future returns from both kinds of activities.

[When social weighting is used, two other discount rates become important, the accounting rate of interest and the consumption rate of interest. Since the analytical system presented here is based on efficiency prices only, these rates need not concern us. They are discussed in Little and Mirrlees (1974) and Squire and van der Tak (1975).]

Note that financial rates of interest, such as government borrowing rates or the prime lending rate, are generally too low to justify their use in economic analysis of projects. Indeed, when the rate of inflation is high, these rates may even be negative in real terms.

Discounting convention for project analysis

In World Bank project analyses, both costs and benefits are discounted beginning with the first project year, and that is the convention adopted in this book. Some international agencies and many private firms begin discounting only with the second project year. Their line of reasoning is that investment must be made before the first year is ended, so how can one say that it should be discounted—that is, that the present worth in the first year is something less than the actual face value? The reasons for the accounting convention adopted here are somewhat arbitrary. First, it is convenient to begin discounting with the first year so that the project years and the discounting periods are the same—that is, project year 1 is discounted using the factor for the first period, and so forth. So long as this accounting convention is consistently observed, it will not introduce a bias or consistent error in the analysis of projects evaluated by discounted measures of project worth. Second, costs in actual practice are paid out during the course of each year, not all on January 1, and to allow for this on something like a day-to-day basis (or even a quarterly basis) is too complicated to be worth any added precision that might be realized.

We may illustrate the effect of the alternative conventions by examining the discounted cost stream laid out in table 9-6. (Note that the factor for discounting period 0 at any discount rate is 1—in other words, year 0 is undiscounted.) We can see that the effect of changing the first application of discounting from year 1 to year 2 is to increase the sum of the stream of present worths by the proportion of the discount factor, in this case by 12 percent [(22.47 − 20.06) ÷ 20.06 × 100 = 12)].

Derivation of Incremental Net Benefit
(Incremental Cash Flow)

When we consider a project, we see it as earning a gross benefit stream from which we must deduct the capital investment and pay the operating costs—the costs of machinery, fertilizer, pesticides, hired labor, management, consultants, and the like. What is then left over is a residual (which will likely be negative in the early years of the project) that is available to recover the investment made in the project (the return *of* capital) and to compensate for the use of the resources invested in the project (the return

Table 9-6. *Discounting from Project Year 1*
and from Project Year 2 Compared
(currency units)

Project year	Amount	Discounting from year 1			Discounting from year 2		
		Discounting period	Discount factor 12%	Present worth 12%	Discounting period	Discount factor 12%	Present worth 12%
1	1.09	1	0.893	0.97	0	1.000	1.09
2	4.83	2	0.797	3.85	1	0.893	4.31
3	5.68	3	0.712	4.04	2	0.797	4.53
4	4.50	4	0.636	2.86	3	0.712	3.20
5	1.99	5	0.567	1.13	4	0.636	1.27
6	0.67	6	0.507	0.34	5	0.567	0.38
7	0.97	7	0.452	0.44	6	0.507	0.49
8	1.30	8	0.404	0.53	7	0.452	0.59
9	1.62	9	0.361	0.58	8	0.404	0.65
10–30	1.95[a]	10–30	2.727[b]	5.32	9–29	3.054[c]	5.96
Total	63.60		8.056	20.06		9.022	22.47

a. Annual amount for years 10 through 30 inclusive. To reach column total, this amount must be included 21 times.

b. Present worth of an annuity factor for years 10 through 30 inclusive. See the subsection on "Present worth of a stream of future income" for method of computation.

c. Present worth of an annuity factor for years 9 through 29 inclusive. See the subsection on "Present worth of a stream of future income" for method of computation.

to or *on* capital). This residual is the net benefit stream. Deducting the without-project net benefit gives the incremental net benefit stream. These streams are commonly called cash flows because discounted measures of project worth were originally developed for use in business. The net benefit flow was distinguished from the profit of the business partly by the fact that no allowance for depreciation was taken from the benefit stream, which thus included all the cash generated.

The definition of incremental net benefit or incremental cash flow applies specifically to investment analysis. Accountants often have a somewhat different definition in mind when they use the term. In accounting, the cash flow is essentially the sum of the profit plus the depreciation allowance, usually computed after payment of taxes.

The major characteristic of the incremental net benefit stream or incremental cash flow is that it includes, without differentiating, both the return *of* capital and the return *to* capital. In other words, to compute the incremental net benefit or cash flow we do *not* deduct from the gross benefit any allowance for depreciation (that is, return *of* capital) nor any allowance for interest on the capital employed that has been supplied by the entity for which we are doing the analysis.

We do not deduct depreciation because the incremental net benefit stream already allows for the return *of* capital over the life of the project. Depreciation is an accounting concept necessary when accounts are to be prepared for one year at a time (not prepared as a projection over the life of the project) and must include an allowance for the capital use during each year. (How the discounted cash flow methodology automatically allows for the return of capital in determining the worth of a project and thus eliminates the need for year-to-year depreciation is illustrated in more detail in the section "What Happened to Depreciation?," below.)

We do not deduct interest on the capital supplied by the entity for which we are doing the analysis because in effect the result of a discounted cash flow analysis *is* the allowance for the return *to* the entity's capital. If we compute net present worth, we are determining what would be left over after allowing for some specified rate of return to the entity's own capital—the interest, if you like. When we compute an internal rate of return, this *is* the return to the entity's own capital and, in a sense, *is* the interest which that capital earns. (More precisely, it is the weighted average return to the entity's own capital engaged over the life of the project.) When we calculate the net benefit-investment ratio, we are comparing the present worth of the benefit we expect to gain with the present worth of the investment. Thus, interest is not a *cost* in deriving the cash flow. Rather, it is the *return* we assume when we discount to obtain the net present worth or the net benefit-investment ratio and, in the case of internal rate of return, it is the *answer* we obtain from our calculations.

There are two important differences in the manner in which we derive the incremental net benefit when we are carrying out an economic, as opposed to a financial, analysis. The first is that in economic analysis taxes are transfer payments within the society, not payments for resources used in production (see chapter 7). Hence, taxes are not deducted as a cost when deriving the incremental net benefit stream as the basis on which to compute the productivity of capital. To the whole economy, taxes are a part of the "benefit" available to the society as a result of the capital invested in the project, and they may be channeled by the society toward whatever purpose the society decides is best.

In contrast, in financial analysis duties and other indirect taxes are a cost that the individual entity must pay before arriving at the amount available to recover its capital and to compensate it for the use of its capital (that is, its incremental net benefit or incremental cash flow). Hence, duties and other indirect taxes are a cost like any other expenditure, and they are deducted to arrive at the net benefit before financing. This stream then becomes the remuneration for all resources engaged in the project at market prices, without regard to financing or income taxes.

The second important difference in deriving the incremental net benefit in economic as opposed to financial analysis is that in financial analysis we generally must account for outside capital borrowed by the entity that is undertaking the project—whether the entity is a farmer, an individual business, or the shareholders of a corporation taken as a group. In financial analysis, when borrowed capital is received it is usually entered in the account as a kind of "benefit" received or "negative cost." Then, when a repayment of principal or a payment of interest is made to the outside supplier of capital, it is deducted from the gross return as a cost in deriving the incremental net benefit or incremental cash flow after financing. This stream thus becomes the remuneration available for the entity's own capital (its equity) after financing. (Examples may be seen in tables 4-19 and 5-6.) The question of financing does not arise in economic analysis because we assume that all resources employed in the project belong to someone within the society—hence, there are no "outside" suppliers of capital.

Also note that, if the entity pays income taxes, these must then be deducted to arrive at the incremental net benefit after financing and taxes, which is the remuneration for the entity's own capital (equity) after financing and taxes.

There may be occasions when the analyst would like to look at the return to the society from a project funded by borrowed foreign capital. The kind of economic analysis outlined here is a valid indicator of project worth and will give the correct ranking of projects if the money borrowed from abroad may be used for any of a wide range of projects (or at least if the lender agreed to supply a stipulated amount of money contingent on the borrower's spending the money on a particular project selected by joint agreement from a wide range of alternatives). But if a foreign creditor is only prepared to lend for one particular project that it has stipulated in advance, then the project analyst may want to determine the return to the society's own capital from participation in the project. He can do this by treating the society as a kind of corporate entity in which the citizens are the shareholders and by determining the net benefit after financing, from which he can calculate the return to the society's own capital.

Although the incremental net benefit stream as it is derived for project analysis has by convention been called the cash flow, it may include noncash elements. In economic analysis of agricultural projects, the most important of these noncash items are the values of home-consumed production and of wages in kind. These might appear in a settlement project, for example, in which unemployed agricultural laborers are established on small holdings. One cost they might incur would be wages paid in kind. Furthermore, because the settlers could now earn a good living, their income would be considerably above the opportunity cost of their labor. If this is so, the excess value of the home-consumed production over and above the opportunity cost of their labor would represent not a cost of production but an incremental benefit available to remunerate capital and would be included in the cash flow. This would be true even if a settler's family were to eat its entire production (we say nothing in economic analysis based on efficiency prices about who actually receives the incremental net benefit; this point was taken up in more detail in chapters 1 and 7).

It is worth repeating a point made earlier. If cost, including investment cost, is subtracted from benefit during the early years of a project, the result will likely be a negative figure—that is, investment cost and initial operating cost will be larger than the benefit. The project will then have a negative incremental net benefit stream or incremental cash flow. The technical term "negative benefit" may take a bit of getting used to, but it really causes no trouble.

Perhaps the tabulation in figure 9-1 and the examples in tables 9-7 and 9-8 (table 9-8 shows the separate income statements for the income taxes reported in table 9-7) can make the derivation of the incremental net benefit or cash flow clearer. The reader may also wish to review the discussions about how to derive the incremental net benefit from farm budgets (chapter 4) and from processing industry accounts (chapter 5).

Net Present Worth

The most straightforward discounted cash flow measure of project worth is the net present worth (often abbreviated as NPW). This is simply the present worth of the incremental net benefit or incremental cash flow stream. (For a more formal mathematical statement, see the appendix to this chapter.) The net present worth may also be computed by finding the difference between the present worth of the benefit stream less the present worth of the cost stream, with both cost and benefit defined as in the previous section on deriving the incremental net benefit. This, however, requires somewhat more calculation.

Net present worth may be interpreted as the present worth of the income stream generated by an investment. In financial analysis, it is the present worth of the income stream accruing to the individual or entity from whose point of view the analysis is being undertaken—say, the farm family or the processing firm. In economic analysis, it is the present worth of the incremental national income generated by the investment.

Economists are somewhat inconsistent in their terminology for this measure. It is often referred to as the net present value (or NPV). In this book we will refer to it as the net present worth to emphasize the parallel with the discounting technique.

To calculate the net present worth requires determination of the appropriate discount rate along the lines discussed in the previous section (the subsection "Choosing the discount rate").

We may illustrate computation of the net present worth by referring to the costs and benefits of the Philippine Ilocos Irrigation Systems Improvement Project summarized in tables 9-9 and 9-10. (I have slightly modified the figures to make the computations come out even.)

A group of improvements is to be made in several irrigation systems in the Ilocos region of northern Luzon. An investment totaling the equivalent of US$18.09 million is to be made over a period of five years. After that, there is an annual operation and maintenance cost equivalent to US$0.34 million. The benefit arises from increased crop production. We will carry out the analysis assuming a project life of 30 years. (There is little reason to carry it out any further; we will return to this point in the section on "Length of the Project Period," below.)

In table 9-9, the present worth of the gross cost stream discounted at 12 percent is found to be US$20.06 million. Similarly, the present worth of the incremental production stream at 12 percent is found to be US$29.64 million. Subtracting the present worth of the cost stream from the present worth of the benefit stream gives a difference of US$9.58 million,

Figure 9-1. *Elements of Net Benefit*

From the standpoint of *financial analysis* (all prices are market prices including taxes and subsidies):

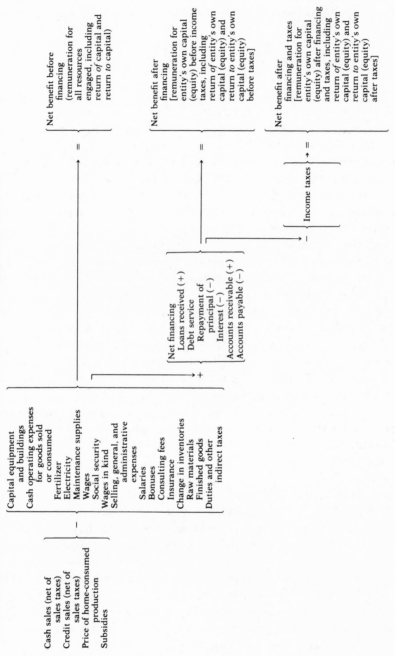

From the standpoint of *economic analysis* (some values may be shadow prices):

$$
\left\{
\begin{array}{l}
\text{Value of output} \\
\quad \text{sold} \\
\text{Value of home-consumed} \\
\quad \text{production}
\end{array}
\right\}
-
\left\{
\begin{array}{l}
\text{Capital equipment and} \\
\quad \text{buildings} \\
\text{Operating expenses for} \\
\quad \text{goods sold or} \\
\quad \text{consumed, including} \\
\quad \text{wages in kind} \\
\text{Selling, general, and} \\
\quad \text{administrative} \\
\quad \text{expenses} \\
\text{Change in inventories}
\end{array}
\right\}
=
\left\{
\begin{array}{l}
\text{Net benefit} \\
\quad \text{(remuneration} \\
\quad \text{for all society's} \\
\quad \text{resources engaged,} \\
\quad \text{including return} \\
\quad \textit{of } \text{capital and} \\
\quad \text{return } \textit{to} \text{ capital)}
\end{array}
\right\}
$$

Table 9-7. *Derivation of Incremental Net Benefit*
(currency units)

	Financial account				Economic account[a]							
	Without project	With project			Using shadow exchange rate				Using standard conversion factor			
					Without project	With project			Without project	With project		
Item		Year 1	Year x	Year z		Year 1	Year x	Year z		Year 1	Year x	Year z
Value of output[b]					*Inflow (gross benefit)*							
Revenue[c]												
Cash sales	1,000	1,000	3,000	3,000	1,200	1,200	3,600	3,600	1,000	1,000	3,000	3,000
Credit sales	100	100	300	300	120	120	360	360	100	100	300	300
Home-consumed production	200	200	300	300	240	240	360	360	200	200	300	300
Off-farm income[d]	200	0	0	0	100	0	0	0	83	0	0	0
Subsidies[e]	50	50	125	125	Omit[f]	Omit	Omit	Omit	Omit	Omit	Omit	Omit
Total inflow	1,550	1,350	3,725	3,725	1,660	1,560	4,320	4,320	1,383	1,300	3,600	3,600
Cash operating expenses					*Outflow (gross cost)*							
Goods and services other than labor												
Fertilizer[g]	50	100	300	300	60	120	360	360	50	100	300	300
Electricity[h]	50	50	100	100	56	56	112	112	47	47	93	93
Maintenance supplies[i]	200	300	550	550	220	330	605	605	183	275	504	504
Remuneration for labor (except that belonging to owners of the entity)												
Wages[j]	100	150	200	200	50	75	100	100	42	62	83	83
Social security[k]	15	22	30	30	Omit	Omit	Omit	Omit	Omit	Omit	Omit	Omit
Payment in kind[l]	25	40	60	60	12	20	30	30	10	17	25	25
Selling, general, and administrative expenses												
Salaries	10	20	20	20	10	20	20	20	8	17	17	17
Bonuses	0	0	0	0	0	0	0	0	0	0	0	0
Consulting and management fees	0	0	0	0	0	0	0	0	0	0	0	0
Insurance	10	15	15	15	10	15	15	15	8	12	12	12
Training and research	0	0	0	0	0	0	0	0	0	0	0	0

	1	2	3	4	5	6	7	8	9	10	11	12
Duties and indirect taxes[m]	0	100	0	0	Omit	Omit	Omit	Omit	Omit	Omit	Omit	Omit
Increase (decrease) in gross fixed assets												
Capital equipment[n]	0	2,000	0	(180)	0	2,400	0	(216)	0	2,000	0	(180)
Site improvement[o]	0	100	0	0	0	100	0	0	0	83	0	0
Increase (decrease) in inventories												
Raw materials[p]	0	100	100	(200)	0	120	120	(240)	0	100	100	(200)
Finished goods[p]	0	250	300	(550)	0	300	360	(660)	0	250	300	(550)
Total outflow	460	3,247	1,675	345	418	3,556	1,722	126	348	2,963	1,434	104
Net benefit before financing												
Total	1,090	(1,897)	2,050	3,380	1,242	(1,996)	2,598	4,194	1,035	(1,663)	2,166	3,496
Incremental	—	(2,987)	960	2,290	—	(3,238)	1,356	2,952	—	(2,698)	1,131	2,461
Financing												
Long-term loans received	0	1,000	0	0	Omit	Omit	Omit	Omit	Omit	Omit	Omit	Omit
Increase (decrease) in short-term loans	0	0	0	0	Omit	Omit	Omit	Omit	Omit	Omit	Omit	Omit
Interest received	0	0	0	0	Omit	Omit	Omit	Omit	Omit	Omit	Omit	Omit
Increase (decrease) in accounts payable and other short-term liabilities	0	60	60	(120)	Omit	Omit	Omit	Omit	Omit	Omit	Omit	Omit
Repayment of long-term loans[q]	0	0	(46)	0	Omit	Omit	Omit	Omit	Omit	Omit	Omit	Omit
Interest payments[q]	0	0	(115)	0	Omit	Omit	Omit	Omit	Omit	Omit	Omit	Omit
Loan commitment fees	0	0	0	0	Omit	Omit	Omit	Omit	Omit	Omit	Omit	Omit
Decrease (increase) in accounts receivable	0	(10)	(10)	20	Omit	Omit	Omit	Omit	Omit	Omit	Omit	Omit
Decrease (increase) in other short-term assets except cash	0	0	0	0	Omit	Omit	Omit	Omit	Omit	Omit	Omit	Omit
Net financing	0	1,050	(111)	(100)	Omit	Omit	Omit	Omit	Omit	Omit	Omit	Omit
Net benefit after financing												
Total	1,090	(847)	1,939	3,280	Omit	Omit	Omit	Omit	Omit	Omit	Omit	Omit
Incremental	—	(1,937)	849	2,190	Omit	Omit	Omit	Omit	Omit	Omit	Omit	Omit
Income taxation												
Income taxes paid[r]	286	77	758	804	Omit	Omit	Omit	Omit	Omit	Omit	Omit	Omit
Net benefit after financing and taxes												
Total	804	(924)	1,181	2,476	Omit	Omit	Omit	Omit	Omit	Omit	Omit	Omit
Incremental	—	(1,728)	377	1,672	Omit	Omit	Omit	Omit	Omit	Omit	Omit	Omit

(Table notes on the following pages.)

(Notes to Table 9-7)

Note: The figures in this table are illustrative and do not represent any real entity. They are assumed to be denominated in local currency. Year 1 is the first year of the project, year *x* is the first full year of operation, and year *z* is the terminal year of the project. The table follows the general format of table 5-6, which may also be consulted. Here and in table 9-8, the accounting convention of indicating negative numbers by parentheses has been adopted.

a. For a discussion of the principles of economic valuation, see chapter 7. The foreign exchange premium is assumed to be 20 percent. Thus, when using the shadow exchange rate to obtain economic values, the financial price of all traded items is multiplied by 1 plus the foreign exchange premium stated in decimal terms, or 1.2 (1 + 0.2 = 1.2). When using the conversion factor to obtain economic values, the financial price of all nontraded items is multiplied by a standard conversion factor of 0.833 (1 ÷ 1.2 = 0.833).

b. All output is assumed to be of tradable items.

c. Sales are shown net of sales discounts and returned goods and net of sales taxes. Credit sales are treated as a real resource use because it is assumed that the output has been consumed.

d. Off-farm income is included to account correctly for the benefit forgone in giving up off-farm income to participate in the project. Although especially applicable to farm accounts, a comparable entry might be included for small firms, in which event salaries would apply only to salaried employees. In the economic account, the off-farm income is assumed to come from unskilled labor services provided by the family and thus to have the same value as hired farm labor; it is shadow-priced at half the market value (see note l).

e. These are direct subsidies. When indirect subsidies operate to change the market prices of items, the financial prices are adjusted to economic values according to the procedures for valuing traded or nontraded items as appropriate.

f. Items marked "Omit" are included in calculating the financial incremental net benefit (incremental cash flow), but they are not included when calculating the economic incremental net benefit.

g. Fertilizer is assumed to be entirely a traded item, although application costs would no doubt require expenditure for nontraded items.

h. For electricity, it is assumed that 60 percent of the value arises from traded sources such as oil and generating equipment and that 40 percent arises from nontraded sources such as labor and local construction materials. Thus, when the shadow exchange rate is used, 60 percent of the value of electricity is treated as a traded item and is multiplied by 1 plus the foreign exchange premium stated in decimal terms, and 40 percent of the value of electricity is treated as a nontraded item and is carried to the economic account unchanged to obtain the economic value of electricity of 56 in the without-project situation [1 + 0.2 = 1.2; (50 × 0.6 × 1.2) + (50 × 0.4) = 56]. Similarly, when the conversion factor is used, 60 percent of the value of electricity is treated as a traded item and is carried to the economic account unchanged, and 40 percent of the value of electricity is treated as a nontraded item and is multiplied by the standard conversion factor of 1 divided by 1 plus the foreign exchange premium stated in decimal terms to obtain the economic value of electricity of 47 in the without-project situation [1 ÷ (1 + 0.2) = 0.833; (50 × 0.6) + (50 × 0.4 × 0.833) = 47].

i. Maintenance supplies are assumed to be half traded and half nontraded. A valuation method parallel to that outlined for electricity in note h is followed. Thus, when the shadow exchange rate is used, the economic value in the without-project situation is 220[(200 × 0.5 × 1.2) + (200 × 0.5) = 220]. When the conversion factor is used, the economic value in the without-project situation is 183 [(200 × 0.5) + (200 × 0.5 × 0.833) = 183]. For convenience, maintenance supplies are shown only as a cash operating expense, although in practice some maintenance would also be included among the selling, general, and administrative expenses.

j. The shadow wage rate is assumed to be half the market wage. Thus, when the shadow exchange rate is used, the market wage used in the financial analysis is multiplied by 0.5 to obtain the economic wage of 50 in the without-project situation (100 × 0.5 = 50). When the conversion factor approach is used, the market wage used in the financial analysis is first multiplied by 0.5 and then multiplied by the standard conversion factor to obtain the economic wage of 42 in the without-project situation (100 × 0.5 × 0.833 = 42).

(Table notes continue on the following page.)

Table 9-8. *Income Statements*
for Income Taxes Reported in Table 9-7
(currency units)

	Without project	With project		
		Year 1	Year x	Year z
Revenue—sales	1,100	1,100	3,300	3,300
Total revenue	1,100	1,100	3,300	3,300
Cash operating expenses	415	622	1,180	1,180
Selling, general, and administrative expenses	20	35	35	35
Noncash operating expenses—depreciation[a]	—	200	200	200
Total operating expenses	435	857	1,415	1,415
Nonoperating income and expenses				
Interest paid	0	0	115	0
Duties and indirect taxes	0	100	0	0
Subsidies	(50)	(50)	(125)	(125)
Total nonoperating expenses	(50)	50	(10)	(125)
Income (profit) before income taxes	715	193	1,895	2,010
Income taxes	286	77	758	804
Net income (profit) after taxes	429	116	1,137	1,206

Note: Income taxes are assumed to be 40 percent of income (profit) before taxes. The format here follows that of table 5-2.

a. Depreciation is allocated on a ten-year, straight-line basis and is charged only on an investment of 2,000.

---

k. Social security is considered to be a direct transfer payment and is omitted from the economic account.

l. Since payment in kind is a form of labor cost, it should be shadow-priced to reflect the opportunity cost of labor. This would mean shadow-pricing the payment in kind in the same manner as for the money wage, in this case at half the financial wage. Since it is the opportunity cost that determines the shadow wage rate, the method of valuing the payment in kind would remain the same even if the payment in kind were made in a tradable commodity such as food grain.

m. Recall that sales are shown net of sales taxes. If this were not the case, there would be an entry for sales taxes received and for sales taxes remitted to the government in the financial account, but these entries would be a direct transfer and thus would not be included in the economic account. Often capital equipment is shown inclusive of duties in financial accounts. If this is the case, duties would be deducted before calculating the economic value and would not appear as a separate entry in the economic accounts.

n. Capital equipment is assumed to be net of duties (which are shown separately) and to consist entirely of traded items, although installation costs would no doubt require expenditure for nontraded items. In year z, the negative entry for the capital equipment represents the residual value.

o. Assumed to involve only nontraded items.

p. Assumed to be entirely traded items.

q. The debt service payments are calculated for the second year of a twelve-year loan of 1,000 at 12 percent interest assuming a constant payment of 161 a year.

r. Income taxes are assumed to be 40 percent of income (profit) before taxes. The pro forma income statements are given in table 9-8 following the format of table 5-2. The depreciation is allocated on a ten-year, straight-line basis and is charged only on an investment of 2,000.

Table 9-9. *Computation of Net Present Worth Subtracting the Present Worth of the Gross Incremental Cost from the Present Worth of the Value of Incremental Production, Ilocos Irrigation Systems Improvement Project, Philippines* (millions of US$)

Year	Incremental cost				Discount factor 12%	Present worth 12%	Value of incremental production (gross benefit)	Discount factor 12%	Present worth 12%
	Capital items	Operation and maintenance	Produc- tion	Gross					
1	1.09	0	0	1.09	0.893	0.97	0	0.893	0
2	4.83	0	0	4.83	0.797	3.85	0	0.797	0
3	5.68	0	0	5.68	0.712	4.04	0	0.712	0
4	4.50	0	0	4.50	0.636	2.86	0	0.636	0
5	1.99	0	0	1.99	0.567	1.13	0	0.567	0
6	0	0.34	0.33	0.67	0.507	0.34	1.67	0.507	0.85
7	0	0.34	0.63	0.97	0.452	0.44	3.34	0.452	1.51
8	0	0.34	0.96	1.30	0.404	0.53	5.00	0.404	2.02
9	0	0.34	1.28	1.62	0.361	0.58	6.68	0.361	2.41
10–30	0	0.34[a]	1.61[a]	1.95[a]	2.727[b]	5.32	8.38[a]	2.727[b]	22.85
Total	18.09	8.50	37.01	63.60	8.056	20.06	192.67	8.056	29.64

Net present worth at 12 percent = US$29.64 − US$20.06 = US$20.06 = US$ + 9.58

US$ U.S. dollars.
Source: Adapted from World Bank, "Philippines: Appraisal of the National Irrigation Systems Improvement Project: I," 1488a (Washington, D.C., 1977; restricted circulation), annex 20, tables 2 and 6.

a. Annual amount for years 10 through 30 inclusive. To reach column total, this amount must be included 21 times.
b. Present worth of an annuity factor for years 10 through 30 inclusive. See the subsection on "Present worth of a stream of future income" for method of computation.

which is the net present worth at a 12 percent discount rate (29.64 − 20.06 = 9.58).

Two points about the layout of tables 9-9 and 9-10 and the computation should be noted. Opposite the entry for the tenth through the thirtieth years, the *annual* amount is entered in the undiscounted cost and benefit columns. To reach the undiscounted total in these columns, the annual amount must be included for each year from the tenth through the thirtieth years, or 21 times. But the present worth entered in the line for the tenth to the thirtieth years is *not* an annual amount; rather, it is the *total* present worth of the stream for the whole twenty-one-year period. This convention for table layout is followed throughout chapters 9 and 10. Note, too, that the total of the discount factors cannot be taken and multiplied by the total of the cost or benefit stream to obtain the present worth. In the gross cost stream in table 9-9, for example, the present worth of US$20.06 million cannot be reached by multiplying the undiscounted total of the gross cost, US$63.60 million, by the total of the discount factors, 8.056 (63.60 × 8.056 ≠ 20.06). The year-by-year procedure must be followed. Including the total of the present worth factors in the tables serves *only* as an internal check. The analyst knows he has determined the factors correctly if they add to the present worth of an annuity factor for the final year of the project.

Although the net present worth may be computed by subtracting the total discounted present worth of the cost stream from that of the benefit stream, it is easier and usual practice to compute it by discounting the incremental net benefit stream or incremental cash flow. Table 9-10 illustrates how this works in the case of the Philippine irrigation example. The gross incremental cost in each year is subtracted from the value of incremental production to obtain the incremental net benefit, or cash flow. Thus, in year 1 the gross incremental cost is US$1.09 million, and there is no incremental production, so the incremental net benefit or cash flow is US$ − 1.09 million (0 − 1.09 = −1.09). As another example, in year 7 the gross incremental cost is US$0.97 million, and the value of incremental production is US$3.34 million, so the incremental net benefit or cash flow is US$ + 2.37 million (3.34 − 0.97 = 2.37). Summing the present worths of the incremental net benefit stream, or cash flow, gives us a value of US$ + 9.58 million. This is exactly the same amount we obtained when we subtracted the present worth of the gross incremental cost from the present worth of the value of incremental production in table 9-9. Deriving the incremental net benefit, or cash flow, first and then discounting, however, is the simpler computational procedure.

A considerable advantage of discounted cash flow measures such as the net present worth, the internal rate of return, or the net benefit-investment ratio is that it makes no difference at all at what point in the computation the netting out takes place. To obtain the incremental net benefit, the analyst may subtract gross cost from gross benefit, the investment cost from the net benefit, or follow any other computational pattern that suits the analyst's analytical needs—provided only that double counting is avoided. In contrast, for the benefit-cost ratio discussed later

Table 9-10. *Computation of Net Present Worth Discounting the Incremental Net Benefit Stream (Cash Flow), Ilocos Project*
(millions of US$)

| Year | Incremental cost | | | | Value of incremental production (gross benefit) | Incremental net benefit (cash flow) | Discount factor 12% | Present worth 12% |
	Capital items	Operation and maintenance	Production	Gross				
1	1.09	0	0	1.09	0	− 1.09	0.893	− 0.97
2	4.83	0	0	4.83	0	− 4.83	0.797	− 3.85
3	5.68	0	0	5.68	0	− 5.68	0.712	− 4.04
4	4.50	0	0	4.50	0	− 4.50	0.636	− 2.86
5	1.99	0	0	1.99	0	− 1.99	0.567	− 1.13
6	0	0.34	0.33	0.67	1.67	+ 1.00	0.507	+ 0.51
7	0	0.34	0.63	0.97	3.34	+ 2.37	0.452	+ 1.07
8	0	0.34	0.96	1.30	5.00	+ 3.70	0.404	+ 1.49
9	0	0.34	1.28	1.62	6.68	+ 5.06	0.361	+ 1.83
10–30	0	0.34[a]	1.61[a]	1.95[a]	8.38[a]	+ 6.43[a]	2.727[b]	+17.53
Total	18.09	8.50	37.01	63.60	192.67	+129.07	8.056	+ 9.58

Net present worth at 12 percent = US$ +9.58

Source: Same as table 9.9.

a. Annual amount for years 10 through 30 inclusive. To reach column total, this amount must be included 21 times.

b. Present worth of an annuity factor for years 10 through 30 inclusive. See the subsection on "Present worth of a stream of future income" for method of computation.

in this chapter, the manner in which costs and benefits are netted out makes a difference in the ratio value. (We will show a numerical illustration of this in the section on the benefit-cost ratio, below.)

Suppose the net present worth had worked out to be negative? Then we would have a case in which, at the discount rate assumed, the present worth of the benefit stream is less than the present worth of the cost stream—that is, insufficient to recover investment. It would be better to put the money in a bank at the assumed interest rate (or, more likely, to invest it in a better project) than to invest it in the project analyzed.

The formal selection criterion for the net present worth measure of project worth is to accept all independent projects with a zero or greater net present worth when discounted at the opportunity cost of capital. (Independent projects are not mutually exclusive; mutually exclusive projects are of a kind that implementing one necessarily precludes implementing another.) An obvious problem of the net present worth measure is that the selection criterion cannot be applied unless there is a relatively satisfactory estimate of the opportunity cost of capital.

No ranking of acceptable, alternative independent projects is possible with the net present worth criterion because it is an absolute, not relative, measure. A small, highly attractive project may have a smaller net present worth than a large, marginally acceptable project. As long as both have a positive net present worth and the administrative capacity and resources exist to implement both (and the projects are not mutually exclusive), this difference is not important. Our selection criterion tells us to undertake both, since there will be enough money if the opportunity cost of capital has been correctly estimated. If because of lack of funds or administrative resources we cannot undertake both, the implication is that the opportunity cost of capital has been estimated to be too low. Then the correct response is to raise the estimate until we have only the selection of projects with net present worths that are zero or positive and for which, in fact, there will be just sufficient investment funds.

Net present worth is also the preferred selection criterion to choose among mutually exclusive projects because of a possible error in applying the internal rate of return measure to such projects (see chapter 10, the section on "Choosing among Mutually Exclusive Alternatives").

Internal Rate of Return

Another way of using the incremental net benefit stream or incremental cash flow for measuring the worth of a project is to find the discount rate that makes the net present worth of the incremental net benefit stream or incremental cash flow equal zero. This discount rate is called the internal rate of return. It is the maximum interest that a project could pay for the resources used if the project is to recover its investment and operating costs and still break even. It is the "rate of return on capital outstanding per period while it is invested in the

Table 9-11. *Computation of Internal Rate of Return, Ilocos Project*
(millions of US$)

Year (1)	Incremental cost			Gross (5)	Discount factor 18% (6)	Present worth 18% (7)	Value of incremental production (gross benefit) (8)	Present worth 18% (9)	Incremental net benefit (cash flow) (10)	Present worth 18% (11)
	Capital items (2)	Operation and maintenance (3)	Produc- tion (4)							
1	1.09	0	0	1.09	0.847	0.92	0	0	− 1.09	− 0.92
2	4.83	0	0	4.83	0.718	3.47	0	0	− 4.83	− 3.47
3	5.68	0	0	5.68	0.609	3.46	0	0	− 5.68	− 3.46
4	4.50	0	0	4.50	0.516	2.32	0	0	− 4.50	− 2.32
5	1.99	0	0	1.99	0.437	0.87	0	0	− 1.99	− 0.87
6	0	0.34	0.33	0.67	0.370	0.25	1.67	0.62	+ 1.00	+ 0.37
7	0	0.34	0.63	0.97	0.314	0.30	3.34	1.05	+ 2.37	+ 0.74
8	0	0.34	0.96	1.30	0.266	0.35	5.00	1.33	+ 3.70	+ 0.98
9	0	0.34	1.28	1.62	0.225	0.36	6.68	1.50	+ 5.06	+ 1.14
10–30	0	0.34[a]	1.61[a]	1.95[a]	1.214[b]	2.37	8.38[a]	10.17	+ 6.43[a]	+ 7.81
Total	18.09	8.50	37.01	63.60	5.516	14.67	192.67	14.67	+129.07	0

Net present worth at 18 percent = US$14.67 − US$14.67 = US$0
Internal rate of return = 18 percent

Source: Same as table 9-9.

a. Annual amount for years 10 through 30 inclusive. To reach column total, this amount must be included 21 times.

b. Present worth of an annuity factor for years 10 through 30 inclusive. See the subsection "Present worth of a stream of future income" for method of computation.

project" (Merrett and Sykes 1963, p. 38). (For a more formal mathematical statement, see the appendix to this chapter.)

The internal rate of return is a very useful measure of project worth. It is the measure the World Bank uses for practically all its economic and financial analyses of projects and the measure used by most other international financing agencies.

To avoid confusion between use of the internal rate of return in financial analysis and use of the same techniques in economic analysis, we will adopt a distinguishing terminology. When the internal rate of return is used in financial analysis, we will refer to the result as the "financial rate of return"; when it is used in economic analysis, we will call the result the "economic rate of return." When the emphasis of our discussion is on methodology, however, we will refer simply to the internal rate of return.

To see how the internal rate of return is calculated, we may take another look at the Philippine Ilocos Irrigation Systems Improvement example for which we derived the incremental net benefit (or incremental cash flow) in table 9-10. But this time, instead of discounting at 12 percent, let us discount at 18 percent, as shown in table 9-11, column 11. By selecting the 18 percent discount rate, we have driven the net present worth of the project down to zero. Put another way, at a discount rate of 18 percent, this project just breaks even—that is, it could earn back all the capital and operating costs expended on it and pay 18 percent for the use of the money in the meantime.

From yet another vantage point, we could have asked ourselves what interest rate this project would earn. In other words, what would be the earning of the money invested in this project? This earning rate of a project is the internal rate of return.

The formal selection criterion for the internal rate of return measure of project worth is to accept all independent projects having an internal rate of return equal to or greater than the opportunity cost of capital.

One word of caution, however. In the case of mutually exclusive projects, direct comparison of internal rates of return can lead to an erroneous investment choice. This danger can be avoided most easily by using the net present worth criterion, but it can also be avoided by discounting the differences in the cash flows of alternative projects. (See chapter 10, the section on "Choosing among Mutually Exclusive Alternatives".)

Note that an internal rate of return of a series of values such as a cash flow can exist *only* when at least one value is negative. If all the values are positive, no discount rate can make the net present worth of the stream equal zero. No matter how high the discount rate, the net present worth of a series would have to be positive if it includes no negative number.

Although the internal rates of return of different projects will vary, projects cannot with confidence be ranked on the basis of the internal rate of return. Only in a very general way will the internal rate of return tell us that one project is better than another, in the sense that it contributes more to national income relative to the resources used. A project with a 25 percent economic rate of return is likely to be a better investment than a project with a 15 percent economic rate of return, but this is at best a rough approximation. To be more precise, we must refer to our formal decision criterion. If the opportunity cost of capital is correctly estimated at 12 percent, we would accept *both* the 15 percent project *and* the 25 percent project. If we have to choose between them because of a limitation of funds or administrative resources, then we should raise the estimate of the opportunity cost of capital until the cut-off rate for the internal rate of return is such that all projects with an internal rate of return greater than the cut-off can be implemented. If we were to raise the cut-off rate in the example above to 18 percent, then the project with a 15 percent economic rate of return would drop out of the investment program. But as long as the estimate of the opportunity cost of capital—hence, the cut-off rate—remains at 12 percent, we cannot know with certainty that the project with 25 percent return contributes relatively more to national income than the one with 15 percent return, and we cannot say with confidence that we should implement the project with the 25 percent rate of return first.

Computing the internal rate of return

Except by lucky accident, one cannot simply choose that discount rate which will make the incremental net benefit stream equal to zero, as was arranged for illustrative purposes in table 9-11. Unhappily, there is no formula for finding the internal rate of return. We are forced to resort to a systematic procedure of trial and error to find that discount rate which will make the net present worth of the incremental net benefit stream equal zero.

The most difficult aspect of the trial and error is making the initial estimate. If the estimate is too far from the final result, then several trials will have to be made to find two rates close enough together to permit accurate interpolation (interpolation is the process of finding a desired value between two other values).

A quick approximation of the discount rate at which to begin the computation may be made by using table 9-12. The variables we must know are: (1) the number of years the incremental net benefit stream (cash flow) is *negative*; (2) the number of years the incremental net benefit stream (cash flow) is *positive*; (3) the annual average incremental net benefit (cash flow) for those years when the stream is *positive*; and (4) the *total* of the incremental net benefit (cash flow) for those years when the stream is *negative* (the negative sign of the sum is ignored).

To illustrate the use of table 9-12, let us again refer to the Philippine irrigation improvement example (table 9-11). Looking at the incremental net benefit stream (cash flow) in column 10, we can see that the incremental net benefit stream is negative during five years. The total incremental net benefit for those years when the stream is positive is US$147.16 million (recall that the annual incremental net benefit of US$6.43 million for years 10 through 30 must be included 21 times.) The annual average incremental net benefit for those years when the stream

Table 9-12. *Method of Computing Initial Estimate of Internal Rate of Return*

First, determine: *Number of years incremental net benefit stream is negative*	Second, determine: *Number of years incremental net benefit stream is positive*	Third, divide: Average annual positive incremental net benefit / Total negative incremental net benefit and use the result to select the proper column here. Then find the initial estimate opposite the appropriate number of years for the negative and the positive incremental net benefit streams.							
		0.1	*0.2*	*0.3*	*0.4*	*0.5*	*0.6*	*0.8*	*1.0*
	5	—	0	12	22	30	38	>50	>50
1	10	0	12	21	28	34	40	50	>50
	20	7	16	23	28	34	38	47	>50
	5	—	0	10	19	25	30	40	49
2	10	0	11	18	24	29	34	42	48
	20	6	14	20	25	29	33	40	46
	5	—	0	9	15	21	25	33	40
3	10	0	10	16	21	26	29	36	41
	20	6	13	18	23	26	29	35	40
	5	—	0	7	13	18	22	28	34
4	10	0	9	15	19	23	26	31	36
	20	6	12	17	21	24	26	31	35
	5	—	0	7	12	16	19	25	29
5	10	0	8	13	17	21	23	28	32
	20	5	12	16	19	22	24	28	31

This table assumes standardized incremental net benefit streams with this general time profile:

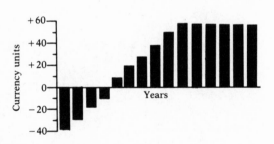

Source: Adapted from Schaefer-Kehnert (1979).

is positive is thus US$5.89 million (147.16 ÷ 25 = 5.89). The total of the incremental net benefit in those years when the stream is negative is US$ − 18.09 million. We will ignore the sign and take the sum to be simply US$18.09 million. Dividing the annual average positive incremental net benefit by the total negative incremental net benefit gives us 0.33 (5.89 ÷ 18.09 = 0.33).

In table 9-12 we can find the group of figures opposite the entry for a negative period of five years and for a positive period of twenty years, the

Table 9-13. *Computation of Internal Rate of Return Illustrating Interpolation, Ilocos Project*
(millions of US$)

| Year | Incremental cost | | | | Value of incremental production (gross benefit) | Incremental net benefit (cash flow) | Discount factor 16% | Present worth 16% | Discount factor 20% | Present worth 20% |
	Capital items	Operation and maintenance	Produc-tion	Gross						
1	1.09	0	0	1.09	0	− 1.09	0.862	− 0.94	0.833	−0.91
2	4.83	0	0	4.83	0	− 4.83	0.743	− 3.59	0.694	−3.35
3	5.68	0	0	5.68	0	− 5.68	0.641	− 3.64	0.579	−3.29
4	4.50	0	0	4.50	0	− 4.50	0.552	− 2.48	0.482	−2.17
5	1.99	0	0	1.99	0	− 1.99	0.476	− 0.95	0.402	−0.80
6	0	0.34	0.33	0.67	1.67	+ 1.00	0.410	+ 0.41	0.335	+0.34
7	0	0.34	0.63	0.97	3.34	+ 2.37	0.354	+ 0.84	0.279	+0.66
8	0	0.34	0.96	1.30	5.00	+ 3.70	0.305	+ 1.13	0.233	+0.86
9	0	0.34	1.28	1.62	6.68	+ 5.06	0.263	+ 1.33	0.194	+0.98
10–30	0	0.34[a]	1.61[a]	1.95[a]	8.38[a]	+ 6.43[a]	1.570[b]	+10.10	0.948[b]	+6.10
Total	18.09	8.50	37.01	63.60	192.67	+129.07	6.176	+ 2.21	4.979	−1.58

Internal rate of return (economic rate of return) = $16 + 4[2.21 \div (2.21 + 1.58)] = 16 + 4(2.21 \div 3.79) = 16 + 4(0.58) = 18.32 = 18$ percent

Source: Same as table 9-9.

a. Annual amount for years 10 through 30 inclusive. To reach column total, this amount must be included 21 times.

b. Present worth of an annuity factor for years 10 through 30 inclusive. See subsection on "Present worth of a stream of future income" for method of computation.

longest given in the table. In the column under 0.3 we find an initial estimate of the internal rate of return of 16 percent, and under the column for 0.4 an initial estimate of 19 percent. Because our estimate of the annual average positive incremental net benefit divided by the total negative incremental net benefit was 0.33, we must interpolate between 16 and 19 percent. Since 0.33 is three-tenths of the interval between 0.3 and 0.4, we must take three-tenths of the interval between 16 and 19 percent, or about 0.9 percent, and this gives us an initial estimate for the internal rate of return of 16.9 percent, which we would round to the nearest whole percentage point, or 17 percent. (We round at this point because we want to use this estimate for our initial discount rate, and discounting tables most often do not have appropriate fractional discount rates.)

It is characteristic, as in this example, that our initial estimate of the internal rate of return will be somewhat in error; and, unlike this example, no whole percentage discount rate will drive the incremental net benefit stream (cash flow) down to exactly zero. Instead, we will have to find a whole percentage discount rate that is somewhat too low and another that is somewhat too high and then interpolate between the two to find our internal rate of return.

We may proceed as indicated in table 9-13. We use our initial estimate of the internal rate of return to determine the present worth of the incremental net benefit stream. If we were using detailed discounting tables such as *Compounding and Discounting Tables for Project Evaluation* (Gittinger 1973), we would do our initial discounting at 17 percent. If, however, we wish to use the summary three-place tables in appendix B, we will have to choose between 16 percent and 18 percent to do our initial discounting, since there is no column for 17 percent. Our initial estimate was 16.9 percent, which is closer to 16 percent than to 18 percent, so we choose to do our initial discounting at 16 percent. In this instance, we find the present worth at 16 percent to be US$ + 2.21 million. When the discounted present worth of the incremental net benefit stream is positive, we know that, at this discount rate, the present worth of the project benefit is greater than the present worth of the cost. The project could pay a higher rate of interest and still recover the resources invested. Hence, we know that 16 percent is too low an estimate of the internal rate of return for this project. Now we need another estimate of the internal rate of return that is on the high side. In practice, it is better never to interpolate between intervals greater than about five percentage points because wider intervals can easily introduce an interpolation error. Five additional percentage points would give us an estimate of the internal rate of return of 21 percent. Since the tables in appendix B contain no entry for 21 percent, if we wish to base our computation on them we must choose either 20 or 22 percent. If we discount at 20 percent, we obtain a present worth for the incremental net benefit stream of US$ − 1.58 million. When the present worth of the incremental net benefit stream is negative, we know that at that discount rate the present worth of the cost stream is greater than the present worth of the benefit stream. The project cannot pay such a high rate of interest and still recover the resources invested.

Just where does the real internal rate of return lie? We could find out by successively narrowing down our limits until finally we find the discount rate that will make the sum exactly zero, but this would require much repetitive computation and the use of fractional discount factors for which no tables exist. Instead, we use interpolation to estimate the true value. (Again, interpolation is simply finding the intermediate value between two discount rates we have chosen. Many readers may have learned how to interpolate when they studied trigonometry in secondary school; the procedure outlined here is exactly the same.)

The rule for interpolating the value of the internal rate of return lying between discount rates too high on the one side and too low on the other is:

$$
\begin{array}{l} \text{Internal} \\ \text{rate of} \\ \text{return} \end{array} = \begin{array}{l} \text{Lower} \\ \text{discount} \\ \text{rate} \end{array} + \begin{array}{l} \text{Difference} \\ \text{between the} \\ \text{discount rates} \end{array} \left(\dfrac{\begin{array}{l}\text{Present worth of incre-}\\\text{mental net benefit}\\\text{stream (cash flow) at}\\\text{the lower discount rate}\end{array}}{\begin{array}{l}\text{Sum of the present worths}\\\text{of the incremental net bene-}\\\text{fit streams (cash flows)}\\\text{at the two discount rates,}\\\text{signs ignored}\end{array}} \right)
$$

This procedure has been applied at the bottom of table 9-13. The lower discount rate is 16 percent. The difference between the two discount rates is the difference between 16 percent and 20 percent, or 4 percent. The present worth of the incremental net benefit stream at the lower discount rate of 16 percent is US$2.21 million. The present worth at the higher discount rate of 20 percent is US$ − 1.58 million. The sum of the present worths of the streams at the two discount rates, ignoring the signs, is US$3.79 million (2.21 + 1.58 = 3.79). Hence:

Internal rate of return = 16 + 4 (2.21 ÷ 3.79) = 16 + 4(0.58) = 18.32 = 18 percent.

As noted earlier, it is better not to try interpolation between a spread wider than about five percentage points. The economic or financial rates of return should always be rounded to the nearest whole percentage point, since the underlying projections never can justify the implication of greater precision.

Interpolation between discount rates that bracket the true internal rate of return always somewhat overstates the true return. This is so because our linear interpolation technique makes the implicit assumption that, as we move from one discount rate to another, the internal rate of return will change following a straight line; actually, the true value of the internal rate of return follows a concave curvilinear function, as indicated in figure 9-2. The error introduced by interpolation is usually

Figure 9-2. *Interpolation Error, Jatiluhur Irrigation Project, Indonesia*

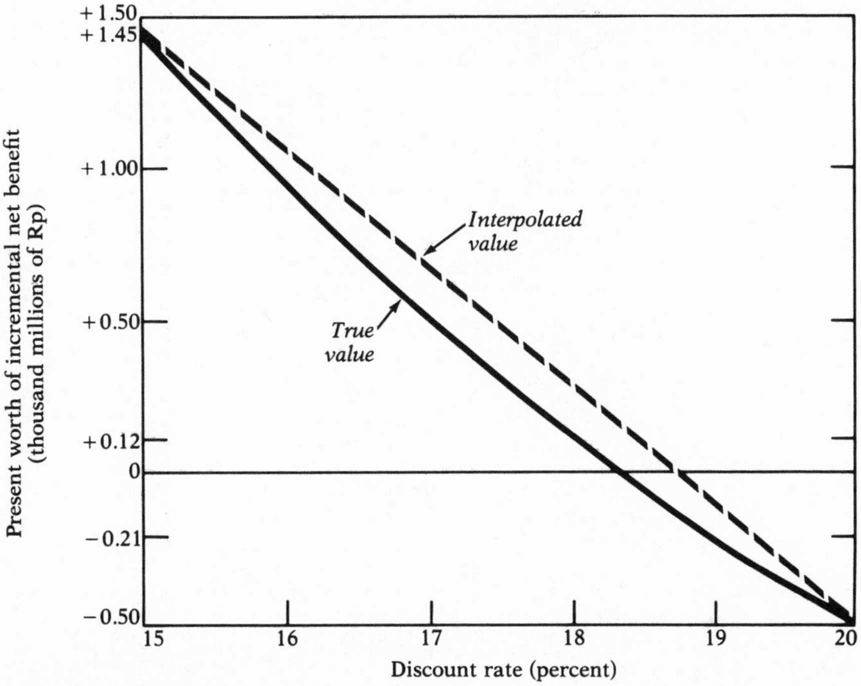

Rp Indonesian rupiahs.
Source: Adapted from World Bank, "Djatiluhur Irrigation Project," PA-37 (Washington, D.C., 1970; restricted circulation), p. 26 and annex 10, p. 1. Since this report was submitted, a spelling reform has changed the spelling of the project area to Jatiluhur.

slight and disappears when the result is rounded to the nearest whole percentage point. Nevertheless, a final figure for the rate of return should always be verified. This can be done most easily by taking advantage of the fact that the interpolation error becomes less and less as we approach one of the discount rates between which we are interpolating. Thus, a verification procedure that reduces the computational burden is to use the internal rate of return estimated by interpolation to discount the incremental net benefit stream once again. We can then interpolate between our estimated internal rate of return and the lower of the discount rates we previously used. This procedure is illustrated in table 9-14 with reference to the Jatiluhur Irrigation Project in Indonesia. Interpolating between 15 percent and 20 percent gives us an estimated internal rate of return of 19 percent. Discounting the incremental net benefit stream at 19 percent shows the present worth to have a negative value of Rp −0.21 thousand million. (The symbol for Indonesian rupiahs is Rp.) Interpolating again, this time between 15 percent and 19 percent, we find the estimate to be 18.48 percent, which would be rounded to the nearest whole percentage point of 18 percent. Because we know that the interpolation process introduces very little error at this point but nonetheless does slightly overestimate the true rate of return and be-

Table 9-14. Computation of Internal Rate of Return Illustrating Interpolation, Jatiluhur Project, Indonesia
(thousand millions of Rp)

Year	Incremental cost	Incremental benefit[a]	Incremental net benefit (cash flow)	Discount factor 15%	Present worth 15%	Discount factor 18%	Present worth 18%	Discount factor 19%	Present worth 19%	Discount factor 20%	Present worth 20%
1	0.5	—	– 0.5	0.870	–0.44	0.847	–0.42	0.840	–.042	0.833	–0.42
2	2.1	0.4	– 1.7	0.756	–1.29	0.718	–1.22	0.706	–1.20	0.694	–1.18
3	3.7	0.7	– 3.0	0.658	–1.97	0.609	–1.83	0.593	–1.78	0.579	–1.74
4	3.7	1.3	– 2.4	0.572	–1.37	0.516	–1.24	0.499	–1.20	0.482	–1.16
5	2.0	1.9	– 0.1	0.497	–0.05	0.437	–0.04	0.419	–0.04	0.402	–0.04
6	0.5	2.2	+ 1.7	0.432	+0.73	0.370	+0.63	0.352	+0.60	0.335	+0.57
7–30	0.5[b]	2.6[b]	+ 2.1[b]	2.782[c]	+5.84	2.019[c]	+4.24	1.825[c]	+3.83	1.653[c]	+3.47
Total	24.5	68.9	+44.4	6.567	+1.45	5.516	+0.12	5.234	–0.21	4.978	–0.50

Internal rate of return interpolating between 15 percent and 20 percent: $15 + 5(1.45 \div 1.95) = 15 + 5(0.74) = 15 + 3.70 = 18.70 = 19$ percent

Internal rate of return interpolating between 15 percent and 19 percent: $15 + 4(1.45 \div 1.66) = 15 + 4(0.87) = 15 + 3.48 = 18.48 = 18$ percent

Internal rate of return interpolating between 18 percent and 19 percent: $18 + (0.12 \div 0.33) = 18 + 0.36 = 18.36 = 18$ percent

Rp Indonesian rupiahs.
Source: Same as figure 9-2.
a. Assumes only an improvement in water control; that is, no accompanying increase in the use of modern inputs.

b. Annual amount for years 7 through 30 inclusive. To reach column total, this amount must be included 24 times.
c. Present worth of an annuity factor for years 7 through 30 inclusive. See the subsection on "Present worth of a stream of future income" for method of computation.

cause we have rounded to the lower whole percentage value, we could confidently stop at this point. For purposes of illustration, however, one further verification is made in table 9-14, by interpolating between 18 and 19 percent. At 18 percent we have a positive present worth, and at 19 percent a negative present worth, so we know that the internal rate of return rounded to the nearest whole percentage point must be either one or the other value. Since the interpolated value between 18 and 19 percent is 18.36 percent, and we know that to be above the true rate by some small amount, we can say with certainty that the internal rate of return rounded to the nearest whole percentage point must be 18 percent.

Reinvestment of returns

A frequent criticism of the internal rate of return is that there is an implicit assumption that all returns from the project will be reinvested at the internal rate of return. This is not, in fact, the case. Instead, as we have noted, the internal rate of return is correctly interpreted as being "the rate of return on capital outstanding per period while it is invested in the project" (Merrett and Sykes 1963, p. 38). Returns withdrawn from a project may be reinvested at any other rate or consumed without affecting the internal rate of return of the project.

In some instances, the reinvestment criticism relates to projects of different duration. If there are two projects, one of ten years' duration that yields 40 percent and another of twenty years' that yields 20 percent, which is preferable? Straight comparison would indicate the higher-yielding alternative for the shorter period. But if it were assumed that there would be no high-yielding project in which to reinvest the funds generated by the project of shorter duration, then it is possible for returns over the whole twenty years to be maximized by investing in the project with lower yield but longer duration. The investment decision in this instance will rest on the analyst's assumption about possible project opportunities ten years hence. The investment decision could be guided by determining the net present worth or internal rate of return of expected costs and returns over the full twenty years, say one twenty-year project versus two ten-year projects.

More than one possible internal rate of return

Under certain circumstances—exceedingly rare in agricultural projects—it is possible that more than one discount rate will make the present worth of the incremental net benefit stream equal zero. This possibility has been the source of considerable (and generally exaggerated) criticism of the internal rate of return as a discounted measure of project worth. (No similar problem exists with the other measures of project worth discussed in this chapter.)

More than one solution in determining the internal rate of return can exist *only* when, following a period of positive cash flows sizable enough

Table 9-15. *Internal Rate of Return Calculation Illustrating Multiple Solutions, Oil Well Project*
(thousands of US$)

Year	Incremental net benefit (cash flow)	Discount factor 20%	Present worth 20%	Discount factor 25%	Present worth 25%	Discount factor 40%	Present worth 40%	Discount factor 45%	Present worth 45%
1–4	+ 50	2.589	+129	2.362	+118	1.849	+ 92	1.720	+ 86
5	−750	0.402	−302	0.328	−246	0.186	−140	0.156	−117
6–20	+100	1.879	+188	1.265	+126	0.462	+ 46	0.345	+ 34
Total	+950	4.870	+ 15	3.955	− 2	2.497	− 2	2.221	+ 3

Source: Grant and Ireson (1964, p. 509).

that the cumulative present worth up to that point is positive, there then occur negative cash flows such that the present worth at t_0 of the cash flow from a given year onward (discounted in the normal way) is negative. Under such circumstances there *may* be more than one discount rate that will bring the present worth of the cash flow down to zero, although this will not necessarily be the case.

Negative incremental net benefits for particular years are sometimes found in agricultural projects. They can arise, for instance, when pumps must be replaced in an irrigation system or at the beginning of a replanting cycle in a crops project. Usually, however, the negative incremental net benefit flows late in the project will have to be quite large for there to be multiple solutions. An occasional negative year, or a final year or two of negative incremental net benefits, will almost never give rise to multiple solutions.

The kind of situation in which there are large negative cash flows after the initial investment phase of the project, although it is rare in agriculture, can be found in natural resources projects. To illustrate a multiple solution, we may consider an example of such a natural resources project given by Grant and Ireson (1964, pp. 509–10). Take the case of an oil company that is offered a lease on a group of wells for which the primary oil reserves are close to exhaustion. The major condition of the purchase is that the oil company must agree to undertake the injection of water into the underground reservoir to make possible a secondary recovery at the time the primary reserves are exhausted. The lessor will receive a standard royalty from all oil produced from the property whether from the primary or secondary reserves. No immediate payment from the oil company is required. The company estimates it will realize US$50 thousand a year for five years before exhausting the primary reserves. Then it must expend US$800 thousand for the water-injection project— the large negative cash flow—after which it will realize US$100 thousand a year for the following fifteen years. The internal rate of return calculation for this example is shown in table 9-15.

From the standpoint of agricultural project analysis, this is a curiosity of internal rate of return theory that has virtually no practical importance. In fact, I have been unable to find an agricultural example from a real project that illustrates the point, and I would appreciate learning of such an example should the reader find one. If such a case exists in an agricultural project, the analytical problem can be resolved by using either the "extended yield" method or the "auxiliary interest rate" method. A discussion of these methods can be found in Merrett and Sykes (1973, pp. 158–65) and Grant and Ireson (1970, pp. 546–65).

Point in time for internal rate of return calculations

Internal rate of return calculations can be done from any point in time, and all points will give the same return. In our illustrations we always calculate from t_0 into the future because this simplifies the calculation. But if we chose the end of the project, for example, we could increase by

Table 9-16. *Benefit-Cost Computation Comparing Gross Benefit with Gross Cost, Ilocos Project*
(millions of US$)

Year	Incremental cost				Discount factor 12%	Present worth 12%	Value of incremental production (gross benefit)	Discount factor 12%	Present worth 12%
	Capital items	Operation and maintenance	Production	Gross					
1	1.09	0	0	1.09	0.893	0.97	0	0.893	0
2	4.83	0	0	4.83	0.797	3.85	0	0.797	0
3	5.68	0	0	5.68	0.712	4.04	0	0.712	0
4	4.50	0	0	4.50	0.636	2.86	0	0.636	0
5	1.99	0	0	1.99	0.567	1.13	0	0.567	0
6	0	0.34	0.33	0.67	0.507	0.34	1.67	0.507	0.85
7	0	0.34	0.63	0.97	0.452	0.44	3.34	0.452	1.51
8	0	0.34	0.96	1.30	0.404	0.53	5.00	0.404	2.02
9	0	0.34	1.28	1.62	0.361	0.58	6.68	0.361	2.41
10–30	0	0.34[a]	1.61[a]	1.95[a]	2.727[b]	5.32	8.38[a]	2.727[b]	22.85
Total	18.09	8.50	37.01	63.60	8.056	20.06	192.67	8.056	29.64

Benefit-cost ratio at 12 percent = US$29.64 ÷ US$20.06 = 1.48

Net present worth at 12 percent = US$29.64 − US$20.06 = US$+9.58

Source: Same as table 9-9.

a. Annual amount for years 10 through 30 inclusive. To reach column total, this amount must be included 21 times.

b. Present worth of an annuity factor for years 10 through 30 inclusive. See the subsection "Present worth of a stream of future income" for method of computation.

compound interest factors all values in the incremental net benefit stream and find the interest rate that just makes the stream equal zero. If we were to designate a point midway through the project period as t_0, we could increase all values before the time from which we choose to work (say from t_{-5} to t_{-1}) by compound interest factors and draw down all future values (say from t_{+1} to t_{+14}) by using discount factors. Again, we would be looking for that interest rate which makes the value of the incremental net benefit stream at t_0 equal zero.

Benefit-Cost Ratio

A third discounted measure of project worth is the benefit-cost ratio. This is the ratio obtained when the present worth of the benefit stream is divided by the present worth of the cost stream. (For a more formal mathematical statement, see the appendix to this chapter.)

Incidentally, economists are quite inconsistent in their use of benefit-cost ratio. About half the time they say "cost-benefit" ratio. Here, however, I will stick to benefit-cost ratio to emphasize the computation by which the measure is worked out.

The benefit-cost ratio is not commonly used in developing countries. This is because the value of the ratio will change depending on where the netting out in the cost and benefit streams occurs. (Further on in this section we will illustrate how this works.) The benefit-cost ratio was the first of the discounted measures of project worth to become well known. It is extensively employed in the United States for water resource projects, although it is now increasingly being replaced by a variation of the net present worth criterion. Many economists in developing countries who have studied in the United States or who are familiar with U.S. practice will know of the benefit-cost measure. By the time discounted measures of project worth began to be applied in developing countries, the discounted cash flow measures of net present worth and internal rate of return had become well known and were being widely used for private investment. Since discounted cash flow measures do not change when different conventions for netting out are used, they are easier to apply and were thus adopted by development economists.

We return to the Philippine Ilocos Irrigation Systems Improvement Project analyzed in tables 9-9 through 9-11 to show how the benefit-cost ratio is calculated. In table 9-16, the gross benefit is compared with the gross cost. The present worth of the gross incremental cost stream at 12 percent is found to be US$20.06 million, whereas the present worth of the value of incremental production or gross benefit stream is found to be US$29.64 million. Dividing the present worth of the gross benefit stream by the present worth of the gross cost stream, we find the benefit-cost ratio to be 1.48 (29.64 ÷ 20.06 = 1.48).

Had the benefit-cost ratio worked out to be less than 1, then the present worth of the costs at this discount rate would have exceeded the present

Table 9-17. *Benefit-Cost Computation Comparing Net Benefit with Investment plus Operation and Maintenance Cost, Ilocos Project*
(millions of US$)

	Incremental cost					Value of incremental production (gross benefit)	Incremental production cost	Net value of incremental production	Discount factor 12%	Present worth 12%
Year	Capital items	Operation and maintenance	Total	Discount factor 12%	Present worth 12%					
1	1.09	0	1.09	0.893	0.97	0	0	0	0.893	0
2	4.83	0	4.83	0.797	3.85	0	0	0	0.797	0
3	5.68	0	5.68	0.712	4.04	0	0	0	0.712	0
4	4.50	0	4.50	0.636	2.86	0	0	0	0.636	0
5	1.99	0	1.99	0.567	1.13	0	0	0	0.567	0
6	0	0.34	0.34	0.507	0.17	1.67	0.33	1.34	0.507	0.68
7	0	0.34	0.34	0.452	0.15	3.34	0.63	2.71	0.452	1.22
8	0	0.34	0.34	0.404	0.14	5.00	0.96	4.04	0.404	1.63
9	0	0.34	0.34	0.361	0.12	6.68	1.28	5.40	0.361	1.95
10–30	0	0.34[a]	0.34[a]	2.727[b]	0.93[a]	8.38[a]	1.61[a]	6.77[a]	2.727[b]	18.46
Total	18.09	8.50	26.59	8.056	14.36	192.67	37.01	155.66	8.056	23.94

Benefit-cost ratio at 12 percent = US$23.94 ÷ US$14.36 = 1.67
Net present worth at 12 percent = US$23.94 − US$14.36 = US$+9.58

Source: Same as table 9-9.
a. Annual amount for years 10 through 30 inclusive. To reach column total, this amount must be included 21 times.
b. Present worth of an annuity factor for years 10 through 30 inclusive. See the subsection "Present worth of a future stream of income" for method of computation.

344

worth of the benefits, and we would not have recovered our initial expenditure plus the return on our investment from the project.

Note that the absolute value of the benefit-cost ratio will vary depending on the interest rate chosen. The higher the interest rate, the smaller the resultant benefit-cost ratio, and, if a high enough rate is chosen, the benefit-cost ratio will be driven down to less than 1.

The formal selection criterion for the benefit-cost ratio measure of project worth is to accept all independent projects with a benefit-cost ratio of 1 or greater when the cost and benefit streams are discounted at the opportunity cost of capital. In the case of mutually exclusive projects, the benefit-cost ratio can lead to an erroneous investment choice. The danger can be avoided most easily by using the net present worth criterion for mutually exclusive projects.

One convenience of the benefit-cost ratio is that it can be used directly to note how much costs could rise without making the project economically unattractive. In table 9-16, for example, we can tell by inspection that costs could rise by 48 percent before the benefit-cost ratio would be driven down to 1. With a little manipulation—taking the reciprocal of the benefit-cost ratio and subtracting it from 1—we can tell that benefits could fall by 32 percent before the ratio would be driven down to one $[1 - (1 \div 1.48) = 0.32; 29.64 - (29.64 \times 0.32) = 20.16; 20.16 \div 20.06 = 1.00]$. In effect, this is a quick means to estimate two "switching values." (A switching value is the amount an element of a project can change before the project becomes an unacceptable investment—see the section devoted to this topic in chapter 10.)

In practice, it is probably more common not to compute the benefit-cost ratio using gross cost and gross benefit, but rather to compare the present worth of the net benefit with the present worth of the investment cost plus the operation and maintenance cost. This reflects U.S. government practice. More specifically, the ratio is computed by taking the present worth of the gross benefit less "associated" cost and then comparing it with the present worth of the "project economic cost." The associated cost is "the value of goods and services over and above those included in project costs needed to make the immediate products or services of the project available for use or sale." Project economic cost is "the sum of installation costs; operation, maintenance, and replacement costs; and induced costs." The induced cost is "uncompensated adverse effects caused by the construction and operation" of the project. Table 9-17 illustrates how the benefit-cost ratio may be computed using this convention. (It is assumed there are no induced effects.) You will note one result of computing the benefit-cost ratio using this convention of netting out is to make it larger than when the gross cost is compared to the gross benefit. [The terms cited above, and further details of U.S. government practice, can be found in "Procedures for Evaluation of National Economic Development Benefits and Costs in Water Resources Planning" (U.S. Government 1979).]

We may use tables 9-16 and 9-17 to illustrate the point made earlier about the advantage discounted cash flow measures have with regard to the netting-out convention. When we changed the netting-out convention from comparing gross benefit with gross cost in table 9-16 to comparing the net benefit with investment plus operation and maintenance cost in table 9-17, we found that the benefit-cost ratio increased from 1.48 to 1.67. But the net present worth did not change when we changed the netting-out convention. It remained US$9.58 million in both cases.

Although in practice projects with higher benefit-cost ratios are often regarded as being preferable (other things being equal), ranking by benefit-cost ratio can lead to an erroneous investment choice. The benefit-cost ratio discriminates against projects with relatively high gross returns and operating costs, even though these may be shown to have a greater wealth-generating capacity than that of alternatives with a higher benefit-cost ratio. McKean (1958, pp. 107–16) discusses this point with illustrative examples.

Although different conventions for netting out costs and benefits may have been used for different projects, no matter how the netting out is done the same group of projects will be accepted if the benefit-cost ratio criterion, strictly construed, is used. In other words, the same group of projects will have benefit-cost ratios of 1 or greater. But a different netting-out convention can change the value of the ratio, as we have seen when two alternative conventions were applied to the same project in tables 9-16 and 9-17. These points are proven true by observation. If the present worth of the benefit stream exceeds the present worth of the cost stream, then the benefit-cost ratio will obviously be greater than 1. However, moving a cost from the denominator and subtracting it from the numerator—as we did when we omitted the production cost from the gross cost stream and instead deducted it from the gross benefit stream—will change the ratio value (and perhaps the rank of a project in comparison with alternatives), although the ratio will, of course, remain greater than 1.

When the benefit-cost ratio is used as a criterion for evaluating projects in a country, it is desirable that all analysts working in the country follow a common netting-out convention to derive their cost and benefit streams. If they do, they can greatly reduce the chances of a misleading indication of choice should administrators rank projects by their ratio values (as they have a tendency to do, despite the restrictions of the formal choice criterion).

Net Benefit-Investment Ratio

We have noted that none of the three discounted measures of project worth we have thus far examined can be relied upon to rank projects. The formal selection rule for each is to accept *all* projects that meet the criterion—a net present worth of zero or greater at the opportunity cost of capital, an internal rate of return equal to or greater than the opportunity cost of capital, or a benefit-cost ratio of 1 or greater at the opportunity cost of capital. Yet in many instances it is convenient to have a reliable measure to rank projects to determine the order in which projects should be undertaken. Such a need is common in practice. Decision-makers often ask that projects be ranked, and a need for ranking arises, for example, when the capital budget is not sufficient to implement immediately all projects being considered. If projects could be ranked, then the ones with highest priority could be chosen for implementation.

A suitable and very convenient criterion for ranking independent projects (that is, those which are not mutually exclusive) that is reliable in all but the most extreme cases is the net benefit-investment ratio (also called the N/K ratio). This is simply the present worth of the net benefits divided by the present worth of the investment; it is a form of the benefit-cost ratio. (For a more formal mathematical statement, see the appendix to this chapter.) The net benefit-investment ratio has been infrequently used in project analysis, perhaps because it has been common practice to rank projects using the internal rate of return or the benefit-cost ratio. As the limitations of these other discounted measures of project worth for ranking projects become better appreciated, it is probable that the net benefit-investment ratio or some close variant will become more widely used.

The net benefit-investment ratio is simple to determine when an incremental net benefit, or cash flow, has been calculated for a project. This is so because the net benefit may be taken to be the net present worth of the incremental net benefit stream in those years after the stream has turned positive, and investment may be taken to be the present worth of the incremental net benefit stream in those early years of the project when the stream is negative. Thus, to calculate this measure, simply divide the sum of the present worths after the incremental net benefit stream has turned positive by the sum of the present worths of the negative incremental net benefits in the early years of the project.

Our discussion of the net benefit-investment ratio will concentrate on its application. A more extensive and formal discussion can be found in Helmers (1979, pp. 99–117).

We may illustrate computation of the net benefit-investment ratio by again referring to the Ilocos irrigation example from the Philippines that we have used to illustrate other discounted measures of project worth. The computation is laid out in table 9-18. The present worth of the incremental net benefit stream at 12 percent after the stream has turned positive is US$22.43 million (0.51 + 1.07 + 1.49 + 1.83 + 17.53 = 22.43). This, then, is the present worth of the net benefit. The present worth of the negative incremental net benefits at 12 percent in the early years of the project, which is the present worth of the investment, is US$12.85 million (0.97 + 3.85 + 4.04 + 2.86 + 1.13 = 12.85). We may ignore the negative signs, since the net benefit-investment ratio is stated as a positive expression. The net benefit-investment ratio thus is 1.75 (22.43 ÷ 12.85 = 1.75).

An incremental net benefit stream usually will be negative for the first few years of a project and then turn positive each year thereafter for the remaining life of the project. This is the case, for example, in the Philip-

Table 9-18. *Net Benefit-Investment (N/K) Ratio Computation, Ilocos Project*
(millions of US$)

	Incremental cost				Value of incremental production (gross benefit)	Incremental net benefit (cash flow)	Discount factor 12%	Present worth 12%
Year	Capital items	Operation and maintenance	Production	Gross				
1	1.09	0	0	1.09	0	− 1.09	0.893	− 0.97
2	4.83	0	0	4.83	0	− 4.83	0.797	− 3.85
3	5.68	0	0	5.68	0	− 5.68	0.712	− 4.04
4	4.50	0	0	4.50	0	− 4.50	0.636	− 2.86
5	1.99	0	0	1.99	0	− 1.99	0.567	− 1.13
6	0	0.34	0.33	0.67	1.67	+ 1.00	0.507	+ 0.51
7	0	0.34	0.63	0.97	3.34	+ 2.37	0.452	+ 1.07
8	0	0.34	0.96	1.30	5.00	+ 3.70	0.404	+ 1.49
9	0	0.34	1.28	1.62	6.68	+ 5.06	0.361	+ 1.83
10–30	0	0.34[a]	1.61[a]	1.95[a]	8.38[a]	+ 6.43[a]	2.727[b]	+17.53
Total	18.09	8.50	37.01	63.60	192.67	+129.07	8.056	+ 9.58

$$\text{N/k ratio at 12 percent} = \frac{\text{Present worth of net benefits at 12 percent}}{\text{Present worth of investments at 12 percent}}$$

$$= \frac{\text{Present worth of positive incremental net benefit at 12 percent}}{\text{Present worth of negative incremental net benefit at 12 percent}}$$

$$= \frac{\text{US\$0.51 + US\$1.07 + US\$1.49 + US\$1.83 + US\$17.53}}{\text{US\$0.97 + US\$3.85 + US\$4.04 + US\$2.86 + US\$1.13}} = \frac{\text{US\$22.43}}{\text{US\$12.85}} = 1.75$$

Source: Same as table 9-9.

a. Annual amount for years 10 through 30 inclusive. To reach column total, this amount must be included 21 times.

b. Present worth of an annuity factor for years 10 through 30 inclusive. See the subsection on "Present worth of a stream of future income" for method of computation.

pine irrigation illustration in table 9-18. It might happen, however, that an investment in the project at some later year would be large enough to turn the incremental net benefit for that year negative. An example might be the year when the pumps are replaced in an irrigation project. This does not affect the means of calculating the net benefit-investment ratio. The net benefit will be the present worth of the incremental net benefit stream after the stream has turned positive, and the negative incremental net benefit that occurs later in the project is simply included in the net present worth of the benefit stream—reducing the stream, obviously, below what it would otherwise have been. The reason for calculating the net benefit-investment ratio in this manner is that we are interested in an investment measure that selects projects on the basis of return to investment during the initial phases of a project. An occasional negative incremental net benefit later in the life of a project does not increase the capital needed during the investment phase of the project.

The formal selection criterion for the net benefit-investment ratio measure of project worth is to accept all projects with a net benefit-investment ratio of 1 or greater when they are discounted at the opportunity cost of capital—in order, beginning with the largest ratio value and proceeding until available investment funds are exhausted.

Selecting independent projects in the order of their net benefit-investment ratio maximizes the return per unit of available investment. This, in turn, maximizes the net present worth of the group of projects chosen, and thus maximizes the income stream that is the objective of the program of project investments.

If the net benefit-investment ratio is used to rank projects, some limitations should be kept in mind. First and most important, the net benefit-investment ratio can be used to rank mutually exclusive projects only when the net benefit-investment ratios of all projects in the investment program are known. Because in practice this would either be impossible or analytically very complex, it is better practice to select among mutually exclusive projects by using the net present worth criterion. Second, there can be instances when the net benefit-investment ratio can indicate incorrect investment decisions, but they are so extreme that they may be ignored when any real project is under consideration. Finally, the net benefit-investment ratio does not hold if one is undertaking what is called dynamic optimization—optimizing project investment over time. Dynamic optimization, however, requires knowledge of all future budget constraints and investment opportunities and so is not a practical methodology to apply in real project investment decisions.

The net benefit-investment ratio is very convenient to use in real-life project investment decisions. It may be used to rank projects in those instances in which, for one reason or another, sufficient funds are not available to implement all projects. It thus satisfies a frequent request of decisionmakers that projects be ranked in the order in which they should be undertaken. It is suitable for use when there is incomplete knowledge of all projects in all periods; when budget constraints will vary in magnitude in the future; and when it is very difficult or costly to redesign projects in future periods—for example, to change the height of a dam—conditions that make it impossible to attempt dynamic optimization.

In a manner similar to that described for the benefit-cost ratio, the net benefit-investment ratio may be used to make a quick estimate of how much the investment cost could rise without making the project economically unattractive. In table 9-18, for example, we can tell by inspection that the investment cost could rise as much as 75 percent before the net benefit-investment ratio would be driven down to one [(22.43 − 12.85) ÷ 12.85 × 100 = 75; 22.43 ÷ (12.85 × 1.75) = 1.00]. By taking the reciprocal of the net benefit-investment ratio and subtracting it from 1, we can quickly tell that the net benefit could fall by almost 43 percent before the ratio would be driven down to one {[1 − (1 ÷ 1.75)] × 100 = 43; [22.43 − (22.43 × 0.43)] ÷ 12.85 = 0.99 }. Thus, again, we have a quick means of estimating two switching values, which are discussed further in the next chapter.

Selecting among Project Alternatives

To illustrate how discounted measures of project worth can be applied to help choose among project alternatives, we return to the four hypothetical investments in pump irrigation presented at the beginning of this chapter and set out in table 9-1 to illustrate undiscounted measures of project worth. In the analysis laid out in table 9-19, we have calculated the net present worth at a 12 percent discount rate, the internal rate of return, the benefit-cost ratio at a 12 percent discount rate, and the net benefit-investment ratio at a 12 percent discount rate.

It is clear that we would reject both projects I and II at the 12 percent discount rate. We would accept project II only if our discount rate were 8 percent or lower, when it would have a net present worth of zero or greater, an internal rate of return at or above the cut-off rate, and a net benefit-investment ratio of 1 or greater. At the 12 percent discount rate we would accept *both* projects III and IV, since both have positive net present worths, internal rates of return above the cut-off rate, and benefit-cost and net benefit-investment ratios greater than 1. If, however, our investment funds were limited to some 30 million currency units (and ignoring any problem of the cash flow within year 2), we would have to choose between projects III and IV. We can see that, by increasing the discount rate, an unambiguous choice would be made. If we set the discount rate at 15 percent, we would accept only project IV, which would have a positive net present worth and an internal rate of return just above the cut-off rate. We would have just used all our investment funds, so our selection criterion would be clear. Alternatively, and more simply, we could select project IV on the basis that it has the higher net benefit-investment ratio at a 12 percent discount rate. (Because of the very simplified figures we have used for illustration, the net present worth, the internal rate of return, and the benefit-cost ratio also rank the projects in the same order as would the net benefit-investment ratio and the formal selection criterion of raising the discount rate. This is only a coincidence. At any given discount rate, we cannot with confidence use the net present worth, or the internal rate of return, or the benefit-cost ratio as ranking measures; our criteria tell us only to accept all projects which meet the selection criteria for these three measures. The net benefit-investment ratio is the only measure of the ones we have discussed that can be used with confidence to rank directly.)

What Happened to Depreciation?

We may now consider a question that sometimes vexes people who are trying to use discounted measures of project worth.

In determining the costs used to calculate discounted measures of project worth, we have not included depreciation. When we discussed the incremental net benefit stream or cash flow, we noted that it was an undifferentiated combination of two things: return *of* capital (which would include depreciation) and returns paid for the use of capital (such as dividends, profits, and the like)—returns *to* capital. We did not subtract depreciation as a cost. Depreciation does not appear in the gross cost computation for the benefit-cost ratio. Yet net present worth determines if a project can earn *more* than some stated amount of return to capital, the internal rate of return is a measure of the interest a project can pay, and the net benefit-investment ratio determines if the project will have a net benefit greater than the investment at some stated amount of return to capital. The question is, what happened to depreciation?

The easiest way to go about illustrating what happens to depreciation in discounted measures of project worth is to compute the net present worth, the internal rate of return, the benefit-cost ratio, and the net benefit-investment ratio of a hypothetical example such as that shown in table 9-20. In this case, we are analyzing a project that does not exactly lose money, but does not make money either. In other words, its net present worth at zero discount rate is zero, its internal rate of return is zero, its benefit-cost ratio at zero rate of interest is just exactly 1, and the net benefit-investment ratio at a zero discount rate is 1.

The question we are concerned with here is, did we get our money back? The answer, obviously, is yes. We spent 1,200 thousand currency units over the five years of the project, and by the end of the fifth year we have received just exactly 1,200 thousand back. So we didn't lose any of our capital, and we recovered all of our other costs.

Did we earn anything on this project? Clearly, no. Both the net present worth and the internal rate of return of this project were simply zero, and the benefit-cost and net benefit-investment ratios had to be computed at a zero rate of interest to have them come out to 1.

Therefore, return *of* capital is realized (that is, depreciation is covered and fully accounted for) when the net present worth of the project at a zero discount rate is zero or greater, when the project earns an internal

Table 9-19. *Ranking of Four Hypothetical Pump Irrigation Projects Using N/K Ratio*
(thousands of currency units)

Project I

Year	Gross cost	Value of incremental production (gross benefit)	Incremental net benefit (cash flow)	Discount factor 12%	Present worth 12%	Discount factor 0%	Present worth 0%	Rank
1	30,000	—	−30,000	0.893	−26,790	1.000	−30,000	
2	5,000	20,000	+15,000	0.797	+11,955	1.000	+15,000	
3	5,000	20,000	+15,000	0.712	+10,680	1.000	+15,000	
4	—	—	—	—	—	—	—	
Total	40,000	40,000	0	2.402	−4,155	3.000	0	4

Net present worth at 12 percent = −4,155,000
Internal rate of return = 0 percent
Benefit-cost ratio at 12 percent = 0.88[a]
N/k ratio at 12 percent = 22,635 ÷ 26,790 = 0.84

Project II

Year	Gross cost	Value of incremental production (gross benefit)	Incremental net benefit (cash flow)	Discount factor 12%	Present worth 12%	Discount factor 8%	Present worth 8%	Rank
1	30,000	—	−30,000	0.893	−26,790	0.926	−27,780	
2	5,000	20,000	+15,000	0.797	+11,955	0.857	+12,855	
3	5,000	20,000	+15,000	0.712	+10,680	0.794	+11,910	
4	5,000	9,100	+4,100	0.636	+2,608	0.735	+3,014	
Total	45,000	49,100	+4,100	3.038	−1,547	3.312	−1	3

Net present worth at 12 percent = 1,547,000
Internal rate of return = 8 percent
Benefit-cost ratio at 12 percent = 0.96[a]
N/k ratio at 12 percent = 25,243 ÷ 26,790 = 0.94

Project III

						Discount factor 14%	Present worth 14%
1	30,000	—	−30,000	0.893	−26,790	0.877	−26,310
2	5,000	7,000	+ 2,000	0.797	+ 1,594	0.769	+ 1,538
3	5,000	19,000	+14,000	0.712	+ 9,968	0.675	+ 9,450
4	5,000	31,000	+26,000	0.636	+16,536	0.592	+15,392
Total	45,000	57,000	+12,000	3.038	+ 1,308	2.913	+ 70

2

Net present worth at 12 percent = 1,308,000
Internal rate of return = 14 percent
Benefit-cost ratio at 12 percent = 1.03[a]
N/k ratio at 12 percent = 28,098 ÷ 26,790 = 1.05

Project IV

						Discount factor 16%	Present worth 16%
1	30,000	—	−30,000	0.893	−26,790	0.862	−25,860
2	5,000	7,000	+ 2,000	0.797	+ 1,594	0.743	+ 1,486
3	5,000	31,000	+26,000	0.712	+18,512	0.641	+16,666
4	5,000	19,000	+14,000	0.636	+ 8,904	0.552	+ 7,728
Total	45,000	57,000	+12,000	3.038	+ 2,220	2.798	+ 20

1

Net present worth at 12 percent = 2,220,000
Internal rate of return = 16 percent
Benefit-cost ratio at 12 percent = 1.06[a]
N/k ratio at 12 percent = 29,010 ÷ 26,790 = 1.08

Source: Table 9-1.
a. The derivation of the benefit-cost ratio is not given in this table.

Table 9-20. *Treatment of Depreciation in Discounted Measures of Project Worth*
(thousands of currency units)

Year	Incremental cost			Value of incremental production (gross benefit)	Incremental net benefit (cash flow)	Discount factor 0%	Present worth 0%
	Capital items	Production	Gross				
1	1,000	0	1,000	0	−1,000	1.000	−1,000
2	—	50	50	300	+ 250	1.000	+ 250
3	—	50	50	300	+ 250	1.000	+ 250
4	—	50	50	300	+ 250	1.000	+ 250
5	—	50	50	300	+ 250	1.000	+ 250
Total	1,000	200	1,200	1,200	0	5.000	0

Net present worth at 0 percent = 0
Internal rate of return = 0 percent
Benefit-cost ratio at 0 percent = 1,200 ÷ 1,200 = 1.00
N/k ratio at 0 percent = 1,000 ÷ 1,000 = 1.00

rate of return of zero or greater, and when the benefit-cost ratio or net benefit-investment ratio is 1 at a zero or greater rate of interest. We do not need to include depreciation separately as a "cost" in analyzing our project. It is automatically taken care of in the computational process. (There is another convenience—we do not need to make any decision about what depreciation schedule to use, a notoriously difficult and arbitrary choice that is essentially an accounting, not an economic, problem.)

Of course, if the net present worth at zero discount rate is less than zero, if the internal rate of return is less than zero, or if the benefit-cost ratio or the net benefit-investment ratio at zero rate of interest is less than 1, then we not only would have earned nothing, but actually would not even have recovered all our costs.

Length of the Project Period

For how long a period should the analyst carry out the economic analysis? The general rule is to choose a period of time that will be roughly comparable to the economic life of the project.

If the project requires a fairly sizable initial capital investment in one kind of asset, such as tubewells or an orchard, a convenient starting point for establishing the period of the analysis is the technical life of the major investment item. In some projects, however, the technical life of the major investment may be quite long, but the economic life of the item is expected to be much shorter because of technological obsolescence. This may be a problem in industrial projects and in some kinds of transport projects, but it is rather uncommon in agricultural projects. Even so, the analyst might expect that the economic life of a processing plant that produces frozen foods would be shorter than the technical life of the equipment, or even that the equipment for producing broiler chickens might become obsolete before it is completely worn out. In most agricultural projects, however, we do not anticipate that rapidly changing technology will make a major investment obsolete over a period of twenty to twenty-five years.

When the economic life of the project is not limited by considerations of obsolescence, and the technical life of the major investment asset extends beyond about twenty-five years, another consideration comes into play that helps to establish a reasonable economic life for the project and, hence, for the economic project analysis. At the discount rates we are talking about and the opportunity costs for capital we think exist in developing countries, any return to an investment beyond about twenty-five years will probably make no difference in project selection. As a result, few agricultural project analyses need to be carried out beyond twenty-five years. But if the technicians working on the project feel the analyst should carry out the economic analysis for a longer period because coconuts will bear for forty years or because a dam can reasonably be expected to last fifty years, then it may be easier for the analyst simply to run the calculations through to a period that satisfies the technicians rather than to discuss the matter further. It is better to save the discussion for the difficult problems of project design and implementation.

To illustrate that extending the economic analysis beyond twenty-five years makes little difference in project selection, we may take two approaches: looking at the discount factors themselves and running an illustrative internal rate of return.

First, the discount factors. Suppose the proposed project is a large dam. We can reasonably expect the dam to last well over fifty years, even though its effectiveness after fifty years may be greatly reduced because of silting. Yet look at the effect on the present worth (and, hence, on present decisionmaking) of that distant benefit. At 14 percent, any benefit received in the fiftieth year is worth today only one-thousandth of its face value—a thousand currency units of return in fifty years is worth only one currency unit today. Beyond fifty years, this dwindles to such a minor amount that it is even difficult to find a table that gives the discount factors.

Even if we are talking about extending the period of analysis from twenty-five to fifty years, the difference these additional twenty-five years make is rather minor. Again, looking at the discount factors:

Present worth of an annuity factor for fifty years at 14 percent	7.133
Less present worth of an annuity factor for twenty-five years at 14 percent	−6.873
Present worth of an annuity factor for twenty-sixth through fiftieth years at 14 percent	0.260

Doubling the life of the project by adding twenty-five years to the analysis only increases the total present worth of the project by about one-fourth of one year's annual net benefit. Put another way, the net benefit from the twenty-sixth to the fiftieth year is worth today only about three months' worth of the same net benefit during the first year.

The calculation in table 9-21, drawn from the Lilongwe Development Program in Malawi, shows the effect on the internal economic return of extending the length of the project period. (The symbol for Malawi pounds is M£. Since this project was prepared, the currency unit of Malawi has been changed to kwachas, MK.) Doubling the assumed life of the project (and assuming no more investment) increases the economic rate of return by only 1 percent, from 13 percent to 14 percent. Given the probable error in estimating yields, prices, and rate of acceptance by farmers, this difference is meaningless.

How Far to Carry Out Computations of Discounted Measures

In agricultural projects, it is misleading to carry out the computations of discounted measures very far. The underlying estimates of the data are

Table 9-21. *Effect on Economic Rate of Return of Doubling Project Life from Twenty-five to Fifty Years, Lilongwe Development Program, Malawi* (thousands of M£)

Year	Incremental net benefit (cash flow)	Discount factor 10%	Present worth 10%	Discount factor 15%	Present worth 15%
	Assuming project life of twenty-five years				
1	− 920	0.909	− 836	0.870	−800
2	− 569	0.826	− 470	0.756	−430
3	− 556	0.751	− 418	0.658	−366
4	− 492	0.683	− 336	0.572	−281
5	− 360	0.621	− 224	0.497	−179
6	− 164	0.564	− 92	0.432	− 71
7	+ 30	0.513	+ 15	0.376	+ 11
8	+ 372	0.467	+ 174	0.327	+122
9	+ 563	0.424	+ 239	0.284	+160
10	+ 650	0.386	+ 251	0.247	+161
11	+ 710	0.350	+ 248	0.215	+153
12	+ 751	0.319	+ 240	0.187	+140
13	+ 781	0.290	+ 226	0.163	+127
14–25	+ 884[a]	1.974[b]	+1,745	0.881[b]	+779
Total	+11,404	9.077	+ 762	6.465	−474
	Economic rate of return = 10 + 5(762 ÷ 1,236) = 13 percent				
	Assuming project life of fifty years				
1–25[c]	+11,404	9.077	+ 762	6.465	−474
26–50	+ 884[d]	0.838[e]	+ 741	0.197[e]	+174
Total	+33,504	9.915	+1,503	6.662	−300
	Economic rate of return = 10 + 5(1,503 ÷ 1,803) = 14 percent				

M£ Malawi pounds (since this project was prepared, the currency unit in Malawi has been changed to kwachas, or MK).

Source: Adapted from World Bank, "Lilongwe Development Program," TO-610a (Washington, D.C., 1968; restricted circulation), annex 4.

a. Annual amount for years 14 through 25 inclusive. To reach column total, this amount must be included 12 times.

b. Present worth of an annuity factor for years 14 through 25 inclusive. See the subsection on "Present worth of a stream of future income" for method of computation.

c. From total line in first section of the table.

d. Annual amount for years 26 through 50 inclusive. To reach column total, this amount must be included 25 times.

e. Present worth of an annuity factor for years 26 through 50 inclusive. See the subsection on "Present worth of a stream of future income" for method of computation.

so inaccurate at best that carrying out the computations to many decimal places implies a spurious precision.

For net present worth, it is normal to report the result in the nearest thousand or million currency units, although in smaller projects the result may sometimes be given in the nearest unit.

Financial and economic rates of return are best rounded to the nearest whole percentage point. Since extremely high internal rates of return are difficult to interpret on theoretical grounds, it is better to report them simply as being very high. As a practical limit, I would suggest not giving internal rates of return greater than 50 percent. Above that value, financial or economic rates of return may be reported as "over 50 percent."

In general, benefit-cost and net benefit-investment ratios are best rounded to the nearest hundredth of a ratio value. Thus, a benefit-cost or a net benefit-investment ratio for which the computation results in a value of 1.434 would be reported as 1.43.

To determine discounted measures of project worth at these levels of accuracy, discount factors of three decimal places are sufficient. This being so, the summary tables in appendix B may be used conveniently and with confidence to determine discounted measures of project worth and to perform most other project computations in which use of such tables is appropriate.

When the analyst includes discounted measures of project worth in a project report, it is unnecessary to show the details of the discounting computation in the summary presentations (such details may be included in an annex to the report). A notation in the main text and at the bottom of the summary tables about the net present worth, the economic or financial rate of return, the benefit-cost ratio, or the net benefit-investment ratio is enough. If how the analyst arrived at the cash flow or the gross cost and benefit is clearly presented, those who are familiar with the analytical techniques will be able to understand how the discounting computation was carried out.

If the analyst is presenting the results of a financial analysis to show a financial rate of return, the point of view assumed in the analysis must be clearly specified. The entry should read "financial rate of return to all resources engaged," "financial rate of return to equity before income taxes," "financial rate of return to the farmer's own resources," or some similar, specific statement.

Comparisons among Discounted Measures

The interrelations of the four discounted measures of project worth can be clearly specified. The internal rate of return is that discount rate which just makes the net present worth of the project equal zero and the benefit-cost ratio and net benefit-investment ratio equal 1.

Taking the opportunity cost of capital as the discount or cut-off rate, from any array of possible project alternatives all four discounted measures of project worth will identify exactly the same group of projects for implementation, although (as discussed above) mutually exclusive projects will have to be subjected to further tests if the internal rate of return, benefit-cost ratio, or net benefit-investment ratio criteria are used. For net present worth, internal rate of return, and benefit-cost ratio, the formal criterion is to accept all projects that meet the test—that is, that have a positive net present worth at the opportunity cost of capital, have an internal rate of return above the opportunity cost of capital, or have a benefit-cost ratio of 1 or greater at the opportunity cost of capital. For the net benefit-investment ratio, the formal selection criterion is to accept projects discounted at the opportunity cost of capital in order, beginning with the largest ratio value and continuing until all investment funds have been exhausted.

Which discounted measure the analyst chooses will depend on the practice in the country in which he is working or on the preference of the financing agency that will be approached to lend for the project. Many project analysts prefer the net present worth criterion for its simplicity, unambiguous quality, and straightforward way of selecting among mutually exclusive projects. They reject the argument that the necessity to establish a reasonable estimate of the opportunity cost of capital before the net present worth can be calculated is a valid objection to use of this measure. They argue that in any event a nation should face up to this task. Some analysts prefer the internal rate of return criterion because it is more easily understood by those not familiar with the discounted measures. The internal rate of return can readily be explained as the maximum rate of interest that a project could pay if all resources were borrowed; it thus can be explained as a measure of the return on the resources engaged in the project. The World Bank has tended to use the internal rate of return as its principal discounted measure because the internal rate of return avoids making a close comparison of the opportunity cost of capital in the Bank's various member countries or setting a worldwide opportunity cost of capital. The net benefit-investment ratio provides a means of ranking independent (not mutually exclusive) projects. As noted earlier, the benefit-cost criterion is infrequently used in developing countries.

In virtually all actual project analyses, the practice is to work out a project and to make the best estimate of the results expressed in one of the discounted measures. Then the project may be selected if it has a net present worth of zero or greater, an internal rate of return equal to or above the cut-off rate, or a benefit-cost ratio or a net benefit-investment ratio of 1 or greater. The criteria, thus, are used on a "go–no-go" basis. Many administrators, however, intuitively tend to rank projects on the basis of the internal rate of return or the benefit-cost ratio. We have noted that, although in a very rough sense projects can be ranked in this manner, it is better not to do this, for it can lead to an erroneous investment decision. It is preferable to use the net benefit-investment ratio to rank projects. The fact of the matter is that ranking is generally unnecessary and so is much better avoided. Rarely can a nation afford to have a "shelf" of fully prepared projects ready to implement and in need of ranking. The demands of economic development are too urgent and the costs of preparing projects too great. Choice among projects that meet the formal criteria of acceptance is related not to the rank of the projects by a discounted measure of worth but on other, noneconomic grounds— including the ability to implement the projects. Given these realities, the ranking issue is a false one. It is sufficient for economic analysis to establish a realistic opportunity cost of capital and accept for implementation those projects which meet such other criteria as regional and sectoral balance, effect on low-income farmers, or administrative feasi-

Table 9-22. *Comparison of Discounted Measures of Project Worth*

Item	Net present worth (NPW)	Internal rate of return (IRR)	Benefit-cost (B/C) ratio	Net benefit-investment (N/K) ratio
Selection criterion	Accept all independent projects with NPW of zero or greater when discounted at opportunity cost of capital (see "Mutually exclusive alternatives," below)	Accept all independent projects with IRR equal to or greater than opportunity cost of capital	Accept all independent projects with B/C ratio of 1 or greater when discounted at opportunity cost of capital	Accept all independent projects with N/K ratio of 1 or greater when discounted at opportunity cost of capital in order of ratio value until available investment funds are exhausted
Ranking	Gives no ranking for order of implementation	May give incorrect ranking among independent projects	May give incorrect ranking among independent projects	May be used to rank independent projects
Mutually exclusive alternatives	Accept alternative with largest NPW when discounted at opportunity cost of capital (NPW is the preferred selection criterion for mutually exclusive alternatives)	Cannot be used directly; must discount differences between incremental net benefit flows of mutually exclusive alternative projects	Cannot be used directly	Cannot be used directly
Discount rate	Must determine a suitable discount rate, generally the opportunity cost of capital	Determined internally; must determine opportunity cost of capital to use as a cut-off rate	Must determine a suitable discount rate, generally the opportunity cost of capital	Must determine a suitable discount rate, generally the opportunity cost of capital

bility and which also are economically attractive as indicated by one of the discounted measures of project worth.

In summary, and for easy reference, some of the contrasts among the net present worth, the internal rate of return, the benefit-cost ratio, and the net benefit-investment ratio are compared in table 9-22.

Appendix. Mathematical Formulations of Discounted Measures of Project Worth

The formal mathematical statements of the discounted measures of project worth discussed in this chapter are given below.

Net present worth:

$$\sum_{t=1}^{t=n} \frac{B_t - C_t}{(1 + i)^t}.$$

Internal rate of return:
The discount rate i such that

$$\sum_{t=1}^{t=n} \frac{B_t - C_t}{(1 + i)^t} = 0.$$

Benefit-cost ratio:

$$\frac{\displaystyle\sum_{t=1}^{t=n} \frac{B_t}{(1 + i)^t}}{\displaystyle\sum_{t=1}^{t=n} \frac{C_t}{(1 + i)^t}}.$$

Net benefit-investment (N/K) ratio:

$$\frac{\displaystyle\sum_{t=1}^{t=n} \frac{N_t}{(1 + i)^t}}{\displaystyle\sum_{t=1}^{t=n} \frac{K_t}{(1 + i)^t}}.$$

In the four mathematical formulations,

B_t = benefit in each year
C_t = cost in each year
N_t = incremental net benefit in each year after stream has turned positive
K_t = incremental net benefit in initial years when stream is negative
t = 1, 2, . . . , n
n = number of years
i = interest (discount) rate.

10

Applying Discounted Measures of Project Worth

When applying discounted measures of project worth in financial and economic analysis of proposed projects, the analyst may encounter some practical questions about their use. I will address several of these questions in this chapter.

Sensitivity Analysis (Treatment of Uncertainty)

One of the real advantages of careful economic and financial project analysis is that it may be used to test what happens to the earning capacity of the project if events differ from guesses made about them in planning. How sensitive is a project's net present worth at financial prices and economic values, or its financial and economic rate of return or net benefit-investment ratio, to increased construction costs? To an extension of the implementation period? To a fall in prices? Reworking an analysis to see what happens under these changed circumstances is called sensitivity analysis. It is one means of drawing attention to a central reality of project analysis: projections are inevitably subject to a high degree of uncertainty about what will actually happen.

Facing page: Plucking tea in Java, Indonesia.

All projects should be subjected to sensitivity analysis. In agriculture, projects are sensitive to change in four principal areas. These, and the technique of sensitivity analysis, are considered below.

Price

Probably every agricultural project should be examined to see what happens if the assumptions about the sale price of the project's product prove wrong. For this the analyst can make alternative assumptions about future prices and see how these affect the net present worth, the financial and economic rates of return, or the net benefit-investment ratio (often abbreviated as N/K ratio).

Testing a project to see what will happen to the measures of project worth when different shadow prices are assumed is also a kind of sensitivity analysis. The analyst could examine a project to see the effect of using the market wage for labor or a shadow price, the official exchange rate or a foreign exchange premium, and so forth. Because of the difficulties in establishing shadow prices, if the project turns out to be relatively insensitive to shadow pricing, it may be better to present the analysis in market prices and to note that the net present worth, the economic rate of return, and the net benefit-investment ratio are relatively insensitive to shadow prices.

Delay in implementation

Delay in implementation affects most agricultural projects. Farmers may fail to adopt new practices as rapidly as anticipated, or they may find it harder to master new techniques than was thought. Other technical difficulties may be underestimated. There may be delays in ordering and receiving new equipment. Unavoidable administrative problems and requirements may delay the project. Testing to determine the effects of delay on the net present worth, the financial and economic rates of return, and the net benefit-investment ratio of a proposed agricultural investment is an important part of the sensitivity analysis.

Cost overrun

Almost every agricultural project should be tested for sensitivity to cost overrun. Projects tend to be very sensitive to cost overrun—especially for construction—because so often the costs are incurred early in the project when they weigh heavily in the discounting process and are for facilities that must be complete before any benefit can be realized. A project that has a quite attractive return if the estimated cost is in fact realized may be only marginally acceptable or unacceptable if costs early in the implementation phase rise significantly.

Cost estimates often are not very firm—one more reason projects should be tested for cost overrun. In many project analyses there is considerable uncertainty about the prices that actually will have to be paid for supplies and equipment. There is a tendency, too, for technicians and project analysts to make their cost estimates on the basis of overoptimistic implementation schedules and assumptions about prices for project inputs.

It is projects with substantial construction components that must be most carefully tested for cost overrun. We noted under "Accuracy of Agricultural Project Analyses. Implementation experience" in chapter 1 that it is large-scale groundwater projects, with their substantial construction element that must be completed before any water can flow, that have the worst record for cost overrun among the principal kinds of projects assisted by World Bank financing. Characteristically, these projects are very sensitive to cost overrun. Agricultural projects are less likely to be as sensitive to production costs that arise later in the life of the project, although in these instances, again, overruns for production costs may make an otherwise quite good project much less attractive.

A test that shows a project to be very sensitive to cost overrun may signal to those who must make investment decisions that it is important to have firm cost estimates before proceeding with the final decision, even if obtaining firm estimates may mean a delay in the start of project implementation. If a project is particularly sensitive to cost overrun, it is also a signal to the project manager and those to whom he reports that it is important to contain costs if the project is to make its expected contribution to increasing national income.

Yield

The analyst may wish to test a proposed project for its sensitivity to errors in estimated yield. There is a tendency in agricultural projects to be optimistic about potential yields, especially when a new cropping pattern is being proposed and the agronomic information is based mainly on experimental trials. A test to determine how sensitive the project's net present worth, financial and economic rates of return, or net benefit-investment ratio are to lower yields not only may provide information useful in deciding whether to implement the project, but also may emphasize the need to ensure sufficient extension services if the project is to be as high-yielding as could reasonably be expected.

Technique of sensitivity analysis

The technique of sensitivity analysis is not complicated. The analyst simply calculates the measure of project worth over again using the new estimates for one or another element of cost or return. The technique is illustrated in tables 10-1 through 10-3 for the Jatiluhur Irrigation Project in Indonesia. In this case, the most probable outcome of the project was listed (table 10-1), and then the project was tested for its sensitivity to a 30 percent cost overrun (table 10-2) and to a 10 percent fall in the price of rice (table 10-3). In these as in earlier tables of this kind, a convention has been adopted that lists the *annual* amount for each year when that

Table 10-1. *Sensitivity Analysis, Jatiluhur Irrigation Project, Indonesia: Most Probable Outcome*
(thousand millions of Rp)

Year	Incremental cost	Incremental benefit[a]	Incremental net benefit (cash flow)	Discount factor 12%	Present worth 12%	Discount factor 20%	Present worth 20%	Discount factor 25%	Present worth 25%
1	0.5	—	− 0.5	0.893	−0.45	0.833	−0.42	0.800	−0.40
2	2.1	0.4	− 1.7	0.797	−1.35	0.694	−1.18	0.640	−1.09
3	3.7	0.8	− 2.9	0.712	−2.06	0.579	−1.68	0.512	−1.48
4	3.7	1.4	− 2.3	0.636	+1.46	0.482	−1.11	0.410	−0.94
5	2.0	2.1	+ 0.1	0.567	+0.06	0.402	+0.04	0.328	+0.03
6	0.5	2.5	+ 2.0	0.507	+1.01	0.335	+0.67	0.262	+0.52
7–30	0.5[b]	2.9[b]	+ 2.4[b]	3.944	+9.47	1.653	+3.97	1.044	+2.51
Total	24.5	76.8	+52.3	8.056	8.14	4.978	+0.29	3.996	−0.85

Net present worth at 12 percent = Rp+ 8.14

Economic rate of return = 20 + 5(0.29 ÷ 1.14) = 20 + 5(0.25) = 21 percent

Net benefit-investment (N/k) ratio at 12 percent = Rp12.00 ÷ Rp3.86 = 3.11

Rp Indonesian rupiahs.
Source: Adapted from World Bank, "Djatiluhur Irrigation Project—Indonesia," PA-37 (Washington, D.C., 1970; restricted circulation), p. 26 and annex 10, p. 1. Since this report was published, a spelling reform has changed the spelling of the project area to Jatiluhur.

a. Assumes only an improvement in water control; that is, no accompanying increase in the use of modern inputs.

b. Annual amount for years 7 through 30 inclusive. To reach column total, this amount must be included 24 times. This same convention is adopted wherever it is relevant for all tables in this chapter.

Table 10-2. *Sensitivity Analysis, Jatiluhur Project: Assuming 30 Percent Cost Overrun*
(thousand millions of Rp)

Year	Incremental cost	Incremental benefit[a]	Incremental net benefit (cash flow)	Discount factor 12%	Present worth 12%	Discount factor 15%	Present worth 15%	Discount factor 20%	Present worth 20%
1	0.6	—	− 0.6	0.893	−0.54	0.870	−0.52	0.833	−0.50
2	2.7	0.4	− 2.3	0.797	−1.83	0.756	−1.74	0.694	−1.60
3	4.8	0.8	− 4.0	0.712	−2.85	0.658	−2.63	0.579	−2.32
4	4.8	1.4	− 3.4	0.636	−2.16	0.572	−1.94	0.482	−1.64
5	2.6	2.1	− 0.5	0.567	−0.28	0.497	−0.25	0.402	−0.20
6	0.6	2.5	+ 1.9	0.507	+0.96	0.432	+0.82	0.335	+0.64
7–30	0.6	2.9	+ 2.3	3.944	+9.07	2.782	+6.40	1.653	+3.80
Total	30.5	76.8	+46.3	8.056	+2.37	6.567	+0.14	4.978	−1.82

Net present worth at 12 percent = Rp+2.37

Economic rate of return = $15 + 5(0.14 \div 1.96) = 15 + 5(0.07) = 15$ percent

N/K ratio at 12 percent = Rp10.03 ÷ Rp7.66 = 1.31

Source: Same as table 10-1.

a. Assumes only an improvement in water control; that is, no accompanying increase in the use of modern inputs.

Table 10-3. *Sensitivity Analysis, Jatiluhur Project: Assuming 10 Percent Lower Price of Rice*
(thousand millions of Rp)

Year	Incremental cost	Incremental benefit[a]	Incremental net benefit (cash flow)	Discount factor 12%	Present worth 12%	Discount factor 15%	Present worth 15%	Discount factor 19%[b]	Present worth 19%
1	0.5	—	− 0.5	0.893	−0.45	0.870	−0.44	0.840	−0.42
2	2.1	0.4	− 1.7	0.797	−1.35	0.756	−1.29	0.706	−1.20
3	3.7	0.7	− 3.0	0.712	−2.14	0.658	−1.97	0.593	−1.78
4	3.7	1.3	− 2.4	0.636	−1.53	0.572	−1.37	0.499	−1.20
5	2.0	1.9	− 0.1	0.567	−0.06	0.497	−0.05	0.419	−0.04
6	0.5	2.2	+ 1.7	0.507	+0.86	0.432	+0.73	0.352	+0.60
7–30	0.5	2.6	+ 2.1	3.944	+8.28	2.782	+5.84	1.825	+3.83
Total	24.5	68.9	+44.4	8.056	+3.61	6.567	+1.45	5.234	−0.21

Net present worth at 12 percent = Rp + 3.61

Economic rate of return = 15 + 4(1.45 ÷ 1.66) = 15 + 4(0.87) = 18 percent

N/K ratio at 12 percent = Rp9.14 ÷ Rp5.53 = 1.65

Source: Same as table 10-1.

a. Assumes only an improvement in water control; that is, no accompanying increase in the use of modern inputs.

b. For a discussion of the interpolation interval, see the subsection on "Choosing the discount rate," chapter 9.

amount is constant over several years. Thus, to reach the total incremental net benefit in table 10-1 of Rp52.3 thousand million, the annual amount of Rp2.4 thousand million must be included 24 times [− 0.5 − 1.7 − 2.9 − 2.3 + 0.1 + 2.0 + 24(2.4) = 52.3]. (The symbol for Indonesian rupiahs is Rp.)

Note what happened to the wealth-generating potential of the project under this sensitivity test. When a 30 percent cost overrun was assumed (table 10-2), the net present worth, assuming a 12 percent opportunity cost of capital, fell 71 percent, from Rp8.14 thousand million to Rp2.37 thousand million [(8.14 − 2.37) ÷ 8.14 × 100 = 71]; the economic rate of return fell by 29 percent, from 21 percent to 15 percent [(21 − 15) ÷ 21 × 100 = 29]; and the net benefit-investment ratio, also assuming a 12 percent opportunity cost of capital, fell by a factor of 2.37 (3.11 ÷ 1.31 = 2.37). When a 10 percent reduction in the price of rice was assumed (table 10-3), the net present worth fell 56 percent, from Rp8.14 thousand million to Rp3.61 thousand million [(8.14 − 3.61) ÷ 8.14 × 100 = 56]; the economic rate of return fell by 14 percent, from 21 percent to 18 percent [(21 − 18) ÷ 21 × 100 = 14]; and the net benefit-investment ratio was cut in half [(3.11 − 1.65) ÷ 3.11 = 0.47]. With these possible outcomes known, whoever must make the project decision may now ask whether it is worth running the risk of that large a drop in the worth of the project, given how likely the cost overrun (or the lower price) will be.

The higher the expected yield, the more sensitive the project. Projects will also be more sensitive to earlier items than to later ones—a direct consequence of the time value of money. Thus, in general, projects tend to be more sensitive to cost overruns that occur early in the project life than to price changes that occur later. Usually, too, a given proportionate change in a major cost or return item will have a more than proportionate effect on the measures of project worth. In the Jatiluhur project in tables 10-1 through 10-3, for example, a 10 percent fall in the price of rice reduced the net present worth by 56 percent, the economic rate of return by 14 percent, and the net benefit-investment ratio by half. No general rule about these relations can be cited. Each sensitivity analysis must be undertaken separately to estimate the effect of a change in assumptions on the worth of the project, and then a judgment must be made about how likely that change will be.

Sensitivity analysis not only has important implications for investment decisions, it also has very important implications for project management. Suppose a project turns out to be particularly sensitive to delay. If senior decisionmakers are aware of how sensitive the project is and how much delay will cost the nation in lost opportunities to generate wealth, these decisionmakers may be willing to cut "red tape"—to ensure that there will not be unnecessary delays in processing financing and other requests from the project and that prompt cooperation will be forthcoming from the agencies that must support the project. Or, it may be decided that the likelihood of delay is so substantial—no matter how effective the project manager is—that it is better to redesign the project to make it more manageable and to permit postponing some costs if

Table 10-4. Switching Values, Cotton Processing and Marketing Project, Kenya: Most Probable Outcome
(thousands of KSh)

Fiscal year	Incremental cost	Incremental benefit	Incremental net benefit (cash flow)	Discount factor 12%	Present worth 12%	Discount factor 20%	Present worth 20%	Discount factor 25%	Present worth 25%
1982	93,004	5,761	− 87,243	0.893	− 77,908	0.833	− 72,673	0.800	− 69,794
1983	101,140	22,833	− 78,307	0.797	− 62,411	0.694	− 54,345	0.640	− 50,116
1984	98,049	46,177	− 51,872	0.712	− 36,933	0.579	− 30,034	0.512	− 26,558
1985	56,135	71,119	+ 14,984	0.636	+ 9,530	0.482	+ 7,222	0.410	+ 6,143
1986	25,385	80,385	+ 55,000	0.567	+ 31,185	0.402	+ 22,110	0.328	+ 18,040
1987	31,804	91,348	+ 59,544	0.507	+ 30,189	0.335	+ 19,947	0.262	+ 15,601
1988	24,308	94,178	+ 69,870	0.452	+ 31,581	0.279	+ 19,494	0.210	+ 14,673
1989	24,032	96,915	+ 72,883	0.404	+ 29,445	0.233	+ 16,982	0.168	+ 12,244
1990	23,962	98,097	+ 74,135	0.361	+ 26,763	0.194	+ 14,382	0.134	+ 9,934
1991	21,314	98,097	+ 76,783	0.322	+ 24,724	0.162	+ 12,439	0.107	+ 8,216
1992	26,145	98,097	+ 71,952	0.287	+ 20,650	0.135	+ 9,714	0.086	+ 6,188
1993	22,476	98,097	+ 75,621	0.257	+ 19,435	0.112	+ 8,470	0.069	+ 5,218
1994	23,289	98,097	+ 74,808	0.229	+ 17,131	0.093	+ 6,957	0.055	+ 4,114
1995	24,641	98,097	+ 73,456	0.205	+ 15,058	0.078	+ 5,730	0.044	+ 3,232
1996	18,797	98,097	+ 79,300	0.183	+ 14,512	0.065	+ 5,155	0.035	+ 2,776
1997	26,164	98,097	+ 71,933	0.163	+ 11,725	0.054	+ 3,884	0.028	+ 2,014
1998	23,622	98,097	+ 74,475	0.146	+ 10,873	0.045	+ 3,351	0.023	+ 1,713
1999	24,641	98,097	+ 73,456	0.130	+ 9,549	0.038	+ 2,791	0.018	+ 1,322
2000	22,124	98,097	+ 75,973	0.116	+ 8,813	0.031	+ 2,355	0.014	+ 1,064
2001	19,030	98,097	+ 79,067	0.104	+ 8,223	0.026	+ 2,056	0.012	+ 949
Total	730,062	1,685,880	+955,818	7.471	+142,134	4.870	+ 5,987	3.955	−33,027

Net present worth at 12 percent = KSh +142,134

Economic rate of return = 20 + 5(5,987 ÷ 5,987 + 33,027) = 20 + 5(0.15) = 21 percent

N/K ratio = 319,386 ÷ 177,252 = 1.80

KSh Kenyan shillings.
Source: Adapted from World Bank, "Kenya, Cotton Processing and Market-ing Project, Staff Appraisal Report," 3355-KE (Washington, D.C., 1981; re-stricted circulation), pp. 50 and 62.

necessary so that the project is less sensitive to delay. This may be desirable even though redesigning the project may somewhat reduce the overall net present worth, rate of return, or net benefit-investment ratio.

Sensitivity analysis is a straightforward (but often quite sufficient) means of analyzing the effects of risk and uncertainty in project analysis. A much more elaborate technique of risk analysis using probability theory and requiring use of a computer is outlined by Reutlinger (1970) and Pouliquen (1970). That approach is generally called "probability analysis." In contrast, the techniques we have been discussing (including sensitivity analysis) are usually called "most probable outcome analysis."

Switching Value

A variation of sensitivity analysis is the "switching value." In straightforward sensitivity analysis we choose an amount by which to change an important element in the project analysis and then determine the impact of that change on the attractiveness of the project. In contrast, when we calculate a switching value we ask how much such an element would have to change in an unfavorable direction before the project would no longer meet the minimum level of acceptability as indicated by one of the measures of project worth. Then those responsible for determining whether to proceed with the project can ask themselves how likely they feel it is that there will be a change of that magnitude.

We may illustrate computation of the switching value with an illustration taken from the Kenya Cotton Processing and Marketing Project. The project provides for improved purchasing and transport of seed cotton and for better ginning facilities. The opportunity cost of capital in Kenya at the time of the analysis was estimated to be 12 percent.

The most probable outcome estimate, laid out in table 10-4, shows that the project would have a net present worth of KSh + 142,134 at a 12 percent opportunity cost of capital, an economic rate of return of 21 percent, and a net benefit-investment ratio of 1.80 at the opportunity cost of capital. (The symbol for Kenyan shillings is KSh.)

One switching-value test the analyst undertook was to determine by what proportion the benefit would have to be reduced before the net present worth would fall to zero—the zero value, of course, would make the economic rate of return exactly 12 percent and the net benefit-investment ratio exactly 1. The computation is laid out in table 10-5. The analyst determined the net present worth at various assumed levels of benefit shortfall. At a 25 percent shortfall, the net present worth at a 12 percent opportunity cost of capital is KSh + 11,985. At a 30 percent shortfall, however, the project has a negative net present worth of KSh − 14,044. To determine the shortfall that would make the net present worth just equal zero, the analyst interpolated between the positive net present worth at 25 percent and the negative net present worth at 30 percent in a manner analogous to the interpolation done to determine the

Table 10-5. *Switching Values, Kenya Cotton Project: Assuming Benefit Shortfall*
(thousands of KSh)

Fiscal year	Assuming 25% shortfall in benefit			Assuming 30% shortfall in benefit			Assuming 27% shortfall in benefit		
	Incremental benefit[a]	Incremental net benefit (cash flow)[b]	Present worth 12%	Incremental benefit[a]	Incremental net benefit (cash flow)[b]	Present worth 12%	Incremental benefit[a]	Incremental net benefit (cash flow)[b]	Present worth 12%
1982	4,321	− 88,683	−79,194	4,033	− 88,971	−79,451	4,206	− 88,798	−79,297
1983	17,125	− 84,015	−66,960	15,983	− 85,157	−67,870	16,668	− 84,472	−67,324
1984	34,633	− 63,416	−45,152	32,324	− 65,725	−46,796	33,709	− 64,340	−45,810
1985	53,339	− 2,796	− 1,778	49,783	+ 6,352	− 4,040	51,917	− 4,218	− 2,683
1986	60,289	+ 34,904	+19,791	56,270	+ 30,885	+17,512	58,681	+ 33,296	+18,879
1987	68,511	+ 36,707	+18,610	63,944	+ 32,140	+16,295	66,684	+ 34,880	+17,684
1988	70,634	+ 46,326	+20,939	65,925	+ 41,617	+18,811	68,750	+ 44,442	+20,088
1989	72,686	+ 48,654	+19,656	67,841	+ 43,809	+17,699	70,748	+ 46,716	+18,873
1990	73,573	+ 49,611	+17,910	68,668	+ 44,706	+16,139	71,611	+ 47,649	+17,201
1991	73,573	+ 52,259	+16,827	68,668	+ 47,354	+15,248	71,611	+ 50,297	+16,196
1992	73,573	+ 47,428	+13,612	68,668	+ 42,523	+12,204	71,611	+ 45,466	+13,049
1993	73,573	+ 51,097	+13,132	68,668	+ 46,192	+11,871	71,611	+ 49,135	+12,628
1994	73,573	+ 50,284	+11,515	68,668	+ 45,379	+10,392	71,611	+ 48,322	+11,066
1995	73,573	+ 48,932	+10,031	68,668	+ 44,027	+ 9,026	71,611	+ 46,970	+ 9,629
1996	73,573	+ 54,776	+10,024	68,668	+ 49,871	+ 9,126	71,611	+ 52,814	+ 9,665
1997	73,573	+ 47,409	+ 7,728	68,668	+ 42,504	+ 6,928	71,611	+ 45,447	+ 7,408
1998	73,573	+ 49,951	+ 7,293	68,668	+ 45,046	+ 6,577	71,611	+ 47,989	+ 7,006
1999	73,573	+ 48,932	+ 6,361	68,668	+ 44,027	+ 5,724	71,611	+ 46,970	+ 6,106
2000	73,573	+ 51,449	+ 5,968	68,668	+ 46,544	+ 5,399	71,611	+ 49,487	+ 5,740
2001	73,573	+ 54,543	+ 5,672	68,668	+ 49,638	+ 5,162	71,611	+ 52,581	+ 5,468
Total	1,264,414	+534,352	+11,985	1,180,119	+450,057	−14,044	1,230,695	+500,633	+ 1,572

Proportionate fall that will make net present worth equal zero at 12 percent opportunity cost of capital
$= 25 + 5[11,985 ÷ (11,985 + 14,044)] = 25 + 5(0.46) = 27$ *percent*

Source: Same as table 10-4.

a. Most probable incremental benefit in table 10-4 reduced by appropriate proportion.

b. Most probable incremental cost from table 10-4 less incremental benefit here.

c. For a discussion of interpolation methodology, see the subsection on "Computing the internal rate of return" in chapter 9.

internal rate of return (see the subsection on "Computing the internal rate of return" in chapter 9). The computation is given at the bottom of table 10-5; it shows that the net present worth equals zero at 27 percent, rounded to the nearest whole percentage point. To verify, the net present worth is recomputed assuming a 27 percent benefit shortfall, and this gives a net present value of KSh + 1,572, not quite zero because the shortfall is rounded to the nearest whole percentage point. The analyst, thus, was able to note that "the project would have to suffer a shortfall in benefits by more than one-fourth (27 percent) before the rate of return fell to the opportunity cost of capital."

Another switching value determined for the Kenya project was to find the maximum benefit delay before the net present worth of the project would fall to zero. The computation is laid out in table 10-6. The analyst computed the net present worth assuming the benefit to be delayed by one, two, and three years. When the benefit is delayed by two years, the net present worth at a 12 percent opportunity cost of capital is KSh + 19,375, so the project would still be acceptable. If the benefit were to be delayed for three years, however, the net present worth would become negative, with a value of KSh − 32,327, and the project would not be acceptable if judged solely on economic grounds. The analyst was thus able to report that "benefits would have to be lagged by more than two years without lagging costs at all before the rate of return would fall below 12 percent."

Choosing among Mutually Exclusive Alternatives

Quite often in project design, and not infrequently in evaluating complete projects, analysts are faced with having to choose among mutually exclusive alternatives—project design options or whole projects of a nature that if one is chosen the other cannot be undertaken. This can apply to such cases as development of surface irrigation and not tubewell irrigation, river development upstream rather than downstream, and plants in alternative locations but serving the same limited market. It can also apply to such design issues as the choice among different scales for projects in which one size precludes implementing a similar project of another size, the time phasing of what is essentially the same project, the different designs for project components, or the purposes of a multi-purpose project. The need to compare mutually exclusive design options is one of the principal reasons to apply economic analysis early in the project cycle.

The preferred discounted measure of project worth for choosing among mutually exclusive projects or project options is the net present worth. Direct comparison of the internal rates of return, the benefit-cost ratios, or the net benefit-investment ratios can lead to an incorrect investment decision. This is so because undertaking a small, high-paying project may preclude generating more wealth through a moderately remunerative but larger alternative.

Table 10-6. *Switching Values, Kenya Cotton Project: Assuming Benefit Delay*
(thousands of KSh)

Fiscal year	Most probable outcome				Benefit delayed 2 years			Benefit delayed 3 years		
	Incremental cost	Incremental benefit	Incremental net benefit (cash flow)	Present worth 12%	Incremental benefit	Incremental net benefit (cash flow)	Present worth 12%	Incremental benefit	Incremental net benefit (cash flow)	Present worth 12%
1982	93,004	5,761	− 87,243	− 77,908	—	− 93,004	− 83,053	—	− 93,004	− 83,053
1983	101,140	22,833	− 78,307	− 62,411	—	− 101,140	− 80,609	—	− 101,140	− 80,609
1984	98,049	46,177	− 51,872	− 36,933	5,761	− 92,288	− 65,709	—	− 98,049	− 69,811
1985	56,135	71,119	+ 14,984	+ 9,530	22,833	− 33,302	− 21,180	5,761	− 50,374	− 32,038
1986	25,385	80,385	+ 55,000	+ 31,185	46,177	+ 20,792	+ 11,789	22,833	− 2,552	− 1,447
1987	31,804	91,348	+ 59,544	+ 30,189	71,119	+ 39,315	+ 19,933	46,177	+ 14,373	+ 7,287
1988	24,308	94,178	+ 69,870	+ 31,581	80,385	+ 56,077	+ 25,347	71,119	+ 46,811	+ 21,159
1989	24,032	96,915	+ 72,883	+ 29,445	91,348	+ 67,316	+ 27,196	80,385	+ 56,353	+ 22,767
1990	23,962	98,097	+ 74,135	+ 26,763	94,178	+ 70,216	+ 25,348	91,348	+ 67,386	+ 24,326
1991	21,314	98,097	+ 76,783	+ 24,724	96,915	+ 75,601	+ 24,344	94,178	+ 72,864	+ 23,462
1992	26,145	98,097	+ 71,952	+ 20,650	98,097	+ 71,952	+ 20,650	96,915	+ 70,770	+ 20,311
1993	22,476	98,097	+ 75,621	+ 19,435	98,097	+ 75,621	+ 19,435	98,097	+ 75,621	+ 19,435
1994	23,289	98,097	+ 74,808	+ 17,131	98,097	+ 74,808	+ 17,131	98,097	+ 74,808	+ 17,131
1995	24,641	98,097	+ 73,456	+ 15,058	98,097	+ 73,456	+ 15,058	98,097	+ 73,456	+ 15,058
1996	18,797	98,097	+ 79,300	+ 14,512	98,097	+ 79,300	+ 14,512	98,097	+ 79,300	+ 14,512
1997	26,164	98,097	+ 71,933	+ 11,725	98,097	+ 71,933	+ 11,725	98,097	+ 71,933	+ 11,725
1998	23,622	98,097	+ 74,475	+ 10,873	98,097	+ 74,475	+ 10,873	98,097	+ 74,475	+ 10,873
1999	24,641	98,097	+ 73,456	+ 9,549	98,097	+ 73,456	+ 9,549	98,097	+ 73,456	+ 9,549
2000	22,124	98,097	+ 75,973	+ 8,813	98,097	+ 75,973	+ 8,813	98,097	+ 75,973	+ 8,813
2001	19,030	98,097	+ 79,067	+ 8,223	98,097	+ 79,067	+ 8,223	98,097	+ 79,067	+ 8,223
Total	730,062	1,685,880	+955,818	+142,134	1,489,686	+759,624	+19,375	1,391,589	+661,527	−32,327

Net present worth at 12 percent assuming benefit delayed 2 years = KSh +19,375
Net present worth at 12 percent assuming benefit delayed 3 years = KSh −32,327

Source: Same as table 10-4.

374

Sometimes what may at first be posed as a pair of mutually exclusive projects can, instead, be seen as successive phases of development. If a small project can be expanded by phases to become a larger alternative, no analytical problem is posed. To implement a small, first-phase project does not preempt a larger, phase-two project; both phases can be undertaken, with each phase judged by any of the measures of project worth.

Although net present worth is the preferred criterion for choosing among mutually exclusive alternatives, it is possible to manipulate the internal rate of return to use it to choose among mutually exclusive alternatives. The net benefit-investment ratio can be used to rank mutually exclusive projects only when the ratios of all projects in the investment program are known; therefore it is not a practical measure to use for this purpose.

To use the internal rate of return to choose between two mutually exclusive alternatives, the cash flow of the smaller alternative is subtracted year by year from the cash flow of the larger alternative. This stream of differences is then discounted to determine the internal rate of return of the stream. This is the financial or economic rate of return to the additional resources necessary to implement the larger alternative as opposed to the smaller one. (Students of economics will recognize that we are, in effect, finding the marginal return for the marginal cost incurred.) How this method is applied will be illustrated in the course of our discussion of the kinds of mutually exclusive projects, below.

When there are several mutually exclusive alternatives, determining the net present worth of each enables us to choose directly the best among them. In contrast, discounting the differences between cash flows of alternatives can only be applied to select between a single pair of alternatives. To use the internal rate of return criterion when there are more than two alternatives, one can proceed by determining the rate of return to the stream of the differences between any pair of alternatives. If the return is above the cut-off rate, the larger alternative is selected; if the return is below, the smaller is selected. The procedure is then repeated by testing the alternative chosen against another alternative, the better of this second pair is selected, and so forth in a kind of elimination tournament until all alternatives have been tested and the best identified.

We will take up five instances of mutually exclusive alternatives:

1. The most general case is where we have entirely different alternative projects that are mutually exclusive—say, a choice between a small irrigation project that preempts a site and a larger one using the same site.
2. We will discuss the scale of a project as a variation of mutually exclusive alternatives, viewing a large project as a mutually exclusive alternative to a small version of the same project.
3. Another instance is the special case of timing—whether it would be better to begin a project now or later. In effect, postponing a project is a mutually exclusive alternative to undertaking it immediately.
4. Yet another special case involves the choice of alternative tech-

Table 10-7. *Measures of Project Worth of Alternative Irrigation Schemes: Small-scale Alternative*
(thousands of currency units)

Project year	Gross cost	Discount factor 12%	Present worth 12%	Gross benefit	Present worth 12%	Incremental net benefit (cash flow)	Present worth 12%	Discount factor 25%	Present worth 25%	Discount factor 30%	Present worth 30%
1	500.0	0.893	446.5	—	—	− 500.0	−446.5	0.800	−400.0	0.769	−384.5
2	5.0	0.797	4.0	140.0	111.6	+ 135.0	+107.6	0.640	+ 86.4	0.592	+ 79.9
3	5.0	0.712	3.6	140.0	99.7	+ 135.0	+ 96.1	0.512	+ 69.1	0.455	+ 61.4
4	5.0	0.636	3.2	140.0	89.0	+ 135.0	+ 85.9	0.410	+ 55.4	0.350	+ 47.2
5	5.0	0.567	2.8	140.0	79.4	+ 135.0	+ 76.5	0.328	+ 44.3	0.269	+ 36.3
6–20	5.0	3.864	19.3	140.0	541.0	+ 135.0	+521.6	1.265	+170.8	0.880	+118.8
Total	595.0	7.469	479.4	2,660.0	920.7	+2,065.0	+441.2	3.955	+ 26.0	3.315	− 40.9

Net present worth at 12 percent = +441.2

Economic rate of return = 25 + 5(26.0 ÷ 66.9) = 25 + 5(0.39) = 27 percent

N/K ratio at 12 percent = 887.7 ÷ 446.5 = 1.99

nologies, in which selection of one technology rules out its alternative.

5. The final case is that of additional purposes in multipurpose projects—the river basin project to control floods and generate hydropower that also includes an irrigation purpose is a mutually exclusive alternative to the same project without the irrigation purpose.

Entirely different projects

Occasionally in agriculture we may be faced with the choice between two mutually exclusive alternative projects of an entirely different nature, one small and high-yielding and the other large but low-yielding. At a given location we may have a choice either of constructing a small irrigation project that is limited to the best land and uses rather simple equipment or of building a considerably larger project that involves a more extensive area and more costly, complicated engineering works. If the small scheme is built, it preempts the site so that the larger project cannot be built. When mutually exclusive alternatives of this nature are met, we can choose between them by selecting the project that has the larger net present worth when discounted at a suitable opportunity cost of capital.

Tables 10-7 through 10-9 illustrate how these computations work and also why relying on a direct comparison of the internal rates of return or net benefit-investment ratios can lead to an erroneous investment decision. In table 10-7, we have a highly remunerative, small-scale irrigation scheme costing 500 thousand currency units in project year 1 that preempts the site available. At a 12 percent opportunity cost of capital, it has a net present worth of 441.2 thousand currency units. An alternative large-scale project costing 2,500 thousand currency units in project years 1 and 2 is presented in table 10-8. The large-scale project has a net present worth at a 12 percent opportunity cost of capital of 683.1 thousand currency units, and on the basis of the net present worth criterion we would select it. If we choose the smaller scheme, we would forgo a net present worth of 241.9 thousand currency units that would otherwise be available to the society (683.1 − 441.2 = 241.9). Recall that if the opportunity cost of capital is set correctly we would be able to implement *all* projects having a positive net present worth at that opportunity cost. Although this approach requires an acceptable estimate of the opportunity cost of capital, if one is available then the method tells us easily and unambiguously which mutually exclusive alternative to accept.

But if we compare the internal rates of return of the two projects, we find that the smaller project has an internal rate of return of 27 percent compared with 16 percent for the larger project. On this basis, we would choose the smaller project. A similar outcome would occur if we tried to use the net benefit-investment ratio to select between these mutually exclusive alternative projects. The smaller project has the larger net

Table 10-8. *Measures of Project Worth of Alternative Irrigation Schemes: Large-scale Alternative*
(thousands of currency units)

Project year	Gross cost	Discount factor 12%	Present worth 12%	Gross benefit	Present worth 12%	Incremental net benefit (cash flow)	Present worth 12%	Discount factor 15%	Present worth 15%	Discount factor 20%	Present worth 20%
1	1,500.0	0.893	1,339.5	—	—	−1,500.0	−1,339.5	0.870	−1,305.0	0.833	−1,249.5
2	1,000.0	0.797	797.0	—	—	−1,000.0	−797.0	0.756	−756.0	0.694	−694.0
3	100.0	0.712	71.2	350.0	249.2	+250.0	+178.0	0.658	+164.5	0.579	+144.8
4	100.0	0.636	63.6	450.0	286.2	+350.0	+222.6	0.572	+200.2	0.482	+168.7
5	100.0	0.567	56.7	550.0	311.8	+450.0	+255.2	0.497	+223.6	0.402	+180.9
6–20	100.0	3.864	386.4	660.0	2,550.2	+560.0	+2,163.8	2.907	+1,627.9	1.879	+1,052.2
Total	4,300.0	7.469	2,714.4	11,250.0	3,397.4	+6,950.0	+683.1	6.260	+155.2	4.869	−396.9

Net present worth at 12 percent = +683.1

Economic rate of return at 12 percent = $15 + 5(155.2 \div 552.1) = 15 + 5(0.28) = 16$ percent

N/K *ratio at 12 percent* = $2,819.6 \div 2,136.5 = 1.32$

benefit-investment ratio of 1.99, so we would select it over the larger project, which has a net benefit-investment ratio of only 1.32. But we know from the discussion of the application of the net present worth criterion that this would be an erroneous choice because we would be forgoing the additional wealth the larger project could create. When we use the internal rate of return criterion, we can avoid this error if we discount the differences between the cash flows of the two projects as is done in table 10-9. There we find that the internal rate of return to the stream of the differences is 14 percent. In other words, if we expand the project from the smaller alternative to the larger, the return to our additional investment is 14 percent. The proper choice criterion, then, is whether the return to our additional investment is above the cut-off rate. Since the cut-off rate in this example is taken to be 12 percent, the return on the additional investment would still be above the cut-off, and we would reject the smaller project in favor of the larger.

Different scales of a project

Sometimes we may wish to choose between a smaller version of a project and a larger version of the same project. Such a case arose in a Brazilian forestry project. The smaller version of the project consisted simply of cutting logs and exporting the round wood; it had a positive net present worth, quite a high economic rate of return, and an attractive net benefit-investment ratio. A somewhat larger version of the project included a sawmill; it had a larger net present worth than the smaller version, but a lower economic rate of return and a smaller net benefit-investment ratio. We could consider the larger version a mutually exclusive alternative to the smaller version.

Applying the net present worth criterion, we would correctly choose the larger version. Note, however, that simply applying directly the economic rate of return or net benefit-investment ratio criterion would have led to an erroneous investment decision.

In this case, undertaking the small project does not preempt the site. We can choose, if we wish, to undertake the small project and then proceed to expand it. Under these circumstances, we do our analysis not of the small version versus the large version, as if the two were mutually exclusive projects, but of the small version as the first phase of a two-phase program. By the net present worth criterion, we know from our earlier discussion that the smaller version, now called phase i, has a positive net present worth, so we would accept it. Then, if we tested the expansion necessary to reach the larger version, now called phase ii, we would find that this phase also has a positive net present worth, and so we would accept it, too. If we wanted to use the internal rate of return approach, the economic rate of return of the second phase of the program would be the economic rate of return of the differences between the incremental net benefit streams of the two versions. Similarly, the net benefit-investment ratio of the phase-ii project would be the net benefit-investment ratio of the differences of the incremental net benefit streams

Table 10-9. *Measures of Project Worth of Alternative Irrigation Schemes: Differences between Alternatives*
(thousands of currency units)

Project year	Cash flow of large-scale scheme	Cash flow of small-scale scheme	Differences between cash flows	Discount factor 12%	Present worth 12%	Discount factor 15%	Present worth 15%
1	−1,500.0	− 500.0	−1,000.0	0.893	− 893.0	0.870	− 870.0
2	−1,000.0	+ 135.0	−1,135.0	0.797	− 904.6	0.756	− 858.1
3	+ 250.0	+ 135.0	+ 115.0	0.712	+ 81.9	0.658	+ 75.7
4	+ 350.0	+ 135.0	+ 215.0	0.636	+ 136.7	0.572	+ 123.0
5	+ 450.0	+ 135.0	+ 315.0	0.567	+ 178.6	0.497	+ 156.6
6–20	+ 560.0	+ 135.0	+ 425.0	3.864	+1,642.2	2.907	+1,235.5
Total	+6,950.0	+2,065.0	+4,885.0	7.469	+ 241.8	6.260	− 137.3

Net present worth at 12 percent of the differences
between incremental net benefit streams = +241.8
Economic rate of return of the differences between
incremental net benefit streams
$$= 12 + 3(241.8 \div 379.1) = 12 + 3(0.64) = 14 \text{ percent}$$

of the two versions. Breaking a project down into phases is the more direct approach and the more easily understood. Such an approach permits us to apply any of our measures of project worth directly without further manipulation.

Of course, if we have sufficient administrative and other resources, we may very well implement two phases—or even more—of a project simultaneously. By analyzing each phase separately, we can tell directly from our analysis how large the project can be before we reach a phase that has a negative net present worth, an economic rate of return below our cut-off rate, or a net benefit-investment ratio less than that of alternative project opportunities.

Different timing of a project

A special case of the choice among mutually exclusive projects is the question of whether to begin a project immediately or to postpone it. The same project begun today or at some future time may be considered, from an analytical standpoint, to be two different, mutually exclusive projects.

Postponing a project can be advantageous *only* if the potential benefit or cost stream will increase independently of when a project is begun. In most agricultural production projects, this is not the case. Rather, it is assumed that costs and benefits will come at some given period of time after the start of the project. If the project is postponed, both costs and benefits will also be postponed and for the same period of time.

Questions of the best time to begin implementation can arise in agricultural projects when there is a processing facility to be constructed. We may want to establish sugar beets in a new area. We have an idea of the maximum rate at which we can expand the area for sugar beets given the limitations imposed by extension work, rates at which farmers will adopt new practices, and the like. We have a choice between shipping the beets to another area for processing—incurring both a transport cost and a loss of sucrose because of natural deterioration in the raw material—or building a new factory of a minimum economic size. Here we have a case where timing should be assessed. The potential benefit of the project grows independently of the beet factory up to its capacity because the benefit is dependent upon the rate at which farmers increase their output of beets. In the first years of the project it might be too expensive to provide for local processing, but at some point the savings in transport cost and sucrose loss will make it economic to build the factory. The problem is when is it most economic to begin.

There are two general approaches commonly employed to determine the optimal time to begin a project. The simplest timing test to calculate, and probably the most widely used in practice, is the "first-year return" method. This technique makes an implicit assumption that once benefits begin they will be rising or constant, but this is the most common situation in all kinds of projects and so is not a serious drawback. In this test, the net benefit stream in the first year the stream is positive is divided by the total of the net benefit stream in those years it is negative. The result expressed in percentage terms is the first-year return. The optimal time to begin the project is the earliest year for which the net benefit stream for a project begun in that year has a first-year return exceeding the opportunity cost of capital. If the project begins earlier, for at least the first year it will fail to earn the opportunity cost of capital, and so it would be better to postpone implementation and use the money elsewhere. If the project begins later, a chance to earn the opportunity cost of capital on the initial investment will be passed by.

The second timing test, somewhat more difficult to calculate than the first-year return test but the easiest test to interpret, is to compute the net present worth of the project by assuming it will begin in different years and by discounting at the opportunity cost of capital. (The same year is taken as t_0 for all of the alternative net present worth computations.) The project should begin in that year when the net present worth is the greatest. Before that time, postponing the project will increase its net present worth at the given opportunity cost of capital; after that time, the net present worth of the project will be less than it need be.

A very common instance of the need to determine optimal timing occurs in relation to traffic growth in road projects. The application of the methods of determining the optimal time to begin a project can be illustrated by the Kenya feeder road example laid out in table 10-10. The cost of constructing the road, divided equally between two years, is estimated at K£760.0 thousand. (The symbol for Kenyan pounds is K£. Since this analysis was made, the unit of currency used in budgeting in Kenya has been changed from pounds to shillings, or KSh.) The road is assumed to have an economic life of thirty years. The earliest the project could have begun was 1970. Once the road was complete, there would be a two-year period while the traffic built up rapidly as people learned about the new road and new traffic was generated. After that, the traffic level would be determined by the general economic conditions of the area and was assumed to grow by 9 percent a year until 1991 and to be constant thereafter for the balance of the economic life of the road. The incremental net benefit streams given in table 10-10 are based on the benefit stream derived from the traffic estimates. (The traffic estimates were made on the basis of growth over 20 years on the assumption that the road was begun in 1970. It will be seen that, even if traffic were assumed to continue to grow after 1991, the optimal time to begin the project would not change.) A residual value was assumed that was based on linear depreciation in those cases where the benefit stream does not last a full thirty years. An opportunity cost of capital of 12 percent is assumed.

To illustrate the first-year return method, we may consider the effect of beginning the road in 1973. The first year the net benefit stream is positive, it amounts to K£79.7 thousand. This is only 10 percent of the investment cost (taken to be the sum of the negative values of the net present worth stream), an indication that it is too soon to begin the project [79.7 ÷ (380.0 + 380.0) × 100 = 10]. If we test for beginning the road in 1974, the net benefit stream in the first year the net present worth is positive amounts to K£86.4, which is only 11 percent of the investment, and it is still too early to begin [86.4 ÷ (380.0 + 380.0) × 100 = 11]. But now if we test for beginning the road in 1975, when the net benefit stream the first year it is positive amounts to K£94.5 thousand, we find the first year return to be 12 percent [94.5 ÷ (380.0 + 380.0) × 100 = 12]. Since 12 percent is our opportunity cost of capital, the first-year return method indicates that 1975 is the optimal year to begin the project.

To determine the optimal time to begin the project using the net present worth method, the net present worth of the road was computed for each timing alternative from 1970 through 1977. The calculation took 1969 as t_0 (that is, 1970 = t_1). The net present worth reaches its greatest value of K£300.6 if the road were to be postponed five years and construction begun in 1975. This, then, is the optimal timing alternative, a result consistent with that we obtained using the first-year return method. Beginning the road either before or after 1975 would result in a lower net present worth.

In this example of mutually exclusive timing alternatives, an investment decision based only on a simple economic rate of return computation would have led to an erroneous choice. Beginning the project in 1970 would yield an overall economic rate of return from the project as a whole of 15 percent. Since this is well above the opportunity cost of capital, at first glance it might seem justifiable to proceed with the project. But we know from our first-year return analysis that if the project is begun in 1970 the return to the capital invested in the first year a positive benefit is received is only 8 percent, and it would thus be better to postpone the investment. Choosing the optimal starting year of 1975 means that the project will have an economic rate of return of 19 percent. If we postpone the project still further, we know that the present worth of the project at the opportunity cost of capital falls—but note that the simple economic rate of return to the project as a whole continues to rise, and this might be misleading to the unwary or ill-advised project analyst.

The internal rate of return criterion can be manipulated to indicate the optimal timing by discounting the differences between the cash flows in each succeeding year until the internal rate of return to the incremental cash flow just equals the opportunity cost of capital. This calculation, however, is complex and more difficult to interpret than either the first-year return or the net present worth approach.

In the Kenya example, the net benefit-investment ratio also indicates the optimal timing directly, but since the net benefit-investment ratio cannot in general be relied on to choose between mutually exclusive projects, its use to determine optimal timing is inadvisable.

Choice between technologies (crossover discount rate)

When there are technological alternatives by which we can realize the same result when designing a project, we have an instance of mutually

Table 10-10. Determination of Optimal Timing, Third Highway Loan Project, Feeder Road Number 10, Kenya (thousands of K£)

Year	Incremental net benefit assuming construction to begin in:							
	1970	1971	1972	1973	1974	1975	1976	1977
1970	−380.0	—						
1971	−380.0	−380.0	—					
1972	+61.0	−380.0	−380.0	—				
1973	+69.1	+67.0	−380.0	−380.0	—			
1974	+77.7	+75.3	+73.0	−380.0	−380.0	—		
1975	+84.7	+84.7	+82.7	+79.7	−380.0	−380.0	—	
1976	+92.3	+92.3	+92.3	+89.7	+86.4	−380.0	−380.0	—
1977	+100.6	+100.6	+100.6	+100.6	+97.8	+94.5	−380.0	−380.0
1978	+109.7	+109.7	+109.7	+109.7	+109.7	+106.9	+102.6	−380.0
1979	+119.6	+119.6	+119.6	+119.6	+119.6	+119.6	+116.0	+111.8
1980	+130.3	+130.3	+130.3	+130.3	+130.3	+130.3	+130.3	+126.4
1981	+142.0	+142.0	+142.0	+142.0	+142.0	+142.0	+142.0	+142.0
1982	+154.8	+154.8	+154.8	+154.8	+154.8	+154.8	+154.8	+154.8
1983	+168.8	+168.8	+168.8	+168.8	+168.8	+168.8	+168.8	+168.8
1984	+183.9	+183.9	+183.9	+183.9	+183.9	+183.9	+183.9	+183.9
1985	+200.5	+200.5	+200.5	+200.5	+200.5	+200.5	+200.5	+200.5
1986	+218.5	+218.5	+218.5	+218.5	+218.5	+218.5	+218.5	+218.5
1987	+238.2	+238.2	+238.2	+238.2	+238.2	+238.2	+238.2	+238.2

1988	+259.7	+259.7	+259.7	+259.7	+259.7	+259.7	+259.7
1989	+283.0	+283.0	+283.0	+283.0	+283.0	+283.0	+283.0
1990	+308.5	+308.5	+308.5	+308.5	+308.5	+308.5	+308.5
1991–2000	+336.3	+336.3	+336.3	+336.3	+336.3	+336.3	+336.3
2001	+361.6[a]	+386.9[b]	+412.2[c]	+437.5[d]	+462.8[e]	+488.1[f]	+513.4[g]
Present worth at 12 percent	+262.2	+279.1	+290.8	+297.6	+300.6	+299.6	+295.4
First-year return (percent)	9	10	10	11	12	14	15
Economic rate of return (percent)	16	16	17	18	19	20	21
N/k ratio	1.35	1.37	1.38	1.39	1.40	1.39	1.39

Note: first data column also reads — 1988 +259.7; 1989 +283.0; 1990 +308.5; 1991–2000 +336.3; 2001 +336.3; Present worth at 12 percent +238.9; First-year return (percent) 8; Economic rate of return (percent) 15; N/k ratio 1.31.

Source: Adapted from World Bank, "Appraisal of a Third Highway Project, Kenya," PTR-24a (Washington, D.C., 1969). Since this analysis was made, the unit of currency used in budgeting in Kenya has been changed from pounds to shillings (KSh).

a. Includes residual value of K£25.3 thousand.
b. Includes residual value of K£50.6 thousand.
c. Includes residual value of K£75.9 thousand.
d. Includes residual value of K£101.2 thousand.
e. Includes residual value of K£126.5 thousand.
f. Includes residual value of K£151.8 thousand.
g. Includes residual value of K£177.1 thousand.

exclusive alternatives because the choice of one technology precludes the use of another for the same purpose. The alternative we choose will be the one with the lower present worth—but, if the total undiscounted cost of using the different alternatives is different and they have differing time profiles, the alternative we choose may depend on the opportunity cost of capital.

Suppose we have a choice between two grain storage systems—one that uses silos and bulk handling and that has the lower undiscounted cost, and the other that uses warehouses and bags. The bulk handling system involves a high initial investment for silos but has low upkeep. The alternative system based on warehouses and bagging has a much lower construction cost but will entail substantial annual operating cost. At a low discount rate, the silo system with its high initial cost but low operating cost will have the lower present worth. Thus, it would be preferred. At a high discount rate, however, the warehouse and bagging system with its low initial cost but high operating cost will have the lower present worth. At some discount rate, both alternatives will have the same present worth, and we will be indifferent on economic grounds which alternative we choose. This is known as the "crossover (or equalizing) discount rate," and it can be found either graphically or by discounting the differences between the cost streams. If the cost of capital or cut-off rate is below the crossover discount rate, we will prefer the alternative that entails the higher initial capital outlay but lower expenditure in the future. Above the crossover discount rate, we will prefer the technological alternative with the lower initial cost, even though this involves higher operating cost later.

We may illustrate this with a forestry project in Tunisia; the analysis is laid out in tables 10-11 through 10-13 and in figure 10-1. It was proposed to clear an area covered with maquis, a scrubby underbrush found in the Mediterranean region, at the rate of 400 hectares a year for five years to prepare the ground for reforestation. Two technological alternatives

Table 10-11. *Choice between Manual and Mechanical Land Clearing in Tunisia: Manual Clearing Alternative*
(US$)

Project year	Wages[a]	Other cost[a]	Total cost	Present worth 10%	Present worth 15%
1	44,050	3,800	47,850		
2	44,050	3,800	47,850		
3	44,050	3,800	47,850	181,399	160,393
4	44,050	3,800	47,850		
5	44,050	3,800	47,850		
Total	220,250	19,000	239,250	181,399	160,393

US$ U.S. dollars.

Source: Personal communication from Mr. Hans Warvinge, Swedish International Development Authority (December 1971).

a. All values at market prices.

Table 10-12. *Choice between Manual and Mechanical Land Clearing in Tunisia: Mechanical Clearing Alternative*
(US$)

Project year	Equipment cost[a]	Operation and maintenance[a]	Total cost	Present worth 10%	Present worth 15%
1	90,700[b]	21,586	112,286	102,068	97,689
2	0	25,134	25,134	20,761	19,001
3	0	25,134	25,134	18,876	16,538
4	0	26,227	26,227	17,913	15,002
5	0	26,227	26,227	16,287	13,035
Total	90,700	124,308	215,008	175,905	161,265

Source: Same as table 10-11.
a. All values at market prices.
b. Tractor and clearer c.i.f. Tunis, taxes included.

were available. The land could be cleared manually at a cost of US$47,850 per year spread evenly over the five-year period for an undiscounted total cost of US$239,250 (table 10-11). Alternatively, tractors and clearing equipment could be purchased and the area cleared mechanically at a lower undiscounted total cost of US$215,008 (table 10-12). The mechanical clearing alternative involved a large initial capital expenditure of US$90,700; after that, however, operation and maintenance costs would only be some US$25,000 a year.

The proper choice between these two alternatives must allow for the time value of money. If a discount rate of 10 percent is assumed, we find the mechanical alternative continues to be cheaper and has the lower present worth. At 15 percent, however, we find the manual method has the lower present worth and, hence, costs less. If we subtract year by year the cost stream of the cheaper undiscounted alternative (in this case, the mechanical clearing) from the more expensive undiscounted alternative (the manual clearing) and then find the discount rate that brings the stream of the differences between the cost streams to zero, we will find that discount rate at which the present worths of the two alternatives are equal (hence, the term "equalizing discount rate"). From an economic standpoint, at this rate we are indifferent about the alternatives. As shown in table 10-13 for the Tunisian example, this crossover or equalizing discount rate is 14 percent. (This discount rate may also be derived graphically as illustrated in figure 10-1.) If our opportunity cost of capital were 10 percent, we would prefer the mechanical clearing alternative, assuming that our criteria were based strictly on cost grounds. If the opportunity cost of capital were 15 percent, we would prefer the manual clearing alternative, even though this is the more expensive alternative in absolute (undiscounted) terms. If the opportunity cost of capital were 14 percent, on economic grounds we would be indifferent about the alternatives.

In Tunisia, where the opportunity cost of capital was probably not much, if any, less than 14 percent, the manual alternative would doubt-

Table 10-13. *Choice between Manual and Mechanical Land-clearing Alternatives in Tunisia: Crossover Discount Rate*
(US$)

Project year	Differences between cost streams	Present worth 10%	Present worth 15%
1	−64,436	−58,572	−56,059
2	+22,716	+18,763	+17,173
3	+22,716	+17,060	+14,947
4	+21,623	+14,769	+12,368
5	+21,623	+13,428	+10,747
Total	+24,242	+5,448	− 824

Crossover discount rate = 10 + 5[5,448 ÷ (5,448 + 824)] = 10 + 5(0.87) = 14 percent

Source: Same as table 10-11.

lessly be chosen if for no other reason than the employment effect manual clearing would have. Note, too, that the example uses market prices. If we were to shadow-price labor at 50 percent of its wage, the undiscounted cost of the manual clearing alternative falls to US$129,125 [(220,250 × 0.50) + 19,000 = 129,125], which makes it well below the undiscounted cost of the mechanical alternative even if we reduce the cost of the tractor and clearing equipment by the amount of duties and taxes. At the shadow wage, there would be no case at all for the mechanical alternative in this example. In other projects, however, the effect of the shadow wage would be to reduce the crossover discount rate—possibly to move it below a cut-off rate so that a labor-intensive alternative that would not be attractive at market prices might prove to be the preferable alternative if shadow prices were used in the economic analysis.

This Tunisian example shows vividly how low (perhaps subsidized) interest rates and high wages (perhaps the result of minimum wage regulations) can encourage mechanization and reduce employment.

Additional purposes in multipurpose projects

A variation of the problem of mutually exclusive alternatives arises in multipurpose projects. In these, a project design that includes one group of purposes is a mutually exclusive alternative to another project design that includes a different group of purposes. The problem is frequently met in rural development projects, and another common example is found in river basin development projects.

The reason we are interested in multipurpose projects, of course, is that often it is possible to provide a group of related goods and services more cheaply from a single project than it is to provide the same benefits from the most economic, alternative single-purpose projects. But there is a danger that a very beneficial purpose (flood control, perhaps) may drive up the overall economic rate of return and thus hide another purpose (irrigation, perhaps) that should be omitted.

Figure 10-1. *Graphic Derivation of Crossover Discount Rate,*
Choice between Mechanical and Manual Land-clearing
Alternatives in Tunisia

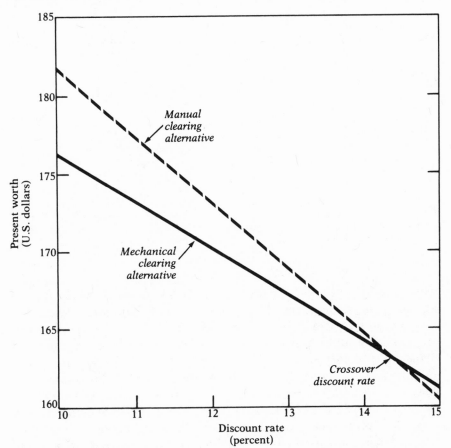

Source: Tables 10-11 through 10-13.

Projects may conveniently be tested for the desirability of an additional purpose by determining the net present worth of the alternative groups of purposes at the opportunity cost of capital. If the project has a greater net present worth with an additional purpose than without it, then the additional purpose is justified. But if the net present worth is reduced by including an additional purpose, then obviously it would be undesirable to include the additional purpose in the project.

The method of analysis is illustrated in tables 10-14 through 10-16. A multipurpose river basin project can be built to provide only flood control and power benefits, or it can be expanded to include an irrigation component. The separable cost wholly attributable to each purpose is given in the first part of table 10-14. These indicate the extent to which the cost of the project would be reduced were one component omitted. In this instance, omitting irrigation reduces the cost of the project by US$18,965 thousand. The alternative cost of providing each benefit in the project by means of the most economic alternative single-purpose proj-

Table 10-14. *Separable and Alternative Costs,*
Multipurpose River Basin Project, United States
(thousands of US$)

Project year	Flood control	Irriga-tion	Power
Separable cost			
1	84	1,132	600
2	1,244	1,970	1,530
3	907	2,865	2,085
4–100	5	134	61
Total	2,720	18,965	10,132
Alternative cost			
1	2,380	1,880	715
2	4,740	5,270	2,100
3	1,370	2,565	1,495
4–100	22	220	226
Total	10,624	31,055	26,232

Source: Adapted from U.S. Government, Department of the Interior, Bureau of Reclamation, *Reclamation Instruction Series 110, Project Planning* (Washington, D.C., 1959), p. 116.5.19.

ect is given in the second part of table 10-14. If the present worth of providing the same purpose by a single-purpose alternative were less than the present worth of the separable cost for providing that same purpose in the multipurpose project, there would be no grounds for including that purpose in the multipurpose project. In table 10-15, discounting at 2.5 percent (the rate in use at the time this analysis was done) shows that the net present worth of the project increases from US$8,273 thousand to US$10,935 thousand when the irrigation component is added. The investment decision, then, would be to include the irrigation component in the project. Had the net present worth with irrigation been less than US$8,273 thousand, the investment decision would have been to omit the irrigation component.

The same investment decision would have been reached if the method of discounting the differences between the cash flows had been used, although this involves more calculation and more chance of error. This approach is illustrated in table 10-16. There the economic rate of return to the irrigation component is found to be 4 percent. Since this is greater than the opportunity cost of capital or cut-off rate of 2.5 percent, the investment decision would be to accept the irrigation component. Note, however, that if one were simply to calculate an internal rate of return for the two versions of the project, with irrigation and without irrigation, the version without irrigation has a slightly higher internal rate of return. If one were not careful about the method of analysis using the internal rate of return for mutually exclusive projects, the wrong investment decision might be made. (Note the relation between the net present worth analysis in table 10-15 and the analysis discounting the differences between cash flows in table 10-16. The differences of the net present worths of the cash flows discounted at 2.5 percent in table 10-15 is US$2,662 thousand

Table 10-15. *Measures of Project Worth without and with Irrigation,*
U.S. Multipurpose River Basin Project
(thousands of US$)

Project year	Cost	Benefit Flood control	Benefit Irriga-tion	Benefit Power	Incremental net benefit (cash flow)	Discount factor 2.5%	Present worth 2.5%
			Without irrigation				
1	2,456	—	—	—	− 2,456	0.976	− 2,397
2	6,218	—	—	—	− 6,218	0.952	− 5,920
3	1,983	—	—	—	− 1,983	0.929	− 1,842
4–100	72	271	—	347[a]	546	33.758	+18,432
Total	17,641	26,287	—	33,659	+42,305	36.615	+ 8,273

Net present worth at 2.5 percent without irrigation = US$+8,273
Internal rate of return without irrigation = 4.8 percent[b]
N/K *ratio at 2.5 percent without irrigation = US$18,432 ÷ US$10,159 = 1.81[b]*

			With irrigation				
1	3,588	—	—	—	− 3,588	0.976	− 3,502
2	8,188	—	—	—	− 8,188	0.952	− 7,795
3	4,848	—	—	—	− 4,848	0.929	− 4,504
4–100	206	271	380	347[a]	+ 792	33.758	+26,736
Total	36,606	26,287	36,860	33,659	60,200	36.615	+10,935

Net present worth at 2.5 percent with irrigation = US$+10,935
Internal rate of return with irrigation = 4.5 percent[b]
N/K *ratio at 2.5 percent with irrigation = US$26,736 ÷ US$15,801 = 1.69[b]*

Source: Same as table 10-14.
a. See the text for a discussion about valuing the power benefit.
b. See the text for a discussion about interpreting these measures.

(10,935 − 8,273 = 2,662), which is exactly the net present worth of the
differences of the streams of cash flows discounted at 2.5 percent as
shown in table 10-16.)

For illustrative purposes, the net benefit-investment ratio has been
included in table 10-15. Note that the net benefit-investment ratio without irrigation, 1.81, is larger than the net benefit-investment ratio with
irrigation, 1.69. Once again we find that the net benefit-investment ratio
cannot be relied on to choose between mutually exclusive alternatives.

A complication arises in regard to the benefit of the power component.
The economic benefit of electricity is generally considered not possible to
estimate. What *is* the benefit of electricity, especially if much of it goes for
household use? In economic analysis of single-purpose projects, this
difficulty is usually resolved by assuming that alternative projects generating the same amount of electricity will have an equivalent benefit and
by simply choosing the one for which the present worth of the cost is
lowest. In analyzing projects such as this multipurpose one, however, a
different approach to valuing power is conveniently adopted. It may be
assumed that if power consumers are willing to pay the price that would
have to be charged to provide the same amount of electricity by the most
economic single purpose as indicated in the second part of table 10-14,
then the economic value of the power component in the multipurpose

Table 10-16. *Discounting Differences between Cash Flows, With and Without Irrigation, U.S. Multipurpose River Basin Project*
(thousands of US$)

Project year	Incremental net benefit (cash flow) with irrigation	Incremental net benefit (cash flow) without irrigation	Differences between cash flows	Discount factor 2.5%	Present worth 2.5%	Discount factor 5%	Present worth 5%
1	− 3,588	− 2,456	− 1,132	0.976	− 1,105	0.952	− 1,078
2	− 8,188	− 6,218	− 1,970	0.952	− 1,875	0.907	− 1,787
3	− 4,848	− 1,983	− 2,865	0.929	− 2,662	0.864	− 2,475
4–100	+ 792	+ 546	+ 246[a]	33.758	+ 8,304	17.125	+ 4,213
Total	+ 60,200	+ 42,305	+ 17,895	36.615	+ 2,662	19.848	− 1,127

Internal rate of return of irrigation component $= 2.5 + 2.5(2,662 \div 3,789) = 4$ *percent*[b]

Source: Same as table 10-14.
a. See the text for a discussion about valuing the power benefit.
b. See the text for a discussion about interpreting this measure.

project is at least that much. That being the case, we may take the annual benefit of the power to be at least the annual equivalent of the net present worth of the cost of providing the power by means of the most economic single-purpose alternative.

In this instance, if we discount the stream of costs for the most economic single-purpose power alternative as given in the second part of table 10-14 at the opportunity cost of capital of 2.5 percent, we reach a net present worth of US$11,715 thousand. To convert this net present worth to an annual equivalent, we need the capital recovery factor for the period from the 4th through the 100th year of the project, since power from the single-purpose alternative is assumed to begin to flow in the 4th year. This cannot be determined conveniently from a commonly used set of compounding and discounting tables such as those in Gittinger (1973). We can, however, calculate the capital recovery factor directly by determining the present worth of an annuity factor for the 4th through the 100th years and by then taking the reciprocal of that, since the capital recovery factor is the reciprocal of the present worth of an annuity factor. (This method is discussed in more detail in the section on "Joint Cost Allocation" in chapter 6.) The present worth of an annuity factor at 2.5 percent for 100 years is 36.614 105. This may be obtained from a detailed set of compounding tables, from calculation along the lines of the discussion in the last section of this chapter, or from the formula in appendix B. The present worth of an annuity factor for 2.5 percent for 3 years is 2.856 024, so that the present worth of an annuity factor at 2.5 percent for the 4th through the 100th years is 33.758 081 (36.614 105 − 2.856 024 = 33.758 081). The capital recovery factor for the 4th through the 100th years at 2.5 percent can then be obtained by taking the reciprocal of the present worth of an annuity factor, or 0.029 623 (1 ÷ 33.758 081 = 0.029 623). We then apply that factor to the net present worth at 2.5 percent of the stream of costs of providing the power by the most economic single-purpose alternative, US$11,715 thousand. The result is the annual value of the cost of providing the power by the single-purpose alternative, US$347 thousand (11,715 × 0.029 623 = 347). This value can then be used to estimate the present worth of the multipurpose project with and without the irrigation component. A fuller discussion of valuing electricity will be found in van der Tak (1969).

Applying Contingency Allowances

For many estimates of project costs, especially costs of those projects in which there is a considerable element of construction in the earlier years, the engineers will often include a contingency allowance. We noted in chapter 2 that physical contingency allowances and contingency allowances intended to reflect relative price changes are real costs in both financial and economic analysis and should be incorporated directly into the project accounts even when the analyst is working in constant prices.

The contingency allowance intended to allow for general inflation, however, does not enter into the project accounts, either financial or economic, when the analyst is working in constant prices. This means that when inflation is expected to be significant, a separate financing plan will be needed to give those responsible for making budget allocations a better idea of the amounts in current terms that they will be asked to make available.

Because future price increases can affect costs only until work is completed, the overall contingency allowance for inflation is built up by applying the appropriate compounding factors to the amount to be expended each year. Suppose we take a project with an expected total cost of US$390 thousand in constant terms as of the beginning of the project, or t_0. Construction costs are to be incurred equally each year over a three-year construction period. We expect inflation to be 8 percent a year during construction. We can lay out the computation as follows (costs are in thousands of U.S. dollars):

Year	Project cost in constant terms		Compounding factor for 1 at 8 percent		Project cost in current terms
1	130	×	1.080	=	140
2	130	×	1.166	=	152
3	130	×	1.260	=	164
Total	390				456

The total cost for the project in current terms would thus be US$456 thousand, and the price contingency would be 17 percent [(456 − 390) ÷ 390 × 100 = 17]. This, of course, is quite different from the 26 percent price contingency we would obtain if we were to compound the whole project cost in constant terms over the three-year period [390 × 1.260 = 491; (491 − 390) ÷ 390 × 100 = 26].

Contingency allowances are usually not included for the operating costs of a project once the initial investment stage is passed. Rather, problems such as higher than anticipated production expenditures are customarily analyzed by using sensitivity analysis, and a judgment is then made about whether to change the design of the project or to abandon it.

In agricultural credit projects, it is generally not necessary to include contingency allowances. Changes in unit costs for this kind of project will primarily affect the number of loans that can be made with the funds available rather than the economic justification of the project itself. Contingencies in agricultural credit projects usually will, however, be treated in the discussion of the economic justification of the project, perhaps in conjunction with the sensitivity analysis.

Contingency allowances are best shown separately in project tables, with appropriate explanations of how they were calculated included in the accompanying text and notes. To avoid double counting, any contingency allowances already included in the basic material used to prepare the project analysis should be eliminated. The amount of contingency provision will vary with the nature of the project and the general components of the project. Contingency allowances should be determined item by item for each project, not based on some national standard allowance. In general, contingency allowances should not be large enough to cover almost any cost overrun, since the possibility of so large a change occurring is small. Such excessive prudence will reduce the pressure for careful cost estimation, relax pressure for tight cost control during project execution, and result in misleading underestimates of the net present worth, the financial and economic return, or the net benefit-investment ratio.

Physical contingency allowances usually are estimated separately for each major category of cost and separately for local and foreign exchange costs. Projects that include large civil engineering works require higher contingency allowances than projects that cover only the supply and erection of equipment. The cost of engineering works will be influenced by such factors as the topography and geology of the project area, the amount of field work necessary to prepare the detailed designs, unforeseen technical difficulties (especially if the project involves subsurface work), the risk of underestimating the amount of work actually required, changes in design during construction, and unusually bad weather that may interrupt work. If large amounts of equipment are involved, contingencies may be appropriate to allow for errors in estimating the exact amount of equipment and the quantity of spare parts needed.

Contingency allowances for relative price changes during the early investment phase of a project may reflect anticipated influences arising from domestic price increases, the expected trend of prices in leading supplier countries, price trends for particular kinds of work or kinds of equipment to be used, and the possible effect of the project in exerting a strong upward pull on prices of locally supplied labor and raw materials. [A projected index of international inflation is included in *Price Prospects for Major Primary Commodities* (World Bank 1982a), which may be helpful in estimating price trends in supplier countries and for imported equipment.]

Replacement costs

Many agricultural projects require investments that have different lifetimes. A good example is found in the case of a pump irrigation scheme in which the earthworks and pump platforms may be expected to last twenty-five to fifty years but the pumps themselves may have a life of only seven to fifteen years. In preparing the analysis, allowance must be made for the replacement cost of the pumps during the life of the project.

Treatment of replacement costs is simple. The analyst includes them among the capital items for the appropriate year in the project analysis. In analysis of the net present worth, internal rate of return, and net benefit-investment ratio, the replacement costs are then netted out when the cash flow is computed. This may make the cash flow for that particular year negative, but only rarely in an agricultural project could this introduce analytical complications (see the subsection on "More than one possible internal rate of return" in chapter 9).

Table 10-17. *Treatment of Replacement Cost, Lift Irrigation Project, India*
(thousand of Rs)

Project year	Investment cost	Incremental benefit[a]	Incremental net benefit (cash flow)	Discount factor 12%	Present worth 12%	Discount factor 30%	Present worth 30%	Discount factor 35%	Present worth 35%
1	469	0	− 469	0.893	− 419	0.769	− 361	0.741	− 348
2	223	0	− 223	0.797	− 178	0.592	− 132	0.549	− 122
3	0	155	+ 155	0.712	+ 110	0.455	+ 71	0.406	+ 63
4–8	0	310	+ 310	2.566	+ 795	1.109	+ 344	0.902	+ 280
9	223[b]	310	+ 87	0.361	+ 31	0.094	+ 8	0.067	+ 6
10–15	0	310	+ 310	1.483	+ 460	0.249	+ 77	0.160	+ 50
16	223[b]	310	+ 87	0.163	+ 14	0.015	+ 1	0.008	+ 1
17–22	0	310	+ 310	0.671	+ 208	0.040	+ 12	0.019	+ 6
23	223[b]	310	+ 87	0.074	+ 6	0.002	0	0.001	0
24	0	310	+ 310	0.066	+ 20	0.002	+ 1	0.001	0
25	0	469[c]	+ 469	0.059	+ 28	0.001	0	0.001	0
Total	1,361	7,134	+5,773	7.845	+1,075	3.328	+ 21	2.855	− 64

Net present worth at 12 percent = Rs+1,075

Financial rate of return = 30 + 5[21 ÷ (21 + 64)] = 30 + 5(0.25) = 31 percent

N/K ratio = Rs1,672 ÷ Rs597 = 2.80

Rs Indian rupees.
Source: Adapted from "Report on Lift Irrigation Project in Sangli District, Maharashtra," section 18 of *Selected Agricultural Project Reports* (Pune, Maharashtra: College of Agricultural Banking, 1978), pp. 373–92.
a. The incremental benefit is aggregated from farm budgets. Operation and maintenance of the scheme are recovered by charges to farmers and are deducted from gross output as a production cost.
b. Pump replacement.
c. Includes residual value for pumps of Rs159 thousand; civil works are assumed to have no residual value.

The treatment of replacement costs is illustrated in table 10-17. The project is a lift irrigation scheme proposed for Sangli District in the state of Maharashtra in western India. The scheme would draw water from the Krishna River to serve three villages and would enable the farmers to grow hybrid sorghum, wheat, and sugarcane in addition to their traditional, rainfed crops. The project would take two years to complete. Once in operation, the civil works associated with the pumps could be expected to last at least twenty-five years. The pumps themselves, however, are expected to be replaced every seven years. In table 10-17, the investment column shows Rs223 thousand for pump replacement in years 9, 16, and 23. The project thus allows for pump replacement quite directly by simply including replacement as an investment cost in the years it is expected to occur. (Note that there is a "residual" value to allow for the unexpired life of the last pump cycle in year 25; we will return to this in the next subsection.) In this Indian example (as is generally the case), the investment cost for pump replacement is not large enough to turn the cash flow negative in any year when new pumps are to be installed, so there is no possibility that there will be more than one solution when the internal rate of return is calculated.

Residual value

Often at the end of a project there may reasonably be expected to be some residual (or terminal) value. That is, the capital asset will not have been all used up in the course of the project period, and there will be a "residual asset." The way to handle this is to treat the residual value of any capital item (say a dam or a stand of trees) as a project "benefit" during the last year of the analysis period.

An example of a residual value is found in the analysis of the Indian pump project outlined in table 10-17 and discussed in the previous subsection on replacement costs. The pumps in this project are replaced every seven years. The last pump replacement before the end of the project in year 25 occurs at the end of year 23. The pump, therefore, is expected to have been used for only two years of its seven-year life by the end of the project. The value of the remaining useful life of the pump should not properly be charged as an investment cost to the project; instead, the project should be credited with the residual value in the final year of the project. Thus, in this example the analyst added an amount equal to five-sevenths of the Rs223 thousand investment cost included in year 23 to the incremental benefit in year 25, or Rs159 thousand [$(7 - 2) \div 7 \times 223 = 159$].

On the whole, residual values will not change the net present worth, rate of return, or net benefit-investment ratio significantly unless the period of the analysis is short or the value of the capital items is quite large in relation to the value of the benefit stream. Such might be the case, for instance, in a livestock project in which a very large residual value may build up in the form of a valuable herd. For agricultural projects carried out to 25 years or so, however, the residual value will usually not change the net present worth or the net benefit-investment ratio by more than a very small proportion, or the rate of return by as much as a percentage point. The reasons are the same ones noted in the discussion of the length of the project period. At the earning capacities of the kinds of projects we are considering, the present worth of future benefits (hence, the present worth of residual values) is just not very great. A practical result of this is that projects are quite insensitive to errors in estimating residual values. A rather gross estimate in a twenty-five-year project is adequate. Note that in table 10-17 virtually no error in estimating the salvage value could significantly affect the measures of project worth. Including residual values in the project analysis will forestall criticisms of the project analysis, or attempts to discredit a project with a low initial investment in favor of another with a high initial investment on the grounds that the analyst ignored the residual value. This may be important when discussing irrigation projects or livestock projects because the technicians' concern and attention may be largely focused on the problems associated with the capital investment in the dam or in the buildup of the breeding herd.

Domestic resource cost

In countries where there are balance of payments problems and where import substitution or export promotion is an important objective, it is useful to estimate the cost in the domestic currency required to earn a unit of foreign exchange through a proposed project. The usefulness of doing so might arise, for instance, in preparing an oil palm project in which export or avoidance of vegetable oil imports is the objective or in evaluating a fertilizer plant intended to reduce or avoid future increases in imports. It is not enough just to earn or save foreign exchange. Some idea must be formed of the cost of saving foreign exchange, and a judgment must be made about whether that cost is too high. By expressing the cost of earning or saving a unit of foreign exchange as domestic resource cost, a direct comparison may be made with the official exchange rate and various shadow prices for foreign exchange. Such a comparison is one basis for evaluating a project.

There are many approaches to estimating the domestic resource cost and numerous theoretical problems to be resolved. These have been discussed at length by Bruno (1967), whose name is so closely identified with this topic that the domestic resource cost is often called the Bruno ratio.

Tables 10-18 and 10-19 illustrate a straightforward approach to estimating the domestic resource cost. This approach is suitable for most project purposes. Its major limitations are the tendency for some "domestic" costs to involve imports—the import consumption of workers, for example—and the partial analysis problem that is common to all discounted measures of project worth. Its advantages are its simplicity and the ease with which the result may be interpreted. To calculate the domestic resource cost by this method, it is necessary to know four items:

Table 10-18. *Calculation of Domestic Resource Cost,*
Indian Farmers Fertilizer Cooperative Fertilizer Project,
India: Foreign Exchange Component
(millions of US$)

Year	Value of production	Invest-ment cost	Produc-tion cost	Other cost or saving[a]	Incre-mental saving	Discount factor 12%	Present worth 12%
1970	—	7	—	—	− 7	0.893	− 6
1971	—	15	—	—	− 15	0.797	−12
1972	—	15	—	—	− 15	0.712	−11
1973	12	—	12	—	0	0.636	0
1974	38	—	18	—	+ 20	0.567	+11
1975	43	—	20	—	+ 23	0.507	+12
1976	56	—	26	—	+ 30	0.452	+14
1977	56	—	25	—	+ 31	0.404	+13
1978	56	—	25	—	+ 31	0.361	+11
1979–84	56	—	25	—	+ 31	1.483	+46
Total	597	37	276	—	+284	6.812	+78

Source: Adapted from U.S. Government, U.S. Agency for International Development (USAID), "India: IFFCO Fertilizer Project Proposal and Recommendations for the Review of the Development Loan Committee," AID-DLC/P-851 (Washington, D.C., 1969), annexes 4A and 4B.

a. If applicable, would include such differences in cost or saving as foreign exchange for insurance, domestic currency saving in distribution from avoiding port charges and locating production closer to the point of use, and the like.

Table 10-19. *Calculation of Domestic Resource Cost,*
India Fertilizer Project: Domestic Currency Component
(millions of Rs)

Year	Invest-ment cost	Produc-tion cost	Other cost or saving[a]	Incre-mental cost	Discount factor 12%	Present worth 12%
1970	107	—	—	107	0.893	96
1971	172	—	—	172	0.797	137
1972	56	—	—	56	0.712	40
1973	24	38	—	62	0.636	39
1974	—	81	—	81	0.567	46
1975	—	90	—	90	0.507	46
1976	—	109	—	109	0.452	49
1977	—	109	—	109	0.404	44
1978	—	109	—	109	0.361	39
1979–84	—	108	—	108	1.483	160
Total	359	1,184	—	1,543	6.812	696

$$\text{Domestic resource cost} = \frac{\text{Present worth of domestic currency cost of realizing foreign exchange saving}}{\text{Present worth of net foreign exchange saving}^b} = \text{Rs696} \div \text{US\$78} = 8.92$$

Source: Same as table 10-18.

a. If applicable, would include such differences in cost or saving as foreign exchange for insurance, domestic currency saving in distribution from avoiding port charges and locating production closer to the point of use, and the like.

b. From table 10-18.

(1) the foreign exchange value of the product to be produced; (2) the foreign exchange cost incurred to produce the product (that is, the foreign exchange cost of such things as imported fuels, imported raw materials, and the like); (3) the domestic currency cost of producing the output; and (4) the opportunity cost of capital. The present worth of the net foreign exchange benefit (discounted at the opportunity cost of capital) is compared with the present worth of the domestic cost of realizing these savings. The ratio between the two present worths is the domestic resource cost, and it may be directly compared with the official exchange rate or with shadow exchange rates.

The Indian Farmers Fertilizer Cooperative, Ltd., proposed to build a modern petrochemical fertilizer facility in the state of Gujarat. The economic analysis gives the costs and benefits broken down into their foreign exchange (table 10-18) and domestic currency (table 10-19) components. The domestic resource cost with a 12 percent opportunity cost of capital assumed is Rs8.92 = US$1.

Since the official exchange rate at the time of the analysis was Rs7.50 = US$1, if the official exchange rate is accepted as a true measure of the value of the rupee (and 12 percent is accepted as the opportunity cost of capital), then it would cost more to manufacture through the project a dollar's worth of fertilizer for import substitution than it would to buy the fertilizer from abroad. At the time the analysis was undertaken, however, it was widely considered in India that a foreign exchange premium of at least 25 percent would better reflect the true value of the rupee. This would make the shadow exchange rate Rs9.375 = US$1 (7.50 × 1.25 = 9.375). If this rate is accepted (with 12 percent still the opportunity cost of capital), then it would cost less to produce a dollar's worth of fertilizer than to import it because the domestic resource cost of Rs8.92 = US$1 is a more favorable exchange rate than the shadow exchange rate of Rs9.375 = US$1.

Calculating Measures of Project Worth Using Current Prices

We have often noted that project analyses are usually done at constant prices because the analyst is concerned with the real return to the project when he is looking at the financial analysis and with the real, not monetary, effects of the project when he turns to economic analysis. Thus, it is common practice for the analyst to assume that general inflation will exert the same relative effect on both costs and benefits and to work in constant prices.

Projects can, of course, be analyzed using current prices. If that were done, general inflation would not affect the selection of projects provided that all projects were analyzed using the same assumptions. That is, the same group of projects would be accepted whether the analysis is done on a constant price basis or on a current price basis. Working with constant prices, however, is the analytically simpler approach because it avoids estimating a rate of inflation and simplifies the computations.

If we use net present worth as the measure of project worth, the amount of the net present worth will be different depending on whether we use current or constant prices (and also on whether we use a shadow foreign exchange rate or a conversion factor to allow for the foreign exchange premium). If we estimate the opportunity cost of capital for the analysis correctly, we will still select the same group of projects to implement. The opportunity cost of capital, however, will be higher by an allowance for inflation. If we use net present worth, we may assume a different rate for inflation for each year if that suits our analytical purpose. There is no easy means to compare the net present worth at current prices to the net present worth at constant prices; the present worth computation must be repeated for each stream of values, and all projects being analyzed must use the same assumptions. A similar comment holds for the net benefit-investment ratio. The value of the ratio will change with changing assumptions about inflation and there is no easy way to compare the net benefit-investment ratio at current prices to the net benefit-investment ratio at constant prices.

In contrast, an internal rate of return calculated at current prices, with a uniform general inflation rate assumed, can easily be converted to the rate of return at constant prices by dividing 1 plus the internal rate of return stated in decimal terms for the current prices by 1 plus the rate of inflation stated in decimal terms. This is illustrated in table 10-20 with the figures from the Ilocos, Philippines irrigation project that were given in table 9-11. If we assume constant prices, the economic rate of return is 18 percent. If we assume a uniform inflation rate of 6 percent throughout the life of the project, then we can derive the incremental net benefit (cash flow) in current prices for any given year by multiplying the incremental net benefit (cash flow) in constant prices for that year by the appropriate compounding factor for 1 at 6 percent. If we determine the internal rate of return for the resulting incremental net benefit (cash flow) stream, we find it to be 25 percent. Dividing this result (in the form of 1 plus the internal rate of return stated in decimal terms) by the assumed inflation rate (also stated in the form of 1 plus the inflation rate stated in decimal terms) gives 1.18—or the economic rate of return of 18 percent we found using constant prices ($1.25 \div 1.06 = 1.18$).

Calculator Applications in Project Analysis

We noted earlier that calculations for project analysis are simply too tedious to be done by hand; however, even the simplest electronic calculators readily available in virtually every nation are sufficient for nearly all calculations needed in project analysis. Indeed, they are the basic computational aid used both by national planning agencies and by international lending institutions. Unfortunately, many project analysts do

Table 10-20. *Internal Rate of Return Computation Using Current Prices,*
Ilocos Irrigation Systems Improvement Project, Philippines
(millions of US$)

Project year	Incremental net benefit (cash flow) at constant prices[a]	Discount factor 18%[a]	Present worth 18%[a]	Compounding factor for 1 at 6%	Incremental net benefit (cash flow) at current prices[b]	Discount factor 25%	Present worth 25%	Discount factor 30%	Present worth 30%
1	− 1.09	0.847	−0.92	1.060	− 1.16	0.800	−0.93	0.769	−0.89
2	− 4.83	0.718	−3.47	1.124	− 5.43	0.640	−3.48	0.592	−3.21
3	− 5.68	0.609	−3.46	1.191	− 6.76	0.512	−3.46	0.455	−3.08
4	− 4.50	0.516	−2.32	1.262	− 5.68	0.410	−2.33	0.350	−1.99
5	− 1.99	0.437	−0.87	1.338	− 2.66	0.328	−0.87	0.269	−0.72
6	+ 1.00	0.370	+0.37	1.419	+ 1.42	0.262	+0.37	0.207	+0.29
7	+ 2.37	0.314	+0.74	1.504	+ 3.56	0.210	+0.75	0.159	+0.57
8	+ 3.70	0.266	+0.98	1.594	+ 5.90	0.168	+0.99	0.123	+0.73
9	+ 5.06	0.225	+1.14	1.689	+ 8.55	0.134	+1.15	0.094	+0.80
10	+ 6.43	0.191	+1.23	1.791	+ 11.52	0.107	+1.23	0.073	+0.84
11	+ 6.43	0.162	+1.04	1.898	+ 12.20	0.086	+1.05	0.056	+0.68
12	+ 6.43	0.137	+0.88	2.012	+ 12.94	0.069	+0.89	0.043	+0.56
13	+ 6.43	0.116	+0.75	2.133	+ 13.72	0.055	+0.75	0.033	+0.45

14	+ 6.43	0.099	+0.64	2.261	+ 14.54	0.044	+0.64	0.025	+0.36
15	+ 6.43	0.084	+0.54	2.397	+ 15.41	0.035	+0.54	0.020	+0.31
16	+ 6.43	0.071	+0.46	2.540	+ 16.33	0.028	+0.46	0.015	+0.24
17	+ 6.43	0.060	+0.39	2.693	+ 17.32	0.023	+0.40	0.012	+0.21
18	+ 6.43	0.051	+0.33	2.854	+ 18.35	0.018	+0.33	0.009	+0.17
19	+ 6.43	0.043	+0.28	3.026	+ 19.46	0.014	+0.27	0.007	+0.14
20	+ 6.43	0.037	+0.24	3.207	+ 20.62	0.012	+0.25	0.005	+0.10
21	+ 6.43	0.031	+0.20	3.400	+ 21.86	0.009	+0.20	0.004	+0.09
22	+ 6.43	0.026	+0.17	3.604	+ 23.17	0.007	+0.16	0.003	+0.07
23	+ 6.43	0.022	+0.14	3.820	+ 24.56	0.006	+0.15	0.002	+0.05
24	+ 6.43	0.019	+0.12	4.049	+ 26.04	0.005	+0.13	0.002	+0.05
25	+ 6.43	0.016	+0.10	4.292	+ 27.60	0.004	+0.11	0.001	+0.03
26	+ 6.43	0.014	+0.09	4.549	+ 29.25	0.003	+0.09	0.001	+0.03
27	+ 6.43	0.011	+0.07	4.822	+ 31.01	0.002	+0.06	0.001	+0.03
28	+ 6.43	0.010	+0.06	5.112	+ 32.87	0.002	+0.07	0.001	+0.03
29	+ 6.43	0.008	+0.05	5.418	+ 34.84	0.002	+0.07	0.000	+0
30	+ 6.43	0.007	+0.05	5.743	+ 36.93	0.001	+0.04	0.000	+0
Total	+129.07	5.517	+0.02		+458.28	3.996	+0.08	3.331	−3.06

Internal rate of return (economic rate of return) at current prices = $25 + 5(0.08 \div 3.16) = 25.13 = 25$ percent
Internal rate of return (economic rate of return) at constant prices = $1.2513 \div 1.06 = 1.1805 = 18$ percent

a. See table 9-12.
b. An inflation rate of 6 percent is assumed.

Source: Adapted from World Bank, "Philippines: Appraisal of the National Irrigation Systems Improvement Project: I," 1488a (Washington, D.C., 1977; restricted circulation), annex 20, tables 2 and 6.

not take full advantage of the flexibility that even simple calculators offer.

We will illustrate some of the uses of a calculator in this section. For this purpose we will provide illustrative computations based on a widely sold, inexpensive calculator (see photograph), but the reader should note that calculators do vary in their opera- tion and that these illustrations will probably have to be adapted. The calcu- lator on which this discussion is based has an eight-digit display (indicated by the display window in the photograph). It can perform the four arithmetic func- tions of addition, subtraction, multi- plication, and division. It has one fully addressable memory; that is, one may add to the memory, subtract from the memory, and recall the memory to the display. The calculator can multiply or divide repeatedly by a constant and can perform chain computations. (Although the small calculators generally avail- able are quite accurate, the last two places when the display is fully used fol- lowing multiplication or division can- not be accepted with confidence. All the digits reproduced in the com- putations below are correct because they have been verified with more elaborate equipment; when the reader follows these illustrations on his own calculator, he may find occasions when the final digit or two do not agree with those given here.)

In these illustrations, numbers reproduced in ordinary roman type are pressed and entered on the calculator as indicated. Numbers printed in *italic* type will be displayed automatically and do not need to be entered. An arithmetic sign or a function notation in **boldface** type indicates that this key (button) on the calculator is to be pressed in the order shown. Thus, a 2 indicates a number to be entered and a **+** indicates that the plus button should be pressed. Other notations include **M+** for "add to memory"; **M−** for "subtract from memory"; **R-CM** for "recall memory" when pressed once and "clear memory" when pushed a second time; and **ON/C** for turning the machine on and for clearing the display.

We can illustrate the arithmetic and chain calculations quickly and simply. Recall the example about calculating the economic value of a tractor in chapter 7 (the subsection "Adjusting Financial Prices to Eco- nomic Values. Indirectly traded items"). We discussed the various com- putations needed to go from a market price to an economic value. We were told that in a tractor costing Rs65,000, 30 percent of the cost was for domestic components and 70 percent of the cost was for imported com- ponents. There was a tariff of 15 percent, so the amount of the imported component had to be divided by 1.15 to eliminate the tariff. We wanted to shadow-price the imported component by using a shadow exchange rate of Rs12 = US$1 instead of the official exchange rate of Rs10 = US$1, and this meant that we increased the domestic price of the imported component by the foreign exchange premium of 20 percent, or 1.2 stated in decimal terms. Each step was set forth individually, but we could have combined all the computations into one chain calculation:

R-CM R-CM 65,000 **x** 0.3 **M+** *19,500*
65,000 **x** 0.7 **÷** 1.15 **x** 1.2 **M+** *47,478*
R-CM *66,978.*

The last figure is, of course, the amount we derived when we added the individually calculated portions together.

One very convenient use of a simple calculator is to verify budget tables quickly. In the Paraguay farm budget in table 4-19, during the fourth year the total inflow was ₲426.6 thousand and the total outflow was ₲129.3 thousand, and these gave a net benefit before financing of ₲297.3 thousand. From this was subtracted debt service of ₲98.2 thousand to obtain the net benefit after financing of ₲199.1 thousand. We can quickly check these totals by simply entering the individual inflow and outflow entries in order on the calculator:

R-CM R-CM 340.7 **+** 85.9 **M+** *426.6*
13.4 **+** 112.8 **+** 3.1 **M−** *129.3*
R-CM *297.3*
oN/C − 98.2 **M+ −** *98.2*
R-CM *199.1.*

The use of the constant feature of the calculator is convenient when we have several values we wish to change by some common proportion. In the calculator we are using for illustration, the constant feature is activated after multiplication and division simply by entering a new number and pressing the **=** button, but on many calculators the constant feature is activated by pressing the "arithmetic" button twice before pressing the **=** button. An example of when the use of a constant would be convenient is found in table 7-1, in which we wished to convert all dollar values to their rupee equivalents using a shadow exchange rate. We have dollar values of US$175, US$20, and US$9. The shadow exchange rate is Rs12 = US$1:

R-CM R-CM 12 **x** 175 **=** *2,100*
20 **=** *240*
9 **=** *108.*

One use of even a simple calculator that also takes advantage of the constant feature is to derive the factors for financial computations or for discounting. Suppose we want to find the compounding factor for 1 for 14 percent at the end of five years:

$$1.14 \text{ \textbf{x} } 1 = = = = = \textit{1.925 414 6.}$$

We can verify this by checking in a standard set of tables such as *Compounding and Discounting Tables for Project Evaluation* (Gittinger 1973). Note that in laying out the computation as indicated the **=** button is pressed as many times as the number of years to be calculated, in this case five.

Discount factors can be just as easily calculated. Since we know that the discount factor is the reciprocal of the compounding factor for 1, we could find the discount factor for 14 percent for five years by dividing 1 by 1.925 415 to obtain 0.519 369. We could reach this result more directly by using our calculator to divide 1 repeatedly by 1 plus our discount rate to obtain the discount factor for 14 percent for five years:

$$1.14 \div = = = = = 0.519\ 368\ 7.$$

Again, we may verify this by checking in the tables or, to the nearest third decimal, in compounding and discounting table 6 in appendix B.

Since the present worth of an annuity factor is the running subtotal of the discount factors, we may obtain it by adding together all the discount factors as we compute them. On the least expensive calculators, there may be an accumulating memory that makes this very easy. On the somewhat more complicated calculators with fully addressable memories in which the **M+** activates the constant feature, the computation is also simple. But on the calculator we are using for illustrative purposes, a bit more manipulation is required. Suppose we want the present worth of an annuity factor for 14 percent for five years:

> **R-CM   R-CM** 1.14 $\div$
> = **M+** = **M+** = **M+** = **M+** = **M+**
> **R-CM**   3.433 081 0.

Finally, we may compute the capital recovery factor easily if we recall that it is the reciprocal of the present worth of an annuity factor. Since we have already obtained the present worth of an annuity factor for 14 percent for five years, we could simply divide 1 by 3.433 081 to obtain 0.291 284. We could compute this directly, however:

> **R-CM   R-CM** 1.14 $\div$
> = **M+** = **M+** = **M+** = **M+** = **M+**
> **R-CM** $\div$ = 0.291 283 5.

For project analysis, the ease with which we can compute discount factors using a simple calculator is most significant when we have occasion to use a fractional discount rate. Some standard discounting tables (including Gittinger 1973) do not have fractional intervals, and those which do generally do not have them for higher interest rates. Using a simple calculator, however, we can easily compute our own factors if, for example, we want to calculate a present worth at some fractional discount rate.

In agricultural projects, one use of the calculator to derive factors occurs when we are working out debt service estimates in farm budgets where the credit terms involve fractional interest rates. In the India Cashewnut Project used to illustrate unit activity budgets in chapter 4, tables 4-22 and 4-25, farmers could borrow at 10.5 percent interest to finance tree planting and then repay in six equal annual installments. To calculate the annual payment for years 8 through 13, we need the capital recovery factor for 10.5 percent for six years. We are unlikely to be able to find the factor in a standard discounting table, but we can easily obtain it directly by using our calculator:

R-CM R-CM 1.105 ÷
= M+ = M+ = M+ = M+ = M+ = M+
R-CM ÷ **=** *0.232 981 9.*

Without a fractional discounting table, we cannot verify our result directly, but we can check to make sure it is of the right order of magnitude by comparing it with the capital recovery factor for six years for 10 percent and for 11 percent. For 10 percent the value is 0.229 607; for 11 percent it is 0.236 377. Our capital recovery factor lies roughly halfway between these two values (although not exactly so, of course), so we may be confident that our factor is pretty close to correct. Now, we may multiply the loan principal (including capitalized interest) of Rs4,756 by our factor of 0.232 981 9 to obtain the annual payment of Rs1,108 (4,756 × 0.232 981 9 = 1,108). This, then, is the amount shown for debt service in years 8 through 13 in tables 4-22 and 4-25.

The various factors used in project analysis may also be computed directly quite easily if one has a calculator that can compute powers. (The simple one we have been using for illustration cannot.) Usually this is indicated by a key marked with **x^y** or some similar notation. If we return to the example from the Indian credit project noted above, we may illustrate how to calculate directly the capital recovery factor for 10.5 percent for six years. The formula for the capital recovery factor (given in appendix B) is:

$$\frac{i(1 + i)^n}{(1 + i)^n - 1}.$$

For convenience, we will begin by calculating the denominator first and then put it into the memory. It is also convenient to begin our calculations by determining the value of $(1 + i)^n$ and then subtracting 1:

R-CM R-CM 1 **+** 0.105 **=** *1.105*
1.105 **x^y** 6 **=** *1.820 428 7*
1.820 428 7 **−** 1 **=** *0.820 428 7* **M+**.

Now we may calculate the numerator. Since we know from our previous calculation that the value of $(1 + i)^n$ is 1.820 428 7, we may begin with that value and then multiply it by i, or 0.105:

1.820 428 7 **x** 0.105 **=** *0.191 145 0.*

Proceeding, we may divide 0.191 145 0 by 0.820 428 7, which has been stored in the memory, to obtain our capital recovery factor:

0.191 145 0 **÷** **R-CM** *0.820 428 7* **=** *0.232 981 9.*

This is the same factor we computed before using the much simpler calculator without the **x^y** key.

Rather more elaborate calculators than those we have been discussing here also have a role to play in project analysis. Calculators designed for business use are available that calculate present worth or even internal rate of return directly from a series of numbers keyed into the calculator. Hand-held calculators programmable with magnetic cards have many potential applications. In agricultural projects they may be used to calculate farm budgets and—most conveniently—herd projections (Espadas 1977). A herd projection that may take even a skilled livestock specialist eight hours to calculate using a simple calculator can be prepared in one or two hours using a card-programmable calculator. The implications for sensitivity analysis are obvious.

The use of computers (as opposed to calculators) in agricultural project analysis is still limited, but the use of "minicomputers" is spreading rapidly, and programs for agricultural project analysis are being developed by the Food and Agriculture Organization and the World Bank. One well-known application of large computers is to optimize cropping patterns using linear programming (see Norton and Solis 1982), but this has been limited for the most part to research efforts and has not become common in operational project evaluation. Computer programs are available for herd projections (Powers 1975). The Inter-American Development Bank has published a computer program to appraise farm development projects (Westley 1981). The Food and Agriculture Organization has developed a program for project analysis that is suitable for small computers. A recently developed World Bank program called Computerized Project Analysis Support System, for which the acronym COMPASS has been adopted, is available for use by project analysts who have access to larger computers. The program can prepare pattern farm budgets, develop project cost tables, do financial analyses of nonfarm enterprises, and elaborate other tables unique to the individual project analysis. From these components it can then aggregate to the project cash flow, calculate measures of project worth, and perform sensitivity analyses. One very convenient use of large computers is for "table making." Programs are available that accept information, arrange it, perform calculations with the data supplied, and then print the result in the form of a table that may be photocopied and included directly in a project report. Information about computer programs for project analysis may be obtained by addressing the Director, Information Resource Management Department, World Bank (Washington, D.C. 20433, U.S.A.).

Appendixes

Appendix A

Guidelines for
Project Preparation
Reports

THE GENERAL GUIDELINES in this appendix are intended to give an idea
about the scope and content of a preparation or appraisal report for an
agricultural or rural development project. Most projects in agriculture
and rural development are adaptable to a fairly standard form of presentation. The format outlined here can provide the analyst with a
starting point. It will give the readers of the report a narrative with
supporting tables and annexes that succinctly convey the information
necessary for them to form their own conclusions about the worth of the
proposed project without confounding them with unnecessary or ex-
traneous detail.

These guidelines emerge from the combined experience of the Food
and Agriculture Organization (FAO), the World Bank, and other international lending institutions. They are adapted, often verbatim, from materials prepared by the FAO Investment Centre for the use of project analysts
in developing countries and its own specialists (FAO 1975 and 1977). In
addition, the Investment Centre has prepared a series of specialized
guidelines for particular kinds of projects, which are available from the
center on request. A comprehensive set of outlines for many different
kinds of agricultural projects has also been prepared by the Inter-
American Development Bank (1978).

Facing page: Picking maize in Guatemala.

Clearly, the substance of a project preparation report is more important than its format. Obviously, too, different elements of a report will need different emphasis depending on the kind of project. The analyst will want to vary the format given here according to the type and complexity of the project he is presenting. On the one hand, these general guidelines touch on many more topics than are needed for any but the most complex project, and the topics mentioned tend to overlap. On the other hand, topics essential to understanding many kinds of agricultural projects have been omitted. This is especially true for projects with significant marketing and processing, rural industry, and rural road components. The analyst will want to leave out topics addressed in these guidelines that are not essential to an understanding of the particular project and to include additional topics that are critical to forming a judgment about the project at hand. He will want to deal with any of the relevant topics in only one place in the report so as to avoid excessive repetition.

As a rule of thumb, a project report should aim at a main text of about twenty-five single-spaced typescript pages for a straightforward agricultural project and of no more than fifty pages for a complex rural development project. This should be supported by a series of annexes, possibly in a separate volume and reproduced in fewer copies. Worksheets, detailed assumptions, and the like may be gathered into a project file and kept at some central location where anyone interested may find them. As far as possible, the main text should present the project in a form that a nonspecialist can understand; specialized back-up information—including maps, charts, and detailed tables—should be reserved for the annexes or the project file.

The principal elements of a project preparation or appraisal report are outlined in the following pages in the order in which they normally appear.

1. Summary and Conclusions

The main purpose of this part, generally only a page or two in length, is to give the reader the essential elements of the project very briefly. It should cover the rationale of the project and its priority, purpose, location and size, beneficiaries, main components, investment period, costs, organization, financial and economic effects, and main issues.

2. Introduction

This part, which is a nontechnical one, usually mentions the arrangements through which the project report was prepared. It can indicate the origin of the project concept in the national development plan, in a sector survey, or by a project identification mission. It might mention the government agencies and other organizations involved in the preparation and any external assistance received. It can acknowledge the team that prepared the project and the report and can mention the period in which they worked. None of the information needs to be given in much detail.

3. Background

To the greatest extent possible, background material should be annexed to the report. A well-thought-out and properly constructed background discussion, however, can do much toward establishing the framework of the project and making it intelligible in a broader economic and social perspective. The analyst needs to be very discriminating when choosing material for this part. The only general guidance is that there should be a clear relation between this material and the contents of other sections of the report. The tendency to ramble is usually more pronounced here than in other parts of the report.

3.1 *Current economic situation*

This discussion could mention per capita income, dependence on particular imports and exports, balance of payments considerations, and the like. It should cover only those features of recent economic developments that have a bearing on the project and on studies of the possible alternatives to the project.

3.2 *The agricultural sector*

This section might describe the main characteristics of the agricultural sector of the country, including constraints to overall development and a description of relevant subsectors.

3.3 *Development and social objectives*

This section might outline development and social objectives as expressed in national plans and official policy statements. It could note the main elements of the national strategy for agricultural development and mention significant government policies, including price and interest rate subsidies, supply of inputs, targets for rural income, regional balance, and the like.

3.4 *Income distribution and poverty*

If a project is designed to benefit a particular group of the rural poor, a discussion of income distribution and poverty would be appropriate in the background section. The information should establish a framework for the eventual justification for selecting a particular region or line of action for priority attention under the project. It should cover information about income distribution on a national basis and give a regional or social dimension to the data.

3.5 *Institutions*

This paragraph might describe the institutions concerned with development and financing in the sectors covered by the project. These might include the ministry of agriculture, the agricultural development bank, the livestock development authority, and the like.

4. Project Rationale

This part should make a persuasive argument for selecting this project for priority attention. Against the background of the previous part, it should fully discuss the development opportunities and constraints within the relevant sectors. It should also explain why a particular development strategy has been decided for this project and establish the technical, social, and economic reasons for the selection of this particular project in preference to possible alternatives. This may also be the best point at which to indicate the scale of the proposed project and to explain why a certain size has been chosen. Finally, there should be a discussion of the project risks and the steps that have been taken in project formulation and that should be taken in project implementation to minimize them.

5. Project Area

The objective of this part, and the details in the supporting annexes and maps, is to present a description of the existing status of the area where the project will be located and to give the basis from which the project starts. These descriptive data should be presented in the relevant physical, agricultural, social, economic, institutional, and legal terms. The part should evaluate, in a narrower sense than the discussion of the agricultural development strategy and the project concept, the development opportunities and potentials as well as the limitations the area presents, focusing throughout on the project description that follows.

5.1 *Physical features*

This section will deal with the main geographical and topographical features of the area and relate the area to important features of the country as a whole. The principal objective is to show that the climate and soils are suitable for the crop and livestock production proposed.

5.1.1 GEOGRAPHICAL LOCATION. The general location of the project area within the country is identified, and then the area is defined more precisely in relation to administrative boundaries and other criteria. The project area might, for example, be a province, a district, a watershed, the command area of a dam, or a combination of these. A tree-crop rehabilitation project might be concerned with particular estates or plantations. Some projects will concern only farmers who produce particular crops but may be spread over a large area.

5.1.2 CLIMATE. This section should cover rainfall, including monthly and annual totals, intensity and variability, temperatures, humidity, evapotranspiration, and the like. Available records and more technical information may be summarized in the annexes. For a dryland farming project, the objective is to show that the amount and timing of rainfall is appropriate for the cropping pattern proposed. For irrigation projects, the rainfall record supports conclusions about when irrigation water is needed and in what volume.

5.1.3 GEOLOGY, SOILS, AND TOPOGRAPHY. Information in this section should support conclusions about the land in the project—its agricultural potential, its suitability for irrigation, its needs for drainage, and the like. Judgment will be required about the scale of the maps of soil and land classification to be included in the report. In project preparation, detailed maps will be needed; in the annexes to the preparation or appraisal report, simply a reference to the detailed maps (kept on file) and a summary map of quite small scale may suffice.

5.1.4 WATER RESOURCES. Surface and underground water resources should be described to the extent they are relevant to project decisions. Usually this is done from the viewpoint of irrigation and drainage, but it may also have a bearing on provision of water for domestic use.

5.2 *Economic base*

This section should cover the main economic features of the project region. It may tend to overlap with some of the social aspects in the following section (5.3). Duplication, of course, should be avoided.

5.2.1 AGRICULTURAL AND LIVESTOCK RESOURCES. The agricultural and livestock resources of the region should be described briefly and the major features quantified. The importance of these sectors in the economy of the region, the proportion of people employed in these activities, the area and output of major products, and an approximate estimate of the value of these products may be given. Recent trends should be noted, and the relative importance of the sector to be assisted under the project should be emphasized.

5.2.2 LAND USE, FARMING SYSTEMS, AND CROPPING PATTERNS. The present land use should be described. This will include information about land tenure, farm size, cropping patterns, crop varieties and livestock breeds, crop yields and livestock production, and inputs. Much of this material can be presented in tabular form in the annexes and only a commentary given in the main text. A short description of agricultural practices and level of technology for each main farming system may be in order. Results achieved on experimental stations in the area may be mentioned, and the performance of individual farmers who have tested the proposed system can be noted to indicate potential production. Constraints should be clearly described, including such factors as social customs, land tenure, technical shortages, and lack of extension that might prevent farmers from reaching acceptable production levels.

5.2.3 INPUT SUPPLY AND PRODUCT MARKETING. A concise description should be given of existing channels for the supply of inputs and of the facilities for marketing farm production. The effects of such government policies as price supports, input subsidies, taxes on products, and the like may be described and evaluated.

5.2.4 OTHER ECONOMIC ACTIVITIES. There may be other economic activities in the area that are important to an understanding of the project. These may include forestry, fishing, rural handicrafts, and processing industries. If data are available, the number of families engaged in secondary activities may be indicated, with at least an approximate indication of their importance to the rural economy.

5.3 *Social aspects*

Social features of the project area should be described under appropriate subheadings. Many topics will overlap with other sections, and a decision will have to be made about where in the report to treat certain topics to avoid duplication.

5.3.1 LAND TENURE AND SIZE OF HOLDINGS. When land tenure is particularly important in a project or where extensive changes are contemplated, it may be more relevant to include land tenure with the discussion of the social aspects than with the discussion of land use (5.2.2). Land tenure should be discussed with reference to the proportion of owner-cultivators, tenant cultivators, and landless labor. If possible, the size of holding may be related to the kind of tenure. The descriptions should refer to any changes in land tenure caused by agrarian reform or settlement.

5.3.2 POPULATION AND MIGRATION. Data may be given that illustrate such aspects of population as density per square kilometer, pressure of population on the cultivated area, dependency ratios, and the literacy rate. It may be relevant to define the rural population, since towns in the project area may be more like large rural villages than small urban centers. When migration is important, annual or seasonal flows may be described and, if possible, quantified. If rural-urban migration is an important issue, its significance and extent may be discussed. A discussion of labor supply may be important if proposed cropping patterns depend on hired labor. A discussion of unemployment and underemployment in the project area or nearby and its seasonality may be relevant. Income levels will have been referred to earlier, but the discussion of the social aspects may include more detailed information about the project area and about other indicators of the quality of rural living such as housing, health, and nutrition. A population projection for the project area over the project life may be included, as well as a discussion of the implications this may have for the project.

5.3.3 SOCIAL SERVICES. When it is important to an understanding of the project and the reasons for its selection, the social services available in the area may be discussed. These services may include primary and secondary schools, dispensaries, and other facilities. Disease problems in the area and possibilities of their control may be discussed. Mention should be made about which social services function well and which may need improvement.

5.4 *Infrastructure*

The treatment given to infrastructure will depend on the extent to which the project itself will have infrastructure-related components. Some projects are concerned exclusively with providing rural infrastructure, in which case, of course, the weight given to this section would be substantial. It may be relevant to quantify the total length of project roads, annual tonnage moved, recent growth in traffic, and the like. The relevance of infrastructure to marketing of project output and to the supply of inputs should be mentioned. Water and electricity services within the region may be briefly described. The number of families served by various infrastructure facilities may be quantified. Ongoing improvement programs may be briefly evaluated.

5.5 *Institutions*

This section, which supplements the discussion of the national situation in the background part of the report (3) should describe the local activities of national agencies or of any special institutions, such as local development authorities, operating in the project region. The main purpose of the section is to provide a basis for understanding the proposals about organization and management of the project that are outlined later. The reader of the report will want to know which institutional arrangements are working satisfactorily and which will need supplementary attention under the project.

6. The Project

Previous parts having set the framework of constraints and opportunities for the project, this part and its supporting annexes should define and describe in detail the objectives of the project and its works and activities—their phasing, their costs, and how they will be financed and procured. As always, the emphasis on particular elements outlined below will vary with the nature of the project, and topics not mentioned may be essential to an understanding of the project. The analyst should adapt this part especially to fit the project.

6.1 *Project description*

This section should give a brief overview of the objectives, location, size, components, and other important features of the project. It serves simply to suggest to the reader of the report what to expect in the more detailed sections that follow. Three or four paragraphs should suffice.

6.2 *Detailed features*

The objective of this section is to describe the proposed project works and other components that make up the project item by item and category by category. It should concentrate on the technical aspects and describe what is to be done in sufficient detail to establish the nature, scope, and cost of the various measures proposed. It should be backed, where necessary, by supporting annexes. Consideration of the costs of implementing the measures is taken up in the section about project costs (6.4), and the manner of implementing them is outlined in the part that discusses organization and management (7), but cross references here may be helpful.

6.2.1 WORKS AND GENERAL FACILITIES. This section includes discussion of irrigation facilities, general infrastructure for settlement projects, access roads, extension facilities, and social infrastructure such as village water supplies, health clinics, schools, and rural electrification. If a development authority is responsible for undertaking construction work, a list of equipment needed for the project may be included here. Similar provision may be made for equipment for operation and maintenance of project works.

6.2.2 ON-FARM INVESTMENT. This section will discuss items such as fencing, farm irrigation and drainage systems, land clearing and leveling, pasture development, and the like. The distinguishing feature of such works is that they are normally carried out by farmers or at the expense of farmers on their own farms, with the project making available credit and perhaps arrangements for the work to be carried out. They are best illustrated by farm budgets that represent the kinds of cropping patterns and livestock enterprises to be undertaken. Farm budgets are also important to the discussion of farm income (8.3) and elsewhere in the project report. As suggested in the discussion of farm income in section 8.3, a centralized analysis is desirable; this probably should be given in an annex.

6.2.3 FARM BUILDINGS AND EQUIPMENT. This section discusses irrigation pumps, sprayers, on-farm storage facilities, tractors, livestock sheds, and a wide range of similar items that in general are made available to farmers through credit arrangements.

6.2.4 CREDIT PROGRAM. If credit is to be provided as part of an overall project, it may conveniently be discussed at this point. This discussion may include the required total amount of credit derived from aggregating farm budgets and the applicable credit terms. If the project is predominantly one to provide credit, only a discussion of the totals involved may be needed here. Detailed discussion of the credit program may be reserved for the section on credit administration (7.1) and the specialized annexes.

6.2.5 PROCESSING AND PRODUCT-MARKETING FACILITIES. Processing and marketing facilities needed under the project may be described in this section. If processing facilities are a large component of the project, this section may be limited to a general description. The detailed discussion can be concentrated, as appropriate, in the sections devoted to marketing structure (7.2), to availability of markets (8.2), and to processing industries and marketing agencies (8.4). As is the case with farm budgets and discussion of a credit agency, a separate annex with detailed accounts for processing and marketing enterprises and with a full discussion of organizational and other problems may be desirable.

6.2.6 SUPPORTING SERVICES. Special supporting services included in the project may be described here. Of particular importance is provision for extension. The number, grade, and availability of additional extension officers may be mentioned, as may their requirements for transport, office equipment, and housing. If the project includes components to train staff or farmers, the relationship of these to national facilities may be described and any facilities such as classrooms and dormitories outlined.

6.2.7 SOCIAL SERVICES. Any social services envisioned under the project should be included in the description of the detailed features. Health services and disease control may be important project activities. The particular actions anticipated should be described and quantities given if new staff or facilities are needed. If education is a project component, the new schools should be described and the number of pupils foreseen given, along with the number of teachers needed. A discussion of domestic water facilities and the number of households involved may be in order.

6.3 Project phasing and disbursement period

This section should describe in detail the phasing of the proposed project actions, including works and general facilities, farm development, processing and marketing facilities, supporting facilities, and social services. From this section are derived the justification for the phasing of expenditure and the disbursement pattern of any loan envisioned for the project. In most cases the disbursement and development periods of agricultural projects extend over three to five years, and this section should address this time horizon. Some projects, such as those involving tree crops, entail a longer phasing and disbursement period. This section might be supported by an annex containing a detailed graphic presentation such as a "critical path diagram" to indicate the sequence of project activities and which activities cannot be delayed without delaying the whole project. [For a discussion of critical path diagramming, see Mulvaney (1969).]

6.4 *Cost estimates*

The importance of accurate cost estimates cannot be overemphasized. They are a crucial element in determining the financial and economic viability of the project and also for planning its funding. The main text should give aggregate cost in a summary table; the complete cost breakdown can be given in annexes. There are many ways to group costs, but a common one is to distinguish between capital and recurrent costs. Costs should be broken down to show local and foreign exchange components. The foreign exchange component includes expenditure for both directly and indirectly imported goods and services. Costs in this section would be presented in constant financial, not economic, terms, and they would be shown at market prices. Duties and other taxes would also be shown, but these should be separately indicated, at least in the annexes. Current costs would be given as part of the financing plan (6.5.4).

6.4.1 CAPITAL COST. The headings under which capital cost is summarized and discussed in the main report preferably should correspond to the approach adopted for the physical description of the items. The estimate for civil works should be based on unit rates and quantities. If equipment for construction or operation and maintenance will be procured under the project, the cost of these should be shown separately. The cost of on-farm development works is determined by aggregation from the pattern farm budgets. Often only those items to be financed by credit, or the amount of the credit needed, will appear in this section. To aggregate from the farm budgets to the economic cost of the project, however, the full incremental cost incurred by the farmers will be needed. If land is acquired for project purposes and a cash outlay is required, this outlay should be included in the items of capital cost. But if the government provides the land free of cost, land will not be included as a project cost item; the opportunity cost of the land, however, will be allowed for in the economic analysis.

6.4.2 RECURRENT COSTS. Either in this section or in the section devoted to financing (6.5), provision will have to be made for the recurrent cost needed for project operation. Recurrent cost usually refers only to the budget for the proposed executing agency.

6.4.3 CONTINGENCIES. It is common for the cost estimates to include a physical contingency allowance, usually on the order of 10 or 15 percent. Price contingency allowances are covered in the section on financing (6.5) or in the section on the budget of the government operating agency or project authority (8.5).

6.5 *Financing*

It is important to prepare a financing plan for the project so that the government may be fully aware of the immediate and future budgetary implications of the project. The plan may be summarized in tabular form in the main text of the report, and supporting detail may be included in the annexes or in separate documents. Completion of the full financing plan may need to await completion of negotiations with outside financing agencies, but it may be possible to include in the preparation report totals of at least the most important items, with the notation that some sources of financing remain to be determined. Some of the elements of the financing plan will grow directly out of the project preparation. For example, when the analyst draws up the credit program, a decision will have to be reached about the down payments to be made by farmers and the rate at which they will be required to repay their loans. Similarly, estimating the foreign exchange component of the project tends to put a ceiling on the proportion of total cost to be met by an outside financing agency.

6.5.1 INVESTMENT COST. The amounts needed by the project each year during the investment phase (or disbursement phase, if outside financing is involved) should be tabulated by major category and broken down into domestic currency and foreign exchange. When known, the proportion of total cost to be borne from domestic sources and that to be financed from outside may be indicated.

6.5.2 TAX REVENUE. If the project will generate significant new tax revenue, as might be the case if the project will increase production of a crop on which an export tax is levied, the amount and timing of the new revenue should be detailed.

6.5.3 RECURRENT COST. A projection should be made of the recurrent cost necessary to operate the project once the investment phase and any anticipated receipt of foreign financing ends. This will indicate the continuing burden on the treasury of maintaining the project administration. This projection will need to be related to the section on the budget needs of the project executing agency (8.5) and to the policies outlined in the section on cost recovery (8.6). The net burden allowing for any increased tax revenues may be noted.

6.5.4 CURRENT COST. Since the project cost normally is stated in constant terms, the financing plan should address itself to a tabulation of the investment and recurrent cost in current terms once the project is undertaken. This will become the basis for the budget allocation as the project proceeds. Since this may involve making a politically sensitive judgment about future rates of inflation, this part of the financing plan may appropriately be dealt with in a separate memorandum addressed to the ministry of finance.

6.6 Procurement

Special requirements for procurement may be mentioned in this section. If it is contemplated that financing will be sought from an international lending agency, special procurement regulations may have to be noted.

6.7 Environmental impact

Nations are increasingly concerned about the environmental impact of proposed projects, and decisionmakers will want assurances that proper attention has been paid to environmental considerations and that any adverse ecologic effects have been minimized. If a significant environmental impact is likely, full treatment in an annex may be called for; otherwise, a short explanatory paragraph will suffice.

7. Organization and Management

In general, the part on organization and management is intended to show which entity or entities will be responsible for the various aspects of project execution and operation and how these entities will carry out their responsibilities. The discussion should demonstrate that the executing agencies have adequate powers, staffing, equipment, and finance. It should show that there are adequate arrangements for coordination between and within the administrative groups responsible for the various project activities. If there are deficiencies, the changes and improvements required should be clearly stated.

For each administrative group, this part of the report should give details of legal status, functions and powers, internal organization, staffing, and the like. If the administrative agency is not a government department, it may be desirable to give details about the legal charter and governing board, how the board is appointed, and any special provisions concerning its budget.

When there is more than one agency concerned with a project, the arrangements for coordination, joint representation on boards, joint committees, and joint use of field facilities may be described.

This part should address the ability of the senior management of an implementing agency to decide policies, approve important expenditures, and appoint the project management responsible for day-to-day operations. It should discuss the number and caliber of the project staff and whether their assignment will permit them to devote enough time to the operation of the project. The qualification and experience of the key management staff may be noted either in an annex or in a separate memorandum. The needs of the project for professional technical staff and the expected availability of such staff should be mentioned. Arrangements for recruitment and staff training should be described. Any necessary provision for assistance from expatriates should be noted and details about the qualifications of expatriates given.

Projects with special emphases will require a discussion of the organization and management requirements imposed by the nature of the particular projects. Several of these special requirements are noted in the following sections. In some instances, a detailed discussion in the annexes will be appropriate.

7.1 *Credit administration*

If credit is important in the project or if the project is predominantly an agricultural credit project, particular attention must be paid to the administrative capability and financial status of the credit agency. In the main text only a summary statement may be necessary, but in the annexes it may be desirable to go into considerable detail. Such details should include projected accounts for the credit agency and a thorough analysis of the position of the agency concerning arrears in repayment of loans and interest delinquencies. Other points to be considered are the legal charter, capitalization, powers and functions, direction, management, delegation of authority, internal organization, staffing, accountancy and control, auditing, operating policies, terms and conditions of loans, collateral requirements and their appropriateness for the group the project is intended to benefit, procedures for loan appraisal and disbursement, and the capability of the agency to operate in a timely and effective manner in the project area. Arrangements for administrative improvements and staff training should be mentioned.

7.2 *Marketing structure*

In this section the organizational arrangements, both public and private, for marketing farm production should be described and assessed. Particular attention should be paid to any rigidities or insufficiencies, and to proposals for correcting the situation if these inadequacies are relevant to the project. A separate annex discussing marketing institutions and proposals to improve them may be desirable if marketing is an important component of the project. This section should be related to that dealing with the financial effects of the project on processing industries and marketing agencies (8.4).

7.3 *Supply of inputs*

This section should discuss the responsibility and arrangements for the provision of supplies for farm production and should mention proposals, where necessary, for improved supply of such inputs. If labor availability was not discussed in the section on population and migration (5.3.2), it may be appropriate to address the question here.

7.4 *Land reform*

If the project will involve any change in land tenure or distribution, the agency responsible for such matters should be described and assessed. There should be a discussion of relevant land laws, cadastral aspects, conditions of tenure, and—in settlement projects—farm size and selection of settlers. Particular attention should be paid to the timing and implementation of land reform measures.

7.5 *Research*

If new research or additional field trials are to be needed, the arrangements and staffing should be discussed. If expatriate specialists will be needed, their qualifications and responsibilities should be outlined. Plans for staff training should be mentioned.

7.6 *Extension*

The arrangements to bring new information about production to farmers in the project area should be discussed. Special equipment and facilities should be outlined and justified unless they have been dealt with in the section on supporting services (6.2.6). Staff training, especially for field agents in the project area, should be outlined.

7.7 *Cooperatives*

If it is intended that cooperatives will be used in the project, the relevant legislation, organization, structure, and operating record of the cooperatives and the agencies responsible for encouraging or administering them should be discussed. Proposed measures for development of cooperatives in the project area, including staff training, should be described.

7.8 *Farmer organization and participation*

The responsibility for any other measures to encourage farmers' participation in the project, to establish farmers' associations, and to ensure good relations between farmers and the project administration should be discussed.

8. Production, Markets, and Financial Results

By the time the reader reaches this point in the project report, much ground will have been covered: the national setting for the project and the reasons for its selection; the project itself, including its technical aspects and costs; and the proposed manner of implementation. From here onwards, emphasis is on the financial and economic feasibility of the project. The report should show that the results of project actions will be sufficiently attractive financially to encourage enough farmers to participate. For processing industries or marketing agencies, the report should demonstrate that it will be financially viable for such firms to participate in the project and that their financial return will be sufficiently attractive.

8.1 Production

The primary benefit of an agricultural or rural development project is usually incremental output from project farms. This is generally the basis on which the project is formulated in the first place, and the physical results to be expected are illustrated in the farm models. Project actions may permit introduction of completely new and more valuable crops but more often will be directed toward increasing yields of existing crops or permitting a more intensive form of livestock production. In any case, the assumptions about yield or livestock production, both with and without the project, should be fully supported in the annex materials.

In this section, attention should be directed toward the aggregate increase in production that is expected. Account should be taken of such factors as the number and phasing of the farms included in the project and the build-up of average yields as farmers adopt the improved technology or as new plantings of tree crops approach maturity. A table showing aggregate build-up during the development period of the project may be included in the annex.

8.2 Availability of markets

This section should demonstrate that satisfactory markets exist for the product of the project. The market must be of sufficient size to absorb the production proposed for the project. If the scale of the project is large enough to exert an appreciable influence on the market, this effect will probably require fairly detailed treatment in an annex, but only the salient points need be mentioned in the main text. If an export commodity is involved, attention should be paid to such special situations as preferential treatment, long-term contracts, or quality preferences. Domestic pricing policies should be fully covered, either in the main text or in a special annex, if they are a matter of extensive debate or if significant policy changes will be required for the project. This section will also mention prices for internationally traded commodities and summarize the results of the import and export parity price calculations that are given in more detail in annex text and tables.

8.3 *Farm income*

The effects of the project on farm income are demonstrated through presentation of farm budgets such as those outlined in chapter 4. Because farm budgets are fundamental to any agricultural or rural development project analysis and will also have been referred to in connection with on-farm investment (6.2.2) and the topics of other sections, it is important to present a fully developed analysis in the project report. This probably can be most conveniently done in one annex, which should include farm budgets that indicate the inflow and outflow for each major farm model anticipated in the project, outline financing needs, and project the incremental net benefit the farm family may expect.

8.4 *Processing industries and marketing agencies*

A discussion of the financial effects of the project on processing industries and marketing agencies may be in order if the project contains such components. A summary in the main text may suffice, but detailed projections of balance sheets, income statements, sources-and-uses-of-funds statements, and the incremental cash flow should be included in appropriate annex material along the lines discussed in chapter 5.

8.5 *Government agencies or project authorities*

In some project reports, especially if the project is to be administered by a largely self-supporting project authority, an analysis of finances from the standpoint of the administering agency may be in order. This section could include expected inflows and outflows of the project authority and the government budget amounts required to support the project. It should be related to the cost recovery section below (8.6). Annex materials along the lines suggested in chapter 6 may be included. Care should be taken to avoid duplication with the section on financing (6.5). In some reports, it may be desirable to centralize the financing plan here and simply to cross-reference it in the section on financing. In any case, if much detail is to be included it may conveniently be gathered into an annex to which both sections can refer.

8.6 *Cost recovery*

This may be an appropriate point in the report to mention any arrangements made to recover part of the cost of the project from beneficiaries. (Usually this section will not address recovery of loans; this matter should be discussed in the sections bearing on credit.) Appropriate cross-references may be made to the section on financing (6.5). In most cases, farmers will be called on to share the cost of the initial investment in on-farm works under the financing plan of the project. The question of cost recovery frequently arises in irrigation projects, in which there may be a problem about the extent to which farmers should bear the cost of operation and maintenance. This may involve questions of government policy about income distribution, or even foodgrain prices, and of financial arrangements in other irrigation projects.

9. Benefits and Justification

This is a crucial part of the project report in which all data discussed in previous parts are brought together and an assessment made—all things considered—about whether to proceed with the project.

9.1 Social benefit

A project usually will have benefits beyond those that are simply financial and economic. A general section may be devoted to the effects of the project on food production, import substitution, foreign exchange earnings, and the like. If the project is of interest mainly because of its social benefit, such as its beneficial effect on the incomes of the poorest farmers, this section takes on added importance, and separate sections devoted to one or another significant social aspect may be in order, as noted below. Because these topics will have been discussed in earlier sections, care should be taken to minimize duplication, and only a brief summary may be needed.

9.1.1 INCOME DISTRIBUTION. The extent to which the income of the poorest sector of the rural population is improved as a result of the project may be shown. Reference must be made to the relative improvement in comparison with other groups in the country.

9.1.2 EMPLOYMENT. The extent to which the project reduces underemployment and unemployment may be assessed. This may be quantified in terms of work years created by the project, with distinction made between permanent employment and employment during the investment or construction phase. The number of jobs created might be compared with the expected increase in the labor force of the project area.

9.1.3 ACCESS TO LAND. If the project includes a land settlement or land reform element, the distribution of land rights with and without the project should be demonstrated.

9.1.4 INTERNAL MIGRATION. In countries where rural-urban migration is a serious problem, it may be useful to note the possible effect of the project on rural-urban migration. Quantification will probably prove difficult.

9.1.5 NUTRITION AND HEALTH. If the project is located in an area where serious nutrition or health problems exist, or if the project is directed toward groups with nutrition and health deficiencies, the expected effects of the project on these problems might be mentioned. In some cases, the effect on nutrition may be quantified in the daily intake of calories or protein that is expected as a result of the project.

9.1.6 OTHER INDICATORS OF THE QUALITY OF LIFE. Some projects may have a significant effect on the quality of rural life through improvements in access to domestic water supplies, electricity, schools, and the like. These may be mentioned and the quantities of the new amenities noted.

9.2 Economic benefit

Finally, the economic desirability of the project should be assessed. Economic costs and benefits are valued along the lines discussed in chapter 7, aggregated as discussed in chapter 8, and evaluated using one or more of the measures of project worth as discussed in chapter 9. An integral part of this section will be to demonstrate through sensitivity analysis, as discussed in chapter 10, the effects of different assumptions about efficiency and prices on the project's wealth-generating potential.

10. Outstanding Issues

Almost every project will have outstanding issues that must be resolved after the preparation report is presented. These considerations may relate to project rationale, policy issues affecting the project, management and other staffing issues, and financing arrangements. The most important of these should be set forth explicitly so that they are drawn forcefully to the attention of readers who must take the necessary actions.

11. Annexes

The annexes to the preparation report contain the detailed support for the project. The main text is written with the general reader in mind, but the annexes will generally be examined in detail primarily by specialists and should be written with the specialist in mind. A large proportion of the annex materials probably will be in the form of tables, maps, drawings, charts, diagrams, and photographs. The annexes will vary widely according to the kind and complexity of the project. They usually are presented in the order in which they are referred to in the main text. Often they are published in a separate volume and reproduced in only the number of copies needed to supply the various specialists and agencies directly concerned with project decisions. Among other topics, annexes may include an amplification of the part on the background of the project

(3); surveys, investigation, laboratory results, and data analyses and interpretations to support the part on the project area (5); studies, designs, estimates, and schedules to support the part on the project (6); detailed proposals to support the part on organization and management (7); farm budgets, projected enterprise accounts, market assessments, and other information to support the part on production, markets, and financial results (8); and analytical material, including shadow prices and assumptions about the foreign exchange premium, to support the part on benefits and justification (9).

Appendix B

Three-decimal Discounting Tables

To CALCULATE most discounted measures of project worth the three-decimal discounting tables reproduced (from Gittinger 1973) at the end of this appendix are sufficient. In general, they will permit estimations to three significant digits for net present worth, to the nearest whole percentage point for internal rate of return, and to a hundredth of a ratio point for benefit-cost and net benefit-investment ratios—as much precision as the underlying data will justify in agricultural projects (see the section on "How Far to Carry Out Computations of Discounted Measures" in chapter 9).

There are instances in which the intervals between percentage points in these tables will not permit computation of the internal rate of return to the nearest percentage point (see the section on "Computing the Internal Rate of Return" in chapter 9). There are also cases in which the opportunity cost of capital to be used for computing net present worth, the benefit-cost ratio, or the net benefit-investment ratio is not given in these tables. In these instances resort will have to be made to more detailed tables, or the factors will have to be calculated directly.

A number of suitable, more detailed discounting tables are available. [Gittinger (1973) contains such a set.] The discount factor, the present worth of an annuity factor, and the capital recovery factor can be calcu-

Facing page: Harvesting dates in Tunisia.

431

lated on any inexpensive calculator with memory and repeat features, although the computation can become a bit repetitive. The method is discussed in the last section of chapter 10.

When a somewhat more complex calculator with capability to compute powers is available, the standard formulas below may be used to obtain directly the factors most commonly used in project analysis. Each formula assumes an interest rate of i per period and a term of n periods. P is the present worth, or the amount at the present time, t_0. F is the future worth, or the amount in the future at the end of the nth period. A is the annuity, or the level payment, to be made at the end of each of n periods.

Compounding Factor for 1

The factor is:

$$(1 + i)^n.$$

It is used to calculate the future worth (F) of a present amount (P) at the end of the nth period at the interest rate of i. The formula is:

$$F = P(1 + i)^n.$$

Compounding Factor for 1 per Annum

The factor is:

$$\frac{(1 + i)^n - 1}{i}.$$

It is used to calculate the future accumulated value (F) at the end of the nth period at the interest rate of i, if a sequence of equal payments (the amount of each payment being A) will be made at the end of each of the n periods. The formula is:

$$F = A \frac{(1 + i)^n - 1}{i}.$$

Sinking Fund Factor

The factor is:

$$\frac{i}{(1 + i)^n - 1}.$$

It is used to calculate the amount of each equal payment (A) to be made at the end of each of n periods to accumulate to a given future worth (F) at the end of the nth period at the interest rate of i. The formula is:

$$A = F \frac{i}{(1 + i)^n - 1}.$$

Note that the sinking fund factor is the reciprocal of the compounding factor for 1 per year.

Discount Factor

The factor is:

$$\frac{1}{(1 + i)^n}.$$

It is used to calculate the present worth (P) of a future value (F) at the end of the nth period at the interest rate of i. The formula is:

$$P = F \frac{1}{(1 + i)^n}.$$

Present Worth of an Annuity Factor

The factor is:

$$\frac{(1 + i)^n - 1}{i(1 + i)^n}.$$

It is used to calculate the present worth (P) of a sequence of level payments (the amount of each payment being A) to be made at the end of each of n periods at the interest rate of i. The formula is:

$$P = A \frac{(1 + i)^n - 1}{i(1 + i)^n}.$$

Capital Recovery Factor

The factor is:

$$\frac{i(1 + i)^n}{(1 + i)^n - 1}.$$

It is used to calculate the amount of each level payment (A) to be made at the end of each of n periods to recover the present amount (P) at the end of the nth period at the interest rate of i. The formula is:

$$A = P \frac{i(1 + i)^n}{(1 + i)^n - 1}.$$

Note that the capital recovery factor is the reciprocal of the present worth of an annuity factor.

COMPOUNDING AND DISCOUNTING TABLES

6. Three-decimal Table for Discount Factor, Various Rates

DISCOUNT FACTOR—How much 1 at a future date is worth today.

Year	1%	3%	5%	6%	8%	10%	12%	14%	15%	16%	18%	20%	22%	24%	25%	26%	28%	30%	35%	40%	45%	50%	Year
1	.990	.971	.952	.943	.926	.909	.893	.877	.870	.862	.847	.833	.820	.806	.800	.794	.781	.769	.741	.714	.690	.667	1
2	.980	.943	.907	.890	.857	.826	.797	.769	.756	.743	.718	.694	.672	.650	.640	.630	.610	.592	.549	.510	.476	.444	2
3	.971	.915	.864	.840	.794	.751	.712	.675	.658	.641	.609	.579	.551	.524	.512	.500	.477	.455	.406	.364	.328	.296	3
4	.961	.888	.823	.792	.735	.683	.636	.592	.572	.552	.516	.482	.451	.423	.410	.397	.373	.350	.301	.260	.226	.198	4
5	.951	.863	.784	.747	.681	.621	.567	.519	.497	.476	.437	.402	.370	.341	.328	.315	.291	.269	.223	.186	.156	.132	5
6	.942	.837	.746	.705	.630	.564	.507	.456	.432	.410	.370	.335	.303	.275	.262	.250	.227	.207	.165	.133	.108	.088	6
7	.933	.813	.711	.665	.583	.513	.452	.400	.376	.354	.314	.279	.249	.222	.210	.198	.178	.159	.122	.095	.074	.059	7
8	.923	.789	.677	.627	.540	.467	.404	.351	.327	.305	.266	.233	.204	.179	.168	.157	.139	.123	.091	.068	.051	.039	8
9	.914	.766	.645	.592	.500	.424	.361	.308	.284	.263	.225	.194	.167	.144	.134	.125	.108	.094	.067	.048	.035	.026	9
10	.905	.744	.614	.558	.463	.386	.322	.270	.247	.227	.191	.162	.137	.116	.107	.099	.085	.073	.050	.035	.024	.017	10
11	.896	.722	.585	.527	.429	.350	.287	.237	.215	.195	.162	.135	.112	.094	.086	.079	.066	.056	.037	.025	.017	.012	11
12	.887	.701	.557	.497	.397	.319	.257	.208	.187	.168	.137	.112	.092	.076	.069	.062	.052	.043	.027	.018	.012	.008	12
13	.879	.681	.530	.469	.368	.290	.229	.182	.163	.145	.116	.093	.075	.061	.055	.050	.040	.033	.020	.013	.008	.005	13
14	.870	.661	.505	.442	.340	.263	.205	.160	.141	.125	.099	.078	.062	.049	.044	.039	.032	.025	.015	.009	.006	.003	14
15	.861	.642	.481	.417	.315	.239	.183	.140	.123	.108	.084	.065	.051	.040	.035	.031	.025	.020	.011	.006	.004	.002	15
16	.853	.623	.458	.394	.292	.218	.163	.123	.107	.093	.071	.054	.042	.032	.028	.025	.019	.015	.008	.005	.003	.002	16
17	.844	.605	.436	.371	.270	.198	.146	.108	.093	.080	.060	.045	.034	.026	.023	.020	.015	.012	.006	.003	.002	.001	17
18	.836	.587	.416	.350	.250	.180	.130	.095	.081	.069	.051	.038	.028	.021	.018	.016	.012	.009	.005	.002	.001	.001	18
19	.828	.570	.396	.331	.232	.164	.116	.083	.070	.060	.043	.031	.023	.017	.014	.012	.009	.007	.003	.002	.001	.000	19
20	.820	.554	.377	.312	.215	.149	.104	.073	.061	.051	.037	.026	.019	.014	.012	.010	.007	.005	.002	.001	.001	.000	20
21	.811	.538	.359	.294	.199	.135	.093	.064	.053	.044	.031	.022	.015	.011	.009	.008	.006	.004	.002	.001	.000	.000	21
22	.803	.522	.342	.278	.184	.123	.083	.056	.046	.038	.026	.018	.013	.009	.007	.006	.004	.003	.001	.001	.000	.000	22
23	.795	.507	.326	.262	.170	.112	.074	.049	.040	.033	.022	.015	.010	.007	.006	.005	.003	.002	.001	.000	.000	.000	23
24	.788	.492	.310	.247	.158	.102	.066	.043	.035	.028	.019	.013	.008	.006	.005	.004	.003	.002	.001	.000	.000	.000	24
25	.780	.478	.295	.233	.146	.092	.059	.038	.030	.024	.016	.010	.007	.005	.004	.003	.002	.001	.001	.000	.000	.000	25
26	.772	.464	.281	.220	.135	.084	.053	.033	.026	.021	.014	.009	.006	.004	.003	.002	.002	.001	.000	.000	.000	.000	26
27	.764	.450	.268	.207	.125	.076	.047	.029	.023	.018	.011	.007	.005	.003	.002	.002	.001	.001	.000	.000	.000	.000	27
28	.757	.437	.255	.196	.116	.069	.042	.026	.020	.016	.010	.006	.004	.002	.002	.002	.001	.001	.000	.000	.000	.000	28
29	.749	.424	.243	.185	.107	.063	.037	.022	.017	.014	.008	.005	.003	.002	.002	.001	.001	.000	.000	.000	.000	.000	29
30	.742	.412	.231	.174	.099	.057	.033	.020	.015	.012	.007	.004	.003	.002	.001	.001	.001	.000	.000	.000	.000	.000	30
35	.706	.355	.181	.130	.068	.036	.019	.010	.008	.006	.003	.002	.001	.001	.000	.000	.000	.000	.000	.000	.000	.000	35
40	.672	.307	.142	.097	.046	.022	.011	.005	.004	.003	.001	.001	.000	.000	.000	.000	.000	.000	.000	.000	.000	.000	40
45	.639	.264	.111	.073	.031	.014	.006	.003	.002	.001	.001	.000	.000	.000	.000	.000	.000	.000	.000	.000	.000	.000	45
50	.608	.228	.087	.054	.021	.009	.003	.001	.001	.001	.000	.000	.000	.000	.000	.000	.000	.000	.000	.000	.000	.000	50

Source: Gittinger (1973, pp. 102–03).

COMPOUNDING AND DISCOUNTING TABLES

7. Three-decimal Table for Present Worth of an Annuity Factor, Various Rates

PRESENT WORTH OF AN ANNUITY FACTOR—
How much 1 received or paid annually for X years is worth today.

Year	1%	3%	5%	6%	8%	10%	12%	14%	15%	16%	18%	20%	22%	24%	25%	26%	28%	30%	35%	40%	45%	50%	Year
1	.990	.971	.952	.943	.926	.909	.893	.877	.870	.862	.847	.833	.820	.806	.800	.794	.781	.769	.741	.714	.690	.667	1
2	1.970	1.913	1.859	1.833	1.783	1.736	1.690	1.647	1.626	1.605	1.566	1.528	1.492	1.457	1.440	1.424	1.392	1.361	1.289	1.224	1.165	1.111	2
3	2.941	2.829	2.723	2.673	2.577	2.487	2.402	2.322	2.283	2.246	2.174	2.106	2.042	1.981	1.952	1.923	1.868	1.816	1.696	1.589	1.493	1.407	3
4	3.902	3.717	3.546	3.465	3.312	3.170	3.037	2.914	2.855	2.798	2.690	2.589	2.494	2.404	2.362	2.320	2.241	2.166	1.997	1.849	1.720	1.605	4
5	4.853	4.580	4.329	4.212	3.993	3.791	3.605	3.433	3.352	3.274	3.127	2.991	2.864	2.745	2.689	2.635	2.532	2.436	2.220	2.035	1.876	1.737	5
6	5.795	5.417	5.076	4.917	4.623	4.355	4.111	3.889	3.784	3.685	3.498	3.326	3.167	3.020	2.951	2.885	2.759	2.643	2.385	2.168	1.983	1.824	6
7	6.728	6.230	5.786	5.582	5.206	4.868	4.564	4.288	4.160	4.039	3.812	3.605	3.416	3.242	3.161	3.083	2.937	2.802	2.508	2.263	2.057	1.883	7
8	7.652	7.020	6.463	6.210	5.747	5.335	4.968	4.639	4.487	4.344	4.078	3.837	3.619	3.421	3.329	3.241	3.076	2.925	2.598	2.331	2.108	1.922	8
9	8.566	7.786	7.108	6.802	6.247	5.759	5.328	4.946	4.772	4.607	4.303	4.031	3.786	3.566	3.463	3.366	3.184	3.019	2.665	2.379	2.144	1.948	9
10	9.471	8.530	7.722	7.360	6.710	6.145	5.650	5.216	5.019	4.833	4.494	4.192	3.923	3.682	3.571	3.465	3.269	3.092	2.715	2.414	2.168	1.965	10
11	10.368	9.253	8.306	7.887	7.139	6.495	5.938	5.453	5.234	5.029	4.656	4.327	4.035	3.776	3.656	3.543	3.335	3.147	2.752	2.438	2.185	1.977	11
12	11.255	9.954	8.863	8.384	7.536	6.814	6.194	5.660	5.421	5.197	4.793	4.439	4.127	3.851	3.725	3.606	3.387	3.190	2.779	2.456	2.196	1.985	12
13	12.134	10.635	9.394	8.853	7.904	7.103	6.424	5.842	5.583	5.342	4.910	4.533	4.203	3.912	3.780	3.656	3.427	3.223	2.799	2.469	2.204	1.990	13
14	13.004	11.296	9.899	9.295	8.244	7.367	6.628	6.002	5.724	5.468	5.008	4.611	4.265	3.962	3.824	3.695	3.459	3.249	2.814	2.478	2.210	1.993	14
15	13.865	11.938	10.380	9.712	8.559	7.606	6.811	6.142	5.847	5.575	5.092	4.675	4.315	4.001	3.859	3.726	3.483	3.268	2.825	2.484	2.214	1.995	15
16	14.718	12.561	10.838	10.106	8.851	7.824	6.974	6.265	5.954	5.668	5.162	4.730	4.357	4.033	3.887	3.751	3.503	3.283	2.834	2.489	2.216	1.997	16
17	15.562	13.166	11.274	10.477	9.122	8.022	7.120	6.373	6.047	5.749	5.222	4.775	4.391	4.059	3.910	3.771	3.518	3.295	2.840	2.492	2.218	1.998	17
18	16.398	13.754	11.690	10.828	9.372	8.201	7.250	6.467	6.128	5.818	5.273	4.812	4.419	4.080	3.928	3.786	3.529	3.304	2.844	2.494	2.219	1.999	18
19	17.226	14.324	12.085	11.158	9.604	8.365	7.366	6.550	6.198	5.877	5.316	4.843	4.442	4.097	3.942	3.799	3.539	3.311	2.848	2.496	2.220	1.999	19
20	18.046	14.877	12.462	11.470	9.818	8.514	7.469	6.623	6.259	5.929	5.353	4.870	4.460	4.110	3.954	3.808	3.546	3.316	2.850	2.497	2.221	1.999	20
21	18.857	15.415	12.821	11.764	10.017	8.649	7.562	6.687	6.312	5.973	5.384	4.891	4.476	4.121	3.963	3.816	3.551	3.320	2.852	2.498	2.221	2.000	21
22	19.660	15.937	13.163	12.042	10.201	8.772	7.645	6.743	6.359	6.011	5.410	4.909	4.488	4.130	3.970	3.822	3.556	3.323	2.853	2.498	2.222	2.000	22
23	20.456	16.444	13.489	12.303	10.371	8.883	7.718	6.792	6.399	6.044	5.432	4.925	4.499	4.137	3.976	3.827	3.559	3.325	2.854	2.499	2.222	2.000	23
24	21.243	16.936	13.799	12.550	10.529	8.985	7.784	6.835	6.434	6.073	5.451	4.937	4.507	4.143	3.981	3.831	3.562	3.327	2.855	2.499	2.222	2.000	24
25	22.023	17.413	14.094	12.783	10.675	9.077	7.843	6.873	6.464	6.097	5.467	4.948	4.514	4.147	3.985	3.834	3.564	3.329	2.856	2.499	2.222	2.000	25
26	22.795	17.877	14.375	13.003	10.810	9.161	7.896	6.906	6.491	6.118	5.480	4.956	4.520	4.151	3.988	3.837	3.566	3.330	2.856	2.500	2.222	2.000	26
27	23.560	18.327	14.643	13.211	10.935	9.237	7.943	6.935	6.514	6.136	5.492	4.964	4.524	4.154	3.990	3.839	3.567	3.331	2.856	2.500	2.222	2.000	27
28	24.316	18.764	14.898	13.406	11.051	9.307	7.984	6.961	6.534	6.152	5.502	4.970	4.528	4.157	3.992	3.840	3.568	3.331	2.857	2.500	2.222	2.000	28
29	25.066	19.188	15.141	13.591	11.158	9.370	8.022	6.983	6.551	6.166	5.510	4.975	4.531	4.159	3.994	3.841	3.569	3.332	2.857	2.500	2.222	2.000	29
30	25.808	19.600	15.372	13.765	11.258	9.427	8.055	7.003	6.566	6.177	5.517	4.979	4.534	4.160	3.995	3.842	3.569	3.332	2.857	2.500	2.222	2.000	30
35	29.409	21.487	16.374	14.498	11.655	9.644	8.176	7.070	6.617	6.215	5.539	4.992	4.541	4.164	3.998	3.845	3.571	3.333	2.857	2.500	2.222	2.000	35
40	32.835	23.115	17.159	15.046	11.925	9.779	8.244	7.105	6.642	6.233	5.548	4.997	4.544	4.166	3.999	3.846	3.571	3.333	2.857	2.500	2.222	2.000	40
45	36.095	24.519	17.774	15.456	12.108	9.863	8.283	7.123	6.654	6.242	5.552	4.999	4.545	4.166	4.000	3.846	3.571	3.333	2.857	2.500	2.222	2.000	45
50	39.196	25.730	18.256	15.762	12.233	9.915	8.304	7.133	6.661	6.246	5.554	4.999	4.545	4.167	4.000	3.846	3.571	3.333	2.857	2.500	2.222	2.000	50

Source: Gittinger (1973, pp. 104–05).

Appendix C

Sources of Institutional Assistance for Project Preparation

For SPECIALIZED ASSISTANCE in preparing complex agricultural projects, many governments may wish to turn to one of the bilateral or multilateral international aid agencies or to engage the services of commercial consultants. This assistance should be discussed directly with the agencies, governments, or consultants concerned.

Bilateral Assistance

Some governments may have a special interest in assisting developing countries to prepare particular projects. Information about bilateral assistance of this kind may be obtained from the embassy or equivalent office of the prospective donor country.

Multilateral Assistance

In addition to assistance agreed on by two governments, a government can enter into arrangements for assistance in preparing projects with a variety of international agencies.

Facing page: Cultivating sweet potatoes in Jamaica.

European Community

The European Community through the European Development Fund provides financial aid and technical assistance to sixty-one developing countries that are signatories to the Lome Convention and to some twenty-seven other countries with which it has special agreements. It is the task of the recipient country to prepare projects intended for assistance from the Community, but Community funds may be used to finance studies of, or technical assistance for, project preparation. More information about assistance for preparing projects may be obtained from the European Community delegation in Lome Convention countries and in seven North African and Middle Eastern countries, or from the Directorate General for Development of the Commission of the European Communities in Brussels. The Commission has prepared two documents intended as guides, *Appraisal of Productive Projects in Agriculture: Economic Analysis and Rate of Return* (1980*a*) and the *Manual for Preparing and Appraising Project Dossiers* (1980*b*).

United Nations Development Programme

Within the United Nations system, the principal source of technical assistance, including help for project preparation, is the United Nations Development Programme (UNDP). The UNDP finances preinvestment activities, including surveys of physical resources and of better ways to use them; analyses of national economic sectors, including agriculture, as a basis for formulating coordinated investment programs or for defining priorities; feasibility studies of investment projects; applied research; manpower training; technical education; and the like.

As a rule, the UNDP does not itself carry out the preinvestment activities it finances. Instead, it turns to executing agencies—the United Nations Office of Technical Cooperation, the specialized agencies of the United Nations, the World Bank, regional development banks, and occasionally other institutions. In agriculture, the Food and Agriculture Organization (FAO) normally has been the executing agency. The World Bank has on occasion taken this responsibility, generally in such cases as credit projects for which the World Bank has special experience to offer.

Each developing country that wishes to take advantage of UNDP assistance works out an agreed "Country Programme" that identifies the sectors or activities for which assistance will be used and estimates the amounts needed. This program can be modified by the country in consultation with the UNDP as new information becomes available about the feasibility, priority, content, timing, and required resources for each activity. Most activities undertaken with UNDP assistance require government contributions, either in kind or in local currency.

Once it is agreed that assistance for preparing a particular project will be included in the country program, a tripartite agreement is drawn up between the country receiving assistance, the UNDP, and the executing agency. This specifies the arrangements for carrying out the activity, details of the reports to be prepared, provision for suspension and termination, and details of the financial contributions provided by the UNDP and the government concerned.

More information about assistance for preparing particular projects may be obtained from the UNDP resident representative stationed in most developing countries. The representative can also make available copies of many UNDP preinvestment and feasibility studies that provide examples for those considering similar activities.

Food and Agriculture Organization–development bank cooperative programs

The FAO has established an Investment Centre staffed by a team of multidisciplinary experts who specialize in the formulation of investment projects. The center helps to identify and prepare agricultural projects in close cooperation with the World Bank, the Inter-American Development Bank, the Asian Development Bank, the African Development Bank, the International Fund for Agricultural Development, and several Arab funds. It also has cooperative programs with national banks and financing institutions in developing countries under the FAO/Bankers Programme.

The Investment Centre is especially useful for bringing to bear a comparative knowledge of similar projects in different countries under roughly comparable conditions and for its familiarity with the special requirements of lending institutions. Usually the Investment Centre helps with project identification and preparation in two distinct stages. The first is a preliminary view of the possible project to gain an idea immediately of what activities should or should not be included, to assess the information that is available or would have to be obtained to prepare a sound analysis, to gain an idea of the administrative and organizational problems, and to be sure a project has appropriate priority within the overall development program of the country. An identification mission generally remains in the country about three weeks. If a government then wishes further assistance, the Centre may provide specialists to help with project preparation. At this stage the technicians assist in preparing detailed critical analyses of the technical, financial, and economic data and assumptions. The Centre's specialists help marshall the available data for the financial and economic analysis and for preparing the project for presentation to the financing agency. The time needed for project preparation, of course, is dependent upon the complexity of the project, and the Centre may send several missions to a country in connection with the project preparation, particularly if there are serious data gaps.

The simplest way for a country to obtain assistance under these FAO-bank cooperative programs is to make direct application to the FAO or to the appropriate bank. This may be done either formally to the Director

General of the FAO through the FAO representative in the country, or informally to the director of the FAO Investment Centre directly or through an FAO or bank staff member. The application may be made by letter or by personal contact at convenient opportunities such as the visit of a staff member of the appropriate agency to the country, bank annual meetings, FAO conferences, and the like. There is no fixed timetable for considering and approving applications for assistance, although in the nature of the activity there is generally a considerable lag between the first letter or conversation and the time the project is actually ready for work to begin. It is therefore important to make contacts early and to provide as much background information as possible on the project proposed.

In the case of FAO-bank cooperative programs, the major portion of the cost is usually borne by the international agencies, but in some instances the government involved may be asked to provide local transport and similar services.

World Bank

Under certain circumstances, World Bank assistance may be available to help with project identification and preparation.

World Bank economic missions, sector survey missions, operational missions, and resident missions may bring to a government's attention projects that seem to offer prospects for good returns. Project supervision missions by Bank staff members in the course of work on particular projects may identify later stages of ongoing projects or similar projects for possible investment.

Once potential projects have been identified, the World Bank in some instances is able to assist in preparation. (World Bank assistance of any form in preparing a project does not, however, constitute a commitment of Bank financing for the resulting project.) The Bank may advise on the planning of feasibility studies—specifying the information that has to be gathered (often by providing questionnaires), defining the studies needed to obtain this information, establishing the relative priority and emphasis to be given to different aspects of the studies, and advising about how these studies can best be organized and presented and, when appropriate, financed. In the later stages of preparation, the Bank may also help ensure that the feasibility study is progressing along the right lines and that it will cover the necessary aspects. This assistance may range from occasional visits by Bank staff to the formal participation of Bank staff in steering committees.

Sometimes the World Bank also finances project preparation studies undertaken either by government agencies or by commercial consultants. World Bank financing for a project may include funds for preparing subsequent phases or additional related projects. In a few cases when a large number of potential projects needed study and preparatory work, a separate loan for technical assistance has been extended.

Member countries of the World Bank can occasionally make use of the World Bank's Project Preparation Facility to finance preparation of projects expected to be presented for Bank financing. This assistance is only extended when other alternatives for financing the preparation either are not available or require excessive administrative effort. Funds advanced under this arrangement are repaid from loan or grant proceeds if a loan or grant is made or over a five-year period if the project is not financed by the World Bank. The facility is usually available only to poor countries that could not reasonably be expected to finance the activities from their own resources pending reimbursement out of an eventual loan or grant. The funds may be used to provide additional support for the group responsible for preparing the project or to finance gaps in the project preparation that must be filled before the project can be appraised by the Bank. Examples of the kinds of omission that these funds could be used to rectify include inadequate economic analysis, incomplete market studies, omission of a monitoring system, the need for more complete information about land tenure in the project area, or unforeseen environmental implications of the project that require further study.

Consultants

Many governments will want to engage either individual consultants or consulting firms to assist with project preparation. Sometimes assistance will be sought for only a particular aspect of project preparation, other times for the entire preparation. The United Nations Industrial Development Organization (UNIDO) has prepared an extremely useful *Manual on the Use of Consultants in Developing Countries* (1972b). This contains many helpful suggestions about how to select, engage, and use consultants, especially consulting firms. The World Bank (1981c) has prepared a pamphlet that outlines its own approach to the use of consultants and the use of consultants by governments in connection with Bank-financed projects, as has the Inter-American Development Bank (1981).

There are many reasons why governments may wish to turn to consultants. Many government agencies are already fully occupied and simply do not have the time to devote to proper project preparation. External help can be brought in that can devote its full attention to preparing the project within a specified time. Required skills or specialized know-how may not be available in the country. A problem may arise that calls for the attention of specialists, but it is not expected to repeat itself—hence, it is not worth developing local expertise in the area. Even when the overall project preparation is to be carried out by a government agency, there may be special technical assessments for which outside expertise is desirable—an analysis of soils for an irrigation project, a market analysis for a specialty crop grown for export, or chemical tests on tree species that might be planted for pulpwood. Consultants may be able to use a new or more up-to-date approach in solving problems. They may also be used to provide an outside, impartial view or may be asked for an independent second opinion.

Consultants may be sought from a variety of sources. Many times an individual or a particular firm will have done similar work previously, and a government may wish to engage the services again. Local consultants or consulting firms may already be well known. Individual consultants may come from local universities. The UNIDO *Manual on the Use of Consultants* has a list of professional consulting associations that will make suggestions about possible consultants. Embassies often have lists available of consultants in their countries. The World Bank maintains lists of individuals and firms that have expressed an interest in consulting, but does not keep a list of "approved" consultants. The Bank's general files on consulting firms are available to visiting representatives from Bank borrowers or member governments who need to review and assess the experience and qualifications of consulting firms they are considering for projects.

An increasing number of national consulting firms of suitable competence exist in developing countries. More might grow if more governments were to adopt a conscious policy to encourage them and to assure them an opportunity to compete for suitable work. When national consulting firms are used instead of government agencies, the advantages of having a group of people who can focus on project preparation without the pressures of day-to-day routine administration are realized. At the same time, the specialized skills that such consultants gain in the course of their work remain in the country and can be available again in the future. In cases where a national consulting firm does not have the full range of expertise needed to prepare a project, the national firm can often draw upon a foreign associate for particular specialized skills and use its own resources for less esoteric work. Such links between local and foreign firms are increasingly common in the consulting field. Retaining overall control in local hands means that local conditions can be fully considered while foreign expertise is utilized. Sometimes, however, national firms simply will not have enough of the skills needed to prepare certain kinds of projects, and a government will have to turn to an international consulting firm. When this happens, the terms of reference for the foreign consultant may provide for an association with a local firm and include a planned training program. Through their association with the foreign consulting firm, the national consultants can increase their expertise. Then, as similar projects are prepared in the future, the involvement of the foreign firm can decrease until the national firm is able to undertake these kinds of consulting assignments entirely on its own.

A frequent concern about the use of consultants is the cost. Often the fees of consultants, especially those from abroad, seem very high compared with government salary scales in the country. One way to reduce the cost of consulting services may be to rely more on qualified local consultants. In the final analysis, however, if an individual consultant or a consulting firm can prepare a sizable project well, even what seems a rather high consulting fee may not be unreasonable. Of course, care must be taken to ensure that any consulting fees asked are reasonable given the complexity of the project and the amounts charged for similar work in other instances. Nonetheless, as the UNIDO *Manual on the Use of Consultants* states, "a good job is well worth the cost, and a poor one is a loss, regardless of price" (1972*b*, p. 19). The cost of consulting services to prepare an agricultural project seldom amounts to more than 5 to 10 percent of the project cost. As the UNIDO *Manual* notes, a saving of, say, 10 percent on consulting fees means no more than a saving of 1 percent on the project cost. But poor consulting services and bad engineering can lead to very substantial cost overruns (1972*b*, ibid.).

Bibliography

Adler, Hans A. 1971. *Economic Appraisal of Transport Projects: A Manual with Case Studies.* Bloomington: Indiana University Press.

An introductory manual focusing on transport projects that include rural roads. Includes case examples.

Austin, James E. 1981. *Agroindustrial Project Analysis.* Baltimore, Md.: Johns Hopkins University Press.

A very useful discussion of the elements of formulating projects for industries that use agricultural raw materials. The emphasis is more on the project design than on narrow methodological considerations.

Bacha, Edmar, and Lance Taylor. 1972. "Foreign Exchange Shadow Prices: A Critical Review of Current Theories." In *Benefit Cost Analysis 1971*, edited by Arnold C. Harberger and others, pp. 29–59. Chicago: Aldine-Atherton.

A comprehensive, formal review of the theory of foreign exchange shadow prices.

Bannock, G., R. E. Baxter, and R. Rees. 1972. *The Penguin Dictionary of Economics.* Harmondsworth, U.K.: Penguin Books.

A standard reference for economic terms.

Barnum, Howard N., and Lyn Squire. 1979. *A Model of an Agricultural Household: Theory and Evidence.* Baltimore, Md.: Johns Hopkins University Press.

Facing page: Carrying rice straw from the field in Bangladesh.

Discusses in considerable detail the economics of rural labor supply in a developing country.

Baum, Warren C. 1978. "The Project Cycle." *Finance and Development*, vol. 15, no. 4 (December), pp. 10–17. Also available in pamphlet form (1982) from the World Bank.

An updated version of an earlier article that established "project cycle" as a concept in development economics.

Benjamin, McDonald P. 1981. *The Making of an Agricultural Project: Principles and Case Studies*. London: Longman.

Traces the process of identifying and preparing an agricultural project.

Bergmann, Hellmuth, and Jean-Marc Boussard. 1976. *Guide to the Economic Evaluation of Irrigation Projects*. Rev. version. Paris: Organisation for Economic Co-operation and Development (OECD).

Focusing entirely on irrigation projects, this work devotes considerable attention to the data needed for project evaluation. The analytical method advanced is somewhat different from, but is not incompatible with, that outlined in this book. An interesting set of blank tables for presenting the results of the analysis is included. Well worthwhile for those working on irrigation investments.

Bierman, Harold, Jr., and Seymour Smidt. 1980. *The Capital Budgeting Decision*. 5th ed. New York: Macmillan.

Good introductory text on investment analysis; intended more for engineering and industrial than for agricultural applications.

Bigg, W. W., and R. E. G. Perrins. 1971. *Spicer and Pegler's Bookkeeping and Accounting*. 17th rev. ed. London: English Language Book Society and H.F.L. (Publishers) Ltd.

A standard, university-level introductory text on accounting.

Brown, David W., William F. Litwiller, and Frank Fender. 1974. *Manual for Agricultural Capital Project Analysis*. Washington, D.C.: U.S. Department of Agriculture, Economic Research Service.

Traces the steps in formulating and presenting an agricultural project. Complementary to this book.

Brown, Maxwell L. 1979. *Farm Budgets: From Farm Income Analysis to Agricultural Project Analysis*. Baltimore, Md.: Johns Hopkins University Press.

A basic text discussing in detail preparation of farm budgets for use in agricultural project analyses, including concepts of farm income, partial budgets, farm models, livestock projections, and aggregation.

Bruce, Colin M. F. 1976. *Social Cost-Benefit Analysis: A Guide for Country and Project Economists to the Derivation and Application of Economic and Social Accounting Prices*. World Bank Staff Working Paper no. 239. Washington, D.C.

Explains the derivation of national parameters used to estimate distributional accounting following the methodology of Squire and van der Tak (1975). It contains a very useful set of worksheets and illustrates their application in Thailand.

———. 1980. "The Stages of Project Planning—An Introduction to Project Planning." CN-301. Washington, D.C.: Economic Development Institute (EDI), World Bank.

Introduces the reader to the concepts and purposes of the various stages of project planning through analysis of the nature of planning; discusses the significance and importance of the various stages; and stresses the need for an acceptance of a project planning system with the political, institutional, and methodological components that make for an effective system.

Bruno, Michael. 1967. "The Optimal Selection of Export-Promoting and Import-Substituting Projects." In *Planning the External Sector: Techniques, Problems, and Policies.* Report on the First Interregional Seminar on Development Planning, Ankara, Turkey, 6–17 September 1965, pp. 88–135. ST/TAO/SER.c/91. New York: United Nations.

A thorough summary of the theoretical and practical problems associated with computing domestic resource cost.

Carnemark, Curt, Jaime Biderman, and David Bovet. 1976. *The Economic Analysis of Rural Road Projects.* World Bank Staff Working Paper no. 421. Washington, D.C.

A discussion of the analytical procedures to apply to rural roads that have low levels of traffic. Emphasizes the interdependence of transport and agricultural production systems in the rural environment and suggests that the analysis should focus on the mechanisms by which transport cost savings are translated into increasing agricultural production and income.

Carruthers, Ian, and Colin Clark. 1981. *The Economics of Irrigation.* Liverpool: Liverpool University Press.

Focuses on irrigation; includes much material dealing with the technical, institutional-organizational-managerial, financial, and economic aspects of irrigation projects.

Commission of the European Communities. 1980*a. Appraisal of Productive Projects in Agriculture: Economic Analysis and Rate of Return.* VIII/701/76 Rev. 4. Brussels.

Brief discussion of financial and economic analysis, with particular attention given to the "basic principles to be followed in the economic and financial analysis of the agricultural projects submitted to the Commission for financing." Includes a case study intended as a guide for preparing projects.

————. 1980*b. Manual for Preparing and Appraising Project Dossiers.* VIII/527/79-EN. Brussels.

Outlines are given for projects dealing with general agriculture, livestock, rural roads, rural industries, rural health, rural education, sites and services, slaughterhouses, drinking water supply, and drainage.

Delp, Peter, and others. 1977. "Systems Tools for Project Planning." Bloomington: Indiana University, International Development Institute, Program of Advanced Studies in Institution Building and Technical Assistance Methodology.

Discusses a range of tools for planning and analyzing projects, including many tools suitable for use when quantification is difficult.

Eckstein, Otto. 1958. *Water Resource Development: The Economics of Project Evaluation.* Cambridge, Mass.: Harvard University Press.

A theoretical discussion of the issues and problems of project analysis. Classic in its field, but stiff going (written for professional economists).

Espadas, Orlando T. 1977. "Herd Projection Using Hewlett-Packard 67 Calculator." CN-31. Washington, D.C.: Economic Development Institute, World Bank.

Contains the program and detailed instructions about how to use a programmable calculator for herd projections.

Estes, Ralph. 1981. *Dictionary of Accounting*. Cambridge, Mass.: MIT Press.

Convenient, up-to-date reference on accounting terms helpful for those doing financial analysis of projects.

Food and Agriculture Organization (FAO), FAO/World Bank Cooperative Programme. 1975. *Guidelines for the Preparation of Feasibility Studies: Rural Development Projects*. Rome.

See next reference for comment.

————, Investment Centre. 1977. *Guidelines for the Preparation of Agricultural Investment Projects*. Rome.

Two of a series of guidelines for various kinds of agricultural projects prepared by the FAO Investment Centre.

Gittinger, J. Price, ed. 1973. *Compounding and Discounting Tables for Project Evaluation*. Baltimore, Md.: Johns Hopkins University Press.

Basic financial tables prepared with the needs of projects analysts in mind. Includes six-decimal tables for 1 percent through 50 percent by whole percentage points for compounding factor for 1, compounding factor for 1 per annum, sinking fund factor, discount factor, present worth of an annuity factor, and capital recovery factor; summary present worth tables; narrow-interval compounding tables for compounding factor for 1 by intervals of tenths of 1 percent from 0.0 percent through 10.9 percent; and a discussion with examples of how to use the tables.

Gittinger, J. Price, Prem C. Garg, and Alfred Thieme. 1982. "Current Use of Project Analysis Tools in the World Bank and the Inter-American Development Bank." CN-86. Washington, D.C.: Economic Development Institute, World Bank.

A review of the application of project analysis tools in projects financed by the World Bank and the Inter-American Development Bank (IDB) during 1981.

Grant, Eugene L., and W. Grant Ireson. 1964 (4th ed.) and 1970 (5th ed.). *Principles of Engineering Economy*. New York: Ronald.

A standard, thorough text in the field that discusses many questions of application.

Greenwald, Douglas, ed. 1982. *Encyclopedia of Economics*. New York: McGraw-Hill.

Extensive list of economics terms with substantial discussion and references.

Gregerson, Hans M., and Arnoldo H. Contreras. 1979. *Economic Analysis of Forestry Projects*. FAO Forestry Paper no. 17. Rome: Food and Agriculture Organization.

Discusses many of the same concepts dealt with in this book, but with forestry examples. Limited to economic analysis only.

Hansen, John R. 1978. *Guide to Practical Project Appraisal: Social Benefit-Cost Analysis in Developing Counties*. Project Formulation and Evaluation Series no. 3. Sales no. E.78.II.B.3. New York: United Nations.

Provides an excellent introduction to the United Nations Industrial Development Organization (UNIDO) *Guidelines for Project Evaluation* (1972a). Especially useful for noneconomists.

Hardie, J. D. M. 1976. *A Guide to Basic Agricultural Project Appraisal in Developing Countries.* Miscellaneous Publication no. 12. Aberdeen, U.K.: University of Aberdeen, School of Agriculture.

An introductory text written to meet the needs of junior staff in developing countries.

Harsh, Stephen B., Larry J. Connor, and Gerald D. Schwab. 1981. *Managing the Farm Business.* Englewood Cliffs, N.J.: Prentice-Hall.

A contemporary farm management text.

Helmers, F. Leslie C. H. 1979. *Project Planning and Income Distribution.* Boston: Martinus Nijhoff.

Excellent review and critique of project analysis theory and practice. Presented in language of formal economics.

Inter-American Development Bank (IDB). 1978. "Guidelines for the Preparation of Loan Applications." Washington, D.C.

Comprehensive and detailed outlines for agricultural projects including rural credit, forestry, integrated rural development, research and extension, agro-industry, livestock development, marketing of agricultural products, and irrigation. At present, most outlines are available in Spanish only.

———. 1981. *Use of Consulting Firms by the IDB and Its Borrowers.* Washington, D.C.

Describes the selection and supervision process, policies, and procedures relating to use of services of consulting firms and individual consultants by the Inter-American Development Bank and its borrowers.

Irvin, George. 1978. *Modern Cost-Benefit Methods. An Introduction to Financial, Economic, and Social Appraisal of Development Projects.* London: Macmillan.

Excellent university-level, introductory text that focuses on methodological issues. Discusses measures of project worth and economic valuation in detail and compares proposed systems of distribution weights.

James, L. D., and R. R. Lee. 1970. *Economics of Water Resources Planning.* New York: McGraw-Hill.

Includes a detailed discussion of the separable costs–remaining benefits method of joint cost allocation.

Kalbermatten, John M., DeAnne S. Julius, and Charles G. Gunnerson. 1982. *Appropriate Sanitation Alternatives: A Technical and Economic Appraisal.* Baltimore, Md.: Johns Hopkins University Press.

Chapter 3 contains a discussion of cost-effectiveness analysis.

Kay, Ronald D. 1981. *Farm Management: Planning, Control, and Implementation.* New York: McGraw-Hill.

A contemporary farm management text with emphasis on the management process.

King, John A., Jr. 1967. *Economic Development Projects and Their Appraisal.* Baltimore, Md.: Johns Hopkins University Press.

An early, descriptive presentation of World Bank projects.

Krishna, Raj. 1967. "Agricultural Price Policy and Economic Development." In *Agricultural Development and Economic Growth*, edited by Herman M. Southworth and Bruce F. Johnston, pp. 497–540. Ithaca, N.Y.: Cornell University Press.

A standard summary of research showing that farmers in developing countries are price responsive. Although data are now dated, the conclusions remain valid and the evidence is among the most clearly laid out available.

Kulp, Earl M. 1977. "Designing and Managing Basic Agricultural Programs." Bloomington: Indiana University, International Development Institute, Program of Advanced Studies in Institution Building and Technical Assistance Methodology.

Presents in detail a system for planning and preparing agricultural projects.

Kutcher, Gary P., and Pasquale L. Scandizzo. 1981. *The Agricultural Economy of Northeast Brazil*. Baltimore, Md.: Johns Hopkins University Press.

An example of a programming model applied to agricultural sector planning.

Lee, James A., coordinating author. 1982. *The Environment, Public Health, and Human Ecology: Considerations for Economic Development*. Washington, D.C.: World Bank.

Discusses the identification and measurement of the effects agricultural and other development projects can have on the environment and human health; includes suggestions about how to avoid or mitigate the undesirable effects through appropriate project design and preparation.

Lieftinck, Pieter, A. Robert Sadove, and Thomas C. Creyke. 1968. *Water and Power Resources of West Pakistan*. 3 vols. Baltimore, Md.: Johns Hopkins University Press.

An example of a programming model applied to agricultural sector planning.

Little, I. M. D., and J. A. Mirrlees. 1974. *Project Appraisal and Planning for Developing Countries*. New York: Basic Books.

Extremely influential book on project analysis that presents many seminal ideas. Written for the professional economist.

Loughlin, James C. 1977. "The Efficiency and Equity of Cost Allocation Methods for Multipurpose Water Projects." *Water Resources Research*, vol. 13, no. 1 (February), pp. 8–14.

Proposed modifications of the separable cost–remaining benefits method of joint cost allocation to increase equity through weighting for the relative amounts of the separable costs assigned to each purpose.

McDiarmid, Orville John. 1977. *Unskilled Labor for Development: Its Economic Cost*. Baltimore, Md.: Johns Hopkins University Press.

Discusses in detail concepts of the economic value of labor and applies these concepts to the economies in East and Southeast Asia.

McKean, Ronald N. 1958. *Efficiency in Government through Systems Analysis with Emphasis on Water Resources Development*. New York: Wiley.

A classic in the field that clearly sets forth the issues. Recommends use of internal rate of return rather than benefit-cost ratio.

Mears, Leon A. 1969. *Economic Project Evaluation with Philippine Cases*. 2 vols. Quezon City: University of the Philippines Press.

A basic text, with cases written for teaching in the Philippines—hence, quite applicable in many South and Southeast Asian nations.

Merrett, A. J., and Allen Sykes. 1973. *The Finance and Analysis of Capital Projects.* 2d rev. ed. London: Longman.

Excellent and thorough text on techniques of project analysis, with emphasis on application for private firms. Particularly good for questions of methodology.

Meyn, Klaus, J. Price Gittinger, and Walter Schaefer-Kehnert. 1980. "Herd Projection Exercise. Paraguay: Livestock and Agricultural Development Project." AE-1124-P. Washington, D.C.: Economic Development Institute, World Bank.

A paper recommending a standardized approach to preparation of herd projections; illustrated by the example from the Paraguay Livestock and Agricultural Project used in chapter 4 of this book.

Mishan, E. J. 1971. "The Postwar Literature on Externalities." *Journal of Economic Literature*, vol. 9, no. 1 (March), pp. 1–28.

A highly technical summary of the literature on secondary effects; focuses primarily on the relation of benefits to individual firms rather than to society as a whole.

Mishra, S. N., and John Beyer. 1976. *Cost-Benefit Analysis: A Case Study of the Ratnagiri Fisheries Project.* Delhi: Hindustan Publishing Corp.

Interesting application of benefit-cost analysis to a fisheries project.

Mulvaney, John. 1969. *Analysis Bar Charting: A Simplified Critical Path Analysis Technique.* Bethesda, Md.: Management Planning and Control Systems, Inc. (5825 Rockmere Drive, Md. 20817, U.S.A.).

Excellent, introductory text on critical path analysis technique. Uses "precedence diagramming," a method that puts activities into boxes and uses arrows to connect them; the method is more readily understood than conventional techniques using arrows to indicate activities.

Niswonger, C. Rollin, and Philip E. Fess. 1977. *Accounting Principles.* 12th ed. Cincinnati, Ohio: South-Western.

Thorough text on accounting following American conventions.

Norton, Roger D., and Leopoldo Solis M. 1982. *The Book of CHAC: Programming Studies for Mexican Agriculture.* Baltimore, Md.: Johns Hopkins University Press.

An example of a programming model applied to agricultural sector planning.

Olivares, Jose. 1978. "Evaluacion retrospectiva de proyectos agricolas" [Retrospective evaluation of agricultural projects]. Washington, D.C.: World Bank. Restricted circulation.

A discussion of World Bank agricultural project experience and reasons why some projects fall short of expectations.

Packard, Philip C. 1974. *Project Appraisal for Development Administration.* The Hague: Mouton.

Discusses the methodology of project analysis by referring to illustrative cases drawn from agroindustrial projects in developing countries.

Pouliquen, Louis Y. 1970. *Risk Analysis in Project Appraisal.* Baltimore, Md.: Johns Hopkins University Press.

Applies formal risk analysis techniques, which require machine computation, primarily to problems of transport and public utility projects. Discusses issues of suitable techniques for applying risk analysis.

Powers, Terry A. 1975. *HERDSIM Simulation Model: User Manual.* Papers on Project Analysis no. 2. Washington, D.C.: Inter-American Development Bank.

Presents and discusses a computer program for beef herd projections.

Prest, A. R., and R. Turvey. 1966. "Cost-Benefit Analysis: A Survey." In *Surveys of Economic Theory*, vol. 3, *Resource Allocation*, edited by the American Economics Association and the Royal Economic Society, pp. 155–207. New York: St. Martin's.

The best general survey with which to begin serious exploration of the issues relating to measures of project worth.

Reutlinger, Shlomo. 1970. *Techniques for Project Appraisal under Uncertainty.* Baltimore, Md.: Johns Hopkins University Press.

A sophisticated treatment of uncertainty; requires the use of a computer. Useful where very large investments are involved and suitable, highly skilled manpower can be assigned to the analysis.

Riley, J. Paul, and others. 1978. "Cost Allocation Alternatives for the Senegal River Development Program." Water Resource Planning Series no. UWRL/P-78/06. Logan: Utah State University, Utah Water Research Laboratory.

A careful discussion of joint cost allocation issues and methodologies applied to an international project in West Africa.

Ripman, Hugh. 1964. "Project Appraisal." *Finance and Development*, vol. 1, no. 3 (December), pp. 178–83.

The first published, systematic presentation of the aspects of project analysis.

Ruthenberg, Hans. 1977. "A Framework for the Planning and Evaluation of Agricultural Development Projects." Nairobi: Ministry of Agriculture, Planning Division. [Available in German as *Ein Rahmen zur Planung und Beurteilung landwirtschaftlicher Entwicklungs-projeckte.* 2. Auflage. Frankfurt: DLG-Verlag.]

A very thorough text with considerable emphasis on preparation of projects as well as a discussion of analytical techniques.

Sassone, Peter G., and William A. Schaffer. 1978. *Cost-Benefit Analysis: A Handbook.* New York: Academic.

Written for noneconomists, this is a direct statement of the elements of benefit-cost analysis. It is addressed to readers in developed rather than developing countries and is not intended to deal with a particular sector. Has a good, but not annotated, bibliography.

Schaefer-Kehnert, Walter. 1978. "Time-Adjusted Cash Flow Projections in Farm Investment Analysis." *Zeitschrift fur Auslandische Landwirtschaft* [Quarterly Journal of International Agriculture], vol. 17, no. 3 (July–September), pp. 233–49.

Discusses the rationale for the "time-adjusted" accounting convention for farm investment analysis and the incremental working capital as a percentage of incremental operating expenditure.

———. 1980. "Methodology of Farm Investment Analysis." *Zeitschrift fur Auslandische Landwirtschaft* [Quarterly Journal of International Agriculture], vol. 19, no. 2 (April–June), pp. 105–21; no. 3 (July–September), pp. 250–67.

Distinguishes farm investment analysis (benefit-cost analysis of on-farm investments) from farm income analysis and funds flow analysis and describes the accounting procedures required for a time-adjusted phasing of costs and benefits. The treatment of inflation, performance criteria, and the measurement of small farmers' investment incentives are also discussed.

————. 1981*a*. "Herd Projection Exercise. Tanzania Ranch." AE-1097-P. Washington, D.C.: Economic Development Institute, World Bank.

A self-teaching guide to herd projections that is compatible with the farm budget accounting convention recommended in this book.

————. 1981*b*. "How to Start an Internal Rate of Return Calculation." CN-30. Washington, D.C.: Economic Development Institute, World Bank.

Discusses means to estimate the internal rate of return easily to reduce the calculation burden arising from repeated trials.

Scott, M. FG., J. D. MacArthur, and D. M. G. Newbery. 1976. *Project Appraisal in Practice*. London: Heinemann.

Applies the methodology proposed by Little and Mirrlees (1974) to selected projects in Kenya. Advanced.

Shanner, W. W. 1979. *Project Planning for Developing Economies*. New York: Praeger.

A general text on the methodology of benefit-cost analysis. The book grew out of materials prepared for university instruction. Contains an analysis of a hypothetical supplemental irrigation project.

Sloan, Harold S., and Arnold J. Zurcher. 1970. *Dictionary of Economics*. 5th ed. New York: Barnes & Noble.

A standard reference for economics terms.

Squire, Lyn, and Herman G. van der Tak. 1975. *Economic Analysis of Projects*. Baltimore, Md.: Johns Hopkins University Press.

A methodology for project analysis developed by two World Bank economists and growing from that of Little and Mirrlees (1974) and the UNIDO *Guidelines* (1972*a*). Recommends a more "systematic and consistent estimation and application of shadow prices" than had previously been common in World Bank practice as well as calculation of "rates of return that take explicit account of the impact of the project on the distribution of income both between investment and consumption and between rich and poor" (p. 3).

United Nations Industrial Development Organization (UNIDO). 1972*a*. *Guidelines for Project Evaluation*. Prepared by Partha Dasgupta and others. New York: United Nations.

Proposes a methodology for project analysis that incorporates elements of more systematic shadow pricing and distribution weights. Along with Little and Mirrlees (1974), this work has exerted substantial influence on recent thinking about project analysis methodology.

————. 1972*b*. *Manual on the Use of Consultants in Developing Countries*. New York: United Nations.

Concise, comprehensive guide of immediate practical relevance to administrators in developing countries.

U.S. Government, Water Resources Council. 1979. "Procedures for Evaluation of National Economic Development (NED) Benefits and Costs in Water Resource Planning." *Federal Register*, vol. 44, no. 242 (December 14), pp. 72892–976.

Defines costs and benefits for use by U.S. government agencies and specifies how they are to be used for evaluating water resource projects.

Upper, Jack L., ed. 1979. "Finance for Project Analysis." Washington, D.C.: Economic Development Institute, World Bank.

A collection of training materials that focus on financial analysis of industrial enterprises.

van der Tak, Herman G. 1969. *The Economic Choice between Hydroelectric and Thermal Power Developments*. Baltimore, Md.: Johns Hopkins University Press.

Discusses methodologies to analyze the choice between alternative technologies with very different time profiles for investment and operating costs.

Wall, Albert. 1979. *Environment and Development*. Washington, D.C.: World Bank.

Discusses the relation between project investment and environmental and health problems.

Ward, William A. 1976. "Adjusting for Over-Valued Local Currency: Shadow Exchange Rates and Conversion Factors." CN-28. Washington, D.C.: Economic Development Institute, World Bank.

Intended for practical application in those instances where estimates by the central planning office are not available and project analysts must determine shadow exchange rates or conversion factors for themselves.

Waterston, Albert, Wayne Weiss, and John L. Wilson. 1976. *Managing Planned Agricultural Development*. Washington, D.C.: Government Affairs Institute.

A handbook intended as a source document for those responsible for preparing agricultural projects.

Westley, Glenn D. 1981. *FARMSIM Users Guide: A Model for the Appraisal of Farm Development Projects*. Papers on Project Analysis no. 12. Washington, D.C.: Inter-American Development Bank.

Presents and discusses a computer program for appraising farm development projects.

Woo, S. J. 1982. "Sources of Information on World Prices." CN-26. Washington, D.C.: Economic Development Institute, World Bank.

Comprehensive listing of sources for obtaining world market prices to use in project analysis.

World Bank. 1978, 1980, and 1981a. *Annual Review of Project Performance Audit Results*. Washington, D.C.

Analyzes the strengths and weaknesses of selected World Bank projects for which loan disbursements have been completed during the year to which the report pertains. Published annually.

———. 1981b. *A Handbook on Monitoring and Evaluation of Agricultural and Rural Development Projects*. Washington, D.C.

Discusses the approach to monitoring and evaluation and specific problems that may be encountered in collecting and evaluating data.

———. 1981c. *Guidelines for the Use of Consultants by World Bank Borrowers and by the World Bank as Executing Agency*. Washington, D.C.

Describes the selection and supervision process, policies, and procedures relating to services of consulting firms and individual consultants used by the World Bank and its borrowers.

————. 1982*a*. *Price Prospects for Major Primary Commodities.* Report no. 814/82. Washington, D.C.

An authoritative and convenient projection of prices for major commodities of interest to developing countries. Published biennially in even-numbered years, with updates at six-month intervals between publications.

————. 1982b. "Irrigation Water Charges, Benefit Taxes, and Cost Recovery Policies." CN-88. Washington, D.C.: Economic Development Institute, World Bank.

A discussion of the concepts underlying World Bank procedures for estimating cost recovery and rent recovery indexes.

Glossary-Index

THE SPECIALIZED TERMS most frequently used in agricultural project analysis are defined in this glossary-index as they are used in this book. Definitions follow index entries and appear in *italic* type. When other terms that are also defined in the index are used in a definition or are cross-referenced, they appear in SMALL CAPITALS. Page numbers in *italic* type indicate figures or tables.

Absolute value. *The numerical value of a real number irrespective of sign.*

Accounting convention (time-adjusted)
  compounding interest and, 306
  discounting and, 315
  for farm investment analysis, 95–99
  financial statements and, 190
  herd projection and, 164–65
  repayment of equal amounts of principal and, 151–53

Accounting period. *The interval between successive entries in an account. In* PROJECT ANALYSIS, *the accounting period is generally a year, but it could be any other convenient time period.*

Accounting price. *See* SHADOW PRICE

Accounts
  aggregation methods and, 287–96
  "articulated," 197
  financial statements and, 190–92

Accounts payable. *Amounts owed by an enterprise to the suppliers of goods or services purchased on credit.*
  financial rate of return calculation and, 212
  sources-and-uses-of-funds statement

Facing page: Transplanting rice in Sri Lanka.

457

project delays and projects for, 29
project preparation and, 419, 423
simple interest calculations and,
147–50
sources-and-uses-of-funds statement
and, 202
unit activity budget and, 146
Creditworthiness. *The ability of an indi-*
vidual, firm, or nation to meet its
DEBT SERVICE *obligations. For a firm,*
a judgment about creditworthiness is
often formed on the basis of one or
another FINANCIAL RATIO.
Creditworthiness ratio, 191, 207–09
Critical path diagram. *A diagram that*
plots the sequence of activities for
project planning and scheduling,
shows which activities must be com-
pleted before others can commence,
and indicates which activities cannot
be delayed without delaying the whole
PROJECT. *Variously referred to as*
"critical path method" (CPM), *"pro-*
gram evaluation and review tech-
nique" (PERT), *or "network analysis."*
See Mulvaney (1969).
Cropping intensity. *Total cultivated area*
on a farm divided by total cropland.
When there is MULTIPLE CROPPING, *the*
cropping intensity may be greater
than 1. Often reported as a percen-
tage. Thus, a farm where 7 hectares
are cultivated as a result of multiple
cropping, but where there are only 5
hectares of total cropland, has a crop-
ping intensity of 1.4 (7 ÷ 5 = 1.4),
or 140 percent.
Cropping pattern. *The area devoted to,*
and the sequence of, crops produced
by a farmer or in a region.
Cropping patterns
climate and, 415
computer use and, 408
family labor and, 139
farm investment analysis and, 90, 91,
92, 93
land use analysis and, 100–01
project preparation and, 415–16, 418
unit activity budgets and, 142
with and without project and, 138
Crops
budgets (aggregation) and,
287–89, 291
climate and poor project estimates
for, 36
inappropriate technology and, 30
incremental working capital for, 127
labor use analysis and, 102–03,
105, 111
land use analysis and, 100–01

operating expenditure and, 98, 123
projected farm production and,
112, *113*
response to nitrogen fertilizer example
(Philippines) and, 65–69
separable costs–remaining benefits
method and, 234
unit activity budgets and, 141, 142
Crossover discount rate, 383–88. *The*
DISCOUNT RATE *that equalizes the*
PRESENT WORTHS *of the* COST STREAMS
of two alternatives producing the
same result. Usually used to choose
between two technological alterna-
tives or alternative project designs
having different time streams. The
preferred alternative is the one with
the lowest present worth. At some dis-
count rate, alternatives having differ-
ent time streams may have equal
present worths; at a higher discount
rate, a different alternative is preferred
from that below the rate. Also called
the "equalizing discount rate."–May
be determined graphically by plotting
the present worth of the two alterna-
tives at different discount rates or
may be computed by finding the
INTERNAL RATE OF RETURN *to the dif-*
ferences year by year between the
cash flows of the alternative with the
higher undiscounted COST *less the*
alternative with the lower undis-
counted cost.
Cull. *In livestock husbandry, to remove as*
a result of failure to meet a standard.
Culled animals are animals removed
from a herd because they do not meet
performance standards. A culling rate
is the proportion of animals of a
class removed for failure to meet per-
formance standards; it is generally
stated as a percentage.
Culled animals
defined, 164
rates of, 166–67
Cultural environment, 91
Cumulative surplus (deficit). *In a govern-*
ment cash flow account for a
PROJECT, *the difference between cash*
INFLOW *and cash* OUTFLOW *from the*
beginning of the project through a
given year. Compare with CURRENT
SURPLUS (DEFICIT)
Currency
economic values determination and
domestic, 244
foreign exchange premium and
domestic, 247

Intangible (*continued*)

efit—disease, illiteracy, and so forth—
but may also be such items as environmental degradation, inconveni-
ence, and the like. Intangible benefits
are sometimes valued as being at least
equal to the estimated cost of the best
alternative method of providing the
same benefit. Thus, the benefit of sup-
plying electricity for home lighting
from a MULTIPURPOSE river basin
PROJECT may be taken to be the cost
of providing the electricity by diesel
generators. This method of
ALTERNATIVE COST VALUATION should
be used only in cases where the
alternative actually would be undertaken in the absence of the project.
The TANGIBLE cost of avoiding an intangible cost may be included in the
cost of a project. Thus, the cost of
avoiding downstream pollution from
excessive fertilizer run-off may be included in the cost of a project as a
means of dealing with the intangible
cost of pollution. However, the nature
of intangible costs and benefits is
such that REAL value of the cost to
those bearing it or of the benefit to
project participants cannot be determined. When intangible costs or benefits are encountered in project analysis, the analyst should identify them
and quantify them to the extent possible. Projects in which a substantial
amount of the benefit is intangible
may be evaluated using COST EFFEC-
TIVENESS ANALYSIS. See EXTERNALITY

Integrated rural development project. A
PROJECT in which a conscious
attempt is made not only to increase
agricultural production in a rural
area, but also to improve INPUT and
OUTPUT marketing and the quality of
rural life.

Inter-American Development Bank,
411, 441

Intermediate. *With reference to goods
and services, those goods and services
that are used as an INPUT for further
transformation by some other production activity—not for consumption or
as an addition to the stock of fixed
CAPITAL. Intermediate goods are an
OUTPUT of one economic enterprise
that have not yet reached the final
form in which they will be used as an
item of consumption or as an addition to the stock of fixed capital. Such*

*goods proceed further through the
production system and are used by
other enterprises as an input. Distinguished from FINAL goods and services, which have reached their ultimate form for use in consumption, or
as an addition to fixed capital. A particular good or service may be either
final or intermediate depending on the
use to which reference is made. Thus,
an orange is an intermediate good if
used to make orange juice and a final
good if consumed directly.*

Intermediate goods, market price determination and pricing of, 71–72

Interest. *A payment for use of money,
generally stated as a percentage of the
amount (PRINCIPAL) borrowed. The
rate of interest is also used for
DISCOUNTING; in that use it generally
is referred to as the DISCOUNT RATE.
"Simple interest" is the interest paid
in one period; compound interest is
interest paid not only on the amount
borrowed but on the interest earned
in previous periods. For methods of
computation, see COMPOUNDING
FACTOR FOR 1 and DISCOUNT FACTOR.*

benefit-cost ratio and, 345

capitalized equal installments and,
157–58

compounding of, 305–08

computing debt service and, 147–50

declining real burden of debt service
and, 158, 161–62

economic analysis and, 19

equal installment repayment and,
153–56

foreign exchange flow and, 222

government cash flow and, 219, 220

income statement and, 196–97

internal rate of return and, 331,
335, 343

payments (sources-and-uses-of-funds
statement), 199, 202

project costs and, 54–55

received (sources-and-uses-of-funds
statement), 199

time value of money (discounting
dimension) and, 305–08

unit activity budget and, 146

Internal rate of return, 210, 299, 343,
358, 401. *A discounted MEASURE OF
PROJECT WORTH. The DISCOUNT RATE
that just makes the NET PRESENT
WORTH of the incremental NET
BENEFIT stream, or incremental cash
flow, equal zero. The maximum
INTEREST that a PROJECT can pay for*

Opportunity cost (*continued*)

> INPUT *is adjusted to the point where its marginal value product is equal to its opportunity cost. In project evaluation, for the* FINANCIAL ANALYSIS *the opportunity cost of a purchased input is always its market price. In* ECONOMIC ANALYSIS, *however, the opportunity cost of a purchased input is always either its marginal value product in its best nonproject alternative use, if for* INTERMEDIATE *goods and services, or its* VALUE IN USE *(as measured by* WILLINGNESS TO PAY*), if it is a* FINAL *good or service. Since price is equal to marginal value product in a perfectly competitive market, in an economic analysis if an input is purchased in a reasonably competitive market the price is at least an initial estimate of the marginal value product of the input and, hence, of its opportunity cost. However, if because of market imperfections or other reasons the market price of an input does not closely approximate the marginal value product in its next best alternative nonproject use, the marginal value product is estimated directly, and that estimate becomes the* SHADOW PRICE *of the item. The concept of opportunity cost is a cornerstone of* PROJECT ANALYSIS *and is the central concept underlying valuation of project inputs. See also* OPPORTUNITY COST OF CAPITAL

economic values and, 243, 245

family labor and, 139

farm-gate price calculation of market prices and, 71

foreign exchange premium and, 250

operating expenditure (family labor or land) and, 126

prices as reflection of value and, 68–69

secondary costs and benefits analysis and, 60

tradable but nontraded items and, 264

unit activity budget problems and, 142, 143, 146

valuing labor and, 258, 260, 262

Opportunity cost of capital. *The* OPPORTUNITY COST *of using* INVESTMENT *resources in a* PROJECT *rather than in their next best alternative use; usually expressed in the form of an* INTEREST *rate. The reduction in nonproject* BENEFITS *in relation to project objectives that is a result of*

> *using* CAPITAL *in the project. In practice, usually a weighted average calculation of the* COST *of securing project capital from various sources. In* FINANCIAL ANALYSIS, *the weighted average cost to the firm or farm of* EQUITY *capital and of borrowed capital from likely sources. In* ECONOMIC ANALYSIS, *usually the weighted average cost of capital to the economy as a whole, but sometimes the weighted average cost of capital to the public sector. The rate at which benefits and costs are discounted in calculating the* NET PRESENT WORTH, *the* NET BENEFIT-INVESTMENT RATIO, *or the* BENEFIT-COST RATIO. *The* CUT-OFF RATE *for* PROJECT ANALYSIS, *and hence the minimum acceptable* INTERNAL RATE OF RETURN. *Several methods exist for formulating and for calculating the economic opportunity cost of capital. Difficulty in calculating the opportunity cost of capital is a primary reason for widespread use of the internal rate of return as a* MEASURE OF PROJECT WORTH.

cut-off rate and, 314

discount measures and, 314, 333, 346, 359

internal rate of return and, 332

mutually exclusive projects and, 382, 383

net benefit-investment ratio and, 346

net present worth method and, 382, 383

Tunisian forestry project example and, 387

Optimization of project investment, 349

Organizational aspects of projects, 14

farmers and, 31

project preparation and, 422–24

Outflow. *All payments that are made, or goods and services of value that are consumed or transferred, to other entities and that decrease* NET BENEFIT. *Distinguished from* INFLOW.

Output. *A good or service produced by an activity. In* PROJECT ANALYSIS, *the product of the* PROJECT.

aggregation and, 293

commercial aspects of projects and, 16

loss avoidance and, 59

market price as estimate of economic value and, 255

predicting future prices and, 75

with and without comparisons and, 47–50